WILEY PLUS

www.wileyplus.com

Wiley is committed to making your entire *WileyPLUS* experience productive & enjoyable by providing the help, resources, and personal support you & your students need, when you need it. It's all here: www.wileyplus.com —

TECHNICAL SUPPORT:

- ⊕ A fully searchable knowledge base of FAQs and help documentation, available 24/7
- ⊕ Live chat with a trained member of our support staff during business hours
- ⊕ A form to fill out and submit online to ask any question and get a quick response
- ⊕ **Instructor-only** phone line during business hours: 1.877.586.0192

FACULTY-LED TRAINING THROUGH THE WILEY FACULTY NETWORK:
Register online: www.wherefacultyconnect.com
Connect with your colleagues in a complimentary virtual seminar, with a personal mentor in your field, or at a live workshop to share best practices for teaching with technology.

1ST DAY OF CLASS...AND BEYOND!
Resources You & Your Students Need to Get Started
& Use *WileyPLUS* from the first day forward.

- ⊕ 2-Minute Tutorials on how to set up & maintain your *WileyPLUS* course
- ⊕ User guides, links to technical support & training options
- ⊕ *WileyPLUS for Dummies*: Instructors' quick reference guide to using *WileyPLUS*
- ⊕ Student tutorials & instruction on how to register, buy, and use *WileyPLUS*

YOUR *WileyPLUS* ACCOUNT MANAGER:
Your personal *WileyPLUS* connection for any assistance you need!

SET UP YOUR *WileyPLUS* COURSE IN MINUTES!
Selected *WileyPLUS* courses with QuickStart contain pre-loaded assignments & presentations created by subject matter experts who are also experienced *WileyPLUS* users.

Interested? See and try WileyPLUS in action!
Details and Demo: www.wileyplus.com

Human
Geography

People, Place, and Culture   Ninth Edition

Human
Geography

People, Place, and Culture   Ninth Edition

Erin H. Fouberg
Northern State University

Alexander B. Murphy
University of Oregon

H. J. de Blij
Michigan State University

WILEY

John Wiley & Sons, Inc.

Vice President & Executive Publisher:	Jay O'Callaghan
Executive Editor:	Ryan A. Flahive
Assistant Editor:	Courtney Nelson
Production Manager:	Dorothy Sinclair
Marketing Manager:	Danielle Torio
Senior Production Editor:	Sandra Dumas
Senior Designer:	Kevin Murphy
Senior Media Editor:	Lynn Pearlman
Photo Editor:	Hilary Newman
Photo Researcher:	Elaine Soares
Front cover image:	Alexander B. Murphy
Back cover image:	© Tony Cenicola/The New York Times /Redux Pictures
Production Management Services:	Jeanine Furino/GGS Higher Education Resources

This book was typeset in 10/12 Janson Text by GGS Higher Education Resources, A Divison of PreMedia Global, Inc. and printed & bound by R. R. Donnelley (Jefferson City). The cover was printed by R. R. Donnelley (Jefferson City).

The paper in this book was manufactured by a mill whose forest management programs include sustained yield harvesting of its timberlands. Sustained yield harvesting principles ensure that the number of trees cut each year does not exceed the amount of new growth.

This book is printed on acid-free paper. ∞

ISBN-13 978-0470-38258-5

Printed in the United States of America.

10 9 8 7 6 5 4 3 2 1

Preface

The noted geographer Yi-Fu Tuan once said, "People make places." Places do not exist in a vacuum. Places cannot be catalogued in terms of characteristics or "facts." Places are constantly changing, and people are responsible for these changes. People create cultures, values, aesthetics, politics, economics, and more, and each of these affects and shapes places. In the study of human geography, we are constantly reminded of how people shape their world and of how people and places vary across space.

Globalization factors heavily into the many influences people have on places. Globalization is a set of processes that flow and pulsate across and through country boundaries—processes that have different outcomes in different places and across scales. Our goals in writing the Ninth Edition of *Human Geography: People, Place, and Culture* were, first, to help students appreciate the role people play in shaping places; second, to provide context for the issues we address so that students can better understand their world; third, to give students the tools to grapple with the complexities of globalization; and fourth, to help students think geographically and critically about their world.

Students need to appreciate the complexities of globalization and to think critically about what they see, read, and hear about their world. Students in college today are living in a world that is quite different from what any other generation has experienced; they are living, as geographer Andrew Kirby explains it, "not in a world without boundaries or without limits, but simply a world." Today's college students engage daily with the world, whether or not they are conscious of that fact. Students are part of the world, and many have a global identity. They need to make sense of themselves not just in their home, college, locality, nation, and region, but also in their world. Globalization means that people and places across the world are constantly interacting. For good or for ill, each of us is a part of that interaction. Each of us, therefore, must make sense of who we are and what our role is in this globalized world, and we each must think critically about how we can shape our world.

The pictures on the front and back covers of this textbook illustrate how people make places and, in the process, create their own individual, local, and global identities. The front cover photo, taken recently by Alexander B. Murphy, shows Hindu people in Varanasi, India, gathering at the sacred waters of the Ganges River to perform ritual bathing. The landscape of the Ganges River and the city of Varanasi reflect how people use the river. In Varanasi, miles of steps called *ghats* line the river so that thousands of people can easily walk down the banks of the river to reach the Ganges each day. Through the use of the river, Hindus have made an indelible imprint on the place; at the same time, the people refine their own identities. The act of sharing the river and performing ritual bathing helps people make sense of who they are—in the process strengthening individual identities and fostering a group identity that helps individuals find their place in local communities as well as in the world beyond. The back cover shows a number of objects you may find in your closet—a pair of Converse, a shirt from the Gap, and an iPod. What stands out among these objects is that each is (PRODUCT) RED. If you have a (RED) product in your closet, you are already aware you are living in a global world: the purchases you make and the things you do each day happen in a global context and can have global impacts. You chose a (RED) product because you knew a portion of the profits would go to the Global Fund to help combat AIDS in Subsaharan Africa, and you were making sense of who you are at the global scale—creating your global identity. Globalization has not erased people and places, nor has it covered them all with a blanket of a one-world culture. With globalization, the way people make places and shape their identities has global, local, and individual implications. What people do today, whether making a pilgrimage to a river or buying a (PRODUCT) RED item, happens in a global context.

When students understand the role people play in making places, see the geographic context in which a major issue occurs, learn to think geographically and critically about the world, and appreciate the complexities of globalization, they become geographically literate and are better prepared to confront the challenges of the twenty-first century.

THE NINTH EDITION

In writing the Ninth Edition, we integrated the text, photos, and illustrations to help students understand the role people play in shaping the world, to provide geographic context to the issues we discuss, to teach students to think geographically and critically, and to explain the complexities of globalization. We used our own field experiences and drew from the research and fieldwork of hundreds of others in order to achieve these goals throughout the text.

In the Ninth Edition, we continue to use Key Questions and Thinking Geographically prompts as the outline for each of the 14 chapters in the text. The Key Questions are listed after the opening field note of each chapter and serve as the outline for the chapter. After each Key Question is answered in the chapter, the reader will find a Thinking Geographically question. These questions ask the reader to apply a geographic concept to a real-life example. Readers who complete the Thinking Geographically questions throughout the text will learn to think geographically and to think critically. Instructors can also use the Thinking Geographically questions as lecture launchers by giving each student a few minutes to write his or her own answer to a question and by then generating a class discussion from these answers.

Several features of the Ninth Edition—the opening field notes, the author field notes, and the guest field notes—provide context and help the reader learn to think geographically. Each chapter in this edition starts with an *opening field note*, written by the author team, that provides context for the particular author's experience in the field and pulls the reader into the chapter. Each chapter also includes one or more *author field notes*, in addition to the opening field note. The author field notes serve as models of how to think geographically. We are also excited about the expanded number of *guest field notes* in this edition. Each guest field note was written by a geographer who has spent time in the field, researching the place that is profiled. All the guest field notes include a photograph taken by the author as well as a paragraph focusing on how what the author saw in the field influenced his or her research.

THE TEACHING AND LEARNING PACKAGE

The Ninth Edition of *Human Geography: People, Place, and Culture* is supported by a comprehensive supplements package that includes an extensive selection of print, visual, and electronic materials.

Resources That Help Teachers Teach

People and Place Lecture Launchers. Working closely with Wiley's Media Team, Erin Fouberg created a collection of video lecture launchers that allow instructors to provide a visual context for key concepts, ideas, and terms that they plan to introduce during their lectures. These videos are available in a DVD format that is optimized for in-class presentation as well as in a streaming format that is available online. Streaming videos will also be made available to students in the context of WileyPLUS assignments that can be graded online and added to the WileyPLUS instructor gradebook.

Online Geography on-Location Videos. Because of their enduring popularity, we have digitized many of the videos from the original VHS series. This rich collection of original and relevant footage was taken during H. J. de Blij's travels. These videos cover a wide range of themes; they are available on the instructor website and are also integrated throughout each student's WileyPLUS eBook.

The *Human Geography: People, Place, and Culture* Instructors' Site. This comprehensive website includes numerous resources to help you enhance your current presentations, create new presentations, and employ our premade PowerPoint presentations. These resources include the following:

- **Image Gallery.** We provide online electronic files for the line illustrations and maps in the text, which the instructor can customize for presenting in class (for example, in handouts, overhead transparencies, or PowerPoints).

- A complete collection of **PowerPoint presentations.** These presentations are available in beautifully rendered, four-color format, and images are sized and edited for maximum effectiveness in large lecture halls. The high-quality photos, maps, and figures provide a set of strong, clear images that are ready to be projected into the classroom.

- A comprehensive **Test Bank** with multiple-choice, fill-in, matching, and essay questions. The Test Bank is distributed via the secure Instructor's website as electronic files and can be saved into all major word processing programs.

- A comprehensive collection of **animations and videos**.

WileyPLUS is a course management system that has helped students and instructors achieve positive learning outcomes by combining robust tools with interactive teaching and learning resources—including a complete online version of the text—all in one easy-to-use system. WileyPLUS allows for automated assigning and grading of homework and creates engaging presentations with many tools and resources.

Wiley Faculty Network (WFN). This peer-to-peer network of faculty is ready to support your use of online course management tools and discipline-specific software/learning systems in the classroom. The WFN will help you apply innovative classroom techniques, implement software packages, tailor the technology experience to the needs of each individual class, and provide you with virtual training sessions led by faculty for faculty.

Course Management. Online course management assets are available to accompany the Ninth Edition of *Human Geography: People, Place, and Culture.*

Resources That Help Students Learn

Student Companion Website www.wiley.com/college/deblij. This easy-to-use and student-focused website helps reinforce and illustrate key concepts from the text. It also provides interactive media content that helps students prepare for tests and improve their grades. This website provides additional resources that complement the textbook and enhance your students' understanding of geography:

- **Videos** provide a first-hand look at life in other parts of the world.
- **Action-oriented Activities** are research-based activities that help students contextualize chapter content.
- **Podcasts, Web Cams, and Live Radio** let students see and hear what is happening all over the world in real time.
- **Flashcards** offer an excellent way to drill and practice key concepts, ideas, and terms from the text.
- **Map Quizzes** help students master the place-names that are crucial to their success in this course. Three game-formatted place-name activities are provided for each chapter.
- **GeoDiscoveries Modules** allow students to explore key concepts in greater depth using videos, animations, and interactive exercises.
- **Chapter Review Quizzes** provide immediate feedback to true/false, multiple choice, and short-answer questions.
- **Annotated Web Links** put useful electronic resources into context.
- **Area and Demographic Data** are provided for every country and world realm.

Kuby, Harner, and Gober's *Human Geography in Action, Fourth Edition.* This workbook integrates the most fundamental concepts of human geography with interactive, hands-on applications. Students can manipulate data, create maps, and explore the implications of basic concepts though these activities.

National Geographic College Atlas of the World. We are delighted to be able to offer the National Geographic College Atlas of the World.

Resources for Advanced Placement Courses

Advanced Placement Student Companion. It has been exciting to watch the Advanced Placement Human Geography course grow so quickly. Wiley has supported students and instructors since the very beginning by offering high-quality content and pedagogy that help teachers teach and students learn the concepts, ideas, and terms that they need to perform at the college level. With the Ninth Edition of *Human Geography*, we continue this legacy of support by offering a new and improved AP Student Companion.

Advanced Placement Instructor Resources. In addition to all of the instructor resources listed above, instructors of Advanced Placement Geography classes will have access to Wiley's integrated training course for teaching Advanced Placement Human Geography. We work closely with AP instructors to create our supplements, and we suggest ways they can use our supplements to enhance their lectures and save them time.

ACKNOWLEDGMENTS

In preparing the Ninth Edition of *Human Geography*, we benefited immensely from the advice and assistance of many of our colleagues in geography. Some told us of their experiences using other editions, and others provided insightful comments on individual chapters. The list that follows acknowledges their support, but it cannot begin to measure our gratitude for all of the ways they helped shape this book:

Ian Ackroyd-Kelly	*East Stroudsburg University*
Frank Ainsley	*University of North Carolina Wilmington*
Jennifer Altenhofel	*California State University, Bakersfield*
Charles Amissah	*Hampton University*
James Ashley	*University of Toledo*
Nancy Bain	*Ohio University*
Brad Bays	*Oklahoma State University*
Sarah W. Bednarz	*Texas A&M University*
Sari Bennett	*University of Maryland, Baltimore County*
J. Best	*Frostburg State University*
Brian Blouet	*College of William & Mary*
Mark Bockenhauer	*St. Norbert College*
Margaret Boorstein	*C.W. Post College of Long Island University*

Michael Broadway	*Northern Michigan University*		*Seattle*
Michaele Ann Buell	*Northwest Arkansas Community College*	John M. Morris	*University of Texas, San Antonio*
Fiona M. Davidson	*University of Arkansas*	Garth A. Myers	*University of Kansas*
Evan Denney	*University of Montana*	Darrell Norris	*SUNY Geneseo*
Dimitar Dimitrov	*Virginia Commonwealth University*	Ann Oberhauser	*West Virginia University*
		Kenji Oshiro	*Wright State University*
Steve Driever	*University of Missouri, Kansas City*	Bimal K. Paul	*Kansas State University*
		Gene Paull	*University of Texas at Brownsville*
James Dyer	*Mount St. Mary's College*		
Adrian X. Esparza	*University of Arizona*	Walter Peace	*McMaster University*
Stephen Frenkel	*University of Washington, Seattle*	Virginia Ragan	*Maple Woods Community College*
Juanita Gaston	*Florida A&M University*	Jeffrey Richetto	*University of Alabama*
Matthew J. Gerike	*Kansas State University*	Mika Roinila	*State University of New York, New Paltz*
Lay James Gibson	*University of Arizona*		
Abe Goldman	*University of Florida*	James Saku	*Frostburg State University*
Richard Grant	*University of Miami*	Richard Alan Sambrook	*Eastern Kentucky University*
Alyson Greiner	*Oklahoma State University*	Joseph E. Schwartzberg	*University of Minnesota*
Jeffrey A. Gritzner	*University of Montana*	Gary W. Shannon	*University of Kentucky*
Qian Guo	*Northern Michigan University*	Betty Shimshak	*Towson University*
		Nancy Shirley	*Southern Connecticut State University*
John Heppen	*University of Wisconsin, River Falls*		
		Susan Slowey	*Blinn College*
John Hickey	*Inver Hills Community College*	Andrew Sluyter	*Pennsylvania State University*
Miriam Helen Hill	*Jacksonville State University*	Herschel Stern	*Mira Costa College*
Peter R. Hoffmann	*Loyola Marymount University*	Neva Duncan Tabb	*University of South Florida*
		Thomas Terich	*Western Washington University*
Peter Hugill	*Texas A&M University*		
Jay Johnson	*University of Nebraska— Lincoln*	Donald Thieme	*Georgia Southern University*
		James A. Tyner	*University of Southern California*
Tarek A. Joseph	*Central Michigan University*		
Artimus Keiffer	*Wittenberg University*	David Unterman	*Sierra and Yuba Community Colleges*
Les King	*McMaster University*		
Paul Kingsbury	*Miami University, Ohio*	Barry Wauldron	*University of Michigan— Dearborn*
Frances Kostarelos	*Governors State University*		
Darrell P. Kruger	*Illinois State University*	George W. White	*Frostburg State University*
Paul Larson	*Southern Utah University*	Leon Yacher	*Southern Connecticut State University*
Jess A. Le Vine	*Brookdale Community College*		
Ann Legreid	*Central Missouri State University*	Donald Zeigler	*Old Dominion University*
		Robert C. Ziegenfus	*Kutztown University*
Elizabeth Leppmann	*St. Cloud State University*		
Jose Lopez	*Minnesota State University*		
David Lyons	*University of Minnesota, Duluth*		

In the Ninth Edition, several of our colleagues in geography provided guest field notes that add a wonderful dimension to the text and help the reader appreciate the kinds of things geographers see in the field. The stories these colleagues tell and the brilliant photos they provide will help students better appreciate the role of fieldwork in geographic research:

Patricia Matthews-Salazar	*Manhattan Community College*		
Darrell McDonald	*Stephen F. Austin State University*	Jonathan Leib	*Old Dominion University*
Wayne McKim	*Towson University*	Korine Kolivras	*Virginia Tech*
Ian MacLachlan	*University of Lethbridge*	Elsbeth Robson	*Keele University*
Glenn Miller	*Bridgewater State College*	Jason Dittmer	*University College London*
Katharyne Mitchell	*University of Washington,*		

Steven M. Schnell — *Kutztown University of Pennsylvania*

Richard Francaviglia — *Geo. Graphic Designs*

Ines Miyares — *Hunter College of the City University of New York*

Sarah Halvorson — *University of Montana*

Derek Alderman — *East Carolina University*

Mary Lee Nolan — *Oregon State University*

George White — *Frostburg State University*

Brad Bays — *Oklahoma State University*

Johnathan Walker — *James Madison University*

Rachel Silvey — *University of Toronto*

Judith Carney — *University of California, Los Angeles*

Fiona M. Davidson — *University of Arkansas*

William Moseley — *Macalester College*

Kenneth E. Foote — *University of Colorado at Boulder*

On a day-to-day basis, many people in the extended John Wiley & Sons family provided support and guidance. Vice President and Publisher Jay O'Callaghan put all the pieces together to make the timing of this edition and the vision for the edition work. Ryan Flahive, Executive Editor for Geography, got the ball rolling and stayed involved during his global tour. Courtney Nelson, Assistant Editor for the Geosciences, organized the writing and review process, provided inspiration and ideas, and handled many issues with grace. Hilary Newman showed dedication and persistence in finding the images the author team wanted to convey the story that each of the 40 new photos in this edition tells. Hilary and photo researcher, Elaine Soares, quickly responded to each request. Elaine also tackled the detail-oriented task of coordinating the geographers who contributed guest field notes to the Ninth Edition. Jennifer MacMillan helped out in a pinch. Don Larson, Terry Bush, Ann Kennedy, and Adam Derringer at Mapping Specialists used their cartographic expertise to update or create more than 40 maps and figures in this edition. Senior Production Editor, Jeanine Furino, brought all of our work together, handling input from a variety of sources with ease. Betty Pessagno, Copy Editor, offered feedback to help us tighten several ideas in this edition. Lizbeth Sydnor and Lennea Mueller researched and provided data for dozens of new and revised maps and figures. Graphic Designer Shannon Imbery created a fresh "Thinking Geographically" logo. Designer Kevin Murphy took Alec Murphy's photo of Varanasi and created a beautiful cover design around it. Marketing Manager Danielle Torio led our marketing team and effectively conveyed our message.

We are grateful to our family and friends who supported us faithfully through this edition. Erin Fouberg thanks Barb, Gina, Jackie, Kelly, MeChelle, Susan, Tammy, Judy, Blayne, Joan, Ed, Glenna, Rod, Margaret, Henry, and all her sisters and brothers for their constant support. Erin also thanks colleagues around the country, especially Jan Smith, for their insights. Alec Murphy is grateful to Matthew Landers and Matthew Derrick for technical and research help, and to Susan Hardwick, Andrew Marcus, and several other colleagues for their encouragement and support. We offer a special thanks to Joseph Kerski, Stephen Hanna, and Karen Hartman for answering special requests. As always, our greatest thanks go to our spouses, Robert Fouberg, Susan Gary, and Bonnie de Blij, who through their support, understanding, and patience make us better people and better authors.

Erin H. Fouberg
Aberdeen, South Dakota

Alexander B. Murphy
Eugene, Oregon

H. J. de Blij
Boca Grande, Florida

About the Authors

Erin H. Fouberg

Erin Hogan Fouberg grew up in eastern South Dakota. She moved to Washington, D.C. to attend Georgetown University's School of Foreign Service, where she took a class in Human Geography from Harm de Blij. At Georgetown, Erin found her International Relations classes lacking in context and discovered a passion for political geography. She earned her master's and Ph.D. at the University of Nebraska-Lincoln. After graduating, Dr. Fouberg taught for several years at the University of Mary Washington in Fredericksburg, Virginia, where the graduating class of 2001 bestowed on her the Mary Pinschmidt Award, given to the faculty member who made the biggest impact on their lives.

Professor Fouberg is Associate Professor of Geography at Northern State University (NSU) in Aberdeen, South Dakota. Her research and publications focus on the governance and sovereignty of American Indian tribes and on geography education. Professor Fouberg served as Vice President of Publications and Products of the National Council for Geographic Education. She enjoys traveling, camping, reading, golfing, and watching athletic and theater events at NSU.

Alexander B. Murphy

Alec Murphy grew up in the western United States, but he spent several of his early years in Europe and Japan. He obtained his undergraduate degree at Yale University, studied law at the Columbia University School of Law, practiced law for a short time in Chicago, and then pursued a doctoral degree in geography (Ph.D. University of Chicago, 1987). After graduating, Dr. Murphy joined the faculty of the University of Oregon, where he is now Professor of Geography and holder of the James F. and Shirley K. Rippey Chair in Liberal Arts and Sciences. Professor Murphy is a widely published scholar in the fields of political, cultural, and environmental geography, with a regional emphasis on Europe. His work has been supported by the National Science Foundation, the National Endowment for the Humanities, and the Fulbright-Hays foreign fellowship program.

Professor Murphy served as the President of the Association of American Geographers in 2003. He is also Vice President of the American Geographical Society. For 11 years he was one of the editors of *Progress in Human Geography*; he currently co-edits *Eurasian Geography and Economics*. In the late 1990s, he led the effort to add geography to the College Board's Advanced Placement Program. His interests include hiking, skiing, camping, music, and of course exploring the diverse places that make up our planet.

H. J. de Blij

Harm de Blij received his early schooling in Europe, his college education in Africa, and his higher degrees in the United States (Ph.D. Northwestern, 1959). He has published more than 30 books and over 100 articles, and has received five honorary degrees. Several of his books have been translated into foreign languages.

Dr. de Blij is Distinguished Professor of Geography at Michigan State University. He has held the George Landegger Chair at Georgetown University's School of Foreign Service and the John Deaver Drinko Chair of Geography at Marshall University, and has also taught at the Colorado School of Mines and the University of Miami. He was the Geography Editor on ABC-TV's "Good Morning America" program for seven years and later served as Geography Analyst for NBC News. He was for more than 20 years a member of the National Geographic Society's Committee for Research and Exploration and was the founding editor of its scholarly journal, *National Geographic Research*. He is an honorary lifetime member of the Society.

Professor de Blij is a soccer fan, an avid wine collector, and an amateur violinist. His website is at www.deblij.net.

For

Robert John
who believes in me

and

Margaret Conna and Henry McGregor
who inspire me

Contents

Introduction to Human Geography

Field Note Awakening to World Hunger

Figure 1.1
Kericho, Kenya. Tea plantations established by British colonists in western Kenya. © H. J. de Blij.

Dragging myself out of bed for a 9:00 A.M. lecture, I decide I need to make a stop at Starbucks. "Grande coffee of the day, please, and leave room for cream." I rub my eyes and look at the sign to see where my coffee was grown. Kenya. Ironically, I am about to lecture on Kenya's coffee plantations. Just the wake up call I need.

When I visited Kenya in eastern Africa, I drove from Masai Mara to Kericho and I noticed nearly all of the agricultural fields I could see were planted with coffee or tea (Fig. 1.1). I also saw the poor of Kenya, clearly hungry, living in substandard housing. I questioned, "Why do farmers in Kenya grow coffee and tea when they could grow food to feed the hungry?" Through the process of answering this question, I learned a lot about the complexities of globalization. In a globalized world, connections are many and simple answers are few.

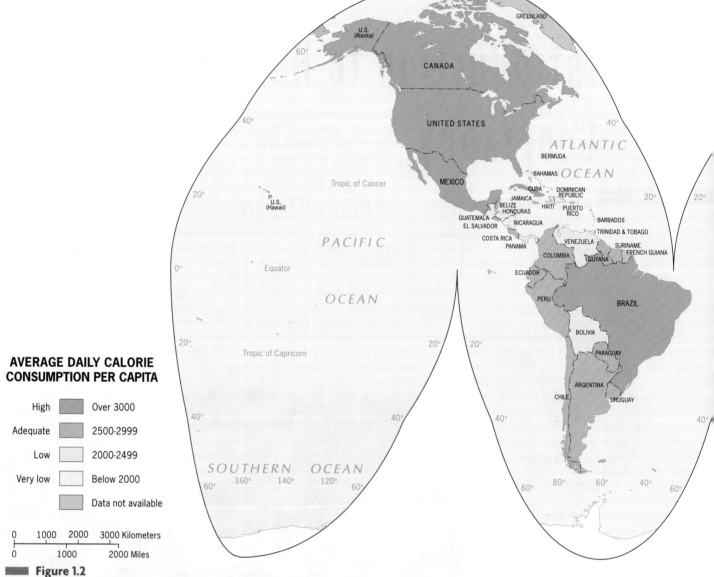

**AVERAGE DAILY CALORIE
CONSUMPTION PER CAPITA**

High		Over 3000
Adequate		2500-2999
Low		2000-2499
Very low		Below 2000
		Data not available

0   1000   2000   3000 Kilometers
0   1000   2000 Miles

Figure 1.2
Average Daily Calorie Consumption Per Capita, 2004. *Data from*: United Nations Food and Agriculture Organization Food Balance Sheets 2004. Note that this map (see Appendix A) is interrupted in the oceans, allowing for maximum clarity of detail on the landmasses.

Major problems in the world, like hunger, may seem easy to solve. Take the total annual food production in the world, divide it by the world's population, and we have plenty of food for everyone. Yet, one-sixth of the world's population is seriously malnourished. The vast majority of the 1 billion malnourished people on Earth are women and children, who have little money and even less power.

[1]Figure 1.2 reveals the wide range of caloric intake throughout the world. Various agencies monitor this index, but their categories differ, and, in recent years, the urgency of their reporting has diminished. As the map indicates, countries are usually grouped into four ranks, ranging from high intake (usually over 3000 calories daily) to very low, or under 2000, but there is no agreement about adequacy. The World Bank regards 2500 calories as adequate, whereas the United Nations uses 2360 as its boundary between adequate and low intake. Such discrepancies (there are others when additional sources are consulted) should raise a caution when you consult Figure 1.2, which is based on data from 2004. The map may effectively portray the global situation by country in general terms. What the map does not reflect is also important: there are nutritional disparities within countries that cannot be shown at this level of scale. For example, diets in western India are

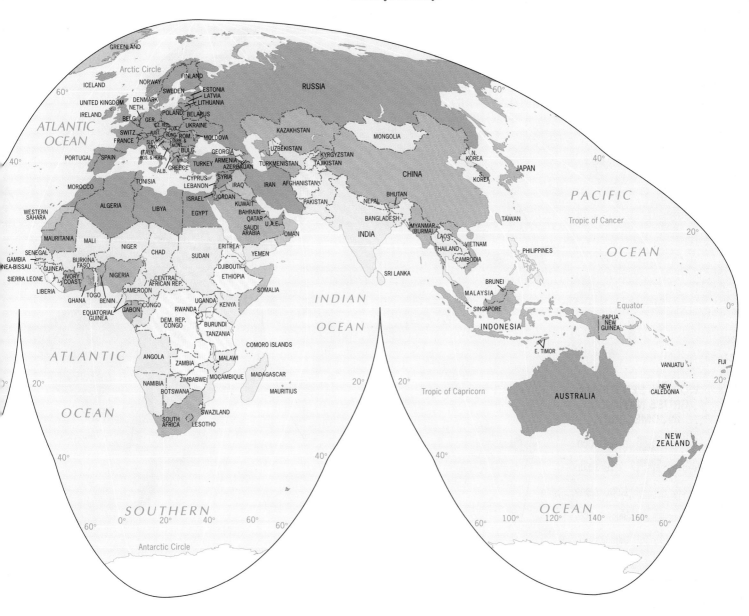

Figure 1.2 shows how food consumption is currently distributed—unevenly.[1] Comparing Figure 1.2 with Figure 1.3 shows that the wealthier countries also are the best fed and that Subsaharan Africa (the part of Africa south of the Sahara Desert) is currently in the worst position, with numerous countries in the lowest categories.

superior to those in eastern India; the intake in northern parts of Sudan is substantially higher than that in its war-ridden south and west. Another factor not shown in Figure 1.2 is dietary balance. With few exceptions, the countries where caloric intake is low are also those where protein is in short supply. Recent studies have indicated that the first six months of life are critical in this respect: inadequate protein intake can damage brain and body for life. Moreover, the food sources that are richest in proteins—meat, fish, and dairy products—are in short supply where they are most needed. It takes food to raise the animals that produce meat, and that food cannot be spared to feed animals when it is needed to sustain the people themselves. And while fish may be obtainable in coastal areas, it becomes less available (and more expensive) in interior Africa and Asia. Thus, even people whose caloric intake is marginally adequate may still be malnourished, and what is often called hidden hunger occurs even in areas mapped as having "adequate calories."

Figure 1.3

Per Capita Gross National Income (in U.S dollars) (GNI), 2007. *Data from:* World Bank, World Development Indicators, 2008.

The major causes of malnourishment are poverty (inability to pay for food), the failure of food distribution systems, and cultural practices that favor men over women and children. Where food does reach the needy, its price may be unaffordable. Hundreds of millions of people subsist on the equivalent of one dollar a day, and many in the vast shantytowns encircling the world's cities must pay rent to landlords who own the plots on which their shacks are built. Too little is left for food, and it is the children who suffer most.

Is solving hunger as simple as each country growing enough food to feed its people? Do the best-fed countries have the most arable (farmable) land? Only 4 percent of Norway is arable land, and more than 70 percent of Bangladesh is arable land (Fig. 1.4). Despite this disparity, Norway is wealthy and well fed, whereas Bangladesh is poor and malnourished. Fortunately for the Norwegians, they are able to overcome their inadequate food production by importing food. Unfortunately for the Bangladeshis, two-thirds of their country is flooded each year during monsoon season, making survival a daily question.

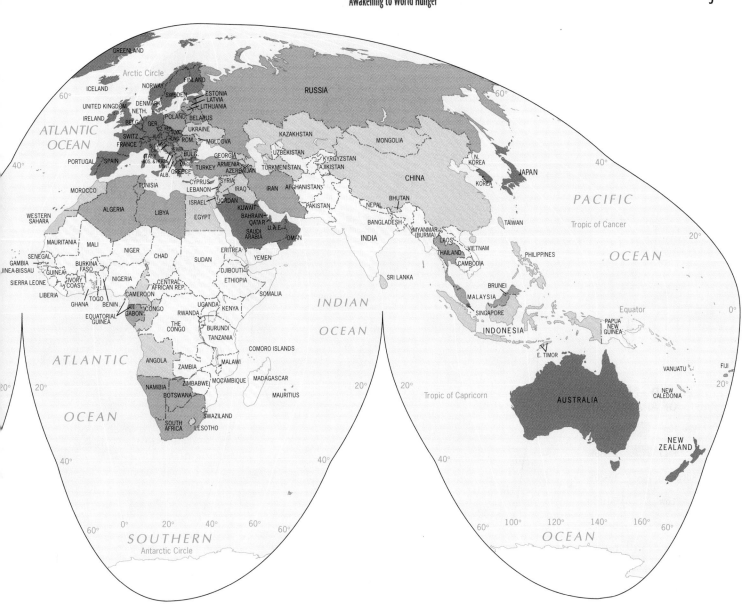

If a poor country has a small proportion of arable land, does that destine its population to a lifetime of malnourishment? It depends on the place. Of all the land classified as arable, some is much more productive than other. For example, only 8 percent of Kenya's land is arable, but the land in the western highlands is some of the most productive agricultural land in the world. Do the Kenyans simply not produce enough food on their lands? Is that what accounts for their malnutrition rate of over 30 percent? No, hunger in Kenya depends much more on what they produce, who owns the land, and how Kenya is tied into the global economy.

The most productive lands of Kenya, those in the western highlands, are owned by foreign coffee and tea corporations. Driving through the open, luxury-crop covered slopes, I saw mostly Kenyan women working the plantations. The lowland plains are dotted by small farms, many of which have been subdivided to the point of making the land unviable. Here, an even higher proportion of the people working the lands are women, but the lands are registered to their husbands or sons because, by law, they cannot own them.

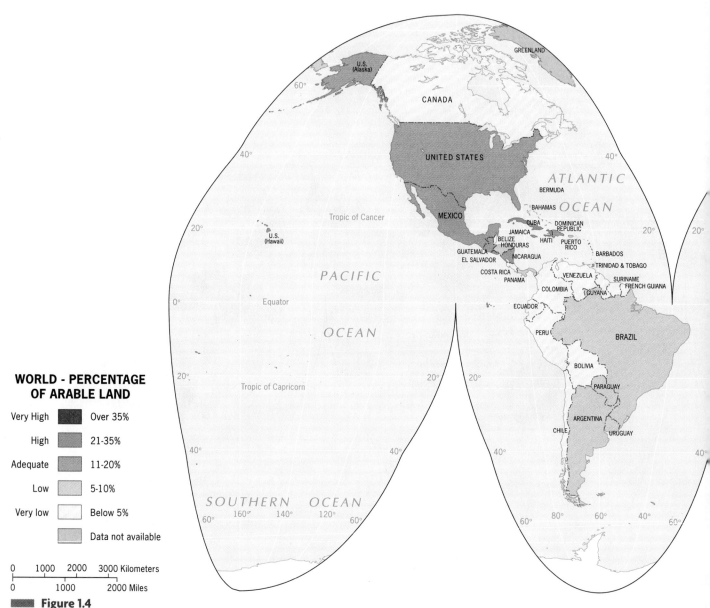

WORLD - PERCENTAGE OF ARABLE LAND

Very High		Over 35%
High		21-35%
Adequate		11-20%
Low		5-10%
Very low		Below 5%
		Data not available

0   1000   2000   3000 Kilometers

0   1000   2000 Miles

Figure 1.4

Percent of Land that is Arable (Farmable), 2005. *Data from:* United Nations Food and Agriculture Organization, 2005.

As I drove through the contrasting landscapes, I continued to question whether it would be better for the fertile highlands to carry food crops that could be consumed by the people in Kenya. I drove to the tea processing center and talked to the manager, a member of the Kikuyu ethnic group, and asked him my question. He said that his country needed foreign income and that apart from tourism, exporting coffee and tea was the main opportunity for foreign income.

As part of the global world-economy, Kenya suffers from the complexities of globalization. With foreign corporations owning Kenya's best lands, a globalized economy that thrives on foreign income, tiny farms that are unproductive, and a gendered legal system that disenfranchises the agricultural labor force and disempowers the caregivers of the country's children, Kenya has multiple factors contributing to the poverty and malnutrition in the country.

To solve one of these problems raises another. If Kenyans converted the richest lands to cash crop production, how would the poor people be able to afford the crops? What would happen to the rest of Kenya's economy and the

government itself if it lost the export revenue from tea and coffee? If Kenya lost its export revenue, how could the country pay loans it owes to global financial and development institutions?

Each of these questions requires its own path of geographic inquiry to answer. Geographers have a long tradition of **fieldwork**: they go out in the field and see what people are doing, and they observe how peoples' actions and reactions vary across space. We, the authors, have countless field experiences, and we will share these with you in order to illustrate that global processes have unique outcomes in different places.

Solving major global problems such as hunger or AIDS is complicated in our interconnected world. Each solution has its own ramifications not only in one place, but also across regions, nations, and the world. Our goals in this book are to help you see the multitude of interconnections in our world, to help you recognize the patterns of human geographic phenomena, to help you understand the uniqueness of place, and to teach you to ask and answer your own geographic questions about this world we call home.

Key Questions For Chapter 1

1. What is human geography?
2. What are geographic questions?
3. Why do geographers use maps, and what do maps tell us?
4. Why are geographers concerned with scale and connectedness?
5. What are geographic concepts, and how are they used in answering geographic questions?

WHAT IS HUMAN GEOGRAPHY?

Human geographers study people and places. The field of **human geography** focuses on how people make places, how we organize space and society, how we interact with each other in places and across space, and how we make sense of others and ourselves in our localities, regions, and the world.

Advances in communication and transportation technologies are making places and people more interconnected. Only 100 years ago, the fastest modes of transportation were the steamship, the railroad, and the horse and buggy. Today, we can cross the globe in record time, with easy access to automobiles, airplanes, and ships.

Aspects of popular culture, such as fashion and architecture, are making many people and places look more alike. Despite all these changes encouraging us to be more alike, our world still encompasses a multitude of ways in which people identify themselves and others. The world consists of nearly 200 countries, a diversity of religions, thousands of languages, and any number of settlement types from small villages to enormous global cities. All of these attributes come together in different ways around the globe to create a world of endlessly diverse places and people. Understanding and explaining this diversity is the mission of human geography.

The word "globalization" is all around us. To make sense of this phenomenon, we first need to define it. **Globalization** is a set of processes that are increasing interactions, deepening relationships, and heightening interdependence without regard to country borders. It is also a set of outcomes that are felt from these global processes—outcomes that are unevenly distributed and differently manifested across the world.

All too often, discussions of globalization focus on the pull between global—seen as a blanket covering the world—and local—seen as a continuation of the traditional despite the blanket of globalization. Geographers are in a place to understand globalization as much more than this. When geographers look at the outcomes of globalization as being distributed unevenly, they are not only talking about the local. Geographers use scale to understand the interrelationships among individual, local, regional, national, and global. What happens at the global scale affects the local, but it also affects the individual, regional and national, and similarly the processes at these scales impact the global. To reduce the world to local and global is to miss much. In this book, we study globalization, and we use scale to understand the effects of globalization and the things that shape globalization (see the discussion of scale later in this chapter).

Globalizing processes occur at the world scale; these processes bypass country borders and include global financial markets or even global environmental change. However, the processes of globalization do not magically appear at the global scale: *what happens at other scales (individual, local, regional, national) helps create the processes of globalization and shape the outcomes of globalization.*

Some argue that understanding globalization is critical to understanding the world today, whereas others maintain that globalization is overhyped. As geographers Ron Johnston, Peter Taylor, and Michael Watts explain, "Whatever your opinion may be, any intellectual engagement with social change in the twenty first century has to address this concept seriously, and assess its capacity to explain the world we currently inhabit." We integrate the concept of globalization into this textbook because processes at the global scale and processes that disregard country borders are clearly changing human geography. At the same time, as we travel the world and continue to engage in fieldwork and research, we are constantly reminded how different places and people are—processes at the individual, local, regional, and national scales continue to change human geography and shape globalization.

No place on Earth is untouched by people. As people explore, travel, migrate, interact, play, live, and work, they make places. People organize themselves into communities, nations, and broader societal networks, establishing political, economic, religious, linguistic, and cultural systems that enable them to function in space. People adapt to, alter, manipulate, and cope with their physical geographic environment. No environment stands apart from human action. Each place we see is affected by and created by people, and each place reflects the culture of the people in that place over time.

Imagine and describe the most remote place on Earth you can think of 100 years ago. Now, describe how globalization has changed this place and how the people there continue to shape it—to make it the place it is today.

WHAT ARE GEOGRAPHIC QUESTIONS?

Geographers study human phenomena such as language, religion, and identity, and they also study physical phenomena, such as landforms, climate, and environmental change. Geographers also examine the interactions between humans and environment. Human geography is the study of human phenomena on Earth, and **physical geography** is the study of physical phenomena on Earth. Geographers are trained in studying both the human and physical worlds, but most focus on one more than the other. We ask similar questions but focus on different phenomena.

Geographer Marvin Mikesell defined geography in shorthand as the "why of where." Why and how do things come together in certain places to produce particular outcomes? Why are some things found in certain places but not in others? To what extent do things in one place influence those in other places? To these questions, we add "so what?" Why does it matter that things are different across space? What role does a place play in its region and in the world, and what does that mean for people there and elsewhere? Questions such as these are at the core of geographic inquiry—whether human or physical—and they are of critical importance in any effort to make sense of our world.

If geography deals with so many aspects of our world, ranging from people and places to coastlines and climates, what do the various facets of this wide-ranging discipline have in common? The answer lies in a perspective that both human and physical geographers use: **spatial**. Whether they are human geographers or physical geographers, virtually all geographers are interested in the spatial arrangement of places and phenomena, how they are laid out, organized, and arranged on the Earth, and how they appear on the landscape.

Mapping the **spatial distribution** of a phenomenon is typically the first step to understanding it. By looking at a map of how something is distributed across space, a geographer can raise questions about how the arrangement came about, what processes create and sustain the particular **pattern** of the distribution, and what relationships exist between different places and things.

Maps in the Time of Cholera Pandemics

In **medical geography**, mapping the distribution of a disease is the first step to finding its cause. In 1854, Dr. John Snow, a noted anesthesiologist in London, mapped cases of cholera in London's Soho District. Cholera is a term used to denote a set of diseases in which diarrhea and dehydration are the chief symptoms.

Cholera is an ancient disease and was confined to India until the beginning of the nineteenth century. In 1816 it spread to China, Japan, East Africa, and Mediterranean Europe in the first of several **pandemics**, a worldwide outbreak of the disease. This initial wave abated by 1823, but by then the very name cholera was feared throughout the world, for it had killed people everywhere by the hundreds, even thousands. Death was horribly convulsive and would come in a matter of days, perhaps a week, and no one knew what caused the disease or how to avoid it.

Soon a second cholera pandemic struck. It lasted from 1826 to 1837, when cholera crossed the Atlantic and attacked North America. During the third pandemic, from 1842 to 1862, England was severely hit, and cholera again spread into North America.

When the pandemic that began in 1842 reached England in the 1850s, cholera swept through the Soho District of London. Dr. Snow mapped the Soho District, marking all the area's water pumps—from which people got their water supply for home use—with a P and marking the residence of each person who died from cholera with a dot (Fig. 1.5). Approximately

■■■ **Figure 1.5**

Cases of Cholera in the Soho District of London, England, 1854. *Adapted with permission from:* L. D. Stamp, *The Geography of Life and Death*, Cornell University Press, 1964.

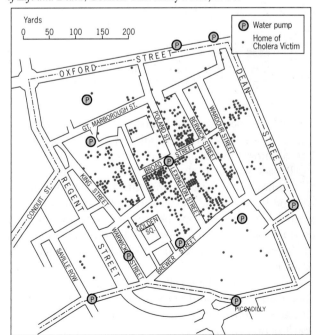

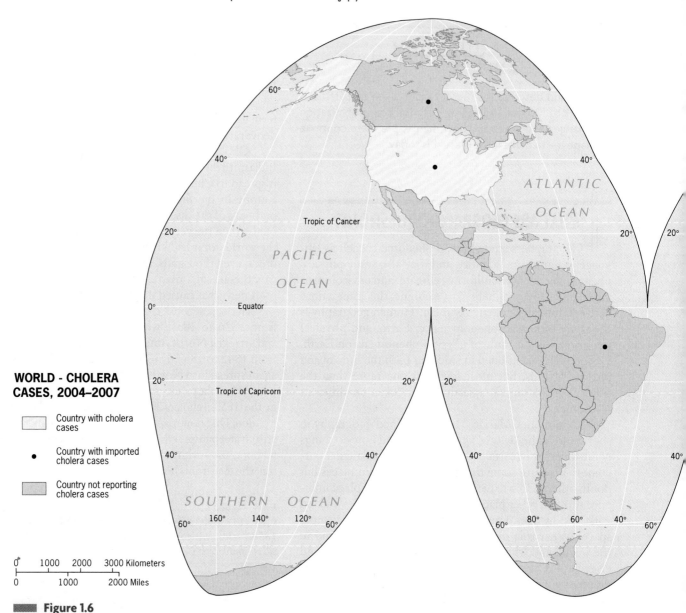

WORLD - CHOLERA CASES, 2004–2007

☐ Country with cholera cases

• Country with imported cholera cases

▨ Country not reporting cholera cases

Figure 1.6
Cases of Cholera and Imported Cholera, 2004–2007. *Reprinted by permission of:* United Nations World Health Organization, 2007.

500 deaths occurred in Soho, and as the map took shape, Snow noticed that an especially large number of those deaths clustered around the water pump on Broad Street. At the doctor's request, city authorities removed the handle from the Broad Street pump, making it impossible to get water from that pump. The result was dramatic: almost immediately the number of reported new cases fell to nearly zero. Snow's theory about the role of water in the spread of cholera was confirmed.

Dr. Snow and his colleagues advised people to boil their water, but it would be a long time before his advice reached all those who needed to know, and in any case many people simply did not have the ability to do so.

Cholera has not been defeated completely, however, and in some ways the risks have been rising in recent years rather than falling (Fig. 1.6). In the teeming shantytowns of the growing cities of the developing world, and in the refugee camps of Africa and Asia, cholera remains a threat. Until the 1990s, major outbreaks remained few and limited (after remaining cholera-free for a half century, Europe had its first reappearance of cholera in Naples in 1972), and Africa reported most cases. But an outbreak in the slums of Lima, Peru, in December 1990 became a fast-spreading **epidemic** (regional outbreak of a disease) that, though confined to the Americas, touched every country in the hemisphere, infected more than 1 million people, and killed over 10,000. In 2006, a cholera outbreak in

Angola spread quickly throughout the country. When the cholera outbreak occurred in 2006, Angola's civil war had ended, which allowed people to move around the country easier and helped spread cholera quickly.

Hygiene prevents cholera, but contaminated water abounds in much of the tropical world's cities. A cholera vaccine exists, but it remains effective for only six months, and it is costly. Dr. Snow achieved a victory through the application of geographical reasoning, but the war against cholera is not yet won.

The fruits of geographical inquiry were life-saving in this case, but the work of geographers typically goes further in life-understanding. Geographers want to understand why people do different things in different places and how the relationship between people and the physical world varies across space.

The Spatial Perspective

Geography, and being geographically literate, involves much more than memorizing places on a map. In this sense, the disciplines of geography and history have much in common. History is not merely memorizing dates. To understand history is to appreciate how events, circumstances, and ideas came together at particular times to produce certain outcomes. Knowledge of how events have developed over time is thought to be critical to understanding who we are and where we are going.

Understanding change over time is critically important, and understanding change across space is equally as important. The great German philosopher Immanuel Kant argued that we need disciplines focused not only on particular phenomena (such as economics and sociology), but also on the perspectives of time (history) and space (geography). The disciplines of history and geography have intellectual cores defined by perspective rather than by subject matter.

Human geographers use a **spatial perspective** as they study a multitude of phenomena ranging from political elections and urban shantytowns to gay neighborhoods and folk music. To bring together the many subfields of human geography and to explain to nongeographers what geographers do, four major geographical organizations in the United States came together in the 1980s and formed the Geography Educational National Implementation Project. The National Geographic Society published their findings in 1986, introducing the **five themes** of geography. The five themes are derived from the spatial perspective of geography.

The Five Themes

The first theme, **location**, highlights how the geographical position of people and things on the Earth's surface affects what happens and why. A concern with location underlies almost all geographical work, for location helps to establish the context within which events and processes are situated.

Some geographers develop elaborate (often quantitative) models describing the locational properties of particular phenomena—even predicting where things are likely to occur. Such undertakings have fostered an interest in **location theory**, an element of contemporary human geography that seeks answers to a wide range of questions—some of them theoretical, others highly practical: Why are villages, towns, and cities spaced the way they are? A geographer versed in location theory might conclude where a SuperTarget should be built (downtown or in a suburb), given the current neighborhoods and new developments, the median income of the people, the locations of other shopping areas, and the existing and future road system. Similarly, a geographer could determine the best location for a wildlife refuge, given existing wildlife habitats and migration patterns, human settlement patterns, and road networks.

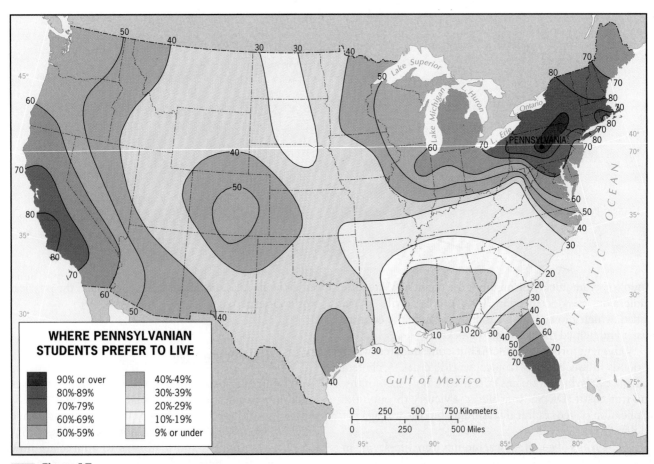

Figure 1.7

Desirable Places to Live.   Where Pennsylvanian college students would prefer to live, based on questionnaires completed by college students.   *Reprinted by permission of:* P. R. Gould and R. White, *Mental Maps*. Harmondsworth: Penguin Books, 1986, pp. 55 and 58.

A spatial perspective invites consideration of the relationship among phenomena in individual places—including the relationship between humans and the physical world. Thus, the second of the five themes concerns **human–environment** interactions. Why did the Army Corps of Engineers alter Florida's physical environment so drastically when they drained part of the Everglades? Have the changes in Florida's environment created an easier path of destruction for hurricanes? Why is the Army Corps of Engineers again changing the course of the Kissimmee River, and what does that mean for farmers around the river and residential developments in the south of Florida? Geographers study the reciprocal relationship between humans and environments.

The third theme of geography is the **region**. Phenomena are not evenly distributed on the surface of the Earth. Instead, features tend to be concentrated in particular areas, which we call regions. Geographers use fieldwork, quantitative, and qualitative methods to develop insightful descriptions of different regions of the world. Novelist James Michener once wrote that whenever he started writing a new book, he first prepared himself by turning to books written by regional geographers about the area where the action was

to occur. Understanding the regional geography of a place allows us to make sense of much of the information we have about places and digest new information about places as well.

The fourth theme is represented by the seemingly simple word **place**. All places on the surface of the Earth have unique human and physical characteristics, and one of the purposes of geography is to study the special character and meaning of places. People develop a **sense of place** by infusing a place with meaning and emotion, by remembering important events that occurred in a place, or by labeling a place with a certain character. Because we experience and give meaning to places, we can have a feeling of "home," when we are in a certain place.

We also develop **perceptions of places** we have never been through books, movies, stories, and pictures. Geographers Peter Gould and Rodney White asked college students in California and Pennsylvania: "If you could move to any place of your choice, without any of the usual financial and other obstacles, where would you like to live?" Their responses showed a strong bias for their home region and revealed that students from both regions had negative perceptions of the South, Appalachia, the Great Plains, and Utah (Fig. 1.7).

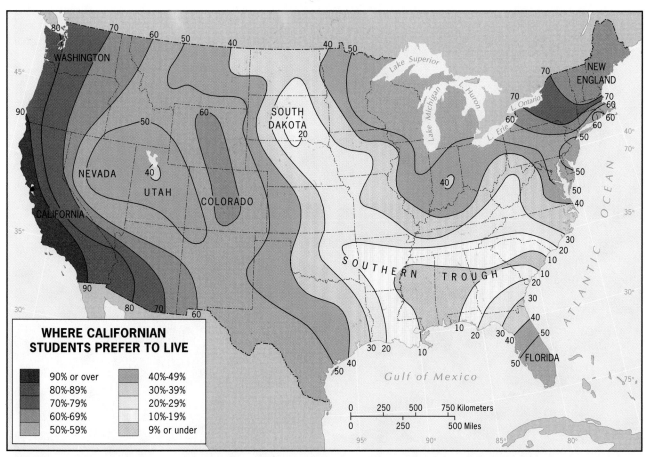

WHERE CALIFORNIAN STUDENTS PREFER TO LIVE

- 90% or over
- 80%-89%
- 70%-79%
- 60%-69%
- 50%-59%
- 40%-49%
- 30%-39%
- 20%-29%
- 10%-19%
- 9% or under

Figure 1.7 (continued)

The fifth theme, **movement**, refers to the mobility of people, goods, and ideas across the surface of the planet. Movement is an expression of the interconnectedness of places. **Spatial interaction** between places depends on the **distances** (the measured physical space between two places) among places, the **accessibility** (the ease of reaching one location from another) of places, and the transportation and communication **connectivity** (the degree of linkage between locations in a network) among places. Interactions of many kinds shape the human geography of the world, and understanding these interactions is an important aspect of the global spatial order.

Cultural Landscape

In addition to the five themes—location, human–environment, region, place, and movement—**landscape** is a core element of geography. Geographers use the term

Field Note

"Hiking to the famed Grinnell Glacier in Glacier National Park brings one close to nature, but even in this remote part of the United States the work of humans is inscribed in the landscape. The parking lot at the start of the six-mile trail, the trail itself, and the small signs en route are only part of the human story. When I arrived at the foot of the glacier, I found myself looking at a sheet of ice and snow that was less than a third the size of what it had been in 1850. The likely reason for the shrinkage is human-induced climate change. If the melt continues at present rates, scientists predict that the glacier will be gone by 2030."

Figure 1.8
Glacier National Park, United States.   © Alexander B. Murphy.

landscape to refer to the material character of a place, the complex of natural features, human structures, and other tangible objects that give a place a particular form. Human geographers are particularly concerned with the **cultural landscape**, the visible imprint of human activity on the landscape. The geographer whose name is most closely identified with this concept is former University of California at Berkeley professor Carl Sauer. In 1927, Sauer wrote an article entitled "Recent Developments in Cultural Geography," in which he argued that cultural landscapes are comprised of the "forms superimposed on the physical landscape" by human activity.

No place on Earth is in a "pristine" condition— humans have made an imprint on every place on the planet (Fig. 1.8). The cultural landscape is the visible imprint of human activity and culture on the landscape. We can see the cultural landscape in the layers of buildings, roads, memorials, churches, fields, and homes that human activities over time have imprinted on the landscape.

Any cultural landscape has layers of imprints from years of human activity. As each group of people arrived and occupied a place, they brought their own technological and cultural traditions and transformed the landscape accordingly. Each new group of residents can also be influenced by what they find when they arrive—and leave some of it in place. In 1929, Derwent Whittlesey proposed the term **sequent occupance** to refer to these sequential imprints of occupants, whose impacts are layered one on top of the other.

The Tanzanian city of Dar es Salaam provides an interesting urban example of sequent occupance. Arabs from Zanzibar first chose the African site in 1866 as a summer retreat. Next, German colonizers imprinted a new layout and architectural style (wood-beamed Teutonic) when they chose the city as the center of their East African colonies in 1891. After World War I, when the Germans were ousted, a British administration took over the city and began yet another period of transformation. The British encouraged immigration from their colony in India to Tanzania. The new migrant Asian population created a zone of three- and four-story apartment houses, which look as if they were transplanted from Bombay, India (Fig. 1.9 left and right). Then, in the early 1960s, Dar es Salaam became the capital of newly independent Tanzania. Thus, the city experienced four stages of cultural dominance in less than one century, and each stage of the sequence remains imprinted in the cultural landscape.

The cultural landscape can be seen as a kind of book offering clues into each chapter of the cultural practices, values, and priorities of its various occupiers. As geographer Peirce Lewis explained in *Axioms for Reading the Landscape* (1979), "Our human landscape is our unwitting autobiography, reflecting our tastes, our values, our aspirations, and even our fears, in tangible, visible form."

Figures 1.9, left and right
Mumbai, India (left) and Dar-es-Salaam, Tanzania (right). Apartment buildings throughout Mumbai (formerly Bombay), India are typically four stories with balconies. In Dar-es-Salaam, Tanzania, this four-story walkup with its laundry and other household items festooned on balconies and in doorways (right) stands where single-family African dwellings once stood, reflecting the sequential occupance of the city.   © Jessica, Poser, University of Illinois at Chicago (left) and Mark Carlson (right).

Like Whittlesey, Lewis recommended looking for layers of history in cultural landscapes, adding that most major changes in the cultural landscape occur after a major event—a war, an invention, an economic depression.

Geographers who practice fieldwork keep their eyes open to the world around them and through practice become adept at reading cultural landscapes. Take a walk around your campus or town and try reading the cultural landscape. Choose one thing in the landscape and ask yourself, "What is that and why is it there?" Take the time to find out the answers!

WHY DO GEOGRAPHERS USE MAPS, AND WHAT DO MAPS TELL US?

Maps are an incredibly powerful geographic tool, and **cartography**, the art and science of making maps, is as old as geography itself. (For details on cartography, see Appendix A at the end of this book.) Maps are used for countless purposes—to wage war, make political propaganda, solve medical problems, locate shopping centers, bring relief to refugees, and warn of natural hazards. **Reference maps** show locations of places and geographic features. **Thematic maps** tell stories, typically showing the degree of some attribute or the movement of a geographic phenomenon.

Reference maps focus on accuracy in showing the **absolute locations** of places, using a coordinate system that allows you to plot precisely where on Earth something is. Imagine taking an orange, drawing a dot on it with a marker, and then trying to describe the exact location of that dot to someone who is holding another orange so she can mark the same spot on her orange. If you draw and number the same coordinate system on both oranges, the task of drawing the absolute location on each orange is not only doable but is simple. Plotting absolute locations to make a reference map is simple with the use of a coordinate system, and the system most frequently used is latitude and longitude. For example, the absolute location of Chicago is 41 degrees, 53 minutes North Latitude and 87 degrees, 38 minutes West Longitude. Using these coordinates, you can plot Chicago on any globe or map that is marked with latitude and longitude.

The establishment of satellite-based **global positioning system (GPS)** allows us to locate things on the surface of the Earth with extraordinary accuracy. Researchers collect data quickly and easily in the field, and low-priced units are encouraging fishers, hunters, and hikers to use GPS in their hobbies. New cars are equipped with GPS units, and dashboard map displays help commuters navigate traffic and travelers find their way. **Geocaching** is a new hobby based on the use of GPS. Geocachers use their GPS units to play a treasure hunt game all over the world. People leave the treasures ("caches") somewhere, mark the coordinates on their GPS, and post clues on the Internet. If you find the cache, you take the treasure and leave a new one.

Relative location describes a place in relation to other human and physical features. Descriptors such as "Chicago is on Lake Michigan, south of Milwaukee" or "Chicago is located where the cross-country railroads met in the 1800s" or "Chicago is the hub of the corn and soybean markets in the Midwest" are all descriptors of Chicago relative to other features. In the southern Wisconsin, northern Illinois, and western Indiana region, all roads lead to Chicago (Fig. 1.10). Within this region, people define much of their lives relative to Chicago because of the tight interconnectedness between Chicago and the region. Northwestern Indiana is so connected to Chicago that they have a time zone separate from the rest of Indiana—allowing people in northwestern Indiana to stay in the same time zone as Chicago.

Absolute locations do not change, but relative locations are constantly modified and change over time. Fredericksburg, Virginia is located halfway between Washington, D.C. and Richmond, Virginia. Today, it is a suburb of Washington, D.C., with commuter trains, van pools, buses, and cars moving commuters between their homes in Fredericksburg and their workplaces in metropolitan Washington, D.C. During the Civil War, several bloody battles took place in Fredericksburg as the North and South fought over the land halfway between their wartime capitals. The absolute location of Fredericksburg has not changed, but its place in the world around it, its relative location, certainly has.

Mental Maps

We all carry maps in our minds of places we have been and places we have merely heard of; these are called **mental maps**. Even if you have never been to the Great Plains of the United States, you may have studied wall maps and atlases or come across the region in books, magazines, and newspapers frequently enough to envision the states of the region (North Dakota, South Dakota, Nebraska, Kansas, Oklahoma, and Texas) in your mind. Even if you have not visited the Great Plains, you will use your mental map of the region. If you hear on the news that a tornado destroyed a town in Oklahoma, you use your mental map of the Great Plains region and Oklahoma to make sense of where the tornado occurred and who was impacted.

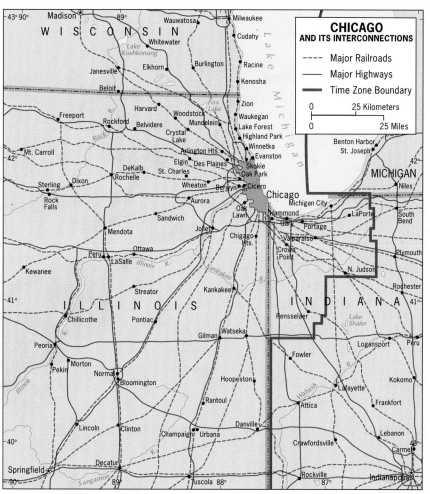

Figure 1.10

All Roads Lead to Chicago. Network of Midwestern roads that lead to Chicago, reflecting the dominance of Chicago in the region.   © E. H. Fouberg, A. B. Murphy, H. J. de Blij, and John Wiley & Sons, Inc.

Our mental maps of the places within our **activity spaces**, those places we travel to routinely in our rounds of daily activity, are more accurate and detailed than places we have never been. If your friend calls and asks you to meet her at the movie theater you go to all the time, your mental map will engage automatically. You will envision the hallway, the front door, the walk to your car, the lane to choose in order to be prepared for the left turn you must make, where you will park your car, and your path into the theater and up to the popcorn stand.

Geographers who study human–environment behavior have made extensive studies of how people develop their mental maps. The earliest humans, who were nomadic, had incredibly accurate mental maps of where to find food and seek shelter. Today, people need mental maps to find their way through the concrete jungles of cities and suburbs.

Geographers have studied the mental map formation of children, the blind, new residents to cities, men, and women, all of whom exhibit differences in the formation of mental maps. To learn new places, women, for example,

tend to use landmarks, whereas men tend to use paths. Activity spaces vary by age, and the extent of peoples' mental maps depends in part on their ages. Mental maps include *terra incognita*, unknown lands that are off-limits. If your path to the movie theater includes driving past a school that you do not go to, your map on paper will likely label the school, but no details will be shown regarding the place. However, if you have access to the school and you are instead drawing a mental map of how to get to the school's cafeteria, your mental map of the school will be quite detailed. Thus, mental maps reflect a person's activity space, what is accessible to the person in his or her rounds of daily activity and what is not.

Generalization in Maps

All maps simplify the world. A reference map of the world cannot show every place in the world, and a thematic map of hurricane tracks in the Atlantic Ocean cannot pinpoint every hurricane and its precise path for the last 50 years.

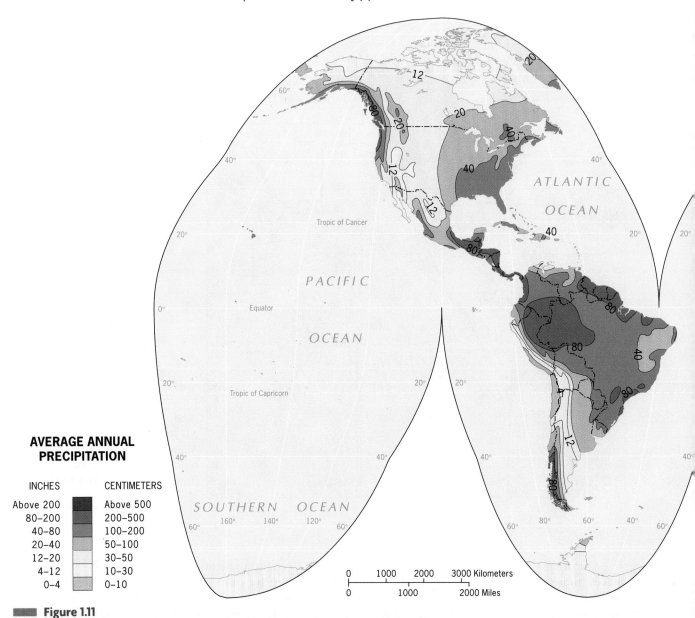

AVERAGE ANNUAL PRECIPITATION

INCHES		CENTIMETERS
Above 200		Above 500
80–200		200–500
40–80		100–200
20–40		50–100
12–20		30–50
4–12		10–30
0–4		0–10

Figure 1.11

Average Annual Precipitation of the World.   A generalized map of the mean annual precipitation received around the world.   © H. J. de Blij, P. O. Muller, and John Wiley & Sons, Inc.

When mapping data, whether human or physical, cartographers, the geographers who make maps, *generalize* the
information they present on maps. Many of the maps in
this book are thematic maps of the world. Shadings show
how much or how little of some phenomena can be found
on a part of the Earth's surface.

Generalized maps help us see general trends, but
we cannot see all cases of a given phenomenon. The
map of world precipitation (Fig. 1.11) is a **generalized map** of mean annual precipitation received around
the world. The areas shaded burgundy, dark blue,
and vibrant green are places that receive the most rain,
and those shaded in orange receive the least rain on average. Take a pen and trace along the equator on the map.
Notice how many of the high-precipitation areas on the
map are along the equator. The consistent heating of the
equator over the course of the entire year brings consistent precipitation to the equatorial region. At the scale
of the world, we can see general trends in precipitation,
such as this, but it is difficult to see the microscale climates of intense precipitation areas everywhere in the
world.

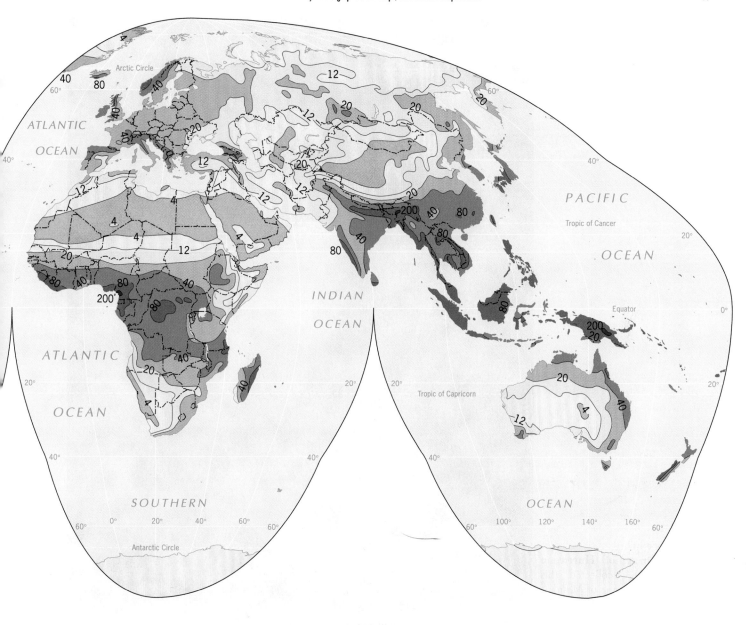

Remote Sensing and GIS

Geographic studies include both long- and short-term environmental change. Geographers monitor the Earth from a distance, using **remote sensing**, using technology that is a distance away from the place being studied. Remotely sensed data are collected by satellites and aircraft (airplanes, balloons) and are almost instantaneously available. After a major weather event, such as the 2008 floods in the Mississippi River Valley or the unprecedented hurricane season in the Gulf of Mexico in 2005, remotely sensed data show us the major areas of impact (Fig. 1.12). A remotely sensed image highlights the eye of a hurricane, and photos taken on the ground show the impact and destruction (Fig. 1.13).

In a government that is harming its citizens or that will not reliably allow foreign aid to help its citizens, remote sensing helps geographers understand the physical and human geography of the place. Google Earth is a free, web-based user-friendly set of remotely sensed images from around the world woven together and accessible to anyone with Internet access. You can think of Google Earth as a quilt of remotely sensed images, taken

Figure 1.12
Satellite image of Hurricane Katrina. NASA collected this image on the morning of Monday, August 29, 2005, shortly before the hurricane made landfall.
© AP/Wide World Photos.

all over the world, coming from several sources, and sewn together—like a patchwork quilt. As a result, the resolution (the measure of the smallest object that can be resolved by the sensor, the degree of detail) of the images (each piece of the quilt) differs.

Remotely sensed images can be incorporated in a map, and absolute locations can be studied over time by plotting change in remotely sensed images for one place over time. Advances in computer technology and data storage, increasing accessibility to locationally based data and GPS technology, and software corporations that tailor products to specific uses have all driven incredible advances in **geographic information systems** (GIS) over the last two decades. Geographers use GIS to compare a

variety of spatial data by creating digitized representations of the environment (Fig. 1.14), combining layers of spatial data, and creating maps in which patterns and processes are superimposed. Geographers also use GIS to analyze data, which can give us new insight into geographic patterns and relationships.

Geographers use GIS for applications in both human and physical geographic research. For example, political geographers use GIS to map layers showing voters, their party registration, their race, their likelihood of voting, and their income in order to determine how to draw voting districts in congressional and state legislative elections. In this case, a geographer can draw a line around a group of people and ask the computer program to tally

how many voters are inside the region, determine what the racial composition is of the district, and show how many of the current political representatives live within the new district's boundaries.

Geographers trained in GIS apply the software technologies in countless fields today. Students who earn undergraduate degrees in geography are employed by software companies, government agencies, and businesses to use GIS in surveying wildlife, mapping soils, analyzing natural disasters, following diseases, assisting first responders, planning cities, plotting transportation improvements, and tracking weather systems. For example, a group of geographers working for one GIS company tailors the GIS software to serve the branches

Figure 1.14
Two Representations of St. Francis, South Dakota.   A) panchromatic raster satellite image collected in 2002 at 10 m resolution during a grassland wildfire; B) vector data—rivers, roads, cities, and land use/land cover digitalized from the image.   Courtesy Joseph J. Kerski using ArcGIS software from Environmental Systems Research Institute, Inc.

of the military and the defense intelligence community. The vast amounts of intelligence data gathered by the various intelligence agencies can be integrated into a GIS and then analyzed spatially. Geographers working in the defense intelligence community can use GIS to query a vast amount of intelligence, interpret spatial data, and make recommendations on issues of security and defense.

The amount of data digestible in a GIS, the power of the location analysis possible with computer hardware, and the ease of analysis with GIS software applications allow geographers to answer complicated questions using GIS. For example, geographer Korine Kolivras analyzed the probability of dengue fever outbreaks in Hawaii using GIS (Fig. 1.15). The maps Kolivras produced may look as simple and straightforward as the cholera maps produced by Dr. John Snow in the 1800s, but the amount of data that went into Kolivras's analysis is staggering in comparison. Dengue fever is carried by a particular kind of mosquito called the Aedes mosquito. Kolivras analyzed the breeding conditions needed for the Aedes mosquito, including precipitation, topography, and several other variables, to predict what places in Hawaii are most likely to experience an outbreak of dengue fever.

A new term of art used in geography is GISc. Geographic information science (GISc) is an emerging research field concerned with studying the development and use of geospatial concepts and techniques to examine geographic patterns and processes. Your school may have a program in GISc that draws across disciplines, bringing together the computer scientists who write the programs, the engineers who create sensors that gather data about the Earth, and the geographers who combine layers of data and interpret them to make sense of our world.

thinking
geographically

Use Google Earth to find a place where a humanitarian crisis is occurring today (such as Myanmar or Darfur) and study the physical and human geography overlaid on Google Earth in this place. How does studying this place on Google Earth change your mental map of the place and/or your understanding of the crisis?

WHY ARE GEOGRAPHERS CONCERNED WITH SCALE AND CONNECTEDNESS?

Geographers study places and patterns at a variety of scales, including local, regional, national, and global. Scale has two meanings in geography: the first is the dis-

tance on a map compared to the distance on the Earth, and the second is the territorial extent of something. Throughout the book, when we refer to scale we are using the second of these definitions. As geographers, the scale of our research or analysis matters because we can make different observations at different scales. We can study a single phenomenon across different scales in order to see how what is happening at the global scale affects localities and how what is happening at a local scale affects the globe. Geographers recognize that phenomena, whether human or physical, happen in a context and that the context looks different at different scales.

The scale at which we study a geographic phenomenon tells us what level of detail we can expect to see. We also see different patterns at different scales. For example, when we study the distribution of wealth at the scale of the globe (see Fig. 1.3), we see the countries in western Europe, Canada, the United States, Japan, and Australia are the wealthiest, and the countries of Subsaharan Africa and Southeast Asia are the poorest. Does that mean everyone in the United States is wealthy and everyone in Indonesia is poor? Certainly not, but on a global-scale map of states, that is how the data appear.

When you shift scales to North America and examine the data for States of the United States and the provinces of Canada (Fig. 1.16), you see that the wealthiest areas are on the coasts and the poorest are in the interior and in the extreme northeast and south. The State of Alaska and the province of the Northwest Territories have high gross per capita incomes that stem largely from oil revenues that are shared among the residents.

Shifting scales again to just one city, for example, metropolitan Washington, D.C. (Fig. 1.17), you observe that suburbs west, northwest, and southwest of the city show the greatest wealth and that suburbs east and southeast have lower income levels. In the city itself, a clear dichotomy of wealth divides the northwest neighborhoods from the rest of the city. Shifting scales again to the individual, if we conducted fieldwork in Washington, DC and interviewed people who live below the poverty line, we would quickly find that each person's experience of poverty and reasons for being in poverty vary—making it difficult to generalize. We would find some trends, such as how women in poverty who have children cope differently than single men or how illegal immigrants cope differently from legal immigrants.

Because the level of detail and the patterns observed change as the scale changes, geographers must be sensitive to their scale of analysis and also be wary of researchers who make generalizations about a people or a place at a particular scale without considering other scales of analysis.

Geographers' concern with scale goes beyond an interest in the scale of individual phenomena to a concern with how processes operating at different scales influence

Guest Field Note

The diffusion of diseases carried by vectors, like the *Aedes* mosquito that transmits dengue, is not solely a result of the environmental factors in a place. I use disease ecology to understand the ways in which environmental, social, and cultural factors interact to produce disease in a place. Through a combination of fieldwork and geographic information systems (GIS) modeling, I studied the environmental habitat of the *Aedes* mosquito in Hawaii and the social and cultural factors that stimulated the outbreak of dengue in Hawaii.

When I went into the field in Hawaii, I observed the variety in the physical geography of Hawaii, from deserts to rainforests. I saw the specific local environments of the dengue outbreak area, and I examined the puddles in streams (Fig. 1.15A) in which the mosquitoes likely bred during the 2001–2002 dengue outbreak. I talked to public health officials who worked so hard to control the dengue outbreak, and I better understood the local environmental factors contributing to the disease. I visited a family who had been heavily affected by dengue, and I saw their home, which, by their choice, lacked walls or screens on all sides. In talking with the family, I came to understand the social and cultural factors that affected the outbreak of dengue in Hawaii.

I created a GIS model of mosquito habitat that considered not only total precipitation in Hawaii (Fig. 1.15B), but also seasonal variations in precipitation (Fig. 1.15C) and temperature (Fig. 1.15D), to help explain where the *Aedes* mosquito is able to breed and survive on the islands. I also studied seasonal fluctuations in streams and population distributions in creating my model of dengue potential areas (Fig. 1.15E).

The GIS model I created can now be altered by public officials in Hawaii to reflect precipitation and temperature variations each year or to incorporate new layers of environmental, social, and cultural data. Officials will be able to better predict locations of dengue outbreaks so they can focus their efforts to combat the spread of the disease.

Credit: Korine N. Kolivras, Virginia Tech

▒ Figure 1.15 A

Maui, Hawaii. *Aedes* mosquitoes breed in artificial and natural water containers, such as the standing puddles left behind when streams dry up during a drought as shown in this photograph along the northeast coast of Maui.

▒ Figure 1.15 B
Total annual precipitation.

▒ Figure 1.15 C
Average June precipitation.

▒ Figure 1.15 D
Average February minimum temperature.

▒ Figure 1.15 E
Dengue potential areas.

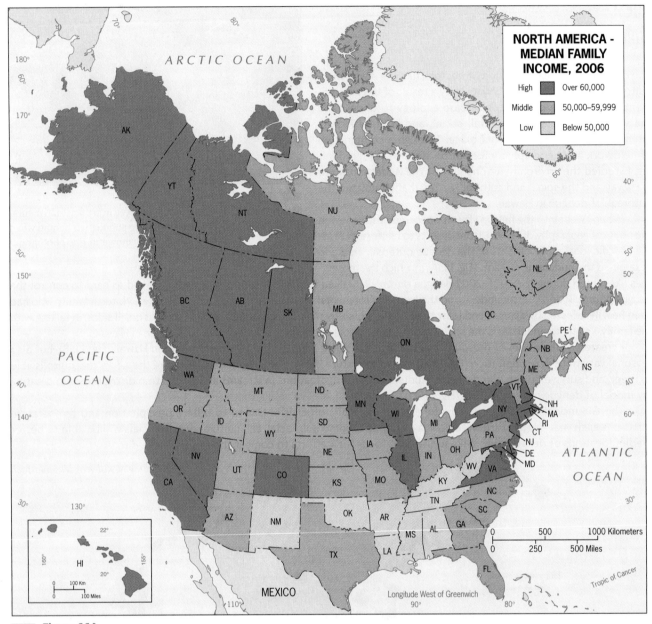

Figure 1.16
Median Family Income (in U.S. dollars), 2006. *Data from:* United States Census Bureau and Census Canada.

one another. If you want to understand the conflict between the Tutsi and the Hutu people in Rwanda, for example, you cannot look solely at this African country. The Rwandan conflict is influenced by developments at a variety of different scales, including patterns of migration and interaction in Central Africa, the economic and political relations between Rwanda and parts of Europe, and the variable impacts of globalization—economic, political, and cultural.

Geographers are also interested in how people use scale politically. Local political movements, such as like the Zapatistas in southern Mexico, have learned to **rescale**

their actions—to involve players at other scales and create a global outcry of support for their position. By taking their political campaign from the individual and local scale to the national scale through their protests against the North American Free Trade Agreement (NAFTA), and then effectively using the Internet to wage a global campaign, the Zapatistas gained attention from the world media, a feat few local political movements achieve.

Geographer Victoria Lawson uses the term *jumping scale* to describe rescaling. She compares the ways in which Western countries, multinational corporations, and the World Trade Organization all take products and ideas

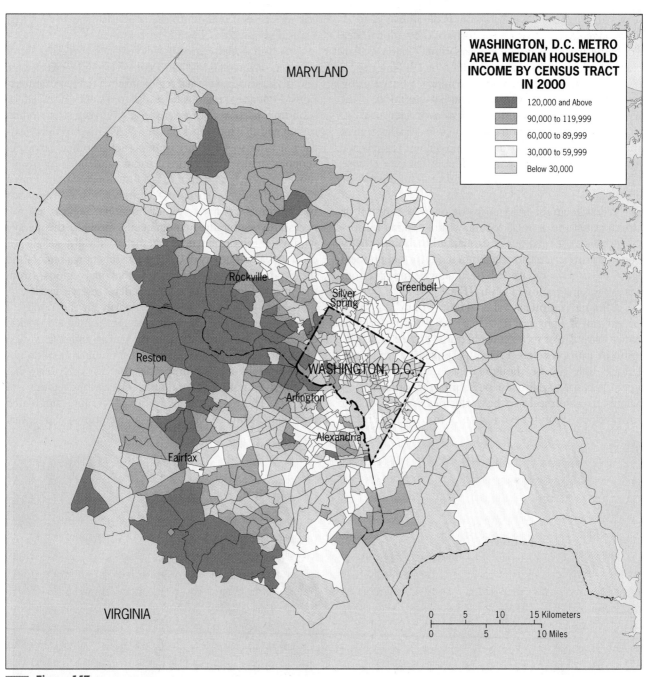

Figure 1.17
Median Family Income (in U.S. dollars), 2000. *Data from:* United States Census Bureau, 2000.

created in Western places and by Western corporations and globalize all rights to profits from them through intellectual property law. Efforts to push European and American views of intellectual property on the globe negate other local and regional views of products and ideas. To the West, rice is a product that can be owned, privatized, and bought and sold. To East Asians, rice is integral to culture, and new rice strains and new ideas about growing rice can help build community, not just profit. Lawson explains that taking a

single regional view and jumping scale to globalize it legitimates that view and negates other regional and local views.

Regions

Geographers often divide the world into regions for analysis. Many colleges offer a course in world regional geography that compares and contrasts major regions of the world. In this book, we use examples from every region of the world, but our focus throughout is on human geography. Nongeographers use some form of the regional idea all the time, even in everyday conversation. When you plan or dream of a vacation in the Rockies, or a hiking trip in New England, or a cruise in the Caribbean, you are using regional notions to convey what you have in mind. Used this way, regions serve as informal frames of reference.

In geography, a region constitutes an area that shares similar characteristics. To identify and delimit regions, we must establish criteria for them. The criteria we choose to define a region can be physical, cultural, functional, or perceptual.

When geographers choose one or more physical or cultural criteria to define a region, we are looking for formal regions. A formal region is marked by homogeneity in one or more criteria or phenomena. A formal physical region is based on a shared physical geographic criterion, such as the karst region of China (Fig. 1.18).

A **formal region** has a shared trait—it can be a shared cultural trait or a physical trait. In a formal cultural region, people share one or more cultural traits. For example, the region of Europe where French is spoken by a majority of the people can be thought of as a French-speaking region. When the scale of analysis shifts, the formal region changes. If we shift scales to the world, the French-speaking formal region expands beyond France into former French colonies of Africa and into the overseas departments that are still associated politically with France.

A **functional region** is defined by a particular set of activities or interactions that occur within it. Places that are part of the same functional region interact to create connections. Functional regions have a shared political, social, or economic purpose. For example, a city has a surrounding region within which workers commute, either to the downtown area or to subsidiary centers such as office parks and shopping malls. That entire urban area, defined by people moving toward and within it, is a functional region. Thus a functional region is a spatial system; its boundaries are defined by the limits of that system. Functional regions are not necessarily culturally homogeneous; instead, the people within the region function together politically, socially, or economically. The city of Chicago is a functional region, and the city itself is part of hundreds of functional regions—from the State of Illinois to the seventh federal reserve district.

Finally, regions may be primarily in the minds of people. **Perceptual regions** are intellectual constructs designed to help us understand the nature and distribution of phenomena in human geography. Geographers do not agree entirely on their properties, but we do concur that we all have impressions and images of various regions and cultures. These perceptions are based on our accumulated knowledge about such regions and cultures. Perceptual

Figure 1.18
Guilin, China.   The South China Karst region, bisected here by the Li River outside Guilin, is an UNESCO World Heritage Site.   © Alexander B. Murphy.

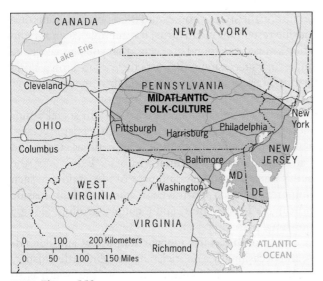

Figure 1.19
Mid-Atlantic Cultural Region. One delimitation of the Mid-Atlantic culture region. *Adapted with permission from:* H. Glassie, *Pattern in the Material Folk Culture of the Eastern United States.* Philadelphia: University of Pennsylvania Press, 1968, p. 39.

regions are not just curiosities. How people think about regions has influenced everything from daily activity patterns to large-scale international conflict. A perceptual region can include people, their cultural traits, such as dress, food, and religion; places and their physical traits, such as mountains, plains, or coasts; and built environments, such as windmills, barns, skyscrapers, or beach houses.

But where is this Mid-Atlantic region? If Maryland and Delaware are part of it, then eastern Pennsylvania is, too. But where across Pennsylvania lies the boundary of this partly cultural, partly physical region, and on what basis can it be drawn? There is no single best answer (Fig. 1.19).

Major news events help us create our perceptual regions by defining certain countries or areas of countries as part of a region. Before September 11, 2001, we all had perceptions of the Middle East region. For most of us, that region included Iraq and Iran but stretched no farther east. As the hunt for Osama bin Laden began and the media focused attention on the harsh rule of the Taliban in Afghanistan, our perceptual region of the Middle East stretched farther east to incorporate Afghanistan and Pakistan. Scholars who specialize in the region had long studied the relationship between these places and areas to the west, but the similarities between Afghanistan and Pakistan and the rest of the Middle East were almost invisible to the general population.

Perceptual Regions in the United States

Cultural geographer Wilbur Zelinsky tackled the enormous, complex task of defining and delimiting the perceptual regions of the United States and southern Canada. In an article titled "North America's Vernacular Regions," he identified 12 major perceptual regions on a series of maps (summarized in Fig. 1.20). When you examine the map, you will notice some of the regions overlap in certain places. For example, the more general term *the West* actually incorporates more specific regions, such as the Pacific Region and part of the Northwest.

The problem of defining and delimiting perceptual regions can be approached in several ways. One is to conduct interviews in which people residing within as well as outside a region are asked to respond to questions about their home and cultural environment. Zelinsky used a different technique; he analyzed the telephone directories of 276 metropolitan areas in the United States and Canada, noting the frequency with which businesses and other enterprises use regional or locational terms (such as "Southern Printing

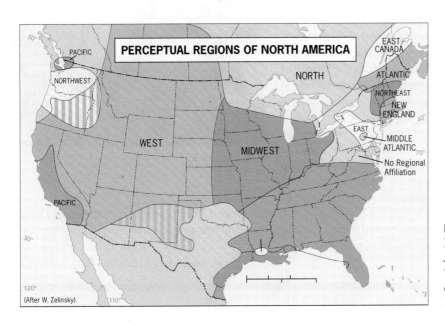

Figure 1.20
Perceptual Regions of North America. *Adapted with permission from:* W. Zelinsky, "North America's Vernacular Regions," *Annals of the Association of American Geographers,* 1980, p. 14.

Company" or "Western Printing") in their listings. The resulting maps show a close similarity between these perceptual regions and culture regions identified by geographers.

Among the perceptual regions shown in Figure 1.20, one, the South, is unlike any of the others. Even today, five generations after the Civil War, the Confederate flag still evokes strong sentiments from both those who revere the flag and those who revile it.

A "New South" has emerged over the past several decades, forged by Hispanic immigration, urbanization, movement of people from other parts of the United States to the South, and other processes. But the South—especially the rural South—continues to carry imprints of a culture with deep historical roots. Its legacy is preserved in language, religion, music, food preferences, and other traditions and customs.

If you drive southward from, say, Pittsburgh or Detroit, you will not pass a specific place where you enter this perceptual region. You will note features in the cultural landscape that you perceive to be associated with the South (such as Waffle House restaurants), and at some stage of the trip these features will begin to dominate the area to such a degree that you will say, "I am really in the South now." This may result from a combination of features in the culture: the style of houses and their porches, items on a roadside restaurant menu (grits, for example), a local radio station's music, the sound of accents that you perceive to be Southern, a succession of Baptist churches in a town along the way. These combined impressions become part of your overall perception of the South as a region.

Such cultural attributes give a certain social atmosphere to the region, an atmosphere that is appreciated by many of its residents and is sometimes advertised as an attraction for potential visitors. "Experience the South's warmth, courtesy, and pace of life," said one such commercial, which portrayed a sun-drenched seaside landscape, a bowing host, and a couple strolling along a palm-lined path.

The South has its vigorous supporters and defenders, and occasionally a politician uses its embattled history to arouse racial antagonism. But today the South is so multifaceted, diverse, vigorous, and interconnected with the rest of the United States that its regional identity is much more complicated than traditional images suggest (Fig. 1.21). This serves as an important reminder that perceptual regions are not static. Images of the South are rapidly changing, and perceptions of the South as a region will change over time.

Guest Field Note

Montgomery, Alabama

Located in a predominately African American neighborhood in Montgomery, Alabama, the street intersection of Jeff Davis and Rosa Parks is symbolic of the debates and disputes in the American South over how the past is to be commemorated on the region's landscape. The Civil War and civil rights movement are the two most important events in the history of the region. The street names commemorate Montgomery's central role in both eras, and they do so in the same public space. Montgomery was the site of the first capital of the Confederacy in 1861 while Jefferson Davis was president. The Alabama capital was also the site of the 1955–1956 Montgomery bus boycott that launched the civil rights movement. The boycott was sparked by Rosa Parks's arrest after she refused to give up her seat on a city bus when ordered to do so by a white person. Most of my research examines the politics of how the region's white and African

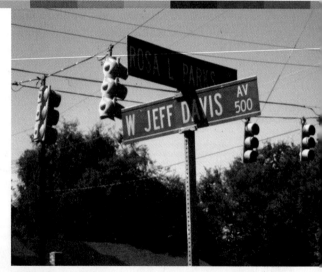

Figure 1.21

Americans portray these separate heroic eras within the region's public spaces, ranging from support for and against flying the Confederate flag to disputes over placing statues and murals honoring the Civil War and the civil rights movement on the South's landscape.

Credit: Jonathan Leib, Old Dominion University

Regions—whether formal, functional, or perceptual—are ways of organizing humans geographically. They are a form of spatial classification, a means of handling large amounts of information so we can make sense of it.

Culture

At the heart of human geography lies the concept of **culture**. Location decisions, patterns, and landscapes are fundamentally influenced by cultural attitudes and practices. Culture refers not only to the music, literature, and arts of a society but also to all the other features of its way of life: prevailing modes of dress; routine living habits; food preferences; the architecture of houses and public buildings; the layout o f fields and farms; and systems of education, government, and law. Culture is an all-encompassing term that identifies not only the whole tangible lifestyle of peoples, but also their prevailing values and beliefs.

The concept of culture is closely identified with the discipline of anthropology, and over the course of more than a century anthropologists have defined it in many different ways. Some have stressed the contributions of humans to the environment, whereas others have emphasized learned behaviors and ways of thinking. Several decades ago the noted anthropologist E. Adamson Hoebel defined culture as

> *[the] integrated system of learned behavior patterns which are characteristic of the members of a society and which are not the result of biological inheritance…culture is not genetically predetermined; it is noninstinctive… [culture] is wholly the result of social invention and is transmitted and maintained solely through communication and learning.*

Hoebel's emphasis on communication and learning anticipated the current view of culture as a system of meaning, not just a set of acts, customs, or material products. Clifford Geertz advanced this view in his classic work, *The Interpretation of Cultures* (1973), which has influenced much recent work in human geography. Hence, human geographers are interested not just in the different patterns and landscapes associated with different culture groups, but in the ways in which cultural understandings affect both the creation and significance of those patterns and landscapes.

Cultural geographers identify a single attribute of a culture as a **culture trait**. For example, the wearing of a turban can be a culture trait of certain Muslim societies; for centuries, it was obligatory for Muslim men to wear this headgear. Although it is no longer required everywhere, the turban continues to be a distinctive trait of many Muslim societies.

Culture traits are not necessarily confined to a single culture. More than one culture may exhibit a particular culture trait, but each will consist of a discrete combination of traits. Such a combination is referred to as a **culture complex**. In many cultures, the herding of cattle is a trait. However, cattle are regarded and used in different ways by different cultures. The Maasai of East Africa, for example, follow their herds along seasonal migration paths, consuming blood and milk as important ingredients of a unique diet. Cattle occupy a central place in Maasai existence; they are the essence of survival, security, and prestige. Although the Maasai culture complex is only one of many cattle-keeping complexes, no other culture complex exhibits exactly the same combination of traits. In Europe, cattle are milked, and dairy products, such as butter, yogurt, and cheese, are consumed as part of a diet very different from that of the Maasai.

A **cultural hearth** is an area where cultural traits develop and from which the cultural traits diffuse. Often a cultural trait, for example, the religion of Islam, can be traced to a single place and time. Muhammad founded Islam in the 500s C.E. (current era) in and around the cities of Mecca and Medina on the Arabian Peninsula. Other culture traits, such as agriculture, can be traced to several hearths thousands of years apart. The term for a trait with many hearths that developed independent of each other is **independent invention**.

Connectedness through Diffusion

Diffusion occurs through the movement of people, goods, or ideas across space. The process of dissemination, the spread of an idea or innovation from its hearth (source area) to other places, is known as **cultural diffusion**. Carl Sauer focused attention on this process in *Agricultural Origins and Dispersals* in which he defined the ancient hearths of agriculture and traced the diffusion of agricultural practices from the hearths. In 1970, Swedish geographer Torsten Hägerstrand published pioneering research on the role of time in the diffusion process. Hägerstrand's research revealed how time, as well as distance, affects individual human behavior and the diffusion of people and ideas. Sauer and Hägerstrand's fascinating research attracted many geographers to the study of diffusion processes. Geographers are still using principles of diffusion to model movement and diffusion through GIS and other geographic techniques.

Whether diffusion of a cultural trait occurs depends, in part, on time and distance from the hearth. The farther a place is from the hearth, the less likely an innovation is to be adopted. Similarly, the acceptance of an innovation becomes less likely the longer it takes to reach its potential adopters. In combination, time and distance cause **time-distance decay** in the diffusion process.

Cultural barriers can also work against diffusion. Certain innovations, ideas, or practices are not acceptable or adoptable in particular cultures because of prevailing attitudes or even taboos. Prohibitions against alcoholic beverages, as well as certain forms of meat, fish, and other foods, restrict their consumption in certain areas. Cultural barriers against other practices, such as the use of contraceptives, also have inhibited diffusion processes. Cultural barriers can pose powerful obstacles to the spread of ideas as well as artifacts.

Expansion Diffusion

Geographers classify diffusion processes into two broad categories: expansion diffusion and relocation diffusion. In the case of **expansion diffusion**, an inno-

vation or idea develops in a hearth and remains strong there while also spreading outward (Fig. 1.22). Later, for example, we will study the spread of Islam from its hearth on the Arabian Peninsula to Egypt and North Africa, through Southwest Asia, and into West Africa. This is a case of expansion diffusion. If we were to draw a series of maps of followers of Islam (Muslims) at 50-year intervals beginning in 620 C.E., the area of adoption of Islam would be larger in each successive period.

Expansion diffusion takes several forms. The spread of Islam is an example of **contagious diffusion**, a form of expansion diffusion in which nearly all adjacent individuals and places are affected. A disease can spread in this way, infecting almost everyone in a population (although not everyone may show symptoms of the disease). However, an idea such as a new fashion or new genre of music may not always spread throughout a contiguous population. For example, the spread of Crocs

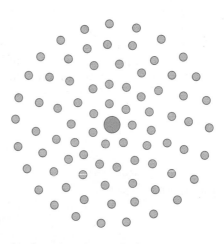

A. Contagious Diffusion

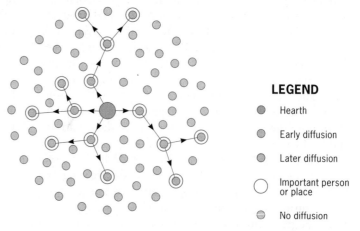

B. Hierarchial Diffusion

LEGEND
- Hearth
- Early diffusion
- Later diffusion
- Important person or place
- No diffusion

■ Figure 1.22
Contagious and Hierarchical Diffusion. © E. H. Fouberg,
A. B. Murphy, H. J. de Blij, and John Wiley & Sons, Inc.

footwear is a case of **hierarchical diffusion**, a pattern in which the main channel of diffusion is some segment of those who are susceptible to (or adopting) what is being diffused. In the case of Crocs, founder Scott Seamans found a clog manufactured by a Canadian company that was created out of the unique croc resin material. Seamans, an avid sailor, put a strap on the back and holes for drainage. He and two co-founders of the crocs company based the company in Boulder, Colorado, had the shoes manufactured, and sold them at boat shows in 2002 and 2003. Crocs footware diffused from boating enthusiasts to gardeners, to the American public—becoming especially popular among children, who adorned their crocs with Jibbitz, or charms designed for crocs. The hierarchy of boaters, gardeners, and then the contagious diffusion that followed helps explain the rapid growth of the crocs brand, which had revenues of over $800 million in 2007.

A third form of expansion diffusion is **stimulus diffusion**. Not all ideas can be readily and directly adopted by a receiving population; some are simply too vague, too unattainable, too different, or too impractical for immediate adoption. Yet, these ideals can still have an impact. They may indirectly promote local experimentation and eventual changes in ways of doing things. For example, the diffusion of mass-produced food items in the late twentieth century—pushed by multinational retailers—led to the introduction of the hamburger to India. Yet the Hindu religion in India prohibits consumption of beef. This was a major cultural obstacle to the adoption of the hamburger (Fig. 1.23). Instead, retailers began selling burgers made of vegetable products—an adaptation that was stimulated by the diffusion of the hamburger but that took on a new form in the cultural context of India.

Relocation Diffusion

Expansion diffusion spreads across space without people physically moving to become "knowers" of the trait or innovation. With expansion diffusion, the people stay put and the innovation, idea, trait, or disease does the moving. **Relocation diffusion**, in contrast, involves the actual movement of individuals who have already adopted the idea or innovation, and who carry it to a new, perhaps distant, locale, where they proceed to disseminate it (Fig. 1.22).

Relocation diffusion occurs most frequently through migration. When migrants move from their homeland, they take their cultural traits with them. Developing an ethnic neighborhood in a new country helps immigrants maintain their culture in the midst of an unfamiliar one. If the homeland of the immigrants loses enough of its population, the cultural customs may fade in the hearth while gaining strength in the ethnic neighborhoods abroad.

▬ Figure 1.23 left and right
New Delhi, India (left) and Vrindavan, India (right).   Hindus believe cows are holy, and in India, evidence of that can be seen everywhere from cows roaming the streets to the menu at McDonald's. In 1996, the first McDonald's restaurant opened in New Delhi, India (left), serving Maharaja Macs and Vegetable Burgers with Cheese. In Indian towns, such as Vrindavan (right), cows are protected and share the streets with pedestrians, bicyclists, and motorists.   © Douglas E. Gurran/AFP/Getty Images (left) and AP/Wide World Photos (right).

Once you think about different types of diffusion, you will be tempted to figure out what kind of diffusion is taking place for all sorts of goods, ideas, or diseases. Please remember that any good, idea, or disease can diffuse in more than one way. Choose a good, idea, or disease as an example and describe how it diffused from its hearth across the globe, referring to at least three different types of diffusion.

WHAT ARE GEOGRAPHIC CONCEPTS, AND HOW ARE THEY USED IN ANSWERING GEOGRAPHIC QUESTIONS?

Geographic concepts include most of the bold-faced words in this chapter, such as relative location, mental map, perceptual region, diffusion, and cultural landscape. In doing geographic research, a geographer thinks of a geographic question, one that has a spatial or landscape component, chooses the scale(s) of analysis, and then applies one or more geographic concepts to conduct research and answer the question. Geographers use fieldwork, remote sensing, GIS, GPS, and qualitative and quantitative techniques to explore linkages among people and places and to explain differences across people, places, scales, and times.

Research in human geography today stems from a variety of theories and philosophies. To understand what geographers do and how they do it, it is easiest to start by defining what geography is not. Today's geography is not environmental determinism.

Rejection of Environmental Determinism

The ancient Greeks, finding that some of the peoples subjugated by their expanding empire were relatively docile while others were rebellious, attributed such differences to variations in climate. Over 2000 years ago, Aristotle described northern European people as "full of spirit … but incapable of ruling others," and he characterized Asian people (by which he meant modern-day Turkey) as "intelligent and inventive … [but] always in a state of subjection and slavery." Aristotle attributed these traits to the respective climates of the regions—the cold north versus the more tropical Mediterranean.

Aristotle's views on this topic were long-lasting. As recently as the first half of the twentieth century, similar notions still had strong support. In 1940, in the *Principles of Human Geography*, Ellsworth Huntington and C.W. Cushing wrote:

> *The well-known contrast between the energetic people of the most progressive parts of the temperate zone and the inert inhabitants of the tropics and even of intermediate regions, such as Persia, is largely due to climate… the people of the cyclonic regions rank so far above those of the other parts of the world that they are the natural leaders.*

The doctrine expressed by these statements is referred to as **environmental determinism**. It holds that human behavior, individually and collectively, is strongly affected by—even controlled or determined by—the physical environment. It suggests that climate is the critical factor in how humans behave. Yet what constitutes an "ideal" climate lies in the eyes of the beholder. For Aristotle, it was the climate of Greece. Through the eyes of more recent commentators from Western Europe and North America, the climates most suited to progress and productiveness in culture, politics, and technology are (you guessed it) those of Western Europe and the northeastern United States.

For a time, some geographers attempted to explain the location of major cultural hearths as solely a function of environment. Quite soon, however, certain geographers doubted whether these sweeping generalizations were valid. They recognized exceptions to the environmental determinists' theories (for example, the Maya civilization in the Americas arose in a tropical climate that most assumed was incapable of complex cultures) and argued that humanity was capable of much more than merely adapting to the natural environment. The many environmentally determinist theories that explain Europe as "superior" to the rest of the world because of the climate and location of the region ignore the fact that for thousands of years, the most technologically advanced civilizations were found outside of Europe in North Africa, Southwest Asia, Southeast Asia, and East Asia.

Chipping away at environmentally determinist theories helped move the geographic study of the relationships between human society and the environment in different directions, but for several decades some geographers still held to environmental determinist positions. In *Climate and the Energy of Nations* (1947), Sidney Markham thought that by tracing the migration of the center of power in the Mediterranean (from Egypt to

Greece to Rome), he could detect the changing climates of that part of Europe during several thousand years of glacial retreat. Markham saw the northward movement of **isotherms**—lines connecting points of equal temperature values—as a key factor in the shifting centers of power in the Ancient World. Basically, he argued that as new places "thawed" after the Ice Age, they became the center of power.

Geographers grew increasingly cautious about such speculative notions, however, and they began asking new questions about human–environment relationships. If generalizations were to be made, they felt they ought to arise from detailed, carefully designed research. Everyone agrees that the natural environment affects human activity in some ways, but people are the decision makers and the modifiers—not just the slaves of environmental forces. People and their cultures shape environments, constantly altering the landscape and affecting environmental systems.

Possibilism

Reactions to environmental determinism produced counterarguments. An approach known as **possibilism** emerged—espoused by geographers who argued that the natural environment merely serves to limit the range of choices available to a culture. The choices that a society makes depend on what its members need and on what technology is available to them. Geographers increasingly accepted the doctrine of possibilism, and geographers increasingly discredited environmental determinism. For those who have thought less carefully about the human–environment dynamic, environmental determinism continues to hold an allure, leading to some highly questionable generalizations about the impact of the environment on humans and a multitude of popular books that use environment as the dominant force in explaining complex histories.

Even possibilism has its limitations because it encourages a line of inquiry that starts with the physical environment and asks what it allows. Human cultures frequently push the boundaries of what is "environmentally possible" through advances in technology—their own ideas and ingenuity. In the interconnected, technologically dependent world we live in today, it is possible to do many things that are at odds with the local environment.

Research today tends to focus on how and why humans have altered environment, and on the sustainability of their practices. In the process, the perspectives of **cultural ecology** (an area of inquiry concerned with culture as a system of adaptation to and alteration of environment) have been supplemented by those of **political ecology**—an area of inquiry fundamentally concerned with the environmental consequences of dominant political-economic arrangements and understandings (see Chapter 13). The fundamental point is that human societies are diverse and the human will is too powerful to be determined by environment.

Today's Human Geography

Human geography encompasses many subdisciplines, including political geography, economic geography, population geography, and urban geography. Human geography also incorporates cultural geography, including cultural traits such as religion, language, and ethnicity.

Cultural geography is both part of human geography and also its own approach to all aspects of human geography. Cultural geography looks at the ways culture is implicated in the full spectrum of topics addressed in human geography. As such, cultural geography can be seen as a perspective on human geography as much as a component of it.

To appreciate more fully the vast topics researched by human geographers, we can examine the multitude of careers human geographers pursue. Human geographers have titles such as location analyst, urban planner, diplomat, remote sensing analyst, geographic information scientist, area specialist, travel consultant, political analyst, intelligence officer, cartographer, educator, soil scientist, transportation planner, park ranger, or environmental consultant. All of these careers and more are open to geographers because each of these fields is grounded in place and is advanced through spatial analysis.

Choose a geographic concept introduced in this chapter. Think about something that is of personal interest to you (music, literature, politics, science, sports), and think about how you could use a geographic concept to study this interest. Think about space and location, your geographic concept, and your interest. Write a geographic question that could be the foundation of a geographic study.

Summary

Our study of human geography will analyze people and places and explain how they interact across space and time to create our world. Chapters 2 and 3 lay the basis for our study of human geography by looking at where people live. Chapters 4–7 focus on aspects of culture and how people use culture and identity to make sense of themselves in their world. The remaining chapters examine how people have created a world in which they function economically, politically, and socially, and how their activities in those realms re-create themselves and their world.

Geographic Concepts

fieldwork	accessibility	culture
human geography	connectivity	culture trait
globalization	landscape	culture complex
physical geography	cultural landscape	cultural hearth
spatial	sequent occupance	independent invention
spatial distribution	cartography	cultural diffusion
pattern	reference maps	time-distance decay
medical geography	thematic maps	cultural barrier
pandemic	absolute location	expansion diffusion
epidemic	global positioning system	contagious diffusion
spatial perspective	geocaching	hierarchical diffusion
five themes	relative location	stimulus diffusion
location	mental map	relocation diffusion
location theory	activity space	geographic concept
human–environment	generalized map	environmental
region	remote sensing	determinism
place	geographic information	isotherm
sense of place	systems	possibilism
perception of place	rescale	cultural ecology
movement	formal region	political ecology
spatial interaction	functional region	
distance	perceptual region	

Learn More Online

About Careers in Geography
www.aag.org
http://www.bls.gov/opub/ooq/2005/spring/art01.pdf

About Geocaching
www.geocaching.org

About Globalization and Geography
www.lut.ac.uk/gawc/rb/rb40.html

About John Snow and His Work on Cholera
http://www.ph.ucla.edu/epi/snow.html

About the State of Food Insecurity in the World
www.fao.org

About World Hunger
www.wfp.org

About Google Earth
www.googleearth.com

Watch It Online

About Globalization
www.learner.org/resources/series180.html#program_descriptions
click on Video On Demand for "One Earth, Many Scales"

CHAPTER 2

Population

Field Note | Where Are the Children?

Figure 2.1
Bordeaux, France. People stroll through the historic streets of Bordeaux, France. © H. J. de Blij.

My mind was on wine. I was in Bordeaux, France, walking down the street to the Bordeaux Wines Museum (Musée des Vins de Bordeaux) with a friend from the city. Having just flown from Dakar, Senegal, after spending several weeks in Subsaharan Africa, I found my current surroundings strikingly different. Observing the buildings and the people around me, I noticed that after having been among so many young children in Subsaharan Africa, the majority of the inhabitants I encountered in Bordeaux were of an aging population.

I turned to my friend and asked, "Where are all the children?" He looked around, pointed, and replied, "There goes one now!"

In Bordeaux, in Paris, in all of France and the rest of Europe, there are fewer children and populations are aging (Fig. 2.1). To reach replacement levels—to keep a population stable over time without immigration—the women of childbearing age in a country need a total fertility rate (TFR) of 2.1. The TFR reports the average number of children born to a woman of childbearing age. At the beginning of this century, more than 60 countries, containing 45 percent of the world's population, had fallen below this replacement level (Fig. 2.2).

In the 1980s, in the midst of a population explosion, Kenya recorded one of the highest TFRs ever, 8.1. Today, parts of Italy are recording the lowest TFRs ever, as low as 0.8 in Bologna. Not a single country in Europe is above replacement levels at present. By 2030, people in Germany over 65 may well account for nearly half the adult population, as compared with one-fifth now. Many other European countries are on a similar trajectory, and even countries with large populations, such as Brazil and China will likely experience substantial aging of the population as their growth rates decline.

Why are women having fewer children? In wealthier countries, more women are choosing to stay in school, work on careers, and marry later, delaying childbirth. Couples worry about the higher cost of raising children and delay starting a family in order to be better prepared financially. In some countries, such as China, governments are administrating lower birth rates. In other countries, such as India, the cultural costs associated with having children, such as providing dowries for girls, are resulting in higher abortion rates, particularly if the woman is pregnant with a girl.

An aging population requires substantial social adjustments. Older people retire and eventually suffer health problems, so they need pensions and medical care. The younger workers in the population must work in order to provide the tax revenues to enable the state to pay for these services. As the proportion of older people in a country increases, the proportion of younger people decreases. Thus, fewer young workers are providing tax revenues to support programs providing services for more retired people. To change the age distribution of an aging country and provide more taxpayers, the only answer is immigration: influxes of younger workers to do the work locals are unable (or unwilling) to do. In recent decades immigrants have come to play a critical role in the United States' economy. Yet immigration can create its own set of social issues, as has already happened in Germany with its large Turkish and Kurdish immigration, in France with its Algerian-Muslim influx, and in the United States with the arrival of immigrants from Latin America.

What will happen when a country resists immigration despite an aging population? Over the next half-century, Japan will be an interesting case study. Japan's population is no longer growing, and projections indicate the Japanese population will decline as it ages, falling from just over 128 million in 2008 to around 100 million in 2050 (some predictions are lower). Japan was a closed society for hundreds of years, and even today, the Japanese government discourages immigration and encourages homogeneity of the population. More than 98 percent of the country's population is Japanese, according to government statistics. The British newspaper *The Guardian* reported that the Japanese government's efforts to maintain the homogeneity of the population are often "lauded domestically as a reason for the country's low crime rate" and strong industrial economy.

Today, TFRs are falling almost everywhere on Earth, in large part because of family planning. In some countries fertility rates are declining dramatically. Kenya's TFR is now down to 4.8; China's fell from 6.1 to 1.75 in just 35 years. Once the government of Iran began to allow family planning, the TFR fell from 6.8 in 1980 to 1.7 in 2008.

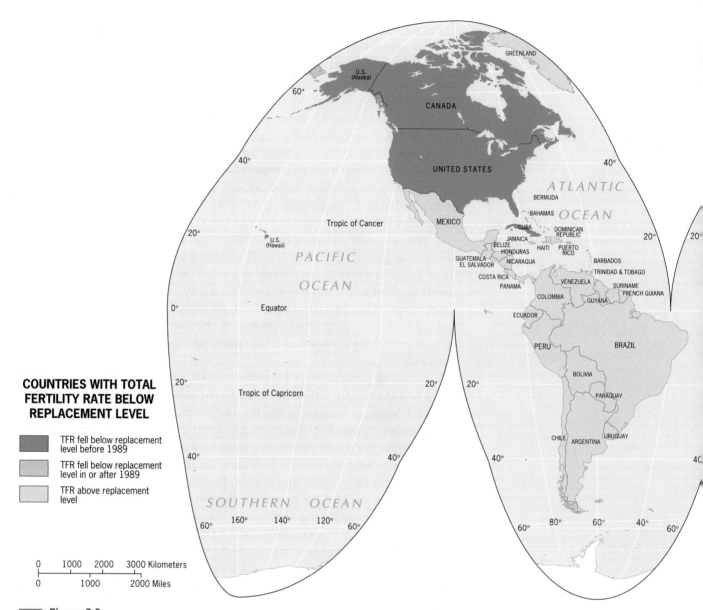

**COUNTRIES WITH TOTAL
FERTILITY RATE BELOW
REPLACEMENT LEVEL**

TFR fell below replacement
level before 1989

TFR fell below replacement
level in or after 1989

TFR above replacement
level

Figure 2.2
Year that Total Fertility Rate among Women Fell below Replacement Levels.
Data from: World Bank, World Development Indicators, 2004.

Having a low TFR was once a status symbol—a goal few governments were able to reach. Realizing now that a young, working population is a necessity for providing tax revenues to support the aging population, governments are getting creative. Countries that desire a larger, younger population, such as Sweden, are providing major financial incentives, like year-long, paid maternity leaves and state-funded daycare, to encourage women to have children.

These programs have had limited success in encouraging sustained population growth. When you walk down the streets of Stockholm, Sweden or Bordeaux, France today, you may ask yourself, "Where are all the children?"

In this chapter, we discuss where people live and why they live where they do. We also examine the rising world population and contrast it with the aging population within particular regions and countries. We look at the ramifications

of population change and of diseases, and we question how governments affect population change.

Key Questions For Chapter 2

1. Where in the world do people live and why?
2. Why do populations rise or fall in particular places?
3. Why does population composition matter?
4. How does the geography of health influence population dynamics?
5. How do governments affect population change?

WHERE IN THE WORLD DO PEOPLE LIVE AND WHY?

When geographers study population, we explain population traits across space. Demography is the study of population, and population geographers work with demographers, asking why demographic problems vary not only from region to region and country to country, but also within countries.

Demographers report the **population density** of a country as a measure of total population relative to land size (Fig. 2.3). Population density assumes an even distribution of the population over the land. The United

States, for example, with a territory of 3,717,425 square miles or 9,629,167 square kilometers (including the surfaces of lakes and ponds and coastal waters up to three nautical miles from shore) had a population of 302.7 million in 2008. This yields an average population density for the United States of just over 81 per square mile (31.5 per square kilometer). This density figure is also known as the country's **arithmetic population density**, and in a very general way it emphasizes the contrasts between the United States and such countries as Bangladesh (2738 per square mile), the Netherlands (1046), and Japan (878).

No country has an evenly distributed population, and arithmetic population figures do not reflect the emp-

Field Note

"An overpass across one of Yangon's busy streets provides a good perspective on the press of humanity in lowland Southeast Asia. Whether in urban areas or on small back roads in the countryside, people are everywhere—young and old, fit and infirm. When population densities are high in areas of

poverty and unsophisticated infrastructure, vulnerabilities to natural hazards can be particularly great. This became stunningly evident in 2008 when a tropical cyclone devastated a significant swath of the Irrawaddy delta south of Yangon, killing some 100,000 people and leaving millions homeless."

Figure 2.3
Yangon, Mayanmar (Burma).   © Alexander B. Murphy.

tiness of most of Alaska and the sparseness of population in much of the West. In other cases, it is actually quite misleading. Egypt, with a population of 78.6 million in 2008, has a seemingly moderate arithmetic population density of 203 per square mile. Egypt's territory of 386,660 square miles, however, is mostly desert, and the vast majority of the population is crowded into the valley and delta of the Nile River. An estimated 98 percent of all Egyptians live on just 3 percent of the country's land, so, the arithmetic population density figure is meaningless in this case (Fig. 2.4 top, bottom).

Physiologic Population Density

A superior index of population density relates the total population of a country or region to the area of *arable* (farmable) land it contains. This is called the **physiological population density**, defined as the number of people per unit area of agriculturally productive land. Take again the case of Egypt. Although millions of people live in its great cities (Cairo and Alexandria) and smaller urban centers, the irrigated farmland is densely peopled as well. When we measure the entire population of Egypt relative to the arable land in the country, the resulting physiologic density figure for Egypt in the year 2008 is 6776 per square mile. This number is far more reflective of Egypt's population pressure, and it continues to rise rapidly despite Egypt's efforts to expand its irrigated farmlands.

Appendix B (at the end of this book) provides complete data on both arithmetic and physiologic population densities, and some of the data stand out markedly. Mountainous Switzerland's high physiologic density should be expected: it is 10 times as high as its arithmetic density. But note Ukraine, with its vast farmlands: its physiologic density is only 1.7 times as high as its arithmetic density. Also compare the high physiologic densities in Middle America (see Puerto Rico) to the moderate data for South America, where Argentina has one of the lowest indices in the world. Furthermore, note that India's physiologic density is the lowest in South Asia despite its huge population (and is less than twice as high as its arithmetic density), whereas China's physiologic density in 2008 was some 40 percent higher. Both China and India have populations well over 1 billion, but according to the physiologic density, India has much more arable land per person than China.

Population Distribution

People are not distributed evenly across the world or within a country. One-third of the world's population lives in China and India. Yet, each country has large expanses of land (the Himalayas in India and a vast interior desert

Field Note

"The contrasting character of the Egyptian landscape could not be more striking. Along the Nile River, the landscape is one of green fields, scattered trees, and modest houses, as along this stretch of the river's west bank near Luxor (Fig. 2.4 top). But anytime I wander away from the river, brown, wind-sculpted sand dominates the scene as far as the eye can see (Fig. 2.4 bottom). Where people live and what they do is not just a product of culture; it is shaped by the physical environment as well."

Figure 2.4 top
Luxor, Egypt. © Alexander B. Murphy.

Figure 2.4 bottom
Luxor, Egypt. © Alexander B. Murphy.

in China) where people are absent or sparsely distributed. In addition to studying population densities, geographers study **population distributions**—descriptions of locations on the Earth's surface where individuals or groups (depending on the scale) live. Geographers often represent population distributions on **dot maps**, in which one dot represents a certain number of a population. At the local scale, a dot map of population can show each individual farm in a sparsely populated rural area. At the global scale, the data are much more generalized. In the following section of this chapter, we study a dot map of the global population.

World Population Distribution and Density

From the beginning of humanity, people have been unevenly distributed over the land. Today, contrasts between crowded countrysides and bustling cities on the one hand and empty reaches on the other hand have only intensified. Historically, people tended to congregate in places where they could grow food—making for a high correlation between arable land and population density. Cities began in agricultural areas, and for most of history, people lived closest to the most agriculturally productive areas. In recent history, advances in agricultural technol-

Figure 2.5
World Population Distribution.   © H. J. de Blij, P. O. Muller, and John Wiley & Sons, Inc.

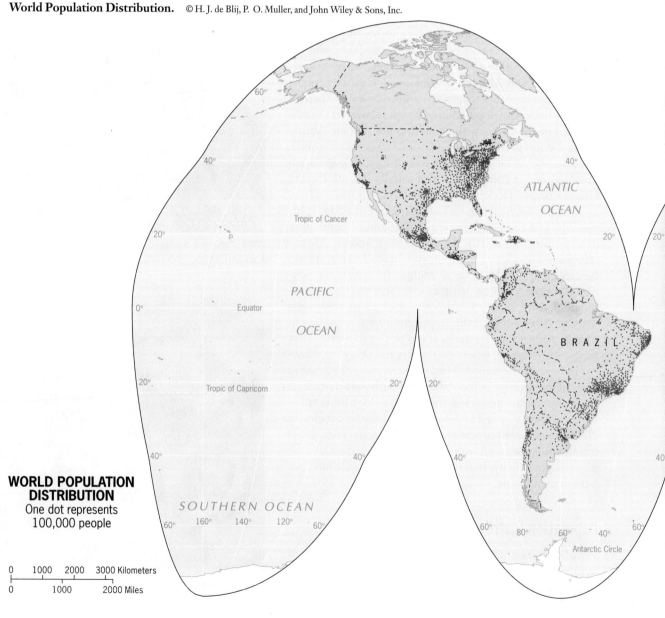

WORLD POPULATION DISTRIBUTION
One dot represents 100,000 people

0   1000   2000   3000 Kilometers
0   1000   2000 Miles

ogy and in transportation of agricultural goods have begun to change this pattern.

At the global scale, where one dot on a map represents 100,000 people, three major clusters of population jump out (Fig. 2.5). Each of the three largest population clusters is on the Eurasian (Europe and Asia combined) landmass. The fourth largest is in North America.

East Asia

Although the distribution map (Fig. 2.5) requires no color contrasts, Figure 2.6 depicts population density through shading: the darker the color, the larger the number of people per unit area. The most extensive area of dark shading lies in East Asia, primarily in China but also in Korea and Japan. Amost one-quarter of the world's population is concentrated here—over 1.3 billion people in China alone.

In addition to high population density in China's large cities, ribbons of high population density extend into the interior along the Yangtze and Yellow River valleys. Farmers along China's major river valleys produce crops of wheat and rice to feed not only themselves but also the population of major Chinese cities such as Shanghai and Beijing.

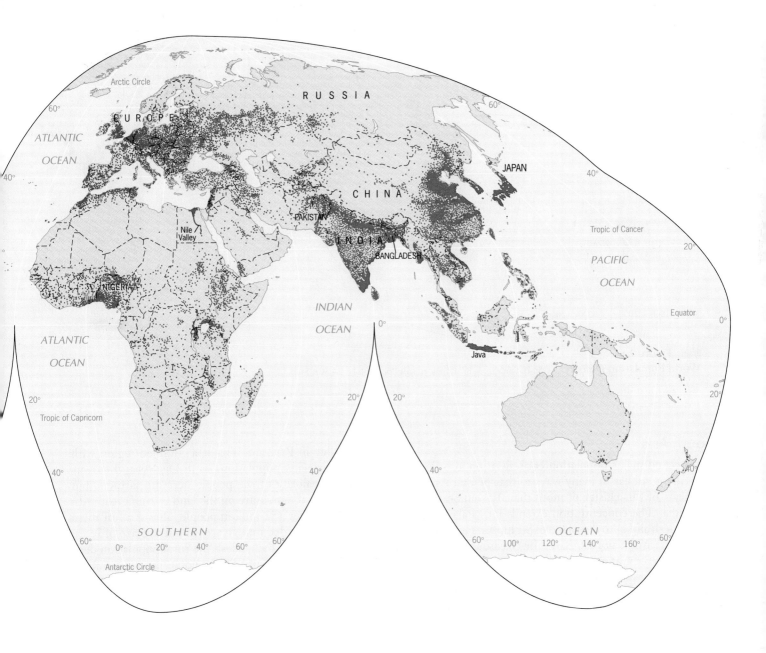

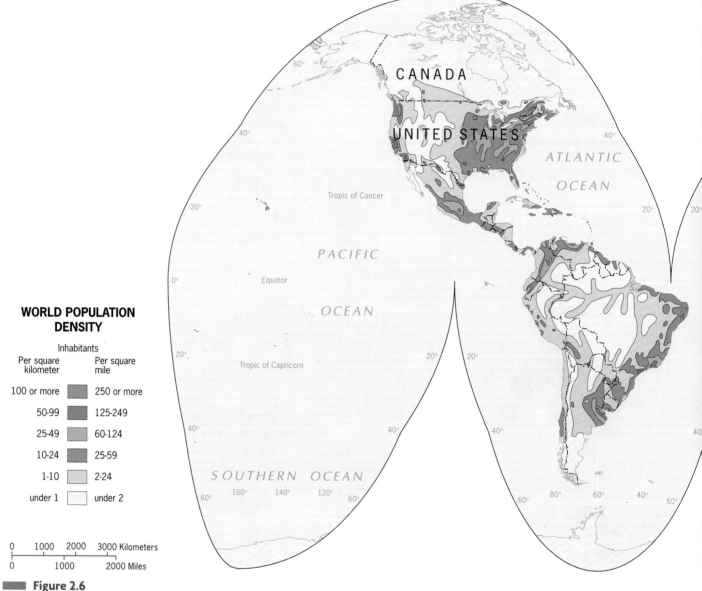

WORLD POPULATION DENSITY

Inhabitants

Per square kilometer		Per square mile
100 or more		250 or more
50-99		125-249
25-49		60-124
10-24		25-59
1-10		2-24
under 1		under 2

0   1000   2000   3000 Kilometers
0   1000   2000 Miles

Figure 2.6
World Population Density.   © E. H. Fouberg, A. B. Murphy, H. J. de Blij, and John Wiley & Sons, Inc.

South Asia

The second major population concentration also lies in Asia and is similar in many ways to that of East Asia. At the heart of this cluster of more than 1.5 billion people lies India. The concentration extends into Pakistan and Bangladesh and onto the island of Sri Lanka. Here, people again cluster in major cities, on the coasts, and along rivers, such as the Ganges and Indus.

Two physical geography barriers create the boundaries of the South Asia population cluster: the Himalaya Mountains to the north and the desert west of the Indus River Valley in Pakistan. This is a confined region with a rapidly growing population. As in East Asia, the overwhelming majority of the people here are farmers, but in South Asia the pressure on the land is even greater. In Bangladesh, over 152 million people, almost all of them farmers, are crowded into an area about the size of Iowa. Over large parts of Bangladesh the rural population density is between 3000 and 5000 people per square mile. By comparison, in 2006 the population of Iowa was just under 3 million people, and the rural population density was well under 30 people per square mile.

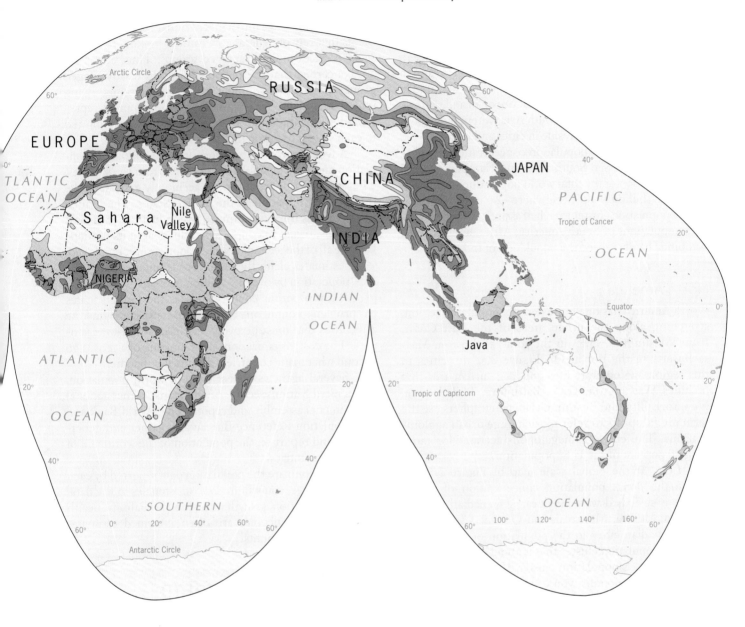

Europe

An axis of dense population extends from Ireland and Great Britain into Russia and includes large parts of Germany, Poland, Ukraine, and Belarus. It also includes the Netherlands and Belgium, parts of France, and northern Italy. This European cluster contains over 715 million inhabitants, less than half the population of the South Asia cluster. A comparison of the population and physical maps indicates that in Europe terrain and environment are not as closely related to population distribution as they are in East and South Asia. For example, note the lengthy extension in Figure 2.5, which protrudes far into Russia. Unlike the Asian extensions, which reflect fertile river valleys, the European extension reflects the orientation of Europe's coal fields. If you look closely at the physical map, you will note that comparatively dense population occurs even in mountainous, rugged country, such as the boundary zone between Poland and its neighbors to the south. A much greater correspondence exists between coastal and river lowlands and high population density in Asia than in Europe generally.

Another contrast can be seen in the number of Europeans who live in cities and towns. The European population cluster includes numerous cities and towns, many of which developed as a result of the Industrial Revolution. In Germany, 88 percent of the people live in urban places; in the United Kingdom, 89 percent; and in France, 74 percent. With so many people concentrated in the cities, the rural countryside is more open and sparsely populated than in East and South Asia (where only about 30 percent of the people reside in cities and towns).

The three major population concentrations we have discussed—East Asia, South Asia, and Europe—account for over 4 billion of the total world population of approximately 6.7 billion people. Nowhere else on the globe is there a population cluster even half as great as any of these. The populations of South America, Africa, and Australia combined barely exceed the population of India alone.

North America

North America has one quite densely populated region, stretching along the urban areas of the East Coast, from Washington, D.C. in the south to Boston, Massachusetts in the north. On Figure 2.5, the cities in this region agglomerate into one large urban area that includes Washington, D.C., Baltimore, Philadelphia, New York City, and Boston. Urban geographers use the term **megalopolis** to refer to such huge urban agglomerations. The cities of megalopolis account for more than 20 percent of the U.S. population.

Look at the global scale map in Figure 2.5 and notice the dense population concentration of megalopolis is stretched west into nearby Canadian cities of Toronto, Ottawa, Montreal, and Quebec City. Adding these Canadian cities to the population of megalopolis creates a population cluster that is about one quarter the size of Europe's population cluster. If you have lived or traveled in megalopolis, you can think about traffic and comprehend what dense population means. However, recognize that the total population of megalopolis is 2.8% of the East Asian population cluster, and that the 5,309 people per square mile density of New York City does not rival the density in world cities like Mumbai, India, with a population density of 76,820 per square mile or Jakarta, Indonesia, with a population density of 27,137 per square mile.

Reliability of Population Data

When the United States planned and conducted its 2000 population **census**, various groups protested the practice of trying to count every single person in the country. Rather, many advocates of homeless, minorities, and others insisted the census practices resulted in a serious undercount of these disadvantaged populations. Much federal government funding depends on population data. If the population of a disadvantaged group is under-

counted, it translates into a loss of dollars for city governments that rely on federal government funding to pay for social services to disadvantaged groups. Thus, advocates are concerned that the people already in disadvantaged groups suffer more so under census undercounts. Being undercounted also translates into less government representation, for the number of congressional seats allotted to each state is based on the census counts.

Advocacy groups urged the census to sample the population and derive population statistics from the samples. They argued this would more accurately represent the true number of people in the United States. The United States Census Bureau continued to conduct its census as it always has, trying to count each individual in its borders. Despite all of the technology and people-power employed, some estimates claim the 2000 census undercounted the U.S. population by over 3.3 million people.

If a prosperous country such as the United States has problems conducting an accurate census, imagine the difficulties that must be overcome in less well-off countries. The cost, organization, and reporting of a census go beyond what many countries can afford or handle.

Several agencies collect data on world population. The United Nations records official statistics that national governments assemble and report. The World Bank and the Population Reference Bureau also gather and generate data and report on the population of the world and of individual countries.

If you compare the population data reported by each of these sources, you will find inconsistencies in the data. Data on population, growth rates, food availability, health conditions, and incomes are often informed estimates rather than actual counts.

As we discussed in the field note at the beginning of this chapter, populations are falling in some parts of the world. How will Figure 2.5 look different 50 years from now? If you were updating this textbook in 50 years, where would the largest population clusters in the world be?

WHY DO POPULATIONS RISE OR FALL IN PARTICULAR PLACES?

In the late 1960s, alarms sounded throughout the world with the publication of Paul Ehrlich's *The Population Bomb*. Ehrlich and others warned that the world's population was increasing too quickly—and was outpacing our food production! We can trace alarms over the burgeoning world population back to 1798, when British economist Thomas Malthus published *An Essay on the Principles of Population*. In this work Malthus warned that the world's population was increasing faster than the food supplies needed to sustain it. His reasoning was that food supplies grew *linearly*, adding acreage and crops incrementally by year, whereas population grew *exponentially*, compounding on the year before. From 1803 to 1826, Malthus issued revised editions of his essay and responded vigorously to a barrage of criticism.

The predictions Malthus made assumed food production is confined spatially—what people can eat within a country depends on what is grown in the country. We now know his assumption does not hold true; countries are not closed systems. Malthus did not foresee how globalization would aid the exchange of agricultural goods across the world. Mercantilism, colonialism, and capitalism brought interaction among the Americas, Europe, Africa, Asia, and the Pacific. Through global interaction, new agricultural methods developed, and commodities and livestock diffused across oceans. In the 1700s, farmers in Ireland grew dependent on a South American crop that was well suited for its rocky soils, the potato. Today, wealthier countries that lack arable land, such as Norway, can import the majority of its foodstuffs, circumventing the limitations of their lands. Each of these examples demonstrates that food production is not confined spatially, as Malthus assumed.

Malthus assumed the growth of food production was linear, but food production has grown exponentially as the acreage under cultivation expands, mechanization of agricultural production diffuses, improved strains of seed are developed, and more fertilizers are used. In the twenty-first century, bioengineering continues to bring new hybrids, genetically modified organisms, and countless herbicides and pesticides that enabled exponential growth in food production.

Nonetheless, Malthus's ideas continue to attract followers. Neo-Malthusians scholars continue to share Malthus's concerns (even if they do not agree with every detail of his argument) and continue to be alarmed at the continuing rise in the world's population. Neo-Malthusians point out that human suffering is now occurring on a scale unimagined even by Malthus. Although many demographers predict the world population will stabilize later in the twenty-first century, neo-Malthusians argue that overpopulation is a real problem that must be addressed now.

Population Growth at World, Regional, National, and Local Scales

Analysis of population growth and change requires attention to scale. In this section, we examine population growth at different scales, but we must be mindful that what happens at one scale can be affected by what is happening at other scales and in other places at the same time.

Keeping in mind that population change in one place can be affected rapidly by what is going on in a neighboring country or at the regional scale, one can gain some insights by looking at population change within the confined territory of a country (or other administrative unit, such as a province or city). To calculate the natural increase in a country's population, simply subtract deaths from births. This is a simple statistic to calculate and comprehend; however, calculating the natural increase misses two other key components in a country's population: immigration, which along with births adds to the total population, and emigration (outmigration), which along with deaths, subtracts from the total population. Using these four components, we can calculate demographic change within a territory.

When we mapped population growth in Figure 2.7, we did not take into account emigration and immigration. Other maps and tables of population growth you see may take into account emigration and immigration. Statistics for each population trait can be calculated globally, by region, by country, or even for smaller locales. When studying population data across scales and across the world, we must constantly remind ourselves of exactly what is being calculated and for where. Otherwise, many of the statistics we read will seemingly be contradictory.

For example, we began this chapter discussing the low and declining TFRs in a number of countries in the world. How can the worldwide population continue to increase when so many countries are experiencing low TFRs and population decline? Despite declining population growth rates and even negative growth rates (growth rates below 0.0) in a number of the world's countries, the global population continues to rise. The worldwide TFR was 2.6 in 2007, above the replacement level of 2.1. The Population Reference Bureau estimates global population will rise to over 9.3 billion by 2050. The low TFRs and low population growth rates enumerated in this chapter are dwarfed by continued additions to the population in countries where growth rates are still relatively high, such as India, Indonesia, Bangladesh, Pakistan, and Nigeria.

One way to easily grasp the growth rate in world population is to compare a population's rate of growth to its **doubling time**. Every rate of growth has a doubling time; for example, if you invest $100 at 10 percent, compounded annually (exponentially), it would take about seven years to double to $200, and then another seven years to become $400, and then another seven years to become $800. When the growth rate is 10 percent, therefore, the doubling time is around seven years.

Two thousand years ago, the world's population was an estimated 250 million. More than 16 centuries passed before this total had doubled to 500 million, the estimated population in 1650. Just 170 years later, in 1820 (when Malthus was still writing), the population had doubled

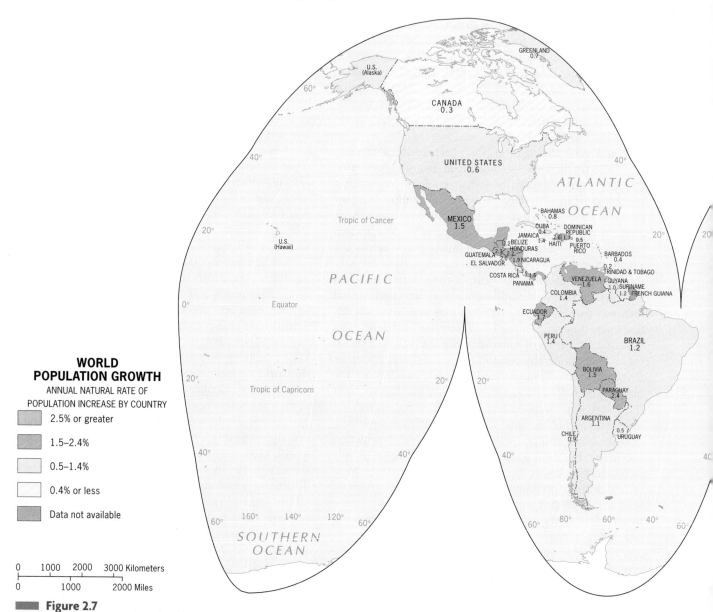

WORLD POPULATION GROWTH
ANNUAL NATURAL RATE OF POPULATION INCREASE BY COUNTRY

- 2.5% or greater
- 1.5–2.4%
- 0.5–1.4%
- 0.4% or less
- Data not available

Figure 2.7
World Population Growth. Annual natural rate of population increase by country. *Data from:* United States Census Bureau, International Data Base, 2008.

again, to 1 billion (Fig. 2.8). And barely more than a century after this, in 1930, it reached 2 billion. The doubling time was down to 100 years and dropping fast; the **population explosion** was in full gear. Only 45 years elapsed during the next doubling, to 4 billion (1975). During the mid-1980s, when the rate declined to 1.8 percent, the doubling slowed to 39 years. Today, world population is doubling in 54 years, and the continuing slowdown in the estimated doubling rate is one of the bright spots in the problematic demographic picture.

For demographers and population geographers who study global population growth today, the concept of doubling time is losing much of its punch. With populations falling in many places, fears of global population doubling

quickly are definitely subsiding. Many indicators, such as the slowing of the doubling time, suggest that the worst may be over, that the explosive population growth of the twentieth century will be followed by a marked and accelerating slowdown during the twenty-first century. The global growth rate is now down to 1.4 percent, perhaps slightly lower. But today the world's population is about 6.7 billion, yielding an increase in world population that still exceeds 80 million annually. Although this does reflect improvement over the 90 million annual increase the world experienced in the late 1980s, the population growth rate of the globe will have to come down well below 1.0 percent to significantly slow down global population growth.

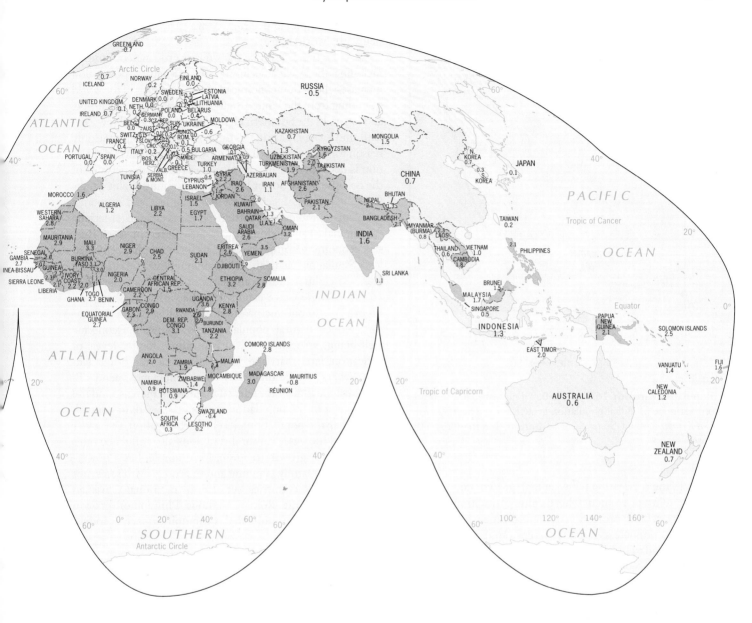

Population Growth at the Regional and National Scales

The world map of population growth rates (Fig. 2.7), displayed by country, confirms the wide range of natural increases in different geographic regions. These variations have existed as long as records have been kept: countries and regions go through stages of expansion and decline at varying times. In the mid-twentieth century, the population of the former Soviet Union was growing vigorously. Thirty years ago, India's population was growing at nearly 3.0 percent, more than most African countries; then India's growth rate fell below that of Subsaharan Africa. Today, Africa's rate of natural increase still is higher than India's

(2.4 percent to 1.7 percent), but now Subsaharan Africa faces the impact of the AIDS epidemic, which is killing millions, orphaning children, reducing life expectancies, and curtailing growth rates.

The map also reveals continuing high growth rates in Muslim countries of North Africa and Southwest Asia. Saudi Arabia has one of the highest growth rates in the world, but some smaller countries in this region are increasing even faster. For some time during the second half of the twentieth century, countries in this region saw their growth rates increase even as those in most of the rest of the world were declining. But more recently several of the fast-growing populations, for example, those of Iran and Morocco, have shown significant declines. Demographers

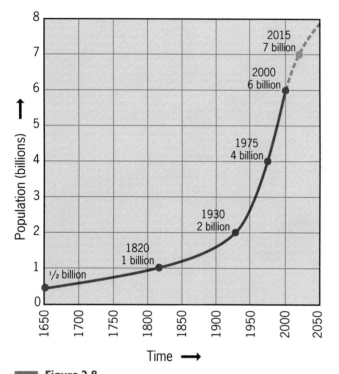

Figure 2.8

Population Growth, 1650 to 2050. The dashed line indicates one estimate of global population growth for the next 50 years. *Data from:* United States Census Bureau, International Data Base, 2007.

point to the correlation between high growth rates and the low standing of women: where cultural traditions restrict educational and professional opportunities for women, and men dominate as a matter of custom, rates of natural increase tend to be high.

South Asia is the most important geographic region in the population growth rate picture. The region includes the country that appears destined to overtake China as the world's most populous: India. Only one country in this region has a growth rate lower than the world average: Sri Lanka. But Sri Lanka's total population is only 20.4 million, whereas the fast-growing countries, Pakistan and Bangladesh, have a combined population exceeding 326 million. India, as the map shows, is still growing well above the world average. The situation in East Asia, the world's most populous region, is different. China's official rate of natural growth has fallen well below 1.0 percent (0.6 in 2008), and Japan's population is no longer growing. Southeast Asia's natural growth rates remain higher, but this region's total population is much lower than either East or South Asia; key countries, such as Indonesia, Thailand, and Vietnam, have declining growth rates.

South America is experiencing significant reductions in natural population growth rates, where those rates were alarmingly high just a generation ago. The region as a whole is still growing at 1.5 percent, but Brazil's population, for example, has declined from 2.9 percent in the mid-1960s to 1.4 percent today. And the populations of Argentina, Chile, and Uruguay are growing at rates well below the world average.

As Figure 2.7 shows, the slowest growing countries—including those with declining rates of natural population increase—lie in the economically wealthier areas of the world extending from the United States and Canada across Europe, and Japan. In the Southern Hemisphere, Australia, New Zealand, and Uruguay are in this category. Wealth is not the only reason for negative population growth rates. Russia's population is declining because of social dislocation in the wake of the collapse of the Soviet Union: deteriorating health conditions, high rates of alcoholism and drug use, and economic problems combine to shorten life expectancies (especially among males) and to lower birth rates (in recent years, Russia's economy has improved, but its birth rate has remained low). Similar problems afflict Ukraine and Kazakhstan, two of Russia's neighbors, which also show slow or negative growth.

No single factor can explain the variations shown on Figure 2.7. Economic prosperity as well as social dislocation reduce natural population growth rates. Economic well-being, associated with urbanization, higher levels of education, later marriage, family planning, and other factors, lowers population growth. In the table in Appendix B, compare the indices for natural population increase and the percentage of the population that is urbanized; in general, the higher the population's level of urbanization, the lower its natural increase. Cultural traditions also influence rates of population growth: religion, for example, has a powerful impact on family planning and thus on growth rates, not only in Islamic countries but also in traditional Christian societies (note the Roman Catholic Philippines' growth rate) and in Hindu-dominated communities (such as India).

Population Growth at the Local Scale

The information provided in Figure 2.7 is based on country-wide statistics. Significant demographic variations also occur *within* countries. In India, for example, some States record population growth rates far above the national average; these States lie mostly in the east of the country (Fig. 2.9). But other States, in the west and southwest region, are growing much more slowly. India is a federation of 28 States and 7 union territories, and the individual States differ greatly both culturally and politically. As in any federation, the will of the federal government cannot be forcibly imposed on the States.

After becoming independent in 1947, India began a population planning program in the 1950s, long before the fear of worldwide overpopulation and a global population bomb spread. In the 1960s, when census numbers revealed the extreme growth rates in parts of the country, the Indian government instituted a national population planning program, encouraging States to join.

Despite the federal effort, rapid population growth continued, especially in the eastern States. Social problems arose in some of the States where governments pursued the campaign vigorously. During the 1970s, the Indian

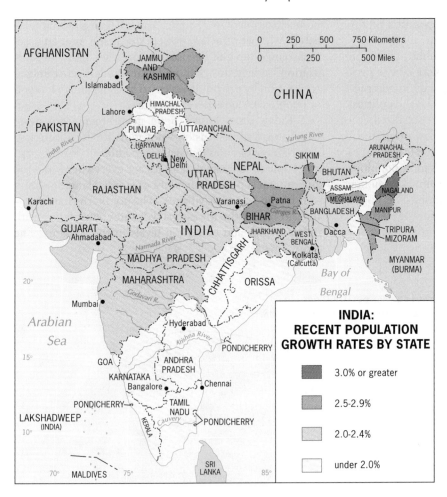

Figure 2.9
Recent Population Growth Rates in India. *Data from:* India Census Bureau, 2001.

Figure 2.10
Maharashtra, India. Above the entrance to a suite of medical offices is a sign announcing that the "free family planning sterilization operation" closed in 1996.
© H. J. de Blij.

government began a policy of forced sterilization of any man with three or more children. The State of Maharashtra sterilized 3.7 million people before public opposition led to rioting, and the government abandoned the program (Fig. 2.10). Other States also engaged in compulsory sterilization programs, with heavy social and political costs—eventually, 22.5 million people were sterilized.

The horrors of the forced sterilization program of the 1970s are haunting India again. In 2004, three districts in the State of Uttar Pradesh (India's most populous State with over 170 million people) instituted a policy of exchanging gun licenses for sterilization. The policy allowed for a shotgun license in exchange for the sterilization of two people and a revolver license in exchange for

the sterilization of five people. Abuse began almost immediately, with wealthy landowners sterilizing their laborers in exchange for gun licenses. Before the "guns for sterilization" policy, districts in Uttar Pradesh encouraged sterilization by providing access to housing and extra food for people who agreed to be sterilized.

Today, most Indian State governments are using advertising and persuasion—not guns for sterilization—to encourage families to have fewer children. Posters urging people to have small families are everywhere, and the government supports a network of family planning clinics even in the remotest villages. The southern States continue to report the lowest growth rates, correlating with higher wealth and education levels in these States. The

Figure 2.11
Crude Birth Rate. Number of Births in a year per 1000 people.
Data from: United States Census Bureau, International Data Base, 2008.

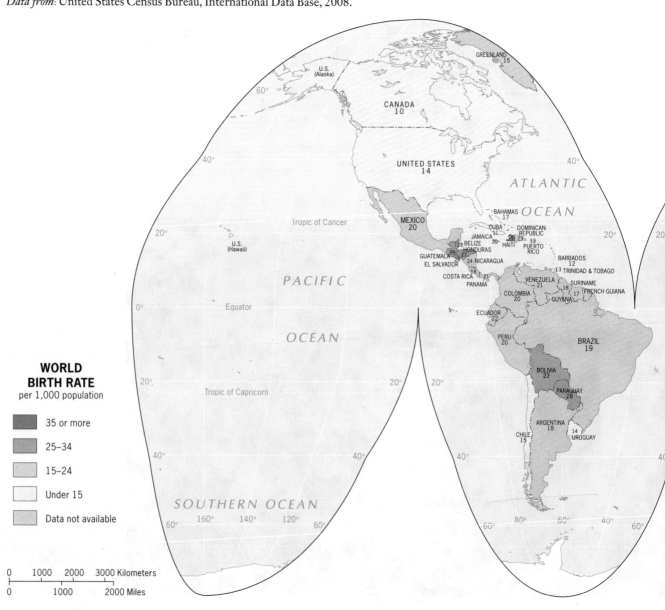

eastern and northern States, the poorer regions of India, continue to report the highest growth rates.

Our world map of growth rates is a global overview, a mere introduction to the complexities of the geography of population. The example of India demonstrates that what we see at the scale of a world map does not give us the complete story of what is happening within each country or region of the world.

The Demographic Transition

The high population growth rates now occurring in many poorer countries are not necessarily permanent. In Europe, population growth changed several times in the last three centuries. Demographers used data on baptisms and funerals from churches in Great Britain to study changes in birth and death rates of the population. They expected the rate of **natural increase** of the population—the difference between the number of births and the number of deaths—to vary over different periods of time. Demographers calculated the **crude birth rate** (CBR), the number of live births per year per thousand people in the population (Fig. 2.11), and the **crude death rate** (CDR), the number of deaths per year per thousand people (Fig. 2.12).

The church data revealed that before the Industrial Revolution began in Great Britain in the 1750s, the country experienced high birth rates and high death rates,

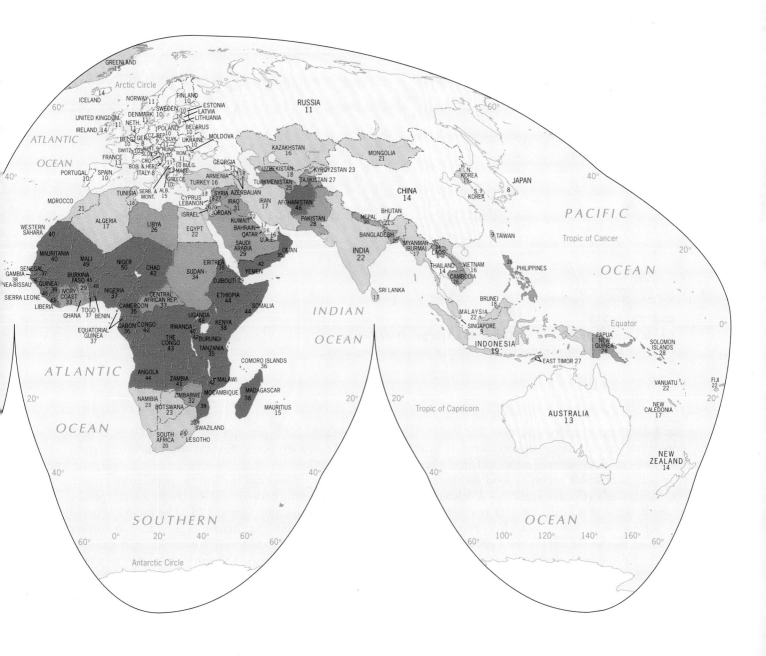

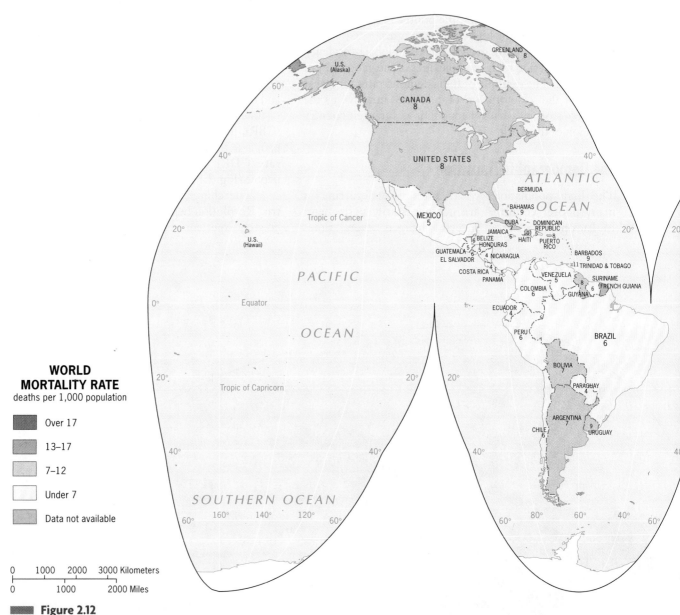

WORLD MORTALITY RATE
deaths per 1,000 population

- Over 17
- 13–17
- 7–12
- Under 7
- Data not available

0   1000   2000   3000 Kilometers
0   1000   2000 Miles

Figure 2.12
Crude Death Rate. Number of Deaths in a Year per 1000 People.
Data from: United States Census Bureau, International Data Base, 2008.

with small differences between the two. The result was low population growth. After industrialization began, the death rates in Great Britain began to fall as a result of better and more stable access to food and improved access to increasingly effective medicines. With a rapidly falling death rate and a birth rate that remained high, Britain's population explosion took place. From the late 1800s through two world wars in the 1900s, death rates continued to fall and birth rates began to fall, but stayed higher than death rates, resulting in continued population growth but at a slower rate. Finally, in recent his-

tory, both the birth rate and death rate in Great Britain declined to low levels, resulting in slow or stabilized population growth.

Demographers call the shift in population growth the **demographic transition**. The transition is typically modeled as shown in Figure 2.13. The model is based on the kind of shift that Britain experienced, but other places either have gone through a similar shift or are in the process of doing so. The initial low-growth phase, which in all places endured for most of human history, is marked by high birth rates and equally high death rates.

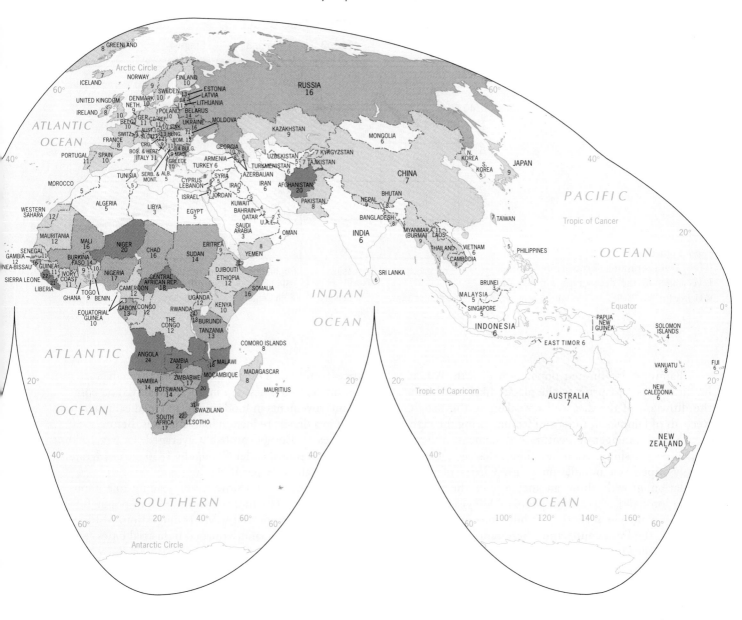

In this phase, epidemics and plagues keep the death rates high among all sectors of the population—in some cases so high that they exceed birth rates. For Great Britain and the rest of Europe, death rates exceeded birth rates during the bubonic plague (the Black Death) of the 1300s, which hit in waves beginning in Crimea on the Black Sea, diffusing through trade to Sicily and other Mediterranean islands, and moving through contagious diffusion and the travel of rats (which hosted the vector, the flea, that spread the plague) north from the Mediterranean.

Once the plague hit a region, it was likely to return within a few years time, creating another wave of human suffering. Estimates of plague deaths vary between one-quarter and one-half of the population, with the highest death rates recorded in the West (where trade among regions was the greatest) and the lowest in the East (where cooler climates and less connected populations delayed diffusion). Across Europe, many cities and towns were left decimated. Historians estimate the population of Great Britain fell from nearly 4 million when the plague began to just over 2 million when it ended.

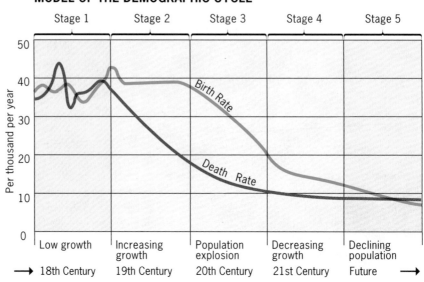

MODEL OF THE DEMOGRAPHIC CYCLE

Famines also limited population growth. A famine in Europe just prior to the plague likely facilitated the diffusion of the disease by weakening the people. Records of famines in India and China during the eighteenth and nineteenth centuries document millions of people perishing. At other times, destructive wars largely wiped out population gains. Charts of world population growth show an increase in the world's population from 250 million people 2000 years ago to 500 million people in 1650 and 1 billion people in 1820. However, the lines connecting these points in time do not trend steadily upward. Rather, they turn up and down frequently, reflecting the impacts of disease, crop failures, and wars.

The beginning of the Industrial Revolution ushered in a period of accelerating population growth in Europe. Before the workers could move from farms to factories, a revolution in agriculture had to occur. The eighteenth century marked the Second Agricultural Revolution, so named because the first occurred thousands of years earlier (see Chapter 11). During the Second Agricultural Revolution, farmers improved seed selection, practiced new methods of crop rotation, selectively bred livestock to increase production and quality, employed new technology such as the seed drill, expanded storage capacities, and consolidated landholdings for greater efficiencies. With more efficient farming methods, the number of people needed in farming decreased and the food supply increased, thereby supporting a higher population overall.

In the 1800s, as the Industrial Revolution diffused through continental Europe, other advances also helped lower the death rates. Sanitation facilities made the towns and cities safer from epidemics, and modern medical

practices diffused. Disease prevention through vaccination introduced a new era in public health. The combined improvements in food supply and medical practice resulted in a drastic reduction in death rates. Before 1750 death rates in Europe probably averaged 35 per 1000 (birth rates averaged under 40), but by 1850 the death rate was down to about 16 per 1000.

Birth rates fell at a slower rate, leading to a population explosion. The increase in the rate of population growth in Europe spurred waves of migration. Millions of people left the squalid, crowded industrial cities (and farms as well) to emigrate to other parts of the world. They were not the first to make this journey. Adventurers, explorers, merchants, and colonists had gone before them. In a major wave of colonization from 1500 through the 1700s, European migrants decimated native populations through conquest, slavery, and the introduction of diseases against which the local people had no natural immunity.

When a second wave of European colonization began in Africa and Asia during the late 1800s, the Europeans brought with them their newfound methods of sanitation and medical techniques, and these had the opposite effect. By the mid-1900s, declining death rates in Africa, India, and South America brought rapid population increases to these regions. At this point, new alarms and cautions of worldwide overpopulation rang.

Although the global alarms continued to ring, they subsided for populations in Europe and North America when population growth rates began to decline in the first half of the 1900s. The cause was a significant decline in birth rates. Populations continued to grow, but at a much slower rate. Many countries in Latin America and Asia experienced falling birth rates later in the twentieth century, which helped slow the global population growth rate.

Why have birth rates declined? Throughout the 1900s, lower birth rates arrived first in countries with greater urbanization, wealth, and medical advances. As more and more people moved to cities, both the economics and the culture of large families changed. Instead of lending a hand on the family farm, children in urban areas were a drain on the family finances. At the same time, new opportunities—especially for women—were often not compatible with large families. Hence, women often delayed marriage and childbearing. Medical advances lowered infant and child mortality rates, lessening the sense that multiple children were necessary to sustain a family. In recent history, the diffusion of contraceptives, the accessibility to abortions, and conscious decisions by many women to have fewer children or to start having children at a later age have all lowered birth rates within a country.

In some parts of the world, countries are now experiencing exceptionally low TFRs. Low birth rates along with low death rates put the countries in a position of negligible, or even negative, population growth. Birth rates are lowest in the countries where women are the most educated and most involved in the labor force.

Future Population Growth

It may be unwise to assume that the demographic cycles of all countries will follow the sequence that occurred in industrializing Europe or to believe that the still-significant population growth currently taking place in Bangladesh, Mexico, and numerous other countries will simply subside. Nonetheless, many agencies monitoring global population suggest that most (if not all) countries' populations will stop growing at some time during the twenty-first century, reaching a so-called **stationary population level** (SPL). This would mean that the world's population would stabilize and that the major problems to be faced would involve the aged rather than the young. In 2004, the United Nations predicted that world population would stabilize at 9 billion in 300 years.

Such predictions require frequent revision, however, and anticipated dates for population stabilization are often moved back. Only a few years ago, the United Nations predicted world population would stabilize at 10 billion in 200 years. The United Nations changed its predictions based on lower fertility rates in many countries. All agencies reporting population predictions have to revise their predictions periodically. In the late 1980s, for example, the World Bank predicted that the United States would reach SPL in 2035 with 276 million inhabitants. Brazil's population would stabilize at 353 million in 2070, Mexico's at 254 million in 2075, and China's at 1.4 billion in 2090. India, destined to become the world's most populous country, would reach SPL at 1.6 billion in 2150.

Today these figures are unrealistic. China's population passed the 1.2 billion mark in 1994, and India's reached 1 billion in 1998. If we were to project an optimistic decline in growth rates for both countries, China's population would "stabilize" at 1.5 billion in 2070 and India's at 1.8 billion in the same year. But population increase is a cyclical phenomenon, and overall declines mask lags and spurts as well as regional disparities.

Examine Appendix B at the end of the book. Study the growth rate column. Which countries have the highest growth rates? Determine what stage of the demographic transition these countries are in, and hypothesize what may lead them to the next stage.

WHY DOES POPULATION COMPOSITION MATTER?

Maps showing the regional distribution and density of populations tell us about the number of people in countries or regions, but they cannot reveal two other aspects of those populations: the number of men and women and their ages. These aspects of population, the **population composition**, are importants because a populous country where half the population is very young has quite different problems from a populous country where a large proportion of the population is elderly. When geographers study populations, therefore, they are concerned not only with spatial distribution and growth rates but also with population composition.

The composition is the structure of a population in terms of age, sex, and other properties such as marital status and education. Age and sex are key indicators of population composition, and demographers and geographers use **population pyramids** to represent these traits visually.

The population pyramid displays the percentages of each age group in the total population (normally five-year groups) by a horizontal bar whose length represents its share. Males in the group are to the left of the center line, females to the right.

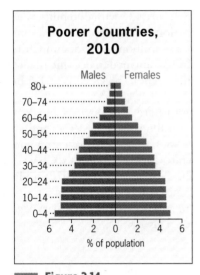

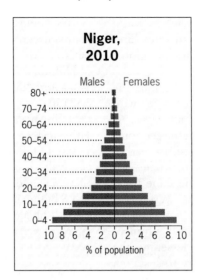

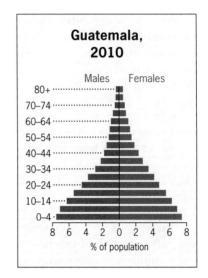

Figure 2.14
Age-Sex Population Pyramids for Countries with High Population Growth Rates.
Data from: United Nations, World Population Prospects: The 2006 Revision.

A population pyramid can instantly convey the demographic situation in a country. In the poorer countries, where birth and death rates generally remain high, the pyramid looks like an evergreen tree, with wide branches at the base and short ones near the top (Fig. 2.14). The youngest age groups have the largest share of the population; in the composite pyramid shown here, the three groups up to age 14 account for more than 30 percent of it. Older people, in the three highest age groups, represent only about 4 percent of the total. Slight variations of this pyramidal shape mark the population structure of such countries as Pakistan, Yemen, Guatemala, The Congo, and Laos. From age group 15 to 19 upward, each group is smaller than the one below it.

In countries with economic wealth, pyramid shapes change. Families become smaller, children fewer. A composite population pyramid for wealthier countries looks like a slightly lopsided vase, with the largest components of the population not at the bottom but in the middle. The middle-age bulge is moving upward, reflecting the aging of the population (Fig. 2.15) and

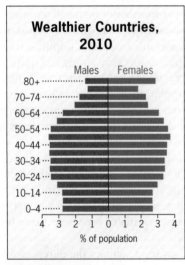

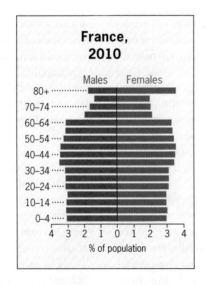

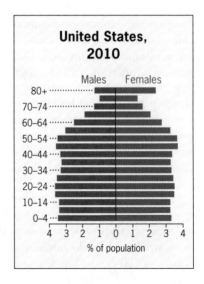

Figure 2.15
Age-Sex Population Pyramids for Countries with Low Population Growth Rates.
Data from: United Nations, World Population Prospects: The 2006 Revision.

the declining TFR. Countries with low TFR and high wealth, such as Italy, France, and Sweden, fit into this pyramid model.

HOW DOES THE GEOGRAPHY OF HEALTH INFLUENCE POPULATION DYNAMICS?

The condition of a country's population requires much more than simply knowing the total population or the growth rate. Also of significance is the welfare of the country's people, across regions, ethnicities, or social classes. Among the most important influences on population dynamics are geographical differences in sanitation, the prevalence of diseases, and the availability of health care.

Infant Mortality

One of the leading measures of the condition of a country's population is the **infant mortality rate** (IMR). Infant mortality is recorded as a baby's death during the first year following its birth (unlike child mortality, which records death between ages 1 and 5). Infant mortality is normally given as the number of cases per thousand, that is, per thousand live births.

Infant and child mortality reflect the overall health of a society. High infant mortality has a variety of causes, the physical health of the mother being a key factor. In societies where most women bear a large number of babies, the women also tend to be inadequately nourished, exhausted from overwork, suffering from disease, and poorly educated. Often, infants die because they are improperly weaned. Demographers report that many children die because their parents do not know how to cope with the routine childhood problem of diarrhea. This condition, together with malnutrition, is the leading killer of children throughout the world. Poor sanitation is yet another threat to infants and children. Estimates are that more than one-fifth of the world's population lacks ready access to clean drinking water or hygienic human waste-disposal facilities.

The map showing the world distribution of infant mortality (Fig. 2.16) reveals high rates in many poorer countries. The map shows infant mortality patterns at five levels ranging from 100 or more per thousand (one death for every eight live births) to fewer than 15. Compare this map to that of overall crude death rate (CDR) in Figure 2.12, and the role of infant mortality in societies with high death rates is evident.

The lowest infant mortality rate among larger populations has long been reported by Japan, with 3.0 deaths per 1000 live births in a country of over 128 million people. Some less populated countries show even lower IMRs. Singapore has over 4.5 million people and an incredibly low IMR of just under 3, and Sweden's nearly 9 million people record an IMR of 2.8.

In 2008, 22 countries still reported an IMR of 100 or more, and several had rates of 125 or higher—that is, one death or more among every eight newborns. Sierra Leone and Afghanistan had the highest IMR: 165. Dreadful as these figures are, they are a substantial improvement over the situation 20 years ago (although they are not much improved since 1997). Globally, infant mortality has been declining, even in the poverty-stricken regions of the world.

Each of these observations about infant mortality rates considers what is happening within an entire country. The IMR varies within countries and gives us a lens into variations in access to health care and health education within a country. A statistic typically varies by region, ethnicity, social class, or other criteria. The IMR of South Africa is 48 per thousand, an average of all the people within the country's borders. The IMR for South African whites is near the European average; for black Africans it is nearer the African average; and for the Coloured and Asian population sectors it lies between these two figures. The reported average for South Africa does not tell ethnic and class differences within South Africa.

In the United States, in 2004, the IMR for African Americans was 13.6, above the countrywide average of 6.8 and the IMR of 5.7 for non-Hispanic whites. The risk factors that lead to a high IMR afflict African Americans at a much higher rate than non-Hispanic whites in the United States. According to the Centers for Disease Control, 88.9 percent of non-Hispanic whites and 76.5 percent of African Americans received prenatal care starting in the first trimester of their pregnancy. Lower education levels for African American women also contributed to the higher IMR. One risk factor that contributes to high IMR, smoking during pregnancy, was higher for non-Hispanic whites. The centers for disease control found that 13.8 percent of non-Hispanic whites smoked cigarettes during pregnancy in 2004, and 8.4 percent of African American women smoked during pregnancy.

The IMR in the United States also varies by region, with the highest IMR in the South and the lowest in the Northeast (Fig. 2.17). Race, ethnicity, social class, education levels, and access to health care also vary by region in the United States, and these correlations are found for many health problems from diabetes to heart disease.

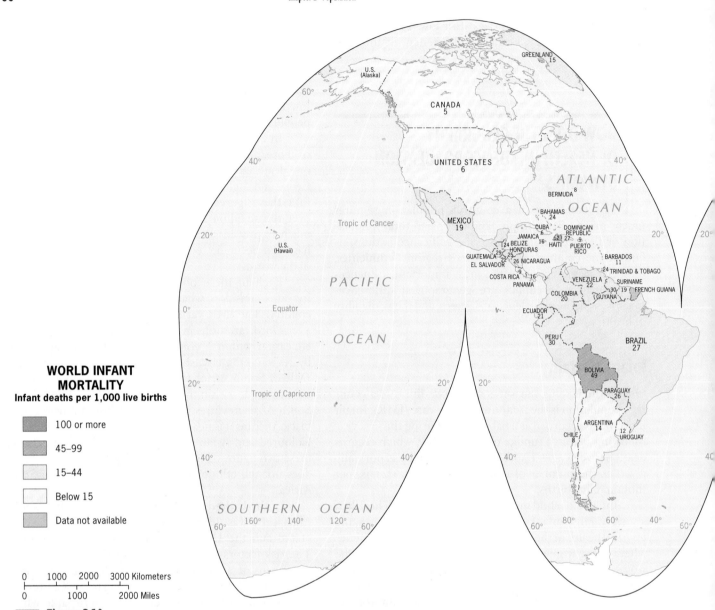

WORLD INFANT MORTALITY
Infant deaths per 1,000 live births

- 100 or more
- 45–99
- 15–44
- Below 15
- Data not available

0   1000   2000   3000 Kilometers
0   1000   2000 Miles

Figure 2.16
Infant Mortality Rate, 2008. *Data from*: CIA World Fact book, 2008 estimate.

According to the Office of Minority Health and Health Disparities at the Centers for Disease Control in the United States, "The leading causes of infant death include congenital abnormalities, preterm/low birth weight, Sudden Infant Death Syndrome (SIDS), problems related to complications of pregnancy, and respiratory distress syndrome. SIDS deaths among American Indian and Alaska Natives is 2.3 times the rate for non-Hispanic white mothers."

Another measurement of the health of children early in life is the newborn death rate, a measurement of the number of children who die in the first month of life out of every 1000 live births. Surprisingly, the United States has the *second highest newborn death rate* in the world. The annual State of the World's Mothers report explains that the high newborn death rate in the United States and in other wealthy countries is typically from premature births and low-birth-rate babies. In the poorer countries

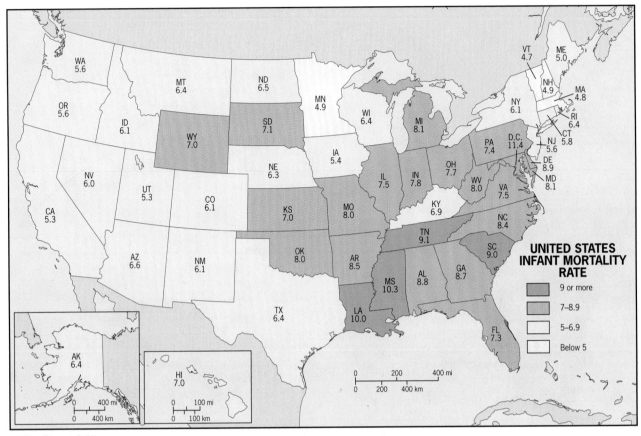

Figure 2.17
Infant Mortality Rate in the United States. Infant deaths per 1,000 live births. *Data from*: Centers for Disease Control, National Vital Statistics Reports, 2007.

of the world, diarrhea and infections cause half of newborn deaths.

Figure 2.18 maps the Mother's Index from the State of the World's Mothers report. The Mother's Index measures 10 barometers of well-being for mothers and children. Although the United States has a high newborn death rate, its position on the Mother's Index is high. The overwhelmingly low measurements for Subsaharan Africa on the Mother's Index confirms that poverty is a huge factor in the health of women and children. Specifically, 99 percent of newborn deaths and 98 percent of maternal deaths (deaths from giving birth) occur in the poorer countries of the world.

In the countries in the world experiencing violent conflict, the Mother's Index plunges, and the chances of newborn survival fall. Examine Figure 2.18 again and note the position of countries that have violent conflict

or a recent history of conflict: Iraq, Afghanistan, Liberia, Sierra Leone, and Angola.

Child Mortality

Infants who survive their first year of life still do not have a long life expectancy in the poorer areas of the world. The **child mortality rate** (CMR), recording the deaths of children between the ages of 1 and 5, remains staggeringly high in much of Africa and Asia, notably in the protein-deficient tropical and subtropical zones. *Kwashiorkor* (also known as protein malnutrition), a malady resulting from a lack of protein early in life, afflicts millions of children; *marasmus*, a condition that results from inadequate protein and insufficient calories, causes the deaths of millions more. In some countries, more than one in five children still die between their first and fifth birthdays, a terrible record in this twenty-first century.

Life Expectancy

Another indicator of a society's well-being lies in the **life expectancy** of its members at birth, the number of years, on average, someone may expect to remain alive. Figure 2.19 shows the average life expectancies of populations by country and thus does not take into account gender differences. Women outlive men by about four years in Europe and East Asia, three years in Subsaharan Africa, six years in North America, and seven years in South America. In Russia today, the difference is approximately 14 years.

The map does reveal huge regional contrasts. At the start of the century, world average life expectancy was 68 for women and 64 for men. Not only are these levels exceeded in the wealthy countries of the Western world, but great progress has also been made in East Asia, where Japan's life expectancies are the highest in the world. With its low infant and child mortality rates and low fertility rates, Japan's life expectancy is predicted to rise to 106 by the year 2300. By contrast, tropical Subsaharan African countries have the lowest life expectancies. In Subsaharan Africa, the spread of AIDS over the past two decades has lowered life expectancies in some countries below 40, a level not seen for centuries.

Life expectancies can change in relatively short order. In the former Soviet Union, and especially in Russia, the life expectancies of males dropped quite precipitously following the collapse of communism, from 68 to 62 years. Today, Russia's life expectancy is only 58 for males; female life expectancy also declined, but only slightly, from 74 to 72.

Life expectancy figures do not mean everyone lives to a certain age. The figure is an average that takes account of the children who die young and the people who survive well beyond the average. The dramatically lower figures for the world's poorer countries primarily reflect high infant mortality. A person who has survived beyond childhood can survive well beyond the recorded life expectancy. The low life expectancy figures for the malnourished countries remind us again how hard hit children are in poorer parts of the world.

Influence on Health and Well-Being

Health and well-being are closely related to location and environment. People who live in Iceland (where mosquitoes are rare) do not need to worry about contract-ing malaria, unless they travel to parts of the tropics where malaria prevails. People who live in close proximity to animals, including livestock, run a greater risk of catching certain diseases than do people who live in cities. When an outbreak of a particular disease occurs (for example "bird flu" in East Asia), its source and diffusion are studied by specialists in medical geography.

Medical geographers study diseases, and they also use locational analysis to predict diffusion and prescribe prevention strategies. A medical geographer can answer questions such as: Where is the bird flu most likely to diffuse and under what time line if an outbreak occurs in New York City? If a country receives enough funding to build 25 clinics for people in rural areas, where should these clinics be located so as to allow a maximum of patients to be able to reach them?

Diseases can be grouped into categories to make it easier to understand the risks they pose. About 65 percent of all diseases are known as **infectious diseases**, resulting from an invasion of parasites and their multiplication in the body. Malaria is an infectious disease. The remainder can be divided into the **chronic** or **degenerative diseases**, the maladies of longevity and old age such as heart disease, and the **genetic** or **inherited diseases** we can trace to our ancestry, that is, the chromosomes and genes that define our makeup. Sickle-cell anemia, hemophilia, and lactose intolerance are among these genetic diseases. These can be of special geographic interest because they tend to appear in certain areas and in particular populations, suggesting the need for special, local treatment.

Three geographic terms are used to describe the spatial extent of a disease. A disease is **endemic** when it prevails over a small area. A disease is epidemic when it spreads over a large region. A pandemic disease is global in scope.

Infectious Diseases

Infectious diseases continue to sicken and kill millions of people annually. Malaria, an old tropical disease, alone still takes more than a million lives annually and infects about 300 million people today. HIV/AIDS, an affliction that erupted in Africa only about 30 years ago, has killed about 25 million people since that time. These two maladies illustrate two kinds of infectious disease: *vectored* and *nonvectored*.

A vectored infectious disease such as malaria is transmitted by a intermediary *vector*, in malaria's case a mosquito. What happens is that the mosquito stings an already-infected person or animal, called a *host*, and sucks up some blood carrying the parasites. These then

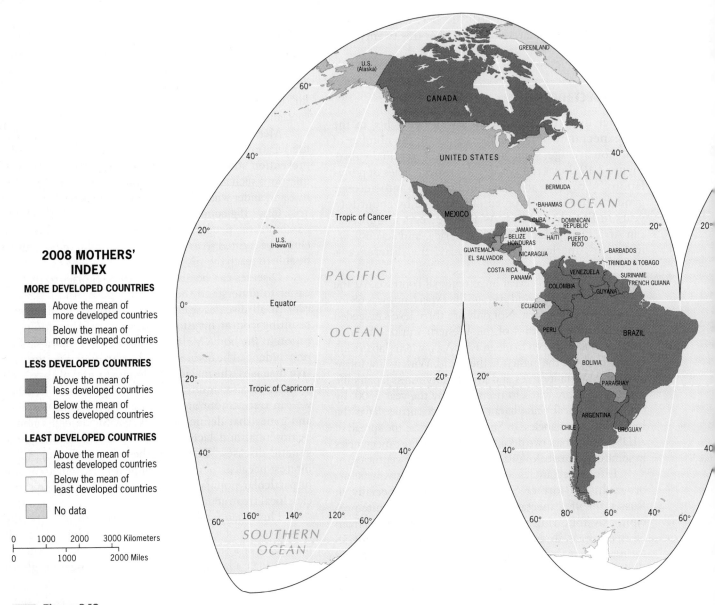

2008 MOTHERS' INDEX

MORE DEVELOPED COUNTRIES

- Above the mean of more developed countries
- Below the mean of more developed countries

LESS DEVELOPED COUNTRIES

- Above the mean of less developed countries
- Below the mean of less developed countries

LEAST DEVELOPED COUNTRIES

- Above the mean of least developed countries
- Below the mean of least developed countries
- No data

0   1000   2000   3000 Kilometers

0   1000   2000 Miles

 Figure 2.18
The Mothers' Index, 2008. Save the children calculates the mothers' index annually, based on 13 indicators, to guage the overall well-being of mothers and their children by country. *Data from:* Save the Children.

reproduce and multiply in the mosquito's body and reach its saliva. The next time that mosquito stings someone, some of the parasites are injected into that person's blood stream. Now that person develops malaria as the parasites multiply in his or her body, and he or she is a host.

Mosquitoes are especially effective vectors of infectious diseases ranging from yellow fever (another historic illness) to dengue fever (a newer disease that is fast spreading—see Chapter 1). But mosquitoes are only one kind of vector. Fleas, flies, worms, snails, and other vectors

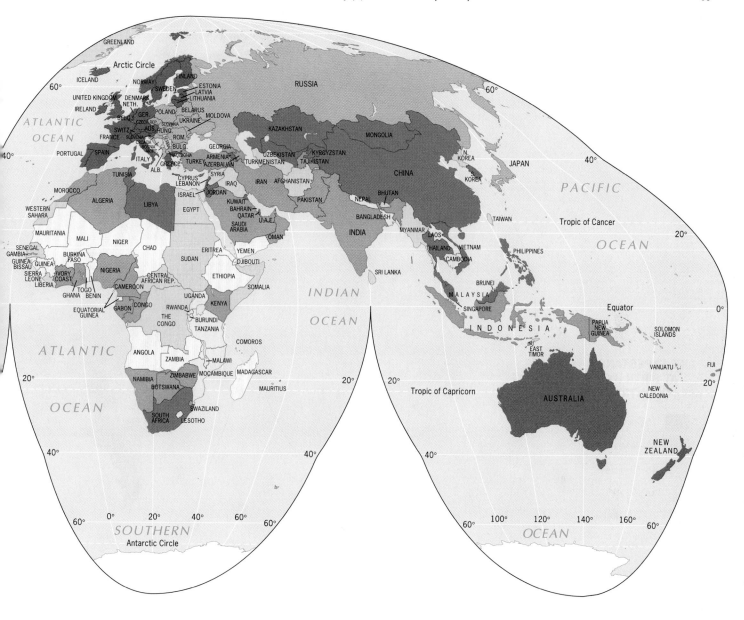

transmit such terrible diseases as sleeping sickness, river blindness, guinea worm, elephantiasis, and numerous others. Tropical climates, where biological activity is most intense, are the worst-afflicted areas of the world, but infectious diseases are a global phenomenon.

No disease in human history has taken more lives than malaria, and the battle against this scourge still is not won. On the day you read this, about 3000 people will die from malaria, the great majority of them in Africa and most of them children. What these numbers do not tell you is that an esti-

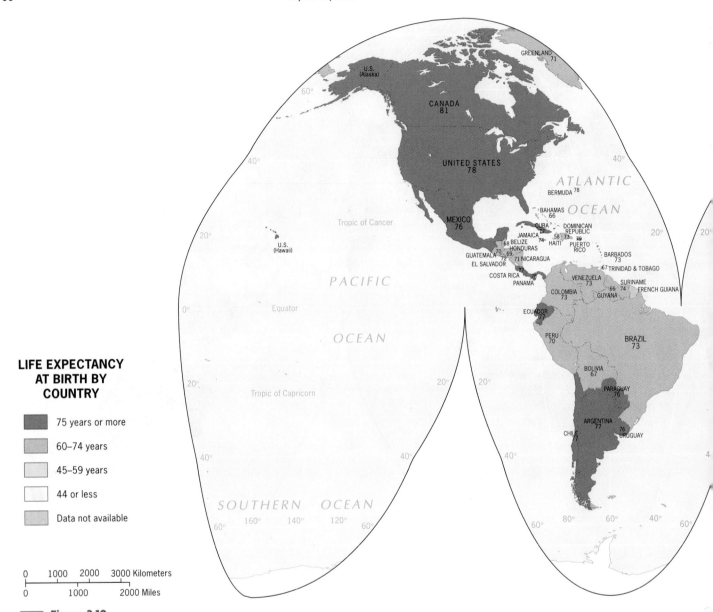

LIFE EXPECTANCY AT BIRTH BY COUNTRY

- 75 years or more
- 60–74 years
- 45–59 years
- 44 or less
- Data not available

| 0 | 1000 | 2000 | 3000 Kilometers |
| 0 | 1000 | 2000 Miles |

Figure 2.19

Life Expectancy at Birth in Years, 2008.   *Data from*: CIA World Factbook, 2008 estimate.

mated 3 to 5 million people live lives that are shortened and weakened by malaria infection. If you do not die from malaria as a youngster, you are likely to be incapacitated or struggle in exhaustion with chronically severe anemia throughout your life (see Chapter 10 for a longer discussion of malaria).

Nonvectored infectious diseases, such as influenza, are transmitted by direct contact between host and victim.

A kiss, a handshake, or even the slightest brush can transmit influenza, a cold, or some other familiar malady. Even standing close to another person so that tiny moisture particles in exhaled air can transmit the disease to you. HIV/AIDS (discussed below) is a nonvectored infectious disease that is transmitted primarily through sexual contact and secondarily through needle sharing in intravenous drug use.

Chronic and Genetic Diseases

Chronic diseases (also called degenerative diseases) are the afflictions of middle and old age, reflecting higher life expectancies. Among the chronic diseases heart disease, cancers, and strokes rank as the leading diseases in this category, but pneumonia, diabetes, and liver diseases also take their toll. In the United States 100 years ago, tuberculosis, pneumonia, diarrheal diseases, and heart diseases (in that order) were the chief killers. Today, heart disease and cancer head the list, with cerebral hemorrhage (stroke) next and accidents also high on the list (Table 2.1). In the early 1900s, tuberculosis and pneumonia caused 20 percent of all deaths; today, they cause fewer than 5 percent.

TABLE 2.1

Leading Causes of Death in the United States, 2005. *Data from*: Center for Disease Control, National Center for Health Statistics, 2008.

Leading Causes of Death in the United States, 2005		
Cause	Total	Percent
1. Heart Disease	652,091	26.6
2. Cancer	559,312	22.8
3. Stroke	143,579	5.9
4. Lung Diseases	130,933	5.3
5. Accidents	117,809	4.8
6. Diabetes	75,119	3.1
7. Alzheimer's Disease	71,599	2.9
8. Influenza and Pneumonia	63,001	2.6
9. Nephritis, Nephritic Syndrome, and Nephrosis	43,901	1.8
10. Septicemia	34,136	1.4

The diarrheal diseases, which were so high on the old list, are now primarily children's maladies. Today, the diarrheal diseases are not even on the list of the 10 leading causes of death.

At the global scale, diseases of infancy have been largely defeated, and such infectious diseases as tuberculosis and pneumonia are less serious threats than they were. The battles against cancer and heart disease, however, are far from won. Recent decades have brought new lifestyles, new pressures, new consumption patterns, and exposure to new chemicals, and we do not know how these affect our health. In order to distribute adequate food supplies to populations in huge urban areas, we add various kinds of preservatives to foods without knowing exactly how they will affect our health in the long run. We substitute artificial flavoring for sugar and other calorie-rich substances, but some of those substitutes have been proven to be dangerous. Despite all the sugar substitutes, obesity plagues a significant percentage of the U.S. population, bringing with it heart disease and diabetes. Even the treatment of drinking water with chemicals is rather recent in the scheme of global population change, and we do not know its long-term effects. Future chronic diseases may come from practices we take for granted as normal now.

Genetic diseases are of particular interest to medical geographers because they are disorders that tend to be transferred from one generation to the next and display clustering that raises questions about environment and long-term adaptation. Prominent among these are metabolic diseases—the body's inability to process all elements of the diet—in which enzymes play a key role. If the body fails to produce enough (or any) of a particular enzyme, that can lead to serious metabolic malfunction. For example, some people suffer from a malady called primary lactose intolerance. If you suffer from this disorder, you do not have an adequate supply of one (or a set) of enzymes that you need to break down the milk sugar lactose.

AIDS

Low life expectancies in some parts of the world are caused by the ravages of diseases such as **AIDS** (Acquired Immune Deficiency Syndrome)—a new disease identified in Africa in the early 1980s. Undoubtedly, AIDS had taken hold in Africa years earlier, perhaps decades earlier. But its rapid diffusion worldwide began in the 1980s, creating one of the greatest health catastrophes of the past century. Nowhere has its impact been greater than in Africa itself.

Medical geographers estimate that in 1980 about 200,000 people were infected with HIV (Human Immunodeficiency Virus, which causes AIDS), all of them Africans. By 2007, the number worldwide exceeded 33.2 million according to the United Nations AIDS Program, with 68 percent (22.5 million) of all cases in Subsaharan Africa! The infection rate has been slowing, and some regions have experienced a downturn, but eastern Europe and central Asia have recently seen a surge in HIV infection.

AIDS is a debilitating disease that weakens the body and reduces its capacity to combat other infections. It is spread through bodily contact that involves the exchange of bodily fluids such as blood or semen. Sexual activity and shared needles among drug users can transmit it but so can blood transfusions. Over a period of years, a person's immune system is impaired, weight loss and weakness set in, and other afflictions, such as cancer or pneumonia, may hasten an infected person's demise.

Over the past two decades, the AIDS pandemic has reached virtually all parts of the world, but its full dimensions are unknown. People infected by HIV do not immediately display visible symptoms of the disease; they can carry the virus for years without being aware of it, and during that period they can unwittingly transmit it to others. In its earliest stages a blood test is needed to confirm HIV's presence, but millions go untested. Add to this the social stigma many people attach to this malady, and it is evident that official statistics on AIDS lag far behind the real numbers.

That is true not only in Africa but in other parts of the world as well; both India and China, for example, long denied that AIDS presents a serious health threat to their populations. Now China is reporting at least 650,000 infected, and the number in India may well exceed 5 million. Estimates of the number of cases in the United States surpass 1 million; in Middle and South America, nearly 2 million are infected. But after Africa, the worst-afflicted geographic realm is Southeast Asia, with as many as 6 million cases.

Nowhere is AIDS having the impact it has had on Subsaharan Africa, however. In 2006, some 24 percent of people aged 15 to 49 were infected in Botswana, 20 percent in Zimbabwe, almost 19 percent in South Africa, and 17 percent in Zambia. These are the official data; medical geographers estimate that 20 to 25 percent of the entire population of several tropical African countries is infected. The United Nations AIDS program reports that more than 1.6 million people died of AIDS in Subsaharan Africa in 2007 alone. Geographer Peter Gould, in his book *The Slow Plague* (1993), calls Africa a "continent in catastrophe," and the demographic statistics support his viewpoint. Life expectancy in Botswana and Swaziland has declined to 34 (and is projected to fall farther), and in Zimbabwe it is 36. In a continent already ravaged by other diseases, AIDS is the leading cause of death.

AIDS is reshaping the population structure of the countries hardest hit by the disease. Demographers look at the projected population pyramids for countries with high rates of infection and no longer see population pyramids—they see population chimneys. The shape of the projected population pyramid is altered to look more like a chimney than a pyramid, reflecting the major impact AIDS plays on the younger population in the country and its future generations (Fig. 2.20). The United States Census Bureau projects that AIDS will cause higher rates of death among young women than young men. In countries with population chimneys, men will take younger and younger brides, thus increasing the rate of AIDS in younger females.

Geographers are engaging in fieldwork to understand the human toll of AIDS locally and within families. Geographer Elsbeth Robson studied the impact of AIDS in hard-hit Zimbabwe. Robson found that global processes like the diffusion of AIDS and reductions in spending on health care (often mandated by structural adjustment programs) "shape young people's home lives and structure their wider experiences." In Subsaharan Africa, the number of children orphaned when parents die from AIDS is growing rapidly (Fig. 2.21). In 2004, UNICEF reported that in just two years, between 2001 and 2003, the number of global AIDS orphans (children who have lost a parent to AIDS) rose from 11.5 million to 15 million. Robson found that in addition to the rising

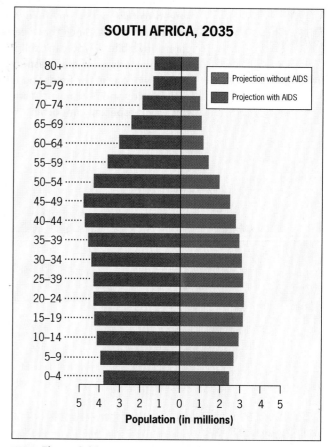

Figure 2.20

Affect of AIDS on the Population Pyramid for South Africa, predicted 2035. Estimated population, male and female, with AIDS and without AIDS. *Data from*: United States Census Bureau, 2005.

number of AIDS orphans, many young children, especially girls, are taken out of school to serve as caregivers for their relatives with AIDS (Figure 2.22). Robson found in her interviews with young caregivers that "more children are becoming young carers as households struggle to cope with income and labor losses through illness and mortality."

There are few positives to report. Uganda, once Africa's worst afflicted country, has slowed the growth of AIDS through an intensive, government-sponsored campaign of propaganda and action—notably the distribution of condoms in even the remotest part of the country. In the world's wealthier countries, remedies have been developed that can stave off the effects of AIDS for many years. But African countries cannot afford such luxuries. United Nations calculations suggest that globally upwards of $50 billion needs to be spent to slow AIDS and treat the infected by 2015; in 2007, only about 10 billion was

Guest Field Note

Marich Village, Kenya

This drawing was done by a Pokot boy in a remote primary school in North Western Kenya. He agreed to take part in my fieldwork some years after I had started researching young carers in Subsaharan Africa. Since those early interviews in Zimbabwe I have been acutely aware of young carers' invisibility—you can't tell who is a young carer just by looking at them. Indeed, invisibility is a characteristic of many aspects of the social impacts of HIV/AIDS. This young person drew himself working in the fields and taking care of cattle. The reasons why African young people help with farming and herding are many, but for young caregivers assisting their sick family members in this way is especially important.

Credit: Elsbeth Robson, Keele University

Figure 2.22

available. The impact of AIDS will be felt in African economies and in African demographics for generations to come. HIV/AIDS will constrain African economic development (see Chapter 10) and require world intervention to overcome.

thinking geographically

Study Figure 2.17, the infant mortality rate (IMR) by state in the United States. Hypothesize why the IMR is low in some regions of the country and high in others. Shift scales in your mind, and take one state and choose one state to consider—how do you think IMR varies within this state—what other factors are involved at this scale and this level of generalization to explain the pattern of IMRs? Use the population Internet sites listed at the end of this chapter to determine whether your hypotheses are correct.

HOW DO GOVERNMENTS AFFECT POPULATION CHANGE?

Over the past century, many of the world's governments have instituted policies designed to influence the overall growth rate or ethnic ratios within the population. Certain policies directly affect the birth rate via laws ranging from subsidized abortions to forced sterilization. Others influence family size through taxation or subvention. These policies fall into three groups: expansive, eugenic, and restrictive.

The former Soviet Union and China under Mao Zedong led other communist societies in **expansive population policies**, which encourage large families and raise the rate of natural increase. Ideological, anticapitalist motives drove those policies, now abandoned. Today, some countries are again pursuing expansive population policies—because their populations are aging and declining. The aging population in Europe has encouraged some countries to embark on policies to encourage

Field Note

"The day was so beautiful and the children's faces so expressive I could hardly believe I was visiting an AIDS hospice village set up for children. The Sparrow Rainbow Village on the edges of Johannesburg, South Africa, is the product of an internationally funded effort to provide children with HIV/AIDS the opportunity to spend what time they have in a clean, safe environment. Playing with the children brought home the fragility of human life and the extraordinary impacts of a modern plague that has spread relentlessly across significant parts of Sub-Saharan Africa."

Figure 2.21
Johannesburg, South Africa. © Alexander B. Murphy.

(through tax incentives and by other fiscal means) families to have more children.

Birth rates in Russia plummeted after the 1991 collapse of the Soviet Union. The total fertility rate (TFR) in Russia in 1980 was 2.04, and now the TFR for Russia is 1.34. Russian Prime Minister Vladimir Putin calls the demographic crisis Russia's greatest current problem. The Russian government offers cash subsidies of $10,000 to women who give birth to a second or third child.

In response to concerns over Russia's aging population, the government of Ulyanovsk Province has held a National Day of Conception each September 12 since 2005. In 2007, government and businesses in Ulyanovsk Province offered the afternoon off for people to participate in the National Day of Conception. The government planned to award a free car to the proud parents of one of the children born 9 months later, on June 12—the Russian National Day. On June 12, 2008 in the Ulyanovsk Province, 87 children were born, about 4 times the average daily birth rate in the province. Russia experienced an increase in TFR in the first half of 2008, but the ability to sustain a high TFR in the country will depend on many factors, including alleviating social problems, stabilizing incomes, and continued government support.

In the past, some governments engaged in **eugenic population policies**, which were designed to favor one racial or cultural sector of the population over others. Nazi Germany was a drastic example of eugenics, but other countries also have pursued eugenic strategies, though in more subtle ways. Until the time of the civil rights movement in

Figure 2.23
Chengdu, China. A large bill-board warning readers to follow China's one-child policy. © H. J. de Blij.

the 1960s, some observers accused the United States of pursuing social policies tinged with eugenics that worked against the interests of African Americans. Some argue that Japan's nearly homogeneous culture is the result of deliberately eugenic social policies. Eugenic population policies can be practiced covertly through discriminatory taxation, biased allocation of resources, and other forms of racial favoritism.

Today the majority of the world's governments seek to reduce the rate of natural increase through various forms of **restrictive population policies**. These policies range from toleration of officially unapproved means of birth control to outright prohibition of large families. China's **one-child policy**, instituted after the end of the Maoist period in the 1970s, drastically reduced China's growth rate from one of the world's fastest to one of the developing world's slowest (Fig. 2.23). Under the one-child policy, families that had more than one child were penalized financially, and educational opportunities and housing privileges were kept from families who broke the one-child mandate.

Population growth rates in China fell quickly under the one-child policy. In the 1970s, China's growth rate was 3 percent; in the mid-1980s it was 1.2 percent; and, today, China's growth rate is 0.7 percent. The main goal of the one-child policy was achieved, but the policy also had several unintended consequences, including an increased abortion rate, an increase in female infanticide, and a high rate of orphaned girls (many of who we were adopted in the United States and Canada).

During the 1990s, under pressure to improve its human rights records and also with the realization that the population was quickly becoming gender (Fig. 2.24) and

age imbalanced (Fig. 2.25), China relaxed its one-child policy. Several caveats allow families to have more than one child. For example, if you live in a rural area and your first child is a girl, you can have a second child, and if both parents of the child are only children, they can have a second child. With these changes, the National Bureau of Statistics of China now estimates that the population growth rate in China will climb again over the next 10 years.

Limitations

Population policies are not independent of circumstances that can influence growth and decline. In the 1980s, the government of Sweden adopted family-friendly policies designed to promote gender equality and boost fertility rates. The programs focused on alleviating much of the cost of having and raising children. In Sweden, couples who work and have small children receive cash payments, tax incentives, job leaves, and work flexibility that last up to eight years after the birth of a child. The policies led to a mini-birth-rate-boom by the early 1990s.

When the Swedish economy slowed shortly thereafter, however, so did the birth rate. The children born in 1991 made up a class of 130,000 students in the Swedish education system. But the children born three years later, in 1994, made up a class of only 75,000 students. The government had to build new classrooms for the temporary population boom, but then faced excess capacity when the boom subsided. Sweden's population policies have helped to produce a natural rate of increase that is a little higher than that in many other European countries,

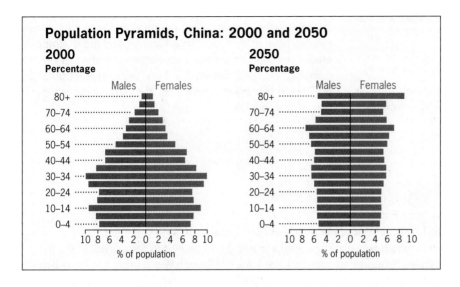

Population Pyramids, China: 2000 and 2050

 **Figure 2.24**
Population Pyramids, China: 2000 and 2050. *Data from:* Population Reference Bureau, 2005.

but these policies can achieve only so much. With a TFR still well below 2, the Swedish government continues to think about new ways to support families and promote birth rates. One imaginative, but not evidently successful, approach was suggested by a spokeswoman for the Christian Democrat Party, who urged Swedish television to show racier programming at night in hopes of returning the population to a higher birth rate!

Contradictions

Some areas of the world with low population growth rates (Fig. 2.9) are in the very heart of the Roman Catholic world. Roman Catholic doctrine opposes birth control and abortion. Adherence to this doctrine appears to be stronger in areas remote from the Vatican (headquarters of the Catholic Church). For example, in the Philippines,

thousands of miles from the Vatican, in Asia's only Roman Catholic country, the still-powerful Catholic Church opposes the use of artificial contraceptives, which the Philippine government supports as a method of controlling population growth. The Church and the Philippine State agree on abortion, as the Philippine constitution prohibits abortion.

Among Islamic countries, the geographic pattern is the opposite. Saudi Arabia, home to Mecca—the hearth of Islam—has one of the world's fastest population growth rates (2.7 percent). But in Indonesia, thousands of miles from Mecca and near the Philippines, the government began a nationwide family planning program in 1970. When fundamentalist Muslim leaders objected, the government used a combination of coercion and inducement to negate their influence. By 2000, Indonesia's family planning program had lowered the growth rate to 1.6 percent, and today it stands at 1.4 percent.

Percent of Total Population

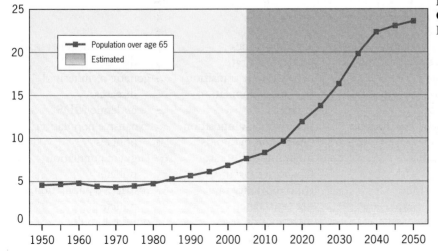

Figure 2.25
Percent of Population over Age 65 in China, 1950–2050. *Data from:* Population Reference Bureau, 2005.

When studying government policies on population, one of the most important things to remember is unintended consequences. Choose one country in the world where women have little access to education and are disempowered. Consider the previous section of this chapter on age composition, and determine how restrictive population policies in this country will alter the population composition of the country.

Summary

In the late 1700s, Thomas Malthus sounded warning bells about the rapidly growing population in Great Britain. He feared a massive famine would soon "check" the growing population, bringing widespread suffering. Although the famine in Great Britain did not take place as he predicted, the rapidly growing worldwide population made many more follow Malthus's trajectory, issuing similar warnings about the population explosion over the last two centuries.

The growth rate of the world population has certainly slowed, but human suffering is not over yet. Dozens of countries still face high death rates and high birth rates. Even in countries where the death rate is low, slowed population growth is often a result of horrid sanitary and medical conditions that lead to high infant and child mortality, diseases such as AIDS that ravage the population and orphan the young, or famines that governments deny and that global organizations cannot ameliorate.

Population pyramids illustrate that as wealthier countries worry about supporting their aging populations, poorer countries have problems of their own. A high birth rate in a poor country does not necessarily mean overpopulation—some of the highest population densities in the world are found in wealthy countries. Even poor countries that have lowered their birth rates and their death rates are constantly negotiating what is morally acceptable to their people and their cultures.

Geography offers much to the study of population. Through geography we can see differences in population problems across space, how what happens at one scale affects what goes on at other scales, and how different cultures and countries approach population questions.

Geographic Concepts

population density
arithmetic population
    density
physiological population
    density
population distribution
dot map
megalopolis
census
doubling time
population explosion
natural increase

crude birth rate
crude death rate
demographic transition
stationary population
    level
population composition
population pyramids
infant mortality rate
newborn mortality rate
child mortality rate
life expectancy
infectious diseases

chronic or degenerative
    diseases
genetic or inherited
    diseases
    endemic AIDS
expansive population
    policies
eugenic population
    policies
restrictive population
    policies
one-child policy

Learn More Online

About Population Growth in the World
www.prb.org

About the Composition of the Population of the United States
www.census.gov

About the Global AIDS Crisis
www.unaids.org/en/
www.npr.org/healthscience/aids2004/

About International Population Programs
www.unfpa.org

Watch It Online

About the Population Transition in Italy
www.learner.org/resources/series85.html#program_descriptions

CHAPTER 3

Migration

Field Note Risking Lives for Remittances

A decade ago, I was on my way to Rosenstiel Marine Center on Virginia Key, off the coast of Miami, Florida. I noticed an overcrowded boat, with about 70 people on board. The Haitians were fleeing the most impoverished country in the Western Hemisphere. Most of the would-be illegal immigrants were men, and there were perhaps half a dozen women and as many children. They jumped overboard prematurely when the Coast Guard approached, and some undoubtedly lost their lives; others made it to the beach and ran for the road.

The Haitians the Coast Guard caught were sent home to Haiti with other illegal Haitian immigrants. The chance of getting caught is high, the travel is treacherous, and hundreds die off the coast of Florida each year. The hope of a job in the United States and the lack of hope in their lives and homes in Haiti compel them to try. The immigrants know that if they make it to shore and can find their way to the homes of friends and family, they can find employment and will live under the radar of the Immigration and Naturalization Service (Fig. 3.1).

■■■ Figure 3.1
Miami, Florida.   A sailboat carrying more than 100 Haitians waits for the United States Coast Guard to pick them up after fleeing Haiti in June 1994.   © AP/Wide World Photos.

Across the world, hundreds of thousands of migrants have fled their homelands by boat, train, car, or foot for opportunities—in North America, Australia, China, and Europe. These immigrants are sometimes welcomed and sometimes turned away. In the United States in the 1970s, the government of the United States welcomed Haitian immigrants because of the growing repressiveness of the government in Haiti at the time and also because most of the Haitian migrants in the 1970s were educated and able to afford travel to the United States. As the political and economic situations in Haiti worsened in the 1980s, the United States changed its policy to one that mandates the automatic deportation of all Haitians the U.S. government catches arriving illegally—by boat or any other method.

Governments greatly impact migration flows by opening and closing doors to migrants. In some cases, the policy is not as simple as the door being open or shut. Since the Clinton administration, the U.S. government has had a "wet foot, dry foot" policy toward Cuban immigrants. If Cuban immigrants are intercepted at sea, they are deported, but if Cuban immigrants make it to land, they have the right to stay.

Why are immigrants willing to risk their lives on overcrowded boats or by crossing treacherous deserts across parts of the United States—Mexico border? Economics provides part of the answer, but it does not explain the whole story. The Pew Hispanic Center found in a 2005 survey that the vast majority of undocumented (illegal) migrants from Mexico "were gainfully employed" in Mexico before they left for the United States. Perception is an overwhelming factor in migration—as long as migrants perceive a better life abroad, they will continue to migrate.

Migration flows vary by region, hometown (rural versus urban), gender, socioeconomic class, age, race, and ethnicity. Geographers who study gender and migration realize that the dynamics of individual households in the sending countries determine who migrates, when they migrate, and where they go.

Today, an estimated 11.3 million illegal immigrants live in the United States, many of whom work in order to send money home to family. Monies migrants send home to family are called **remittances**. Haitians living in the United States, Canada, and the Caribbean sent home over $1 billion in remittances in 2007, a figure equivalent to 30 percent of Haiti's gross domestic product and far outpacing the value of Haitian exports. The 2001 census in Haiti estimates that one in five households in Haiti receives remittances from abroad.

The economies of many poorer countries in the Caribbean, Africa, Central and South America, and Eurasia depend in part on remittances sent to their citizens. In 2007, Mexican immigrants sent $23.98 billion in remittances home, up from $23.05 billion the year before.

Not all immigrants are illegal. Of the estimated 37.9 million immigrants in the United States today, 26.6 million are legal immigrants (Fig. 3.2). Countries recognize the need for immigrant labor, and many have policies allowing—indeed encouraging—legal immigrants to work under temporary visas to fill a need. Thousands of people who work in the United States and Canada are there on temporary visas to fill seasonal jobs in agriculture and forestry. In the United States, over 45,000 agricultural laborers legally enter the country each year under a program that allows unskilled laborers into the country, as long as no Americans want the jobs. Canada began to allow agricultural laborers into the country in 1966. In both Canada and the United States, the vast majority of legal agricultural

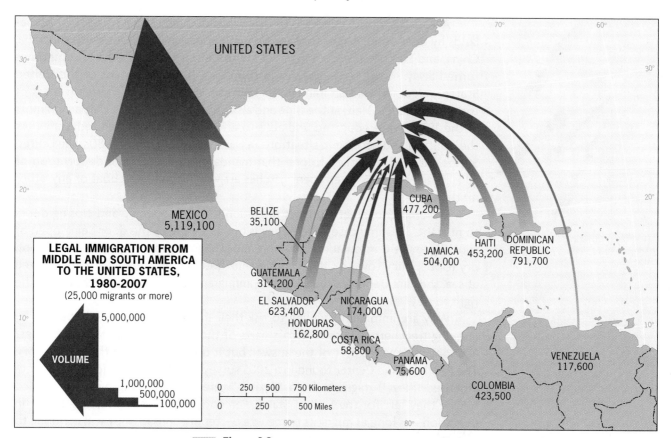

Figure 3.2
Legal Immigration from Middle and South America to the United States, 1980–2007.
Data from: United States Department of Homeland Security, Yearbook of Immigration Statistics, 2007.

laborers come from Mexico. Canadian companies travel to Mexico to recruit agricultural laborers from rural Mexico and laborers for the hotel industry from urban areas of Mexico.

Since September 11, 2001, many countries have cracked down on immigration, making legal and illegal immigration more difficult. The United States has earmarked more money for building fences along its border with Mexico, hiring additional border patrols, and installing new technology to intercept would-be terrorists. The cultural landscape of the border region is changing. The government is erecting specially designed fences that are difficult to climb, while at the same time ensuring the fences have spaces where people across the border can speak with each other. The new fences and security south of San Diego, California, are pushing illegal immigration farther east into the desert. The fences in the desert are marked by empty water bottles and memorials to Mexicans who have died trying to cross the border (Fig. 3.3).

Eventhough globalization has promoted a freer flow of goods across the world, and the North American Free Trade Agreement (NAFTA) has established freer trade among Mexico, the United States, and Canada, the free flow of people is far from realized. Less than a decade ago, the U.S. government commissioned a barrier dividing Nogales, Arizona, from Nogales, Mexico. The *New York Times* reported that the architecture firm that designed the wall followed government requirements that it be aesthetically pleasing to "evoke the friendship" between the two countries while also making it "resistant to physical assault by means such

■ Figure 3.3
Tijuana, Mexico.   Tijuana and San Diego, California are separated by a highly guarded border
infrastructure that in this section includes two walls to discourage illegal crossing. Human rights
activists placed crosses on the wall to memorialize people who died while attempting to cross into
the United States.   © AP/Wide World Photos.

as welding torches, chisels, hammers, firearms, climbing over or penetration with
vehicles." Illegal immigrants go to great lengths to find their way into the United
States; and similarly, the U.S. government goes to great lengths to deter illegal
immigration.

In this chapter, we examine various types of migration and question why
migrants choose to leave a particular place and why they go to a particular place.
We also examine the barriers governments erect to slow human migration, questioning why government policies shift and how policies affect migration flows. By
employing geographic concepts such as scale in our analysis of human migration,
we seek to shed light on the nature and meaning of migration flows and to gain an
appreciation for why people migrate, where they migrate, and how people, places,
and landscapes change as a result.

Key Questions For Chapter 3

1. What is migration?
2. Why do people migrate?
3. Where do people migrate?
4. How do governments affect migration?

WHAT IS MIGRATION?

Movement is inherently geographical. Movement changes people, as well as the way they see themselves in the world. Movement changes places—both the places the people left and the places where they go. Human movement speeds the diffusion of ideas and innovations; it intensifies spatial interaction and transforms regions; and it is often closely linked to environmental conditions.

The movement of humans takes several forms. Mobility ranges from local to global—from the daily to once in a lifetime. Mobility has increased markedly over the past decades. With greater mobility, people broaden their perspectives and widen the horizons of others, thus encouraging further mobility. All movement involves leaving home. The three types of movement we discuss in this section vary based on time away from home. **Cyclic movement** involves shorter periods away from home; **periodic movement** involves longer periods away from home; and **migration** involves a degree of permanence the other two do not: with migration, the mover may never return "home."

Cyclic Movement

Cyclic movement involves journeys that begin at our home base and *bring us back to it*. The great majority of people have a daily routine that takes them through a regular sequence of short moves within a local area. These moves create what geographers call **activity spaces**. The scale of activity space varies across societies. You may go to classes every weekday and perhaps to a job as well, creating a relatively confined and stable activity space, diversified by shopping trips and social activities. The average activity space of a North American covers a greater amount of territory than that of an average African or Southwest Asian.

Commuting is also a cyclic movement. Commuting—the journey from home to work and home again—takes from minutes to hours and can involve several modes of transportation. The average North American commuter travels a greater distance each day than the average Chinese villager does in a year. Advances in transportation technology have expanded daily activity spaces. Cars and vast infrastructure enable people to commute over long distances. In Washington, D.C., commuters combine use of their cars, commuter trains, and the metro to travel upwards of 100 miles each way, each day, commuting not only from the surrounding suburbs, but also from Delaware, West Virginia, and central Virginia. By airplane, commuters arrive at work in Washington, D.C., from New York City. Others, such as members of Congress, commute from their home state, keeping houses there and apartments in the Washington, D.C. area.

Another form of cyclic movement is seasonal movement. Every autumn, hundreds of thousands of travelers leave their homes in Canada and the northern parts of the United States and seek the winter sun in Florida and other "Sunbelt" States, returning in the spring. This seasonal transfer has huge economic consequences (and electoral significance) in depopulated northern towns and burgeoning tourist centers in the South.

This kind of seasonal movement is a luxury. Another type of cyclic movement, **nomadism**, is a matter of survival, culture, and tradition. Nomadism is dwindling across the world, but it can still be found in parts of Asia and Africa. Westerners often envision nomadism as an aimless wandering across steppe and desert by small groups of rootless roamers—people who claim no territory and do not behave territorially. In reality, nomads need to know their territory well in order to find water, food, and shelter in their cyclic movements. Nomadic movement takes place along long-familiar routes repeated time and again. The nomads and their animals visit water sources and pastures that have served their ancestors for centuries. Weather conditions may affect the timing of their route, but barring obstacles such as fenced international borders or the privatization of long-used open country, nomads engage in cyclic movement.

Periodic Movement

Periodic movement, like cyclic movement, involves returning home. Periodic movement involves *a longer period of time* away from the home base than cyclic movement. One common type of periodic movement is **migrant labor**, which involves millions of workers in the United States and tens of millions worldwide. The need for migrant labor in the farm fields of California, Florida, and other parts of the United States creates a large flow of cross-border movers, many of whom eventually become immigrants.

A specialized form of periodic movement is **transhumance**—a system of pastoral farming in which ranchers move livestock according to the seasonal availability of pastures. This is a periodic form of movement because it involves a long period of residential relocation (unlike classic nomadism). In Switzerland, for example, cattle are driven up the mountain slopes to high, fresh pastures during the summer; farm families follow the herds, taking up residence in cottages that are abandoned during the cold winter. In the "Horn" of Northeast Africa, hundreds of thousands of people follow their livestock from highland to lowland and back in search of pastures renewed by seasonal rainfall.

Periodic movement takes on other forms as well. If you leave home to attend a college far away, you are living away from home for four (or more) years. Although you may retain a home address in your place of origin, you now spend the great majority of your time in your new abode (traveling home only for breaks), and your mobility cannot be categorized as cyclic.

Military service is another form of periodic movement. In a given year, as many as 10 million U.S. citizens, including military personnel and their families, are moved to new locations where they will spend tours of duty that can last several years.

Migration

When movement results in permanent relocation across significant distances, it is classified as *migration*. The process of migration involves the long-term relocation of an individual, household, or larger group to a new locale outside the community of origin.

International migration, movement across country borders, is also called transnational migration. When a migrant leaves the home country, he or she is classified as an emigrant (one who migrates out) of the home country. When the same migrant enters a new country, he or she is classified as an immigrant (one who migrates in) of the new country. Emigration subtracts from the total popula-

tion of a country, and **immigration** adds to the total population of a country.

Countries also experience **internal migration**—migration that occurs within a single country's borders. Mapping internal migration routes reveals patterns of well-defined streams of migrants that change over time. Early in the twentieth century, a major migration stream took tens of thousands of African American families from the South of the United States to the industrializing cities of the Northeast and Midwest. Today, major internal migration movements in the United States are carrying migrants to the Sunbelt and the Far West (Fig. 3.4).

Internal migration varies according to the mobility of the population. In mobile societies, internal migration over long distances is common. In the United States, the flow of internal migration is not as simple as rural to urban. Rather, in the past few decades, internal migrants have flocked to the economically dynamic regions of the Sunbelt and Far West. Internal migrants have escaped from large cities and rural areas to move to medium-sized cities for retirement or family-friendly lifestyles; and wealthy individuals who seek solace and space have moved into environmentally attractive rural areas, trying to keep

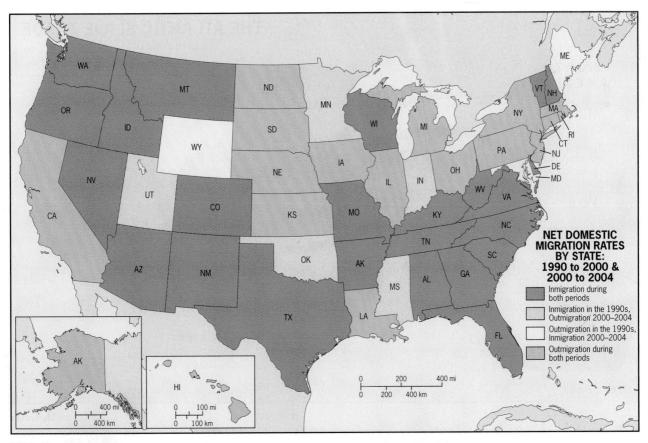

Figure 3.4
Recent Internal Migration in the United States. *Courtesy of:* United States Census Bureau, Population Estimates Program, 2004.

the area "rural," while pushing out farmers. The U.S. population is the most mobile in the world. More than 5 million people move from one State to another every year, and nearly seven times as many—an average of 35 million—move within their State, county, or community. On average, an American citizen moves once about every six years.

Relatively new migrants also migrate internally within their new home country. Since the 1940s, the American Southwest and Florida have attracted millions of migrants from Latin America to the United States. Most migrants stayed in these same basic regions, perhaps migrating part of the year to work in agricultural fields. In 1986, the US government passed the Immigration Reform and Control Act (IRCA), legislation that gave amnesty and permanent residence to 2.6 million migrants who had been living in the United States for a long period of time. The newly legal migrants under IRCA could move anywhere, and during the 1990s, many moved to the Great Plains and Midwest and also to the South (Fig. 3.5). Migrants found the South attractive for the same reasons other Americans were—the growth of

the Sunbelt economy in the 1990s brought numerous job opportunities, and the warm climate year round was also attractive.

In Peru, which is a less mobile society than the U.S. society, the pattern of internal migration is generally from rural to urban. Migrants have left rural areas and moved to Lima, the capital. Global and national investment capital is concentrated in Lima. The capital represents the major focus of economic opportunity for the rural population. Lima receives the vast majority of Peru's migrants, regardless of age, gender, or marital status.

Choose one type of cyclic or periodic movement and then think of a specific example of the kind of movement you chose. Now, determine how this movement changes both the home and the destination. How do these places change as a result of this cyclic or period movement?

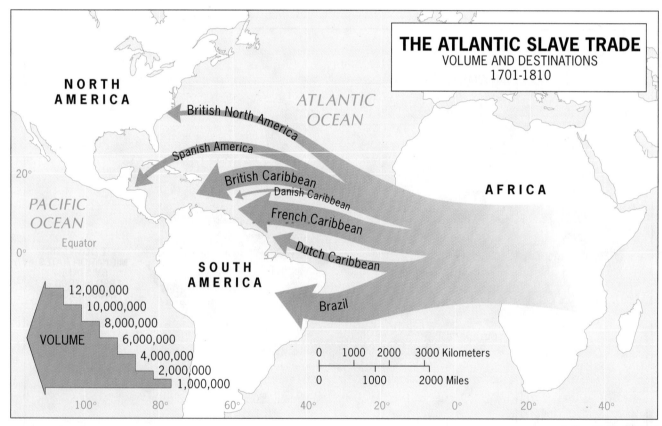

(after P. D. Curtin)

Figure 3.5
The Atlantic Slave Trade. *Adapted with permission from:* Philip D. Curtin, *The Atlantic Slave Trade.* University of Wisconsin Press, 1969, p. 57 and Donald K. Fellows, *Geography.* John Wiley & Sons, Inc., 1967, p. 121.

WHY DO PEOPLE MIGRATE?

Migration can be the result of a voluntary action, a conscious decision to move from one place to the next. It can also be the result of involuntary action, a forced movement chosen by one group of people for another group of people. **Forced migration** involves the imposition of authority or power, producing involuntary migration movements that cannot be understood based on theories of choice. **Voluntary migration** occurs after a migrant weighs options and choices (even if desperately or not so rationally), and can be analyzed and understood as a series of options or choices that result in movement.

The distinction between forced and voluntary migration is not always clear-cut. The enormous European migration to the United States during the nineteenth and early twentieth centuries is often cited as a prime example of voluntary migration. However, some European migration can be construed as forced. The British treatment of the Irish during their colonial rule over Ireland can be seen as political persecution—a cause for forced migration. During British colonialism in Ireland, the British took control of nearly all of the Irish Catholic lands and discouraged the operation of the Catholic Church in Ireland. Until 1829, the British enforced penal laws preventing Irish Catholics from buying land, voting, or carrying weapons. The mass exodus of migrants from Ireland to North America in the mid-1800s can be seen as forced, both because of the British treatment of the Irish and because of the potato famine, but it can also be seen as voluntary in that the Irish chose to go to North America.

At the scale of an individual region or country, we can question whether a decision to migrate is forced or voluntary. At the scale of the household, the decision to migrate is all the more complex. For certain members of a migrating household, the move may be under duress, and for others, the move may be a preferred choice. The neutral title "migrant" veils the complexities of decision making at the household scale. Geographic studies of gender in migration reveal the complexities of migration at the household scale. At the household scale, geographers consider power relationships, divisions of labor, and gender identities in understanding migration flows. Here, decisions are made, in geographer Victoria Lawson's terms, in a "cooperative conflict bargaining process." Who has a say in this process and how much of a say each individual has depend on gendered power relationships and responsibilities in the household.

Studies of gender and migration find that, in many regions, men are more mobile than women and men migrate farther than women. Generally, men have more choices of employment than women, and women earn less than men in the jobs they find at the destination. One study of migration in Mexican households found that strongly patriarchal households shield young women from migration, sending young men out to work. Mexican households without a strong patriarchy send young, unmarried women to the city or another country to gain employment.

Thus, geographers cannot easily describe migration flows in terms of men and women or forced and voluntary. Ultimately, the decision or directive to migrate happens to an individual migrant within a household, place, country, region, and world, each of which has its own dynamics. The key difference between voluntary and forced migration, however, is that voluntary migrants have an option (at the very least—where to go or what to do once there); forced migrants do not.

Forced Migration

The largest and most devastating forced migration in the history of humanity was the Atlantic slave trade, which carried tens of millions of Africans from their homes to South America, the Caribbean, and North America, with huge loss of life. The number of Africans sold into slavery will never be known (estimates range from 12 million to 30 million). Figure 3.5 shows an approximation of the numbers involved, as well as the destinations of the trans-Atlantic African deportees.

Because slavery plays a major role in U.S. history, many students in the United States assume the vast majority of African slaves were forced across the Atlantic and into the southeastern United States. However, as the map shows, a considerable majority of Africans were forced across the Atlantic to the Caribbean region, to coastal Middle America, and to Brazil.

The Atlantic slave trade began during the sixteenth century, when Africans were first brought to the Caribbean. In the early decades of the seventeenth century, they arrived in small numbers on plantations that were developing in coastal eastern North America. Plantation economies from the southeastern United States to Brazil helped drive the slave trade. The wealth promised through plantation agriculture created a demand for slaves by plantation owners, who paid European shippers for slaves, who in turn paid African raiders for slaves. Of all crops produced on plantations in the Americas and Caribbean during the 1700s, sugar was the most important economically. Figure 3.5 reflects the scramble for sugar islands in the Caribbean, as the map names Spanish, British, Danish, French, and Dutch colonies in the Caribbean as destinations for slaves. Add the coffee, fruit, and sugar plantations in Brazil and the cotton plantations of the southeastern United States, and the destinations on the map make sense.

The terror and destruction of slave raiding afflicted large areas of Africa. Much of West Africa was exploited, from Liberia to Nigeria and inland to the margins of the Sahara. So many Africans were taken from the area that is now Benin to Bahia in Brazil that significant elements of the local culture remained intact in the transition. Today there are strong ties between Bahia and Benin, and cultural exchanges are growing stronger. The entire Equatorial African coastal region was victimized as well, and Portuguese slave traders raided freely in the Portuguese domains of Angola and Mozambique. Arab slave raiders were active in East Africa and the Horn, penetrating Equatorial Africa and often cooperating with the Europeans. Zanzibar, off the coast of mainland Tanzania, long was a major slave market.

We know proportionately where slaves ended up, but we can never gauge the full impact of this horrific period. In *A Colonizer's Model of the World*, geographer James Blaut discussed the sheer loss to African civilizations that occurred when significant populations were enslaved. The Atlantic slave trade also changed the Caribbean, where on many islands the vast majority of people are of African-Caribbean descent, and few, if any, indigenous peoples remain. In combination, the slave trade inflicted incalculable damage on African societies and communities, and changed the cultural and ethnic geography of Brazil, Middle America, and the United States.

Although no forced migration in human history compares in magnitude to the Atlantic slave trade, there have been other forced migrations that have changed the world's demographic map. For 50 years beginning in 1788, tens of thousands of convicts were shipped from Britain to Australia, where they had a lasting impact on the continent's population geography. In the 1800s, the U.S. government took lands from thousands of Native Americans and forcibly moved them to other areas of the country—some far from their traditional homelands. In the Soviet Union during Stalin's ruthless rule between the late 1920s and 1953, the government forcibly moved millions of non-Russians from their homes to remote parts of Central Asia and Siberia for political reasons. During the 1930s in Germany, the Nazis were responsible for a significant forced migration of Jews from portions of Western Europe that fell under their control.

Forced migration still happens today. It continues to occur, for example, in the form of countermigration, in which governments send back migrants caught entering their countries illegally. In the 1990s, the United States repatriated Haitian arrivals from Florida. For 30 years, people from Afghanistan have left the country in search of safety from civil war, the Taliban, and the current instability of the Afghan War. Approximately 10 million Afghans have been refugees since 1979, fleeing mainly to Pakistan and Iran. Policies toward these refugees have shifted over time. During the 1980s and the early 1990s, the international community sent substantial aid to Pakistan to help them serve the refugee population.

After the Taliban took control of Afghanistan in 1994, support for Pakistan waned and the Pakistan government forced the repatriation of thousands of Afghans. Since September 11, 2001, the international community, led by the UNHCR has helped Pakistan and Iran repatriate nearly 5 million refugees to Afghanistan. Currently, 3 million Afghans are registered refugees in Iran and Pakistan, and approximately 1 million more Afghans in Pakistan are not registered as refugees. The repatriation of Afghans continues and is complicated by the current war and the fact that over half the Afghan refugees in Pakistan and Iran were born there . . . not in Afghanistan.

Push and Pull Factors in Voluntary Migration

Why do people choose to migrate? Researchers have been intrigued by this question for more than a century. Studies of voluntary migration flows indicate that the intensity of a migration flow varies with such factors as similarities between the source and the destination, the effectiveness of the flow of information from the destination back to the source, and the physical distance between the source and the destination.

Over a century ago, British demographer Ernst Ravenstein sought an answer to the question of why people voluntarily migrate. He studied internal migration in England, and on the basis of his data he proposed several **laws of migration**, many of which are still relevant today including:

1. Every migration flow generates a return or counter-migration.
2. The majority of migrants move a short distance.
3. Migrants who move longer distances tend to choose big-city destinations.
4. Urban residents are less migratory than inhabitants of rural areas.
5. Families are less likely to make international moves than young adults.

Ravenstein also posited an inverse relationship between the volume of migration and the distance between source and destination; that is, the number of migrants to a destination declines as the distance they must travel increases. Ravenstein's idea is an early observation of the **gravity model**, which predicts interaction between places on the basis of their population size and distance between them. The gravity model assumes spatial interaction (such as migration) is directly related to the populations and inversely related to the *distance* between them—an assumption that had more meaning in an age before airplane travel and the Internet. In mathematical terms, the equation for the gravity model is the multiplication of the two populations divided by the distance between them.

Although the gravity model gives us a guide to expected migration, migration is not as simple as a mathematical equation. When a person, family, or group of people makes a voluntary decision to migrate, push and pull factors come into play. **Push factors** are the conditions and perceptions that help the migrant decide to leave a place. **Pull factors** are the circumstances that effectively attract the migrant to certain locales from other places—the decision of where to go. A migrant's decision to emigrate from the home country and migrate to a new country results from a combination of push and pull factors—and these factors play out differently depending on the circumstance and scale of the migration. Because a migrant is likely to be more familiar with his or her place of residence (source) than with the locale to which he or she is moving (destination), a migrant will likely perceive push factors more accurately than pull factors. Push factors include individual considerations such as work or retirement conditions, cost of living, personal safety and security, and, for many, environmental catastrophes or even issues like weather and climate. Pull factors tend to be vaguer and may depend solely on perceptions construed from things heard and read rather than on experiences in the destination place. Often, migrants move on the basis of excessively positive images and expectations regarding their destinations.

When considering pull factors, the principle of **distance decay** comes into play (Fig. 3.6). Prospective migrants are likely to have more complete perceptions of nearer places than of farther ones, which confirms the notion that the intensity of human activity, process, or function declines as distance from its source increases. Since interaction with faraway places generally decreases as distance increases, prospective migrants are likely to feel much less certain about distant destinations than about nearer ones. This leads many migrants to move less far than they originally contemplated.

Many migration streams that appear on maps as long, unbroken routes in fact consist of a series of stages, a phenomenon known as **step migration**. A peasant family in rural Brazil, for example, is likely to move first to a village, then to a nearby town, later to a city, and finally to a metropolis such as São Paulo or Rio de Janeiro. At each stage a new set of pull factors comes into play.

Not all migrants from one place follow the same steps. When 1000 people leave a village and migrate to a town in a given year, most, if not all, of them may dream of making it to—and in—the "big city." But only about 500 may actually move from town to city, and of these, only 200 eventually reach the metropolis that impelled them to move in the first place. Along the way the majority are captured by **intervening opportunity**. This happened when African Americans by the tens of thousands migrated northward after World War I to seek work in growing cities like Chicago and Cleveland. Many found employment in St. Louis and Cincinnati; that is, they encountered intervening opportunities along their northbound routes.

Along any route of migration, whether direct, in steps, or interrupted by intervening opportunity, a voluntary migrant weighs push and pull factors.

Types of Push and Pull Factors

What specific factors impel people to pull up stakes and leave the familiar for the uncertain? What specific factors help migrants choose a destination? Research has shown that typically a combination of factors, not just one, leads to deciding it is time to move and deciding where to go. Any single factor can be either a push for the migrant to leave the home country or a pull to the new country, and which factor matters most depends on the migrant and the circumstances surrounding the decision to migrate.

Legal Status

Migrants can arrive in a country with (legally) or without (illegally) the consent of the host country. Each country around the world gets to determine who is allowed to migrate to their country and under what circumstances. If you apply for and receive a work visa from another country, you are legally allowed to live in the country and work there for the time allotted on the visa (usually a period of months or years). Having a visa makes you a legal migrant because you have your documents, your visa, to show your legal right to be in the place. If you do not have a visa, you are an illegal, or undocumented, migrant in the country.

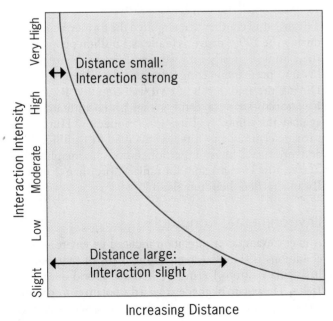

Figure 3.6
Distance Decay. © E.H. Fouberg, A.B. Murphy, H. J. de Blij, and John Wiley & Sons, Inc.

Undocumented or illegal migrants choose quite different options for finding their way into the country than legal migrants do, simply because they do not want to be caught for fear of **deportation** (being sent back home).

Economic Conditions

Poverty has driven countless millions from their homelands and continues to do so. Perceived opportunities in destinations such as Western Europe and North America impel numerous migrants, both legal and illegal, to cross the Mediterranean, the Caribbean, and the Rio Grande in search of a better life. The lower economic position of migrants in their host countries can lead to exploitation by employers and others. The United Nations convention on the Protection of the Rights of All Migrant Workers and Members of Their Families recognizes the precarious position of migrant workers—their need for work and their desire to not be deported. The convention establishes standards of treatment for migrant workers. Although only 22 states have signed onto the convention, its statements on human trafficking and the right of migrant workers to equal wages are influencing states' migration policies.

Power Relationships

Gender, ethnicity, race, and money are all factors in the decision to migrate. The power relationships already embedded in society enable the flow of migrants around the world. Employers who hire migrant workers often have perceptions of what kinds of migrants would best work for them.

Women in the Middle East hire Southeast Asian women to work as domestic servants, housekeepers, and nannies. Geographer Paul Boyle points out that by hiring women from abroad, the female head of household establishes a relationship in which the employee's "ethnicity and citizenship status differentiates them from their female employer and this influences the power relationships that underpin the working arrangements." In their study of placement agencies that help people hire domestic workers, Stiell and England found that certain ethnicities were portrayed according to a scripted stereotype. For instance, workers from the Caribbean went from being portrayed as "docile, jolly and good with children" to being depicted as "difficult, aggressive and selfish," and women from the Philippines are in demand now as they are being portrayed as "'naturally' docile, subservient, hard-working, good natured, domesticated, and willing to endure long hours of housework and child-care with little complaint."

Race is also a factor in the hiring of migrant workers. For example, carpet companies in Dalton, Georgia (the carpet capital of the world) began hiring Mexican workers after the 1986 passage of IRCA because they saw them as hard workers who were loyal to one company. In the same time frame, North and South Carolina have also experienced surges in the Mexican migrant population. Geographer

Jamie Winders cites the work of several researchers in the South whose research "raises the issue of displacement of black workers by Mexican migration—a topic hinted at by many studies but addressed by few." Issues of race and migrant status in hiring can spill over into neighborhoods as they have recently in Raleigh, North Carolina, where in the last 10 years conflicts over affordable housing between the African Americans who lived in the neighborhoods and Mexican migrants who moved into the neighborhoods for the same affordable housing have arisen.

Geographer Paul Boyle also cites the power relationships based on money in the growing migration industry, whereby migration flows are contractually arranged in order to fill labor needs for particular economic sectors throughout the world. Contractors give migrants advances on their income, help them migrate to the new country or region within a country, and then take wages in order to pay for advances and other needs the contractor supplies to the migrants.

Political Circumstances

Throughout history oppressive regimes have engendered migration streams. Desperate migrants fled Vietnam by the hundreds of thousands after the communists took control of the country in 1975. In 1972 Uganda's dictator, Idi Amin, expelled 50,000 Asians and Ugandans of Asian descent from his country. The Cuban communist dictatorship expelled more than 125,000 Cubans in 1980 in the "Mariel Boatlift." Politically driven migration flows are marked by both escape and expulsion.

Armed Conflict and Civil War

The dreadful conflict that engulfed the former Yugoslavia during the 1990s drove as many as 3 million people from their homes, mostly into western Europe. Many people became permanent emigrants, unable to return home. During the mid-1990s, a civil war engulfed Rwanda in Equatorial Africa, a conflict that pitted militant Hutu against the minority Tutsi and "moderate" Hutu. The carnage claimed an estimated 800,000 to 1 million lives and produced huge migration flows into neighboring Zaïre (now Congo) and Tanzania. More than 2 million Rwandans fled their homeland.

Environmental Conditions

A major example of migration induced by environmental conditions is the movement of hundreds of thousands of Irish citizens from Ireland to the New World during the 1840s. The potato blight destroyed the potato crop, creating famine. The famine was exacerbated by a set of political conditions for which the British government has recently apologized—a reminder that environmental conditions rarely operate in a social vacuum. But this migration with an

This photo shows the damage caused by the 1995 eruption of the Sourfriere Hills volcano on the Caribbean Island of Montserrat. In the foreground you can see the grey volcanic ash clogging the roadbed, and in the background the abandoned capital city of Plymouth. Many buildings cannot even be entered because the ash has buried their first floors or caved in their ceilings. This scene illustrated for me the complexities of migration in the face of natural disasters. Many Montserrations fled to the United States when Plymouth was destroyed, and were given "temporary protected" immigration status. The U.S. government told Montserratian refugees to leave in 2005—not because the volcanic crisis was over or because the housing crisis caused by the volcano was solved. Rather, the U.S. government expected the volcanic crisis to last at least 10 more years; so, the Monsterratians no longer qualified as "temporary" refugees.

Credit: Jason Dittmer, University College London

Figure 3.7

environmental component permanently altered the demographics of both Ireland (the source) and the northeastern region of the United States (the chief destination).

Environmental crises such as earthquakes, hurricanes, and volcanic eruptions also stimulate migrations. For example, a surge of migration follows every major earthquake in California and flooding as from Hurricane Katrina or the 2008 floods in the midwestern United States. Because many migrants return, the net outflow generated by such momentary crises is usually small, but not always. New Orleans is estimated to have lost close to 40% of its population as a result of Hurricane Katrina.

Some environmental crises, such as volcanic eruptions, bring long-term environmental changes to the landscape, making return migration difficult, if not impossible. For example, the Caribbean island of Montserrat had a small population of about 10,000 prior to a volcanic eruption that began in 1995. The volcano has been active since then, prompting a migration flow. Geographer Jason Dittmer studied how drastically the physical and cultural landscapes of Montserrat have changed since the onset of volcanic activity. Dittmer explains that roughly half the island has been proclaimed an Exclusion Zone, a region that includes the capital city of Plymouth (Fig. 3.7).

People are not allowed in this zone of active volcanic activity. The people who remained must now live in the northern part of the island where the soils are thin, the land is rocky, and making a living is difficult. Over 7000 people migrated off the island, and the remaining 3000 migrated to the northern coast of the island, where the effects of the volcano are less felt.

Culture and Traditions

People who fear that their culture and traditions will not survive a major political transition, and who are able to migrate to places they perceive as safer, will often do so. When British India was partitioned into a mainly Hindu India and an almost exclusively Muslim Pakistan, millions of Muslim residents of India migrated across the border to the new Islamic state. Similarly, in the 1990s after decades of Soviet obstruction, more than 2 million Jews left the former Soviet Union for Israel and other destinations. And turbulent political conditions in South Africa during the mid-1990s impelled many whites to emigrate to Australia, Europe, and North America.

Technological Advances

For some migrants, emigration is no longer the difficult and hazardous journey it used to be. Although most migrants still move by simple and even difficult means, some use modern forms of transportation and communication, the availability of which can itself encourage migration.

Gone is the time when would-be emigrants waited months, even years, for information about distant places. News today travels faster than ever, including news of job opportunities and ways to reach desired destinations. Television, radio, and telephone stimulate millions of people to migrate by relaying information about relatives, opportunities, and already established communities in destination lands. Advances in communication technology strengthen the role of **kinship links** as push or pull factors. When deciding where to go, a migrant is often pulled to places where family and friends have already found success. Thus, Turks quickly heard about Germany's need for immigrant labor. Algerians knew where the most favorable destinations were in France. Haitians knew that a "Little Haiti" had sprung up in the Miami area.

When migrants move along and through kinship links, they create what geographers call chain migration. **Chain migration** occurs when the migrant chooses a destination and writes, calls, or communicates through others to tell family and friends at home about the new place. The migrant may help create a positive perception of the destination for his family and friends, and may promise help with migration, by providing housing and assistance obtaining a job. Reassuring family and friends that a new community has been formed, a place where they can feel home, encourages further migration along the same chain. Chains of migration built upon each other create **immigration waves**—swells in migration from one origin to the same destination.

Think about a migration flow within your family, whether internal, international, voluntary, or forced. The flow can be one you experienced or one you only heard about through family. List the push and pull factors. Then, write a letter in the first person (if you were not involved, pretend you were your grandmother or whomever) to another family member at "home" describing how you came to migrate to the destination.

WHERE DO PEOPLE MIGRATE?

It is tempting to reduce the flow of migration to simple economics—a chance for a job in another place trumps the lack of a job at home. However, migration is much more complicated. Migration depends on various push and pull factors, ranging from persecution in civil war to environmental disaster, from disempowerment in the home to discrimination in the country, and each migration flow is helped or hampered by existing networks and governmental actions.

In this section of the chapter, we examine where people migrate, that is, what destinations they choose. At the global, regional, and national scales, we can see several major migration flows over the past 500 years, flows where hundreds of thousands of people migrated along the same general path. We focus on where—on the destinations in these major migration flows. A large movement of migrants changes places—both the place the migrants left and the destination. As we discuss migration flows at the global, regional, and national scales in this chapter, remember that these flows give only an overview of migration. At the local and household scales, each individual or family migration required life-altering decisions, and those decisions fostered global change.

Global Migration Flows

Before 1500, long-distance, **global-scale migration** occurred haphazardly, typically in pursuit of spices, fame, or exploration. To put exploration in perspective, we need to remember that a complete map of the world's continents did not exist until the early 1800s. European **explorers**, who included surveyors and cartographers, played a major role in finally mapping the world. On the heels of exploration came European **colonization**—a physical process whereby the colonizer takes over another place, putting its own government in charge and either moving its own people into the place or bringing in indentured outsiders to gain control of the people and the land. First, Europeans colonized the Americas and the coasts of Africa and parts of Asia from the 1500s to the 1800s. Then, Europeans colonized interior Africa and Asia starting in the late 1800s and into the 1900s.

The past five centuries have witnessed human migration on an unprecedented scale, much of it generated by European colonization. The major flows of global migration from 1500 on are shown in Figure 3.8. The migration flows include movements from Europe to North America (1); from Southern Europe to South and Middle America (2); from Britain and Ireland to Africa and Australia (3); from Africa to the Americas during the period of slavery (4); and from India to eastern Africa, Southeast Asia, and Caribbean America (5).

Among the greatest human migrations in recent centuries was the flow from Europe to the Americas. Emigration from Europe (1 and 2 in Fig. 3.8) began slowly. Before the 1830s, perhaps 2.75 million Europeans left to settle overseas. The British went to North America, Australia, New Zealand, and South Africa (3). From Spain and Portugal, many hundreds of thousands of Europeans emigrated to Middle and South America. Early European colonial settlements grew, even in coastal areas of present-day Angola, Kenya, and Indonesia. The rate of European emigration increased sharply between 1835 and 1935, with perhaps as many as 75 million departing for colonies in Africa and Asia, and for economic opportunities in the Americas. Although millions of Europeans eventually returned to their homelands, the net outflow from Europe was enormous, as evidenced by the sheer number of Canadians and Americans who identify themselves as being of European ancestry.

As already discussed, the Americas were the destination of another mass of immigrants: African slaves.

African slaves were among the very first non-American Indian settlers in this country (4). Although this migration is mapped as just one of the eight major migrations, its immense and lasting impact on both sides of the Atlantic sets it apart from all the others.

Even as the Atlantic slave trade was in progress, the European impact was generating other major migrations as well. The British, who took control over South Asia, transported tens of thousands of "indentured" workers from present-day India, Pakistan, and Sri Lanka to East and South Africa (see symbol (5) on Fig. 3.8). Today, people of Indian ancestry form substantial minorities in South Africa, Kenya, and Tanzania and, until their forced migration from Uganda, in that country as well. Their disproportionate share of commerce and wealth is now a major source of ethnic friction.

Long before the British arrived in India, Hindu influences radiated into Southeast Asia, reaching the Indonesian islands of Java and Bali. Later, the British renewed the Indian migration stream, bringing South Asians to the Malay Peninsula (including Singapore) and to their Pacific holdings including Fiji (Fig. 3.8).

The British were also instrumental in relocating Asians, mainly from India, to such Caribbean countries as Trinidad and Tobago and Guyana (the trans-Pacific stream marked 5 in Fig. 3.8). The Dutch brought many Javanese from what is today Indonesia to their former dependency of Suriname along the same route.

Regional Migration Flows

The stories of huge flows of migrants mapped in Figure 3.8 were unprecedented and meet few rivals in terms of sheer number today. Although some global migration flows already discussed were forced and some were voluntary, each occurred across an ocean. Migration also occurs at a **regional scale**, with migrants going to a neighboring country to take advantage of short-term economic opportunities, to reconnect with their cultural group across borders, or to flee political conflict or war.

Economic Opportunities

European colonialism helped establish **islands of development** throughout the world. Islands of development are often coastal cities because their establishment was based on access to trade (Fig. 3.9). Islands of development are places within a region or country where most foreign investment goes, where the vast majority of paying jobs are located, and where infrastructure is concentrated.

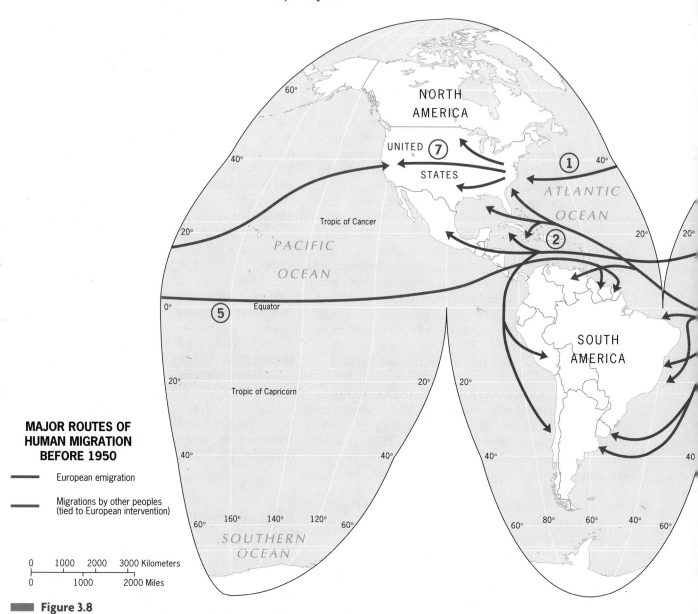

MAJOR ROUTES OF HUMAN MIGRATION BEFORE 1950

European emigration

Migrations by other peoples (tied to European intervention)

0   1000   2000   3000 Kilometers
0   1000   2000 Miles

Figure 3.8
Major Routes of Human Migration before 1950.   © H. J. de Blij, P. O. Muller, and John Wiley & Sons, Inc.

To understand migration flows from one poor country to another, it is not sufficient to analyze the flow at the global scale. We need to understand where the region fits into the global interaction picture, and to see how different locations within the region fit into interaction patterns at both the global and regional scales. For example, within the region of West Africa, the oil-producing areas of Nigeria are islands of development. In the mid-1970s, poor people in Togo, Benin, Ghana, and the northern regions of Nigeria, perceiving

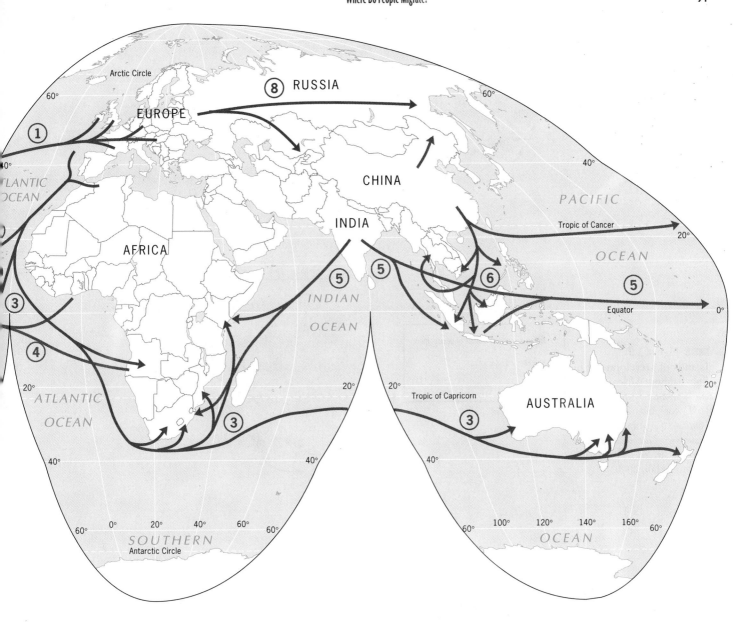

that economic life was better in coastal Nigeria, were lured to the coast for short-term jobs while the oil economy was good. The migrants, usually young men, worked as much as they could and sent almost all of the money they earned home as remittances to support their families. They worked until the oil economy took a fall in the early 1980s, and at that point, the Nigerian government decided the foreign workers were no longer needed. The Nigerian government forcibly pushed out 2 million foreign workers.

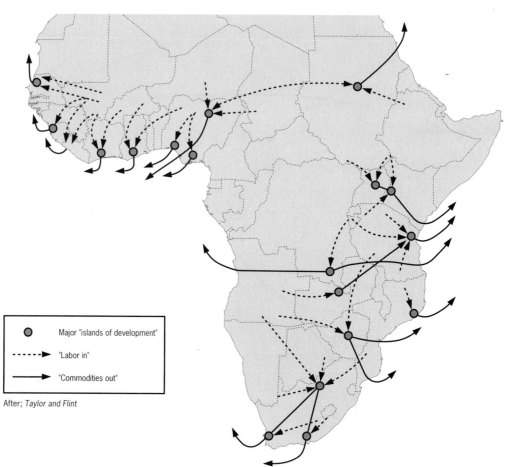

■ **Figure 3.9**
Islands of Development in Sub-Saharan Africa. *Adapted with permission from:* Peter J. Taylor and Colin Flint, *Political Geography: World-Economy, Nation-State and Locality,* 4th ed., New York: Prentice Hall, 2000.

Legend:
- ● Major "islands of development"
- - - - → "Labor in"
- ——→ "Commodities out"

After; *Taylor and Flint*

Global economic processes and the lasting effects of European colonialism certainly played a role in this West African migration flow. If we study such a flow only at the global scale, we see migrants moving from one poor country to another poor country. But if we use both the global and regional scales to study this flow, we understand regional economic influences and the pull of islands of development in Nigeria.

European colonialism also had an impact on regional migration flows in Southeast Asia. Europe's colonial occupation of Southeast Asia presented economic opportunities for the Chinese. During the late 1800s and early 1900s, many Chinese immigrated to cities in the region to work in trade, commerce, and finance (Fig. 3.10). Many remained, and today Chinese minorities in Southeast Asian countries account for substantial portions of national populations: 14 percent in Thailand, 32 percent in Malaysia, and 76 percent in Singapore. The Chinese

minority in Indonesia accounts for only about 3 percent of the total population, but Indonesia has more than 200 million people, so its Chinese minority is one of Southeast Asia's largest clusters.

Reconnection of Cultural Groups

Regional migration flows also center on reconnecting cultural groups across borders. A migration stream with enormous consequences is the flow of Jewish immigrants to Israel. At the turn of the twentieth century, fewer than 50,000 Jewish residents lived in what was then Palestine. From 1919 to 1948, Great Britain held control over Palestine, and Britain encouraged Jews (whose ancestors had fled more than a thousand years earlier from the Middle East to Europe) to return to the region. By 1948, as many as 750,000 Jews resided in Palestine, when the United Nations intervened to partition the

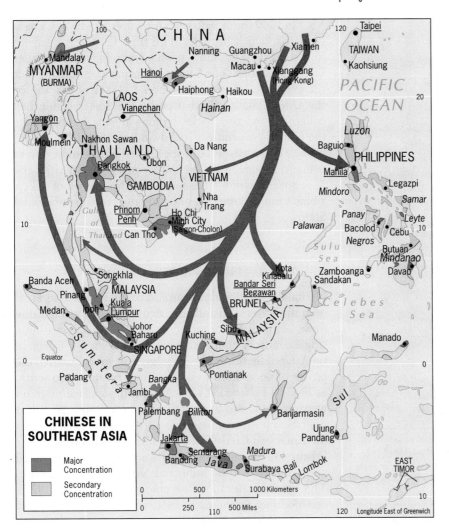

Figure 3.10

Chinese in Southeast Asia. The great majority of Chinese who live in Southeast Asia migrated from southeastern China.
© H. J. de Blij, P. O. Muller, and John Wiley & Sons, Inc.

area and establish the independent state of Israel (the original boundaries of the new state are shown in orange in Fig. 3.11). Following the division of the land between the newly created Israeli state and the state of Palestine, another migration stream began—600,000 Palestinian Arabs fled or were pushed out of Israeli territories. Many sought refuge in neighboring Jordan, Egypt, Syria, and elsewhere.

Through a series of wars, Israel expanded its area of territorial control (Fig. 3.11) and actively built settlements for new Jewish immigrants in Palestinian territories (Fig. 3.12). Jewish immigrants from the Eurasian region continue to migrate to Israel. Following the collapse of the Soviet Union in the early 1990s, thousands of Jews who had been unable to practice their religion in the Soviet Union migrated to Israel. Today Israel's population of 7.4 million (including about 1 million Arab citizens) continues to grow through immigration as well as substantial natural increase.

Conflict and War

At the end of World War II, as many as 15 million Germans migrated westward from their homes in Eastern Europe, either voluntarily or because they were forced to leave. Before the East German government built the Berlin Wall and the Iron Curtain was lowered, several million Germans fled Soviet-controlled East Germany into what was then West Germany. And millions of migrants left Europe altogether to go to the United States (1.8 million), Canada (1.1 million), Australia (1 million), Israel (750,000), Argentina (750,000), Brazil (500,000), Venezuela (500,000), and other countries. As many as 8 million Europeans emigrated from Europe in this postwar stream.

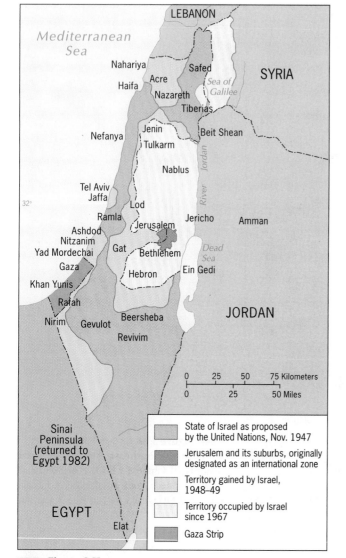

Territory occupied by Israel
since 1967

Figure 3.11

Changing Boundaries of Israel. *Updated and adapted with permission from:* M. Gilbert, *Atlas of the Arab-Israeli Conflict,* New York: Macmillan, 1974, p. 38.

Even before Cuba became a communist state, thousands of Cuban citizens applied annually for residency in the United States. Fidel Castro came to power in Cuba in 1959. During the 1960s, while the Cuban government was establishing the Communist Party of Cuba and formalizing a communist state, the number of Cuban immigration to the United States swelled. The U.S. government formalized the flow as the Cuban Airlift, an authorized movement of persons desiring to escape from a communist government. The vast majority of Cuban immigrants arrived and remained in the greater Miami area. In southern Florida they developed a core of Hispanic culture, and in 1973, Dade County, Florida declared itself bicultural and bilingual.

In 1980 another massive, organized exodus of Cubans occurred, which brought more than 125,000 Cubans to U.S. shores; the migrants qualified for refugee status under U.S. regulations. The Cuban influx persisted throughout the 1980s, and then in 1994, over 30,000 Cubans fled for the United States. By that point, the Soviet Union had collapsed, and the Soviet Union's financial support for the Cuban government had dwindled. The 1994 exodus pushed diplomats in both the United States and Cuba to come to an agreement on Cuban migration. In 1995, the U.S. government established the wet foot–dry foot policy, which stemmed the flow of Cuban migrants to the United States.

National Migration Flows

National migration flows can also be thought of as internal migration flows. Historically, two of the major migration flows before 1950 occurred internally—that is, within a single country rather than across international borders. In the United States, a massive migration stream carried the center of population west (and more recently also south, as Fig. 3.13 shows). As the American populace migrates westward, it is also shifting from north to south, to reflect migration flows from south to north and back again. After the American Civil War, and gaining momentum during World War I, millions of African Americans migrated north to work in the industrial Northeast and Midwest. This internal migration flow continued during the 1920s, declined during the depression years of the 1930s, and then resumed its upward climb.

In the 1970s, the trend began to reverse itself: African Americans began leaving the North and returning to the South. The reversal had several causes. Although the civil rights movement in the 1960s did not change conditions in the South overnight, it undoubtedly played a role in the reverse migration. Disillusionment with living conditions in the urban North and West, coupled with growing economic opportunities in southern cities, also drew African Americans southward. African Americans who lived in northern cities migrated to southern cities, not to rural areas, as the urban economies of the Sunbelt began to grow.

Russia also experienced a major internal migration, but in Russia, people migrated east, from the heartland of the Russian state (near Moscow and St. Petersburg) to the shores of the Pacific. This eastward migration significantly altered the cultural mosaic of Eurasia, and understanding this migration flow helps us understand the modern map of Eurasia. During the czarist (1800s–1910s) and communist periods (1920s–1980s), Russian and Soviet rulers tried to occupy and consolidate the country's far eastern frontier, moving industries eastward, building railroads and

Field Note

"Just a few miles into the West Bank, not far from Jerusalem, the expanding Israeli presence could not be missed. New settlements dot the landscape—often occupying strategic sites that are also easily defensible. These "facts on the ground" will certainly complicate the effort to carve out a stable territorial order in this much-contested region. That, of course, is the goal of the settlers and their supporters, but it is salt on the wound for those who contest the Israeli right to be there in the first place."

Figure 3.12
Jerusalem, Israel. © Alexander B. Murphy.

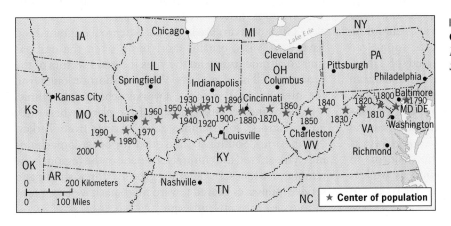

Figure 3.13
Changing Center of Population.
Data from: United States Census Bureau, *Statistical Abstract*, 2001.

feeder lines, and establishing Vladivostok on the Pacific Coast as one of the world's best equipped naval bases. As Russia and then the Soviet Union expanded outward and to the east, the country incorporated numerous ethnic minorities into the country.

During the communist period, the Soviet government also employed a policy of Russification, which sought to assimilate all the people in the Soviet territory into the Russian culture. One way the Soviets pushed for Russification was by encouraging people of Russian heritage to move out of Moscow and St. Petersburg and fill in the country. By 1980, as many as 30 million Russians had moved out toward the borders. After the collapse of the Soviet Union in 1991, some people moved back to their original homelands, but the map will long carry the impact of Russia's eastward expansion.

Mexico offers a more recent example of internal migration. As many as 1 million Mexicans successfully cross into the United States each year, both legally and illegally. Many Mexicans emigrate from the northern areas of Mexico into the southern areas of the United States. In the northern Mexican State of Zacatecas, an estimated one out of every two people is currently living in the United States. As a result, the northern areas of Mexico are experiencing a labor shortage. In response, Mexican workers from areas farther south in the country are migrating northward to fill the labor shortage, especially in Mexico's agricultural sector. Many Mexicans migrating north within the country are Huichol Indians, one of Mexico's indigenous populations. Ironically, the Huichol in northern Mexico are experiencing the same kind of substandard living conditions, lack of acceptance by locals, and exploitation by employers that the Mexicans from the north are experiencing in the United States.

Guest Workers

The countries of Europe that were major participants in World War II lost many young men in this long conflict. After the war, European countries, rebuilding their economies with the help of the U.S.-sponsored Marshall Plan, found themselves in need of laborers. Two flows of migration into Western European countries began: first within the European region, as workers from poorer European countries and regions migrated to economically growing areas, and second from outside of Europe, as millions of foreign workers immigrated from North Africa (the majority to France) and Turkey (mostly to Germany) as well as from the Caribbean region, India, and Africa (many to the United Kingdom).

Western European governments called the labor migrants **guest workers**. The laws allowing guest workers into Europe assumed the workers would fill the void left by those who died during World War II, and then they would return to their home countries. Instead, the guest workers stayed—both because they wanted to and because they were needed. Two to three generations of Turks have now been born in Germany—making them far more than "guests." The German government, which had for decades defined German citizens as those of German descent, only recently allowed Turks to become citizens of the country.

Not only in Germany, but in countries around the world, millions of guest workers live outside of their home country and send remittances from their jobs home. Guest workers often work as agricultural laborers or in service industries (hotels, restaurants, tourist attractions). The home states of these workers are fully aware that their citizens have visas and are working abroad. In many instances, the economies of the home countries come to rely on the remittances, and the home governments work with destination countries and with the international labor organization to protect the rights of the guest workers.

Despite the legal status of guest workers and the work of governments and international organizations to protect them, many employers abuse them because many guest workers are unaware of their rights. Long hours and low pay are common, but guest workers continue to work because the money is better than they would ordinarily receive and because they are supporting families at home.

When the need for labor declines, destination governments can squeeze out guest workers. Nigeria, as noted earlier, did exactly that in the early 1980s when the Nigerian government sent foreign workers from other areas of West Africa home, often by force. Similarly, the government of the home country can pull out its guest workers, bringing them home when conditions in the destination region become perilous. For example, over 30,000 Indonesians were working in the Middle East before the 2003 Iraq War; the Indonesian government decided to pull its workers home just before the war began.

Guest workers are legal (documented) migrants who have work visas, usually short term; often the destination governments extend the visas if certain sectors of the economy still need laborers. Whether short or long term, the international flow of guest workers changes the ethnic, linguistic, and religious mosaic of the places where they go. In Europe, for example, guest workers from Turkey, North Africa, South Asia, and other former colonial holdings have altered the cultural landscape of the region. New temples, mosques, restaurants, grocery stores, shops, and service industries geared toward migrants have taken root in Europe's cultural landscape.

Refugees

You may have seen a story on the televised news showing thousands upon thousands of poor people fleeing a crisis in their home region or country by walking. They put their few earthly possessions and their babies on their backs and walk. They walk to another town. They walk beyond their country's border. They walk to a refugee camp without adequate food, water, or amenities. International agencies attempt desperate relief efforts while disease spreads, dooming infants and children and emaciating adults. As they walk, they remember all they are leaving behind—the only life they have known. But in the midst of war and persecution, it is too hard to hold onto this life. So, they walk.

The world's refugee population has grown steadily since the 1951 establishment of the Refugee Convention, which established an international law specifying who is a refugee and what legal rights they have. The main goal of the 1951 Refugee Convention was to help European refugees following the end of World War II. The United Nations High Commissioner for Refugees (UNHCR) helped to repatriate (return to their homeland) most of the refugees from World War II.

In 1970, the United Nations reported 2.9 million persons were refugees; the majority were Palestinian Arabs dislocated by the creation of the state of Israel and the armed conflicts that followed. In 1980, the refugee total had nearly tripled, to over 8 million. In 2007, the UNHCR reported 11.4 million refugees (not counting Palestinian refugees in Jordan and Syria), forced from their homes and across country borders.

The United Nations agency that monitors the refugee problem is the key organization supporting refugees. It organizes and funds international relief efforts and negotiates with governments and regimes on behalf of the refugees. But UNHCR is not alone in tracking this global problem; other offices often contradict UNHCR's data, arguing that the situation, especially for IDPs, is even worse than the United Nations suggests.

The 1951 Refugee Convention defines a **refugee** as "a person who has a wellfounded fear of being persecuted for reasons of race, religion, nationality, membership of a particular social group, or political opinion." Countries interpret this definition in different ways, especially since the phrase "wellfounded" leaves much room for judgment.

Perhaps the biggest problem with the UN definition has to do with **internally displaced persons** (called IDPs, sometimes called internal refugees). Internally displaced persons are people who have been displaced within their own countries (such as the victims of Hurricane Katrina), but they do not cross international borders as they flee. IDPs tend to remain undercounted

(if not almost invisible). In 2007, UNHCR estimated that 26 million people (in addition to the 11.4 million official refugees) are IDPs—forced to abandon their homes. The United Nations and international law distinguish between *refugees*, who have crossed one or more international borders during their move and encamped in a country other than their own, and *internally displaced persons*, who abandon their homes but remain in their own countries.

Because the status of a refugee is internationally defined and recognized and comes with legal rights, the United Nations High Commissioner for Refugees and states in the world must distinguish between refugees and migrants who may be just as poor or desperate but who do not qualify for refugee status. When a refugee meets the official criteria, he or she becomes eligible for assistance, including possible **asylum** (the right to protection in the first country in which the refugee arrives), to which other migrants are not entitled. Such assistance can extend over decades and become the very basis for a way of life, as has happened in the Middle East. In Jordan, Palestinian refugees have become so integrated into the host country's national life that they are regarded as permanent refugees, but in Lebanon other Palestinians wait in refugee camps for resettlement and still qualify as temporary refugees.

The United Nations helps ensure that refugees and internally displaced persons are not forcibly returned to a homeland where persecution is still continuing. Once the violence subsides in a place and the conditions improve, the UNHCR helps return refugees to their homelands, a process called **repatriation**.

In the 1990s, hostilities broke out between the Hutu and Tutsi ethnic groups in Rwanda that led to a genocide that killed hundreds of thousands and a disastrous exodus of more than one million refugees who fled to neighboring Democratic Republic of the Congo (then called Zaire), Tanzania, and Uganda. The Tutsi–Hutu strife in Rwanda spread to neighboring Burundi and dislocated tens of thousands. After the civil war in Rwanda calmed down in 1996, the UNHCR and the World Health Organization watched and aided as 500,000 Rwandans returned from across the border in The Democratic Republic of Congo (then Zaire) (Fig. 3.14).

Regions of Dislocation

The refugee situation changes frequently as some refugees return home, conditions permitting, and as other, new streams suddenly form. Yet we can make certain generalizations about the overall geography of refugees. In the early twenty-first century, Subsaharan Africa had the largest number of refugees in the world as well as the greatest potential for new refugee flows.

■■■ **Figure 3.14**
Zaire-Rwanda border region.   Hundreds of thousands of mainly Hutu refugees stream out
of a refugee camp in eastern Zaire, heading home to Rwanda in November 1996.
© AP/Wide World Photos.

The second-ranking geographic realm in terms of refugee numbers was Southwest Asia and North Africa,
the realm that includes the Middle East, Iraq, and
Afghanistan. South Asia, as a result of Pakistan's proximity to Afghanistan, ranked third (Fig. 3.15).

Most refugees move without any more tangible
property than they can carry with them. When the United
States and its allies began their retaliatory bombing in
Afghanistan following the terrorist attack on New York
and Washington in September 2001, tens of thousands of
Afghan refugees climbed across mountain passes to reach
the relative safety of Pakistan, unable to bring any but the
barest personal belongings. Most refugees make their first
"step" on foot, by bicycle, wagon, or open boat. Refugees
are suddenly displaced, limiting their options, and most
have few resources to invest in their journey. As a result,

the vast majority of the world's refugees come from relatively poor countries and travel to neighboring countries
that are equally poor. The impact of refugee flows is certainly felt most in the poorest countries of the world.

Africa

Africa's people are severely afflicted by dislocation—
and not just in terms of the 8 million "official" refugees
accounted for by international relief agencies. Many
millions more are internally displaced persons. Of all
regions in the world, Subsaharan Africa is most impacted
by migration because the majority of the world's migration flows are refugees, and the majority of refugees are
in Subsaharan Africa. Add to that the extreme poverty
and devastation of disease in many parts of Subsaharan

Africa, and each day is a humanitarian crisis in parts of the region.

During the last decade of the twentieth century and the first years of the twenty-first, several of the world's largest refugee crises occurred in Subsaharan Africa. In West Africa, civil wars in Liberia and Sierra Leone sent columns of hundreds of thousands of refugees streaming into Guinea and Ivory Coast; in 1997, the UNHCR reported more than 1.5 million refugees in this small corner of Africa. And Angola, strife-torn ever since the days of the Cold War, still has well over 1 million internally displaced persons (some estimates put the total nearer 2 million).

Sudan, which has been in a civil war for two decades, is the site of the worst refugee crisis in Africa today. The conflict in Sudan is between the north, which is largely Arab and Muslim, and the south, which is majority black African and Christian or animist (a follower of a traditional religion). Sudan, a country drawn by European colonialism, is home to traditional religions in the south, Christianity brought by Western missionaries in the south, and Islam brought by North African traders in the north.

Intensifying the struggle between the north and the south was the decision by the Muslim-dominated regime in Khartum to impose Islam's Shari'a religious laws (a judicial code based on the Koran, Islam's holy book) on the entire country. Shari'a laws, especially the criminal code, are harsh (prescribing, for example, the amputation of hands or limbs for theft). In the south, where people are ethnically and culturally different from those in the north, and where Christianity and traditional religions are stronger, that action eliminated any prospect of a compromise.

The war in Sudan has caused immense damage—over 2.2 million people have died in the fighting or have starved as a result of the war. More than 5 million people have been displaced, with over 1.6 million in neighboring Uganda alone. Both sides of the Sudanese civil war have interfered with the efforts of international agencies to help the refugees.

After the north–south civil war began to calm down, the conflict in Sudan moved to the Darfur region in the northwestern part of Sudan. The entire north of Sudan is largely Muslim, but only two-thirds of the northerners speak Arabic as their native language. The other one-third are Muslim but are not ethnically Arab. The non-Arab Muslims are part of at least 30 different ethnic groups in the Darfur region of western Sudan. The Arab Muslim government (located in the north) began a campaign of genocide early in this century against the non-Arab Muslims in Darfur. The government of Sudan funds the militia known as the Janjaweed. The Janjaweed is waging a genocide campaign against the non-Arab, Muslim, darker-skinned Africans in Darfur—a campaign that includes killing over 400,000, raping women and girls, taking lands and homes from Africans, and displacing 2.5 million people (Fig. 3.16).

The U.S. government and the United Nations Security Council are calling the government's actions in Darfur **genocide** (defined in 1948 by the Convention on Genocide as "acts committed with intent to destroy, in whole or in part, a national, ethnical, racial, or religious group"). The international community is trying to negotiate an end to the government-backed campaign in Darfur at the same time that a peace accord between the north and south is close at hand.

The long-lasting refugee crisis in Sudan helps us understand the complexity of political conflict and migration flows in Subsaharan Africa. The Muslim against Muslim conflict in Darfur demonstrates that political conflict is not just religious—it is also ethnic and political.

Mixed into this extremely local conflict are regional and global-scale debates about what to do. Regionally, the African Union, an organization committed to finding African solutions to African problems, has committed Nigerian and Rwandan troops to Darfur to try to solve the crisis. The African Union is supported with American and European monies and military strategizing. At the global scale, the United Nations Security Council met in Kenya in 2004 trying to find a solution and eventually passed a resolution condemning the Sudanese government and threatening punitive damages against the government for their actions in Darfur. Two members of the Security Council, China and Pakistan, abstained from the vote because each of these countries relies on oil imports from Sudan. Under international pressure in 2008, China began to pressure the Sudanese government to end the violence in Darfur, but the Chinese government also refuses to recognize the Janjaweed's relationship with the Sudanese government.

North Africa and Southwest Asia

This geographic region, extending from Morocco in the west to Afghanistan in the east, contains some of the world's longest-lasting and most deeply entrenched refugee problems. A particularly significant set of refugee problems center on Israel and the displaced Arab populations that surround it. Decades of United Nations subventions have more or less stabilized this situation, but many refugees are still in camps.

The Gulf War of 1991 and the current war in Iraq have generated millions of refugees in the region in the last 20 years. In 1991, in the aftermath of the Gulf War that followed Iraq's invasion of Kuwait, a significant percentage of the Kurdish population of northern Iraq, threatened by the surviving military apparatus and under Baghdad's control, abandoned their villages and towns

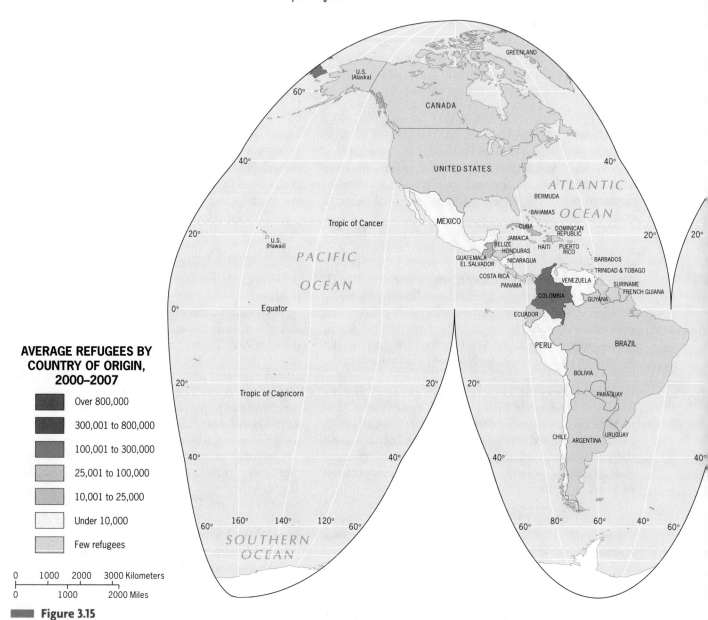

AVERAGE REFUGEES BY COUNTRY OF ORIGIN, 2000–2007

- Over 800,000
- 300,001 to 800,000
- 100,001 to 300,000
- 25,001 to 100,000
- 10,001 to 25,000
- Under 10,000
- Few refugees

0   1000   2000   3000 Kilometers

0   1000   2000 Miles

Figure 3.15

Average Refugee Population between 2000 and 2007 by Country of Origin. *Data from:* World Health Organization, Global Health Atlas, 2008.

and streamed toward and across the Turkish and Iranian borders. The refugee movement of Iraq's Kurds involved as many as 2.5 million people and riveted world attention to the plight of people who are condemned to such status through the actions of others. It led the United States and its allies to create a secure zone for Kurds in northern Iraq in the hope of persuading displaced Kurds in Turkey and Iran to return to their country. But this effort was only partially successful. The Kurdish people of Iraq were severely dislocated by the events surrounding the Gulf War; as Figure 3.14 shows, many remain refugees in Turkey as well as Iran. The current war in Iraq has gener-

ated upwards of 2 million refugees, most of whom are living in neighboring Syria and Jordan.

During the 1980s, Afghanistan was caught in the Soviets' last imperialist campaign and paid an enormous price for it. The Soviet invasion of Afghanistan at the end of 1979, in support of a puppet regime, as well as Afghan resistance, generated a double migration stream that carried millions westward into Iran and eastward into Pakistan. At the height of the exodus, 2.5 million Afghans were estimated to be living in camps in Iran, and some 3.7 million gathered in tent camps in Pakistan's northwestern province and in southern Baluchistan. The Soviet invasion

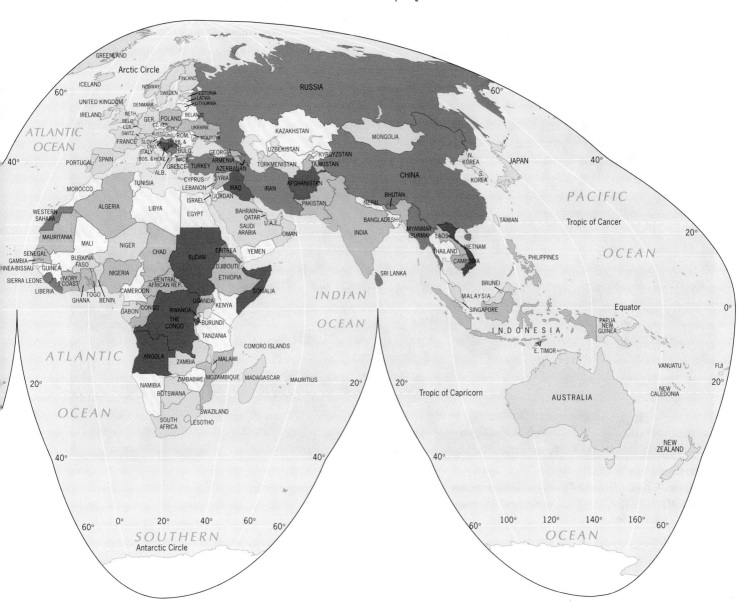

seemed destined to succeed quickly, but the Russian generals underestimated the strength of Afghan opposition. U.S. support for the Muslim forces in the form of weapons supplies helped produce a stalemate and eventual Soviet withdrawal, but this was followed by a power struggle among Afghan factions. As a result, most of the more than 6 million refugees in Iran and Pakistan—about one-quarter of the country's population—stayed where they were.

In 1996, the Taliban, an Islamic Fundamentalist movement that began in northwest Pakistan, emerged in Afghanistan and took control of most of the country, imposing strict Islamic rule and suppressing the factional conflicts that had prevailed since the Soviet withdrawal. Although several hundred thousand refugees moved back to Afghanistan from Pakistan, the harsh Taliban rule created a countermigration and led to further refugee movement into neighboring Iran, where their number reached 2.5 million. Eventually, Afghanistan became a base for anti-Western terrorist operations, which reached a climax in the attack on the United States on September 11, 2001. Even before the inevitable military retaliation began, and despite efforts by both Pakistan and Iran to close their borders, tens of thousands of Afghan refugees flooded across, intensifying a refugee crisis that is now nearly a quarter-century old.

▬ Figure 3.16
Bredjing, Chad. Refugees from the Darfur region of Sudan bake bread near their tent in Chad's largest refugee camp. © Scott Nelson/Getty Images.

Amidst the crises in Israel/Palestine, Iraq, and Afghanistan, nearly every country in Southwest Asia is currently experiencing the impact of refugees.

South Asia

In terms of refugee numbers, South Asia is the third-ranking geographic realm, mainly because of Pakistan's role in accommodating Afghanistan's forced emigrants. During the Soviet intrusion in the 1980s, the UNHCR counted more than 3 million refugees; during the 1990s, the total averaged between 1.2 and 1.5 million. That number rose when Allied retaliation against terrorist bases began in October 2001. Today, Afghanistan has an enormous refugee crisis with 3 million refugees living outside of Afghanistan, mostly in Pakistan and Iran.

The other major refugee problem in South Asia stems from a civil war in Sri Lanka. This conflict, arising from demands by minority Tamils for an independent state on the Sinhalese-dominated and -controlled island, has cost tens of thousands of lives and has severely

damaged the economy. The United Nations reports about 200,000 are now internally displaced.

Southeast Asia

Southeast Asia is a reminder that refugee problems can change quickly. Indochina was the scene of one of the twentieth century's most desperate refugee crises—the stream of between 1 and 2 million people who fled Vietnam in the aftermath of the long war that ended in 1975. In the early 1990s, it was Cambodia that produced an exodus of 300,000 refugees escaping from their country's seemingly endless cycle of violence, ending up in refugee camps on the Thailand side of the border. Today, the largest refugee camps in this realm are internal refugees in Myanmar (formerly Burma), victims of the 2004 tsunami, the 2008 cyclone, and the repressive rule of the generals who are seeking to subjugate the country's minorities. But as the UNHCR states, that figure is an estimate only; information from Myanmar's closed society is difficult to secure.

Europe

In the 1990s, the collapse of Yugoslavia and its associated conflicts created the largest refugee crisis in Europe since the end of World War II. In 1995, the UNHCR reported the staggering total of 6,056,600 refugees, a number that some observers felt was inflated by the Europeans' unusually liberal interpretations of the United Nations' rules for refugee recognition. Nevertheless, even after the cessation of armed conflict and the implementation of a peace agreement known as the Dayton Accords, the UNHCR still reports as many as 1.6 million internal refugees in the area—people dislocated and unable to return to their homes.

Other Regions

The number of refugees and internally displaced persons in other geographic realms is much smaller. In the Western Hemisphere, only Colombia has a serious internally displaced person problem, numbering between 2 and 3 million people, caused by the country's chronic instability associated with its struggle against narcotics. Large areas of Colombia's countryside are vulnerable to armed attack by "narcoterrorists" and paramilitary units; these rural areas are essentially beyond government control, and thousands of villagers have died in the crossfire. Hundreds of thousands more have left their homes to seek protection.

People who abandon their familiar surroundings because conditions have become unlivable perform an ultimate act of desperation. In the process, the habits of civilization vanish as survival becomes the sole imperative. The Earth's refugee and internally displaced person populations are a barometer of the world's future.

Imagine you are from an extremely poor country, and you earn less than $1 a day. Choose a country to be from, and look for it on a map. Assume you are a voluntarily migrant. You look at your access to transportation and the opportunities you have to go elsewhere. Be realistic, and describe how you determine where you will go, how you get there, and what you do once you get there.

HOW DO GOVERNMENTS AFFECT MIGRATION?

The control of immigration, legal and illegal, the granting of asylum to asylum-seeking refugees, and the fate of cross-border refugees, permanent and temporary, have become hot issues around the world. In Europe, right-wing political parties whip up anti-immigrant sentiment. In California, the state government demands federal monies to provide services for hundreds of thousands of illegal immigrants; if the federal government cannot control its borders, they argue, states should not have to foot the bill. In Cuba, the Castro regime has used migration as a threat: in August 1994, Castro threatened to open Cuba's doors to a flood of emigrants who would invariably all flee to the United States. And in the United States, the federal government faced reproach for preventing tens of thousands of Haitians from entering Florida and millions of Mexicans from illegally crossing into the United States.

Efforts to restrict migrations are nothing new. Media coverage, political debates, and political wrangling only make it seem so. In the fourteenth century, China built the Great Wall in part as a defensive measure but also as a barrier to emigration (by Chinese beyond the sphere of their authorities) and immigration (mainly by Mongol "barbarians" from the northern plains). The Berlin Wall, the Korean DMZ (demilitarized zone), the fences along the Rio Grande—all are evidence of the desire of governments to control the movement of people across their borders.

Legal Restrictions

Typically, the obstacles placed in the way of potential immigrants are legal, not physical. Restrictive legislation appeared in the United States in 1882, when Congress approved the Oriental Exclusion Acts (1882–1907). Congress designed these **immigration laws** to prevent the immigration of Chinese people to California. In 1901, the Australian government approved the Immigration Restriction Act, which ended all nonwhite immigration into the newly united country. In particular, the Australian government was targeting Japanese, Chinese, and South Asian immigrants. The act also prohibited immigration by South Pacific Islanders who worked on Australia's large sugar plantations. The Australian government furthered action against the plantation workers (the Kanakas) by deporting the South Pacific Islanders by the end of 1906. These immigration policies created what is known as the *White Australia Policy*, which remained in effect until modification in 1972 and again in 1979.

Waves of Immigration in the United States

Changes in a country's migration policies are reflected in the number of people entering the country and the origin of the immigrants (see Fig. 3.17). The United States experienced two major waves of immigration before 1930 and

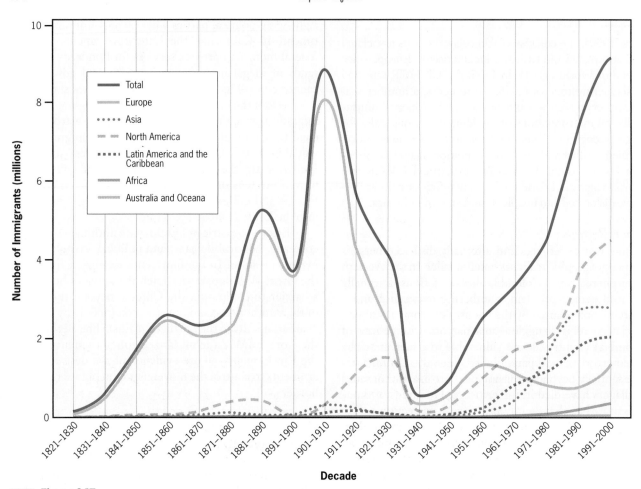

Immigration to the United States by Region, 1820 to 2001. *Data from:* United States Census Bureau, 2002.

is in the midst of another great wave of immigration today. Major changes in the government's migration policies are reflected in this graph. Push factors are also reflected in Figure 3.17, as people in different regions found reasons to leave their home and migrate to the United States.

During the 1800s, the United States opened its doors to immigration, and most of the immigrants arrived from Europe, especially Northern Europe (Scandinavia) and Western Europe (including Ireland, Great Britain, Germany, and France). In the later part of the 1800s, a greater proportion of Europeans who immigrated to the United States came from Southern and Eastern Europe (including Italy, Spain, Portugal, Russia, and Poland).

Following World War I, political tides in the United States turned toward *isolationism*—staying

out of entanglements abroad. In addition, Congress feared growing migration from Eastern and Southern Europe. Many whites in the United States at the time saw migrants hites from Eastern and Southern Europe as darker skinned and as an inferior race of whites. In this context, Congress passed restrictive legislation in 1921, deterring immigration from Southern and Eastern Europe. Congress set immigration **quotas,** whereby each year, European countries could permit the emigration to the United States of 3 percent of the number of its nationals living in the United States in 1910. In 1910, the greatest proportion of immigrants in the United States came from Northern and Western Europe, thus the quotas allowed migration from Northern and Western Europe and severely restricted immigration from Southern and Eastern Europe (Fig. 3.17).

In 1924, Congress altered the Immigration Act by lowering the quota to 2 percent and making 1890 the base year, further reducing the annual total to 150,000 immigrants and further discouraging Eastern and Southern European migration.

The rapid fall in total immigration to the United States is clear in Figure 3.17. Just prior to the Great Depression, Congress passed the National Origins Law in 1929, whereby Congress continued to limit immigration to 150,000 per year. Congress also tied immigration quotas to the national origins of the U.S. population in 1920. As a result of this provision, Congress in effect prevented the immigration of Asians. With these laws in effect and the Great Depression in full swing, immigration slowed to a trickle during the 1930s, and in some years emigration actually exceeded immigration in the United States.

After 1940, Congress modified the restrictions on immigration to the United States. In 1943, Congress gave China equal status to that of European countries, and in 1952 granted Japan a similar status. In 1952, immigration began to rise again (Fig. 3.17) after Congress passed a new Immigration and Nationality Act. Congress designed the act to incorporate all preceding legislation, establishing quotas for all countries and limiting total immigration to 160,000. However, far more than 160,000 immigrants entered the country as refugees, thereby filling quotas for years ahead. Estimates vary, but more than 7 million immigrants may have entered the United States as refugees between 1945 and 1970.

By 1965, Congress recognized the 1952 act as a failure and abolished the quota system. Congress set new limits, which are also reflected in Figure 3.17. The United States allowed 170,000 immigrants per year from countries outside of the Western Hemisphere and 120,000 from countries in the Americas. Refugee policies and guest worker policies over the last three decades allowed many more immigrants than these limitations.

The United States and Australia are not the only countries that have restricted immigration. Many countries practice **selective immigration**, in which individuals with certain backgrounds (criminal records, poor health, subversive activities) are barred from entering.

Other countries have specific requirements. For example, South Africa long demanded "pure" European descent; New Zealand favored persons of British birth and parentage; Australia's assisted passage program favored immigrants from Britain, the Netherlands, Malta, and Italy; Brazil preferred people with a farming background; and Singapore courts financially secure persons of Chinese ancestry. Today South American countries place limits on the number of immigrants who may cross their borders, and several countries are instituting quota systems.

Post–September 11

Since September 11, 2001, government immigration policies have incorporated security concerns. Prior to that date, the U.S. border patrol was concerned primarily with drug trafficking and human smuggling. The new government policies affect asylum-seekers, illegal immigrants, and legal immigrants.

Immediately after September 11, the George W. Bush administration cracked down on asylum-seekers. The U.S. government marked 33 countries as countries where al-Qaeda or other terrorist groups operate, and the government automatically detained anyone from one of these 3 countries who enters the United States looking for asylum (Fig. 3.18).

New government policies also affect illegal immigrants. The Justice Department currently has a policy that allows it to detain any illegal immigrant, even if the person has no known ties to terrorist organizations. This policy stems from the department's concern that terrorists may use Haiti as a "staging point." The idea behind this law is that terrorists could travel to Haiti temporarily and then illegally migrate from Haiti to the United States to commit terrorist attacks. Similarly, the government fence-building along the United States–Mexican border (discussed at the beginning of this chapter) is a response in part to the concern that terrorists will use Mexico as a staging ground to immigrate illegally and commit terrorist attacks.

In addition to focusing on asylum-seekers and illegal immigration, the post–September 11 world is concerned with legal immigration. The 9/11 Commission Report, released in 2004, discusses the issue of terrorists using fabricated or altered papers to migrate to the United States. The 9/11 terrorists entered the United States using visas. The Commission reported that the Federal Aviation Administration flagged more than half of the 9/11 hijackers with the profiling system they had in place. However, the policy at the time was to check the bags of those flagged, not the people themselves. The Commission explains, "For terrorists, travel documents are as important as weapons," and it recommends stepping up inspections and questioning at travel checkpoints, to see these checkpoints as "a chance to establish that people are who they say they are and are seeking access for their stated purpose, to intercept identifiable suspects, and to take effective action."

People and organizations opposed to the post–September 11 policies counter that raising fences and detaining people will not combat terrorism; rather, it will

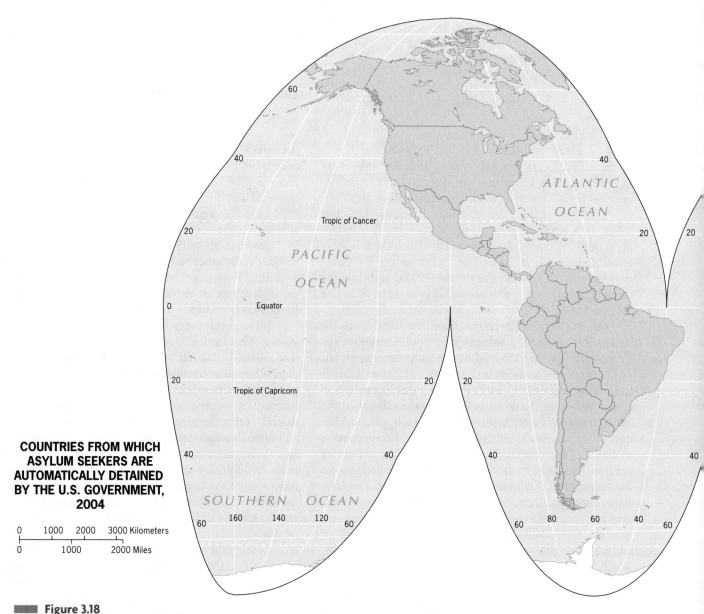

**COUNTRIES FROM WHICH
ASYLUM SEEKERS ARE
AUTOMATICALLY DETAINED
BY THE U.S. GOVERNMENT,
2004**

Figure 3.18
Countries from which Asylum Seekers to the United States are Automatically Detained.
Data from: National Immigration Law Center, http://www.nilc.org/immlawpolicy/arrestdet/
ad064.htm, last accessed June 2005.

intensify hatred of the U.S. government, thus promoting terrorism. Organizations such as Human Rights First, Amnesty International, and the Migration Policy Institute claim that the new government crackdowns have violated civil liberties and have done nothing to make Americans safer. Others opposed to the new border regulations argue the crackdown has only slowed traffic and the flow of business and tourism, and has utterly failed to slow illegal immigration, which along the United States-Mexico border is up from last year.

Regardless of which side of this debate you choose, we can all agree that concern about migration will continue to shape security policy in the United States, Europe, and beyond in the decades to come.

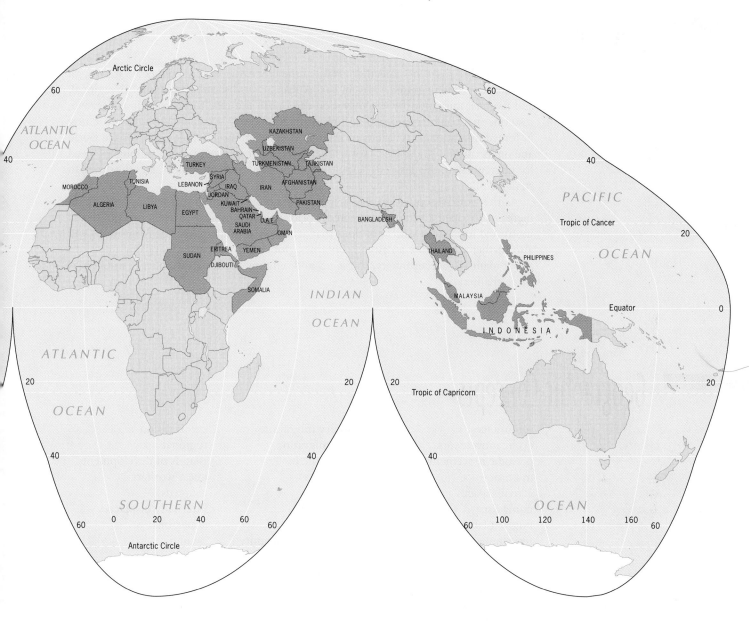

thinking
geographically

One goal of international organizations involved in aiding refugees is repatriation—return of the refugees to their home countries once the threat against them has passed. Take the example of Sudanese refugees. Think about how their land and their lives have changed since they became refugees. You are assigned the daunting task of repatriating Sudanese from Uganda once a peace solution is reached. What steps would you have to take to re-discover a home for these refugees?

Summary

In the last 500 years, humans have traveled the globe, mapped it, connected it through globalization, and migrated across it. In this chapter, we discussed major global, regional, and national migration flows. Migration can occur as a result of a conscious decision, resulting in a voluntary migration flow, or migration can occur under duress, resulting in forced migration. Both kinds of migration have left an indelible mark on the world and on its cultural landscapes. Governments attempt to strike a balance among the need for migrant labor, the desire to help people in desperate circumstances, and the desire to stem the tide of migration.

As the world's population mushrooms, the volume of migrants will expand. In an increasingly open and interconnected world, neither physical barriers nor politically motivated legislation will stem tides that are as old as human history. Migrations will also further complicate an already complex global cultural pattern—raising questions about identity, race, ethnicity, language, and religion, the topics we turn to in the next three chapters.

Geographic Concepts

remittances	voluntary migration	colonization
cyclic movements	laws of migration	regional scale
periodic movement	gravity model	islands of development
migration	push factors	guest workers
activity spaces	pull factors	refugees
nomadism	distance decay	internally displaced
migrant labor	step migration	persons
transhumance	intervening opportunity	asylum
military service	deportation	repatriation
international migration	kinship links	genocide
immigration	chain migration	immigration laws
internal migration	immigration wave	quotas
forced migration	explorers	selective immigration

Learn More Online

About Immigration to the United States
www.uscis.gov

About Refugees
www.unhcr.org

About Geographic Mobility and Movement in the United States
www.census.gov/population/www/socdemo/migrate.html

Watch It Online

About the Migration and Identity
www.learner.org/resources/series85.html#program_descriptions
click on Video On Demand for "A Migrants Heart"

About the United States–Mexico Border Region
www.learner.org/resources/series180.html#program_descriptions
click on Video On Demand for "Boundaries and Borderlands"

Local Culture, Popular Culture, and Cultural Landscapes

Field Note Preserving Culture

The signs with the Tata Corporation's logo were everywhere on the landscape of the city of Hyderabad in India (Fig. 4.1): a Tata corporate building across the street from our flat; Tata emblazoned on the grill of trucks throughout the city; Tata sky satellite dishes bring television into homes; Tata International consulting buildings in the high-tech district of the city.

I asked my host what the Tata Corporation was and where the name came from. He explained, "Tata is a family name. The Tata family are members of the Parsi religion and they own many businesses throughout India and the world."

I was surprised I had not heard of the Tata family before, but I had heard about the Parsi. The Parsi are an ethnic group and a religion. The Parsi are followers of the Zoroastrian religion and came to India from Persia (present-day Iran) somewhere between the eighth and tenth centuries.

According to Indian folklore, the Parsi were looking for a place of refuge as they fled from Iran. They sent word to a Hindu ruler in western India that they wanted to settle there. The Hindu ruler sent the Parsi a bowl full of milk to symbolize that they should not come to India—that the western states were already full. Legend has it that the Parsi leader placed a gold ring in the bowl of milk and returned it—symbolizing they would bring wealth to the region without displacing the people. Around 1500 years ago, the Parsi soon settled in western India, primarily in the city of Bombay.

Figure 4.1
Hyderabad, India. A Tata Corporation building in Hyderabad, India.
© Erin H. Fouberg.

India is overwhelmingly Hindu (85 percent), but the followers of the Parsi religion, who make up 0.0069 percent of the Indian population (fewer than 60,000 Parsi in the Indian population of 1.2 billion people), control a large share of the Indian economy. The Tata Group recorded revenues of $28.8 billion in 2006–2007, while the entire gross national income (GNI) of India for the same time frame was around $800 billion. In addition to the Tata family, the Godrej Group, which produces soap, appliances, and office equipment, and the Wadias Company, which produces textiles and owns an airline, are both companies established and run by Parsi families in India.

How did such a small group of families become such major players first in the Indian economy, and now in the global economy? Some Indian economists point to a positive relationship the Parsi had with the British when India was a colony of Great Britain. Others point to the tight-knit Parsi community that benefited financially early on through the establishment of India's cotton industry and then grew that wealth into many other sectors over time.

The financial success of the Parsi in India cannot be ascribed to a single cause. The tight-knit community of the Parsi and the maintenance of cultural practices that keep the Parsi together and culturally separate from the dominant Hindu culture were definitely factors in the Parsi success. These same traits now threaten to destroy the Parsi culture, and their numbers are beginning to dwindle.

A local culture such as the Parsi is maintained through the preservation of cultural traits and cultural practices. Today, one core cultural practice among the Parsi threatens the existence of the culture itself. According to an edict set down by Parsi religious leaders in 1918, the Parsi religion recognizes only the children who are born of two Parsi parents. Although some Parsi do accept the children who are born to a Parsi father and non-Parsi mother as a member of the Parsi community, children born of Parsi women who are married to non-Parsi (called "outsiders" by the Parsi) are not accepted as community members.

This is significant today because the Parsi have a very high literacy rate in India—98 percent—and many Parsi women are highly educated, have good jobs, and choose either not to marry, to have children late (thus reducing fertility rates), or to marry outside of the Parsi community. In addition, thousands of Parsi, women and men, have migrated to the United States and Europe over the past few decades.

One Parsi high priest sees the historical lack of intermarriage as a major reason the Parsi were able to keep their culture and religion in a world surrounded by Hindu followers. Parsi in India today question whether to count the women married to "outsiders" and the children born to them. Not counting these women and children, the Parsi population in India has declined over the last 30 years from 100,000 to 56,000.

The local culture of the Parsi is highly engaged in the global economy, and today they are struggling to maintain their culture and sustain their numbers in a changing world.

In an era of globalization, popular culture has diffused around the globe— embraced by some and rejected by others—nonetheless, infiltrating every corner of the globe. Local cultures continue to exist around the world, but they face constant pressure from larger cultural groups and from the enveloping popular culture. In the face of these pressures, some members of local cultures have clung more tightly to their customs, some have let go, and others have forged a balance between the two.

Key Questions For Chapter 4

1. What are local and popular cultures?
2. How are local cultures sustained?
3. How is popular culture diffused?
4. How can local and popular cultures be seen in the cultural landscape?

WHAT ARE LOCAL AND POPULAR CULTURES?

A **culture** is a group of belief systems, norms, and values practiced by a people. Although this definition of culture sounds simple, the concept of culture is actually quite complex. A group of people who share common beliefs can be recognized as a culture in one of two ways: (1) the people call themselves a culture or (2) other people (including academics) can label a certain group of people as a culture. Traditionally, academics have labeled cultural groups as folk cultures or as part of popular culture. The idea is that the **folk culture** is small, incorporates a homogeneous population, is typically rural, and is cohesive in cultural traits, whereas **popular culture** is large, incorporates heterogeneous populations, is typically urban, and experiences quickly changing cultural traits. Instead of using this polarity of folk and popular cultures, some academics now see folk and popular cultures as ends of a continuum, defining most cultures as fitting somewhere between folk and popular.

In this chapter, we chose to use the concept of **local culture** rather than folk culture. We find folk culture to be a limiting concept in as much as it requires us to create a list of traits (such as the one in the previous paragraph) and to look for cultures that meet that list of traits. This methodology of defining folk cultures leaves much to be desired. Once we have our list of traits, we must ask ourselves, are the Amish a folk culture? Are the Navajo a folk culture? And it is in this very process that we get frustrated with the concept of folk culture—for it is *how the people define themselves* that matters much more.

A local culture is a group of people in a particular place who see themselves as a collective or a community, who share experiences, customs, and traits, and who work to preserve those traits and customs in order to claim uniqueness and to distinguish themselves from others.

We are much more interested in questions such as, do the Amish have a group identity, and what cultural traits do they share? How do the Amish navigate through popular culture and defend their local customs? Why do a group of Americans in a small town identify themselves as Swedish Americans and hold festivals to commemorate important Swedish holidays, while other Swedish Americans in other parts of the country function completely unaware of the Swedish holidays? Why do certain ethnic holidays such as St. Patrick's Day transcend ethnicity to be celebrated as a part of popular culture?

It is remarkable to note how people in local cultures (folk or not) accept or reject diffusing cultural traits, depending on what works for them. Some local cultures rely primarily on religion to maintain their belief systems, others rely on community celebrations or on family structures, and still others on a lack of interaction with other cultures.

Local cultures are constantly redefining or refining themselves based on interactions with other cultures (local and popular) and diffusion of cultural traits (local and popular). Local cultures also affect places by establishing neighborhoods, by building churches or community centers to celebrate important days, and by expressing their material and nonmaterial cultures in certain places.

The **material culture** of a group of people includes the things they construct, such as art, houses, clothing, sports, dance, and foods. **Nonmaterial culture** includes the beliefs, practices, aesthetics (what they see as attractive), and values of a group of people. What members of a local culture produce in their material culture reflects the beliefs and values of their nonmaterial culture.

Unlike local cultures, which are found in relatively small areas, popular culture is ubiquitous and can change in a matter of days or hours. Popular culture is practiced by a heterogeneous group of people: people across identities and across the world. Like local culture, popular culture encompasses music, dance, clothing, food preference, religious practices, and aesthetic values. The main paths of diffusion of popular culture are the transportation, marketing, and communication networks that interlink vast parts of the world (see Chapter 14 for further discussion of these networks).

A new fashion, such as the Dior Extreme cutout sandal, finds itself on runways in Paris; it will be seen on models in New York within days; days later it will be seen on celebrities (Fig. 4.2); it makes its way to *In Style* magazine within weeks; and it will be found in upscale stores in the same time frame with knockoffs in your local mall weeks after that. The costumers for *Sex and the City: The Movie*, Patricia Fields and Molly Rogers, put the Dior Extreme cutout sandal on actor Sarah Jessica Parker in the 2008 movie in several scenes—rapidly diffusing its popularity and spurring shoe companies to copy the sandal and offer it at a lower price and a broader audience.

In popular culture, as we have seen, fashion trends spread quite quickly through the interconnected world; it through the corporations (such as the media industry) that work to construct popular culture (Fig. 4.3).

Both local cultures and popular cultures are constantly navigating through a barrage of customs diffused from each other and across scales, through a complex of political and economic forces that shape and limit their practices, and through global communications and transportation networks that intricately link certain parts of the world and distance others.

In this chapter, we focus on how local cultures are sustained despite the onslaught of popular culture, how popular culture diffuses and is practiced in unique ways in localities of the world, and how local and popular cultures are imprinted on the cultural landscape.

Employing the concept of hierarchical diffusion, describe how you became a "knower" of your favorite kind of music—where is its hearth, and how did it reach you?

Figure 4.3
Los Angeles, California. Actor Ashton Kutcher wears a red string bracelet while speaking at the Kabbalah center. Kabbalists believe a red string bracelet worn around the left wrist and tied with seven knots will protect the wearer from negative influences. @Ann Johansson /© AP/Wide World Photos

Figure 4.2
New York, New York. Sarah Jessica Parker wears Dior Extreme Cutout sandal in *Sex and the City: The Movie.* ©David Murphy/Newscom/PhotoShot.

is a classic case of **hierarchical diffusion**. The hierarchy in this case is the fashion world. Key cities such as Milan, Paris, and New York are the **hearth** (the point of origin) or the cases of first diffusion. The next tier of places includes the major fashion houses in world cities. Finally, the suburban mall receives the innovation. Hierarchical diffusion can also occur through a hierarchy of people. In this case, the designer is the hearth, the models are the next tier, celebrities and the editors and writers of major magazines follow, and subscribers to fashion magazines follow in close order. Finally, anyone walking through a shopping mall can become a "knower" in the diffusion of this innovation.

We do not see local and popular cultures as being ends of a continuum; rather, we see both operating on the same plane, affecting people and places in different ways across different scales. For example, you may go to a major department store, such as Target or Wal-Mart and see Hutterites or Amish dressed in distinctive local clothing in the midst of the ultimate in popular culture: a major international department store. Traditions, such as painting henna on one's hands or practicing mystical Kabbalah beliefs, are carried from centuries-old customs of local cultures to the global popular culture through a popular culture icon or

HOW ARE LOCAL CULTURES SUSTAINED?

During the 1800s and into the 1900s, the U.S. government had an official policy of **assimilation**. It wanted to assimilate indigenous peoples into the dominant culture—to make American Indians into "Americans" rather than "Indians." Canadians, Australians, Russians, and other colonial powers adopted similar policies toward indigenous peoples, using schools, churches, and government agents to discourage native practices. In the United States, the federal government forced tribal members to settle in one place and to farm rather than hunt or fish. Public and missionary school teachers punished tribal members for using their native language.

Government agents rewarded the most "American" Indians with citizenship and paid jobs. The federal government even employed East Coast women from 1888 until 1938 to live on reservations and show the native women how to be "good housewives" by teaching them Victorian ways of cooking, cleaning, and sewing.

Today, several churches and governments have apologized for assimilation policies. In 2008, the governments of Australia and Canada each officially apologized to their indigenous populations (Aboriginals in Australia and First Nations and Inuit in Canada).

The Australian Parliament unanimously passed a motion stating, "We apologize for the laws and policies of successive parliaments and governments that have inflicted profound grief, suffering and loss on these our fellow Australians." Australian Prime Minister Kevin Rudd apologized specifically for the government's policy of taking Aboriginal children from their homes and placing them in residential schools—a policy that lasted from the 1800s until the late 1960s.

Canadian Prime Minister Stephen Harper likewise cited the disastrous outcomes of the assimilation policies in his apology to Canada's 1.3 million indigenous people. Prime Minister Harper apologized for the abuse and the lasting negative effects of Canada's residential schools, stating: "We now recognize that it was wrong to separate children from rich and vibrant cultures and traditions, that it created a void in many lives and communities, and we apologize for having done this. We now recognize that, in separating children from their families, we undermined the ability of many to adequately parent their own children and sowed the seeds for generations to follow." Speaking to the indigenous people seated in the House of Commons, he continued, "Not only did you suffer these abuses as children, but as you became parents, you were powerless to protect your own children from suffering the same experience, and for this we are sorry."

The United States government has not formally apologized to American Indians for the policy of assimilation. American Indians in the United States are working to push back assimilation and popular culture by reviving the customs of their local cultures. Tribes are teaching younger generations their language, reviving their traditional religion, and eating the foods and herbs of their lands, the foods and herbs on which their ancestors depended.

Local cultures are sustained through customs. A **custom** is a practice that a group of people routinely follows. People have customs regarding all parts of their lives, from eating and drinking to dancing and sports. To sustain a local culture, the people must retain their customs. The customs change in small ways over time, but they are maintained despite the onslaught of popular culture.

Researcher Simon Harrison recognizes that local cultural groups purposefully and often fervently define themselves as unique, creating boundaries around their culture and distinguishing themselves from other local cultures. In the age of globalization, where popular culture changes quickly and diffuses rapidly, Harrison finds that local cultures typically have two goals: keeping other cultures out and keeping their own culture in.

For example, a local culture can create a boundary around itself and try to keep other cultures out—in order to avoid "contamination and extinction." Harrison uses the example of the Notting Hill carnival in London to describe how Londoners from the West Indies (the Caribbean) claimed the festival as their own, in conjunction with an increasing sense of collective West Indies culture. The festival did not begin as a West Indies celebration, but as people from the West Indies shared experiences of "unemployment, police harassment and poor housing conditions" during the 1970s, they began to define themselves as a local culture and redefined the festival as a West Indian celebration.

A local culture can also work to avoid **cultural appropriation**, the process by which other cultures adopt customs and knowledge and use them for their own benefit. In our globalizing world, Harrison explains that cultural appropriation is a major concern for local cultures because aspects of cultural knowledge, such as natural pharmaceuticals or musical expression, are being privatized by people outside the local culture and used to accumulate wealth or prestige. Local cultures can thus work to keep their customs and knowledge to themselves, to avoid cultural appropriation.

Geographers see both of these processes happening with local cultures around the world; local cultures desire to keep popular culture out, keep their culture intact, and maintain control over customs and knowledge. Geographers also recognize that through these actions, *places become increasingly important*. When defining a place (such as a town or neighborhood) or a space for a short amount of time (such as an annual festival) as quintessentially representing the local culture's values, members of a local culture reinforce their culture and their beliefs. In the process, a local culture can reestablish customs, re-create entire towns, or establish urban neighborhoods.

■ Figure 4.4
Stratford, South Dakota. A Hutterite boy who lives in the Hutterville Farm colony near Stratford, South Dakota. © Erin H. Fouberg.

Rural Local Cultures

Members of local cultures in rural areas often have an easier time maintaining their cultures because they are more isolated. By living together in a rural area, members of a local culture can more easily keep external influences on the outside. It is no accident that we find Anabaptist groups, such as the Hutterites, the Amish, and the Mennonites, living in rural areas of South Dakota, Pennsylvania, and Virginia, respectively.

For the past five centuries, many Anabaptist groups have migrated to rural areas beyond these three states (often fleeing persecution) with the expressed purpose of living apart and staying together. During the Protestant Reformation, Anabaptists broke from both the Catholic Church and the new Protestant churches. Followers of the new religion were called Anabaptists (meaning baptized again) because of their belief in adult baptism, despite having been baptized as infants in the Protestant or Catholic religions.

Anabaptists broke from the state as well as the church; they stressed pacifism and soon suffered persecution. Fleeing persecution, Anabaptists migrated east to Moravia and Austria, and then to Russia and the Ukraine. Continually moving to rural areas to live apart, alone, and avoid persecution, a group of Anabaptists called the Hutterites, named for leader Jacob Hutter, eventually migrated to North America in the second half of the 1800s.

Old Order Anabaptist groups are shown in stereotypical ways in the popular media, but major differences exist across Old Order Amish, Mennonites, Hutterites, and Brethren. The Hutterites are the only Anabaptist group who live communally (Fig. 4.4). Rather than living with immediate family on a farmstead, Hutterites live in colonies of about 100 people, with individuals ranging in age from infant to elderly. More than 425 colonies are located in Minnesota, South Dakota, North Dakota, Saskatchewan, Montana, and Alberta (Fig. 4.5). In their book *On the Backroad to Heaven*, Donald Kraybill and Carl Bowman explain that the lynchpin of each colony is the Hutterite religion. Members of the colony join together every night for a 30-minute service as well as on Sundays. The most prominent position in a colony is held by the minister, who speaks in archaic German, reading sermons written in the sixteenth century.

Unlike the Amish, Hutterites readily accept technologies that help them in their agricultural pursuits. However, they do not accept technologies such as televisions, cameras, and cell phones, which encourage individualistic behaviors or undermine the Hutterite religion. Colonies assign separate jobs and tasks to men and women, which reinforces a patriarchal social structure. Kraybill and Bowman explain that marriages happen across colonies, and women move to their husband's colony after marrying. As a result, a single colony is usually composed of only one or two surnames. Moving to their husband's colony perpetuates women's weak political position in the colony. Women are expected to rear many

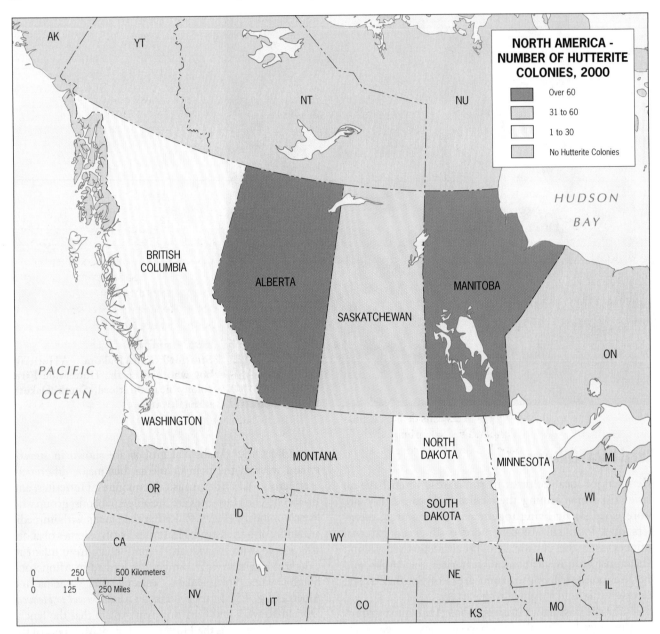

Figure 4.5
Hutterite Colonies in North America. *Data from*: D. B. Kraybill and C. F. Bowman, *On the Backroad to Heaven: Old Order Hutterites, Mennonites, Amish, and Brethren* (Baltimore: Johns Hopkins University Press, 2001), p. 31.

children, averaging five or six currently, but the colony as a whole is responsible for raising and disciplining the child.

Hutterite colonies specialize in diversified agriculture, raising feed, food, and livestock on up to 10,000 acres. Hutterite men often barter with neighboring farmers to fix machinery, trade goods, and lend help. Aside from shopping, interaction with the outside world is uncommon for most in the colony. The minister serves as liaison with the outside world, and he works with lawyers and bankers to keep the colony corporation operating smoothly and profitably. The most economically successful colonies have created products used in agriculture that they produce in their shops and sell to other farmers. One colony produces stainless steel animal

feeders, and another markets its own animal feed. Some colonies also invest hundreds of thousands of dollars in computerized milking systems for their dairy operations and computerized systems for feeding and raising hogs.

Mennonites have migrated from the East Coast of the United States in search of rural farmland. Geographer Dawn Bowen has traced the migration of Mennonites, finding their desire to farm in rural areas leading them to the northern reaches of Alberta, Canada, to turn forestlands into farmlands and as far away as Bolivia to find a place where they can farm, form their own schools, and practice their religion without pervasive pressures from the popular culture. Rurality can make it much easier for local cultures to keep their culture intact by separating themselves from other local cultures and from popular culture as well. Rurality also enables local cultures to define their own space, to create a place, a town that reflects their values, and to practice their customs unfettered in that place.

In rural local cultures, the economic activity, such as whale or bison hunting, can be such a focus of daily life that numerous customs are tied to it. In rural areas, often all members of a local culture engage in the same economic activities. For instance, in the early 1800s in North America, the Plains Indians migrated during the year based on the bison; they made tools, shelter, and clothing out of the bison, and held dances and ceremonies that surrounded the bison hunt. When a local culture discontinues its major economic activity, it faces the challenge of maintaining the customs that depended on the economic activity and, in turn, sustaining its culture. In the modern world, when a local culture decides to reengage in a traditional economic activity or other cultural custom, it must navigate through the limitations and perceptions imposed by different governments and cultures across a variety of scales.

The Makah American Indians

In the late 1990s, the Makah American Indians of Neah Bay, Washington, did what environmentalists considered unthinkable: they reinstated the whale hunt. The Makah hunted whales for 1500 years, but were stopped in the 1920s because the gray whale they hunted became endangered. In 1994, the National Oceanic and Atmospheric Association (NOAA) removed the eastern North Pacific gray whale from the endangered list.

In 1999, when the Makah reinstated the whale hunt, tribal members interviewed by journalists spoke to their traditional culture as their reason for returning to the whale hunt. They needed to return to their past, they said, to understand their ancestors, to re-create and solidify their local culture. In the midst of a popular culture onslaught, the Makah sought refuge in their past.

Although the Makah wanted to hunt whales as their ancestors did, their 1999 hunts took place in a completely different context than the Makah faced a century before. This time, the Makah hunted whales under the watchful eye of the International Whaling Commission; they faced numerous protests by Green Peace and local environmentalists; and they found themselves in federal court with the George W. Bush administration on their side supporting the reinstatement of the whale hunt.

The Makah wanted to hunt with their traditional canoes and harpoons, for they saw the whale hunt as a central focus for their culture (Fig. 4.6). The contemporary whale hunt was not that simple. Actors at the regional, national, and global scale influenced whether the Makah could hunt whales and also the methods the Makah used in their hunt. When the Makah killed a gray whale in May 1999, they did so with a .50 caliber rifle, as dictated by the International Whaling Commission, in hopes of being more humane and finishing the kill more quickly than

█ Figure 4.6
Neah Bay, Washington. Makah American Indians show their support for the return of the whale hunt. © Dan Levine/AFP/Getty Images.

Guest Field Note

Lindsborg, Kansas

Lindsborg, Kansas, founded by Swedish Lutherans in 1869, has remade itself in recent decades as "Little Sweden, U.S.A." Swedish gift shops, restaurants, and ethnic festivals, along with faux-Swedish storefronts, all attract visitors interested in the Swedish American heritage. Here you see a Dala horse, a traditional Swedish folk craft that has been adopted as the town symbol. Note, too, the Swedish and American flags flying in the background. Most visitors to the town assume one of two things: either the town is an island of nineteenth-century culture passed on unchanged for generations, or it is a crock of Disneyesque fakery cooked up to draw in gullible tourists. The fascination of fieldwork is that it undermines any such simplifications. I found ethnicity here to be complex, quirky, ever-changing, and very much a part of the people's lives. Swedishness in Lindsborg has been invented and reinvented time and time again through the decades, as people constantly look for answers to that most basic of questions: who am I?

Credit: Steven M. Schnell, Kutztown University of Pennsylvania

Figure 4.7

their ancestors had. Soon after, the Makah whale hunt was put on hold, as cases calling for a cessation of the hunt made their way through the courts.

American Indians are not the only Americans looking to the customs of their ancestors to reinvigorate their local cultures. Throughout the rural United States, small towns were built by immigrants from Europe, and many local cultures have defined entire small towns as places to maintain their culture and to teach others about their customs and beliefs.

Little Sweden, U.S.A.

The residents of Lindsborg, Kansas, have proclaimed their town Little Sweden, U.S.A. Geographer Steven Schnell asked why a town of 3300, which a few decades ago had little or no sign of Swedishness on its landscape, transformed itself into a place where Swedish culture is celebrated every day in gift stores on Main Street and in buffets in restaurants (Fig. 4.7).

Cynics would argue the reason is purely economic, but there is more to it than that. Certainly, Lindsborg benefits economically from tourists who flock to buy Swedish trinkets and celebrate Swedish festivals. But, as Schnell found, on a daily basis, the people of Lindsborg benefit from promoting a sense of a shared history, a common place in this world. In the 1930s, the townspeople began to share stories about the roles of Swedes in American history and the importance of their Swedishness to Lindsborg. From that base, the townspeople began to celebrate their Swedish heritage in the 1950s, highlighting the "everyday existence" (the local culture) of the Swedes who immigrated to Lindsborg. During festivals today, the townspeople (whether Swedish or not) dress up in the peasant clothes Swedish immigrants wore in the 1800s. Geographer James Shortridge refers to this as **neolocalism**, seeking out the regional culture and reinvigorating it in response to the uncertainty of the modern world.

The Makah, the Hutterites, and the people of Lindsborg have something in common: each is inundated with a pulsating popular culture that challenges their place in the world. Each has chosen to maintain or reconnect with its local culture. For the Hutterites, the goal is to maintain, what they have, to adopt only those technologies that advance their agricultural pursuits and ban those that challenge their religion. Central concerns for the Makah include thinking in their own language, embracing their history, and coming to know who they are despite what others have done to subvert their identity. The people of Lindsborg, seek to celebrate the Swedish immigrants who made the place unique and connect with others around them.

Urban Local Cultures

Some local cultures have successfully built a world apart, a place to practice their customs, within a major city by constructing tight-knit **ethnic neighborhoods**. Hasidic Jews in Brooklyn, New York, and Italian Americans in the North End of Boston, Massachusetts, are able to maintain their distinct local cultures in urban environments.

Runners of the New York City Marathon can see the ethnic neighborhoods of New York City's boroughs firsthand. Running through Brooklyn, they see a predominantly Mexican neighborhood full of Mexican flags and mariachi bands, followed in sharp contrast by a Hasidic Jewish neighborhood with streets lined with men and boys on one side and women and girls on another all dressed in clothes modeled after eighteenth-century Russian and Polish clothing (Fig. 4.8).

Field Note

"One of the most amazing aspects of running the New York City marathon is seeing the residents of New York's many ethnic neighborhoods lining the streets of the race. Running through the Hasidic Jewish neighborhood in Williamsburg, Brooklyn was striking: even before noticing the traditional dress of the neighborhood's residents, I noticed the crowd was much quieter—the people were not yelling, they were clapping and quietly cheering."

Figure 4.8
Williamsburg, Brooklyn, New York.   © Martha Cooper/Peter Arnold, Inc.

In the North End of Boston, the Italian community still celebrates the feast days of Italian saints. This area is home to 12 religious societies, each focusing on an Italian saint. Between June and September, each of the 12 societies holds a celebration for its saint. Members of the society march through the North End holding a statue of their saint, collecting money and adorning the saint with it. Each society is led by the Romaband, an Italian band that has played since 1919. The march ends with a street celebration, including vendors selling everything from fried calamari to hot dogs.

Having their own ethnic neighborhood enables members of a local culture in an urban area to set themselves apart and practice their customs. Schools, houses of worship, food stores, and clothing stores all support the aesthetics and desires of members of the local culture. The greatest challenge to local cultures in cities is the migration of members of the popular culture or another local culture or ethnic group into their neighborhood. Members of local cultures in both Brooklyn and the North End are being challenged by young artists and professionals, who are moving into the respective neighborhoods. Rents and housing costs are climbing in each neighborhood, and the cultural landscapes are starting to reflect the neighborhood's new residents. A new arts community is inundating the Hasidic neighborhood of Brooklyn called Williamsburg. Today, you will find art galleries, artistically painted old warehouses converted into residences, and even a new brewery. In Boston's North End, young professionals are taking advantage of the neighborhood's favorable location, choosing apartments in the North End so they can walk to their jobs in the city center. Today, you will find apartments being renovated to appeal to the North End's new residents.

Local Cultures and Cultural Appropriation

Local cultures, whether rural or urban, often find themselves trying to keep their customs for themselves, to prevent others from appropriating their customs for economic benefit. Anthropologists and geographers have studied how others are using local cultural knowledge, customs, and even names. For example, a brewery that produced Crazy Horse beer was sued by the estate of Crazy Horse (a Lakota Indian leader).

The process through which something (a name, a good, an idea, or even a person) that previously was not regarded as an object to be bought or sold becomes an object that can be bought, sold, and traded in the world market is called **commodification**. One need look no further than eBay to see commodification. Newspapers frequently report on bizarre objects, such as California Governor Arnold Schwarzenegger's cough drop or a person's vote for a London mayoral election, being commodified in Internet space.

Commodification affects local cultures in numerous ways. First, their material culture, their jewelry and clothing, their food and games, can be commodified by themselves or by nonmembers. Similarly, their nonmaterial culture, their religion, language, and beliefs, can be commodified, often by nonmembers selling local spiritual and herbal cures to ailments. Local cultures may be commodified as a whole, with tourist buses "observing" the Amish culture of Lancaster, Pennsylvania, or trekking with "traditional" Nepalese guides on spiritual journeys through the Himalayas.

When commodification occurs, the question of **authenticity** follows. When local cultures or customs are commodified, usually one image or experience is typecast as the "authentic" image or experience of that culture, and it is that image or experience that the tourist or buyer desires. However, local cultures are dynamic, and places and people change over time. To gain an "authentic" sense of place, people need to experience the complexity of a place directly rather than the stereotype of a place. An "authentic" local culture does not fit into a single experience or image; rather, an "authentic" local culture is one that is complex and not stereotyped.

The act of stereotyping local culture is quite confusing for the members of the local culture, for rarely is there consensus that all things must be done in one traditional way. Tourists in Lancaster County, for example, may be disappointed to see some Amish driving tractors across their fields. European, Canadian, American, or Australian trekkers in Nepal desire the same "authentic" experience that a travel pamphlet shows when trekking across the Himalayas.

Authenticity of Places

During the process of colonization, Europeans tagged the cultures they encountered as either savage or mystic. "Authentic" tourist destinations are designed to exploit the mystical in local cultures. A new South African theme park, The Lost City (built on the site of the resort Sun City), capitalizes on *mystical images of Africa described in a legend*, thereby "freezing" the continent to a time that never existed (Fig. 4.9).

A local culture need not be "mystical" in order to create an authentic place. The city of Branson, Missouri, is capitalizing on a local culture in the Ozarks that melds a number of people and perceptions in one place so that tourists can consume the place. Geographer Johnathan Bascom studied the processes by which the city of Branson has effectively tapped its local customs, such as food preferences, history, and music, to create an "authentic" identity for Branson that sets it apart from neighboring towns. Branson becomes "authentic," and surrounding towns that try to capitalize on their rural, country heritage become "copies."

■ **Figure 4.9**
Sun City, South Africa. The Lost City resort in Sun City evokes the mystical images of Africa described in a legend. © Lindsay Hebberd/Corbis.

Guinness and the Irish Pub Company

Theme parks and entertainment venues overtly choose a stereotype and perpetuate it, but a discerning tourist or consumer may be aware of what is occurring. Often, the act of corporations commodifying the mystique of local cultures to drive profits is less obvious to the consumer. The Guinness Brewing Company of Dublin, Ireland, created a business plan nearly 20 years ago aimed at capitalizing on the global mystique of the traditional Irish pub. Guinness saw the sales of its stout beer declining in Ireland and the United Kingdom and decided to go global.

Guinness formed a partnership with the Irish Pub Company, which has offices in Dublin, Atlanta, the United Arab Emirates, and Australia. The Irish Pub Company studied traditional Irish pubs and created five Irish pub prototypes—including Irish Country Cottage, Victorian Dublin, traditional pub, Gaelic (based on what pubs would have looked like had they existed over 2000 years ago in Ireland), and Irish Brewery. For example, a hotel owner in Naples, Florida, or a businessperson in Dubai, United Arab Emirates (Fig. 4.10), works with the Irish Pub Company to choose a good site and to choose the pub type. The specifications are sent to Ireland, and the pub itself is built in Ireland and shipped abroad. Along with the pub, the Irish Pub Company provides food recommendations, training, music suggestions, and notably, Irish bartenders trained in their Dublin "pub school." The Irish Pub Company also sells bric-a-brac (Irish antiques and reproductions) to give the place the feel of an Irish pub. Of course, every pub has Guinness on tap. All of these components create what the Irish Pub Company refers to as ambience that leads to *craic* (Irish for fun).

■ **Figure 4.10**

Dubai, United Arab Emirates. An old Irish truck marks the entrance to an Irish Pub Company pub in Dubai. © Alamy.

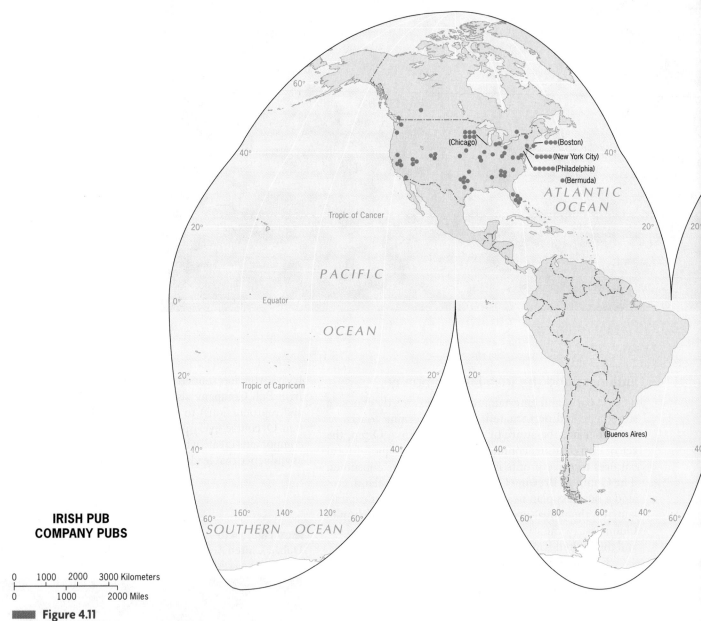

IRISH PUB COMPANY PUBS

0   1000   2000   3000 Kilometers

0   1000   2000 Miles

Figure 4.11
Irish Pubs Designed by the Irish Pub Company.   *Data from*: Irish Pub Company, by email and http://www.irishpubcompany.com/pubsworldwide.asp, last accessed July 2008.

Guinness and the Irish Pub Company have built over 400 pubs in 40 countries around the world (Fig. 4.11). Remarkably, dozens of the pubs are in Ireland proper. The most enigmatic of the pubs is in Las Vegas, Nevada. The Irish Pub Company designed and built a pub called Nine Fine Irishmen that spans 9000 square feet in the New York-New York Hotel and Casino and spills an additional 20,000 square feet onto Las Vegas Boulevard. The "authentic" Irish pub in "authentic" New York in the "Disneyfied" Las Vegas is one we can chew on for a while.

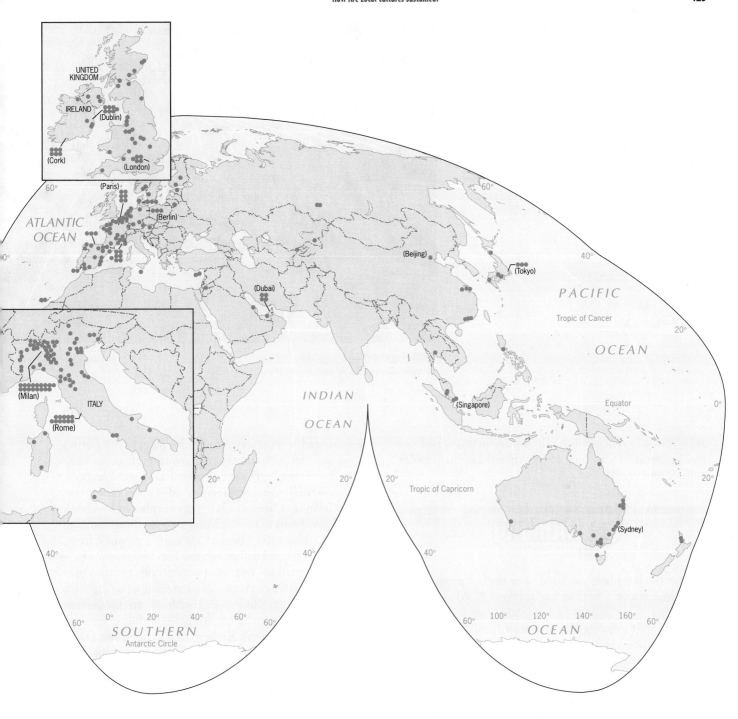

The commodification of local customs freezes customs in place and time for consumption, with claims of "authenticity" abounding. The search for "authentic" local cultures implies an effort to identify peoples who are seemingly untouched by change or external influence. However, all local cultures (rural and urban) are dynamic, and all have been touched by external influences throughout their existence (Fig. 4.12). The search for an "authentic" local culture merely perpetuates myths about local cultures. Members of local cultures

Field Note

"The Dingle Peninsula in Ireland was long one of the more remote parts of the country, and even its largest town, Dingle, was primarily an agricultural village just a few decades ago. As I walked through the streets of town, I noticed the colorful inns and houses of the older town. The 'Little Bridge Pub' on the corner of this intersection in the older town is an 'authentic' pub, the kind that the Irish Pub Company works to replicate."

Figure 4.12
Dingle, Ireland   © Alexander B. Murphy.

are constantly renegotiating their place in this world and making sense of who they are in the midst of the popular culture onslaught.

What is the last place you went to or the last product you purchased that claimed to be "authentic?" What are the challenges of defending the authenticity of this place or product while refuting the authenticity of other similar places or products?

HOW IS POPULAR CULTURE DIFFUSED?

Extraordinary changes have occurred over the past century in the time it takes for people, innovations, and ideas to diffuse around the globe. The innovation of agriculture took nearly 10,000 years to diffuse around the world. In much more recent times, the diffusion of developments such as the printing press or the Industrial Revolution was measured over the course of 100 years or more.

During the past century, however, the pace of diffusion shrank to months, weeks, days, and in some cases even hours. Simultaneously, the spatial extent of diffusion has expanded, so that more and more parts of the Earth's surface are affected by ideas and innovations from far away places. For example, the social networking site Facebook has over 40 million subscribers and adds many new members each day. In Canada in 2007, the number of Facebook subscribers doubled to 7 million in just three months. With that many subscribers and instant communication, news can travel quickly through the Facebook network.

Transportation and communication technologies have altered **distance decay**. No longer does a map with a bull's-eye surrounding the hearth of an innovation describe how quickly the innovation will diffuse to areas around it (Fig. 4.13 top). Rather, what geographer David Harvey called **time–space compression** explains how quickly innovations diffuse and refers to how interlinked two places are through transportation and communication technologies (Fig. 4.13 bottom).

In the past few decades, major world cities have become much closer to each other as a result of modern technologies, including airplanes, high-speed trains, expressways, wireless connections, fax machines, e-mail, and telephone. Places that lack transportation and communications technologies are now more removed from interconnected places than ever. All of the new technologies create the infrastructure through which innovations diffuse. Because the technologies link some places more closely than others, ideas diffuse through interconnected places rapidly rather than diffusing at constant rates across similar distances.

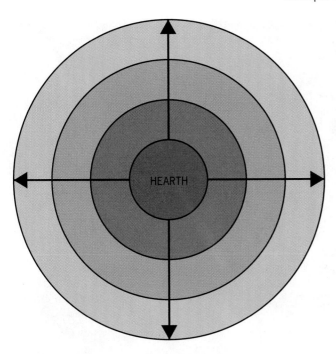

A. DISTANCE DECAY

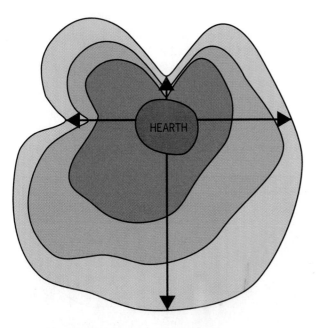

B. TIME-SPACE COMPRESSION

Figure 4.13a, b
Distance Decay and Time–Space Compression. With distance decay, the likelihood of diffusion decreases as time and distance from the hearth increases. With time–space compression, the likelihood of diffusion depends on the connectedness (in communications and transportation technologies) among places.
© E. H. Fouberg, A. B. Murphy, H. J. de Blij, and John Wiley & Sons, Inc.

Hearths of Popular Culture

Popular culture diffuses hierarchically in the context of time–space compression, with diffusion happening most rapidly across the most compressed spaces. As we saw in the last section, even local customs practiced for centuries in one place can be swept up into popular culture. How does a custom, idea, song, or object become part of popular culture? It is relatively easy to follow the communications, transportation, and marketing networks that account for the diffusion of popular culture, but how do we find the hearths of popular culture, and how do certain places establish themselves as the hearths of popular culture?

Establishing a Hearth

All aspects of popular culture—music, sports, television, and dance—have a hearth, a place of origin. Typically, a hearth begins with contagious diffusion: developers of an idea or innovation may find they have followers who dress as they do or listen to the music they play. A multitude of American musical groups (REM, Hootie and the Blowfish, Vertical Horizon) began as college bands or in college towns. They play a few sets in a campus bar or at a campus party and gain followers. The group starts to play to bars and campuses in nearby college towns, and soon they sell self-made compact discs at their concerts.

Bands that begin on college campuses or in college towns and build from their base typically follow the path of building a hearth for their sound's diffusion first through contagious diffusion and then through hierarchical diffusion. Towns like Athens, Georgia, Burlington, Vermont, Seattle, Washington, Charlottesville, Virginia, and other college towns are the perfect nesting spaces for new bands. The Dave Matthews Band created and perfected their sound in Charlottesville, Virginia in the early 1990s. Lead singer and guitarist Dave Matthews was born in South Africa and landed in Charlottesville as a young adult, after living in Johannesburg, New York, and London (Fig. 4.14).

Matthews was a bartender at Miller's in Charlottesville when he met Ross Hoffman, a local songwriter who mentored Matthews in song writing. The Dave Matthews Band was formed when Matthews invited Carter Beuford (drums), LeRoi Moore (saxophone, who died in 2008), Stefan Lessard (bass), and Boyd Tinsley (violin) to join him in creating a demo of some of his songs. The Dave Matthews Band's first live show was in Charlottesville on Earth Day in April 1991. The band played bars throughout the Charlottesville area from 1991 through 1993. Manager Coran Capshaw followed the path of diffusion carved by the Grateful Dead and Phish, through a grassroots campaign of word of mouth (contagious diffusion).

Hierarchical diffusion of the band soon followed, through the hierarchy of college towns in the United States

Figure 4.14
Randalls Island, New York. Boyd Tinsley and Dave Matthews of the Dave Matthews Band. ©James Devaney/GettyImages.

(Fig. 4.15). The Dave Matthews Band played 200 nights a year in fraternities, sororities, bars, and clubs throughout the American Southeast, following the same circuit as college band Hootie and the Blowfish. The band encouraged fans to record their music and send it to friends, helping to establish audiences for the band in college towns far removed from Charlottesville.

Their first album, released in 1993, was on the band's own independent label. It hit the college charts, and a union with RCA soon followed with their second album, *Under the*

Figure 4.15
World Distribution of Dave Matthews Band concerts. *Data from:* http://www.bmbalmanac.com, last accessed July 2008. Compiled by Liz Sydnor and Lennea Mueller.

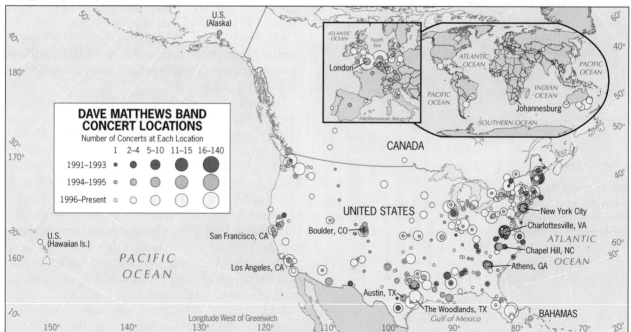

Table and Dreaming, released in 1994. As *Entertainment* magazine explained in 1995, "By playing nearly 200 gigs a year and releasing their own CDs, they built up such a zealous following that when Under the Table entered the album chart at No. 34, neither MTV nor most of America had even heard of them." The band's first video was not released until three months after the song "What Would You Say" hit the Billboard charts.

The band became broadly popular after 1995 and began playing large arenas throughout the United States and in Australia. The band continues to rely on its fan base for support. Manager Capshaw and the Dave Matthews Band were early adopters of the Internet to stay connected with fans. Today, the official Dave Matthews Band fan club has over 80,000 online members (each of whom pay $35 a year to belong).

The music of groups such as the Dave Matthews Band, Phish, Grateful Dead, and Jimmy Buffet also diffuses relocationally, as fans follow the musicians along their concert routes, living in their cars and selling tie-died shirts and beaded necklaces out of the backs of their cars in the parking lots of concert venues. The action of following the bands for years (an estimated 500 to 1000 fans traveled to *every* Grateful Dead concert) leads fans to create their own customs and culture. Like other acts of pilgrimage (see Chapter 7 on religion), environmental effects can be grave. Prior to their final concert, Phish (breaking up for the second time), used their website to plead to fans to leave their beloved rural Vermont as they found it. Today, Reverb, a nonprofit organization, helps bands, including the Dave Matthews Band, create environmentally conscious concerts—having bands purchase carbon offset credits for each of their concerts, supporting recycling, selling eco-friendly merchandise, and setting up Reverb Eco-Villages at concert venues to encourage eco-friendly behaviors among fans.

Manufacturing a Hearth

The question of whether a college band "makes it" depends greatly on the choices and actions of record producers and music media corporate giants. Certain corporations, such as Viacom, the parent company of MTV, generate and produce popular culture, pushing innovations in popular culture through the communications infrastructure that links them with the rest of the world (Fig. 4.16). Geographer Clayton Rosati studied the infrastructure of MTV and its role in the production of popular culture and geographies of popular culture. In his study, he found that MTV produces popular culture by opening globalized spaces to local culture, thereby globalizing the local. Rosati explained that "MTV's incorporation of rap music and Hip Hop expressive forms into its production since 1997" helped produce music celebrities and opened the MTV space to "artists and forms that were often formerly relegated to street corners, block parties and mixtapes—broadening the unification of popular aspirations with the machinery of the industrial production of culture."

A 2001 documentary produced by PBS entitled *The Merchants of Cool* looks at the roles corporations and marketing agencies play in creating popular culture. By conducting focus groups with teenagers (the main demographic for innovations in popular culture), by amassing enormous databases of what

Figure 4.16
New York, New York. The Times Square Studios of MTV's Total Request Live (TRL) show. ©James Leynse/Corbis.

teenagers do and like, by sending "cool hunters" ("cool" kids themselves) out to talk with other "cool" kids about what is "cool," and by rummaging through teenagers' bedrooms (as Rosati noted MTV does for casting its reality shows), MTV and marketing companies are creating what is cool, what is new in popular culture. In the process of producing *The Merchants of Cool*, producers interviewed Sharon Lee, one of the founding partners of Look-Look, a research company specializing in youth culture. Lee explained how trends in popular culture are spread from the hearth:

> *Actually it's a triangle. At the top of the triangle there's the innovator, which is like two to three percent of the population. Underneath them is the trend-setter, which we would say is about 17 percent. And what they do is they pick up on ideas that the innovators are doing and they kind of claim them as their own. Underneath them is an early adopter, which is questionable exactly what their percentage is, but they kind of are the layer above mainstream, which is about 80 percent. And what they do is they take what the trend-setter is doing and they make it palatable for mass consumption. They take it, they tweak it, they make it more acceptable, and that's when the mass consumer picks up on it and runs with it and then it actually kills it.*

This description is a perfect story of the hierarchical diffusion of traits and trends in popular culture.

With these kinds of infrastructure behind the production of popular culture, we may expect popular culture to act as a blanket, evenly covering the globe. Even as popular culture has diffused throughout the world, it has not blanketed the world, hiding all existing local cultures underneath it. Rather, one aspect of popular culture (such as music or food) will take on new forms when it encounters a new locality and the people and local culture in that place. Geographers and anthropologists call this the **reterritorialization** of popular culture: a term referring to a process in which people start to produce an aspect of popular culture themselves, doing so in the context of their local culture and place, and making it their own.

Reterritorialization of Hip Hop

Hip Hop and rap grew out of the inner cities of New York and Los Angeles during the 1980s and 1990s. Places such as Compton (Los Angeles) and the Bronx and Harlem (New York) came to represent the hearths of Hip Hop. These neighborhoods (as well as places in Detroit and Atlanta that later served as the basis for the midwestern and southern hearths) became the authentic spaces of Hip Hop and rap. Neighborhood venues became the best place to enjoy an authentic performance, and the lyrics reflected the importance of local places to the music itself.

The Hip Hop from these hearths diffused abroad, especially to major cities in Europe. MC Solaar, Die Fantastischen Vier, and Jovanotti each made Hip Hop their own by writing music that connected with the youth of their country (France,

Germany, and Italy, respectively). As Hip Hop diffused throughout Europe, it mixed with existing local cultures, experiences, and places, reterritorializing the music to each locale.

In Southeast Asia, Indonesia serves as a good example of the process of reterritorialization. Imported Hip Hop diffused first to a small group of people in Indonesia; then, Indonesians began to create Hip Hop music. Through the creation of their own music, Indonesian Hip Hop artists integrated their local culture with the practices of the "foreign" Hip Hop hearth to create a hybrid that was no longer foreign.

As Hip Hop has diffused and grown, artists have addressed the major concerns of their local cultures in their lyrics. Hip Hop artists in the United States wrote about social issues in the 1980s and 1990s, and some wrote about violence, crime, and surviving during the gangsta rap of the 1990s. Some artists write more about having fun and partying. In France and Germany, American Hip Hop music diffused first to immigrants living in major cities. In France, for example, some of the first Hip Hop artists were African, Arab, and Spanish immigrants writing about the racism they experienced in France.

The results of reterritorialization are seen in the ways Hip Hop artists around the world use the texts and music from their own local cultures, national cultures, and libraries to sample (mix) in their music. Hip Hop artists outside of the United States typically write and perform in their own language or dialect with reference to Hip Hop terms used by artists in the United States.

Replacing Old Hearths with New: Beating Out the Big Three in Popular Sports

Baseball, football, and basketball are historically the big three sports in the United States. During the 1800s and 1900s, they all benefited from advances in transportation technology, communication technology, and institutionalization. First, the railroad interconnected cities across the country, allowing baseball teams to compete and baseball to diffuse. The telegraph enabled newspapers to report baseball scores, which added to the sport's following. In the late 1880s, electric lighting made basketball a nighttime spectator sport, played inside gymnasiums. The founding of the National Football League in 1920 helped institutionalize (by creating institutions to support it, formalize it, and regulate it) the sport of football, with rules that have changed relatively little over the last century.

During much of the twentieth century, the big three dominated sports popular culture. Figures such as Mark McGwire, Michael Jordan, and Brett Favre found their ways onto Wheaties boxes and to icon status. In the last decades of the twentieth century, advertising contracts and corporate sponsors padded and eventually surpassed the salaries of the biggest sports heroes.

While the big three continued to draw millions of fans and huge crowds to their venues, a growing number of alternative sports began to capture the imagination of young sports fans. Popular films (including *Endless Summer*) of the 1960s immortalized the freedom of surfing. In the 1970s, sidewalk surfing, now known as skateboarding, diffused from its hearth in Southern California. In the 1980s, snowboarding found a following and met strong resistance on ski slopes in the United States.

The organization of ESPN's X Games (debuting in 1995) and the proliferation of video games involving extreme sports propelled previously alternative sports into popular culture. Video games sparked interest in the sports for kids who had never shown any interest in sports. Tony Hawk, the famous vert (a skateboarding ramp that looks like an enormous pipe cut in half—also called a halfpipe) skateboarder, worked with Activision to create several versions of Tony Hawk's Pro Skater, with average annual sales of $180 million. In 2001, sales relating to video games were higher than the movie industry's box office receipts. That same year, baseball took a back seat to skateboarding, with more children under the age of 18 skateboarding than playing baseball.

Extreme sports greats, like Tony Hawk, gain corporate sponsors, create their own brands, and sign lucrative advertising deals. Hawk reportedly earns more than $10 million a year through his skateboards and clothing line, his video games, and his stints as spokesperson for Heinz, Hershey, and Frito-Lay (Fig. 4.17). Hawk has even combined popular sports with popular music, creating his Boom Boom Huck Jam tour that features famous skateboarders, BMX bike riders, and motorcycle stunt drivers, neatly choreographed and enhanced by alternative live music.

The expansion of extreme sports into the mainstream of popular culture has been driven by advertisers who court the 12–34 age demographic, fans looking for athletes who are outside of the excess of major league sports, and fans who desire a sport that is different from their parents' sport. Researchers Maureen Smith and Becky Beal studied how masculine identities are created through MTV's television show "Cribs." They found that in the current economy, "marketing lifestyles and desires is central to selling products, which has opened new and multiple masculinity markets." Marketers use sports to "sell trucks, beer, fast food, financial advice, and a number of other products and lifestyles, including fashion and skin care."

Like new music or other forms of popular culture, extreme sports become more popular, mainstream, and commodified. Once that happens, the fan base turns its attention to a new extreme sport, and the corporate sponsors begin to tap into the new popular sport, helping it follow the same path to popular, mainstream, and commodified status.

One of the best known recent examples of this trend is the popularization of Ultimate Fighting. In the early 1990s, advertising executives and sports promoters drew from a long history of mixed martial arts fights in Brazil to produce

▬▬▬ Figure 4.17

Los Angeles, California.   Professional skateboarder Tony Hawk has led the charge of extreme sports by performing tricks such as this one, where he completed a 900 to win the Skateboard Vert Best Trick at the ninth X Games.   © Matt A. Brown/X Games/IX/NewSport/Corbis.

a series of fights in the United States among different martial arts and boxing experts to see who was the best fighter. The new fights, called mixed martial arts, grew a fan base through live matches and pay per view on cable television. The early mixed martial arts fights had few rules (such as no headbutting) and no weight classes.

The fan base grew quickly, and by 1993, the Ultimate Fighting Championship (UFC) was formed to serve as a professional organization for mixed martial arts. The sport continued to grow during the 1990s, with the establishment of rules over time allotments for matches, the institutionalization of promotions and marketing, and the growth in popularity of a reality television show called *The Ultimate Fighter*. The UFC has diffused to over 100 countries, and the rules of the UFC, including specifications for the fighting arena called "the Octagon" or "the Cage," are being institutionalized as the basis for ultimate fighting worldwide. References to ultimate fighting and ultimate fighters (such as Chuck Liddell's appearance on HBO's *Entourage*) are diffusing into other aspects of popular culture, spreading both the commodification and the popularization of the sport (Fig. 4.18).

Figure 4.18
Culver City, California. Ultimate Fighting Championship (UFC) fighter Chuck Liddell at Spike TV's Guys Choice Awards. © Frederick M. Brown/Getty Images.

Identity and the desire to remain outside of popular culture will continue to spur the creation of extreme sports to rival the "big three." In discussing MTV's production of culture, Rosati explained that the foundation of industrial capitalism is not simply "meeting the existing needs of the public." Rather, industrial capitalism demands that corporations continue to produce goods that "become socially *desirable*." The need for corporations to create the "new" so that they have something to sell that is "socially desirable" applies to MTV and the music industry, as well as to major sports promoters and marketers. Skateboarding and ultimate fighting will be followed by the next extreme sport and the next, as long as corporations can spur the consumption of the new.

Stemming the Tide of Popular Culture— Losing the Local?

The policies of assimilation practiced by the American, Canadian, Russian, Australian, and New Zealand governments were official policies designed for the express purpose of disrupting and changing indigenous, local cultures. Western, democratic governments no longer have official policies of assimilation. Yet, for people in many local cultures and in regions that are not hearths of popular culture, popular culture itself can feel like a policy of assimilation.

Popular media such as music, television, and film from the United States and the United Kingdom diffuse quickly. American, and to a lesser extent British, products can now be seen and heard around the world. If you turn on the television in Harare, Zimbabwe, you can easily find reruns of a 10-year-old American television show, or a contemporary CNN broadcast. If you walk down the street in Seoul, South Korea, you might hear a radio broadcasting a song recorded by the Beatles, Madonna, or Justin Timberlake. If you go to a cinema in Santiago, Chile, you can choose among several recently released American films.

The influence of Europe, the United States, and Japan in global popular culture makes many people feel threatened by cultural homogenization. At the global scale, North America, western Europe, and Japan exert the greatest influence on global popular culture at present. Each region acts as a major hearth for certain aspects of popular culture. North America influences western Europe and Japan in music, sports, and fast food; Japan influences North America and western Europe in children's television programs and electronic games; and western Europe influences North America and Japan in fashion, art, and philosophy.

The rapid diffusion of popular culture can cause consumers to lose track of the hearth of a good or idea. For example, Americans may think of the Nintendo Wii as an American product because of its popularity throughout the country. The Nintendo Wii, like most video game consoles and games, was created in Japan. Japanese video designer Shigeru Miyamoto, who also created Donkey Kong, Mario Brothers, and the Legend of Zelda, led the design of the interactive Wii for Nintendo. The diffusion of the Wii into households and even retirement homes throughout North America was embraced by Americans and Canadians alike, because it has not been seen as a threat to local culture.

The diffusion of popular culture, when it displaces or replaces local culture, usually will be met with resistance. In response to the influx of American and British film, the French government heavily subsidizes its domestic film industry. French television stations, for example, must turn over 3 percent of their revenues to the French cinema. The French government also stemmed the tide of American and British music on the radio by setting a policy in the 1990s requiring 40 percent of on-air time to be in French. Of the 40 percent, half must be new artists. These policies directly benefited the French Hip Hop industry. By performing in French, the new artists received quite a bit of air time on French radio. Through policies and funding, the French government has helped maintain its cultural industries, but in countless other cases, governments and cultural institutions lack the means or the will to promote local cultural productions.

Concern over the loss of local distinctiveness and identity is not limited to particular cultural or socioeconomic settings. We find such concern among the dominant societies of wealthier countries, where it is reflected in everything from the rise of religious fundamentalism to the establishment of semiautonomous communes in remote locations. We find this concern among minorities (and their supporters) in wealthier countries, where it can be seen in efforts to promote local languages, religions, and customs by constructing barriers to the influx of cultural influences from the dominant society. We find it among political elites in poorer countries seeking to promote a nationalist ideology that is explicitly opposed to cultural globalization. And we find it among social and ethnic minorities in poorer countries who seek greater autonomy from regimes promoting acculturation or assimilation to a single national cultural norm.

Geographers realize that local cultures will interpret, choose, and reshape the influx of popular culture. People interpret individual cultural productions in very different ways, depending on the cultural context in which they view them. What people choose to adopt from popular culture, how they reterritorialize it, and what they reject help shape the character and culture of people, places, and landscapes.

Think about your local community (your college campus, your neighborhood, or your town). Determine how your local community takes one aspect of popular culture and makes it your own.

HOW CAN LOCAL AND POPULAR CULTURES BE SEEN IN THE CULTURAL LANDSCAPE?

The tension between globalized popular culture and local culture can be seen in the **cultural landscape**—the visible imprint of human activity on the landscape. Human imprint includes everything from how people have changed and shaped the environment to the buildings, signs, fences, and statues people erect. Cultural landscapes reflect the values, norms, and aesthetics of a culture. On major roadways in North American towns and suburbs, the landscape is a series of big box stores, gas stations, and restaurants that reflect popular culture (Fig. 4.19). As you drive down one of these roadways, one place

Figure 4.19

Roseville, Minnesota. A series of signs advertising national chains creates a nondescript landscape on Snelling Avenue in this St. Paul suburb. Across the street from where this photo was taken is the site of T-1, the first Target store ever built (which was recently torn down and replaced with the largest Target store in the world).   © Bridget Hogan Hoye.

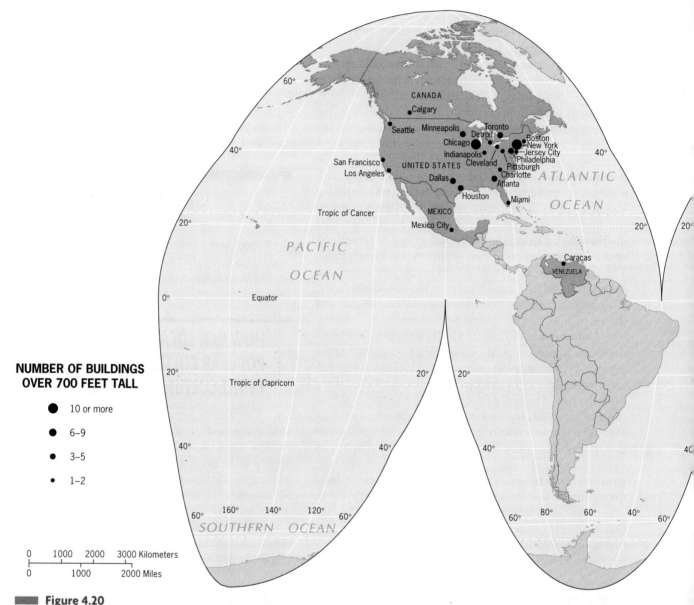

Figure 4.20
World Distribution of Skyscrapers.   Number of skyscrapers that are taller than 700 feet. *Data from*: Emporis Inc., 2005.

looks like the next. You drive past TGIFridays, Applebees, Wal-Mart, Target, and McDonald's. Then, several miles down the road, you pass another conglomeration (clustering) of the same stores. Geographer Edward Relph coined the word **placelessness** to describe the loss of uniqueness of place in the cultural landscape to the point that one place looks like the next.

Cultural landscapes begin to blend together, converging cultural landscapes in three dimensions: (1) particular architectural forms and planning ideas have diffused around the world; (2) individual businesses and products have become so widespread that they now leave a distinctive landscape stamp on far-flung places; and (3) the wholesale borrowing of idealized landscape images,

though not necessarily fostering convergence, promotes a blurring of place distinctiveness.

The global diffusion of the skyscraper provides a clear illustration of the first point—particular architectural forms and planning ideas have diffused around the world (Fig. 4.20). In the second half of the 1800s, with advancements in steel production and improved costs and efficiencies of steel use, architects and engineers created the first skyscrapers (the Home Insurance Building of Chicago is typically pointed to as the first skyscraper). The fundamental difference between a skyscraper and another building is that the outside walls of the skyscraper do not bear the major load or weight of the building; rather, the internal steel structure or skeleton of the building bears most of the load.

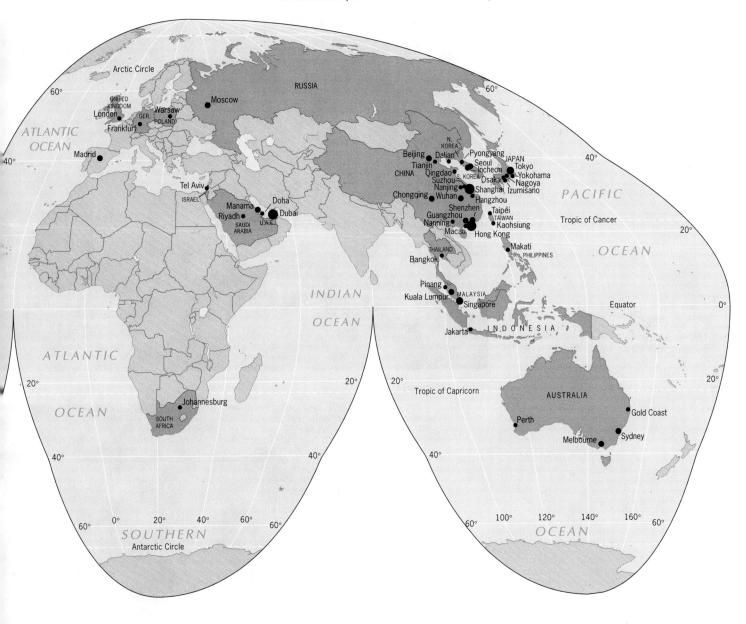

From Singapore to Johannesburg and from Caracas to Toronto, the commercial centers of major cities are dominated by tall buildings, many of which have been designed by the same architects and engineering firms. With the diffusion of the skyscraper around the world, the cultural landscape of cities has been profoundly impacted. Skyscrapers require substantial land clearing in the vicinity of individual buildings, the construction of wide, straight streets to promote access, and the reworking of transportation systems around a highly centralized model. Skyscrapers are only one example of the globalization of a particular landscape form. The proliferation of skyscrapers in Taiwan, Malaysia, and China in the 1990s marked the integration of these economies into the major players in the world economy. Today, the growth of skyscrapers in Dubai, United Arab Emirates signals the world city status of the place (Fig. 4.21).

Reading signs is an easy way to see the second dimension of cultural landscape convergence: the far-flung stamp of global businesses on the landscape. Walking down the streets of Rome, you will see signs for Blockbuster and Pizza Hut. The main tourist shopping street in Prague hosts Dunkin' Donuts and McDonald's. A tourist in Munich, Germany, will wind through streets looking for the famed beer garden, the Hofbräuhaus, and will happen upon the Hard Rock Café, right next door (Fig. 4.22). Marked landscape similarities such as these can be found everywhere from international airports to shopping centers. The

Figure 4.21
Taipei City, Taiwan. The Taipei 101 Building, the World's tallest building. ©José Fuste Raga /Age Fotostock America, Inc.

Figure 4.22
Munich, Germany. In modern-day Munich, the famed Hofbräuhaus shares a street corner with the Hard Rock Cafe.
© Courtesy Munich Tourist Office.

global corporations that develop spaces of commerce have wide-reaching impacts on the cultural landscape. Architectural firms often specialize in building one kind of space—performing arts centers, medical laboratories, or international airports. Property management companies have worldwide holdings and encourage the Gap, the Cheesecake Factory, Barnes and Noble, and other companies to lease space in all of their holdings. Facilities, such as airports and college food courts, begin to look the same even though they are separated by thousands of miles.

The third dimension of cultural landscape convergence is the wholesale borrowing of idealized landscape images across the world. As you study the cultural landscape, you may notice landscape features transplanted from one place to another—regardless of whether the landscape feature even "fits."

The strip in Las Vegas, Nevada, represents an extreme case of this tendency, with various structures designed to evoke different parts of the planet. The popular Venetian Hotel and Casino in Las Vegas replicates the Italian city of Venice, including canals. The Las Vegas Sands Corporation, a casino developer and owner, recently built a new Venetian Hotel and Casino—across the Pacific from Las Vegas in Macao (a former port of Portugal that became part of China again in 1999). The Venetian Macao Resort cost $2.4 billion and is three times the size of the largest casino in Las Vegas (Fig. 4.23). Gambling is illegal in mainland China, but Macao's recent incorporation into China and its special status allow gambling to grow on the small island.

The borrowing of landscape is not confined to grand-scale projects like the Venetian. A more common borrowed landscape in North America is the town center. Town centers popping up in suburbia in North America have a similar look—one that is familiar if you have walked on Main Street, U.S.A. at Disneyland or Disney World, or if you have visited the centers of any number of "quaint" historic towns on the eastern seaboard. Each town center is designed to make you think of all things American and to feel immediately "home" in the place.

In less obvious ways, cultural borrowing and mixing is happening all around the world. This idea is behind the **global-local continuum** concept. This notion emphasizes that what happens at one scale is not independent of what happens at other scales. Human geography is not simply about documenting the differences between places; it is also about understanding the processes unfolding at different scales that produce those differences. What happens in an individual place is the product of interaction across scales. People in a local place mediate and alter regional, national, and global processes, in a process called **glocalization**. The character of place ultimately comes out of a multitude of dynamic interactions among local distinctiveness and wider-scaled events and influences.

Figure 4.23
Top: UNESCO World Heritage site, **Venice, Italy.** © Cindy Milter Hopkins/Danita Delimont. Middle: The Venetian Hotel Casino in **Las Vegas, Nevada.** © David Noble Photography/Alamy. Bottom: The Venetian Hotel and Casino in **Macau, China.** © Paul Yeung/ Reuters/Landov

Cultural Landscapes of Local Cultures

What makes travel interesting for most people is the presence of variety in the cultural landscape. Travel beyond the tourist sites and the main roads, and one will easily find landscapes of local cultures, even in wealthy countries such as the United States and Canada. By studying local cultural landscapes, you can gain insight into the social structures of local cultures. In everything from the houses to the schools to the churches to the cemeteries, a local cultural landscape reveals its foundation.

The Mormon landscape of the American West was created by the founders of the Church of Jesus Christ of Latter-day Saints as they moved westward under persecution and in search of a place where they could practice their religion freely. The Mormon Church began in Vermont, and then John Smith and his followers moved westward to Independence, Missouri. From there, Mormons migrated westward to present-day Salt Lake City, Utah. The easiest place to see the foundations of the Mormon cultural landscape are in the small towns established by Mormons throughout Utah and stretching into Arizona, Nevada and Idaho (Fig. 4.24).

Geographers, including Donald Meinig, Richard Francaviglia, and Allen Noble have studied the Mormon landscape and discerned the roots of the Mormon culture in the local landscape. If you drove from Chicago west to Las Vegas and traveled through the rural areas of Nebraska and Utah on your path, you would immediately notice one fundamental difference in the landscape: farmsteads versus farming villages. In the Great Plains, farms were established as single farmsteads, where a farm family lived alone on their 160 acres and the nearest neighbor was down the dirt road. In the rural Mormon landscape, early settlers established farming villages where houses clustered together and crop lands surrounded the outskirts of the village (Fig. 4.25). Clustering houses together in a farming village allowed Mormons to protect each other (because the religious followers were experiencing persecution in the east and because the settlers' fears were raised by stories of Indians attacking villages in the west) and equally importantly, to join together for services in each village's chapel.

Figure 4.24

The Mormon Cultural Region. *Adapted with permission from*: D.W. Meinig, "The Mormon Culture Region: Strategies and Patterns in the Geography of the American West, 1847–1964," Annals of the Association of American Geographers, 55, 2 (1965), p. 196.

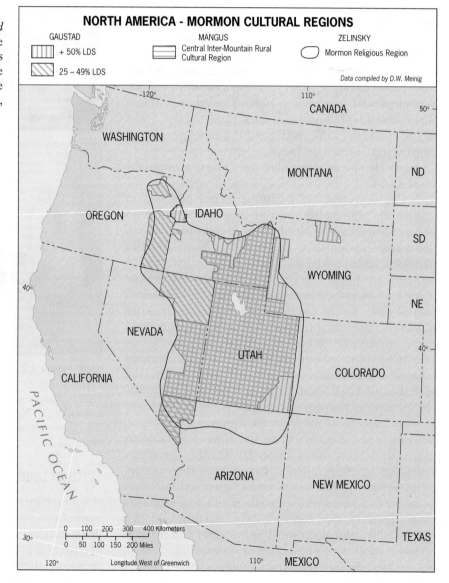

Guest Field Note

Paragonah, Utah

I took this photograph in the village of Paragonah, Utah in 1969, and it still reminds me that field work is both an art and a science. People who know the American West well may immediately recognize this as a scene from "Mormon Country," but their recognition is based primarily on their impressions of the place. "It is something about the way the scene looks," they may say, or "it feels like a Mormon village because of the way the barn and the house sit at the base of those arid bluffs." These are general impressions, but how can one prove that it is a Mormon scene? That is where the science of field work comes into play. Much like a detective investigating a crime scene, or a journalist writing an accurate story, the geographer looks for proof. In this scene, we can spot several of the ten elements that comprise the Mormon landscape. First, this farmstead is not separate from the village, but part of it—just a block off of Main Street, in fact.

Figure 4.25
Paragonah, Utah. Photo taken in 1969.

Next we can spot that central-hall home made out of brick; then there is that simple, unpainted gabled-roof barn; and lastly the weedy edge of a very wide street says Mormon Country. Those are just four clues suggesting that pragmatic Mormons created this cultural landscape, and other field work soon confirmed that all ten elements were present here in Paragonah. LIke this forty-year old photo, which shows some signs of age, the scene here did not remain unchanged. In Paragonah and other Mormon villages, many old buildings have been torn down, streets paved, and the landscape "cleaned up"—a reminder that time and place (which is to say history and geography) are inseparable.

Credit: Richard Francaviglia, Geo.Graphic Designs, Salem, Oregon

Geographer Richard Francaviglia offers several factors that delimit the Mormon landscape in western United States and Canada, including symmetrical brick houses that look more similar to houses from the East Coast than to other pioneer houses, wide streets that run due north-south and east-west, ditches for irrigation, poplar trees for shade, bishops storehouses for storing food and necessities for the poor, and unpainted fences. Because the early Mormons were farmers and were clustered together in villages, each block in the town was quite large, allowing for one-acre city lots where a farmer could keep livestock and other farming supplies in town. The streets were wide so that farmers could easily turn a cart and horses on the town's streets.

The morphology (the size and shape of a place's buildings, streets, and infrastructure) of a Mormon village tells us a lot, and so too, can the shape and size of a local culture's housing. In Malaysia, the Iban, an indigenous people, live along the Sarawak River in the Borneo region of Malaysia. Each long house is home to an extended family of up to 200 people. The family and the long house function as a community, sharing the rice farmed by the family, supporting each other through frequent flooding of the river (the houses are built on stilts), and working together on the porch that stretches the length of the house. The rice paddies surrounding each long house are a familiar shape and form throughout Southeast Asia, but the Iban long house tells you that you are experiencing a different kind of place—one that reflects a unique local culture.

Focus on the cultural landscape of your college campus. Think about the concept of placelessness. Determine whether your campus is a "placeless place" or if the cultural landscape of your college reflects the unique identity of the place. Imagine you are hired to build a new student union on your campus. How could you design the building to reflect the uniqueness of your college?

Summary

Advances in transportation and communications technology help popular culture diffuse at record speeds around the world today. Popular culture changes quickly, offering new music, foods, fashions, and sports. Popular culture envelopes and infiltrates local cultures, presenting constant challenges to members of local cultures. Some members of local cultures have accepted popular culture, others have rejected it, and still others have forged a balance between the two.

Customs from local cultures are often commodified, propelling them into popular culture. The search for an "authentic" local culture custom generally ends up promoting a stereotyped local culture or glorifying a single aspect of that local culture. Local culture, like popular culture, is dynamic, and the pursuit of authenticity disregards the complexity and fluidity cultures.

Geographic Concepts

culture	assimilation	time–space compression
folk culture	custom	reterritorialization
popular culture	cultural appropriation	cultural landscape
local culture	neolocalism	placelessness
material culture	ethnic neighborhood	global-local continuum
nonmaterial culture	commodification	glocalization
hierarchical diffusion	authenticity	folk-housing regions
hearth	distance decay	diffusion routes

Learn More Online

About the Irish Pub Company
www.irishpubcompany.com

About the Makah Tribe
www.makah.com

About the City of Lindsborg
www.lindsborg.org

About the Hutterites
www.hutterites.org

Watch It Online

Merchants of Cool
www.pbs.org/wgbh/pages/frontline/shows/cool/

The Way the Music Died
www.pbs.org/wgbh/pages/frontline/shows/music

CHAPTER 5

Identity: Race, Ethnicity, Gender, and Sexuality

Field Note   Building Walls

Traveling on the Indonesian island of Bali, I saw a brick-making facility and stopped to visit. Boys and women were building bricks by hand, in the hot sun. I watched young boys scoop wet mud from a quarry by a creek into their wheelbarrows. They poured the mud into wooden forms. Once the bricks began to dry and harden in the sun, someone had to turn the bricks repeatedly to prevent them from cracking.

The woman in Fig. 5.1 worked ten hours a day, six days a week, turning, stacking, and restacking bricks to prevent them from cracking. For her work, she earned about 45 cents (U.S.) per hour.

More than a century ago, bricks were made this way in the United States. Today, the brick-making industry in the United States makes use of a great deal of technology and robotics to manufacture bricks. Instead of using the sun to bake the bricks, brick-making factories in the United States employ enormous tunnel-shaped kilns. The *Mississippi Business Journal* described how bricks are made in one factory: "Clay and water go in one end of the new 590 foot tunnel kiln and brick pallets will roll out the other end as robots and employees work side by side."

What hit me harder than the difference in technology between the two countries is the difference in labor. In Bali, women and boys make bricks. In the United States, the vast majority of brick-makers are men, who are aided by machines (one company estimated that 98 percent of its operations' employees in

Figure 5.1
Bedugul, Indonesia. This woman working at a brick-making facility in the village of Bedugul on the Indonesian island of Bali makes about 45 cents (U.S.) per hour and works 10 hours a day, 6 days a week.   © H. J. de Blij.

the factory are men). What makes brick-making a job for women and boys in Bali and a job for men and robots in the United States? *Does being a brick-maker mean different things in each of these places?*

Throughout the world, different cultures and societies have different ideas about what jobs are appropriate for men and what jobs are appropriate for women. Geographers, especially those who study gender, realize people have created divisions of labor that are *gendered*. Geographers Mona Domosh and Joni Seager define **gender** as "a culture's assumptions about the differences between men and women: their 'characters,' the roles they play in society, what they represent." Divisions of labor are one of the clearest ways in which societies are gendered.

In Bali, brick-making is still done by hand by boys and women. The industry is not technologically sophisticated, and bricks are made one by one. Even beyond brick-making facilities, most of the factory jobs in Indonesia and in poorer countries of the world, go to women instead of men. Factory managers in these areas often hire women over men because they see women as an expendable labor pool. Researcher Peter Hancock studied gender relations and women's work in factories in Indonesia and reported, "Research in different global contexts suggests that factory managers employ young women because they are more easily exploited, less likely to strike or form membership organizations, are comparatively free from family responsibilities, and more adept at doing repetitive and delicate tasks associated with assembly line work."

In many societies in poorer countries, families see young women as financial supporters of their families. Thus, many women migrate from rural areas and travel to cities or central industrial locales (such as export production zones—EPZs) to produce and earn a wage that is then sent home to support the schooling of their brothers and younger sisters (until these girls are also old enough to leave home and work). In Indonesia and in neighboring Malaysia and the Philippines, many women temporarily migrate to the Middle East to work as domestics (cooking, cleaning, and providing childcare) in order to send money home to support the family. In the United States, rarely does an oldest daughter migrate to the city (while her family stays behind in a rural region) to labor in a factory so she can pay for her younger brothers' schooling.

Although public education in the United States is free and open to boys and girls, American society still has gendered divisions of labor. The few women who work in brick-manufacturing facilities in the United States are typically assigned to tasks that require little lifting—such as gluing pieces of the various types of brick the company produces to boards so that salespeople can use them as samples. The dominant assumption in American society is that work that requires heavy lifting needs to be completed by men and that the good-paying, unionized jobs need to go to the "head of the household." In the United States, the dominant assumption is that the head of household is a man.

Society creates boxes in which we put people and expect them to live. These boxes are in a sense stereotypes embodying assumptions we make about what is expected *from* or *assumed about* women, men, members of certain races or ethnic groups, and people with various sexual preferences. In the creation of these boxes, society can place entire professions or certain tasks into the "woman" box, thereby gendering the division of labor. Places—notably the kitchen of a home or a store in the mall—can also be gendered. At any point in time, people negotiate their personal identities, find their ways through all the expectations placed on them by the boxes society puts around them, and they modify and reinforce the social relations that create the places in which they work and live.

Rarely do the social relations that create gendered divisions of labor focus only on gender. The social relations in a place also create boxes for other identities. In this chapter, we focus on gender, race, ethnicity, and sexuality. We examine how people and society construct identities, how place factors into identity, and how geography reflects and shapes power relationships among different groups of people.

Key Questions For Chapter 5

1. What is identity, and how are identities constructed?
2. How do places affect identity, and how can we see identities in places?
3. How does geography reflect and shape power relationships among groups?

WHAT IS IDENTITY, AND HOW ARE IDENTITIES CONSTRUCTED?

A man gets off the airplane, walks to the baggage carousel to find his suitcase, and is greeted by dozens of black suitcases. He walks to the parking garage to find his car and sees a sea of black cars that all look the same. The narrator intones," Maintain your identity. Drive a Saab."

Identities are marketed through cars, clothing, memberships, jewelry, and houses. Advertisers tell us we can purchase our identity. Yet, identity is much more personal than what we drive, wear, belong to, or where we live. Geographer Gillian Rose defines **identity** as "how we make sense of ourselves." How do each of us define ourselves? We *construct* our own identities through experiences, emotions, connections, and rejections. We work through derivations and delinations to find an identity that meshes with who and where we are at any given point in time. An identity is a snapshot—an image of who we are at that moment. Identities are fluid, constantly changing, shifting, becoming. Place and space are integral to our identities because our experiences in places and perceptions of places help us make sense of who we are.

In addition to defining ourselves, we define others and others define us. One of the most powerful ways to construct an identity is by **identifying against**. To identify against, we first define the "other," and then we define ourselves as "not the other." Edward Said wrote thoughtfully about how Europeans, over time, constructed an identity for the region that is now more commonly called the Middle East and Asia, and how Europeans defined the region as the "Orient," as a mystical place through paintings and writings. Geographer James Blaut wrote eloquently about how Europeans defined Africans and Americans as "savage" and also as "mystical." Through these definitions of

the "other" during European exploration and colonialism, Europeans defined themselves as "not mystical" or "not savages" and therefore as "civilized." These ideas of identities still influence our vernacular speech today, through phrases such as "the civilized world" or "before civilization." Phrases such as these invariably mean someone is defining the "other" and in the process is defining himself or herself as superior.

One of the most powerful foci of identity in the modern world is the state. State nationalism has been such a powerful force that in many contexts people think of themselves first and foremost as French, Japanese, or American. Nationalist identities are a product of the modern state system, so we defer consideration of this form of identity to the chapter focused on the rise of the state system (Chapter 8). But nationalist identities coexist with all sorts of other identities that divide humanity—identities that can trump state nationalism in certain contexts and certain scales of interaction. Language and religion can function as foci of identity, and we will turn to these in the next two chapters. This chapter takes up several other important axes of identity: race, gender, ethnicity, and sexuality. We look at issues of identity construction, place and scale through an analysis of race. We examine ethnicity and sexuality as identities that are shaped by and that shape place. Our concluding discussion in this chapter looks at power relationships through the lenses of gender and ethnicity.

Race

Race is a constructed identity and is a perfect example of how identities are built geographically. Biologically, all people are part of the same race, the human race. The various "races" to which people refer are not biologically based. Yet, countless times during our lives, we fill out census forms, product warranty information, surveys, medical forms, and application forms that ask us to "check" the box next to our "race" (Fig. 5.2).

Where did society get the idea that humans fall into different categories of race? Throughout history, societies in different parts of the world have drawn distinctions among peoples based on their physical characteristics, but many of societies' modern assumptions about race grew out of the period of European exploration and colonialism. Benedict Anderson argues that differences in socioeconomic classes fueled the concept of superiority attached to race, **racism**. Anderson notes that even before exploration and colonialism, wealthy Europeans defined themselves as superior to those living elsewhere. During exploration and colonialism, the nonwealthy in colonizing countries defined themselves as superior to the people in the colonies. Anderson explains:

Colonial racism was a major element in that conception of "Empire" which attempted to weld dynastic legitimacy and national community. It did so by generalizing a principle of innate, inherited superiority on which its own domestic position was (however shakily) based to the vastness of the overseas possessions, covertly (or not so covertly) conveying the idea that if, say, English lords were naturally superior to other Englishmen, no matter: these other Englishmen were no less superior to the subjected natives.

The stories the commoners heard about the "mystical" and "savage" "others" fostered feelings of superiority. One of the easiest ways to define the "other" is through skin color because it is visible. In building our own identities, an easy way to determine who we are identifying against is by the color of skin.

What society typically calls a "race" is in fact a combination of physical attributes in a population. Differences in skin color, eye color, and hair color are variations within the human race. The differences likely result from a long history of adaptation to different environments. Sunlight stimulates the production of *melanin*, which protects skin from damaging ultraviolet rays; the more melanin that is present, the darker the skin will be. Many believe that this helps to explain why, over the millennia, humans living in low latitudes—from tropical Africa through southern India to Australia—had darker skins. Another (not incompatible) theory holds that the production of vitamin D (a vitamin necessary to live a healthy life) is stimulated by the penetration of ultraviolet rays. Over the millennia, natural selection in areas with shorter days in winter and more indirect sun angles (the higher latitudes) favored those with the least amount of pigmentation, those who most easily absorb ultraviolet rays and in turn produce vitamin D.

Whatever may be said about the link between environment and the development of particular physical characteristics, it is important to recognize that skin color is *not* a reliable indicator of genetic closeness. The indigenous peoples of southern India, New Guinea, and Australia, for example, are about as dark-skinned as native Africans, but native Africans, southern Indians, and Aboriginal Australians are not closely related genetically (Fig. 5.3). No biological basis for dividing the human species into four or five groups based on skin color exists. Instead, racial categories are the product of how particular cultures have *viewed* skin color.

The racial distinctions used in a place today are drawn from categories of skin color that are rooted in the cultural history, power relationships, and politics of a place over the past few centuries. Geographer Benjamin Forest gives us a global overview of racial distinctions:

In Britain, the term "black" refers not only to Afro-Caribbeans and Africans, but also to individuals from the Indian subcontinent. In Russia, the term "black" is used to describe "Caucasians," that is, people such as Chechens from the Caucasus region. In many parts of Latin America, particularly Brazil, "racial" classification is really a kind of class placement, in which members of the wealthy upper class are generally considered as "white," members of the middle class as mixed race or Mestizo, and members of the lower class as "black." Indeed, because racial classifications are based on class standing and physical appearance rather than ancestry, "the designation of one's racial identity need not be the same as that of the parents, and siblings are often classified differently than one another."

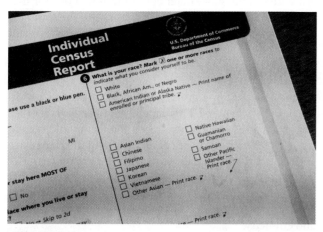

▪▪ Figure 5.2
United States.   Although biologically there is only one human race, we are constantly asked to choose race "boxes" for ourselves. This page of the 2000 United States Census asks the individual, "What is your race?" and directs the individual to "Mark one or more races to indicate what you consider yourself to be."   © Marilyn Angel Wynn/Nativestock Pictures.

Field Note

"We were traveling in Darwin, Australia in 1994 and decided to walk away from the modern downtown for a few hours. Darwin is a multicultural city in the midst of a region of Australia that is largely populated by Aboriginals. At the bus stops on the outskirts of the city, Aboriginals reached Darwin to work in the city or to obtain social services only offered in the city. With a language barrier between us, we used hand gestures to ask the man in the white shirt and his son if we could take their picture. Gesturing back to us, they agreed to the picture. Our continued attempts at sign language soon led to much laughter among the people waiting for the next bus."

Figure 5.3
Darwin, Australia.   © H. J. de Blij

In each of these cases, and in countless others, people have constructed racial categories to justify power, economic exploitation, and cultural oppression.

Racism in the United States

Unlike a local culture or ethnicity to which we may *choose* to belong, race is an identity that is more often *assigned*. Benjamin Forest explains, "In many respects, racial identity is not a self-consciously constructed collection of characteristics, but a condition which is imposed by a set of external social and historical constraints." In the United States, racial categories are imposed on people through residential segregation, racialized divisions of labor, and the categories of races recorded by the United States Census Bureau (and other government and nongovernmental agencies).

Definitions of races in the United States have historically focused on dividing the country into "white" and "nonwhite." Congress and the public have defined and redefined different groups of migrants as either "white" or "nonwhite" depending on the winds of political and economic change at the time. For example, when immigration to the United States shifted from northern and western Europe to southern and eastern Europe, the United States government and the public at large had to redefine what is "white" to allow people with olive-colored skin from the Mediterranean to count as "white."

Through migration and through differences in fertility rates among peoples in the United States, the country is becoming increasingly "nonwhite." How Americans define the "races" in the United States is increasingly being contested. In 2000, the United States Census categorized "Hispanic" as an ethnicity rather than a race. In the boxes provided by the United States Census Bureau, a person can now be "White, non-Hispanic," "White, Hispanic," "Black, non-Hispanic," "Black, Hispanic," and so forth (Table 5.1). Note that even with the new set of boxes, the American population can still be separated into "White, non-Hispanic" and "everyone else." According to the data projections provided in Table 5.2, the population of "everyone else" will surpass (in numbers) the "White, non-Hispanic" population around 2050.

Residential Segregation

Racism has affected the distribution of African Americans, American Indians, and others throughout the history of the United States. During the past century, some of the most dramatic geographic impacts of racism are found at the neighborhood scale. Historically, states, cities, and towns passed laws outlining residential segregation, disallowing the migration of certain racial groups into neighborhoods. Laws passed during and after the civil rights movement of the 1960s in the United States made it illegal to legislate residential segregation. Despite these changes, many cities in the United States remain extremely segregated residentially.

Geographers Douglas Massey and Nancy Denton defined **residential segregation** as the "degree to which two or more groups live separately from one another, in different parts of the urban environment." Massey and

TABLE 5.1

Population of the United States by Race, 2000. In 2000, the United States Census Bureau allowed Americans to categorize themselves as one race or more than one race.

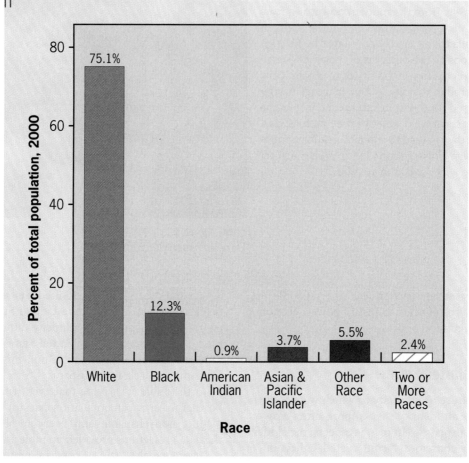

Courtesy of: United States Census Bureau, 2001.

Denton defined different kinds of residential segregation in a 1988 article, explaining that residential segregation is complex because:

> *groups may live apart from one another and be "segregated" in a variety of ways. Minority members may be distributed so that they are overrepresented in some areas and underrepresented in others, varying on the characteristic of evenness. They may be distributed so that their exposure to majority members is limited by virtue of rarely sharing a neighborhood with them. They may be spatially concentrated within a very small area, occupying less physical space than majority members. They may be spatially centralized, congregating around the urban core, and occupying a more central location than the majority. Finally, areas of minority settlement may be tightly clustered to form one large*

> *contiguous enclave, or be scattered widely around the urban area.*

A special report issued by the United States Census Bureau in 2002 statistically analyzed, charted, and mapped residential segregation in metropolitan areas of the country, using the following five statistical measurements of segregation: evenness, exposure, concentrated, centralized, and clustered. These five measurements directly correspond to the five types of segregation outlined by Massey and Denton.

In the 2002 Census Bureau report, the authors reported on the levels of residential segregation in metropolitan areas of the United States between 1980 and 2000. They found that overall residential segregation by race/ethnicity is on the decline. For each of the four identities they researched—Amerian Indians and Alaska

TABLE 5.2

Estimated Percentage of United States Population by Race and Ethnicity until 2050. In 2000, the United States Census Bureau calculated race and Hispanic origin separately, allowing people to place themselves in one or more race categories plus one of two Hispanic origin categories (Hispanic or Non-Hispanic). According to the race categories provided in these Census estimates, starting in 2050, the "White, non-Hispanic" population will no longer be the majority population in the United States.

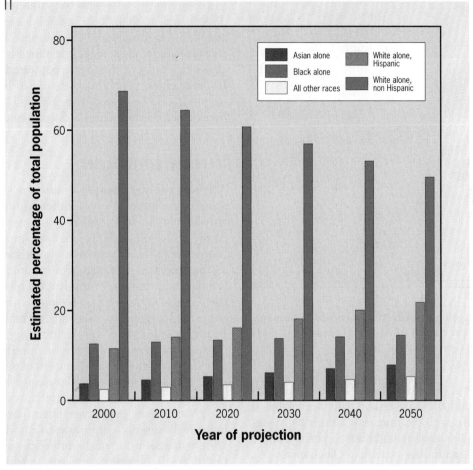

Data from: United States Census Bureau, 2001.

Natives; Asians, Native Hawaiians, and Pacific Islanders; Black/African Americans; and Hispanics/Latinos—they calculated five statististical measures of residential segregation.[1]

<hr/>

[1]We chose to use the term *Hispanic* in this chapter, recognizing that the term is as inaccurate a descriptor as "Latino" for people from Mexico, Central America, South America, and the Caribbean. Whenever possible, we use the place from which people come, for example, Mexicans or Puerto Ricans, rather than the broad term *Hispanic* (you can read more of an argument for using this method in Daniel D. Arreola, ed., *Hispanic Spaces, Latino Places* (Austin: University of Texas Press, 2004). Similarly, we use the term *American Indian* rather than *Native American*, whenever possible using a tribal name, for example, Lakota Tribe or Cheyenne River Sioux Tribe rather than the broad term *American Indian*.

The researchers reported that all five measures of residential segregation showed a decrease in residential segregation for African Americans between 1980 and 1990 and another such decrease between 1990 and 2000. Residential segregation did increase in some of the 220 metropolitan areas that have at least 3 percent of the population who self-identify as African American. The most residentially segregated large metropolitan area for African Americans is Milwaukee, Wisconsin (Fig. 5.4), and close behind is Detroit, Michigan. For African Americans, the least residentially segregated large metropolitan area is Orange County, California, followed by San Jose, California.

When using an average of all five measures of segregation, the most residentially segregated metropolitan

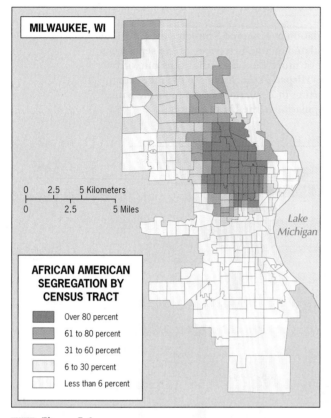

■■■ Figure 5.4
Residential Segregation of African Americans in Milwaukee, Wisconsin. Percent African American by census tract. *Data from*: United States Census Bureau, 2000.

area for American Indians and Alaska Natives is Phoenix-Mesa, Arizona, and the least residentially segregated is Oklahoma City. In fact, the four least residentially segregated metropolitan areas (with at least 3 percent of the population American Indian) were all in Oklahoma.

Grouping Asians, Native Hawaiians, and Pacific Islanders, the researchers reported 30 metropolitan areas with at least 3 percent of the population fitting one of these identities. Based on calculations for all five statistics of residential segregation, the most residentially segregated metropolitan area for Asians/Pacific Islanders is San Francisco, followed by New York and Los Angeles. The least residentially segregated cities for Asians/Pacific Islanders are Naussau-Suffolk (New York) and Baltimore, Maryland (Fig. 5.5).

In addition, Baltimore is the least residentially segregated city for Hispanics/Latinos. The researchers found that the cities with the highest number of Hispanic residents experienced the greatest amount of residential segregation. They focused their analysis on the 36 large metropolitan areas with an Hispanic population accounting for at least 3 percent of the total urban population. The city with the greatest amount of residential segregation for Hispanics was New York.

The numbers and maps produced by the Census Bureau show the outcomes of a variety of stories, but they do not tell us the stories. Why does residential segregation persist in some places and not in others? In some of the most segregated cities, people know where the "other" lives and will purposefully choose to live in neighborhoods with people like them instead of the "other." Real estate agents and community leaders may consciously or subconsciously direct people to their "own" neighborhoods (blockbusting and redlining are discussed in Chapter 9). In some cities, race is related to class, making it difficult to afford a higher class neighborhood that is also populated by another race. In other cities, people may choose to live in a blighted neighborhood because it is their neighborhood, one they have helped create and that reflects their culture.

Identities across Scales

The way we make sense of ourselves in this globalized world is complex. We have different identities at different scales: individual, local, regional, national, and global. At the individual scale, we may see ourselves as a son, a brother, a golfer, or a student. At the local scale, we may see ourselves as members of a community, leaders of a campus organization, or residents of a neighborhood. At the regional scale, we may see ourselves as Southerners, as north Georgians, as Atlantans, as Yankees living in the South, or as migrants from another region of the world. At the national scale, we may see ourselves as American, as college students, or as members of a national political party (Fig. 5.6). At the global scale, we may see ourselves as Western, as educated, as relatively wealthy, or as free.

A common way geographers have envisioned an individual's various identities is to describe the identities as nested, one inside of the other; the appropriate identity is revealed at the appropriate scale. In this vein, each larger territorial extent of geographic space has its own corresponding set of identities. Today, more geographers see identities as fluid and intertwined rather than as neatly nested. Identities affect each other in and across scales, and the ways places and peoples interact across scales simultaneously affect identities within and across scales.

The Scale of New York City

One way scale affects identity is by helping shape what is seen—what identity is apparent to others and to ourselves at different scales. To demonstrate this idea, we can shift our focus from residential segregation in all large metropolitan areas in North America to one enormous metropolitan area, New York City. New York has a greater number and diversity of immigrants than any other city in the United States. At the scale of New York, we can see how identities change so that we are no longer

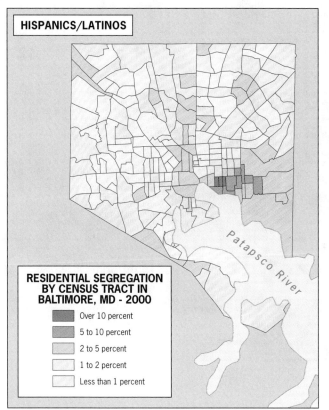

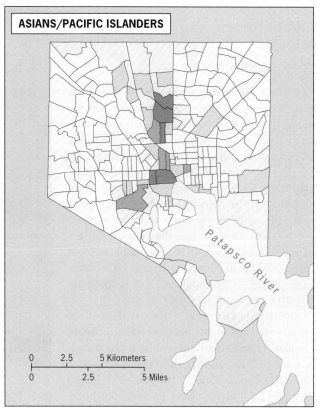

Figure 5.5
Residential Segregation of Hispanics/Latinos and Asians/Pacific Islanders in Baltimore, Maryland. Percent of Hispanics/Latinos and Asian/Pacific Islanders by census tract. *Data from*: United States Census Bureau, 2000.

Figure 5.6
Cedarburg, Wisconsin. A supporter of Barack Obama (who holds plans for Hillary Clinton on her sign) stands among supporters of John McCain at a McCain campaign event. © Robyn Beck/AFP/ Getty Images.

Guest Field Note

Washington Heights, New York

It is a warm humid September morning, and the shops along Juan Pablo Duarte Boulevard are already bustling with customers. The Dominican flag waves proudly from each corner's traffic signal. Calypso and salsa music ring through the air, as do the voices of Dominican grandmothers negotiating for the best prices on fresh mangos and papayas. The scents of fresh *empanadas de yuca* and *pastelitos de pollo* waft from street vendor carts. The signage, the music, the language of the street are all in Spanish and call out to this Dominican community. I am not in Santo Domingo but in Washington Heights in upper Manhattan in New York City.

Whenever I exit the "A" train at 181st Street and walk toward St. Nicholas Avenue, renamed here Juan Pablo Duarte Boulevard for the founding father of the Dominican Republic, it is as if I have boarded a plane to the island. Although there are Dominicans living in most neighborhoods of New York's five boroughs, Washington

Figure 5.7

Heights serves as the heart and soul of the community. Dominicans began settling in Washington Heights in 1965, replacing previous Jewish, African American, and Cuban residents through processes of invasion and succession. Over the past 40 years they have established a vibrant social and economic enclave that is replenished daily by transnational connections to their homeland. These transnational links are pervasive on the landscape, and include travel agencies advertising daily flights to Santo Domingo and Puerto Plata and stores handling *cargas, envios,* and *remesas* (material and financial remittances) found on every block, as well as *farmacias* (pharmacies) selling traditional medicines and *botanicas* selling candles, statues, and other elements needed by practitioners of Santería, a syncretistic blending of Catholicism and Yoruba beliefs practiced among many in the Spanish Caribbean.

Credit: Ines Miyares, Hunter College of the City University of New York

---

simply Hispanic (as the Census enumerates us); we are Puerto Rican or Mexican or Dominican from a certain neighborhood.

The people in New York who are defined by Census as Hispanic are much more diverse than this one box would indicate. In a chapter called "Changing Latinization of New York City," geographer Inés Miyares describes the importance of Caribbean culture in the Hispanic population of New York. The majority of New York's 2.2 million Hispanics are Puerto Ricans and Dominicans (together accounting for over 65 percent of Hispanics in the city). Historically, the Caribbean culture has made the greatest Hispanic imprint on New York's cultural landscape.

New immigrants to a city often move to areas occupied by older immigrant groups, in a process called **succession**. In New York, Puerto Ricans moved into the

immigrant Jewish neighborhood of East Harlem in the early twentieth century, successively assuming a dominant presence in the neighborhood. With the influx of Puerto Ricans, new names for the neighborhood developed, and today it is frequently called Spanish Harlem or El Barrio (meaning "neighborhood" in Spanish). As the Puerto Rican population grew, new storefronts appeared, catering to the Puerto Rican population, such as travel agencies (specializing in flights to Puerto Rico), specialty grocery stores, and dance and music studios.

Like the immigrant flow from Puerto Rico, the large-scale immigrant flow from the Dominican Republic that began in 1965 resulted in a distinct neighborhood and cultural landscape. Dominican immigrants landed in the Washington Heights/Inwood neighborhood of upper Manhattan, a neighborhood previously occupied by immigrant Jews,

African Americans, Puerto Ricans, and Cubans. Miyares reports that although a Jewish cultural landscape persists, including a Jewish university, synagogues, and Jewish delicatessens, the cultural landscape of Washington Heights is clearly Dominican—from store signs in Spanish to the presence of the colors of the Dominican flag (Fig. 5.7).

New York is unique because of the shear number and diversity of its immigrant population. The city's cultural landscape reflects its unique population. Miyares explains:

> *Since the overwhelming majority of New York City's population lives in apartments as opposed to houses, it is often difficult to discern the presence of an ethnic group by looking at residential housescapes. However every neighborhood has a principal commercial street, and this is often converted into an ethnic main street. It is commonly through business signs that immigrants make their presence known. Names of businesses reflect place names from the home country or key cultural artifacts. Colors of the national flag are common in store awnings, and the flags themselves and national crests abound in store décor. Key religious symbols are also common. Immigrants are so prevalent and diverse that coethnic proprietors use many kinds of visual clues to attract potential customers.*

Throughout the process, new immigrants need not change the facades of apartment buildings to reflect their culture. New immigrants focus their attention on the streetscapes, creating businesses to serve their new community and reflect their culture.

Popular belief in parts of New York holds that the Caribbean presence in the city is so strong that new Hispanic migrants to New York City simply acculturate into the Caribbean culture. Miyares cautions, however, that not all Hispanics in the city are categorically assimilated into the Caribbean culture. Rather, the local identities of the Hispanic populations in New York vary by "borough, by neighborhood, by era, and by source country and entry experience." In the last 10 to 15 years, the greatest growth in the Hispanic population of New York has been Mexican. Mexican migrants have settled in a variety of ethnic neighborhoods, with new Chinese immigrants in Brooklyn and with Puerto Ricans in East Harlem. The process of succession continues in New York, with Mexican immigrants moving into and succeeding other Hispanic neighborhoods, sometimes creating contention between and among the local cultures.

Taking a step back to the United States as a whole, we find that the Census Bureau defines over 2 million New Yorkers as Hispanic. In New York and in specific neighborhoods such as East Harlem, the word *Hispanic* does little to explain the diversity of the city. At these scales, different identities are claimed and assigned, identities that reflect local cultures and neighborhoods.

Recall the last time you were asked to check a box for your race. Does that box factor into how you make sense of yourself individually, locally, regionally, nationally, and globally?

HOW DO PLACES AFFECT IDENTITY, AND HOW CAN WE SEE IDENTITIES IN PLACES?

The processes of constructing identities and identifying against, just like any other social or cultural process, are rooted in places. When we construct identities, part of what we do is infuse place with meaning by attaching memories and experiences to the place. This process of infusing a place "with meaning and feeling" is what geographer Gillian Rose and countless other geographers refer to as developing a sense of place. We develop a **sense of place**, and like identities, our sense of place is fluid; it changes as the place changes and as we change.

What is of particular interest to geographers is how people define themselves through places. Our sense of place becomes part of our identity, and our identity affects the ways we define and experience place. Rose explains:

> *One way in which identity is connected to a particular place is by a feeling that you belong to that place. It's a place in which you feel comfortable, or at home, because part of how you define yourself is symbolized by certain qualities of that place. The geographer Relph, for example, has even gone so far as to claim that "to be human is to live in a world that is filled with significant places: to be human is to have to know your place."*

The uniqueness of a place can become a part of who we are.

Ethnicity and Place

Ethnicity offers a good example of how identities affect places and how places affect identities. The idea of **ethnicity** as an identity stems from the notion that people are closely bounded, even related, in a certain place over time. The word *ethnic* comes from the ancient Greek word *ethnos*, meaning "people" or "nation." Geographer Stuart Hall explains, "Where people share not only a culture but an *ethnos*, their belongingness or binding into group and place, and their sense of cultural identity, are very strongly defined." Hall explains that ethnic identity is "historically constructed like all cultural identities" and is often considered natural because it implies ancient relations among a people over time.

This definition may sound simple, but the concept of ethnicity is not. In the United States, for example, a group of people may define their ethnicity as Swiss American. Switzerland is a state in Europe. The people in Switzerland speak four major languages and other minor ones. The strongest identities in Switzerland are most often at the *canton* level—a small geographically defined area that distinguishes cultural groups within the state. So, which Swiss are Swiss Americans? The way Swiss Americans see Switzerland as part of who they are *may not exist in Switzerland proper* (Fig. 5.8). Ethnicity sways and shifts across scales, across places, and across time. A map showing all recognizable ethnic areas would look like a three-dimensional jigsaw puzzle with thousands of often-overlapping pieces—some no larger than a neighborhood, others as large as entire countries.

Ethnic identity is greatly affected by scale and place. Several years ago, the *Washington Post* published an article

Figure 5.8

New Glarus, Wisconsin. The town of New Glarus was established by immigrants from Switzerland in 1845. The Swiss American town takes pride in its history and culture, as the artwork on this sign welcoming visitors reveals.   © New Glarus Chamber of Commerce.

about the thriving South Asian community in Fairfax County, Virginia, a suburb of Washington, D.C. In South Asia, the countries of Pakistan and India have a history of animosity, and they identify themselves by region within a country and, more powerfully, by country within the region. However, in Fairfax County, Virginia, a world apart from India and Pakistan, many South Asians identify with each other. A South Asian video rental store rents both Pakistani and Indian movies. South Asian grocery stores carry foods from both countries and regions throughout them. The geographical context affected the South Asian identity.

Cultural groups often invoke ethnicity when race cannot explain differences and antagonism between groups. Just as "racial conflicts" are rooted in perceptions of distinctiveness based on differences in economics, power, language, religion, lifestyle, or historical experience, so too are "ethnic conflicts." A conflict is often called ethnic when a racial distinction cannot easily be made. For example, using physical appearance and skin color, an observer cannot distinguish the ethnic groups in many of the conflicts around the world. The adversaries in recent conflicts in Northern Ireland, Spain, the former Yugoslavia, Sri Lanka, Ivory Coast, or Rwanda cannot be identified racially; so, the parties in the conflicts use "ethnicity" to identify themselves and others.

Ethnicity is also invoked when a distinct cultural group is clustered in one area. Thus, the term *ethnicity* is often reserved for a small, cohesive, culturally linked group of people who stand apart from the surrounding culture (often as a result of migration). Like other aspects of culture, ethnicity is a dynamic phenomenon that must be understood in terms of the geographic context and scales in which it is situated.

Chinatown in Mexicali

The border region between the United States and Mexico is generally seen as a cultural meeting point between Mexicans and Anglo Americans. The ethnic composition of people in the border region is more varied than Mexican and Anglo. Through migration, people from Germany, Russia, India, China, Japan, and countless other places also live in the cities and rural areas of the United States–Mexico border region. Some of the migrants to this region have blended into the larger community over time, and others have created distinct patterns of settlement and ethnically imprinted cultural landscapes.

The town of Mexicali is the capital of the State of Baja California (located in Mexico, just south of the State of California in the United States). Not far from the central business district of Mexicali lies one of the largest Chinatowns in Mexico. A 1995 study of the Mexicali Chinatown by geographer James R. Curtis showed that it has been the crucible of Chinese ethnicity in the Mexicali Valley throughout much of the twentieth century. Chinese began arriving in 1902, and by 1919 more than 11,000 Chinese were either permanent or temporary residents of the valley. They established a thriving Chinatown in the

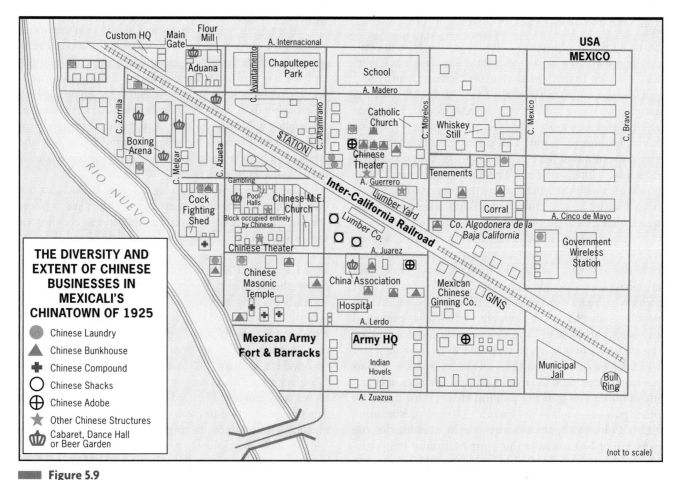

Figure 5.9

Chinatown in Mexicali, Mexico. The diversity and extent of Chinese businesses in Mexicali's Chinatown of 1925 is shown in this map. *Adapted with permission from*: J. R. Curtis, "Mexicali's Chinatown," *The Geographical Review*, 85 (1995), p. 344.

heart of Mexicali that served as the uncontested center of Chinese life in the region for decades (Fig. 5.9).

The Chinese of Mexicali were prominent players in the social and economic life of the city during the twentieth century. They owned and operated restaurants, retail trade establishments, commercial land developments, currency exchanges, and more. By 1989 they owned nearly 500 commercial or service properties. In an effort to sustain their cultural traditions and add to the cultural life of the city, they established the China Association, which plays an active role in Mexicali's social and civic life.

Mexicali's Chinatown is experiencing a transformation, as Chinese residents have dispersed to the edges of the city and beyond (many because they can afford to move out of town now). Relatively few Chinese continue to live in the city's Chinatown; some have even moved across the border to Calexico (a city of 27,000 on the California side of the border), while retaining business interests in Mexicali. Yet Mexicali's Chinatown continues to play an important symbolic and functional role for individuals of Chinese ancestry in the area, who are still shaping the region's social and economic geography. Even in regions where an ethnic population is small in number, if they have a group identity and consciousness, they can have a lasting effect on the cultural landscape.

Identity and Space

Another way of thinking about place is to consider it as a cross section of space. Doreen Massey and Pat Jess define **space** as "social relations stretched out" and **place** as "particular articulations of those social relations as they have come together, over time, in that particular location." Part of the social relations of a place are the embedded assumptions about ethnicity, gender, and sexuality, about what certain groups "should" and "should not" do socially, economically, politically, even domestically. Geographers who study identities, such as gender, ethnicity, race, and sexuality, realize that when people make places, they do so in the context of surrounding social relationships. We can, for example, create places that are **gendered**—places designed for women or for men. A building can be constructed with the goal of creating gendered spaces within, or a building can become gendered by the way people use it and interact within it.

Sexuality and Space

Sexuality is part of humanity. Just as gender roles are culturally constructed, so too do cultures decide what is "normal" sexually. In their installment on "Sexuality and Space" in *Geography in America at the Dawn of the 21ˢᵗ Century*, geographers Glen Elder, Lawrence Knopp, and Heidi Nast argue that most social science (across disciplines) is written in a heteronormative way. This means that the default subject in the minds of the academics who write studies is heterosexual, white, and male. These geographers and many others are working to find out how the contexts of local cultures and the flow of global culture and politics affect the sexual identities of people—beyond the heteronormative.

Geographers' initial forays into the study of sexuality focused largely on the same kinds of questions posed by those who first took up the study of race, gender, and ethnicity: where people with shared identity cluster, what they do to create a space for themselves, and what kinds of problems they have. For example, early studies examined gay neighborhoods in San Francisco and London, focusing on how gay men created the spaces as their own and what the space means to their identities. Specific studies have also focused on the role of gay pride parades in creating communities and the political struggle for access to other parades (such as St. Patrick's Day parades in some cities). Other studies in urban geography examine the role gays and lesbians play in the gentrification of neighborhoods in city centers (a topic we revisit in Chapter 9).

More recent studies on gay and lesbian neighborhoods question the purpose and goal of the neighborhoods. Previous studies all assumed that gay and lesbian neighborhoods are built in opposition to the dominant culture. According to geographer Natalie Oswin, newer studies see gay and lesbian neighborhoods as "extending the norm, not transgressing or challenging it." In a 2006 study, geographer Catherine Jean Nash studied Toronto's gay village and the debate over the meaning of homosexual identity and how that played out in the Toronto neighborhood.

Today, geographers studying sexuality are focusing not only on the distributions and experiences of people in places but also on the theories behind the experiences—the theories that explain and inform our understanding of sexuality and space. Many of the geographers who study sexuality today are employing queer theory in their studies. By calling the theory **queer theory**, Elder, Knopp, and Nast explain that social scientists (in geography and other disciplines) are appropriating a commonly used negative word in society and turning it to describe a theory that "highlights the contextual nature" of opposition to the heteronormative and focuses on the "political engagement" of "queers" with the heteronormative. Geographers are also concentrating on extending fieldwork on sexuality and space beyond the Western world of North America and Europe to the rest of the world, exploring and explaining the local contexts of political engagement.

In 2000, the United States Census Bureau counted the number of same-sex households in the United States. These

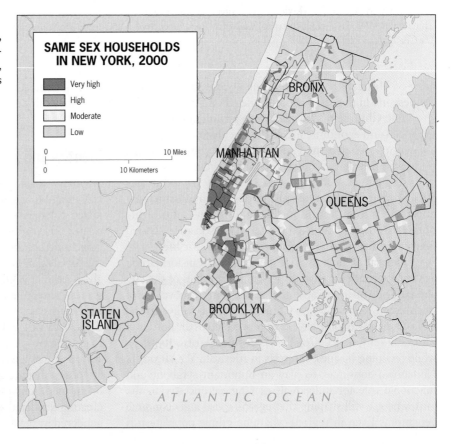

Figure 5.10

Same Sex Households in New York, 2000. The map shows the concentrations of same-sex households in New York, by census tract. *Data from*: United States Census Bureau, 2000.

data, by census tract (a small area in cities and larger area in rural America) made it possible for Gary Gates and Jason Ost to publish *The Gay and Lesbian Atlas*. Their detailed maps of major cities in the United States show concentrations of same-sex households in certain neighborhoods of cities, such as Adams-Morgan and DuPont Circle in Washington, D.C., and the West Village and Chelsea in Manhattan (Fig. 5.10). Taking the Census data by county, we can see a pattern of same-sex households in the United States, with concentrations in cities with well-established gay and lesbian neighborhoods. And we can also see the presence of same-sex households throughout the country, throughout states where same-sex unions are illegal.

In the 2000 Census, the government tallied the number of *households* where a same-sex couple (with or without children) lived. Study the map of same-sex households by census tract in Figure 5.10. What gay men and lesbian women are not being counted on this map? How would the map change if sexuality were one of the "boxes" *every* person filled out on the census?

HOW DOES GEOGRAPHY REFLECT AND SHAPE POWER RELATIONSHIPS AMONG GROUPS OF PEOPLE?

Power relationships (assumptions and structures about who is in control and who has power over others) affect identities directly and the nature of those affects depends on the geographical context in which they are situated. Power relationships also affect cultural landscapes—determining what is seen and what is not. Massey and Jess explain that the cultural landscape, the visible human imprint on the landscape, reflects power relationships. "The identities of both places and cultures, then, have to be made. And they may be made in different, even conflicting ways. And in all this, power will be central: the power to win the contest over how the place should be seen, what meaning to give it; the power, in other words, to construct the dominant imaginative geography, the identities of place and culture."

Power relationships do much more than shape the cultural landscape. Power relationships can also subjugate entire groups of people, enabling society to enforce ideas about the ways people should behave or where people should be welcomed or turned away—thus altering the distribution of peoples. Policies created by governments can limit the access of certain peoples—for example, the Jim Crow laws in the United States that separated "black" spaces from "white" spaces, right down to public drinking fountains. Even without government support, *people create places where they limit the access of other peoples*. For example, in Belfast, Northern

Ireland, Catholics and Protestants have defined certain neighborhoods as excluding the "other" through the painting of murals, the hanging of bunting, and the painting of curbs (Fig. 5.11). In major cities in the United States, local governments do not create or enforce laws defining certain spaces as belonging to members of a certain gang, but the people themselves create spaces, much like the people of Belfast do, through graffiti, murals, and building colors.

Just Who Counts?

The statistics governments collect and report reflect the power relationships involved in defining what is valued and what is not. Think back to the Constitution of the United

Figure 5.11
Belfast, Northern Ireland.   Signs of the conflict in Northern Ireland mark the cultural landscape throughout Belfast. In the Ballymurphy area of Belfast, where Catholics are the majority population, a woman and her children walk past a mural in support of the Irish Republican Army. The mural features images of women who lost their lives in the conflict, including Maureen Meehan, who was shot by the British Army and Anne Parker, who died when the bomb she planned to detonate exploded prematurely.   © AP/Wide World Photos.

States prior to the Fourteenth Amendment, when the government enumerated a black person as three-fifths of a white person. Until 1924, the U.S. government did not recognize the right of all American Indians to vote (even though the Fifteenth Amendment recognized the right to vote regardless of race in 1870). The U.S. government separated American Indians into those who were "civilized" enough to be citizens and those who were not ("Indians not taxed") until 1924 when it recognized the citizenship of all American Indians born in the United States. Not until 1920 did States ratify the Nineteenth Amendment to the Constitution, recognizing the right of all Americans to vote, regardless of sex. Despite progress in counting people of all races, ethnicities, and sex, some charge that the United States Census Bureau continues to undercount minority populations (see Chapter 2), and throughout the world, the work of women is largely undervalued and uncounted.

When the United States and other *state* governments began to count the value of goods and services produced within state borders, they did so with the assumption that the work of the household is reserved for women and that this work does not contribute to the productivity of the state's economy. The most commonly used statistic on productivity, the gross national income (the monetary worth of what is produced within a country plus income received from investments outside the country), does not evaluate work in the home. The gross national income (GNI) includes neither the unpaid labor of women in the household nor, usually, the work done by rural women in less developed countries.

Scholars estimate that if women's productivity in the household alone were given a dollar value (for example, by calculating what it would cost to hire people to perform these tasks), the world's total annual GNI (that is, the gross national income for all countries combined) would grow by about one-third. In poorer countries, women produce more than half of all the food; they also build homes, dig wells, plant and harvest crops, make clothes, and do many other things that are not recorded in official statistics as being economically productive (Fig. 5.12).

Despite these conditions, the number of women in the "official" labor force is rising. In 1990, the United Nations estimated that there were 828 million women in the labor force. All but one geographic region showed increases between 1970 and 1990: in the wealthier countries of the world, from 35 to 39 percent of the labor force; in Middle and South America, from 24 to 29 percent. In East and Southeast Asia the figure rose very slightly, to 40 and 35 percent, respectively. In Subsaharan Africa, the percentage of women in the labor force actually declined from 39 percent in 1970 to 37 percent in the 1990s. These statistics reveal that, in stagnating or declining economies, women are often the first to suffer from job contraction.

Even though women are in the official labor force in greater proportions than ever before, they continue to be paid less and have less access to food and education than men in nearly all cultures and places around the world. A 2004 report from the United Nations stated that two-thirds of the 880 million illiterate adults in the world are women and that women account for 70 percent of the world's poorest citizens.

In most of Asia and virtually all of Africa, the great majority of wage-earning women still work in agriculture. In Subsaharan Africa, nearly 80 percent of wage-earning women work on plantations and farms; in Asia, the figure is over 50 percent. Although the number of women working in industries in these areas is comparatively small, it is rising. The increase has been slowed by the global economic downturn of the early 2000s, as well as by mechanization, which leads to job reductions and hence to layoffs of women workers. In the *maquiladoras* of northern Mexico (see Chapter 10), for example, many women workers lost their jobs when labor markets contracted between 2001 and 2002.

As the foregoing discussion has highlighted, many women engage in "informal" economic activity—that is, private, often

▆▆ Figure 5.12
South Korea. The women in this photo sat near one of the ancient temples in southern Korea, selling the modest output from their own market gardens. This activity is one part of the informal economy, the "uncounted" economy in which women play a large role.
© Alexander B. Murphy.

Guest Field Note

One of the leading causes of mortality and morbidity among children under the age of five in developing countries is waterborne disease. My research has focused on building an understanding of the factors that contribute to the vulnerability of young children to this significant public health problem. I have conducted my research in communities located in the relatively remote Karakoram Range of northern Pakistan. Of particular interest to me is the microenvironment of water-related disease risk, and in particular, the factors at the household scale that make the prevalence of childhood illness more or less severe. One of the primary methodological strategies that I employ in this research involves household microstudies, which entail in-depth interviews with family members (primarily mothers who are the principal child health providers), child health histories, and structured observations. One of the most important findings of this research in mountain communities, in my opinion, is that the education, social support, and empowerment of women is critical to breaking the cycle of disease impacts and to ensuring long-term child survival.

Figure 5.13

Credit: Sarah J. Halvorson, University of Montana

home-based activity such as tailoring, beer brewing, food preparation, and soap making. Women who seek to advance beyond subsistence but cannot enter the formal economic sector often turn to such work. In the migrant slums on the fringes of many cities, informal economic activity is the mainstay of the community. As with subsistence farming, however, it is difficult to assess the number of women involved, their productivity, or their contribution to the overall economy.

Statistics showing how much women produce and how little their work is valued are undoubtedly interesting. Yet, the work geographers who study gender have done goes far beyond the accumulation of such data. Over the last two decades, geographers have asked why society talks about women and their roles in certain ways and how these ideas, heard and represented throughout our lives, affect the things we say, the ways we frame questions, and the answers we derive. For example, Ann Oberhauser and her co-authors explained that people in the West tend to think that women are employed in the textile and jewelry-making fields in poorer countries because the women in these regions are "more docile, submissive, and tradition bound" than women in the core. A geographer studying gender asks where these ideas about women come from and how the ideas themselves bind women to certain jobs and certain positions in society—key elements in making places what they are.

Vulnerable Populations

Power relations can have a fundamental impact on which populations or areas are particularly vulnerable to disease, death, injury, or famine. Geographers use mapping and spatial analysis to predict and explain what populations or people will be impacted most by natural hazards, such as earthquakes, volcanoes, hurricanes, and tsunamis or by environmental policies. Vulnerability theory tells us that not all people are affected in the same way by social, political, economic, or environmental change. Rather, the nature and spatial character of existing social structures influence which populations are the most vulnerable.

Fieldwork is the best way to understand how power structures in society create vulnerable groups and how those vulnerable groups are affected by change. Through fieldwork and interviews, geographers can see differences in vulnerability within groups of people.

Geographer Sarah Halvorson studied differences in the vulnerabilities of children in northern Pakistan. She examined vulnerability of children to diarrheal diseases by paying attention to "constructions of gender, household politics, and gendered relationships that perpetuate inherent inequalities and differences between men and women and within and between social groups."

Halvorson studied 30 families, 15 of whom had low frequency of diarrhea and dysentery and 15 of whom had high frequency of these diseases. Through her fieldwork, Halvorson came to understand that several tangible resources (such as income and housing) and several intangible resources (including social status and position within the family structure) all factored into the vulnerability of children to diarrheal diseases in northern Pakistan. Halvorson found that people with higher incomes generally had lower disease rates, but that income was not the only factor (Fig. 5.13). The least vulnerable children and women were those who had higher incomes and an established social network of support. In cases where income was low, if a woman had a strong social network, she could still help her children into the low disease group.

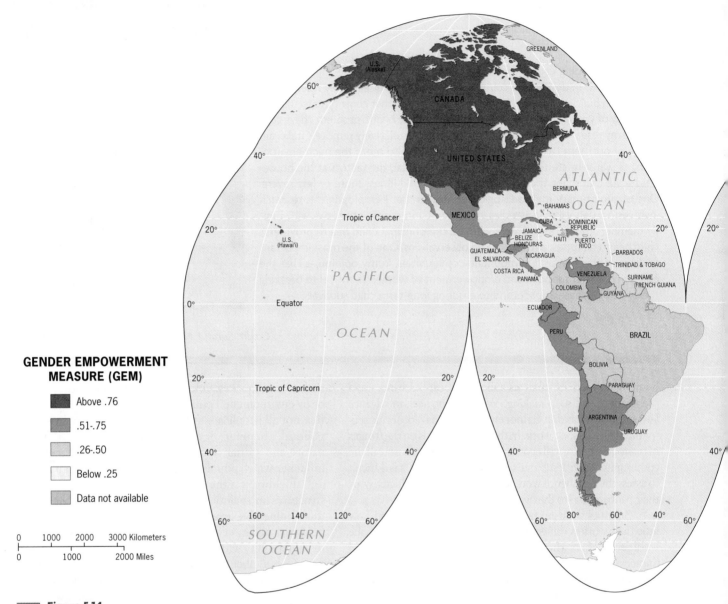

GENDER EMPOWERMENT MEASURE (GEM)

- Above .76
- .51-.75
- .26-.50
- Below .25
- Data not available

Figure 5.14
Gender Empowerment Measure (GEM) by country.   The GEM value is derived from a number of statistics measuring womens' access to political and economic decision making. Data from: United Nations Development Program, Human Development Report 2007–2008.

Geographer Joseph Oppong recognized that the spatial analysis of a disease can reveal what populations are most vulnerable in a country. In North America and Europe, HIV/AIDS is much more prevalent among homosexual and bisexual men than among heterosexual men and women. In Subsaharan Africa, women have much higher rates of HIV/AIDS than men. Oppong explains that "AIDS as a global problem has unique local expressions that reflect the spatial distribution and social networks of vulnerable social groups."

According to Oppong, in most of Subsaharan Africa, HIV/AIDS rates are highest for women in urban areas, and for women who work as sex workers. In Ghana, HIV/AIDS rates were lower for women in the urban area of Accra. Oppong postulates that women in Accra have lower HIV/AIDS rates because they have greater access

to health care than women in rural areas. Women in rural areas who were not treated for malaria had higher incidences of HIV/AIDS, according to his research. Oppong also found that women in polygamous relationships in the Muslim part of northern Ghana had lower HIV/AIDS rates. Oppong offers two theories as to why women Muslims in polygamous relationships had lower HIV/AIDS rates: first, Muslims have a cultural practice of avoiding sexual promiscuity, and second, Muslims in Ghana practice circumcision, which helps lower the rate of HIV/AIDS transmission in that part of the country.

Fieldwork helps geographers apply vulnerability theory to understand how existing spatial structures, power relationships and social networks affect the impacts of disease and hazards around the world.

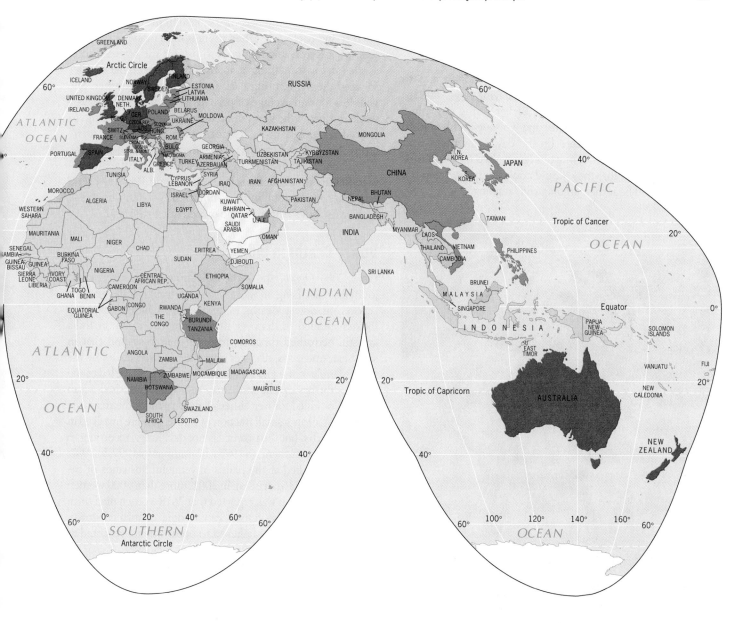

Women in Subsaharan Africa

Migration flows, birth rates, and child mortality rates affect the gender composition of cities, states, and regions. Some regions of the world have become male-dominated, whereas other regions of the world have become female-dominated—at least in number.

Much of Subsaharan Africa, especially rural areas, is dominated numerically by women. In this region of the world, most rural to urban migrants are men. Domosh and Seager explain that men leave rural areas to work in heavy industry and mines in the cities, "while women are left behind to tend the farms and manage the household economy. Indeed parts of rural South Africa and Zimbabwe have become feminized zones virtually depopulated of men." Although women populate much of rural Subsaharan Africa, society and governments work in conjunction to subjugate the women. Women in Subsaharan Africa have heavy responsibilities, few rights, and little say (Fig. 5.14). They produce an estimated 70 percent of the realm's food, almost all of it without the aid of modern technology. Their backbreaking hand-cultivation of corn and other staples is an endless task. As water supplies decrease, the exhausting walk to the nearest pump gets longer (Fig. 5.15). Firewood is being cut at ever-greater distances from the village, and the task of hauling it home becomes more difficult every year. As the men leave for the towns, sometimes to marry other wives and have other children, the women left in the villages struggle for survival.

Field Note

"A woman and her daughter came walking along the path to a village near Kanye, Botswana, carrying huge, burlap-wrapped bundles on their heads. Earlier in the day, I had seen the women fetching water and working in the field to weed the maize (corn). Later in the day, I saw them with batches of firewood that must have weighed 60 pounds or more. In the evening, they would cook the meal. From the village, I could hear men arguing and laughing."

Figure 5.15
Kanye, Botswana.   © H. J. de Blij

Even though a woman in this position becomes the head of a household, when she goes to the bank for a loan she is likely to be refused; banks throughout much of Africa do not lend money to rural women. Not having heard from her husband for years and having reared her children, she might wish to apply for title to the land she has occupied and farmed for decades, but land titles usually are not awarded to women. Only a small percentage of African women have the legal right to own property.

Young girls soon become trapped in the cycle of female poverty and overwork. Often there is little money for school fees; what is available first goes to pay for the boys. As soon as she can carry anything at all, the girl goes with her mother to weed the fields, bring back firewood, or fetch water. She will do so for an average of perhaps 12 hours a day, 7 days a week, during all the years she remains capable of working. In East Africa, cash crops such as tea are sometimes called "men's crops" because the men trade in what the women produce. When the government of Kenya tried to increase the productivity on the tea plantations in the 1970s and 1980s, the government handed out bonuses—not to the women who did all of the work but to the men who owned title to the land!

Dowry Deaths in India

On a 2004 *Oprah!* show, the talk show queen interviewed journalist Lisa Ling about her travels through India and her reports on dowry deaths in India. The Chicago audience looked stunned to discover that thousands of girls in India are still betrothed through arranged marriages and that in some extreme cases, disputes over the price to be paid by the bride's family to the groom's father (the dowry) have led to the death of the bride. The bride may be brutally punished (often burned) or killed for her father's failure to fulfill the marriage agreement. Only a small fraction of India's girls are involved in **dowry deaths**, but the practice is not declining. According to the Indian government, in 1985, the number was 999; in 1987, 1786 women died at the hands of vengeful husbands or in-laws; in 1989, 2436 perished; in 2001, more than 7000 women died; and in 2006, it was reported that 7618 women died from dowry deaths. These figures report only confirmed dowry deaths; many more are believed to occur but are reported as kitchen accidents or other fatal domestic incidents.

The power relationships that placed women below men in India cannot be legislated away. Government entities in India (federal as well as State) have set up legal aid offices to help women who fear dowry death and seek assistance. In 1984, the national legislature passed the Family Courts Act, creating a network of "family courts" to hear domestic cases, including dowry disputes. But the judges tend to be older males, and their chief objective, according to women's support groups, is to hold the family together—that is, to force the threatened or battered woman back into the household. Hindu culture attaches great importance to the family structure, and the family courts tend to operate on this principle.

Recognizing that movement away from arranged marriages and dowries among the Indian population is slow in coming, the journalist and talk show host took the issue of dowry deaths *to the global scale*—to generate activism in the West and create change at the local scale in India. Ling explained that the place of women in India has changed little. She described women as a financial burden on the bride's family, who must save for a sizable dowry to marry off the woman. Ling describes the dowry as a financial transaction, through marriage the burden of the woman moves from the bride's family to her husband's family. As the American media typically does when talking about social ills, Winfrey and Ling interviewed a woman in India to show that global change can help make local change possible. Nisha Sharma was to marry in front of 1500 guests in a town just outside of the capital of New Delhi. On her wedding day, the groom's family demanded $25,000 in addition to the numerous luxury items they had already received as dowry (including washing machines, a flat screen TV, and a car) (Fig. 5.16). Nisha's father refused to pay, the man's family became violent, and Nisha called the police on her cell phone. She has become a local hero and is also an example in the West of how to beat the dowry deaths using global technology, in this case, a cell phone.

Unfortunately, not all women in India (or in many other places around the world) feel empowered enough to stand up to injustices committed against women, nor do they have education, paying jobs, and cell phones (Nisha Sharma had all three). Despite the laws against dowry deaths, women remain disempowered in much of Indian society. Some pregnant women undergo gender-determining tests (ultrasound and amniocentesis) and elect to have abortions when the fetus is a girl. Girls who make it to birth may suffer female infanticide as many parents fear the cost of dowries and extend little social value to girls. In all of these cases, moving issues to the global scale has the potential to draw attention to the social ills. Yet, for the social ills to be cured, power in social relationships must shift at the family, local, regional, and national scales.

Shifting Power Relationships among Ethnic Groups

In Chapter 4, we discussed local cultures that define themselves ethnically. The presence of local ethnic cultures can be seen in the cultural landscapes of places we discussed in Chapter 4—notably Little Sweden in Kansas or the Italian North End in Boston. In many places, more than one ethnic group lives in a place, creating unique cultural landscapes and revealing how power relationships factor into the ways ethnicities are constructed, revised, and solidified, where ethnic groups live, and who is subjugating whom.

Three urban geographers—John Frazier, Florence Margai, and Eugene Tettey-Fio—tracked the flow of people and shifts in power relationships among the multiple ethnicities that have lived in Alameda County, California, in their book *Race and Place: Equity Issues in Urban America*. The county borders San Francisco and includes the geographic areas of Berkeley and Oakland. The region was populated mainly by Hispanics prior to the Gold Rush. After 1850, migrants from China came to the county. The first Asian migrants to the county lived in a dispersed settlement pattern, but the first African Americans lived in a segregated area of the county.

A common story from areas with multiple ethnicities is an ebb and flow of acceptance. When the economy is booming, residents are generally more accepting of each other. When the economy takes a downturn, residents often begin to resent each other and can blame the "other" for their economic hardship (for example, "they" took all the jobs). In Alameda County, much of the population resented Chinese migrants when the economy took a downturn in the 1870s. The first Chinese Exclusion Act (prohibiting immigration of Chinese) was passed in 1882. Chinese exclusion efforts persisted for decades afterward in Alameda County and resulted in the city of Oakland moving Chinatown several times.

During the 1910s, the economy of the region grew again, but the city of Oakland limited the Chinese residents to Chinatown, using ethnic segregation to keep them apart from the rest of the population. Frazier, Margai, and

▮▮▮ Figure 5.16
Noida, India. Nisha Sharma sits in front of the dowry her father planned to give her groom's family. Sharma made national and global headlines when she refused to marry her groom after his family demanded an even larger dowry. © AP/Wide World Photos.

Tettey-Fio described how Oakland's Chinatown was dictated by law and not elected by choice:

> *At a time when the Chinese were benefiting from a better economy, the "whites only" specifications of local zoning and neighborhood regulations forced separatism that segregated the Oakland Chinese into the city's Chinatown. What today is sometimes presented as an example of Chinese unity and choice was, in fact, place dictated by law.*

Until World War II, the Chinese lived segregated from the rest of Oakland's population. When the war began, residents of Alameda County, like much of the rest of the United States, focused on the Japanese population in the county, persecuting, segregating, and blaming them. After World War II, the ethnic population of Asians in Alameda County became much more complex. The Asian population alone doubled in the decade between 1980 and 1990 and diversified to include not only Chinese and Japanese but also Koreans, Vietnamese, Cambodians, and Laotians. In Alameda County today, as in much of the rest of the United States, the first wave of immigrants from Asia (mainly from China, India, and Korea), who came to the region already educated, are not residentially segregated from the white population. However, the newer immigrants from Asia (mainly Southeast Asia—during and following the Vietnam War) are segregated from whites residentially, mixing much more with the African American population in the inner-city neighborhoods. Here, Asians experience a high rate of poverty, much like the Hispanic and African American populations in the same regions of the county do.

In California (and in much of the rest of the United States), the "Asian" box is drawn around a stereotype of what some call the "model minority." Frazier and his colleagues explain the myth of the model minority: the myth "paints Asians as good, hardworking people who, despite their suffering through discrimination, harassment, and exclusion, have found ways to prosper through peaceful means." Other researchers have debunked the myth by statistically demonstrating the different levels of economic success experienced by various Asian peoples, with most success going to the first wave of migrants and lower paying jobs going to newer migrants. Both groups are burdened with a myth that stereotypes them as the "model minority."

Power Relations in Los Angeles

Over the last four decades, the greatest migration flow into California and the southwestern United States has come from Latin America and the Caribbean, especially Mexico. In the 2000 Census, the city of Los Angeles had nearly 3.7 million people, over 46 percent of whom were Hispanic, over 11 percent black or African American, and 10 percent Asian (using Census categories for race and ethnicity). The Hispanic population in the city grew from 39.32 percent of the population in 1990 to 46 percent by 2000.

The area of southeastern Los Angeles County is today "home to one of the largest and highest concentrations of Latinos in Southern California," according to a study by geographer James Curtis. Four decades ago, this area of Los Angeles was populated by working-class whites who were segregated from the African American and Hispanic populations through discriminatory policies and practices. Until the 1960s, southeastern Los Angeles was home to corporations such as General Motors, Bethlehem Steel, and Weiser Lock. During the 1970s and 1980s, the corporations began to close as the process of deindustrialization (see Chapter 11) fundamentally changed where and how goods are produced. As plants closed and white laborers left the neighborhoods, a Hispanic population migrated into southeastern Los Angeles. A housing crunch followed by the 1980s, as more and more Hispanic migrants headed to southeastern Los Angeles. With a cheap labor supply now readily available in the region again, companies returned to southeastern Los Angeles, this time focusing on smaller-scale production of textiles, pharmaceuticals, furniture, and toys. In addition, the region attracted industrial-toxic waste disposal and petrochemical refining facilities.

In his study of the region, Curtis records the changes to the cultural landscape. He calls the change in neighborhoods whereby the Hispanic population jumped from 4 percent in 1960 to over 90 percent Hispanic in 2000 a process of **barrioization** (referring to *barrio*, the Spanish word for neighborhood). With the ethnic succession of the neighborhood from white to Hispanic, the cultural landscape changed to reflect the culture of the new population. The structure of the streets and the layout of the housing remained largely the same, giving the Hispanic population access to designated parks, schools, libraries, and community centers built by the previous residents and rarely found in other barrios in Southern California. However, the buildings, signage, and landscape changed as "traditional Hispanic housescape elements, including the placement of fences and yard shrines as well as the use of bright house colors" diffused through the barrios. Curtis explains that these elements were added to existing structures, houses, and buildings originally built by the white working class of southeastern Los Angeles.

The influx of new ethnic groups into a region, the replacement of one ethnic group by another within neighborhoods, changes to the cultural landscape, the persistence of myths such as the "model minority" myth of Asians, and an economic downturn can create a great deal of volatility in a city.

On April 29–30, 1992, the city of Los Angeles, California, became engulfed in one of the worst incidents of civil unrest in United States history. During the two days of rioting 43 people died, 2383 people were injured, and 16,291 people were arrested. Property damage was estimated at approximately $1 billion, and over 22,700 law enforcement personnel were deployed to quell the unrest. According to the media, the main catalyst for the mass upheaval was the announcement of a "not guilty" verdict in the trial of four white Los Angeles police officers accused of using excessive force in the videotaped arrest of Rodney King, a black motorist. To the general public, the Los

Angeles riots became yet another symbol for the sorry state of race relations between blacks and whites in the United States. Yet, a geographic perspective on the Los Angeles riots suggests they were more than a snap response to a single event; they were localized reactions not only to police brutality, but also to sweeping economic, political, and ethnic changes unfolding at regional and even global scales.

The riots took place in South Central Los Angeles. Like the region of southeast Los Angeles (described above), the South Central area was once a thriving industrial region with dependable, unionized jobs employing the resident population. In the 1960s, however, the population of South Central Los Angeles was working-class African American, and the population of southeastern Los Angeles was

▬▬▬ Figure 5.17
The Changing Ethnic Composition of South-Central Los Angeles, 1960–1980. *Adapted with permission from*: J. H. Johnson, Jr., C. K. Jones, W. C. Farrell, Jr., and M. L. Oliver. "The Los Angeles Rebellion: A Retrospective in View," *Economic Development Quarterly*, 6, 4 (1992), pp. 356–372.

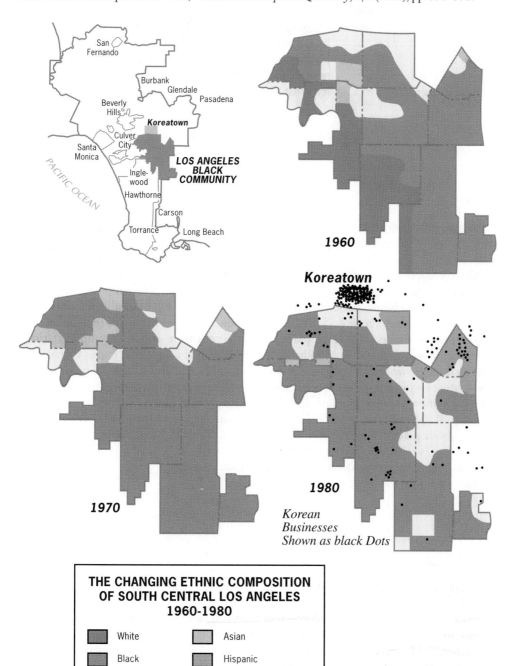

working-class white. After 1970, South Central Los Angeles experienced a substantial decrease in the availability of high-paying, unionized manufacturing jobs when plants closed and relocated outside of the city and even outside the country. The people of South Central Los Angeles lost over 70,000 manufacturing jobs between 1978 and 1982 alone!

Geographer James Johnson and his colleagues explored the impact of economic loss on the ethnic and social geography of South Central Los Angeles. They found that the population of the area was over 90 percent African American in 1970, and by 1990, the population was evenly split between African Americans and Hispanics. This change in population composition was accompanied by a steady influx of Korean residents and small-business owners who were trying to find a niche in the rapidly changing urban area (Fig. 5.17).

Johnson and his colleagues argued that the Los Angeles riots were more than a spontaneous reaction to a verdict. They were rooted in the growing despair and frustration of different ethnic groups competing for a decreasing number of jobs in an environment of declining housing conditions and scarce public resources. Their work shows the importance of looking beyond the immediate catalysts of particular news events to the local, national, and global geographical contexts in which they unfold.

Geographers who study race, ethnicity, gender, or sexuality are interested in the power relationships embedded in a place from which assumptions about "others" are formed or reinforced. Consider your own place, your campus, or locality. What power relationships are embedded in this place?

Summary

Identity is a powerful concept. The way we make sense of ourselves is a personal journey that is mediated and influenced by the political, social, and cultural contexts in which we live and work. Group identities such as gender, ethnicity, race, and sexuality are constructed, both by self-realization and by identifying against and across scales. When learning about new places and different people, humans are often tempted to put places and people into boxes, into myths or stereotypes that make them easily digestible.

The geographer, especially one who spends time in the field, recognizes that how people shape and create places varies across time and space and that time, space, and place shape people, both individually and in groups. James Curtis ably described the work of a geographer who studies places: "But like the popular images and stereotypical portrayals of all places—whether positive or negative, historical or contemporary—these mask a reality on the ground that is decidedly more complex and dynamic, from both the economic and social perspectives." What Curtis says about places is true about people as well. What we may *think* to be positive identities, such as the myths of "Orientalism" or of the "model minority," and what we know are negative social ills, such as racism and dowry deaths, are all decidedly more complex and dynamic than they first seem.

Geographic Concepts

gender	residential segregation	place
identity	succession	gendered
identifying against	sense of place	queer theory
race	ethnicity	dowry deaths
racism	space	barrioization

Learn More Online

About the Gay and Lesbian Atlas
www.urban.org/pubs/gayatlas/

About Racial and Ethnic Segregation in the United States, 1980–2000
http://www.census.gov/hhes/www/housing/resseg/papertoc.html

About the Murals in Northern Ireland
http://cain.ulst.ac.uk/mccormick/intro.htm

Watch It Online

About Ethnicity and the City
http://www.learner.org/resources/series180.html#program_descriptions
click on Video On Demand for "Boston: Ethnic Mosaic"

About Ethnic Fragmentation in Canada
www.learner.org/resources/series180.html#program_descriptions
click on Video On Demand for "Vancouver: Hong Kong East" and "Montreal: An Island of French"

About Migration and Identity
http://www.learner.org/resources/series85.html#program_descriptions
click on Video on Demand for "A Migrant's Heart"

Language

Field Note   What should I say?

In stores throughout Brussels, Belgium, you can see the capital city's bilingualism all around you—literally. From McDonald's (Fig. 6.1) to the metro, signs in Brussels are posted in duplicate, with one in Flemish (a variant of Dutch) and one in French.

Walking into a travel agency in Brussels one afternoon, I immediately noticed the signs in duplicate: two signs towered over the woman behind the counter; two signs advertised a new budget airline carrier that would be serving the Brussels airport; two signs labeled the restrooms; and two signs announced the travel agency's hours of operation.

I debated for a minute whether to speak to the person behind the counter in French or Flemish. She was speaking Flemish with the person in front of me, but I decided to use French since my knowledge of that language is better. The student from Italy who stood behind me in line apparently had no such debate. She stepped up to the counter, asked her question in English, and received a reply in excellent English.

Many geographers are initially drawn to the discipline through maps. However, maps, especially at the world or continental scale, generalize so much information that they hide the complexities of everyday life. Once you become a geographer, you begin to question every map you examine. Look at the European map of languages (Fig. 6.2), and zero in on Belgium. The map shows a neat line dividing Flemish speakers (a Germanic language) in the northern region of Flanders from French speakers (a Romance language) in the southern region of Wallonia.

Behind this neat line on the language map lies a complicated, at times contentious, linguistic transition zone. To understand language patterns in Belgium, we must also study the issue at the local scale. Although the bilingual capital of Brussels is located in the Flemish-speaking north (Flanders), for an estimated 85 percent of the locals, French is the mother tongue (Fig. 6.3).

In Belgium, language has been a divisive issue for generations. During the nineteenth century, French speakers controlled the industrial economy and government of the country. The concentration of industry in southern Belgium strengthened their position. The French-speaking elite in Brussels and other Flemish cities began a process of "Frenchification." They promoted French and used it when interacting with their counterparts in other countries. By the twentieth century, a majority of the people in Brussels spoke French, although people in the areas surrounding Brussels continued to speak Flemish.

Many in northern Belgium (surrounding Brussels) opposed the growing Frenchification of Flanders. The leaders of the Flemish movement initially sought linguistic rights—the right of Flemish speakers to use their language in public affairs, court proceedings, and schools. Yet they were constantly frustrated with the opposition of French speakers to their demands. By the 1920s, the Flemish leadership began calling for the country to be partitioned along linguistic lines so that those living in northern Belgium could control their own affairs.

By the 1960s, a fixed partition scheme came into being—dividing the country into Flemish-speaking Flanders in the north and French-speaking Wallonia in the south. The government recognizes Brussels as a distinct region—a bilingual capital—but places strict limits on the use of French in the rest of northern Belgium.

The partitioning process produced upheavals throughout the country. The experience helped strengthen the sense of Flemish identity and fueled a counter-movement among the French Walloons. With language-group identity on the rise, conflicts between linguistic "communities" became a central feature of Belgian political life. After the 1960s, Belgian heavy industry became less competitive, and the country's economy began a shift to high technology, light industry, and

LANGUAGES OF EUROPE

Major Indo-European Branches	Other Indo-European Branches	Uralic Language Family	
Germanic group	**Celtic group**	**Finno-Ugric group**	Areas with significant concentrations of other languages (usually adjacent national languages).

Major Indo-European Branches

Germanic group

WESTERN GERMANIC
1 Dutch
2 German
3 Frisian
4 English

NORTHERN GERMANIC
5 Danish
6 Swedish
7 Norwegian
8 Icelandic
9 Faeroses

Romance group

10 Portuguese 14 French
11 Spanish 15 Italian
12 Catalan 16 Rhaeto-Romance
13 Provençal 17 Romanian

Slavic group

WEST SLAVONIC
18 Polish
19 Slovak
20 Czech
21 Sorbian

EAST SLAVONIC
22 Russian
23 Ukrainian
24 Belarusian

SOUTH SLAVONIC
25 Slovene
26 Serbo-Croatian
27 Macedonian
28 Bulgarian

Other Indo-European Branches

Celtic group

BRITTANIC
29 Breton
30 Welsh

GAULISH
31 Irish Gaelic
32 Scots Gaelic

Baltic group

33 Latvian 34 Lithuanian

Hellenic

35 Greek

Thracian/Illyrian group

36 Albanian

Thracian/Illyrian group

37 Romani

Uralic Language Family

Finno-Ugric group

38 Ginnish 41 Estonian
39 Karelian 42 Hungarian
40 Saami

Samoyedic group

44 Samoyedic

Altaic Language Family

Turkic group

45 Turkish

Other Languages

Basque

46 Basque

Areas with significant concentrations of other languages (usually adjacent national languages).

---- Boundary between languages.

—— Boundary between Indo-European and non-Indo-European languages.

Figure 6.2

Languages of Europe. Generalized map of language-use regions in Europe. *Adapted with permission from*: A. B. Murphy, "European Languages," T. Unwin, ed., *A European Geography*. London: Longman, 1998, p.38.

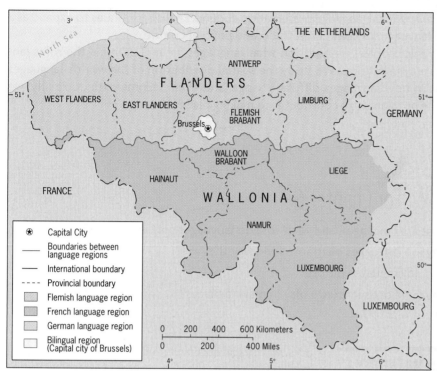

Figure 6.3
Divided Belgium. Flemish, French, and German dominate the different administrative areas in Belgium. *Adapted with permission from*: A. B. Murphy, "Belgium's Regional Divergence along the Road to Federation," in G. Smith, ed., *Federalism: The Multiethnic Challenge*. London: Longman, 1995, p. 82.

services—much of it concentrating in Flemish-speaking Flanders. As a result, the economic power in Belgium flipped, with the French-speaking industrial south taking a back seat to the Flemish-speaking north. Today, Wallonia has an unemployment rate of 17 percent, whereas Flanders has one of the lower unemployment rates in Europe.

Currently, the vast majority of power and decision making rests with the individual governments of Flanders and Wallonia rather than in a centralized government in Brussels. With their newfound wealth, many in Flanders wanted to see a greater federalization of the country, which would put even more power in each of the two regions. Today, no political party in Belgium operates at the national scale. Wallonia and Flanders each have their own political parties that vie for power in their respective regions. Under the circumstances, it is not surprising that it took Belgium nine months to form a government after the spring 2007 elections.

Brussels is going in another direction entirely, serving as the principal capital of the European Union (EU). Brussels is home to the EU Council and Commission. Moreover, much of the committee work done by the European Parliament takes place in Brussels (the formal home of the Parliament is in Strasbourg, France). The role Brussels serves as the European Union capital may prevent Belgium from splitting into two countries. Both Flanders and Wallonia have vested interests in Brussels, so neither would abandon it lightly. And the French-speaking majority in Brussels has little interest in casting its lot with the region in which it is situated—Flanders. Some have proposed making Brussels a capital district for the European Union, like the District of Columbia (Washington, D.C.), in the United States.

The example of Belgium gives us a multitude of insights into language. Language questions are often politicized. Language frequently is tied to other identity issues such as socioeconomic status. And while all of the debates about national and local language preservation abound, English continues to expand as a global language for commerce, trade, and popular culture.

In this chapter, we question what languages are and examine the roles languages play in cultures. We study the spatial distribution of the world's languages and learn how languages diffuse, change, and even become extinct. Finally, we examine how language contributes to making places unique.

Key Questions For Chapter 6

1. What are languages, and what role do languages play in cultures?
2. Why are languages distributed the way they are?
3. How do languages diffuse?
4. What role does language play in making places?

WHAT ARE LANGUAGES, AND WHAT ROLE DO LANGUAGES PLAY IN CULTURES?

A scene in Quentin Tarantino's cult classic movie *Pulp Fiction* shows Vincent and Jules in the front seat of the car talking about France. Vincent, trying to demonstrate his knowledge of French culture, turns to Jules and says, "You know what they call a....a....a quarter pounder with cheese in Paris?" Jules replies, "They don't call it a quarter pounder with cheese?" Vincent, ever the expert, explains in a few choice words that France uses the metric system and that the French would not know what a quarter pounder is. Then, he explains, "They call it a 'royale' with cheese." Jules, surprised, asks, "What do they call a Big Mac?" Vincent explains, "Well a Big Mac is a Big Mac, but they call it 'Le Big Mac.'"

This humorous exchange shows the juxtaposition of two opposing forces in our globalized world: globalization of culture and preservation of local and national culture. Are the two contradictory, or can we have globalization of restaurants, food, music, and culture while preserving local languages?

Language is a fundamental element of local and national culture. The French government has worked diligently, even aggressively, to protect the French language, dating back to 1635 and the creation of the Académie Française, an institution charged with standardizing and protecting the French language. In the last few decades, diffusion of globalized terms into France has posed a huge challenge for the Académie Française.

With the support of many French people, the French government passed a law in 1975 banning the use of foreign words in advertisements, television, and radio broadcasts, and official documents, unless no French equivalent could be found. In 1992, France amended its constitution to make French the official language. In 1994, the French government passed another law to stop the use of foreign (mainly English) words in France, with a hefty fine imposed for violators. The law mandates French translations for globalized words, requiring the use of official French terms in official communications rather than le meeting, le weekend, le drugstore, or le hamburger. The Internet, where more than 85 percent of all websites are in English (Fig. 6.4), has posed another set of challenges for the Académie Française. Some of the translations the Académie requires are somewhat cumbersome—for example, the official translation of e-mail is "courrier electronique" and the official translation of hacker is "pirate informatique."

In addition to demonstrating the conflicting forces of globalized language and local or national language, the example of France reveals that language is much more than a way of communicating. A **language** is a set of sounds and symbols that is used for communication. But language is also an integral part of culture, reflecting and shaping it.

Language and Culture

Language is one of the cornerstones of culture; it shapes our very thoughts. We can use vast vocabularies to describe new experiences, ideas, and feelings, or we can create new words that represent these things. Who we are as a culture, as a people, is reinforced and redefined moment by moment through shared language. Language reflects where a culture has been, what a culture values,

INTERNET CONTENT, BY LANGUAGE

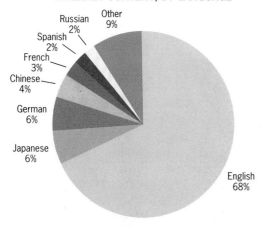

INTERNET USERS, BY LANGUAGE SPOKEN

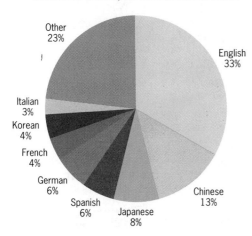

TOP 10 LANGUAGES, BY MILLIONS OF SPEAKERS

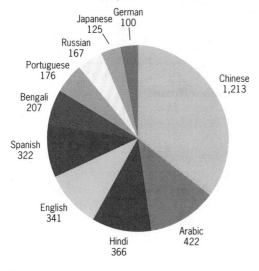

■ **Figure 6.4**

Languages used on the Internet.   Adapted with permission from: World Resources Institute (WRI) in collaboration with United Nations Development Program, United Nations Environment Program, and World Bank. 2005. *World Resources 2005: The wealth of the Poor-Managing Ecosystems to Fight Poverty.* Washington, DC: WRI.

even how people in a culture think, describe, and experience things.

Perhaps the easiest way to understand the role of language in culture is to examine people who have experienced the loss of language under pressure from others. During colonization, both abroad and within countries, colonizers commonly forced the colonized people to speak the language of the colonizer. These language policies continued in many places until recently and were enforced primarily through public (government) and church (mission) schools.

American, Canadian, Australian, Russian, and New Zealand governments each had policies of forced assimilation during the twentieth century, including not allowing indigenous peoples to speak native languages. For example, the United States forced American Indians to learn and speak English. Both mission schools and government schools enforced English-only policies in hopes of assimilating American Indians into the dominant culture. In an interview with the producers of an educational video, Clare Swan, an elder in the Kenaitze band of the Dena'ina Indians in Alaska, eloquently describes the role of language in culture:

> *No one was allowed to speak the language—the Dena'ina language. They [the American government] didn't allow it in schools, and a lot of the women had married non-native men, and the men said, "You're American now so you can't speak the language." So, we became invisible in the community. Invisible to each other. And, then, because we couldn't speak the language*—what happens when you can't speak your own language is you have to think with someone else's words, and that's a dreadful kind of isolation *[emphasis added]*.

Shared language makes people in a culture visible to each other and to the rest of the world. Language helps to bind a cultural identity. Language is also quite personal. Our thoughts, expressions, and dreams are articulated in our language; to lose that ability is to lose a lot.

Language can reveal much about the way people and cultures view reality. Some African languages have no word or term for the concept of a god. Some Asian languages have no tenses and no system for reporting chronological events, reflecting the lack of cultural distinction between then and now. Given American culture's preoccupation with dating and timing, it is difficult for many in the United States to understand how speakers of these languages perceive the world.

Language is so closely tied to culture that people use language as a weapon in cultural conflict and political strife. In the United States, where the Spanish-speaking population is growing (Fig. 6.5), some Spanish speakers and their advocates are demanding the use of Spanish in

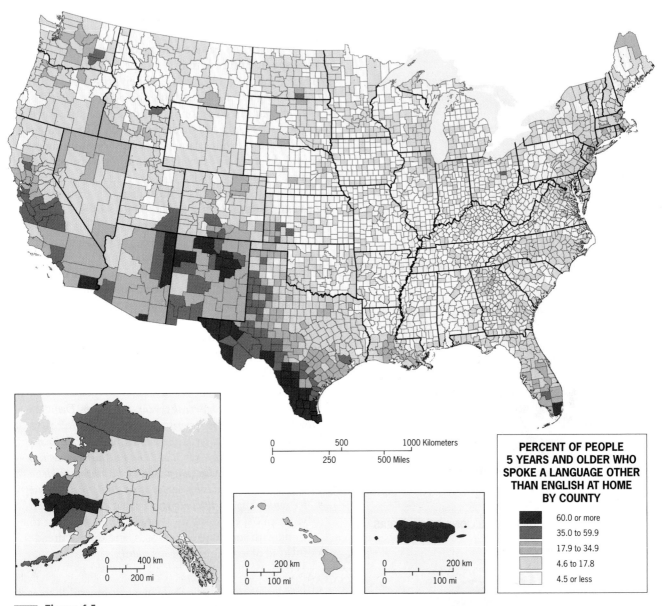

Figure 6.5
**Percent of People 5 Years and Older Who Speak a Language Other than English at Home
in the United States.**   The data presented include all non-English languages by county. *Data
from:* United States Census Bureau, 2000.

public affairs. In turn, people opposed to the use of Spanish in the United States are leading countermovements to promote "Official English" policies, where English would be the official language of government. Of course, Spanish is not the only non-English tongue spoken in the United States, but it overshadows all others and is therefore the focus of the English first movement (Table 6.1). During the 1980s, over 30 different States considered passing laws declaring English the State's official language. Some 30 States today have declared English the official language of the State either by statute or by amending the State constitution (one law was subsequently overturned by the courts). A few States have passed English-plus laws,

encouraging bilingualism for non-English speakers, and a few other States are officially bilingual, such as Hawai'i (Hawai'ian and English), and New Mexico has bilingual education (Spanish and English).

In Quebec, Canada, the focus is on passing laws that promote the use of the province's distinct version of the French language. The country of Canada is officially bilingual, a reflection of the colonial division of the country between France and Great Britain. Government documents and even scholarly journals are printed in both English and French. Most of the country's French speakers live in the province of Quebec. The majority of people in Quebec speak French at home.

TABLE 6.1
Top Ten Languages Spoken at Home by Non-English Speakers in the United States.

TOP TEN LANGUAGES SPOKEN AT HOME BY NON-ENGLISH SPEAKERS		
Language	**Total**	**Percent**
1. Spanish	28,101,052	59.9
2. Chinese	2,022,143	4.3
3. French	1,643,838	3.5
4. German	1,382,613	2.9
5. Tagalog	1,224,241	2.6
6. Vietnamese	1,009,627	2.1
7. Italian	1,008,370	2.1
8. Korean	894,063	1.9
9. Russian	706,242	1.5
10. Polish	667,414	1.5

Data from: United States Census Bureau.

In recent history, the Quebecois (people of Quebec) have periodically called for more independence for their province within Canada, even voting on secession at times. Although a majority has never voted for secession, the provincial government has passed several laws requiring and promoting the use of French in the province. In 1977, the Quebec government compelled all businesses in the province to demonstrate that they functioned in French. Upon passage of this law, many businesses and individuals moved out of the province of Quebec into neighboring Ontario. In 1993, the Quebec government passed a law requiring the use of French in advertising (Fig. 6.6). The Quebec law allows the inclusion of both French and English (or another language) translations on signage, as long as the French letters are twice the size of the other language's letters.

Not all of Quebec's residents identify with the French language. Within the province, a small proportion of people speak English at home, others speak indigenous languages, and still others speak another language altogether—one

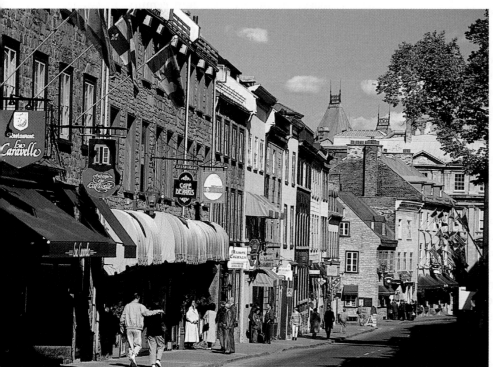

Figure 6.6
Quebec Province, Quebec. The imprint of the French Canadian culture is evident in the cultural landscape of Rue Saint-Louis in Quebec. Here, the architecture and store signs confirm that this region is not simply Canadian; it is French Canadian. © Michelle Burgess/SUPERSTOCK.

associated with their country of origin. When the Quebec Parliament passed several laws promoting French during the 1980s and 1990s, members of Canada's First Nations, such as the Cree and Mohawk (who live in Quebec), expressed a desire to remain part of Canada should Quebec secede from the country. During the same period, Quebec has experienced a flow of international migrants, many of whom seek residence in Quebec as a way to enter Canada and North America at large. These new immigrants must learn French under Quebec law.

Quebec, like any other place, is susceptible to change. Calls for independence in Quebec are waning, as the separatist political party has captured fewer seats in recent parliamentary elections for the province. Nonetheless, the Quebecois still feel a connection to France. The province even has a presence in Paris in the *Maison Quebec* (House of Quebec), an embassy-like entity of the province. As people, ideas, and power flow through the province, change will continue. Yet, the province's laws, programs, presence in France, and the desire of the Quebecois to remain loyal to their French language will at the very least keep the language alive as the province continues to experience change.

What Is a Language?

Many geography textbooks differentiate languages based on a criterion of mutual intelligibility. **Mutual intelligibility** means that two people can understand each other when speaking. The argument goes that if two of us are speaking two different languages, say Spanish and Portuguese, we will not be able to understand each other, but if we are speaking two dialects of one language, we will achieve mutual understanding. Yet linguists have rejected the criterion of mutual intelligibility as strongly as geographers have rejected environmental determinism.

First, mutual intelligibility is almost impossible to measure. Even if we used mutual intelligibility as a criterion, many languages would fail the test. Famous linguist Max Weinreich once said: "a language is a dialect with an army." Think about it. How could we possibly see Mandarin Chinese and Cantonese Chinese as dialects of the same language, when two people speaking the language to each other cannot understand what each other is saying? Both can read the standard form of Chinese that has been built up by a strongly centralized Chinese government. But the spoken dialects are not mutually intelligible. Yet, we see Chinese as one language because of the weight of political and social institutions that lie behind it.

A further complication with the mutual intelligibility test is revealed in Scandinavia, where, for example, a Danish speaker and a Norwegian speaker (at least if they come from Oslo) will be able to understand what each other is saying. Yet we think of Danish and Norwegian as distinct languages. Having a Norwegian language helps Norwegians identify themselves as Norwegians rather than as Danes or Scandinavians. Other languages that are recognized as separate but are mutually intelligible in many (or nearly all) aspects are Serbian and Croatian, Hindi and Urdu, Spanish and Portuguese, and Navajo and Apache.

Given the complexities of distinguishing languages from dialects, the actual number of languages in use in the world remains a matter of considerable debate. The most conservative calculation puts the number at about 3000. However, most linguists and linguistic geographers today recognize between 5000 and 6000 languages, including more than 600 in India and over 1000 in Africa.

Standardized Language

Language is dynamic: new discoveries, technologies, and ideas require new words. Technologically advanced societies are likely to have a **standard language**, one that is published, widely distributed, and purposefully taught. In some countries, the government sustains the standard language through official state examinations for teachers and civil servants. Ireland promotes the use of the Irish (Celtic) language by requiring all government employees to pass an Irish-language examination before they can be hired. The phrase "the King's English" is a popular reference to the fact that the English spoken by well-educated people in London and its environs is regarded as British Received Pronunciation (BRP) English—that is, the standard.

Who decides what the standard language will be? Not surprisingly, the answer has to do with influence and power. In France, the Académie Française chose the French spoken in and around Paris as the official, standard language during the sixteenth century. In China, the government chose the Northern Mandarin Chinese heard in and around the capital, Beijing, as the official standard language. Although this is China's official standard language, the linguistic term *Chinese* actually incorporates many variants. The distinction between the standard language and variations of it is not unique to China; it is found in all but the smallest societies. The Italian of Sicily is quite different from the Italian spoken north of Venice, and both tongues differ from the standard Italian spoken in Florence and Tuscany, the region where many leaders of the Italian Renaissance wrote and published in what became the standard Italian language.

Dialects

Variants of a standard language along regional or ethnic lines are called **dialects**. Differences in vocabulary, syntax (the way words are put together to form phrases), pronunciation, cadence (the rhythm of speech), and even the pace of speech all mark a speaker's dialect. Even if the written form of a statement adheres to the standard language, an accent can reveal the regional home of a person who reads the statement aloud. In the United States, the words "horse" and "oil" are written the same way in New England and in the South, but to the Southerner, the New Englander may be saying "hahse," and to the New Englander, the Southerner seems to be saying "all."

Linguists think about dialects in terms of **dialect chains**, distributed across space. Dialects nearest to each other geographically will be the most similar (greater spatial interaction), but as you travel across the space, the dialects become less intelligible to each other because less interaction occurs. If all of these dialects are part of one language, which one of the dialects is *the language*? This question points to another challenge in defining languages. Is one of the many English dialects in the world the one, true English? Language is actually an umbrella for a collection of dialects, and we tend to see one of these dialects as the "true" language only because it is the one we speak or because it is the one a government claims as the standard.

Frequently, dialects are marked by actual differences in vocabulary. A single word or group of words can reveal the source area of the dialect. Linguistic geographers map the extent of particular words, marking their limits as isoglosses. An **isogloss** is a geographic boundary within which a particular linguistic feature occurs, but such a boundary is rarely a simple line. Usually, outlying areas of usage extend beyond the isogloss. Fuzzy isoglosses may signify that the dialect has expanded or contracted. Linguists who study dialects examine pronunciations, vocabularies, use of colloquial phrases, and syntax to determine isoglosses.

Linguistic geographer Hans Kurath published atlases of dialects in the United States, defining Northern, Southern, and Midland dialect in the eastern part of the country. In the mid-1900s, Kurath drew distinct isoglosses among the three dialects, based on pronunciation of certain sounds and words. A more recent study of American dialects by linguist Bert Vaux used a 122-question online survey to map dialects in the United States. Maps of the soda, pop, and coke question (Fig. 6.7) and the hero, sub, poor-boy question reveal the prominent dialects of New England and the deep South, the fuzzy border between the two regions (Kurath's Midland dialect), the mixture of dialects in much of the rest of the country, and a few scattered areas outside the dialect regions where one or the other dialect dominates.

Figure 6.7
Common Name for a Soft Drink in the United States, by State, 2002. *Data from*: Bert Vaux, Harvard Survey of North American Dialects. http://cfprod01.imt.uwm.edu/Dept/FLL/linguistics/dialect/last accessed September 2005.

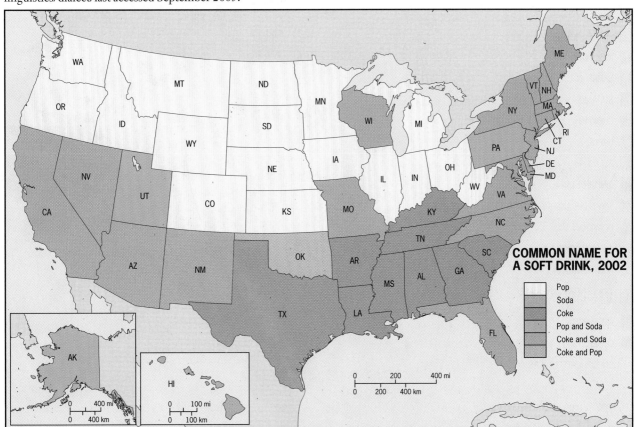

Linguist Bert Vaux's study of dialects in American English points to the differences in words for common things such as soft drinks and sandwiches. Describe a time when you said something and a speaker of another dialect did not understand the word you used. Where did the person with whom you were speaking come from? Was the word a term for a common thing? Why do you think dialects have different words for common things, things found across dialects, such as soft drinks and sandwiches?

WHY ARE LANGUAGES DISTRIBUTED THE WAY THEY ARE?

The first step in mapping the distribution of world languages is to classify languages. Linguists and linguistic geographers classify languages in terms that are also used in biology and for the same reasons: like species, some languages are related and others are not. At the global scale, we classify languages into **language families**. Within a single language family, the languages have a shared but fairly distant origin. We break language families into **subfamilies** (divisions within a language family), where the

Figure 6.8
Language Families of the World.   Generalized map of the world distribution of language families. *Adapted with permission from*: Hammond, Inc., 1977.

LANGUAGE FAMILIES OF THE WORLD

1	INDO-EUROPEAN
2	AFRO-ASIATIC
3	NIGER-CONGO
4	SAHARAN
5	SUDANIC
6	KHOISAN
7	URALIC
8	ALTAIC
9	SINO-TIBETAN
10	JAPANESE AND KOREAN
11	DRAVIDIAN
12	AUSTRO-ASIATIC
13	AUSTRONESIAN
14	TRANS-NEW GUINEA AND AUSTRALIAN
15	AMERINDIAN
	OTHERS
	UNPOPULATED AREAS

commonalities are more definite and the origin is more recent. Completing the categorization are individual languages, covering a smaller extent of territory, and dialects, covering the smallest extent of territory.

The world map of languages, Figure 6.8, actually maps 20 major *language families*. The Indo-European language family stretches across the greatest extent of territory and also claims the greatest number of speakers. Within the Indo-European language family, English is the most widely spoken language (of all languages in the world, Chinese claims even more speakers than English). Speakers of English encircle the world, with 300 million in North America, 64 million in Great Britain and Ireland,

and 22 million in Australia and New Zealand. Hundreds of millions of people in India, Europe, and Africa use English as a second language.

The world map of language families shows several language families spoken by dwindling, often marginally located or isolated groups. The Indo-European languages of European colonizers surround the language families of Southeast Asia. Languages in the Austro-Asiatic language family survive in the interior of eastern India and in Cambodia and Laos. Languages in the Austronesian family are numerous and quite diverse, and many of the individual languages are spoken by fewer than 10 million people. Remoteness helps account for the remaining

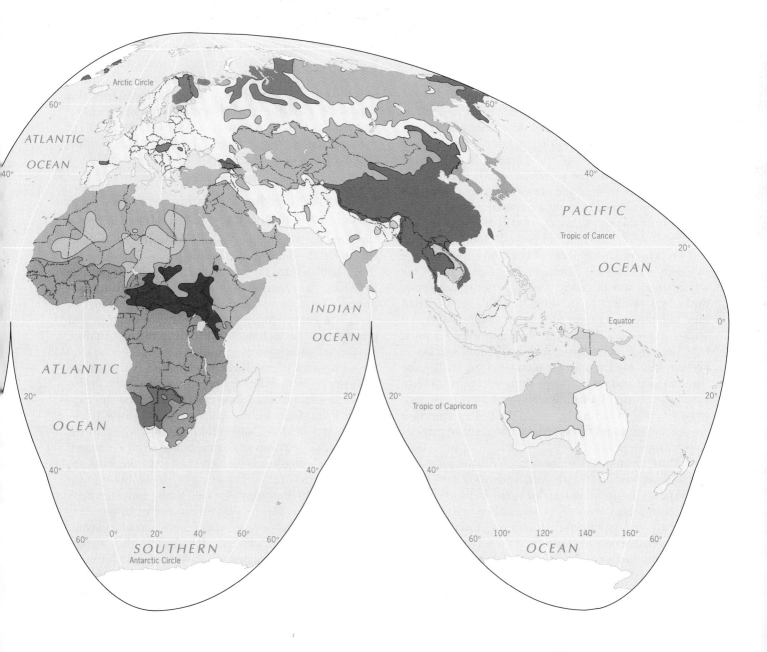

languages in the Amerindian language family. These languages remain strongest in areas of Middle America, the high Andes, and northern Canada.

If we look carefully at the map of world language families, some interesting questions arise. Consider, for example, the island of Madagascar off the East African coast. The primary languages people in Madagascar speak belong not to an African-language family but to the Austronesian family, the languages of Southeast Asia and the Pacific Islands. Why is a language from this family spoken on an island so close to Africa? Anthropologists have found evidence of seafarers from the islands of Southeast Asia crossing the Indian Ocean to Madagascar. At the time, Africans had not sailed across the strait to Madagascar, so no African languages diffused to the island, preserving the Southeast Asian settlements and language for centuries. Later, Africans began to come to Madagascar, but by that time the language and culture of Southeast Asia had been well established.

Language Formation

In the process of classifying languages, linguists and linguistic geographers study relationships among languages, looking for similarities and differences within and among languages. One way to find and chart similarities among languages is to examine particular words, looking for sounds shifts over time and across languages. A **sound shift** is a slight change in a word across languages within a subfamily or through a language family from the present backward toward its origin. For example, Italian, Spanish, and French are all members of the Romance language subfamily of the Indo-European language family. One way linguists and linguistic geographers can determine this is by looking at sound shifts for single words across time (all three languages are derived from Latin) and across languages. For example, the Latin word for milk, *lacte*, became *latta* in Italian, *leche* in Spanish, and *lait* in French. Also, the Latin for the number eight, *oto*, became *otto*, *ocho*, and *huit*, respectively. Even if linguists did not already know that Italian, Spanish, and French are languages rooted in Latin, they could deduce a connection among the languages through the sound shifts of particular words.

More than two centuries ago William Jones, an Englishman living in South Asia, undertook a study of Sanskrit, the language in which ancient Indian religious and literary texts were written. Jones discovered that the vocabulary and grammatical forms of Sanskrit bore a striking resemblance to the ancient Greek and Latin he learned while in college. "No philologer [student of words] could examine all three," Jones wrote, "without believing them to have sprung from some common source, which,

perhaps, no longer exists." His idea was a revolutionary notion in the 1700s.

During the nineteenth century Jakob Grimm, a scholar and a writer of fairy tales, suggested that sound shifts might prove the relationships between languages in a scientific manner. He explained that related languages have similar, but not identical, consonants. He believed these consonants would change over time in a predictable way. Hard consonants, such as the *v* and *t* in the German word *vater*, softened into *vader* (Dutch) and *father* (English). Using Grimm's theory that consonants became softer as time passed and sounds shifted, linguists realized that consonants would become harder as they went "backwards" toward the original hearth and original language.

From Jones's notions and Grimm's ideas came the first major linguistic hypothesis, proposing the existence of an ancestral Indo-European language called **Proto-Indo-European**. Discovery of a Proto-Indo-European language would give us the hearth of ancient Latin, Greek, and Sanskrit. A single Proto-Indo-European hearth would link modern languages from Scandinavia to North Africa and from North America through parts of Asia to Australia. Several research tasks followed from this hypothesis. First, the vocabulary of the proposed ancestral language had to be reconstructed. Second, the hearth of the language had to be located. Third, the routes of diffusion needed to be traced.

Reconstructing the Vocabulary of Proto Indo-European and Its Ancient Ancestor

Linguists use a technique called **backward reconstruction** to track sound shifts and hardening of consonants "backward" toward the original language. If it is possible to deduce a large part of the vocabulary of an **extinct language** (a language without any native speakers), it may be feasible to go even further and re-create the language that preceded it. This technique, called **deep reconstruction**, has yielded some important results.

The work of two Russian scholars in particular has had great impact on the deep reconstruction of the Proto-Indo-European language and even the ancestral language of the Proto-Indo-European language. Vladislav Illich-Svitych and Aharon Dolgopolsky began working in the 1960s, each using deep reconstruction to re-create ancient languages. Using words they assumed to be the most stable and dependable parts of a language's vocabulary, such as those identifying arms, legs, feet, hands, and other body parts, and terms for the sun, moon, and other elements of the natural environment, they reconstructed an inventory of several hundred words. Remarkably, they worked independently, each unaware of the other's work for many years. When they finally met and compared their inventories, they found that the inventories were amazingly similar. The scholars agreed that they had established some key characteristics not only of the Proto-Indo-European language but also of its ancient ancestor, the **Nostratic** language.

The Nostratic vocabulary the researchers reconstructed revealed much about the lives and environments of its speakers. Apparently, they had no names for domesticated plants or animals, so Nostratic speakers were hunter-gatherers, not farmers. The Nostratic words for dog and wolf turned out to be the same, suggesting that the domestication of wolves may have been occurring at the time people were speaking Nostratic. The oldest known bones of dogs excavated at archaeological sites date from about 14,000 years ago, so Nostratic may have been in use at about that time, well before the First Agricultural Revolution.

Nostratic is believed to be the ancestral language not only of Proto-Indo-European, and thus the Indo-European language family as a whole, but also of the Kartvelian languages of the southern Caucasus region, the Uralic-Altaic languages (which include Hungarian and Finnish, Turkish and Mongolian), the Dravidian languages of India, and the Afro-Asiatic language family, in which Arabic is dominant (Fig. 6.8).

Locating the Hearth of Proto-Indo-European

German linguist August Schleicher was the first to compare the world's language families to the branches of a tree (Fig. 6.9). In the mid-nineteenth century, he suggested that new languages form through **language divergence**, which occurs when spatial interaction among speakers of a language breaks down and the language fragments first into dialects and then into discrete tongues. The process of language divergence has happened between Spanish and Portuguese and is now happening with Quebecois French. Each new language becomes a new leaf on a tree, its branches leading back to the hearth, the trunk of the tree. Through backward reconstruction, linguists and linguistic geographers can find how languages fit together and where the branches were once joined. Tracing backward far enough, linguists and linguistic geographers can find the hearth of a language family.

If linguists and linguistic geographers can find the hearth of the Proto-Indo-European language, they will find a major part of the tree's trunk. Finding the trunk is a daunting task, as reconstructing even a small branch of the language tree is complicated. Languages do not change only through divergence (the splitting of branches); they also change through convergence and extinction. If peoples with different languages have consistent spatial interaction, **language convergence** can take place, collapsing two languages into one. Instances of language convergence create special problems for

researchers because the rules of reconstruction may not apply or may be unreliable. Language extinction creates branches on the tree with dead ends, representing a halt in interaction between the extinct language and languages that continued. Languages become extinct either when all descendants perish (which can happen when an entire people succumb to disease or invaders) or when descendants choose to use another language, abandoning the language of their ancestors. The process of language extinction does not occur overnight; typically, it takes place across generations, with degrees of bilingualism occurring in the interim.

Tracking the divergence, convergence, extinction, and locations of the languages derived from Proto-Indo-European, linguists theorize that the hearth of the Proto-Indo-European language was somewhere in the vicinity of the Black Sea or east-central Europe. From this hearth, Proto-Indo-European speakers dispersed, vocabularies grew, and linguistic divergence occurred, spurring new languages. By analyzing the vocabulary of the Proto-Indo-European language, linguists and geographers can discern the environment and physical geography of the language's hearth and also deduce aspects of the peoples' culture and economy. Judging from the reconstructed vocabulary of Proto-Indo-European, it appears that the language dates back to a people who used horses, had developed the wheel, and traded widely in many goods.

British scholar Colin Renfrew developed his own theory regarding the diffusion of Proto-Indo-European and agriculture. He proposed that three areas in and near the agricultural hearth of the Fertile Crescent gave rise to three language families (Fig. 6.10). The **Renfrew hypothesis** claims that from Anatolia (present-day Turkey—to which agriculture diffused early from the nearby Fertile Crescent) diffused Europe's Indo-European languages; from the western arc of the Fertile Crescent came the languages of North Africa and Arabia; and from the Fertile Crescent's eastern arc ancient languages spread into present-day Iran, Afghanistan, Pakistan, and India, later to be replaced by Indo-European languages.

Others now contrast Renfrew's location of the hearth of the Proto-Indo-European language and even the role of agriculture in its diffusion. Using genetic evidence, Stephen Oppenheimer argues that people came out of Central Africa, following now-flooded coastlines of East Africa, the southern Arabian Peninsula, and into India about 80,000 years ago. Oppenheimer's research supports theories by some linguists indicating that the hearth of the Proto-Indo-European language could lie in India. He claims that people from India migrated into Europe and Renfrew's hearths less than 50,000 years ago. If additional research supports this hypothesis, other linguists may rethink the origins and hearth of the Proto-Indo-European language.

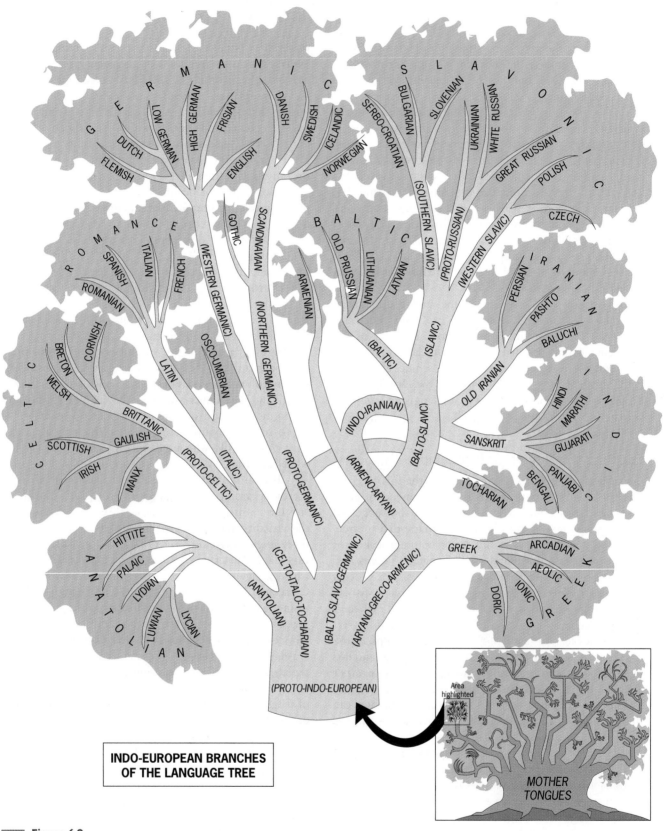

**INDO-EUROPEAN BRANCHES
OF THE LANGUAGE TREE**

■■■ **Figure 6.9**

Indo-European Branches of the Language Tree. *Adapted with permission from*: T. V. Gamkrelidze and V. V. Ivanov. "The Early History of Indo-European Languages," *Scientific American*, March 1990, p. 111.

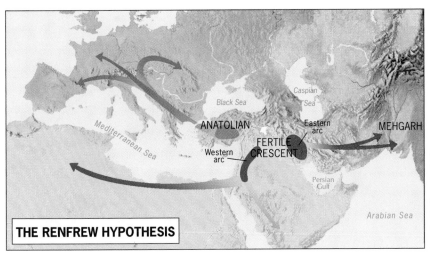

Figure 6.10
The Renfrew Hypothesis. The Renfrew Hypothesis proposes that three sources of agriculture each gave rise to a major language family. *Adapted with permission from*: "The Origins of Indo-European Languages," *Scientific American*, 1989, p. 114.

Tracing the Routes of Diffusion of Proto-Indo-European

Several major theories hypothesize how, why, and where languages diffuse over time. Each theory varies according to the main impetus for diffusion, and each theory leads us back to different hearths. One commonality among the theories is a focus on Europe. When studying the diffusion of Proto-Indo-European, the focus is typically on Europe for two reasons: one, it is clear the language diffused into Europe over time; and two, there is a significant body of historical research and archaeology focused on the early peopling of Europe.

The presence of Europe's oldest languages (Celtic) in the far west supports the idea that newer languages arrived from the east. But how and where did they spread through Europe? The **conquest theory** provides one explanation. This theory holds that early speakers of Proto-Indo-European spread from east to west on horseback, overpowering earlier inhabitants and beginning the diffusion and differentiation of Indo-European tongues. The sound shifts in the derivative languages represent a long period of divergence in languages as one moves west through Europe.

An alternative agricultural theory proposes that Proto-Indo-European diffused westward through Europe with the diffusion of agriculture. Citing the archaeological record, Luca Cavalli-Sforza and Albert Ammerman proposed that for every generation (25 years) the agricultural frontier moved approximately 18 kilometers (11 miles). This means farmers would have completely penetrated the European frontier in about 1500 years, which is close to what the archaeological record suggests. But some of the nonfarming societies in their path held out, and their languages did not change. Thus, Etruscan did not become extinct until Roman times, and Euskera (the Basque language) survives to this day as a direct link to Europe's prefarming era.

In 1991, the agriculture theory received support from analyses of the protein (that is, gene) content of individuals from several thousand locations across Europe. This research confirmed the presence of distance decay in the geographic pattern: certain genes became steadily less common from southern Turkey across the Balkans and into western and northern Europe. This pattern was interpreted as showing that the farming peoples of Anatolia moved steadily westward and northward (Fig. 6.11). With established farming providing a more reliable food supply, population could increase. As a result, a slow but steady wave of farmers dispersed into Europe and mixed with nonfarming peoples, diluting their genetic identity as the distance from their source area increased.

Despite the genetic gradient identified in Europe, some linguistic geographers continue to favor the **dispersal hypothesis**, which holds that the Indo-European languages that arose from Proto-Indo-European were first carried eastward into Southwest Asia, next around the Caspian Sea, and then across the Russian-Ukrainian plains and on into the Balkans (Fig. 6.12). As is so often the case, there may be some truth in each hypothesis. If Anatolia were the hearth, the diffusion of Proto-Indo-European could have occurred both westward across southern Europe and in the broad arc shown in Figure 6.12.

We still do not know where the Proto-Indo-European language was born, or the location of its hearth. Like all other languages that gave rise to language families, Proto-Indo-European has deeper roots that link it to languages outside of the Indo-European family. Some scholars have even suggested that Nostratic (and its contemporaries, variously named Eurasiatic, Indo-Pacific, Amerind, and Austric) is a direct successor of a proto-world language that goes back to the dawn of human history, but this notion is highly speculative. The inset in Figure 6.9 reminds us how little of the human language tree we know with any certainty.

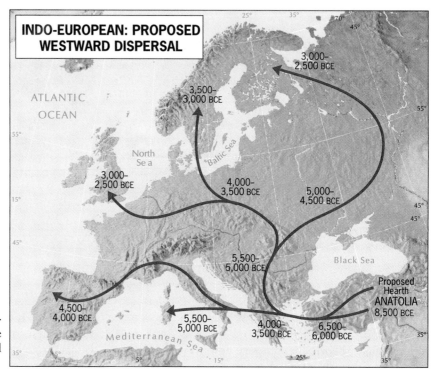

Figure 6.11
Indo-European Language Family: Proposed Westward Dispersal.   Approximate timings and routes for the westward dispersal of the Indo-European languages.

Figure 6.12
Indo-European Language Family: Proposed Hearth and Dispersal Hypothesis.   This theory proposes that the Indo-European Language Family began in the Caucasus Mountain region and dispersed eastward before diffusing westward. *Adapted with permission from*: T. V. Gamkrelidze and V. V. Ivanov, *Scientific American*, March 1990, p. 112.

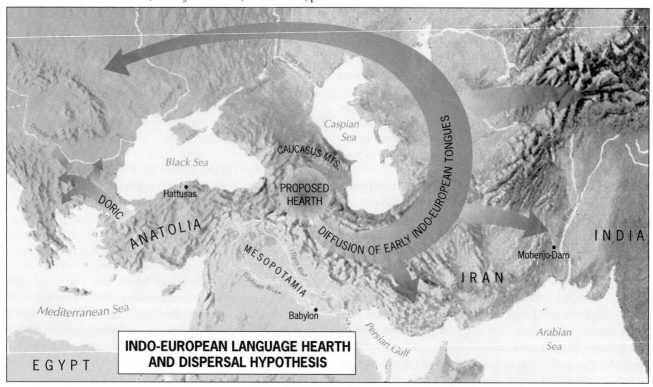

The Languages of Europe

The map of world languages (Fig. 6.8) demonstrates how widely spread the Indo-European language family is across the globe, dominating Europe, significant parts of Asia (including Russia and India), North and South America, Australia, and portions of Southern Africa. About half the world's people speak Indo-European languages. The Indo-European language family is broken into subfamilies such as Romance, Germanic, and Slavic. And each subfamily is broken into individual languages, such as English, German, Danish, and Norwegian within the Germanic subfamily.

The language map of Europe (Fig. 6.2) shows that the Indo-European language family prevails in this region, with pockets of the Uralic family occurring in Hungary (the Ugric subfamily) and in Finland and adjacent areas (the Finnic subfamily), and a major Altaic language, Turkish, dominating Turkey west of the Sea of Marmara. Celtic people brought Indo-European tongues into Europe when they spread across the continent over 3000 years ago. Celtic speech survives at the western edges of Europe, but in most places Celtic tongues fell victim to subsequent migrations and empire building. These historical developments led to the creation of a European linguistic pattern characterized by three major subfamilies: Romance, Germanic, and Slavic.

The **Romance languages** (French, Spanish, Italian, Romanian, and Portuguese) lie in the areas that were once controlled by the Roman Empire but were not subsequently overwhelmed. The **Germanic languages** (English, German, Danish, Norwegian, and Swedish) reflect the expansion of peoples out of northern Europe to the west and south. Some Germanic peoples spread into areas dominated by Rome, and at the northern and northeastern edges of the Roman Empire their tongues gained ascendancy. Other Germanic peoples spread into areas that were never part of an ancient empire (present-day Sweden, Norway, Denmark, and the northern part of the Netherlands). The Germanic character of English bears the imprint of a further migration—that of the Normans into England in 1066, bringing a Romance tongue to the British Isles. The essential Germanic character of English remained, but many new words were added that are Romance in origin. The **Slavic languages** (Russian, Polish, Czech, Slovak, Ukrainian, Slovenian, Serbo-Croatian, and Bulgarian) developed as Slavic people migrated from a base in present-day Ukraine close to 2000 years ago. Slavic tongues came to dominate much of eastern Europe over the succeeding centuries. They, too, overwhelmed Latin-based tongues along much of the eastern part of the old Roman Empire—with the notable exception of an area on the western shores of the Black Sea, where a Latin-based tongue either survived the Slavic invasion or was reintroduced by migrants. That tongue is the ancestor of the modern-day Romance language: Romanian.

A comparison of Europe's linguistic and political maps shows a high correlation between the languages spoken and the political organization of space. The Romance languages, of Romanic-Latin origin, dominate in five countries, including Romania. The eastern boundaries of Germany coincide almost exactly with the transition from Germanic to Slavic tongues. Even at the level of individual languages, boundaries can be seen on the political map: between French and Spanish, between Norwegian and Swedish, and between Bulgarian and Greek.

Although Figure 6.2 shows a significant correlation between political and linguistic boundaries in Europe, there are some important exceptions. The French linguistic region extends into Belgium, Switzerland, and Italy, but in France, French coexists with Basque in the southwest, a variant of Dutch in the north, and a Celtic tongue in the northest. The Celtic languages survive in the western region of France called Brittany (Breton), in the northern and western parts of Wales (Welsh), in western Ireland (Irish Gaelic), and in the western Highlands and islands of Scotland (Scots Gaelic). The use of Romanian extends well into Moldavia, signifying a past loss of national territory. Greek and Albanian are also Indo-European languages, and their regional distribution corresponds significantly (though not exactly) with state territories. Figure 6.2 underscores the complex cultural pattern of eastern Europe: German speakers in Hungary; Hungarian speakers in Slovakia, Romania, and Yugoslavia; Romanian speakers in Greece and Moldavia; Turkish speakers in Bulgaria; and Albanian speakers in Serbia.

Although the overwhelming majority of Europeans and Russians speak Indo-European languages, the Uralic and Altaic language families are also represented. Finnish, Estonian, and Hungarian are major languages of the Uralic family, which, as Figure 6.8 shows, extends across Eurasia to the Pacific Coast. The Altaic family to which Turkish belongs is equally widespread and includes Turkish, Kazakh, Uigur, Kyrgyz, and Uzbek languages.

One language on the map of Europe stands out for two reasons: first, it covers a very small land area, and second, it is *in no way related to* any other language family in Europe. Did you find it? This tantalizing enigma is the Basque language, Euskera. Isolated in the Andorra Mountain region between Spain and France, the Basque people and their Euskera language survived the tumultuous history of Europe for thousands of years—never blending with another language or diffusing from the Andorra region. (Some recent genetic evidence points to a link between Euskera and an extinct language in the Middle East, but this is uncertain.) The Basques have a strong identity tied to their language and independent history, an identity that was cemented by the horrid treatment they received under fascist dictator Francisco Franco, who ruled Spain during and after World War II. After Franco died in 1975, a Basque separatist group demanded autonomy within Spain. The Spanish government recognized Basque autonomy in its 1979 constitution, granting the Basque region its own parliament, giving their language official status, and transferring some taxation and education powers from the capital to the Basque region. A group of Basque separatists continue to demand more, waging a campaign of violence against Spanish targets and even moderate Basque leaders (Fig. 6.13).

Languages of Subsaharan Africa

The world map of language families masks the extreme fragmentation of languages in parts of the world such as Subsaharan Africa. In Subsaharan Africa, the map of world language families reflects the dominance of the Niger-Congo language family. By including language subfamilies, we can gain a more meaningful picture of Subsaharan Africa's linguistic diversity (Fig. 6.14).

Figure 6.13
San Sebastián, Spain.   Graffiti on the wall of this building uses the English language, "Freedom for the Basque Country," to show support for the Basque separatist movement.   © Denise Powell.

Figure 6.14
Language Families of Africa.   Regional classification of African Language Families. *Adapted with permission from*: Hammond, Inc., 1977.

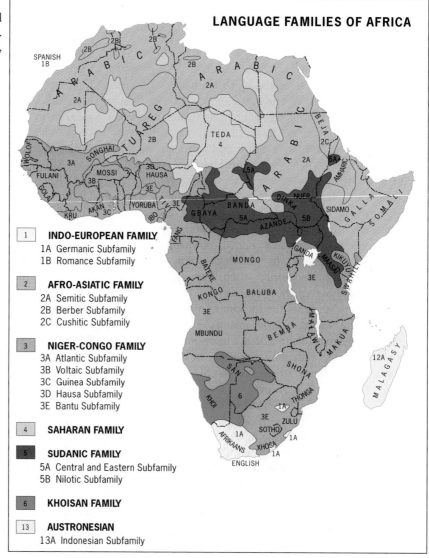

Studying language subfamilies helps us understand migration and settlement patterns in Subsaharan Africa. The oldest languages of Subsaharan Africa are the Khoisan languages, which include a "click" sound. Although they once dominated much of the region, Khoisan languages were marginalized by the invasion of speakers of the Bantu languages. Studying the languages in the Bantu subfamily, we can see that the languages are still closely related, with similar prefixes and vocabularies. Similarities among the Bantu languages mean that the languages have been in Subsaharan Africa for a shorter time—typically, the longer a language has been in a place, the more likely sounds will have shifted and languages splintered.

Linguistic diversity is evident not just at the world regional scale, but at the country scale. Nigeria encompasses several subfamilies of the Niger-Congo family, and its population includes speakers of two major Subsaharan African language families. Indeed, Nigeria's 141 million people speak more than 500 different languages. The three most prominent languages are distributed regionally: Hausa is in the north and is spoken by some 35 million, Yoruba is in the southwest and is spoken by 25 million speakers, and Ibo is in the southeast and is spoken by more than 25 million people (Fig. 6.15). Of the remaining languages spoken in Nigeria, the vast majority are spoken by fewer than one million people. These minor languages persist because daily survival, community, and culture are tied closely to the local scale in Nigeria. Even people who leave their hometowns for work send money back to their hometown associations to support their culture and economy.

Were it not for British colonialism, the country of Nigeria would never have existed. The diverse people of this place have been amalgamated into the Nigerian borders for less than a century. European colonists are responsible for the arbitrary borders of most of Africa—borders that ignore cultural divides. When Nigeria gained its independence in 1962, the government decided to adopt English as the "official" language, as the three major regional languages are too politically charged and thus unsuitable as national languages.

When Nigeria's children go to school, they first must learn English, which is used for all subsequent instruction. Certainly, the use of English has helped Nigeria avoid some conflicts based on language, but Nigerian educators are having second thoughts about the policy. Upon entering school, children who have grown up speaking a local language are suddenly confronted with a new, unfamiliar tongue. The time and energy spent learning English are taken away from learning other subjects. Moreover, for many students, knowledge of English is irrelevant when they emerge from school (as many do after only six years) unable to function in local Nigerian society. Nigeria is having serious doubts about its relationship with the English language brought there by the colonists who arbitrarily established their multilinguistic and multiethnic country in the first place.

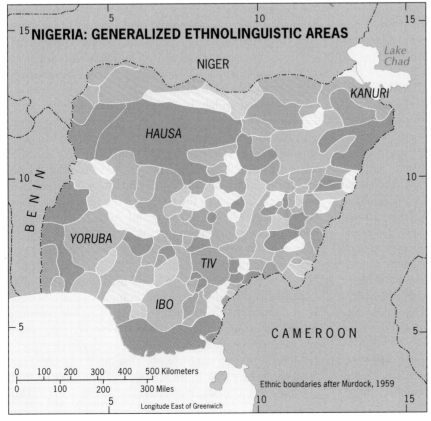

Figure 6.15

Nigeria: Generalized Ethnolinguistic Areas. This map demonstrates the mosaic of languages in Nigeria by shading each of the country's ethnolinguistic areas. The colors represent diversity; they do not show associations among ethnolinguistic areas. *Data from*: ethnolinguistic area boundaries are based on a map in G. P. Murdock, *Africa: Its Peoples and Their Culture History*. New York: McGraw-Hill, 1972.

Education also affects the distribution of languages across the globe and within regions and countries. Thinking about different regions of the world, consider how education plays a role in the distribution of English speakers. Who learns English in each of these regions and why? What role does education play in the global distribution of English speakers?

HOW DO LANGUAGES DIFFUSE?

Just a few thousand years ago most habitable parts of the Earth were characterized by a tremendous diversity of languages. With the rise of empires, of larger-scale, more technologically sophisticated literate societies, some languages began to spread over larger areas. By 2000 years ago, languages such as Chinese and Latin had successfully diffused over large regions. The Han Empire in China and the Roman Empire in Europe and North Africa knit together large swaths of territory, encouraging the diffusion of one language over the regions. The most powerful and wealthiest people were the first to learn Chinese and Latin in these empires, as they had the most to lose by not learning the languages. Local languages and illiteracy continued among the poor in the empires, and some blending of local with regional languages occurred. When the Roman Empire disintegrated, places within the region discontinued interaction, prompting a round of linguistic divergence.

In the late Middle Ages, the invention of the Gutenberg printing press and the rise of nation-states worked to spread literacy and stabilize certain languages through widely distributed written forms. Johann Gutenberg perfected the printing press, inventing the movable type printing press, the Gutenberg press, in Germany in 1440. In 1452, Gutenberg printed the first Gutenberg Bible (the sacred text for Christians), which brought the scriptures out of churches and monasteries. The Gutenberg press diffused quickly in the century following—throughout Europe and beyond. The printing press allowed for an unprecedented production of written texts, in languages besides Latin. Gutenberg's press made it possible to print the Bible in one's own language, such as French or German, rather than Latin, helping to standardize European languages. The Luther Bible played this role for German, as did the King James Bible for English.

The rise of relatively large independent states was equally important (see Chapter 8), for these political entities had a strong interest in promoting a common culture, often through a common language (such as French or Dutch). Political elites who were literate and had access to written texts brought peoples together and played a key role in distributing printed texts. Moreover, as the leaders of countries such as England and Spain sought to expand their influence overseas through mercantilism and colonialism, they established networks of communication and interaction, helping to diffuse certain languages over vast portions of the Earth's surface.

Over the last 500 years, the world's people have had innumerable opportunities for spatial interaction, and thus contact between and among languages. The increasing contact among people has encouraged the formation of new languages to bridge linguistic gaps in trade and commerce, has spurred language replacement (one language replaces another), and has encouraged language extinction (a language with no native speakers). The modern world also provides technology to preserve and stabilize languages and supports institutions that teach languages to large numbers of people.

Lingua Franca

Even before the expansion of trade encouraged the global diffusion of languages such as English and Spanish, regional trade encouraged people speaking different tongues to find ways to communicate with one another. A **lingua franca** is a language used among speakers of different languages for the purposes of trade and commerce. A lingua franca can be a single language, or it can be a mixture of two or more languages. When people speaking two or more languages are in contact and they combine parts of their languages in a simplified structure and vocabulary, we call it a **pidgin language**.

The first widely known lingua franca was a pidgin language. During the 1200s seaborne commerce in the Mediterranean Sea expanded, and traders from the ports of southern France (the Franks) revitalized the ports of the eastern Mediterranean. But the local traders did not speak the seafarers' language. Thus began a process of convergence in which the tongue of the Franks was mixed with Italian, Greek, Spanish, and Arabic. The mixture came to be known as the Frankish language, or lingua franca, and it served for centuries as the common tongue of Mediterranean commerce.

The term *lingua franca* is still used to denote a common language used for trade and commerce that is spoken by peoples with different native tongues. Arabic became a lingua franca during the expansion of Islam, and English did so in many areas during the colonial era. English is the only linguistic common denominator that binds together multilingual India—both in India itself and among those from subcontinent who have migrated to other areas (Fig. 6.16).

Figure 6.16
Dubai, United Arab Emirates.   The message on the back of the bench is written in the lingua franca known to virtually all Indian migrants to the Arabian Peninsula.   © Alexander B. Murphy.

A different sort of a lingua franca in wide use today is Swahili, the lingua franca of East Africa. Through centuries of trade and interaction, Swahili developed from an African Bantu language mixed with Arabic and Persian, encompassing 100 million speakers from southern Somalia to northern Mozambique and from coastal Kenya and Tanzania to Uganda and the East African Great Lakes region. Swahili has a complex vocabulary and structure, and while millions of East Africans communicate in the language, most still learn and speak a local language as their first or primary language.

Over time a pidgin language may gain native speakers, becoming the first language children learn in the home. When this happens, we call it a creolized or Creole language. A **Creole language** is a pidgin language that has developed a more complex structure and vocabulary and has become the native language of a group of people. The word *Creole* stems from a pidgin language formed in the Caribbean from English, French, and Portuguese languages mixed with the languages of African slaves. The language became more complex and became the first language of people in the region, replacing the African languages.

Pidgin and Creole languages are important unifying forces in a linguistically divided world. They tend to be simple and accessible, and therefore disseminate rapidly. In Southeast Asia a trade language called Bazaar Malay is heard from Myanmar (Burma) to Indonesia and from the Philippines to Malaysia; it has become a lingua franca in the region. A simplified form of Chinese also serves as a language of commerce even beyond the borders of China.

Multilingualism

Widespread diffusion and mixing of languages over the last 500 years, combined with the division of the world into more than 200 countries, has left the idea of a single language being spoken in a single country unrealizable. For that to happen, we would need a world of contiguous, discrete languages territorially divided into upwards of 3000 countries.

Only a few **monolingual states**—countries in which only one language is spoken—exist. They include Japan in Asia; Uruguay and Venezuela in South America; Iceland,

Denmark, Portugal, and Poland in Europe; and Lesotho in Africa. Even these countries, however, have small numbers of people who speak other languages; for example, more than a half-million Koreans live in Japan. In fact, as a result of migration and diffusion, no country is truly monolingual today. English-speaking Australia has more than 180,000 speakers of Aboriginal languages. Predominantly Portuguese-speaking Brazil has some 1.5 million speakers of Amerindian languages.

Countries in which more than one language is in use are called **multilingual states**. In some of these countries, linguistic fragmentation reflects strong cultural pluralism as well as divisive forces. This is true in former colonial areas where colonizers threw together peoples speaking different languages, as happened in Africa and Asia.

Multilingualism takes several forms. In Canada and Belgium, the two major languages each dominate particular areas of the country. In multilingual India, the country's official languages generally correspond with the country's States (Fig. 6.17). In Peru, centuries of acculturation have not erased the regional identities of the American Indian tongues spoken in the Andean Mountains and the Amazonian interior, and of Spanish, spoken on the coast.

Official Languages

Countries with linguistic fragmentation often adopt an **official language** (or languages) to tie the people together. In former colonies, the official language is often one that ties them to their colonizer, as the colonizer's language invariably is one already used by the educated and politically powerful elite. States adopt official language in the hope of promoting communication and interaction among peoples who speak different local and regional languages.

Many former African colonies have adopted English, French, or Portuguese as their official language, even though they have gained independence from former imperial powers. Thus, Portuguese is the official language of Angola, English is the official language of Nigeria and Ghana, and French is the official language of Côte d'Ivoire.

Such a policy is not without risks. As we noted earlier in this chapter in the case of Nigeria, the long-term results of using a foreign language may not be positive. In some countries, including India, citizens objected to using a language (English in India) that they associated with colonial repression. Some former colonies chose not just one but two official languages: the European colonial language

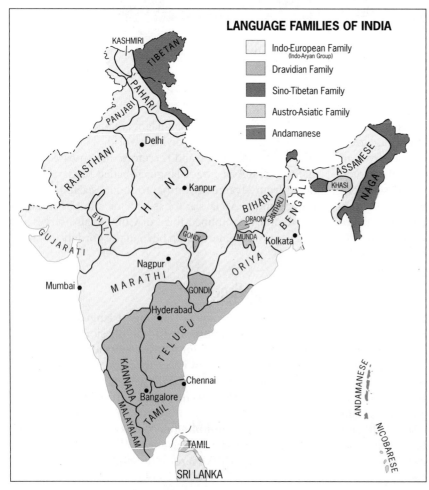

Figure 6.17

Language Families of India. Regional classification of Indian Language Families. India's states generally coincide with a major language family or language. *Adapted with permission from*: Hammond, Inc., 1977.

plus one of the country's own major languages. English and Hindi are official languages of India. Similarly, English and Swahili are official languages of Tanzania. In Mauritania, French and Arabic are official languages. But this solution was not always enough. When India gave Hindi official status, riots and disorder broke out in non-Hindi areas of the country. Kenya, which at first made English and Swahili its official languages, decided to drop English in the face of public opposition to rules requiring candidates for public office to pass a test of their ability to use English.

The official languages in a country are a reflection of the country's history. In Peru, Spanish and the Amerindian language Quechuan have official status and are found in distinct regions. In the Philippines, English (spoken primarily in Manila) and a creolized Spanish called Pilipino are both official languages. Tiny Singapore, the city-state at the tip of the Malay Peninsula, has four official languages: English, Chinese, Malay, and Tamil (an Indian tongue). India is the country with the largest number of official languages—22 if we include both official languages listed in the country's constitution and official languages proclaimed by States within India.

The European Union is not a country, but it recognizes 23 official languages, and the United Nations has 6 official languages. In each of these cases, the international organization offers simultaneous translation among the official languages to any member of the parliament (European Union) or the general assembly (United Nations) who requests it. Each international organization also publishes paper documents and maintains its website in all official languages.

Global Language

What will the global language map look like 50 years from now? More and more people are using English in a variety of contexts. English is now the standard language of international business and travel (the lingua franca), much of contemporary popular culture bears the imprint of English, and the computer and telecommunications revolution relies heavily on the use of English terminology. Does this mean that English is on its way to becoming a global language?

If global language means the principal language people use around the world in their day-to-day activities, the geographical processes we have examined so far emphatically do not point to the emergence of English as a global tongue. Population growth rates are generally lower in English-speaking areas than they are in other areas, and little evidence shows people in non-English speaking areas willing to abandon their local language in favor of English. Indeed, since language embodies deeply held cultural views and is a basic feature of cultural identity, many people actively resist switching to English.

Yet if **global language** means a common language of trade and commerce used around the world, the picture looks rather different. Although not always welcomed, the trend throughout much of the world is to use English as a language of cross-cultural communication—especially in the areas of science, technology, travel, and business. Korean scholars are likely to communicate with their Russian counterparts in English; Japanese scientific journals are increasingly published in English; Danish tourists visiting Italy may use English to get around; and the meetings of most international financial and governmental institutions are dominated by English. Under these circumstances, the role of English as an international language of commerce will grow.

We must be careful in this conclusion, however. Anyone looking at the world 200 years ago would have predicted French as the principal language of cross-cultural communication in the future. Times are different now, of course. The role of English in the computer revolution alone makes it hard to imagine a fundamental shift away from the dominance of English in international affairs. Yet, economic and political influences on language use are always in flux, and nothing is inevitable.

Choose a country in the world. Imagine you become a strong leader of a centralized government in the country. Pick a language used in the country other than the tongue spoken by the majority. Determine what policies you could put in place to make the minority language an official language of the country. What reactions would your initiative generate? Who would support it and who would not?

WHAT ROLE DOES LANGUAGE PLAY IN MAKING PLACES?

Over a decade ago, geographer Yi-Fu Tuan researched the importance of language in making places. He emphasized how people use language as a tool to give meaning to points on the Earth's surface. Each **place** is a unique location—a reflection of people's activities, ideas, and tangible creations.

Tuan explains that by simply naming a place, people call the place into being and impart a certain character to it. Geographers call place names **toponyms**. People are responsible for making places; places do not exist in a vacuum, nor are they organic. The social processes going on in a place determine whether a toponym is passed down or changed, how the people will interpret the history of a place, and how the people will see a place. Tuan contrasts the examples of "Mount Prospect" and "Mount Misery" to help us understand that a name alone can color the character of a place and even the experiences of people in a place. If you planned to travel to "Mount Prospect," your expectations and even your experiences might well be quite different than a trip to "Mount Misery."

A toponym can give us a quick glimpse into the history of a place. Simply by knowing who named the place and how the name was chosen helps us understand the uniqueness of a place. In his book, *Names on the Land: A Historical Account of Place-Naming in the United States* (1982), English professor George Stewart recognized that certain themes dominate American toponyms. Stewart developed a classification scheme focused on ten basic types of place-names, including: *descriptive* (Rocky Mountains); *associative* (Mill Valley, California); *commemorative* (San Francisco); and *commendatory* (Paradise Valley, Arizona). Toponyms also reflect *incidents* (Battle Creek, Michigan); a claim of *possession* (Johnson City, Texas); or a *folk* culture (Plains, Georgia). Stewart explains that some of the most interesting toponyms are *manufactured*, such as Truth or Consequences, New Mexico, or are simply *mistakes*, such as Lasker, North Carolina, named after the State of Alaska. Stewart's final category of toponyms is *shift names*. Shift names include relocated names, such as those found in migrant communities (Lancaster, England to Lancaster, Pennsylvania) and double names, which occur when a place has two names that mean the same thing (Alpine Mountains).

Knowing Stewart's ten categories of toponyms at the very least helps us understand that a story lies behind every toponym we encounter in our travels. The stories of toponyms quite often have their roots in migration, movement, and interaction among people. When languages diffuse through migration, so too do toponyms. Studying the toponyms in a place can tell us much about the historical migration of peoples. George Stewart's classic book on toponyms reveals many clusters of migrants and corresponding toponyms. Often the toponyms remain long after the migrants moved on. Clusters of Welsh toponyms in Pennsylvania, French toponyms in Louisiana, and Dutch toponyms in Michigan reveal migration flows and also can provide insight into language change and evolution of dialects.

Brazil provides an interesting case study of migration flows and toponyms. Most Brazilian toponyms are Portuguese, reflecting the Portuguese colonization of the land. Amid the Portuguese toponyms sits a cluster of German toponyms in the southern state of Santa Catarina. The map of the state is marked by the place-naming activities of German immigrants. For example, the German word for flower is "Blume," and several last names in German begin with "Blum." The German immigrants had a fondness for the tropical flowers they saw in Brazil: southern Brazil is therefore dotted with towns named Blumenau, Blumberg, Blumenhof, Blumenort, Blumenthal, and Blumenstein. Brazilian toponyms also reveal the enormous flow of forced migration from West Africa to Brazil during the slave trade. The Brazilian State of Bahia has a number of toponyms that originated in West Africa, especially Benin and Nigeria.

The toponyms we see on a map depend in large part on who produced the map. Some embattled locales have more than one name at the same time. Argentineans refer to a small cluster (archipelago) of islands off the southeast coast of South America as the Malvinas, but the British call the same cluster of islands the Falkland Islands. In 1982, Argentina invaded the Malvinas, but the British forces fought back, and the islands remain under British control. British, American, and other allies call and map the islands as the Falklands, but Argentineans continue to call and map the islands as the Malvinas. The war ended in a matter of weeks, but the underlying dispute lingers, and so do both names.

In the United States, an agency called the United States Board on Geographic Names, established by President Benjamin Harrison in 1890, is responsible for deciding what toponyms appear on government-produced maps. The board anglicizes place-names from around the world. Some translations have the same spelling as the foreign country, such as Paris and London. Others are off a letter or more, resulting in some confusion for American tourists when they are looking for the train to Rome or Prague but only find trains to Roma or Praha.

Changing Toponyms

Tuan explained that when people *change the toponym* of a place, they have the power to "wipe out the past and call forth the new." For example, people in a small town in Wales feared the loss of the Welsh language and despised the role the English had played in diminishing the use of the Welsh language. They also wanted to boost their local economy by attracting tourists to their town. A century ago, the people renamed their town with a Welsh word unpronounceable by others: Llanfairpwllgwyngyllgog erychwyrndrobwllllantysiliogogogoch (Fig. 6.18). The name accurately describes the town in northern Wales, "The Church of St. Mary in the hollow of white hazel near the rapid whirlpool by the church of St. Tysilio of the red cave." For the last two decades, Wales has had an official policy of teaching both Welsh and English in the schools in order to preserve and boost usage of the Welsh language. Pronouncing the name of this town correctly is now a benchmark for students learning Welsh, and the residents of the town take pride in their ability to pronounce it.

Toponyms are part of the cultural landscape. Changes in place-names give us an idea of the layers of history, the layers of cultural landscape in a place. For example, on the Kenai Peninsula in Alaska, where Clare Swan (whom we cited earlier in this chapter) is from, the changing place-names give us insight into identity questions in the place. Natives in one

Figure 6.18
Llanfairpwllgwyngyllgogerychwyrndrobwllllantysiliogogogoch, Wales. The town with the self-proclaimed longest name in the world attracts hordes of tourists each year to a place whose claim to fame is largely its name.   © Alexander B. Murphy.

town on the Kenai Peninsula called their home Nanwalek in the early 1800s; when the Russians came in and took over the peninsula, they changed the name to Alexandrof. Americans mapped Alaska and then made it a State, and in the process, they changed the name to English Bay. Recently, the townspeople changed the name of their home back to Nanwalek. When you arrive in Nanwalek, you will see native people, see signs of the Russian Orthodox religion, hear them speak English, and then talk with the native people who are reviving their native language and culture. The changes in the place-name provide insight into the cultural landscape.

Post-Colonial Toponyms

The question of changing toponyms often arises when power changes hands in a place. When African colonies became independent countries, many of the new governments immediately changed the toponyms of places named after colonial figures. The new governments renamed several countries: Upper Volta to Burkina Faso, Gold Coast to Ghana, Nyasaland to Malawi, and Northern and Southern Rhodesia to Zambia and Zimbabwe, respectively. Countries in Asia also chose new toponyms to mark their independence and separate themselves from their past: East Pakistan became Bangladesh, and the Netherlands East Indies became Indonesia.

Newly independent countries also changed the names of cities and towns to reflect their independence. Thus, Leopoldville (named after a Belgian king) became Kinshasa,

capital of the Congo; Salisbury, Zimbabwe, named after a British leader, became Harare; and Lourenço Marques, Mozambique, commemorating a Portuguese naval hero, became Maputo. However, newly independent countries did not wipe all colonial names and references from their maps. Etoile (the Congo), Colleen Bawn (Zimbabwe), and Cabo Delgado (Mozambique) remain on the postcolonial map.

Post-revolution Toponyms

Independence prompts name changes, and so too do changes in power through coups and revolutions. During his reign, authoritarian dictator, General Mobutu Sese Seko, changed the name of the Belgian Congo in Subsaharan Africa to Zaïre. At first, other governments and international agencies did not take this move seriously, but eventually they recognized Mobutu's Zaïre. Governments and companies changed their maps and atlases to reflect Mobutu's decision. The government of Zaïre changed the name of their money from the franc to the zaïre, and they even changed the name of the Congo River to the Zaïre.

In 1997, the revolutionary leader Laurent Kabila ousted Mobutu and established his regime in the capital, Kinshasa. Almost immediately, he renamed the country. Zaïre became the Democratic Republic of the Congo (reflecting the colonial name). Again, governments and companies reacted, changing their maps and atlases to reflect Kabila's decision.

Recent revolutions in power in Russia and South Africa led to many changes in toponyms in these countries. When the Soviet Union began, the communist government changed many places named for czars who were in power before them, replacing them (of course) with Soviet names. Once the Soviet Union collapsed, a new round of name changes occurred, often going back to Czarist-era names. In the new Russia, Leningrad reverted to St. Petersburg, Sverdlovsk went back to Yekaterinburg (its name under the czars), and Stalingrad was renamed Volgograd (for the river). Reformers, nationalists, and lingering communists argued bitterly over the toponym changes, and many people continued to address their mail according to their city's former name.

In the same time frame, South Africa experienced a major revolution that also resulted in a fundamental change in governance. Today, the government of South Africa is wrestling with pressures for and against toponym changes. The government restructured the country's administrative framework, creating nine provinces out of four and giving some of the new provinces African names (Mpumalanga for the new Eastern Transvaal, Gauteng for a new central province). One of the old provinces, Natal, has become Kwazulu-Natal. The government also changed some names of towns and villages, but South Africa's map still includes many names from the Boer-British and Apartheid periods. Name changes can evoke strong reactions from people, and the South African government is trying to move slowly and carefully to avoid arousing emotions in their still-divided country.

Memorial Toponyms

People can choose to change a toponym to memorialize an important person or event. Hundreds of parks in the United States are named Memorial Park for hundreds of such persons and events. Towns or government agencies can vote to change the name of a school, a library, or a public building to memorialize people who have played a role in shaping the place or who have had an enormous influence on people in the place.

Certain events such as decolonization or a political revolution can spur changes in toponyms, and so too can revolutions in thought and behavior. The civil rights movement of the 1960s in the United States left many lasting impressions of people and events, especially in the South, where many protests, sit-ins, and marches occurred. Geographer Derek Alderman explains that, in recent decades, African Americans in the South have "taken a particularly active role in reconstructing commemorative landscapes—from calling for the removal of Confederate symbols from public places to the building of memorials and museums honoring the civil rights movement." Streets are often the focal point of commemoration in the cultural landscape because so many people travel along them daily, serving as a constant reminder of the person or event being memorialized.

Alderman studied the practice of changing street names to memorialize Martin Luther King Jr. (MLK), the major African American leader of the civil rights movement. Although streets named after MLK are found throughout the United States, the greatest concentration of memorial streets are in the South, especially in Georgia (King's home state) and Mississippi (Fig. 6.19). Alderman studied the distribution of MLK streets in the South, comparing their locations with census data on race and socioeconomics. He found that although MLK streets are found in both cities and rural areas, "MLK streets are located—whether by choice or by force—in census areas that are generally poorer and with more African Americans than citywide averages." (Fig. 6.20) Alderman tempers this

▬▬ Figure 6.19

Cities in the United States with a Street Named for Martin Luther King Jr. *Data from:* Data drawn from several sources by Derek Alderman, Matthew Mitchelson, and Chris Philamy, East Carolina University, 2003.

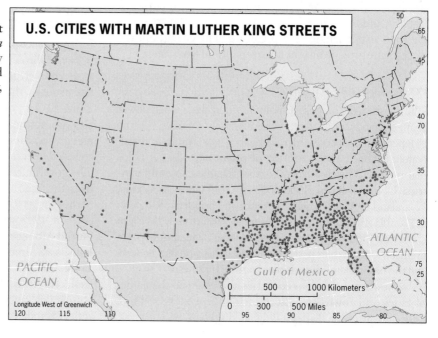

Guest Field Note

Greenville, North Carolina

Greenville, North Carolina changed West Fifth Street to Martin Luther King Jr. Drive in 1999. Originally, African American leaders wanted all of Fifth Street renamed—not just part of it—but residents and business owners on the eastern end strongly opposed the proposal. After driving and walking down the street, I quickly realized that King Drive marked an area that was predominantly black with limited commercial development, whereas East Fifth was mostly white and more upscale. When I interviewed members of Greenville's African American community, they expressed deep frustration over the marginalization of the civil rights leader. In the words of one elected official, "The accomplishments of Dr. King were important to all Americans. A whole man deserves a whole street!" Naming streets for King is a controversial process for many cities, often exposing continued racial tensions and the potential for toponyms to function as contested social boundaries within places.

Figure 6.20

Credit: Derek Alderman, East Carolina University

finding with a caution that not all MLK streets are located in poorer areas of cities. Even when MLK streets are located in depresssed areas, the African American population may have purposefully chosen a street because it runs through an African American neighborhood. Alderman's subsequent studies explore the scale of the city and the contested views of what kinds of streets should be named for MLK—be they residential, commercial, major thoroughfares (perhaps those that connect white and African American neighborhoods), or residential streets in largely African American neighborhoods.

The presence of streets named for civil rights leaders in the cultural landscapes of the American South creates a significant counterbalance to the numerous places of commemoration named for leaders of the Confederacy during the Civil War (see Chapter 1).

Commodification of Toponyms

The practice of commodifying (buying, selling, and trading) toponyms is growing, especially in areas largely within the fold of popular culture. International media corporations that reach across the globe bring known names to new places, drawing consumers to the place based on what they have heard or experienced elsewhere. For example, the Disney Corporation opened Tokyo Disneyland in 1983 and Disneyland Paris in 1990, both places that capitalize on the success of Disneyland and Disneyworld in the United States. As corporations spread their names and logos to other places, they seek to "brand" places, creating or re-creating places that consumers associate with places of the same brand.

In recent years, the activities of corporations with a global reach have been stamped on the landscape. Stadiums are especially susceptible to this form of commodification: FedEx Field, MCI Center, Fleet Center, and Coors Field are perfect examples. In 2004, the Metropolitan Transit Authority in New York City proposed renaming the metro stops, bridges, and tunnels after corporate sponsors. Instead of the Lincoln Tunnel, we could be traveling through the Target Tunnel, and instead of stopping at Times Square, we could be stopping at Disney Times Square (which, ironically is already named for a company—the *New York Times*).

thinking geographically

This place was first named by Gabrielino Indians. In 1769, Spanish Franciscan priests renamed the place. In 1850, English speakers renamed the place. Do not use the Internet to help you. Use only maps in this book or in atlases to help you deduce what this place is. Maps of European exploration and colonialism will help you the most. Look at the end of the chapter summary for the answer.

Summary

The global mosaic of languages reflects centuries of divergence, convergence, extinction, and diffusion. Linguists and linguistic geographers have the interesting work of uncovering, through deep reconstruction, the hearths of the world's language families. Some languages, such as Basque, defy explanation. Other languages are the foci of countless studies, many of which come to differing conclusions about their ancient origins.

As certain languages, such as English and Chinese, gain speakers and become global languages, other languages become extinct. Some languages come to serve as the lingua franca of a region or place. Governments choose official languages, and through public schools, educators entrench an official language in a place. Some countries, faced with the global diffusion of the English language, defend and promote their national language. Whether requiring signs to be written a certain way or requiring a television station to broadcast some proportion of programming in the national language, governments can preserve language, choose a certain dialect as the standard, or repel the diffusion of other languages.

Regardless of the place, the people, or the language used, language continues to define, shape, and maintain culture. How a person thinks about the world is reflected in the words used to describe and define it.

Answer to Final Thinking Geographically Question: Los Angeles, California.

Geographic Concepts

language	backward reconstruction	Slavic languages
culture	extinct language	lingua franca
mutual intelligibility	deep reconstruction	pidgin language
standard language	Nostratic	Creole language
dialects	– language divergence–	monolingual states
dialect chains	language convergence	multilingual states
isogloss	Renfrew hypothesis	official language
language families	conquest theory	global language
subfamilies	dispersal hypothesis	place
sound shift	Romance languages	toponym
Proto-Indo-European	Germanic languages	

Learn More Online

About Bert Vaux's Survey of American Dialects:
http://www4.uwm.edu/FLL/linguistics/dialect/

About Learning Foreign Languages On-Line:
http://www.bbc.co.uk/languages/

Watch It Online

About the Loss of Native Languages in Alaska
www.learner.org/resources/series85.html#program_descriptions
click on Video On Demand for "Alaska: The Last Frontier?"

CHAPTER 7

Religion

Field Note   Dying and Resurrecting

Figure 7.1
Vyshniyvolochek, Russia.   A Russian Orthodox church lies in ruins in this small village in 1964.   © H. J. de Blij.

When I made my first trip to the Soviet Union in 1964, the world was divided into West and East in the Cold War. I was cataloging the unique cultural landscape in my mind as my group drove along a road from Leningrad to Moscow: I was looking for evidence of communism on the landscape. The rural areas were filled with state and collective farms. To me, the most interesting aspect of the landscape was the multitude of churches in ruins.

In every town we passed, and in many villages along the way, churches lay in ruins, their roofs collapsed, their steeples toppled. The bells were gone; where stained-glass windows once adorned the churches there were now gaping holes (Fig. 7.1). My host did not want me to photograph the churches.

"Why let them collapse?" I asked, "Why not remove them altogether?" He pointed his finger to emphasize his point, "Religion causes conflict. We had many religions in the Soviet Union, and they set Soviet against Soviet. And the Orthodox

Church opposed our communist victory. That's what these useless relics are for. They remind the people of our victory and their freedom."

When the Soviet Union came into being in the 1920s, the government sought to knit together diverse lands stretching from Eastern Europe to the Pacific Ocean. People already lived in all of these lands and had their own cultures and their own religions. At its height of territorial expansion, the Soviet Union included 15 Republics (each of which was an independent country before being annexed) and more than 100 ethnically distinct territories (the Republic of Russia itself included 70 distinct territories).

To diminish the religious diversity of the Soviet people, the government chose an official policy of atheism and discouraged religious practice among its citizens. In Russia, the state seized church bells and other religious paraphernalia and demolished many churches, converting others to secular uses. In the Muslim republics and territories, the Soviets tolerated Islamic practice among the old but not among the young. Time, they believed, would erase the imprints of both Christianity and Islam.

Soviet policies had an impact on religion but not always in expected ways. In some cases, religious practices went underground. Some religions thrived in this environment, whereas others disappeared all together. The example of Armenia and Azerbaijan shows how Soviet policies failed to diminish differences in the long run. Along the border between Christianity and Islam in the area between the Caspian and Black seas lie two republics infused with religion: Christian Armenia on the Black Sea and Shi'ite Muslim Azerbaijan on the Caspian Sea.

The Soviets believed that the people in this region would show less allegiance to their republics and more allegiance to the Soviet Union if power rested at the local rather than republic scale. The Soviet Union drew boundaries for local control, creating a layout that separated ethnic groups within small areas (Fig. 7.2). In the middle of Muslim Azerbaijan, the Soviets drew a border around Christian Armenians and called it Nagorno-Karabakh. Similarly, to the southwest of Christian Armenia, along the border with Iran, the Soviets drew a border around Muslim Azerbaijanis and called it Nakhichevan.

The divide-and-diminish plan functioned only as long as the Soviet Union controlled both republics. When the Soviet Union dissolved in 1991 and the repub-

Figure 7.2
Nagorno-Karabakh and Nakhichevan. This map shows the Muslim Azerbaijani Nakhichevan, cut off by Christian Armenia, and the Christian Armenian Nagorno-Karabakh, surrounded by Muslim Azerbaijan.
© H. J. de Blij, A. B. Murphy, E. H. Fouberg, and John Wiley & Sons, Inc.

lics became independent states, ethnic strife broke out almost immediately. Azerbaijani Muslims, long cut off from their Iranian Shi'ite counterparts, broke through the southern border, acquiring weapons in the process. Soon Muslims and Christians were locked in combat, and Armenian refugees were streaming from Nagorno-Karabakh westward and even fleeing by boat across the Caspian Sea. More than 70 years of Soviet domination had done little to soften Armenian-Christian memories of Islamic oppression or to lessen the intensity of Azerbaijani-Muslim disdain for Christian "unbelievers."

As Russia formed from the rubble of the Soviet Union, religion came above ground. In 1996, the Russian Orthodox Church rebuilt the Cathedral of Christ the Savior two blocks from the Kremlin. The Soviet government destroyed the cathedral in 1931 to build a palace commemorating Soviet leaders, but the palace was never built. According to Russian geographer Dmitri Sidorov, during Soviet times, what stood in the place of the cathedral was a large pit. In the first half of the 1990s, the pit served as "Russia's most famous geographical symbol for the failed communist endeavor."

In this chapter, we consider the sources, diffusion, and transformation of the world's great religions, their regional patterns, and their cultural landscapes. Like language, religion can be a strong unifying force, but it can also divide and foster conflict. In this chapter, we study religious strife in Northern Ireland, the former Yugoslavia, the Middle East, the Horn of Africa, and beyond.

Key Questions For Chapter 7

1. What is religion, and what role does it play in culture?
2. Where did the world's major religions originate, and how do religions diffuse?
3. How is religion seen in the cultural landscape?
4. What role does religion play in ethnic conflict?

WHAT IS RELIGION, AND WHAT ROLE DOES IT PLAY IN CULTURE?

Religion and language lie at the foundation of culture: both confer and reflect identity. Like languages, religions are constantly changing. Although religious leaders and bureaucracies sometimes attempt to slow the pace of change, religions nevertheless change over time.

Interaction among people can cause one language to become extinct and another to thrive. The same is true for religion, where interaction can sometimes lead to conversion. Through conversion, migration, missionary efforts, and conquest, major religions of the world have diffused across cultural barriers and language boundaries.

The cultural landscape is marked by religion—most obviously by churches and mosques, cemeteries and shrines, statues and symbols (Fig. 7.3). Other more subtle markers of religion dot the landscape as well. The presence or absence of stores selling alcohol or of signs depicting the human form in particular ways reflect prevailing religious views. Religion is also proclaimed in modes of dress (veils, turbans) and personal habits (beards, ritual scars). The outward display of religious beliefs often reveals the inward structure of a religion. For example, in the Islamic Republic of Pakistan, in 1991, the government proclaimed that possessing a beard would be a condition for the appointment of judges. The beard requirement is an outward display of religion, and it also shows the inward structure of Islam in Pakistan, where women are not in a place of power.

Religion is an extraordinarily difficult concept to define. In the chapter "Geography of Religion and Belief Systems," written for *Geography in America*, geographers Robert Stoddard and Carolyn Prorak define religion as "a system of beliefs and practices that attempts to order

Field Note

"Each religion approaches the disposition of the deceased in different ways, and cultural landscapes reflect religious traditions. In largely Christian, western regions, the deceased are buried in large, sometimes elaborate cemeteries. The Hindu faith requires cremation of the deceased. Wherever large Hindu communities exist outside of India, you will see crematoriums, the equivalent of a Hindu funeral home."

Figure 7.3
Mombasa, Kenya.   © H. J. de Blij.

life in terms of culturally perceived ultimate priorities." Stoddard and Prorak explain that the idea of "perceived ultimate priorities" is often expressed in terms of "should": people explain and justify how they and others "should" behave based on their religious beliefs. From eating habits to dress codes, religions set standards for how adherents "should" behave. "Shouldness" goes beyond religion to other belief systems, but in this chapter we focus on formal religions, their distribution, and their role in making and shaping places and cultures. The idea that a "good" life has rewards and that "bad" behavior risks punishment has an enormous influence on cultures, on how people behave, and on how people perceive and evaluate the behavior of others.

Religion manifests itself in many different ways. We can see religion in the worship of the souls of ancestors who are thought to inhabit natural objects such as mountains, animals, or trees; in the belief that a certain living person possesses special abilities granted by a supernatural power; and in the belief in a deity or deities, as in the great

world religions. In some places, societies are so infused with religion that religious tradition strongly influences behaviors during waking hours through ritual and practice and even during periods of sleep in prescribing the orientation of the body.

Across the multitude of religions, some religious practices such as ritual and prayer are common. Rituals may mark important events in people's lives: birth and death, attainment of adulthood, or marriage. Rituals are typically expressed at regular intervals in a routine manner, as is done on certain days in the Christian and

Figure 7.4
Antwerp, Belgium.   The cathedral in Antwerp was built beginning in 1352 and still dominates the central part of town. © Alexander B. Murphy.

Jewish worlds, certain times of the day in the Muslim world, or according to certain astronomical events in the Jewish, Hindu, Muslim, and Christian worlds. A common ritual is prayer, whether at mealtime, at sunrise and sundown, at night upon retiring, or in the morning when arising.

Although religious beliefs and prescriptions influence many societies, **secularism** now prevails in some societies. In these places, religion, at least in its organized form, has become less significant in the lives of most people. But even in secular societies, religion permeates art, history, customs, and beliefs (Fig. 7.4). Indeed, no matter what society you come from, what you eat, when you work, when you shop, and what you are allowed to do are influenced by religion.

In short, organized religion has a powerful effect on human societies. It has been a major force in combating social ills, sustaining the poor, promoting the arts, educating the deprived, and advancing medical knowledge. However, religion has also blocked scientific study, encouraged the oppression of dissidents, supported colonialism and exploitation, and condemned women to an inferior status in many societies. Religion is, if nothing else, one of the most complex—and often controversial—aspects of the human condition.

Describe how religion and language affect and change each other to shape cultures. (Consider what happens to a society's religion and language when a different religion or language diffuses to the place.)

WHERE DID THE MAJOR RELIGIONS OF THE WORLD ORIGINATE, AND HOW DO RELIGIONS DIFFUSE?

Despite the wide variety of religions found around the world, they are commonly classified into three categories based on their approaches to the concept of divinity. Adherents of **monotheistic religions** worship a single deity, a God or Allah. Believers in **polytheistic religions** worship more than one deity, even thousands. **Animistic religions** are centered on the belief that inanimate objects, such as mountains, boulders, rivers, and trees, possess spirits and should therefore be revered.

Throughout much of human history, virtually all religions were either animistic or polytheistic, or both. Somewhere around 3500 years ago, however, a monotheistic religion developed in Southwest Asia called Zoroastrianism. (The Parsi we talked about at the beginning of Chapter 4 are Zoroastrians who moved to India.) Some believe that the monotheism of late Judaism, Christianity, and Islam can be traced to Zoroastrian influences. Others believe that Judaism itself was the first monotheistic religion. Whichever the case, the eventual diffusion of religions influenced by monotheism—Christianity and Islam—spread monotheistic ideas throughout much of the world and marked a major theological shift from the long dominance of polytheistic and animist beliefs in most places.

By 500 BCE (Before the Common Era), four major hearths of religion and philosophy were developed in the world (Fig. 7.5). The hearth of Greek philosophy is along the northern shores of the Mediterranean Sea. From a hearth in South Asia, along the Indus River Valley, came Hinduism; from a hearth on the eastern Mediterranean came Judaism; and from a hearth on the Huang He River Valley in China

Figure 7.5

Hearths of Major World Religions. *Adapted with permission from*: Albert M. Craig, William M. Graham, Donald Kagan, Stephen Ozment, and Frank M. Turner. *The Heritage of World Civilizations*, Seventh Edition. New York: Prentice Hall, 2006.

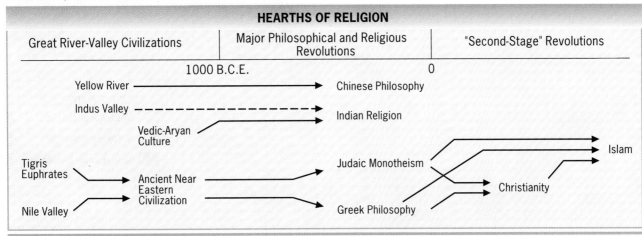

came Chinese philosophies. These early-established religions and philosophies profoundly impacted other religions, as the arrows in Figure 7.5 demonstrate. Philosophies and religions diffused from their hearths, affecting one another and influencing the ways founders established newer religions. The two religions with the greatest number of adherents in the world today, Christianity and Islam, were both influenced by Judaism and Greek philosophy.

The World Map of Religions Today

The map in Figure 7.6 provides a global overview of the distribution of the world's major religions. Any map of world religions is a generalization, and caution must be used when making observations from the map. First, the shadings on the map show the major religion in an area, thereby masking minority religions, many of which have a significant number of followers. India, for example, is depicted as a Hindu region (except in the northwest), but other religions, such as Islam and Sikhism, attract millions of adherents in India (150 million Muslims live in India). Second, some of the regions shown as belonging to a particular religion are places where faiths have penetrated relatively recently and where traditional religious ideas influence the practice of the dominant faith. Many Christian Africans, for example, continue to believe in traditional powers even as they profess a belief in Christianity. Finally, in a number of areas many people have moved away from organized religion entirely. Thus, France appears on the map as a Roman Catholic country,

Figure 7.6

Religions of the World.   *Data from:* Several sources, including Hammond, Inc, 1977, H. J. de Blij, P. O. Muller, and A. Winkler Prins, *The World Today*, 4e, 2008 State Department Religious Freedom Report, CIA World Factbook, Pew Forum on Religion and Public Life, and author observations.   © E. H. Fouberg, A. B. Murphy, H. J. de Blij, and John Wiley & Sons, Inc.

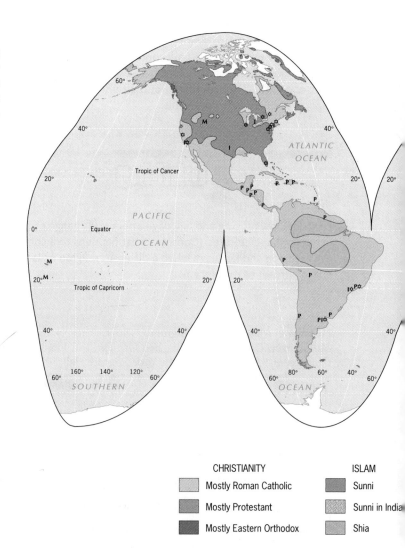

CHRISTIANITY

Mostly Roman Catholic

Mostly Protestant

Mostly Eastern Orthodox

ISLAM

Sunni

Sunni in India

Shia

yet a significant number of French people profess adherence to no particular faith.

Despite the limitations of the map of world religions, it illustrates how far Christian religions have diffused (2.1 billion adherents worldwide), the extent of the diffusion of Islam (1.34 billion), the connection between Hinduism (950 million adherents) and one of the world's major population concentrations, and the continued importance Buddhism (347 million followers) plays in parts of Asia. Many factors help explain the distributions shown on the map, but each of the widespread religions shares one characteristic in common: they are all universalizing religions. **Universalizing religions** actively seek converts because they view themselves as offering belief systems of universal appropriateness and appeal. Christianity, Islam, and Buddhism all fall within this category, and their universalizing character helps explain their widespread distribution (Table 7.1).

Universalizing religions are relatively few in number and of recent origin. Throughout much of human history, most religions have not actively sought converts. Rather, a given religion has been practiced by one particular culture or ethnic group. In an **ethnic religion**, adherents are born into the faith and converts are not actively sought. Ethnic religions tend to be spatially concentrated—as is the case with traditional religions in Africa and South America (250 million followers). The principal exception is Judaism (13 million adherents), an ethnic religion whose adherents are widely scattered as a result of forced and voluntary migrations.

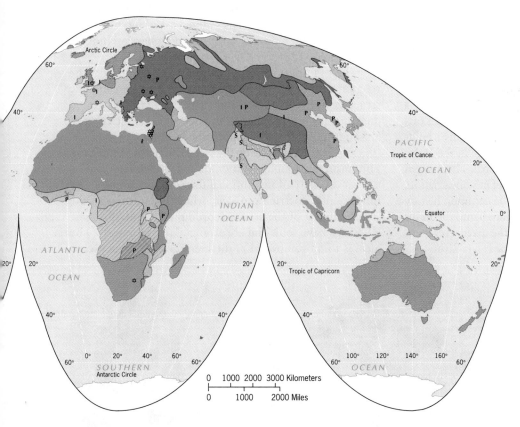

RELIGIONS OF THE WORLD

▢ HINDUISM	▢ CHINESE RELIGIONS and BUDDHISM – MAHAYANA	✡ JUDAISM
▢ BUDDHISM – TANTRAYANA	▢ SHINTOISM and BUDDHISM – MAHAYANA	S SIKH
▢ BUDDHISM – THERAVADA	▢ TRADITIONAL and SHAMANIST RELIGIONS	M MORMONISM
▨ TRADITIONALIST MIXED		P EVANGELICAL PROTESTANTS
		I ISLAM

TABLE 7.1
Adherents to Major World Religions

Religion	Number of Adherents	Percent of Total Global Adherents
Christianity	2.1 billion	41.79%
Islam	1.34 billion	26.67%
Hinduism	950 million	18.91%
Buddhism	347 million	6.90%
Traditional beliefs	250 million	4.97%
Sikhism	24 million	.48%
Judaism	13 million	.26%

Data from *The Atlas of Religion*, Joanne O'Brien and Martin Palmer, University of California Press, 2007.

From the Hearth of South Asia

Hinduism

In terms of number of adherents, **Hinduism** ranks third after Christianity and Islam as a world religion. Hinduism is one of the oldest religions in the modern world, dating back over 4000 years, originating in the Indus River Valley of what is today part of Pakistan. Hinduism is unique among world religions in a number of ways. The religion does not have a single founder, a single theology, or any agreement on its origins. The common account of the history of Hinduism holds that the religion is based on ancient practices in the Indus River cities of Mohenjo-Daro and Harappa. The ancient practices included ritual bathing and belief in reincarnation, or at least a long journey after death. The common history says that Aryans invaded (some say migrated) into the Indus region and gave the name Hinduism to the diverse religious practices of the people who lived along the Indus River.

Despite the ambiguous beginnings of Hinduism, one thing is certain: Hinduism is no longer associated with its hearth in Pakistan. Pakistan is primarily a Muslim country, and as Figure 7.6 demonstrates, Hinduism is found mainly in India. In fact, one of the most sacred places for Hindus is the Ganges River, in India.

Just as there is no consensus on Hinduism's origins, there is a lack of agreement on defining Hinduism relative to other major world religions. Many define Hinduism as a polytheistic religion because of the presence of many gods. However, many Hindus define their religion as monotheistic. The one god is Brahman (the universal soul), and the other gods in the religion are various expressions of Brahman. Similarly, Western academics define Hinduism today as an ethnic religion because Hindus do not actively seek converts. At the same time, historical evidence shows Hindus migrating into Southeast Asia and diffusing their religion (as a universalizing religion would) before the diffusion of Buddhism and Islam into Southeast Asia (Fig. 7.7). Although Hinduism is now more of an ethnic religion, the religion has millions of adherents in the populous region of South Asia, extending beyond India to Bangladesh, Myanmar, Sri Lanka, and Nepal.

The Hindu religion is not centrally organized. The religion does not have an administrative or bureaucratic structure like Christianity and Islam. The Hindu religion does not have a prophet or a single book of scriptures, although most Hindus recognize the sacredness of the *Vedas* (the four texts that make up the sacred books of Hinduism). Hinduism is a conglomeration of beliefs characterized by a great diversity of institutional forms and practices. The fundamental doctrine is *karma*, which has to do with the transferability of the soul. According to Hindu doctrine, all beings have souls and are arranged in a hierarchy. The ideal is to move upward in the hierarchy and then escape

■ Figure 7.7
Angkor Wat, Cambodia. The extensive, walled structure at the temple complex in Angkor Wat marks the earliest period of Hinduism's diffusion into Southeast Asia. Eventually, Buddhism supplanted Hinduism in Cambodia, and many Hindu temples such as this now suffer from neglect and destruction. © H. J. de Blij.

from the eternal cycle of *reincarnation* through union with Brahman (the universal soul). A soul moves upward or downward according to the individual's behavior in the present life. Good deeds and adherence to the faith lead to a higher level in the next life, whereas bad behavior leads to demotion to a lower level. All souls, those of animals as well as humans, participate in this process. The principle of reincarnation is a cornerstone of Hinduism.

Hinduism's doctrines are closely bound to Indian society's caste system, for castes themselves are steps on the universal ladder. However, the **caste system** locks people into particular social classes and imposes many restrictions, especially in the lowest of the castes, the Dalits. Until a generation ago, the Dalits could not enter temples, were excluded from certain schools, and were restricted to performing the most unpleasant tasks. The coming of other religions to India, the effects of modernization during the colonial period, and especially the work of Mahatma Gandhi helped loosen the social barriers of the caste system and somewhat improved the lot of the 80 million Dalits.

Diffusion of Hinduism

Hinduism was born in the western part of the Indian subcontinent and spread eastward through processes that are not well understood. Before the advent of Christianity, Hinduism had diffused into Southeast Asia. It first attached itself to traditional faiths and then slowly replaced them. Later, when Islam and Christianity appeared and were actively spread in Hindu areas, Hindu thinkers attempted to integrate certain new teachings into their own religion. For example, elements of the Sermon on the Mount (Jesus's

sermon in which he described God's love for the poor and the peacemakers) now form part of Hindu preaching, and Christian beliefs contributed to the weakening of caste barriers. In other instances, the confrontation between Hinduism and other faiths led to the emergence of a compromise religion. Islam stimulated the rise of Sikhism, whose followers disapproved of the worship of idols and disliked the caste system, but retained the concepts of reincarnation and karma.

As Figure 7.8 shows, Hinduism evolved in what is today Pakistan, reached its fullest development in India, and spread into Southeast Asia. Given its current character as an ethnic religion, it is not surprising that Hinduism's geographical extent is relatively small. Indeed, throughout most of Southeast Asia, Buddhism and Islam overtook the places where Hinduism had diffused during its universalizing period. In overwhelmingly Muslim Indonesia, the island of Bali remains a Hindu outpost. Bali became a refuge for Hindu holy men, nobles, and intellectuals during the sixteenth century, when Islam engulfed neighboring Java, which now retains only architectural remnants of its Hindu age. Since then, the Balinese have developed a unique faith, still based on Hindu principles but mixed with elements of Buddhism, animism, and ancestor worship. The caste system prevails, but the lower castes outnumber the higher castes by nearly 10 to 1—producing less divisiveness than in India. Religion plays an extremely important role in Bali. Temples and shrines dominate the cultural landscape, and participation in worship, festivals, and other ceremonies of the island's unique religion is almost universal. Religion is so much at the heart of Balinese culture that it is sometimes described as a celebration of life.

Figure 7.8

Diffusion of Four Major World Religions.   The hearths and major routes of diffusion are shown on this map. It does not show smaller diffusion streams: Islam and Buddhism, for example, are gaining strength in North America, although their numbers are still comparatively small.

©E. H. Fouberg, A. B. Murphy, and H. J. de Blij, John Wiley & Sons, Inc.

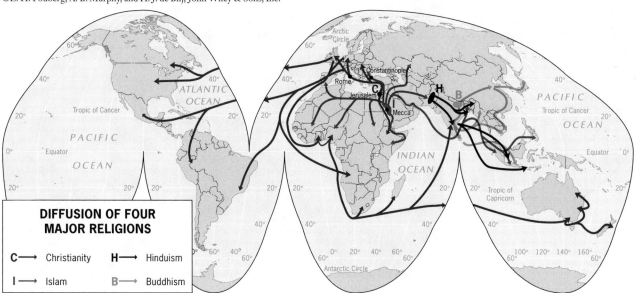

Outside South Asia and Bali, Hinduism's presence is relatively minor. Over the last two centuries, Hinduism has diffused to small parts of the world through migration. During British colonialism, the British transported hundreds of thousands of Hindu adherents from their colony of India to their other colonies in East and South Africa, the Caribbean, northern South America, and the Pacific Islands. Because Hinduism is not a universalizing religion today, the relocation diffusion has produced pockets rather than regions of Hinduism.

Buddhism

Buddhism splintered from Hinduism over 2500 years ago. Buddhism and several other religions appeared in India as a reaction to questions about Hinduism's teachings at the time. Reformers questioned Hinduism's strict social hierarchy that protected the privileged and kept millions in poverty. Prince Siddhartha, who was heir to a wealthy kingdom in what is now Nepal, founded Buddhism. Siddhartha was profoundly shaken by the misery he saw around him, which contrasted sharply with the splendor and wealth in which he had been raised. Siddhartha came to be known as Buddha

(the enlightened one). He may have been the first prominent Indian religious leader to speak out against Hinduism's caste system. Salvation, he preached, could be attained by anyone, no matter what his or her caste. Enlightenment would come through knowledge, especially self-knowledge; elimination of greed, craving, and desire; complete honesty; and never hurting another person or animal.

After Buddha's death in 489 BCE at the age of 80, the faith grew rather slowly until the middle of the third century BCE, when the Emperor Asoka became a convert. Asoka was the leader of a large and powerful Indian state that extended from the Punjab to Bengal and from the Himalayan foothills to Mysore. He not only set out to rule his country in accordance with the teachings of Buddha; he also sent missionaries to carry Buddha's teachings to distant peoples (Fig. 7.9). Buddhism spread as far south as Sri Lanka and later advanced west toward the Mediterranean, north into Tibet, and east into China, Korea, Japan, Vietnam, and Indonesia, over a span of about ten centuries (Fig. 7.8). Although Buddhism diffused to distant lands, it began to decline in its region of origin. During Asoka's rule there may have been more Buddhists than Hindu adherents in India, but after that period the strength of

■■■ Figure 7.9

Borobudur, Indonesia. Built about 800 CE when Buddhism was spreading throughout Southeast Asia, Borobudur was abandoned and neglected after the arrivals of Islam and Christianity and lay overgrown until uncovered and restored under Dutch colonial rule in 1907–1911. The monument consists of a set of intricately carved, walled terraces; the upper terraces are open. In the upper terraces stand six dozen stupas, each containing a sculpture of the Buddha in meditation, visible when you peer through the openings.   © H. J. de Blij.

Hinduism began to reassert itself. Today Buddhism is practiced by relatively few in India, but still thrives in Sri Lanka, Southeast Asia, Nepal, Tibet, and Korea. Along with other faiths, it also survives in Japan.

Like Christianity and Islam, Buddhism changed as it grew and diffused, and now the religion is strongly regional-assuming different forms in different regions. Buddhism's various branches have an estimated 347 million adherents, with Mahayana Buddhism and Theravada Buddhism claiming the most adherents. Theravada Buddhism is a monastic faith that survives in Sri Lanka, Myanmar (Burma), Thailand, Laos, and Cambodia. It holds that salvation is a personal matter, achieved through good behavior and religious activities, including periods of service as a monk or nun. Mahayana Buddhism, which is practiced mainly in Vietnam, Korea, Japan, and China, holds that salvation can be aided by appeals to superhuman, holy sources of merit. The Buddha is regarded as a divine savior. Mahayana Buddhists do not serve as monks, but they spend much time in personal meditation and worship. Other branches of Buddhism include the Lamaism of Xizang (Tibet), which combines monastic Buddhism with the worship of local demons and deities, and Zen Buddhism, the contemplative form that is prevalent in Japan.

Buddhism has become a global religion over the last two centuries, diffusing to many areas of the world. However, the faith has suffered in Southeast Asia. Militant regimes have attacked the religion in Cambodia, Laos, and Vietnam. In Thailand, Buddhism has been under pressure owing to rising political tensions. Nevertheless, the appeal of Buddhism's principles has ensured its continued diffusion, most recently in the Western world.

Shintoism

Buddhism is mixed with a local religion in Japan, where **Shintoism** is found. This ethnic religion, which is related to Buddhism, focuses particularly on nature and ancestor worship (Fig. 7.10). The Japanese emperor made Shintoism the state religion of Japan in the nineteenth century, according himself the status of divine-right monarch. At the end of World War II, Japan separated Shintoism from the emperor, taking away the state sanctioning of the religion. At the same time, the role of the emperor in Japan was diminished and given a ceremonial status. The number of adherents in Japan is somewhere between 105 and 118 million, depending on the source. The majority of Japanese observe both Buddhism and Shintoism.

From the Hearth of the Huang He River Valley

Taoism

While the Buddha's teachings were gaining converts in India, a religious revolution of another kind was taking place in China. Two major schools of Chinese philosophy, Taoism and Confucianism, were forming. The beginnings of **Taoism** are unclear, but scholars trace the religion to an older contemporary of Confucius, Lao-Tsu, who published a volume titled *Tao-te-ching*, or "Book of the Way." In his teachings, Lao-Tsu focused on the proper form of political rule and on the oneness of humanity and nature: people, he said, should learn to live in harmony with nature. This gave rise to the concept of **Feng Shui**—the art and science of organizing living spaces in order to channel the life forces that exist in nature in favorable ways. According to

Figure 7.10

Kyoto, Japan. In Japan, both Buddhism and Shintoism make their marks on the cultural landscape. This Shinto shrine, with its orange trim and olive-green glazed tiles, is visible after passing under a torii—a gateway usually formed by two wooden posts topped by two horizontal beams turned up at their ends—which signals that you have left the secular and entered the sacred world. © H. J. de Blij.

tradition, nothing should be done to nature without consulting the *geomancers*, people who know the desires of the powerful spirits of ancestors, dragons, tigers, and other beings occupying the natural world and can give advice on how to order things according to Feng Shui.

Among the Taoist virtues are simplicity and spontaneity, tenderness, and tranquility. Competition, possession, and even the pursuit of knowledge are to be avoided. War, punishment, taxation, and ceremonial ostentation are viewed as evils. The best government, according to Lao-Tsu, is the least government.

Thousands of people began to follow Taoism. Lao-Tsu himself was worshiped as a god, something of which he would have disapproved. People, animals, even dragons became objects of worship.

Confucianism

Confucius lived from 551 to 479 BCE, and his followers constructed a blueprint for Chinese civilization in almost every field, including philosophy, government, and education. In religion, Confucius addressed the traditional Chinese tenets that included belief in heaven and the existence of the soul, ancestor worship, sacrificial rites, and shamanism. He held that the real meaning of life lay in the present, not in some future abstract existence, and that service to one's fellow humans should supersede service to spirits.

Confucianism is mainly a philosophy of life, and like Taoism, Confucianism had great and lasting impacts on Chinese life. Appalled at the suffering of ordinary people at the hands of feudal lords, Confucius urged the poor to assert themselves. He was not a prophet who dealt in promises of heaven and threats of hell. He denied the divine ancestry of China's aristocratic rulers, educated the landless and the weak, disliked supernatural mysticism, and argued that human virtues and abilities, not heritage, should determine a person's position and responsibilities in society.

Despite these views, Confucius came to be revered as a spiritual leader after his death in 479 BCE, and his teachings diffused widely throughout East and Southeast Asia. Followers built temples in his honor all over China. From his writings and sayings emerged the Confucian Classics, a set of 13 texts that became the focus of education in China for 2000 years. Over the centuries, Confucianism (with its Taoist and Buddhist ingredients) became China's state ethic, although the Chinese emperor modified Confucian ideals over time. For example, one emperor made worship of and obedience to the emperor part of Confucianism. In government, law, literature, religion, morality, and many other ways, the Confucian Classics were the guide for Chinese civilization.

Diffusion of Chinese Religions

Confucianism diffused early into the Korean Peninsula, Japan, and Southeast Asia, where it has long influenced the practice of Buddhism. More recently, Chinese immigrants expanded the influence of the Chinese religions in parts of Southeast Asia and helped to introduce their principles into societies ranging from Europe to North America.

The diffusion of Chinese religions even within China has been tempered by the Chinese government's efforts to suppress religion in the country. Like the Soviet government, the communist government that took control of China in 1949 attempted to ban religion, in this case Confucianism, from public practice. But after guiding all aspects of Chinese education, culture, and society for 2000 years, Confucianism did not fade easily from the Chinese consciousness. Confucianism and Taoism are so entrenched in Chinese culture that the government's anti-religion initiatives have not had their desired effect. For example, a Chinese government policy in the 1950s that ran counter to the teachings of Feng Shui met much resistance by tradition-bound villagers. Feng Shui geomancers in China have the responsibility of identifying suitable gravesites for the deceased—gravesites that leave the dead in perfect harmony with their natural surroundings. The Chinese created burial mounds for their dead at these chosen gravesites. The pragmatic communist Chinese government saw the burial mounds as a barrier to efficient agriculture, so they leveled the burial mounds during the communalization program. Tradition-bound villagers strongly opposed the practice; they harbored a reserve of deep resentment that exploded much later in the revolutionary changes of the 1970s.

Geomancy is still a powerful force in China today, even in urban areas with large populations. Geographer Elizabeth Teather studied the rise of cremation and columbaria (resting places for ashes) in Hong Kong, investigating the impact Feng Shui has had on the structures and the continued influence of Chinese religious beliefs on burial practices in the extremely densely populated city of Hong Kong. Traditional Chinese beliefs favor a coffin and burial plot aligned with Feng Shui teachings. However, with the growth of China's population, the government has highly encouraged cremation over the past few decades. The availability of burial plots in cities like Hong Kong is quite low, and the costs of burial plots have risen in turn.

Teather explains that although cremation is on the rise in Hong Kong, traditional Chinese beliefs are dictating the final resting places of ashes. Most Chinese people, she states, have a "cultural need to keep ancestral remains appropriately stored and in a single place." In North America and Europe, a family often chooses to scatter the ashes of a cremated loved one, but a Chinese family is more likely to keep the ashes together in a single identifiable space so that they can return to visit the ancestor during Gravesweeping Festivals (an annual commemoration of ancestors during which people visit and tend the graves of their ancestors). Teather describes how Feng Shui masters are consulted in the building of columbaria and how Feng Shui helps dictate the price placed on the niches

Field Note

"Many cities in Europe have distinct Jewish neighborhoods with active synagogues and communities. Others, such as Prague, also have historical Jewish neighborhoods, marked with cemeteries and synagogues that have become historical sites or museums. The Old Jewish Cemetery in Prague was built in the 1400s and the last person was buried there in 1787. The jumbled mass of tombstones in the cemetery is a result of layers of people (up to 12 layers) being buried within the confines of the cemetery over the centuries."

Figure 7.11
Prague, Czech Republic.   © Erin H. Fouberg.

for sale in the columbaria (with the lowest prices for the niches near the "grime of the floor").

From the Hearth of the Eastern Mediterranean

Judaism

Judaism grew out of the belief system of the Jews, one of several nomadic Semitic tribes living in Southwest Asia about 4000 years ago. The roots of Jewish religious tradition lie in the teachings of Abraham (from Ur), who is credited with uniting his people to worship only one God. According to Jewish teaching, Abraham and God have a covenant in which the Jews agree to worship only one God, and God agrees to protect his chosen people, the Jews.

The history of the Jews is filled with upheaval. Moses led them from Egypt, where they had been enslaved, to Canaan, where an internal conflict developed and the nation split into two branches, Israel and Judah. Israel was subsequently wiped out by enemies, but Judah survived longer, only to be conquered by the Babylonians and the Assyrians. The Jews regrouped to rebuild their headquarters, Jerusalem, but then fell victim to a series of foreign powers. The Romans destroyed their holy city in 70 CE (Common Era) and drove the Jews away, scattering the adherents to the faith far and wide. Jews retained only a small presence on the eastern shores of the Mediterranean until the late nineteenth century.

Our map shows that unlike other ethnic religions, Judaism is not limited to a small territorial extent. Rather, Judaism is distributed throughout parts of the Middle East and North Africa, Russia, Ukraine, Europe, and parts of North and South America (Fig. 7.6). According to *The Atlas of Religion*, of all the world's 18 million Jews, 40.5 percent live in the United States, 40.2 percent live in Israel, and then in rank order, less than 5 percent live in France, Canada, the United Kingdom, Russia, and Argentina. Judaism is one of the world's most influential religions, although it claims only 18 million adherents.

During the nineteenth century, a *Reform* movement developed with the objective of adjusting Judaism and its practices to current times. However, many feared that this reform would cause a loss of identity and cohesion, and the *Orthodox* movement sought to retain the old precepts. Between those two extremes is a sector that is less strictly orthodox but not as liberal as that of the reformers; it is known as the *Conservative* movement. Significant differences in ideas and practices are associated with these three branches, but Judaism is united by a strong sense of ethnic distinctiveness.

Diffusion of Judaism

The scattering of Jews after the Roman destruction of Jerusalem is known as the **diaspora**—a term that now signifies the spatial dispersion of members of any ethnic group. The Jews who went north into Central Europe came to be known as *Ashkenazim*, and the Jews who scattered across North Africa and into the Iberian Peninsula (Spain and Portugal) are called *Sephardim*. For centuries, both the Ashkenazim and the Sephardim were persecuted, denied citizenship, driven into ghettos, and massacred (Fig. 7.11).

In the face of constant threats to their existence, the Jews were sustained by extraordinary efforts to maintain a sense of community and faith. The idea of a homeland for the Jewish people, which became popular during the nineteenth century, developed into the ideology of **Zionism**. Zionist ideals are rooted in the belief that Jews should not be absorbed into other societies. The horrors of the Nazi campaign against Jews from the 1930s through World War II, when the Nazis established concentration camps and killed some six million Jews, persuaded many Jews to adopt Zionism. Jews from all over the world concluded that their only hope of survival was to establish a strongly defended homeland on the shores of the eastern Mediterranean. Aided by sympathetic members of the international community, the Zionist goal of a Jewish state became a reality in 1948, when two states, Israel and Palestine, were carved out of the territory of the eastern Mediterranean in a United Nations resolution.

While adherents to Judaism live across the world, many Jews have moved to Israel since its establishment. The Israeli government passed the Law of Return in 1950, which recognizes the rights of every Jew to immigrate to Israel. In 2004, over 10,000 Jews left the former Soviet Union for Israel, along with nearly 4000 Jews from Africa and over 2000 from each of western Europe and North America.

Christianity

Christianity can be traced back to the same hearth in the Mediterranean as Judaism, and like Islam, Christianity stems from a single founder, in this case, Jesus. Christian teachings hold that Jesus is the son of God, placed on Earth to teach people how to live according to God's plan. Christianity split from Judaism, and it, too, is a monotheistic religion. Jesus of Nazareth was born in Bethlehem, and during his lifetime, he traveled through the eastern Mediterranean region preaching, performing miracles, and gaining followers. Christians celebrate Easter as the day Jesus rose from the dead after being crucified three days prior (Good Friday). According to Christian teaching, the crucifixion of Jesus fulfilled an ancient prophecy and changed the fate of Jesus' followers—giving them eternal life.

The first split in Christianity, between Roman Catholicism and Eastern Orthodox, developed over a number of centuries. At the end of the third century, the Roman Emperor Diocletian attempted to keep the empire together by dividing it for purposes of government. His divisions left a lasting impression. When the Roman Empire fell and broke up, the western region, centered on Rome, fell on hard times. The eastern region, with Constantinople (now Istanbul in Turkey) at its heart,

became the new focus of the Byzantine Empire (Fig. 7.12). Christianity thrived there and radiated into other areas, including the Balkan Peninsula. This split into west and east at the end of the Roman Empire became a cultural fault line over time. It was formally recognized in 1054 CE when the Roman Catholic Church (centered in Rome) and the Eastern Orthodox Christian Church (centered in Constantinople) separated.

The **Eastern Orthodox Church** suffered blows when the Ottoman Turks defeated the Serbs in Kosovo in 1389, when the Turks took Constantinople in 1453, and when the Soviet Union suppressed Eastern Orthodox churches in the twentieth century. Today, the Eastern Orthodox Church remains one of the three major branches of Christianity and is experiencing a revival in former Soviet areas.

The **Roman Catholic Church** claims the most adherents of all Christian denominations (more than 1 billion). Centered in Rome, Catholic theology teaches the infallibility of the pope in interpreting Jesus' teachings and in formulating ways to navigate through the modern world. The power of the Roman Catholic Church peaked in the Middle Ages, when the Church controlled sources of knowledge and worked in conjunction with monarchs to rule much of western Europe.

During the Middle Ages, Roman Catholic authorities often wielded their power in an autocratic manner and distanced themselves from the masses. The widespread diffusion of the Black Death during the 1300s and the deaths that resulted caused many Europeans to question the role of religion in their lives. The Roman Catholic Church itself also experienced divisions within its hierarchy, as evidenced by the Western Schism during the early 1300s, which at one point resulted in three people claiming to be the pope. Reformers to the Church soon followed. During the fifteenth and sixteenth centuries, John Huss, Martin Luther, John Calvin, and others challenged fundamental teachings of Roman Catholicism, leading to the Protestant Reformation and challenging the practices of the Church's leaders. The **Protestant** sects of Christianity compose the third major branch of Christianity. Like Buddhism's challenge to Hinduism, the Protestant Reformation affected Roman Catholicism, which answered some of the challenges to its theology in the Counter-Reformation. Some countries in Europe such as Switzerland (Fig. 7.13) are still divided into Catholic and Protestant regions.

Christianity is the largest and globally the most widely dispersed religion. Christian churches claim more than 1.5 billion adherents, including some 430 million in Europe and the former Soviet Union; approximately 355 million in North and Middle America; approximately 310 million in South America; perhaps 240 million in Africa; and an estimated 165 million in Asia. Christians

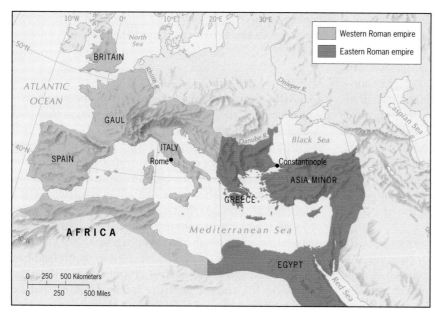

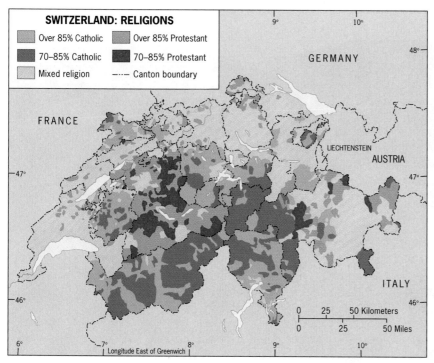Figure 7.12
Figure 7.12
The Roman Empire, divided into west and east.   This map reflects the split in the empire, with the western empire focusing on Rome and the eastern empire focusing on Constantinople.   © H. J. de Blij, A. B. Murphy, and E. H. Fouberg, and John Wiley & Sons, Inc.

thus account for nearly 40 percent of the members of the world's major religions. Roman Catholicism, as noted earlier, is the largest segment of Christianity. Figure 7.6 reveals the strength of Roman Catholicism in party of Europe and North America, and throughout much of Middle and South America. Among religious adherents in significant parts of North America, Australia, New Zealand, and South Africa, Protestant churches prevail. Eastern Orthodox churches have as many as 180 million

followers in Europe, Russia and its neighboring states, Africa (where a major cluster exists in Ethiopia), and North America.

Diffusion of Christianity

The dissemination of Christianity occurred as a result of expansion combined with relocation diffusion. In western Europe, Christianity declined during the centuries

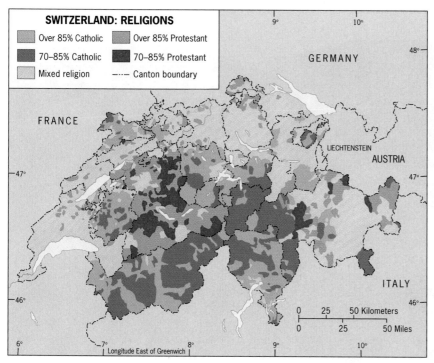

Figure 7.13
Religions in Switzerland. These data show the concentration of religions by canton and commune in Switzerland. Two cantons, Neuchatel and Geneva, separated religion from the commune government; thus, religion is no longer taught in the public schools in these two cantons. In Switzerland's other 24 cantons, religious matters (including taxes of individuals and businesses to support churches) are handled by the canton governments. *Adapted with permission from:* Bundesamt fur Statistik, Office federal de la statistique, Switzerland, 2005.

immediately after the fall of the Roman Empire. Then a form of contagious diffusion took place as the religious ideas that had been kept alive in remote places such as coastal Ireland and Scotland spread throughout western Europe. In the case of the Eastern Orthodox faith, contagious diffusion took place from the religion's hearth in Constantinople to the north and northeast. Protestantism began in several parts of western Europe and expanded to some degree through contagious diffusion. Much of its spread in northern and central Europe, however, was through hierarchical diffusion, as political leaders would convert—sometimes to escape control from Rome—and then the population would gradually accept the new state religion.

The worldwide diffusion of Christianity occurred during the era of European colonialism beginning in the sixteenth century. Spain invaded and colonized Middle and South America, bringing the Catholic faith to those areas. Protestant refugees, tired of conflict and oppression in Europe, came to North America in large numbers. Through the efforts of missionaries, Catholicism found adherents in Congo, Angola, Mozambique, and the Philippines. The Christian faith today has over 33,000 denominations. Hundreds of these denominations engage in proselytizing (purposeful spreading of religious teachings) around the world, creating an incredibly complex geographical distribution of Christians within the spaces of the world map that are shaded in "Christian" (Fig. 7.6).

The Christian faith has always been characterized by aggressive and persistent proselytism, and Christian missionaries created an almost worldwide network of

conversion during the colonial period that endures and continues to expand today (Fig. 7.14).

Islam

Like Christianity, **Islam**, the youngest of the major religions, can be traced back to a single founder, in this case, Muhammad, who was born in Mecca in 571 CE. According to Muslim belief, Muhammad received the truth directly from Allah in a series of revelations that began when the Prophet was about 42 years old. During these revelations, Muhammad spoke the verses of the Qu'ran (Koran), the Muslims' holy book. Muhammad admired the monotheism of Judaism and Christianity; he believed Allah had already revealed himself through other prophets including Judaism's Abraham and Christianity's Jesus. However, Muhammad came to be viewed as the one true prophet among Muslims.

After his visions, Muhammad had doubts that he could have been chosen to be a prophet but was convinced by further revelations. He subsequently devoted his life to the fulfillment of the divine commands. In those days the eastern Mediterranean and the Arabian Peninsula were in religious and social disarray, with Christianity and Judaism coexisting with polytheistic religions. Muhammad's opponents began to combat his efforts. The Prophet was forced to flee Mecca, where he had been raised, for Medina, and he continued his work from this new base.

In many ways, the precepts of Islam revised Judaic and Christian beliefs and traditions. The central precept is that there is but one god, who occasionally reveals himself through the prophets, such as Abraham, Jesus, and Muhammad. Another key precept is that Earthly matters

Figure 7.14
La Chinantla, Mexico. Catholic missionaries (of the Marianist order) interact with people in the Uxpanapa Valley in Mexico. © Randall Hyman, Photographer.

are profane; only Allah is pure. Allah's will is absolute; he is omnipotent and omniscient. Muslims believe that all humans live in a world that was created for their use but only until the final judgment day.

Adherents to Islam are required to observe the "five pillars" of Islam (repeated expressions of the basic creed, frequent prayer, a month of daytime fasting, almsgiving, and, if possible, at least one pilgrimage to Mecca in one's lifetime). The faith dictates behavior in other spheres of life as well. Islam forbids alcohol, smoking, and gambling. In Islamic settlements, the people build mosques to observe the Friday prayer and to serve as social gathering places (Fig. 7.15).

Islam, like all other major religions, is divided—principally between **Sunni** Muslims (the great majority) and the **Shi'ite** or *Shiah* Muslims (concentrated in Iran). Smaller sects of Islam include Wahhabis, Sufis, Salafists, Alawites, Alevis, and Yazeedis. The religion's main division between Sunni and Shi'ite occurred almost immediately after Muhammad's death, and it was caused by a

conflict over his succession. Muhammad died in 632 CE, and to some, the rightful heir to the Prophet's caliphate (area of influence) was Muhammad's son-in-law, Ali. Others preferred different candidates who were not necessarily related to Muhammad. The ensuing conflict was marked by murder, warfare, and lasting doctrinal disagreements. The Sunni Muslims eventually prevailed, but the Shi'ite Muslims, the followers of Ali, survived in some areas. Then, early in the sixteenth century, an Iranian (Persian) ruling dynasty made Shi'ite Islam the only legitimate faith of that empire—which extended into what is now southern Azerbaijan, southeastern Iraq, and western Afghanistan and Pakistan. This gave the Shi'ite branch unprecedented strength and created the foundations of its modern-day culture region centered on the state of Iran.

Sunni Muslims believe in the effectiveness of family and community in solving life's problems; Shi'ites believe that the imam is the sole source of true knowledge. *Imams* are Shi'ite Muslim leaders whose appointments they regard as sanctioned by Allah. Shi'ites believe imams are without sin and infallible, making imams a potent social as well as political force. Shi'ite Islam has influenced Sunni Islam in several ways. The veneration of Ali has diffused throughout Sunni Islam and is reflected in the respect all Muslims show to Ali's descendants, the *sayyids* of East Africa and the *sharifs* of North Africa.

Diffusion of Islam

At the time of Muhammad's death in 632 CE, Muhammad and his followers had converted kings on the Arabian Peninsula to Islam. The kings then used their armies to spread the faith across the Arabian Peninsula through invasion and conquest. Moving west, in waves of invasion and conquest, Islam diffused throughout North Africa. By the early ninth century, the Muslim world included emirates extending from Egypt to Morocco, a caliphate occupying most of Spain and Portugal, and a unified realm encompassing Arabia, the Middle East, Iran, and most of what is today Pakistan. Ultimately, the Arab empire extended from Morocco to India and from Turkey to Ethiopia. Through trade, Muslims later spread their faith across the Indian Ocean into Southeast Asia (Fig. 7.16). As Muslim traders settled trading ports in Southeast Asia, they established new secondary hearths of Islam and worked to diffuse the religion contagiously from the secondary hearths. Recent diffusion of Islam into Europe (beyond Spain and Portugal), South Africa, and the Americas has largely been a result of migration—of relocation diffusion.

Today, Islam, with more than 1.3 billion followers, ranks second to Christianity in global number of adherents. Islam is the fastest growing of the world's major religions, dominating in Northern Africa and Southwest Asia, extending into Central Asia, the former Soviet Union and

Figure 7.15
Kota Kinabalu, Malaysia. The soaring minaret of the Sabah State Mosque creates a strong Muslim imprint on the cultural landscape of the city. © H. J. de Blij.

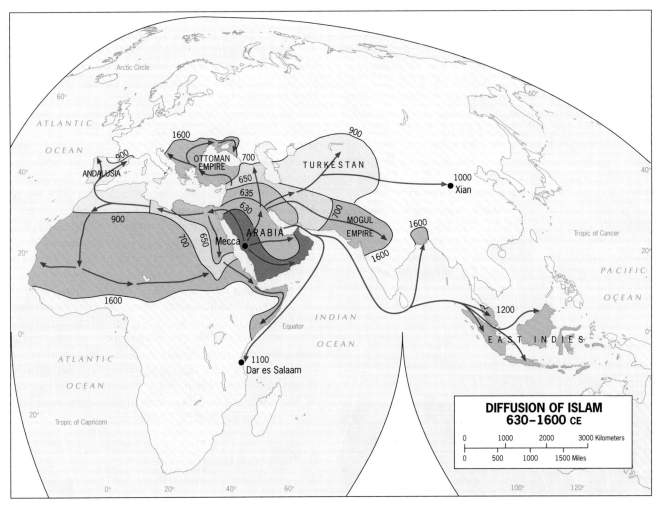

Figure 7.16

Diffusion of Islam. This map shows the diffusion of Islam from 600 CE to 1600 CE   © H. J. de Blij,
P. O. Muller, and John Wiley & Sons, Inc.

China, and including clusters in Indonesia, Bangladesh, and southern Mindanao in the Philippines. Islam is strongly represented in India, with over 150 million adherents, and in Subsaharan Africa, with approximately 190 million adherents. Islam has followers in Bosnia and Albania and has substantial numbers of adherents in the United States and western Europe (Fig. 7.17). The largest Muslim country is actually outside of the Middle East, in Southeast Asia. Indonesia has nearly 200 million adherents. In fact, of Islam's 1.3 billion followers, more than half live outside Southwest Asia and North Africa. And not everyone in Southwest Asia and North Africa is Muslim. The region is home to millions of Christians, Jews, and other smaller religious sects.

Indigenous and Shamanist

Finally, Figure 7.6 identifies large areas in Africa and several other parts of the world as "Indigenous and Shamanist." **Indigenous religions** are local in scope, usually have a rev-

erence for nature, and are passed down through family units and groups (tribes) of indigenous peoples. No central tenet or belief can be ascribed to all indigenous religions. We do not group indigenous religions because they share a common theology or belief system. Instead, we group indigenous religions because they share the same pressures from the diffusion of global religions- and they have survived (Fig. 7.18).

Shamanism is a community faith in which people follow their shaman—a religious leader, teacher, healer, and visionary. Shamans have appeared at various times to various peoples in Africa, Native America, Southeast Asia, and East Asia. These appearances had similar effects on the cultures of widely scattered peoples. Perhaps if these shamanist religions had developed elaborate bureaucracies and sent representatives to international congresses, they would have become more similar and might have evolved into another world religion. Unlike Christianity or Islam, the shamanist faiths are small and comparatively isolated.

Shamanism is a traditional religion, an intimate part of a local culture and society, but not all traditional

Figure 7.17
Paris, France. This large mosque in Paris attests to the significance of Islamic migration to France over the past several decades. Global religions are not found in neat geographical spaces; they are now found side-by-side all over the world.   © Alexander B. Murphy.

religions are shamanist. Many traditional African religions involve beliefs in a god as creator and provider, in divinities both superhuman and human, in spirits, and in a life hereafter. Christianity and Islam have converted some followers of traditional religions, but as the map indicates, they have failed to convert most African peoples, except in limited areas. Figure 7.6 shows where the adherents to traditional religions remain in the majority.

The Rise of Secularism

The world map of religion might mislead us into assuming that all or even most of the people in areas portrayed as Christian or Buddhist do in fact adhere to these faiths. This is not the case. Even the most careful analysis of worldwide church and religious membership produces a total of about 4 billion adherents—in a population of over 6 billion. Hundreds of millions of peoples are not counted in this figure because they practice traditional religions. But even when they are taken into account, additional hundreds of millions do not practice a religion at all. Moreover, even church membership figures do not accurately reflect the number of *active members* of a church. When polled about their church-going activities, fewer than 3 percent of the people in Scandinavia reported frequent attendance, and in France and Great Britain, less than 10 percent reported attending church at least once a month. The lack of members-active or otherwise underscore the rise of **secularism**, indifference to or rejection of organized religious affiliations and ideas.

Figure 7.18
Indigenous Religions.   Adapted from: *The Atlas of Religion*, Joanne O'Brien and Martin Palmer. University of California Press, 2007.

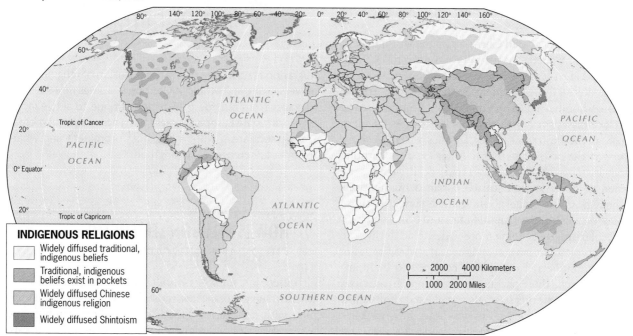

INDIGENOUS RELIGIONS
- Widely diffused traditional, indigenous beliefs
- Traditional, indigenous beliefs exist in pockets
- Widely diffused Chinese indigenous religion
- Widely diffused Shintoism

The level of secularism throughout much of the Christian and Buddhist worlds varies from country to country and regionally within countries. In North America, for instance, a poll in 2002 asked whether people felt religion was very important to them. Only 30 percent of Canadians agreed with this statement, whereas 59 percent of Americans felt religion was very important to them. In France, the government recently banned the wearing of overt religious symbols in public schools. The French government wanted to remove the "disruption" of Muslim girls wearing hijab (head scarves), Jewish boys wearing yarmulke (skullcaps), and Christian students wearing large crosses to school. The French government took the position that banning all religious symbols was the only egalitarian approach.

Looking at polls that ask about the importance of religion for people in a country does not give us the complete picture, however. Canada's 30 percent rate would be much, much lower if we removed recent or second-generation immigrants from the tally. Immigrants often hold onto their religion more fervently to help them ease into a new place and to link into a community in their new home. Buddhists and Hindus on Canada's west coast and Muslims in the eastern part of Canada have a higher rate of adherence to their religion than many long-term residents of the country.

In some countries, antireligious ideologies are contributing to the decline of organized religion. Church membership in the former Soviet Union, which dropped drastically during the twentieth century under communist rule, rebounded, after the collapse of the Soviet system but to much lower numbers. Maoist China's drive against Confucianism was, in part, an antireligious effort, and China continues to suppress some organized religious practices, as reports of religious persecution continue to emanate from China.

In many areas labeled Christian on the world map of religions, from Canada to Australia and from the United States to western Europe, the decline of organized religion as a cultural force is evident. In the strongly Catholic regions of Southern Europe and Latin America, many people are dissatisfied with the papal teachings on birth control, as the desire for larger families wanes in these regions of the world. In Latin America, the Catholic Church is being challenged by rapid social change, the diffusion of other Evangelical Christian denominations into the region, and sexual abuse scandals similar to those that have occured in the United States and Canada.

Secularism has become more widespread during the past century. People have abandoned organized religion in growing numbers. Even if they continue to be members of a church, their participation in church activities has declined. Traditions have also weakened. For example, there was a time when almost all shops and businesses were closed on Sundays, preserving the day for sermons, rest, and introspection. Today, shopping centers are mostly open as usual, and Sunday is increasingly devoted to business and personal affairs, not to church. To witness the rise of secularism among Christians in America first-hand, explore your town, city, or suburb on a Sunday morning: how many people are wearing casual clothes and hanging out at the coffee shop reading newspapers, and how many people are attending church services?

At the same time that secularism is on the rise in the United States, many people who do follow their religion seem to be doing so more fervently. Religious traditions are stronger in some cultural regions of the United States than in others, and Sunday observance continues at a high level, for example, in the Mormon culture area of the United States. Even though Catholic dioceses are closing churches and declaring bankruptcy in some parts of the Northeast, other Catholic dioceses are building new churches and enormous activity halls in other parts of the country. Moreover, Evangelical and other alternative churches are growing rapidly in some parts of the United States and western Europe. Entire industries, such as Christian music and Christian publications, depend on the growing commitment of many Americans and Europeans to their religion.

The division between secularism and fervent adherence is not confined to the Christian world. Secularism is growing in South Korea, where half of the population does not profess adherence to any particular religion. Although major faiths are experiencing an overall decline in adherence, several smaller religions are growing in importance: Baha'i, Cao Dai, Jainism, and the Spiritual Church of Brazil.

Migration plays a large role in the diffusion of religions, both universalizing and ethnic. As Europe becomes more secular, migrants from outside of Europe continue to settle in the region. Imagine Europe 30 years from now. Predict where in Europe secularism will be the most prominent and where religious adherence will strengthen.

HOW IS RELIGION SEEN IN THE CULTURAL LANDSCAPE?

Religion marks cultural landscapes with houses of worship such as churches, mosques, synagogues, and temples; with cemeteries dotted with religious symbols and icons; with stores designated to sales of religious goods;

Guest Field Note

Ardmore, Ireland

At St. Declan's Holy Well in Ireland, I found a barbed wire fence substituting for the more traditional thorn tree as a place to hang scraps of clothing as offerings. This tradition, which died out long ago in most parts of Continental Europe, was one of many aspects of Irish pilgrimage that led me to speculate on "Galway-to-the-Ganges" survival of very old religious customs on the extreme margins of an ancient Indo-European culture realm. My subsequent fieldwork focused on contemporary European pilgrimage, but my curiosity about the geographical extent of certain ancient pilgrimage themes lingered. While traveling in Asia, I found many similarities among sacred sites across religions. Each religion has formation stories, explanations of how particular sites, whether Buddhist monasteries or Irish wells, were recognized as sacred. Many of these stories have similar elements. And, in 1998, I traveled across Russia from the remote Kamchatka Peninsula to St. Petersburg. Imagine my surprise to find the tradition of hanging rag offerings on trees alive and well all the way across the Russian Far East and Siberia, at least as far as Olkon Island in Lake Baikal.

Figure 7.19

Credit: Mary Lee Nolan, Oregon State University

---

and even with services provided to religious adherents who travel to sacred sites. When adherents voluntarily travel to a religious site to pay respects or participate in a ritual at the site, the act of travel is called a **pilgrimage**. Geographers who study religion are interested in the act of pilgrimage and its impacts on place, people, religion, culture, and environment.

Sacred sites are places or spaces people infuse with religious meaning. Members of a religious group may define a space or place as sacred out of either reverence or fear. If a sacred site is held with reverence, adherents may be encouraged to make a pilgrimage to the sacred site for rejuvenation, reflection, healing, or fulfillment of a religious commitment.

In ancient human history, sacred spaces were typically features in the physical geographic landscape, such as buttes, mountain peaks, or rivers. In more recent history, as universalizing religions diffused across the world, sacred sites were abandoned, usurped, or altered. Geographer Mary Lee Nolan studied Irish sacred sites and observed that many of the remote physical geographic features of the Irish landscape were sacred to the Celtic people (Fig. 7.19). When Roman Catholicism diffused to Ireland, the Catholic Church usurped many of these features,

infusing them with Christian meaning. Nolan described the marriage of Celtic sacred sites and Christian meaning:

The early Celtic Church was a unique institution, more open to syncretism of old and new religious traditions than was the case in many other parts of Europe. Old holy places, often in remote areas, were "baptized" in the new religion or given new meaning through their historical, or more often legendary, association with Celtic saints. Such places were characterized by sacred site features such as heights, insularity, or the presence of holy water sources, trees, or stones.

Nolan contrasted Irish sacred sites with those in continental Europe, where sacred sites were typically built in urban, accessible areas. In continental Europe, Nolan found that the "sacred" (bones of saints or images) was typically brought to a place in order to infuse the place with meaning.

In many societies, features in the physical geographic landscape remain sacred to religious groups. Access to and use of physical geographic features are constrained by private ownership, environmental concerns, and the act of designating certain sacred spaces as public recreational or tourist areas. Geographer Kari Forbes-Boyte studied Bear

Butte, a site sacred to members of the Lakota and Cheyenne people in the northern Great Plains of the United States and a site that became a state park in the 1960s. Bear Butte is used today by both Lakota and Cheyenne people in religious ceremonies and by tourists who seek access to the recreational site. Nearby Devils Tower, which is a National Monument, experiences the same pull between religious use by American Indians and recreational use by tourists.

Places such as Bear Butte and Devils Tower experience contention when one group sees the sites as sacred and another group does not. In many parts of the world, sacred sites are claimed as holy or significant to adherents of more than one religious faith. In India several sites are considered sacred by Hindus, Buddhists, and Jains. Specifically, Volture Peak in Rajgir in northeastern India is holy to Buddhists because it is the site where Buddha first proclaimed the Heart Sutra, a very important canon of Buddhism. Hindus and Jains also consider the site holy because they consider Buddha to be a god or prophet. Fortunately, this site has created little discord among religious groups. Pilgrims of all faiths peacefully congregate in the place year after year. Other sacred sites are not so fortunate. Some of the most contentious sites are in Jerusalem, a city seen as holy by three major world religions: Judaism, Christianity, and Islam.

Sacred Sites of Jerusalem

The ancient city of Jerusalem is sacred to Jews, Christians, and Muslims. Jews saw Jerusalem as sacred before the birth of Jesus, but most Jews fled from the city and surrounding area during the diaspora. For Jews, Jerusalem remained sacred even though they did not control it, and when the Zionist movement gained strength, Jews set their sights on controlling the sacred city once again. The most important sacred site for Jews is the Western Wall (also called the Wailing Wall), at the edge of the Temple Mount in Jerusalem (Fig. 7.20). The Temple Mount was the site of the two great temples of the Jewish people. Occupying the top of a modest hill where, according to the Torah (the sacred book of Judaism that is also part of the Old Testament of Christianity's sacred book, the Bible), Abraham almost sacrificed his son Isaac. On this hill, Jews built two temples, each of which was destroyed by invaders. The Western Wall is all that remains of the second temple, and Jews gather in the place to remember the story of Abraham and the destruction of the temples and to offer prayers. The name "Wailing Wall" evokes the sounds of mourning over the temple's demise (and the suffering of Jews over time) made by Jewish pilgrims.

For Christians, Jerusalem is sacred both because of the sacrifice Abraham was willing to make of his son at the Temple Mount and because Jesus' crucifixion took place outside of the city's walls. Jesus was then buried near the Cross (Jews only allowed kings to be buried inside the city walls) in a tomb Roman Emperor Constantine marked with a basilica that is now the Church of the Holy Sepulchre (Fig. 7.21). Christians believe that from that tomb Jesus rose from the dead on Easter. For centuries the Roman, and then the

Figure 7.20
Jerusalem, Israel. The Western Wall, which is sacred to Jews, stands right next to the Dome of the Rock, which is sacred to Muslims.
© Alexander B. Murphy.

the sacred land of Jerusalem. Between 1095 and 1199, European political and religious leaders organized a series of Crusades to retake the so-called Holy Land. The first Christian crusaders captured Jerusalem in 1099, ruling the city for almost 100 years. As the first crusaders made their way across what is modern-day Turkey on their way to Jerusalem, they also left a series of conquests in their wake—laying claim to the city of Antioch and a number of other strategically important sites. Some of the crusaders returned to western Europe, but many settled, mingled, and intermarried with the local people. Muslims ultimately retook Jerusalem in 1187, and later Christian crusaders were unable to conquer it again. The Crusades helped cement a commitment by Christians to protect the Church of the Holy Sepulchre. Similarly, the Crusades and then Zionism cemented a commitment by Muslims to protect the Dome of the Rock and by Jews to protect the Western Wall. The commitment by three major religions to protect and control their sacred sites has led to political turmoil that echoes far beyond Jerusalem, as we will see in the next section of this chapter.

Landscapes of Hinduism and Buddhism

Traditional Hinduism is more than a faith; it is a way of life. Pilgrimages follow prescribed routes, and rituals are attended by millions of people. Festivals and feasts are frequent, colorful, and noisy. Hindus believe that the erection of a temple, whether modest or elaborate, bestows merit on the builder and will be rewarded. As a result, the Hindu cultural landscape—urban as well as rural—is dotted with countless shrines, ranging from small village temples to structures so large and elaborate that they are virtually holy cities. The location of shrines is important because Hindus prescribe that such holy places should minimally disrupt the natural landscape. Whenever possible, a Hindu temple is located in a "comfortable" position, for example, under a large, shady tree. Hindus also want their temples to be near water because many gods will not venture far from water and because water has a holy function, *ritual bathing*, in Hinduism (Fig. 7.22). A village temple should face the village from a prominent position, and followers must make offerings frequently. Small offerings of fruit and flowers lie before the sanctuary of the deity honored by the shrine.

The cultural landscape of Hinduism is the cultural landscape of India, its main culture region. As one travels through India, the Hindu faith is a visual as well as an emotional experience. Temples and shrines, holy animals by the tens of millions, distinctively garbed holy men, and the sights and sounds of long processions and rituals all contribute to a unique atmosphere (Fig. 7.23).

Figure 7.21
Jerusalem, Israel. The Church of the Holy Sepulchre is sacred to Christians who believe it is the site where Jesus Christ was crucified. Inside the church, a Christian worshipper lights a candle at Jesus Christ's tomb. © Reuters/Corbis Images.

Byzantine, Empire controlled the city and protected their sacred site.

In the seventh century, Muslim armies took control over the city from the Byzantine Empire. Muslims constructed a mosque called the Dome of the Rock adjacent to the Western Wall to mark the site where Muslims believe Muhammad arrived from Mecca and then ascended into heaven (Fig. 7.20). The site Jews call Temple Mount is called al-Haram al-Sharif (the Noble Sanctuary) by Muslims.

Christians and Muslims fought the Crusades of the Middle Ages over the question of who should control

Figure 7.22
Varanasi, India. Hindus perform morning rituals in the Ganges River at one of Hinduism's most sacred places, the city of Varanasi, known as the city of Lord Shiva.   © Alexander B. Murphy.

Field Note

"In the summer of 2007, the newer, Hi-Tec city area of Hyderabad, India was under construction. Migrant workers built new roads, new apartment houses, and new office buildings throughout the city. Beautiful new homes reflected the new wealth accrued among many in the city's newly wealthy. In front of the new homes, I could see Hinduism in the cultural landscape, as many owners built temples for their favorite Hindu god. In the oldest parts of the city, I visited Golconda Fort, built more than 1500 years ago. On the day I was there, the Hindu women of the city were participating in the Bonalu Festival as an act of honoring Mother Goddess. The women climbed nearly 400 steps to the top of the fort, carrying with them offerings of food. At the top, I was welcomed into the temple. I took off my shoes and took part in a festival that began in the mid-1800s, when the Hindu women began the festival to ward off the anger of the gods, as the city stood under the siege of the bubonic plague."

Figure 7.23
Hyderabad, India.   © Erin H. Fouberg.

When Buddha received enlightenment, he sat under a large tree, the Bodhi (enlightenment) tree at Bodh Gaya in India. The Bodhi tree now growing on the site is believed to be a descendant of the original tree. The Bodhi tree has a thick, banyan-like trunk and a wide canopy of leafy branches. Because of its association with the Buddha, the tree is revered and protected. Buddhists make pilgrimages to Bodh Gaya and other places where Buddha may have taught beneath Bodhi branches. With Buddhism, the Bodhi tree diffused as far as China and Japan, its purposeful planting marking the cultural landscape of numerous villages and towns.

Buddhism's architecture includes some magnificent achievements, especially the famed structures at Borobudur in central Java (Indonesia). Buddhist shrines include *stupas*, bell-shaped structures that protect burial mounds. Buddhists also construct temples that enshrine an image of Buddha in his familiar cross-legged pose, as well as large monasteries that tower over the local landscape. The pagoda is perhaps Buddhism's most familiar structure. Its shape is derived from the relic (often funeral) mounds of old. Every fragment of its construction is a meaningful representation of Buddhist philosophy (Fig. 7.24).

Along with the religious structures such as temples, we can see evidence of religion in the cultural landscapes of the dead. Traditionally, Hindus, and more recently Buddhists, and Shintoists cremate their dead. Thus, wherever a large pocket of Hindus, Buddhists, or Shintoists live, a crematorium will be nearby. The Hindu crematorium in Kenya stands in stark contrast to much of the rest of the cultural landscape and signals the presence of a large Hindu population (Fig. 7.3).

The cultural landscapes of South Asian religions extend into Southeast Asia, where several religions that began in the South Asian hearth (including Hinduism and Buddhism) diffused into Southeast Asia. Later, Islam replaced the South Asian religions in many of these places, and even later Christian missionaries gained adherents in Southeast Asia when Christian governments encouraged the migration of their people and their religion to their colonies in these areas. Today, we can stand in Singapore, study the cultural landscape, and see the influences of Christianity, Buddhism, Hinduism, and Islam.

Field Note

"To reach the capital of Myanmar (Burma) we had to transfer to a ferry and sail up the Rangoon River for several hours. One of Southeast Asia's most spectacular Buddhist shrines is the golden Shwedogon Pagoda in the heart of Yangon. The golden dome (or *chedi*) is one of the finest in Southeast Asia, and its religious importance is striking: eight hairs of the Buddha are preserved here. Vast amounts of gold have gone into the creation and preservation of the Shwedogon Pagoda; local rulers often gave the monks their weight in gold—or more. Today, the pagoda is a cornerstone of Buddhism, drawing millions of faithful to the site. Myanmar's ruling generals have ruined the country's economy and continue to oppress Buddhist leaders who try to convey public grievances to the regime, even blocking international aid following the devastating impact of cyclone Nargis in May 2008. The generals have a powerful ally in the Chinese, who are building bridges and laying pipelines but who exercise little influence over the military junta."

Figure 7.24
Yangon, Myanmar. © H. J. de Blij

Landscapes of Christianity

The cultural landscapes of Christianity's branches reflect the changes the faith has undergone over the centuries. In medieval Europe the cathedral, church, or monastery was the focus of life. Other buildings clustered around the tower, steeple, and spire of the church that could be seen (and whose bells could be heard) for miles in the surrounding countryside (Fig. 7.25). In the square or plaza in front of the church, crowds gathered for ceremonies and festivals, and the church was always present—even if the event was not primarily religious. Good harvests, military victories, public announcements, and much else took place in the shadow of the symbol of religious authority. As a result of mercantilism and colonialism, Europeans exported the ornate architecture of European Christian churches wherever they settled (Fig. 7.26).

Figure 7.26
Singapore. Built beginning in 1834, St. Andrew's Cathedral stands on spacious grounds between Singapore's commercial center and hotel district. The church was built by the Church of England and stands in the midst of a city that is predominantly Chinese with Buddhist, Hindu, and Muslim minorities. © H. J. de Blij.

Figure 7.25
Bordeaux, France. Built beginning in 1472, St. Michael's Tower rises over Bordeaux, France, marking the importance of the Catholic Church in Bordeaux's history and culture. © H. J. de Blij.

The Reformation, the rise of secularism, and the decline of organized religion are reflected in the cultural landscape as well. Many of the ornate churches in the town squares of medieval cities now function as museums instead of serving active congregations. Other churches in secular regions are closing their doors or significantly reducing the number of religious services offered. Yet, not all of Europe's sacred sites have become secularized. Famous cathedrals continue to hold services while tourists peruse the interior of the vast churches. And other sacred sites of Christianity, such as churches for specific saints,

Figure 7.27
Vatican City. Pope John Paul II greeted pilgrims at a general audience in St. Peter's Square. Thousands gathered each week to see the pope and hear him greet visitors in multiple languages. © Erin H. Fouberg.

places where significant events occurred, and Vatican City in Rome, are still major pilgrimage sites in Europe. When in Rome, the leader of the Catholic Church, the pope, holds an outdoor service for pilgrims to Vatican City, attracting thousands of followers to St. Peter's Square each week (Fig. 7.27).

Cities in Europe are also home to centuries-old Christian cemeteries. Traditionally, Christians bury, rather than cremate, their dead, and in cities, the cemeteries are often crowded with tombstones. Outside of European cities and in North America, Christian cemeteries can resemble large parks. These cemeteries often reflect class differences: some graves are marked by simple tombstones, whereas others are elaborate structures. With rising land-use pressures and the associated costs of burial, however, cremation is becoming increasingly common among Christians—particularly in North America and western Europe.

Religious Landscapes in the United States

The United States, a predominantly Christian country, demonstrates considerable diversity in its religious cultural landscapes. In *The Cultural Geography of the United States*, geographer Wilbur Zelinsky constructed a map identifying religious regions in the country. Figure 7.28 presents a modified version of Zelinsky's map. The religious regions on the map are familiar to anyone who has even the most general impression of cultural differences in the United States.

The New England region is strongly Catholic; the South's leading denomination is Baptist; the Upper Midwest has large numbers of Lutherans; and the Southwest is predominantly Spanish Catholic. The broad midland region extending from the Middle Atlantic to the Mormon region (in the Western United States) and has a mixture of denominations in which no single church dominates; this is also true of the West. As Figure 7.28 shows, some regions represent local clustering, such as the French Catholic area centered in New Orleans and the mixed denominations of Peninsular Florida, where a large Spanish Catholic cluster has emerged in metropolitan Miami.

More interesting than the simple regionalization of religions in the United States is the variation in cultural landscapes within regions. In a 2008 study, geographers Barney Warf and Mort Winsberg used data on religious adherents by county in the United States to discern what counties and regions of the country have the most and the least religious diversity. Warf and Winsberg defined religious diversity as having a variety of religions within a small spatial unit, in this case a county. One way the authors mapped religious diversity is presented in Figure 7.29, a map showing counties with the least religious diversity in the darkest colors. In counties with the darkest shading, one religion accounts for 64 percent or more of all religious adherents in the county. In comparing Figure 7.29 to 7.28, we can see that the Mormon region in Utah and southern Idaho, the Southern Baptist region in the South, and the Catholic region of the Northeast are some of the least diverse regions in the country. In these regions, you can expect to see the imprint of one major religion throughout the cultural landscape. By contrast, religious regions characterized by many lightly colored counties have a rich religious mix.

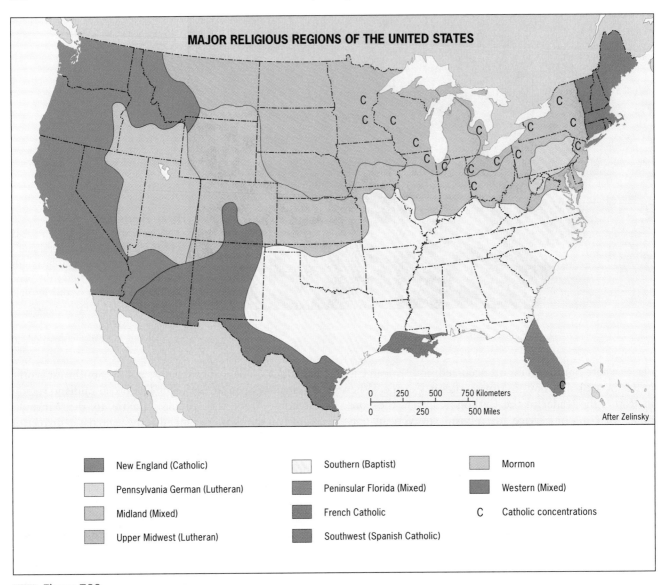

Figure 7.28
Major Religious Regions of the United States. A generalized map of the religious regions of the United States shows concentrations of the major religions. *Adapted with permission from*: W. Zelinsky, *The Cultural Geography of the United States*, revised edition. Englewood Cliffs, NJ: Prentice Hall, 1992, p. 96.

The plain white churches of the South and Lutheran Upper Midwest coincide with the Protestant Church's pragmatic spending of church money—not on art and architecture as the Catholic Church historically did (Fig. 7.30). Conversely, many Catholic churches in the United States, both in the Northeast and in Chicago, as well as in other immigrant-magnet cities, were built by immigrants who lived in ethnic neighborhoods. Immigrants spent their own money and used their own building skills to construct more ornate churches and dozens of cathedrals that tied them back to their country of origin and demonstrated their commitment to their faith (Fig. 7.31).

Landscapes of Islam

Elaborate, sometimes magnificently designed mosques whose balconied minarets rise above the townscape dominate Islamic cities, towns, and villages. Often the mosque is the town's most imposing and most carefully maintained building. Five times every day, from the towering **minarets**, the faithful are called to prayer. The sounds emanating from the minarets fill the streets as the faithful converge on the holy place to pray facing Mecca.

At the height of Islam's expansion into eastern North Africa and southern Europe, Muslim architects incorporated

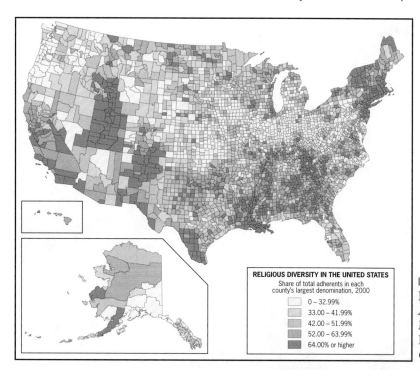

Figure 7.29

Religious Diversity in the United States. *Adapted with permission from*: B. Warf and M. Winsberg, "The Geography of Religious Diversity in the United States," *Professional Geographer*, 2008.

Figure 7.30

Brown County, South Dakota. Scandinavian Lutheran Church was founded by immigrants from northern Europe. The simple architecture of the church is commonly found in Protestant churches in the Great Plains. © Erin H. Fouberg.

Figure 7.31

Zell, South Dakota. St. Mary's Catholic Church was built by nuns in 1875 to serve Catholic immigrants and American Indians. The more ornate architecture and stained glass of St. Mary's Church is commonly found in Catholic churches in the Great Plains. © Erin H. Fouberg.

Figure 7.32
Isfahan, Iran. The dome of this mosque demonstrates the geometric art evident in Muslim architecture.
© Alexander B. Murphy.

earlier Roman models into their designs. The results included some of the world's greatest architectural masterpieces, such as the Alhambra Palace in Granada and the Great Mosque of Cordoba in Spain. Islam's prohibition against depicting the human form led to the wide use of geometric designs and calligraphy—the intricacy of which is truly astounding (Fig. 7.32). During the eleventh century, Muslim builders began glazing the tiles of domes and roofs. To the beautiful arcades and arched courtyards, they added the exquisite beauty of glass-like, perfectly symmetrical cupolas. Muslim architecture represents the unifying concept of Islamic monotheism: the perfection and vastness of the spirit of Allah.

Islam achieved its greatest artistic expression, its most distinctive visible element, in architecture. Even in the smallest town, the community helps build and maintain its mosque. The mosque symbolizes the power of the faith and its role in the community. Its primacy in the cultural landscape confirms the degree to which, in much of the Muslim world, religion and culture are one.

One of the most well-known pilgrimages in the modern world is the Muslim pilgrimage to Mecca, the **hajj**. One of the five pillars of Islam, the hajj requires all Muslims (if financially and physically able) to make the pilgrimage to Mecca at least once during their lifetime. Each year, over 1.3 million Muslims from outside of Saudia Arabia and over 1 million from inside the country make the hajj (Fig. 7.33). The pilgrimage requires the

faithful to follow certain steps of reverence in a certain order and within a certain time frame. As a result, the pilgrims move from Mecca through the steps of the hajj en masse. In 2004, over 250 pilgrims were trampled to death as hordes of people followed the steps of the pilgrimage, and in 1990 over 1400 pilgrims suffered the same fate. The Saudi government now restricts the number of visas granted each year to Muslims from outside of the country. Yet, the number of pilgrims continues to climb, and the services needed for Muslim pilgrims during the hajj and during the rest of the year now employ four times as many people in Saudi Arabia as the oil industry does. The landscape around Mecca reflects the growing number of pilgrims year round, as towers of apartment buildings and hotels encircle the sacred city.

Geographer Surinder Bhardwaj has studied non-hajj pilgrimages in Islam, which include "visits to sacred shrines of holy men, the graves of saints and Imams, and the tombs of martyrs of the faith." Although some sects of Islam see non-hajj pilgrimage as non-Islamic, the *ziarats* (non-hajj pilgrimages) are important to a growing number of Muslims. Bhardwaj points out that the hajj is obligatory but the ziarat is voluntary. He explains that study of the ziarat helps geographers understand the many variations and regional forms of Islam in the world today. For example, Bhardwaj describes how the ziarat in Indonesia (the country with the largest number of

Figure 7.33
Mecca, Saudi Arabia. Pilgrims circle the holy Kaaba in the Grand Mosque in Mecca during the hajj. © AP/Wide World Press.

Muslims) reflects the continued influence of pre-Islamic ways. Especially in the interior of Indonesia, Islam has mixed with Buddhism and Hinduism, both of which stress the importance of pilgrimage. Similar to Ireland, where the Catholic Church usurped Celtic sacred sites, Bhardwaj found that many sites in Indonesia that were sacred under Hinduism and Buddhism *were* usurped by Islam, which changed the object of pilgrimage from non-Muslim to Muslim.

geographically

Choose a pilgrimage site, such as Mecca, Vatican City, or the Western Wall, and describe how the act of pilgrimage (in some cases by millions) alters this place's cultural landscape and environment.

WHAT ROLE DOES RELIGION PLAY IN POLITICAL CONFLICTS?

Religious beliefs and histories can bitterly divide peoples who speak the same language, have the same ethnic background, and make their living in similar ways. Such divisions arise not only between people adhering to different major religions (as with Muslims and Christians in the former Yugoslavia) but also among adherents of the same religion. Some of the most destructive conflicts have pitted Christian against Christian and Muslim against Muslim.

Religious conflicts usually involve more than differences in spiritual practices and beliefs. Religion often functions as a symbol of a wider set of cultural and political differences. The "religious" conflict in Northern Ireland is not just about different views of Christianity, and the conflict between Hindus and Sikhs in India has a strong political as well as religious dimension. Nevertheless, in these and other cases religion serves as the principal symbol around which conflict is organized.

Conflicts along Religious Borders

A comparison between Figure 7.6 and a political map of the world (see Fig. 8.3) reveals that some countries lie entirely within the realms of individual world religions, whereas other countries straddle **interfaith boundaries**, the boundaries between the world's major faiths. Many countries that lie astride interfaith boundaries are subject to potentially divisive cultural forces—particularly when the people see their religious differences as a source of social division within their country. This is the case in several countries in Africa that straddle the Christian-Muslim interfaith boundary (Fig. 7.34). Other countries with major religious disputes straddle **intrafaith boundaries**, the boundaries within a single major faith. Intrafaith boundaries include divisions between

Christian Protestants and Catholics, divisions between Muslim Sunni and Shi'ite, and the like. This is the case in Northern Ireland, where Protestants and Catholics, who both worship in the Christian tradition, have a long history of conflict.

Interfaith and intrafaith boundaries can be peaceful, or they can spur enormously violent political conflict. Israel/Palestine, the Horn of Africa, and the former Yugoslavia provide examples of interfaith conflicts, and Northern Ireland is an example of an intrafaith conflict. In each case, religious difference is not the only factor, but it certainly plays an important symbolic and perceptual role.

Israel and Palestine

Earlier in this chapter, we discussed the history of the conflict over the sacred space of Jerusalem. The region of Israel and Palestine is home to one of the most contentious

Figure 7.34
African Transition Zone. Percent Muslim by State. © H. J. de Blij, P. O. Muller, and John Wiley & Sons, Inc.

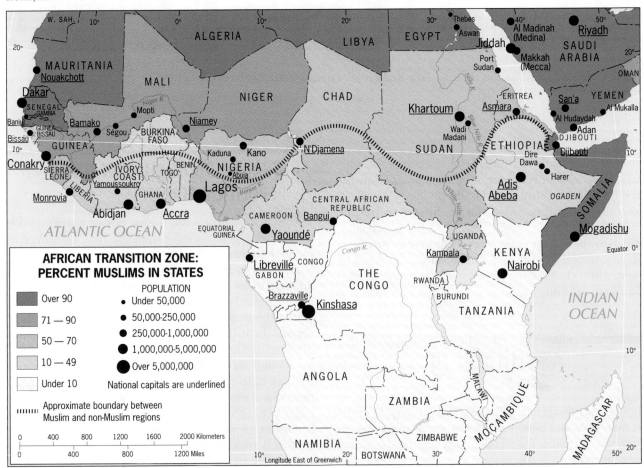

religious conflicts in the world today. In the aftermath of World War I, European colonialism came to a region that had previously been controlled and fought over by the Jews, Romans, Christians, Muslims, and Ottomans. A newly formed League of Nations (a precursor to the United Nations) recognized British control of the land, calling the territorial mandate Palestine. At that point, the vast majority of people living in the land were Muslim Palestinians. The goal of the British government was to meet Zionist goals and to create, in Palestine, a national homeland for the Jewish people (who had already begun to migrate to the area). The British explicitly assured the world that the religious and civil rights of existing non-Jewish peoples in Palestine would be protected. The British policy did not produce a peaceful result, however. Civil disturbances erupted almost immediately, and, by 1947–1948, Jews and Palestinians engaged in open warfare.

In the wake of World War II and the Holocaust, many more Jews moved to the region. Shortly after the war, the British mandate ended, and the newly formed United Nations voted to partition Palestine—creating independent Israeli and Palestinian states. From the drawing of the first map, the partitioning plan was set for failure (see Fig. 3.11). Palestinians and Israelis were to live in noncontiguous states. Surrounding Arab states reacted violently against the new Jewish state. Israel survived through numerous wars in which Palestinians lost their lands, farms, and villages. As a consequence of war and the consolidation of the Israeli state, Palestinians migrated or fled to refugee camps in neighboring Arab states. ANUSES

In the 1967 Arab-Israeli War, Israel gained control of the Palestinian lands in Gaza, the West Bank, and the Golan Heights. The international community calls these lands the Occupied Territories. The Jewish presence in Gaza has always been small. But over the last three decades, the Israelis built Jewish housing settlements throughout the West Bank and have expanded the city of Jerusalem eastward into the West Bank (razing Palestinian houses along the way) to gain more control of territory. The Israeli government severely restricts new building by Palestinians, even on lands in the Palestinian zones of the West Bank. Events in the early and mid-1990s began to change this religious-political mosaic as self-government was awarded to Gaza and to small areas inside the West Bank. Palestinian Arabs were empowered to run their own affairs within these zones. Stability and satisfactory coexistence could lead to further adjustments, some thought—and eventually a full-fledged Palestinian state. In 1995, the parties hammered out a peace accord that would have created a substantial Palestinian state. In 2000, Palestine rejected the peace terms and the Oslo framework, which many saw as the best chance for peace in the region.

In September 2005, the Israeli government shifted its policy toward the Gaza Strip. Israel evacuated the settlements that had been built there, burned down the buildings that remained (Fig. 7.35), and then granted autonomy to Gaza. The Palestinians living in the Gaza Strip rejoiced—visiting the beaches that were previously open only to Israeli settlers and traveling across the border into Egypt to purchase goods. Within days, the border with Israel was closed—making it impossible for many Palestinians to travel to their places of work in Israel. The border with Egypt was closed as well. Although Palestinians now have greater freedom within the Gaza Strip, they are economically isolated and the standard of living has dropped.

The Israeli government tightly controls the flow of Palestinians and goods into and out of the West Bank and Gaza Strip. Gaza is surrounded by fences, and in some places a wall—with land mines in certain areas and dust road to show footprints. Most controversially, however, the Israelis have set about constructing a security fence in the West Bank, which does not follow the 1947 West Bank border but dips into the West Bank to include some of the larger Israeli Settlements on Israel's side of the fence. This may greatly complicate any future territorial settlement, and some Israelis are opposed to it. But many others argue that Palestinians continue to fight a war against the Israelis—with terrorism. Palestinian attacks against Israelis threaten the everyday lives of the Israeli people; no bus, coffee shop, restaurant, or sidewalk is safe from the threat of terrorist attack. Similarly, in the aftermath of a terrorist attack, the Israeli military hunts the suspects, shedding blood in Palestinian neighborhoods.

The situation in Israel and Palestine today does not reflect a simple interfaith boundary. The tiny region has a multitude of interfaith boundaries, especially in the West Bank (Fig. 7.36). The settlements in the West Bank have produced many miles of interfaith boundaries within a small political territory.

The Economist recently summed up the prospects for peace in the region, saying that despite some signs that violence by both sides is abating, "there is not a flicker of hope, in the short run, that even a truce is in the offing." At the same time that Israel withdrew from the Gaza Strip, the government was erecting a new security fence in the West Bank and was building new Israeli housing in the West Bank. In 2005, *The Economist* explained that an Israeli human rights group, B'Tselem, believes the new security fence will "still separate many Palestinians (particularly around Jerusalem) from their farmland and cut deep into the West Bank around the main Israeli settlements—in effect joining them to Israel proper while nearly dividing any future Palestinian state into enclaves."

The conflict over the small territory of the Holy Land is amplified by the sentiment of both Israelis and

Figure 7.35
Erez Crossing, Gaza Strip. The Israeli Army withdrew from the Gaza Strip in 2005, after occupying the territory for 38 years. Israeli troops demolished the Israeli Army liason offices on September 9, 2005, in preparation for completing the Israeli retreat from the Gaza Strip on September 11, 2005. © AP/Wide World Photos.

Palestinians that they have a historic (in the minds of some, even a divine) right to the land; by the violence inflicted on each other by both sides; and by, as Stoddard and Prorok put it, the belief and emotional conviction by both parties that the "territory belongs to them."

The Horn of Africa

The religions in the Horn of Africa include Islam, ancient Christian sects, and Christian sects of European colonizers (Fig. 7.37). Over the last 2000 years, the small coun-

try of Eritrea, on the Red Sea coast, has changed hands a multitude of times. Along with diversity in religion, this region, like the rest of Africa, incorporates a very high level of linguistic diversity.

At the heart of the Horn of Africa lies mountainous Ethiopia, the cultural core area of Amharic (Coptic) Christians. For centuries, the Amharics in the mountains of Ethiopia used their nearly impregnable natural fortress to control the lowlands beyond the borders of what is today Ethiopia. As Islam diffused into North Africa, Muslims converted some people at the base of the mountains, but the Amharic rulers maintained control of most

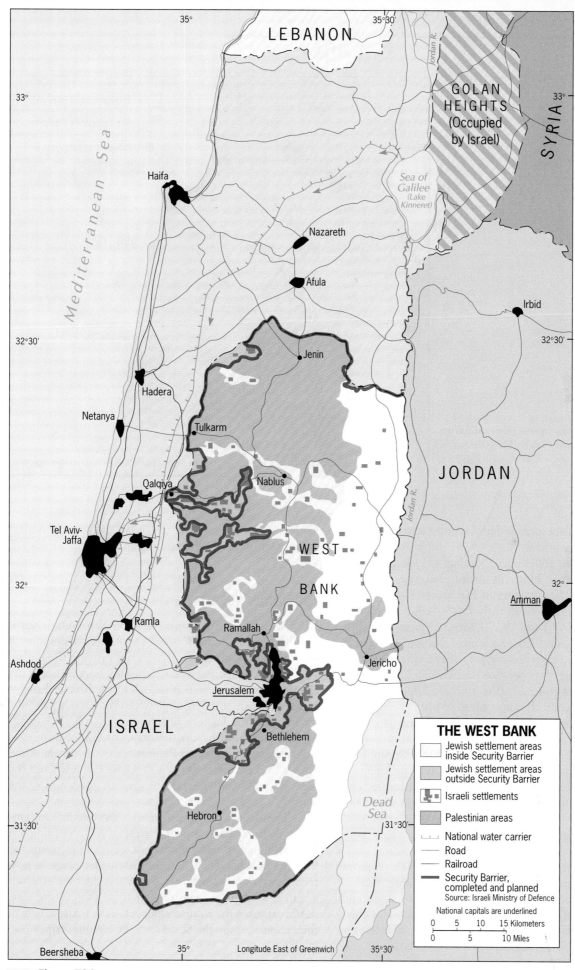

Figure 7.36
The West Bank. *Adapted with permission from*: C. B. Williams and C. T. Elsworth, *The New York Times*, November 17, 1995, p. A6. © The New York Times.

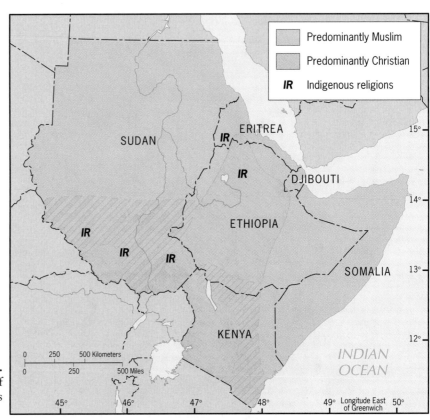

Figure 7.37
Religious Regions in the Horn of Africa.
Data from: United States Department of State, International Report on Religious Freedom, 2004.

of the region. Islam surrounded the Amharics to the north, northeast, and southeast.

During the 1600s, the Ottoman (Muslim) Empire extended into the Horn of Africa, but the Amharics remained. With the coming of European colonialism to Africa, in the late 1800s to early 1900s, Italy took Eritrea as a colony. After World War II, Great Britain controlled the region, and in 1950, the United Nations decided it was best for Eritrea to become part of Ethiopia. The marriage was not one of consent, and the Muslim Eritreans did not easily accept control by the Amharic Ethiopians. The Amharic rulers controlled not only the Muslim Eritreans in the north, but also the Muslim Somalis in the east, together with a huge arc-shaped region of traditional and other sects of Christianity to the west and south. The Amharics continued to control these areas, even after the kingdom of Ethiopia was overthrown by a military dictatorship. The Eritreans' war for independence lasted for 30 years, and finally ended in 1991 with the Eritreans reaching their goal of independence. But the situation has remained tense with border conflicts erupting in the early 2000s.

Eritrea's secession did not end Ethiopia's religious multiculturalism. Ethiopia still contains a large Muslim population of Somalis in its eastern zone; the south and west are non-Muslim; and Amharic Christians still cluster in their highland domain. The separation of Eritrea is likely to be only one step in a series of changes that underscore the difficulties of straddling an interfaith border.

The Former Yugoslavia

No discussion of the impact of interfaith boundaries is complete without the former Yugoslavia. A number of religious and linguistic fault lines run through the Balkan Peninsula. We discussed one of the fault lines earlier in the chapter when we looked at the fall of the Roman Empire and the subsequent division between the Roman Catholic Church and the Eastern Orothodox Church. The dividing line between the two branches of Christianity runs right through the Balkan Peninsula. The Slovenians and Croats in the west of the peninsula are Catholic, and the Serbians and Montenegrans in the east and south of the peninsula are Eastern Orthodox.

The Balkan Peninsula is also a dividing line for language in Europe, with people west of the line using the Roman alphabet and people east of the line using the Cyrillic alphabet. The Serbo-Croatian language is now recognized as two languages, Serbian and Croatian. Even when these languages were recognized as a single language, the Croats used the Roman alphabet in the written form of their language, and the Serbs used the Cyrillic script.

These divisions in religion and language were complicated by the entry of another universalizing religion during the 1300s. The Ottoman Turks, a Muslim empire, brought soldiers to their northwestern military frontier and converted some Serbian communities to Islam. The Ottomans took control of the region by force, beginning with the bloody battle of Kosovo in 1389, which was the Serbian homeland during the European Middle Ages. From that point on, the region has had pockets of Muslims in the middle and south of the peninsula, creating numerous interfaith boundaries. Even by the early 1990s, the clusters of Muslims on the peninsula were quite large, in terms of both territorial extent and population. Muslims had a strong presence in Bosnia and in its capital, Sarajevo, as well as in Kosovo and Macedonia.

Yugoslavia is another example of a country thrown together and left wrestling with significant diversity. The name "Yugoslavia" means land of the South Slavs. The country was formed in the chaotic aftermath of World War I before 1920. When World War II began, many Serbs already resented the Muslim presence in the region, harking back to the time when the Ottomans defeated the Serbs. During World War II, the Croats, who supported the German Nazis, fought the anti-Nazi Serbs. Croats, with the might of the Nazis behind them, sought to rid their territories of Serbs, who lived in Croatia and Bosnia during the war. After 1945, Yugoslavia came under the control of a communist dictator, Josip Broz Tito. For decades, Tito ran Yugoslavia as a centralized country with six republics. During his reign, he stopped nationalist movements in Croatia and among Muslim Albanians in Kosovo. Tito never healed the ethnic divides in Yugoslavia; he simply suppressed them and pushed them out of view during his control. After his death in 1980, Serbian nationalist leader Slobodan Milosevic ruled for the benefit of Serbs until Yugoslavia was swept up in the winds of change produced by the disintegration of the Soviet Union in the late 1980s. Slovenia was the first republic to declare its independence from the rest of the country, followed closely by Croatia and Bosnia.

Serbia, led by Milosevic, tried to force the republics to stay in a Serb-dominated Yugoslavia. The multiethnic republic of Bosnia and Herzegovina was caught in the middle when war broke out between the Croats and Serbs (Fig. 7.38). The Muslims in Bosnia and Herzegovina were soon attacked by both camps. The term **ethnic cleansing** came into use to describe the ouster of Bosnian Muslims and others from their homes and lands—and sometimes their slaughter. Serbs and Croats also sought to "cleanse" each other's territories. In the midst of war, the Croats and Muslims formed a coalition to fight against the Serbs. More than 2.5 million Bosnians were driven from their homes, and hundreds of thousands were injured or killed. Atrocities became so rampant that other countries agreed to form a war crimes tribunal while the war was ongoing.

The international community belatedly became involved, and a partition plan was put in place. New countries joined the United Nations: Slovenia, Croatia, Serbia and Montenegro, Macedonia, and Bosnia and Herzegovina. The plan divided Bosnia and Herzegovina into two republics: one for Croats and Muslims and one for Serbs. The future of Bosnia and Herzegovina is quite uncertain. The central government has little power, and the wounds of war are still raw. The long line dividing the two republics was secured by 60,000 NATO peacekeepers from Europe and the United States, but oversight has now been transferred to a European Union force (Fig. 7.39).

In 2003, the name Yugoslavia disappeared from the maps and was replaced by the name Serbia and Montenegro for the former Yugoslavia. The splintering of the Balkan Peninsula continued in 2006 when Montenegro voted for independence in a referendum. The United States and the European Union recognized Montenegro's statehood, and in the same year, Montenegro joined the United Nations.

A final development of significance began to unfold in the second half of the 1990s, when a group of ethnically Albanian Muslims in Kosovo (an autonomous region in southwestern Serbia) demanded autonomy. The Serbian leadership responded with a campaign of ethnic cleansing against Kosovo Albanians in 1999. They razed whole villages, drove out people in great numbers, and killed many. The international community was once again slow to intervene. This time the North Atlantic Treaty Organization (NATO), led by the United States, initiated a bombing campaign against Serbia that brought hostilities to a halt and paved the way for the introduction of a peacekeeping force. After failed attempts to reach a negotiated agreement on independence, in 2008 the Kosovars unilaterally declared the founding of the new independent state of Kosovo. Many countries, including the United States, recognized the new state, but others—notably Russia, and of course, Serbia—did not.

Northern Ireland

A number of western European countries, as well as Canada and the United States, have large Catholic communities and large Protestant communities, and often these are reflected in the regional distribution of the population. In most places, the split between these two sects of Christianity creates little if any rift today. The most notable exception is Northern Ireland.

Today Northern Ireland and Great Britain (which includes England, Scotland, and Wales) form the United Kingdom of Great Britain and Northern Ireland (the UK). This was not always the case. For centuries, the island of

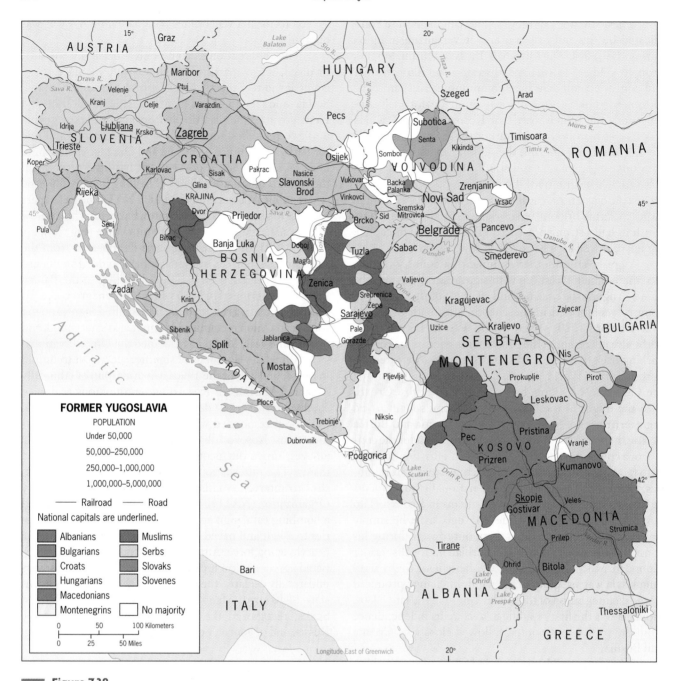

Figure 7.38
The Former Yugoslavia. This map shows the generalized distribution of ethnic groups in Yugoslavia before the war. *Adapted with permission from*: Office of the Geographer of the United States Department of State, Washington, D.C., 1991.

Ireland was its own entity, marked by a mixture of Celtic religious practices and Roman Catholicism. As early as the 1200s, the English began to infiltrate the island of Ireland, taking control of its agricultural economy. Colonization began in the sixteenth century, and by 1700, Britain controlled the entire island. During the 1800s, the Irish colony produced industrial wealth for Britain in the shipyards of the north. Protestants from the island of Great Britain (primarily Scotland) migrated to Ireland during the 1600s and

1700s to control the farms. During the 1700s, Protestants migrated particularly to Northern Ireland to take advantage of the political and economic power granted to them in the colony. During the 1800s, migrants were drawn to northeastern Ireland where industrial jobs and opportunities were greatest. During the colonial period, the British treated the Irish Catholics harshly, taking away their lands, depriving them of their legal right to own property or participate in government, and regarding them as second-class citizens.

Figure 7.39
Bosnia and Herzegovina. The map shows the Muslim-Croat Federation, the Serb Republic, and the Dayton Accord partition line.   © H. J. de Blij, *Power of Place.*

In the late 1800s, Irish Catholics began reinvigorating their Celtic and Irish traditions; this strengthening of their identity fortified their resolve against the British. In the early 1900s, the Catholic Irish rebelled against British colonialism. In 1922, Britain partitioned Ireland to protect the Protestants in the northeast. Twenty-six counties formed the Republic of Ireland, with a vast Irish Catholic majority. And the six counties of the north voted to form Northern Ireland, which became part of the United Kingdom. The six counties that compose Northern Ireland are home to both Catholics and Protestants (Fig. 7.40). The substantial Catholic minority in Northern Ireland felt unprotected as part of the United Kingdom.

The Protestant majority in Northern Ireland, constituting about two-thirds of the total population (about 1.6 million), possessed most of the economic and political advantages. As time went on, economic stagnation for both populations worsened the situation, and the Catholics in particular felt they were being repressed. Charges of discrimination and repression of Catholics were underscored by Irish Republican Army (IRA) terrorist acts, bringing British troops into the area in 1968. Although the Republic of Ireland was sensitive to the plight of Catholics in the North, no official help was extended to those who were engaging in violence.

Catholics and Protestants in Northern Ireland segregated their lives and homes from one another. The cultural landscape marks the religious conflict, as each group clusters in its own neighborhoods and celebrates either impor-

tant Catholic or Protestant dates (see Fig. 6.11). Irish geographer Frederick Boal wrote a seminal work in 1969 on the Northern Irish in one area of Belfast. Boal used fieldwork to mark Catholic and Protestant neighborhoods on a map, and he interviewed over 400 Protestants and Catholics in their homes. Boal used the concept of **activity space** to demonstrate how Protestants and Catholics had each chosen to separate themselves in their rounds of daily activity. Boal found that each group traveled longer distances to shop in grocery stores tagged as their respective religion, walked further to catch a bus in a neighborhood belonging to their own religion, gave their neighborhood different toponyms, read different newspapers, and cheered for different football (soccer) teams.

The ongoing conflict between Protestants and Catholics in Northern Ireland made little sense to either Protestants or Catholics who live outside of this region in peace. Although religion is the tag-line by which we refer to the Troubles in Northern Ireland, the conflict is much more about economics, oppression, access to opportunities, terror, civil rights, and political influence. But religion and religious history are the banners beneath which the opposing sides march, and church and cathedral have become symbols of strife rather than peace.

In the 1990s, Boal updated his study of Northern Ireland and found hope for a resolution. Boal found that religious identities were actually lessening in intensity among the younger generation and among the more educated. In Belfast, the major city in Northern Ireland, Catholics and

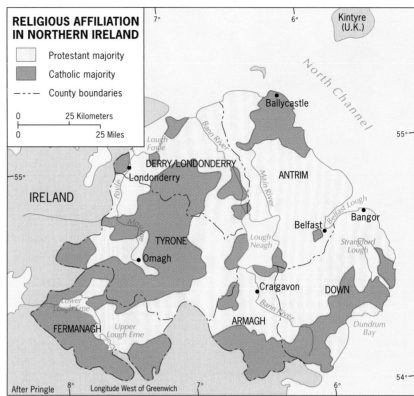

RELIGIOUS AFFILIATION IN NORTHERN IRELAND

Protestant majority
Catholic majority
- - - - County boundaries

0 _____ 25 Kilometers
0 _____ 25 Miles

Figure 7.40
Religious Affiliation in Northern Ireland. Areas of Catholic and Protestant majorities are scattered throughout Northern Ireland. *Adapted with permission from*: D. G. Pringle, *One Island, Two Nations?* Letchworth: Research Studies Press/Wiley, 1985, p. 21.

Protestants are now intermixing in spaces such as downtown clubs, shopping centers, and college campuses.

Boal's observations were right, and a movement toward resolution among the population along with the British government's support for devolution (see Chapter 8) helped fuel the April 1998 adoption of an Anglo-Irish peace agreement known as the Belfast Agreement & Good Friday Agreement, which raised hopes of a new period of peace in Northern Ireland. Following a decade of one step back and two steps back toward peace, Northern Ireland finally realized a tenuous peace in 2007 when the Northern Ireland Assembly (Parliament) was reinstated. Yet the conflict has not gone away. While some of the younger generation may be mixing socially, more "peace walls" (giant barriers between Catholic and Protestant neighborhoods) have been constructed since the signing of the Belfast agreement—raising concerns that segregation may be increasing.

Religious Fundamentalism and Extremism

Today, throughout the world, religious leaders and millions of their followers are seeking to return to the basics of their faith. The drive toward **religious fundamentalism** is often born out of frustration over the perceived breakdown of society's mores and values, lack of religious authority, failure to achieve economic goals, loss of a sense of local control, or a sense of violation of a religion's core territory. Regardless of the religion, a fundamentalist group holds its religious beliefs as nonnegotiable and uncompromising.

People in one society often fear fundamentalism in other societies without recognizing it in their own. In fact, what many call fundamentalism is sometimes better defined as extremism. **Religious extremism** is fundamentalism carried to the point of violence. The attacks on the United States in September 2001 reinforced the tendency of many Americans to equate extremism with Islam. Yet Christian extremism is also a potent force, as witnessed in the United States when religious zealots kill physicians who perform legal abortions. Fundamentalists can be extremists, but by no means are all fundamentalists, whether Christian, Muslim, Jewish, or any other religion, extremists.

Today the forces of globalization affect religions. Education, radio, television, and travel have diffused notions of individual liberties, sexual equality, and freedom of choice—but also consumerism and secularism. In the process, the extent of cultural diffusion and innovation has accelerated. Some churches have managed to change with the times, allowing women to serve as priests and homosexuals to marry, and generally liberalizing their doctrines. Others have gone in the opposite direction, reaffirming fundamental or literalist interpretations of religious texts and trying to block modern influences and external cultural interference.

Christianity

The Roman Catholic Church has long resisted innovations deemed incompatible with the fundamentals of the faith. Among the issues giving rise to disputes are birth control, family planning, and the role of women in the religious bureaucracy. The major religions tend to be male-dominated, and few women have managed to enter the hierarchy. This is true in the Roman Catholic Church, where women are not allowed to serve as priests. The Roman Catholic Church has over 1 billion adherents and has a global diplomatic and political presence, affecting policies in numerous places and on many topics. For example, the Roman Catholic Church preaches against the use of artificial means of birth control as well as abortion. During the September 1994 United Nations Conference on Population and Development, the Roman Catholic Church sought to ally itself with Islamic countries against advocates of population control.

In the United States, certain sects of the Catholic Church continue to hold Mass in Latin and are much more fundamentalist than the rest of the Church. Some of these sects are part of the Catholic Church and continue to operate within the purview of the Church. Others stand apart from the Catholic Church and do not recognize the pope, nor does the Vatican sanction them. For example, actor/director Mel Gibson belongs to the Holy Family Church, which does not recognize the pope, and the Vatican does not recognize that church as part of the Catholic Church. Gibson's church is most associated with the *Traditionalist Catholic Movement*, a fundamentalist

movement that believes the Mass should still be conducted in Latin and that modern popes and clergy are not following the traditional theology and practices of the Church.

In the United States, Christian fundamentalism is also associated with Protestant faiths. Preaching a doctrine of strict adherence to the literal precepts of the Bible, many Protestant Christian fundamentalists believe that the entire character of contemporary society needs to be brought into alignment with biblical principles. Fundamentalist Protestant churches range from tiny churches to enormous warehouse-style churches with thousands of members. Regardless of the size of the congregation, fundamentalist Protestant churches have become increasingly active in political and social arenas—arguing for prayer in public schools, the teaching of creationism in science courses, a strict ban on abortion, and the adoption of laws outlawing gay marriage (Fig. 7.41). In the process, they have gained considerable influence, especially in local politics (school boards and city councils).

Judaism

Like all other major religions, Judaism has fundamentalist sects. The most fundamentalist of the three major sects of Judaism is Orthodox. Yet, the Orthodox sect is divided into several different schools of thought, teachings, and

Figure 7.41

Gay Marriage in the United States.   Data from: BBC, map: Gay marriage across the US. http://news.bbc.co.uk/2/hi/americas/35 16 551.stmlastaccessed: September 2008.

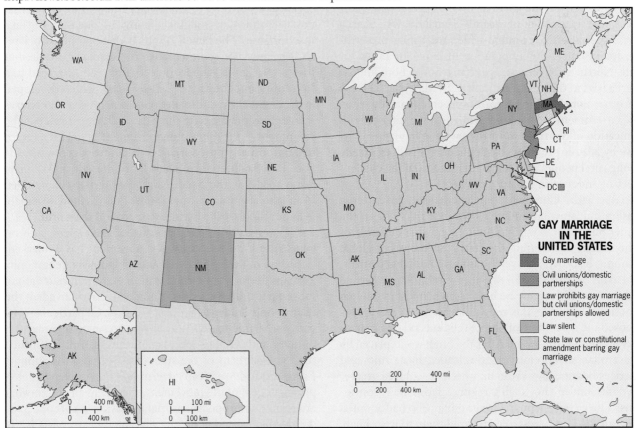

synagogues. Much diversity exists among Orthodox Jews, with varying views on Israel, education, and interaction with non-Orthodox Jews. Fundamentalist Jews who have migrated to Israel tend to vote for more conservative candidates in Israeli elections, affecting election outcomes. Similarly, some fundamentalist Jews who remain in Europe or North America send money to certain politicians in Israel in support of policies such as Israeli settlements on the West Bank.

Judaism also has its extremist element—people whom the majority of Jews denounce and whom the government of Israel has even banned from the country. Among the Jewish extremist groups is the Kach and Kahane Chai—followers of the late American-born, Israeli Rabbi Meir Kahane. Rabbi Kahane espoused anti-Arabism in his teachings, and his followers (Kahane Chai) continue to do so. Members of Kach or Kahane Chai are suspected in several terrorist acts in Isreal.

Islam

Other major faiths must also confront the pressures of change. Not all Muslim communities, for example, adhere precisely to the rules of the Qu'ran prohibiting the use of alcohol. The laws of Islam, which (like some other religions) are very strict when interpreted literally, are not applied with equal force throughout the Muslim world. Such inconsistency, along with concerns over external influence, produces a reaction, not only in the religious bureaucracies but also among many believers.

One sign of the growth of Islamic fundamentalism is the expansion of Islam's **Shari'a laws**. Shari'a laws, especially the criminal code, are harsh, prescribing, for instance, the amputation of hands or limbs for theft. Northern Nigeria and northern Sudan both impose Shari'a laws in their criminal courts. In Malaysia, Chinese and other non-Muslim minorities reacted fearfully when the government considered demands for the general application of Shari'a law. In Indonesia, a fundamentalist drive by Islamic preachers has found fertile soil, especially among rural people who remain remote from the changes affecting Indonesian society elsewhere.

As with Christian fundamentalism, countering Muslim fundamentalism entails political risks. When the former Shah of Iran tried to limit the power of the imams as he sought to integrate the state into the wider global economy, he provoked a religious movement that contributed to his overthrow. (His overthrow in 1979 was also tied to the autocratic regime he headed, which fostered much opposition.) During the revolution in Iran, the imams imposed the most basic of Shi'ite religious rules and practices upon their followers. After the Shah was replaced by an ayatollah, a supreme religious leader, those rules and practices became law. Women, who had acquired greater freedoms under the Shah's regime, faced new restrictions. The government arrested women who had adopted Western modes of dress and required them to wear hijab, veils, and long robes. Many lost positions in commerce and administration, and their political influence declined.

What happened in Iran during the 1970s and 1980s was one of the significant early manifestations of the trend toward fundamentalism. Since then, the government of Iran has used fundamentalism to keep its grip on power. In 2008, the Islamic government of Iran banned all Iranian celebrities (actors and athletes) from appearing in commercials or other advertisements. Prior to September 11, the growth of a different fundamentalist movement, the Taliban in Afghanistan, provided a particularly striking example of how quickly a fundamentalist government can use extremism to change a place. The Taliban regime seized control of much of the country during the 1990s and asserted the strictest fundamentalist regime in the contemporary world. The leadership imposed a wide range of religious restrictions, sought to destroy all statues depicting human forms, required followers of Hinduism to wear identifying markers, and forbade women to appear in public with their head exposed.

The Taliban in Afghanistan also provided a haven for the activities of Islamic extremists who sought to promote an Islamic holy war, or **jihad**, against the West in general and the United States in particular. One of the key figures in the Islamic extremist movement of the past decade, Osama bin Laden, helped finance and mastermind a variety of terrorist activities conducted against the United States, including the destruction of the World Trade Towers, the attack on the Pentagon, and the downing of Flight 93 on September 11, 2001 (Fig. 7.42). Bin Laden and his followers are a product of a revolutionary Islamic movement that now sees the West as a great enemy and one that Muslims must oppose. The beliefs of bin Laden and his associates are certainly not representative of Islam as a whole, but they are religious beliefs. Indeed, they can be traced to a form of Islam, known as *Wahhabi Islam*, which developed in the eighteenth century in opposition to what was seen as sacrilegious practices on the part of Ottoman rulers. The champions of the opposition movement called for a return to a purportedly pure variant of Islam from centuries earlier. The Saudi Arabian state is the hearth of Wahhabi Islam today, as the Saudi Royal family has championed Wahhabi Islam since the 1800s. Saudis fund Wahhabi Islamic schools, called madrasses, around the world.

A variety of forces have fueled the violent path on which the Wahhabi extremist movement has embarked, but some of these forces are unambiguously geographic. Perhaps the most important is the widely held view among movement followers that "infidels" have invaded the Islamic holy land over the past 80 years. Of particular concern to Islamic extremists are the presence of American military and business interests in the Arabian Peninsula, the establishment of the state of Israel, and the support European and American governments have given Israel. A principal goal of the movement is to bring an end to what are seen as improper territorial incursions. A second geographically related concern of Wahhabi extremists is the

Figure 7.42
New York, New York. On September 11, 2001, with the north tower of the World Trade Center already burning, hijacked United Airlines flight 175 flew toward the south tower of the World Trade Center. © CNN via Getty Images News and Sport Services.

diffusion of modern culture and technology and its impact on traditional lifestyles and spiritual practices. Ridding the Islamic world of such influences is also a major goal.

Islamic fundamentalists who have resorted to violence in pursuit of their cause (thereby becoming extremists) are relatively small in number. Yet one of the critical contemporary issues is the extent to which they can or will attract widespread support throughout the Islamic world. The potential for such support is greatest among those who feel that they are the losers in the contemporary global economic order and who feel their cultures are fundamentally threatened. By extension, a key to avoiding the division of the world into mutually antagonistic religious realms is to promote an atmosphere in which such feelings do not become widespread. This, in turn, suggests the importance of non-Islamic cultures conveying an understanding of the gap between mainstream and fundamentalist Islam, and supporting the economic and political efforts of genuinely democratic forces in Islamic countries.

Boal's studies in Northern Ireland demonstrate that solving a religious conflict is typically not about theology; it is about identity. You are assigned the potentially Nobel Prize–winning task of "solving" the conflict either in Northern Ireland or in Israel and Palestine. Using Boal's example, determine how you can alter activity spaces and change identities to create the conditions for long-lasting peace in this conflict zone.

Summary

Religion is a major force in shaping and changing culture. The major world religions today all stem from an area of Eurasia stretching from the eastern Mediterranean to China. Major world religions are distributed regionally, with Hinduism in India; Buddhism, Taoism, Shintoism, and Chinese philosophies in East and Southeast Asia; Islam reaching across North Africa, through the Middle East and into Southeast Asia; Shamanist religions mainly in Subsaharan Africa; and Christianity in Europe, Western

Asia, the Americas, Australia, and New Zealand. Judaism, another major world religion, is not as concentrated. Today, Judaism has a base in Israel and has adherents scattered throughout Europe and the Americas.

As the September 11, 2001, attacks on New York City and Washington, D.C., made clear, religious beliefs can drive people to extremist behaviors. On a day-to-day basis, however, religion more typically drives cultures—shaping how people behave, how people perceive the behaviors of others, and how people across place, scale, and time interact with each other.

Geographic Concepts

religion
secularism
monotheistic religion
polytheistic religion
animistic religion
universalizing religion
ethnic religion
Hinduism
caste system
Buddhism
Shintoism
Taoism
Feng Shui

Confucianism
Judaism
diaspora
Zionism
Christianity
Eastern Orthodox Church
Roman Catholic Church
Protestant
Islam
Sunni
Shi'ite
indigenous religions
Shamanism

secularism
pilgrimage
sacred sites
minarets
hajj
interfaith boundaries
intrafaith boundaries
ethnic cleansing
activity space
relgious fundamentalism
religious extremism
shari'a laws
jihad

Learn More Online

About Devils Tower
http://www.nps.gov/deto/place.htm

About Religions of the World
http://www.bbc.co.uk/religion/religions

About the Sacred Sites in Jerusalem
http://news.bbc.co.uk/hi/english/static/in_depth/middle_east/2000/holy_places/default.stm

Watch It Online

Christianity in European History

Choose among several programs. Click on Video on Demand.
http://www.learner.org/resources/series58.html#program_descriptions

The Confucian Tradition

Choose among three programs. Click on Video On Demand.
http://www.learner.org/resources/series144.html#program_descriptions

Sacred Sites in Jerusalem

Choose program 17 "Jerusalem, Capital of Two States." Click Video on Demand.
http://www.learner.org/resources/series180.html#program_descriptions

CHAPTER 8

Political Geography

Field Note   Independence Is Better Than Servitude

I arrived in Ghana just after an assassination attempt on the country's first president, Kwame Nkrumah. As I drove through the capital city of Accra in 1962, I stopped short when I saw a statue of President Nkrumah in the middle of the street. I have seen plenty of statues of leaders in my travels, but this one was unique. Ghanians had dressed their hospital-ridden president in a hospital gown and bandaged his head!

I stopped the car to take a picture (Fig. 8.1), and I read the proclamations on Nkrumah's statue. Written in English, they said, "To me the liberation of Ghana will be meaningless unless it is linked up with the liberation of Africa" and "We prefer self-government with danger to servitude in tranquility."

Ghana, the first black African colony to become independent, gained its independence in 1960. A wave of decolonization swept through Africa in the 1960s (Fig. 8.2)—fueled by the hope that decolonization would bring political and economic independence. But decolonization did not eliminate political and economic problems for Africa. Former colonies became states, reaching political independence under international law; each new country was now sovereign, legally having the ultimate say over what happened within the borders. New political problems arose within the sovereign countries. Each had to deal with a mixture of peoples, cultures, languages, and religions amalgamated during colonialism. Economically, the new countries found themselves fully intertwined in

Figure 8.1
Accra, Ghana. Statue of Kwame Nkrumah, the first president of Ghana. © H. J. de Blij.

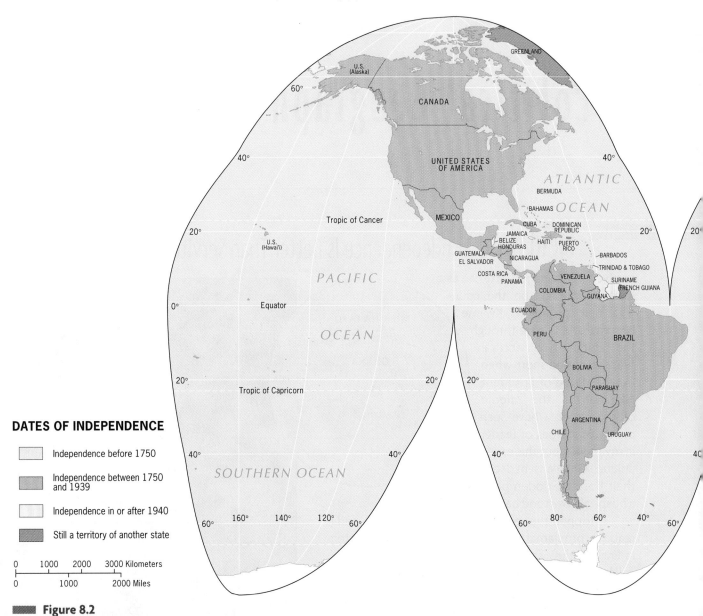

Figure 8.2

Dates of Independence for States, throughout the World.   The first major wave of independence movements between 1750 and 1939 occurred mainly in the Americas. The second major wave of independence movements after 1940 occurred mainly in Africa and Asia. *Data from*: CIA World Factbook, 2008.

the world economy, unable to control fundamental elements of their own economies.

For many of the new African states, Nkrumah's words rang true—independence was better than servitude, even if it meant danger instead of tranquility. Nkrumah, elected in 1960, was overthrown by the military in 1966 and died in exile in 1972.

The story of Ghana and President Nkrumah is a familiar one. After decades of European colonial rule, peoples around the world sought independence; they wanted to have their own country, and they wanted to have a voice in happened in their country. Nkrumah knew the risk was great—danger came with the quick transition and from the inheritance of a political organization that made little sense for Ghana or the people who lived there. European colonialism set the world up as a

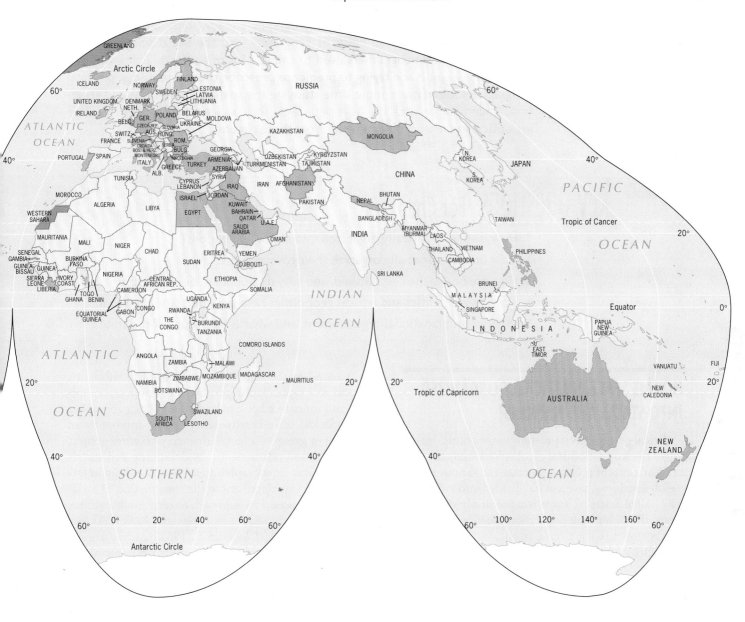

huge functional region for Europe—one where Europe benefited the most economically. Colonialism also brought the European way of politically organizing space to the rest of the world. This system and its lack of fit for most of the world has caused political strife, and yet, peoples still seek to become independent countries because, in Nkrumah's words, they know independence is better than servitude.

Political activity is as basic to human culture as language or religion. Political behavior is expressed by individuals, groups, communities, nations, governments, and supranational organizations. Each desires power and influence to achieve personal and public goals. Whether or not we like politics, each of us is caught up in these processes, with effects ranging from the composition of school boards to the conduct of war.

In this chapter, we examine how geographers study politics, the domain of political geography. Like all fields of geography (and the social sciences, more generally), political geographers used to spend a lot of time explaining why the world is the way it is and trying to predict or prescribe the future. Today, political geographers spend much more time studying the spatial assumptions and structures underlying politics, the ways people organize space, the role territory plays in politics, and what problems result from these circumstances.

Key Questions For Chapter 8

1. How is space politically organized into states and nations?
2. How do states spatially organize their governments?
3. How are boundaries established, and why do boundary disputes occur?
4. How do geopolitics and critical geopolitics help us understand the world?
5. What are supranational organizations, and what is the future of the state?

HOW IS SPACE POLITICALLY ORGANIZED INTO STATES AND NATIONS?

Political geography is the study of the political organization of the world. Political geographers study the spatial manifestations of political processes at various scales. At the global scale, we have a world divided into individual countries called states. A **state** is a politically organized territory with a permanent population, a defined territory, and a government. To be a state, an entity must be recognized as such by other states.

The present-day division of the world political map into states is a product of endless accommodations and adjustments within and between human societies. On the conventional political map, a mosaic of colors is used to represent more than 200 countries and territories, a visualization that accentuates the separation of these countries by boundaries (Fig. 8.3). The political map of the world is the world map most of us learn first. We look at it, memorize it, and name the countries and perhaps each country's capital. It hangs in the front of our classrooms, is used to organize maps in our textbooks, and becomes so natural-looking to us that *we begin to think it is natural.*

The world map of states is anything but natural. The mosaic of states on the map represents a way of politically organizing space (into states) that is less than 400 years old. Just as people create places, imparting character to space and shaping culture, people make states. States and state boundaries are made, shaped, and refined by people, their actions and their history. Even the idea of dividing the world into territorially defined states is one created and exported by people.

Central to the state is the concept of territoriality. Political geographers study territoriality across scales, cultures, and time. In a book published in 1986, geographer Robert Sack defined **territoriality** as "the attempt by an individual or group to affect, influence, or control people, phenomena, and relationships, by delimiting and asserting control over a geographic area." Sack sees human territoriality as a key ingredient in the construction of social and political spaces. His approach to territoriality differs from the approach social anthropologist Robert Ardrey took in *The Territorial Imperative* (1966). Ardrey argued that human territoriality is analogous to the instinct in animals to control and defend territory. Sack, by contrast, argues that human territoriality takes many different forms, depending on the social and geographical context, and that it should not be compared to an animal instinct. Instead, he calls for a better understanding of the human organization of the planet through a consideration of how and why different territorial strategies are pursued at different times and in different places.

Drawing from Sack's observations, political geographers have studied how people have changed the way territoriality is expressed and how ideas of territoriality vary over space and time. Today, territoriality is tied closely to the concept of **sovereignty**. As Sack explained, territorial behavior implies an expression of control over a territory. In international law, the concept of sovereignty is territorially defined. Sovereignty means having the last say (having control) over a territory—politically and militarily. At the world scale, the states of the world have the last say—legally, at least—over their respective territories. When the international community recognizes an entity as a state, it also recognizes the entity as being sovereign within its borders. Under international law, states are sovereign, and they have the right to defend their **territorial integrity** against incursion from other states. These modern ideas of how state, sovereignty, and territory are intertwined began in mid-seventeenth-century Europe and diffused to the rest of the world.

The Modern State Idea

In the 1600s, Europeans were not the only ones who behaved territorially, organized themselves into distinct political units, or claimed sovereignty. Because territoriality manifests itself in different ways, the idea of the state looked different in different regions of the world 400 or 500 years ago. The role territory played in defining the state and the sovereign varied by region.

In North America, American Indian tribes behaved territorially but not necessarily exclusively. Plains tribes shared hunting grounds with neighboring tribes who were friendly, and they fought over hunting grounds with neighboring tribes who were unfriendly. Territorial boundaries were shifting; they were usually not delineated on the ground. Plains tribes also held territory communally—individual tribal members did not "own" land. In a political sense, territoriality was most expressed by tribes within the Plains. Similarly, in Southeast Asia and in Africa, statelike political entities also existed. In all of these places, and in Europe before the mid-1600s, rulers held sway over a people, but there was no collective agreement among rulers about how territory would be organized or what rulers could do within their respective domains.

The European state idea deserves particular attention because it most influenced the development of the modern state system. We can see traces of this state idea more than two millennia ago near the southeastern shores of the Mediterranean Sea, where distinct kingdoms emerged within discrete territories. Greek philosophy on governance and aspects of Ancient Greece and Rome play parts in the modern state idea. Political geographer Rhys Jones studied state formation in the United Kingdom during the European Middle Ages. He found the first states in Wales were small in size but had the attributes of the modern state. In the late Middle Ages, governments constructed more sizable states in what are now the United Kingdom, France, and Spain. We cannot trace a clear evolution in the European state idea, but we can see aspects of the modern state in many places and at many points in European history.

By the early seventeenth century such states as the Republic of Venice, Brandenburg, the Papal States of central Italy, the Kingdom of Hungary, and several minor German states were part of a complicated patchwork of political entities, many with poorly defined borders. The emerging political state was accompanied by **mercantilism**, which led to the accumulation of wealth through plunder, colonization, and the protection of home industries and foreign markets. Rivalry and competition intensified in Europe as well as abroad. Powerful royal families struggled for dominance in eastern and southern Europe. Instability was the rule, strife occurred frequently, and repressive governments prevailed.

The event in European history that marks the beginning of the modern state is the **Peace of Westphalia**, negotiated in 1648 among the princes of the states making up the Holy Roman Empire, as well as a few neighboring states. The treaties that constituted this peace concluded Europe's most destructive internal struggle over religion (the Thirty Years' War). They contained new language recognizing the rights of rulers within defined, demarcated territories. The language of the treaties laid the foundations for a Europe made up of territorially defined states. They originally applied only to the states that were party to the treaty, but they gave rise to a political-territorial order that spread throughout western and central Europe.

The rise of the Westphalian state system marked a fundamental change in the relationship between people and territory. Whereas in previous eras societies had largely defined their territories, in the Westphalian system territories define societies (the French are the people who live in France). Territory is treated as a fixed element of political identification, and states define exclusive, nonoverlapping territories. State rulers are sovereign over their territories and the people that inhabit them.

Even well after the Peace of Westphalia, absolutist rulers controlled most European states. During the later seventeenth and eighteenth centuries, however, the development of an increasingly wealthy middle class proved to be the undoing of absolutism in parts of western Europe. City-based merchants gained wealth and prestige, while the nobility declined. Money and influence were increasingly concentrated in urban areas, and the traditional measure of affluence—land—became less important. The merchants and businessmen demanded political recognition. In the 1780s, a series of upheavals began that would change the sociopolitical face of the continent—most notably the French Revolution of 1789. The revolution, conducted in the name of the French people, ushered in an era in which the foundations for political authority came to be seen as resting with a state's citizenry, not with a hereditary monarch.

Nations

The popular media and press often use the words *nation*, *state*, and *country* interchangeably. Political geographers use *state* and *country* interchangeably (often preferring state), but the word *nation* is distinct. State is a legal term in international law, and the international political community has some agreement about what this term means. *Nation*,

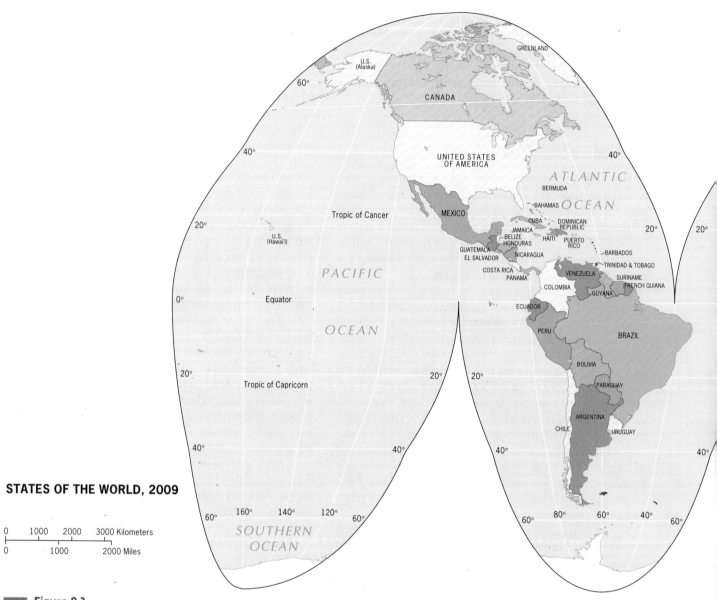

STATES OF THE WORLD, 2009

0   1000   2000   3000 Kilometers
0   1000   2000 Miles

■■■ **Figure 8.3**
States of the World, 2009.   © H. J. de Blij, P. O. Muller, and John Wiley & Sons, Inc.

on the other hand, is a culturally defined term, and few people agree on exactly what it means. Some argue that a nation is simply the people within a state's borders; here, all people who live in Germany would compose the German nation. Yet this approach gives little sense of how politically charged the concept of nation really is.

We define **nation** as a group of people who think of themselves as one based on a sense of shared culture and history, and who seek some degree of political-territorial autonomy. This idea encompasses different kinds of culturally defined nations. Nations variously see themselves as sharing a religion, a language, an ethnicity, or a history. How a nation is defined depends on the people who see themselves as part of the nation. All cultural communities are ultimately mixtures of different peoples. The French

are often considered to be the classic example of a nation, but the most French-feeling person in France today is the product of a melding together of a wide variety of cultural groups over time, including Celts, Ancient Romans, Franks, Goths, and many more. If the majority of inhabitants of modern France belong to the French nation, it is because they claim the French nation as an identity—not because the French nation exists as a primordial group that has always been distinct.

People in a nation tend to look to their past and think, "we have been through much together," and when they look to their future they often think, "whatever happens we will go through it together." A nation is identified by its own membership; therefore, we cannot simply define a nation as the people within a territory. Indeed,

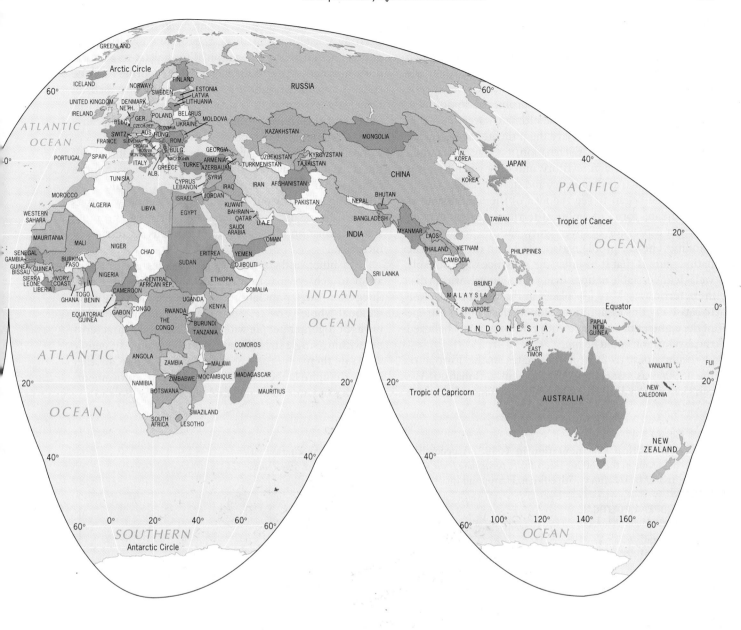

rarely does a nation's extent correspond precisely with a state's borders. For example, in the country of Belgium, two nations—the Flemish and the Walloons—exist within the state borders.

This definition of nation is also workable because it makes room for different views of how nations came to be. Historically, nations were treated as something we were born into, something natural that changes over time. The widely held view was that all people belong to a nation and always have. Recently, scholars have argued that nations are constructed, that people create nations to give themselves an identity at that scale. One of the most widely read scholars on nationalism today, Benedict Anderson, defines the nation as an "imagined community"—imagined because you will never meet all of the people in your nation and

community because, despite that fact, you see yourself as part of a collective.

Nation-State

The European model of the state—the nation-state—became the aspiration of governing elites around the world. Literally, a **nation-state** is a politically organized area in which nation and state occupy the same space. Since few (if any) states are nation-states, the importance of the nation-state concept lies primarily in the idea behind it. States and the governments that run states desire a unified nation within their borders to create stability and to replace other politically charged identities that may challenge the state and the government's control of the state.

The goal of creating nation-states dates to the French Revolution, which sought control by an imagined cultural-historical community of people rather than a monarchy or colonizer. The Revolution initially promoted **democracy**, the idea that the people are the ultimate sovereign—that is, the people, the nation, have the ultimate say over what happens within the state. Each nation, it was argued, should have its own sovereign territory, and only when that was achieved would true democracy and stability exist.

People began to see the idea of the nation-state as the ultimate form of political-territorial organization, the right expression of sovereignty, and the best route to stability. The key problem associated with the idea of the nation-state is that it assumes the presence of reasonably well-defined, stable nations living contiguously within discrete territories. Very few places in the world come close to satisfying this assumption. Nonetheless, in the Europe of the eighteenth and nineteenth centuries, many believed the assumption could be met.

The quest to form nation-states in the Europe of the 1800s was associated with a rise in nationalism. We can view nationalism from two vantage points: that of the people and that of the state. When *people* in a nation have a strong sense of nationalism, they have a loyalty to the nation and a belief in the nation. This loyalty to a nation does not necessarily coincide with the borders of the state. A *state* does not have a strong sense of nationalism; rather, the government of a state is nationalistic. In this sense, the government promotes the nation, and because the government is the representative of the state, it seeks to promote a nation that coincides with the borders of the state. In the name of nationalism, a state with more than one nation in its borders can attempt to build a single national identity out of the divergent people within its borders. In the name of nationalism, a state can promote a war against another state that threatens its territorial integrity.

In nineteenth-century Europe, states used nationalism to achieve a variety of goals. In some cases they integrated their population into an ever more cohesive national whole (France, Spain), and in other cases they brought together people with shared cultural characteristics within a single state (Germany, Italy). Similarly, people who saw themselves as a separate nation within another state or empire launched successful separatist movements and achieved independence (Ireland, Norway, Poland).

▒▒▒ **Figure 8.4**

European Political Fragmentation in 1648. A generalized map of the fragmentation of Western Europe in the 1600s. *Adapted with permission from*: Geoffrey Barraclough, ed. *The Times Concise Atlas of World History*, 5th edition, Hammond Incorporated, 1998.

Guest Field Note

Cluj-Napoca, Romania

To Hungarians, Transylvania is significant because it was an important part of the Hungarian Kingdom for a thousand years. Many of their great leaders were born and buried there, and many of their great churches, colleges, and architectural achievements are located there too. For example, in the city of Cluj-Napoca (Kolozsvár in Hungarian) is St. Michael's Cathedral and next to it is the statue of King Matthias, one of Hungary's greatest kings. Romanians have long lived in the territory too, tracing their roots back to the Roman Empire. To Romanian nationalists, the existence of Roman ruins in Transylvania is proof of their

Figure 8.5

Roman ancestry and their right to govern Transylvania because their ancestors lived in Transylvania before those of the Hungarians. When archaeologists found Roman ruins around St. Michael's Cathedral and King Matthias's statue, they immediately began excavating them, which in turn aggravated the ethnic Hungarians. Traveling in Transylvania made me very aware of how important places are to peoples and how contested they can be.

Credit: George White, Frostburg State University

European state leaders used the tool of nationalism to strengthen the state. The modern map of Europe is still fragmented, but much less so than in the 1600s (Fig. 8.4). In the process of creating nation-states in Europe, states absorbed smaller entities into their borders, resolved conflicts by force as well as by negotiation, and defined borders.

To help people within the borders relate to the dominant national ideal, states provide security, goods, and services to the citizens. States support education, infrastructure, health care, and a military to preserve the state and to create a connection between the people and the state—to build a nation-state. European states even used the colonization of Africa and Asia in the late 1800s and early 1900s as a way to promote nationalism. People could take pride in their state, in their nation, in its vast colonial empire. People could identify themselves with their French, Dutch, or British nation by contrasting themselves with the people in the colonies—people whom they defined as mystical or savage. By identifying against an "other," the state and the people helped identify the traits of their nation—and in so doing, worked to build a nation-state.

Multistate Nations, Multinational States, and Stateless Nations

The sense of belonging to a nation rarely meshes perfectly with state borders. The lack of fit between nation and state creates complications, such as states with more than one nation, nations with more than one state, and nations without a state.

Nearly every state in the world is a **multinational state**, a state with more than one nation inside its borders. The people living in the former state of Yugoslavia never achieved a strong sense of Yugoslav nationhood. Millions of people who were citizens of Yugoslavia never had a Yugoslav nationality—they long identified themselves as Slovenes, Croats, Serbs, or members of other nations or ethnic groups within the state or region. Yugoslavia was a state that always had more than one nation, and eventually the state collapsed.

When a nation stretches across borders and across states, the nation is called a **multistate nation**. Political geographer George White studied the states of Romania and Hungary and their overlapping nations (Fig. 8.5). As he has noted, the territory of Transylvania is currently in the middle of the state of Romania, but it has not always been that way. For two centuries, Hungary's borders stretched far enough east to incorporate Transylvania into the state of Hungary. The Transylvania region today is populated by Romanians and by Hungarians, and both states claim a desire and a right to control the territory. Both states have places within Transylvania that they see as pivotol to the histories of their nations. The desire to control the territory and to stretch the Hungarian state in order to mesh with what Hungarians see as the Hungarian nation requires the movement of state borders. White explains how important territory is to a nation: "The control and maintenance of territory is as crucial as the control and maintenance of a national language, religion, or a particular way of life. Indeed, a language, religion or way of life is difficult to maintain without control over territory." In the case of Romania and Hungary, and in similar states where the identity of the nation is tied to a particular territory, White explains that nations will defend their territories as strongly as they defend their "language, religion, or way of life."

Another complication that arises from the lack of fit between nations and states is that some nations do not have a state; they are **stateless nations**. The Palestinians are an example of a stateless nation. The Palestinian Arabs have gained control over the Gaza Strip and fragments of the Occupied Territories, and these territories may form the foundations of a future state. Well over half of the approximately 8 million Palestinians continue to live in Israel, Jordan, Lebanon, Syria, and other Arab states. The international community does not yet recognize the Palestinian lands as a state.

A much larger stateless nation is that of the over 27 million Kurds who live in an area called Kurdistan that covers parts of six states (Fig. 8.6). In the aftermath of the 1991 Gulf War, the United Nations established a Kurdish Security Zone north of the 36th parallel in Iraq, but subsequent events have dashed any Kurdish hopes that one day this might become a state. The Kurds form the largest minority in Turkey, and the city of Diyarbakir is the unofficial Kurdish capital; however, relations between the 10 million Kurds in Turkey and the Turkish government in Ankara have been volatile. Without the consent of Turkey, establishing a truly independent Kurdish state will be difficult.

European Colonialism and the Diffusion of the Nation-State Model

Europe exported its concepts of state, sovereignty, and the desire for nation-states to much of the rest of the world through two waves of colonialism (Fig. 8.7). In the sixteenth century, Spain and Portugal took advantage of an increasingly well-consolidated internal political order and newfound wealth to expand their influence to increasingly far-flung realms during the first wave of colonialism. Later joined by Britain, France, the Netherlands, and

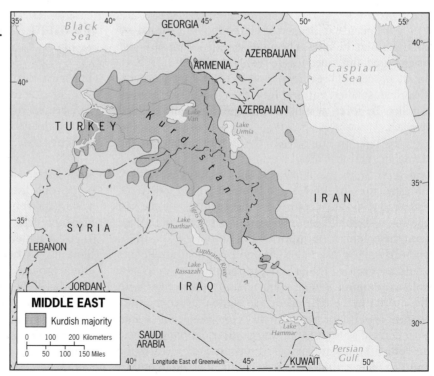

Figure 8.6
Kurdish Region of the Middle East.
© H. J. de Blij, P. O. Muller, and John Wiley & Sons.

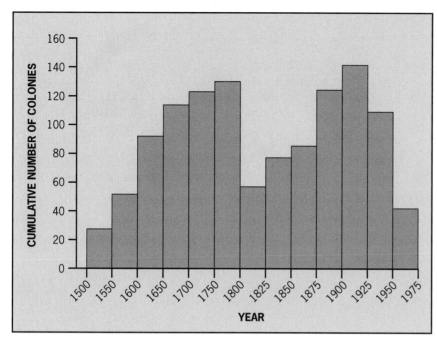

Figure 8.7
Two Waves of Colonialism between 1500 and 1975. Each bar shows the total number of colonies around the world. *Adapted with permission from*: Peter J. Taylor and Colin Flint, *Political Geography: World-Economy, Nation-State and Locality*, 4th ed., New York: Prentice Hall, 2000.

Belgium, the first wave of colonialism established a far-reaching capitalist system. After independence movements in the Americas during the late 1700s and 1800s, a second wave of colonialism began in the late 1800s. The major colonizers were Britain, France, the Netherlands, Belgium, Germany, and Italy. The colonizing parties met for the Berlin Conference in 1884–1885 and arbitrarily laid out the colonial map of Africa. Driven by motives ranging from economic profit to the desire to bring Christianity to the rest of the world, colonialism projected European power and a European approach to organizing political space into the non-European world (Fig. 8.8).

With Europe in control of so much of the world, Europeans laid the ground rules for the emerging international state system, and the modern European concept of the nation-state became the model adopted around the world. Europe also established and defined the ground rules of the capitalist world economy, creating a system of economic interdependence that persists today.

During the heyday of **colonialism**, the imperial powers exercised ruthless control over their domains and organized them for maximum economic exploitation. The capacity to install the infrastructure necessary for such efficient profiteering is itself evidence of the power relationships involved: entire populations were regimented in the service of the colonial ruler. Colonizers organized the flows of raw materials for their own benefit, and we can still see the tangible evidence of that organization (plantations, ports, mines, and railroads) on the cultural landscape.

Despite the end of colonialism, the political organization of space and the global world economy remain. And

while the former colonies are now independent states, their economies are anything but independent. In many cases raw material flows are as great as they were before the colonial era came to an end. For example, today in Gabon, Africa, the railroad goes from the interior forest (which is logged for plywood) to the major port and capital city, Libreville. The second largest city, Port Gentile, is located to the south of Libreville, but the two cities are not connected by road or railroad. Like Libreville, Port Gentile is export-focused, with global oil corporations responsible for building much of the city and its housing, and employing most of its people.

Construction of the Capitalist World Economy

The long-term impacts of colonialism are many and varied. One of the most powerful impacts of colonialism was the construction of a global order characterized by great differences in economic and political power. The European colonial enterprise gave birth to a globalized economic order in which the European states and areas dominated by European migrants emerged as the major centers of economic and political activity. Through colonialism, Europeans extracted wealth from colonies and established the colonized as subservient in the relationship.

Of course, not all Europeans profited equally from colonialism. Enormous poverty persisted within the most powerful European states. Similarly, not all colonizers profited to the same degree. In the late seventeenth century, Spain had a large colonial empire, but the empire

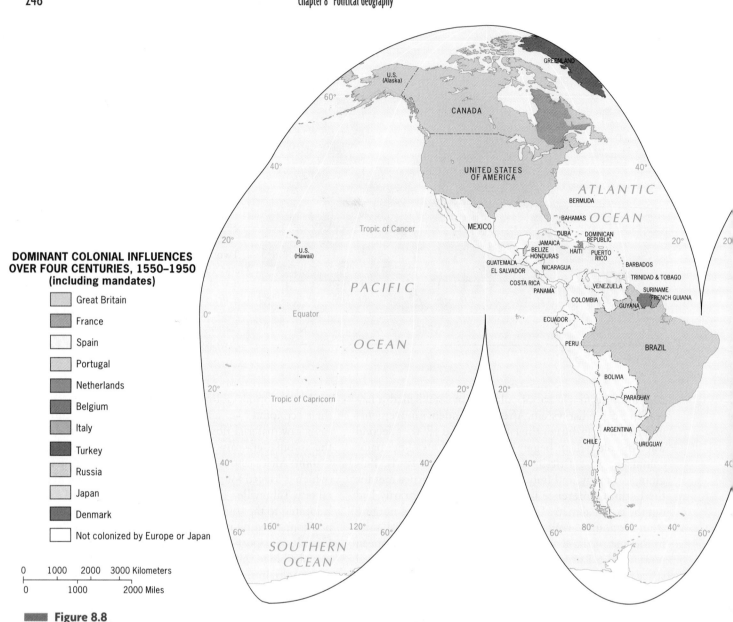

DOMINANT COLONIAL INFLUENCES OVER FOUR CENTURIES, 1550–1950 (including mandates)

- Great Britain
- France
- Spain
- Portugal
- Netherlands
- Belgium
- Italy
- Turkey
- Russia
- Japan
- Denmark
- Not colonized by Europe or Japan

0   1000   2000   3000 Kilometers
0   1000   2000 Miles

Figure 8.8
Dominant Colonial Influences, 1550–1950. The map shows the *dominant* European or Japanese colonial influence in each country over the four centuries.   © H. J. de Blij, John Wiley & Sons.

was economically draining Spain by then. Neither were Europeans the only people to profit from colonialism. During the period of European colonialism (1500–1950), Russia and the United States expanded over land instead of over seas, profiting from the taking of territory and the subjugation of indigenous peoples. Japan was a regional colonial power, controlling Korea and other parts of East and Southeast Asia as well as Pacific Islands through colonization. But the concentration of wealth that colonialism brought to Europe, and to parts of the world dominated by European settlers (such as the United States, Canada, and Australia), is at the heart of the highly uneven global distribution of power that is still with us today.

The forces of colonialism played a key role in knitting together the economies of widely separated areas—giving birth to a global economic order, the world economy. Wealth is unevenly distributed in the world economy, as can be seen in statistics on per capita gross national income (GNI): Haiti's GNI is only $1840, whereas Norway's is $40,420. But to truly understand why wealth is distributed unevenly, we cannot simply study each country, its resources, and its production of goods. Rather, we need to understand where countries fit in the world economy. That is, we need to see the big picture.

Think of a pointillist painting. Specifically, envision the magnificent work of nineteenth-century French

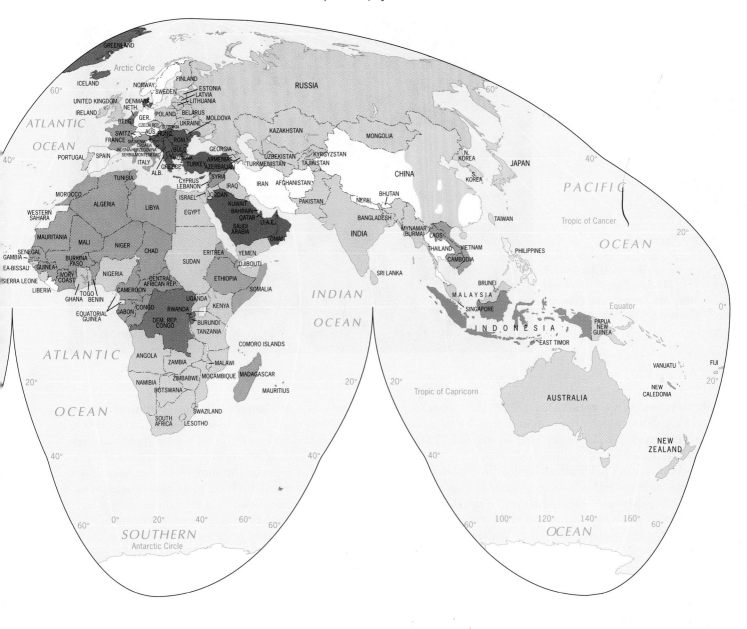

painter Georges Pierre Seurat, *Sunday Afternoon on the Island of La Grande Jatte* (Fig. 8.9). The painting hangs in the Art Institute of Chicago. If you have the opportunity to see the painting and if you stand close enough, you will see Seurat's post-Impressionist method of painting millions of points or dots—single, tiny brush strokes, each a single color. When you step back again, you can gain a sense of how each dot fits into the picture as a whole.[1]

In the last few decades, social scientists have sought to understand how each dot, how each country and each locality, fit into the picture of the world as a whole. To study a single dot or even each dot one at a time, we miss the whole. Even if we study every single dot and add them together, we still miss the whole. We need to step back and see the whole, as well as the individual dots, studying how one affects the other. By now, this should sound familiar—it is one of the ways geographers think about **scale**.

Political geographers took note of one sociologist's theory of the world economy and added much to it. Building on the work of Immanuel Wallerstein, proponents of world-systems theory view the world as much more than

[1] We must give credit to former student Kelsey Lynd, who came up with this metaphor for world-systems theory in a political geography class at the University of Mary Washington in 1999.

Figure 8.9
Chicago, Illinois. Sunday Afternoon on the Island of La Grande Jatte by Georges Pierre Seurat hangs in the Art Institute of Chicago.
© Bridgeman Art Library/SUPERSTOCK.

the sum total of the world's states. Much like a pointillist painting, world-systems theorists hold that to understand any state, we must also understand its spatial and functional relationships within the world economy.

Wallerstein's publications number in the hundreds, and the political and economic geography publications tied to world-systems theory number in the thousands. To simplify the research, we can study the three basic tenets of world-systems theory, as Wallerstein defines them:

1. The world economy has one market and a global division of labor.
2. Although the world has multiple states, almost everything takes place within the context of the world economy.
3. The world economy has a three-tier structure.

According to Wallerstein, the development of a world economy began with capitalist exchange around 1450 and encompassed the globe by 1900. **Capitalism** means that in the world economy, people, corporations, and states produce goods and exchange them on the world market, with the goal of achieving profit. To generate a profit, producers seek the cheapest labor, drawing from the globe. As a result, a corporation can move production of a good from North Carolina to Mexico and then to China, simply to take advantage of cheaper labor. In addition to the world labor supply, producers gain profit

by commodifying whatever they can. **Commodification** is the process of placing a price on a good and then buying, selling, and trading the good. Companies create new products, generate new twists on old products, and create demand for the products through marketing. As children, none of the authors of this book could have imagined buying a bottle of water. Now, we do it all the time.

Second, despite the existence of approximately 200 states, everything takes place within the context of the world economy (and has since 1900). Colonialism set up this system—exporting the politically independent state and also constructing an interdependent global economy. When colonies became independent, gaining the legal status of sovereign states was relatively easy for most colonies; the United Nations Charter even set up a committee to help colonies do so after World War II. But gaining economic independence is simply impossible. The economies of the world are tied together, generating intended and unintended consequences that fundamentally change places.

Lastly, world-systems theorists see the world economy as a three-tiered structure: the core, periphery, and semiperiphery. The core and the periphery are not just places but processes. **Core** processes incorporate higher levels of education, higher salaries, and more technology—core processes generate more wealth in the world economy. **Periphery** processes incorporate lower levels of education, lower salaries, and less technology—peripheral processes generate less wealth in the world economy.

The core and periphery are processes, but these processes happen in places. As a result, some geographers have defined certain places as core and others as periphery in the world economy (Fig. 8.10). Others stress the processes and try to avoid labeling places as core or periphery because processes in places are not static and they are not confined by state borders. From the beginning, Wallerstein defined the **semiperiphery** as places—places where core and periphery processes are both occurring—places that are exploited by the core but in turn exploit the periphery. By taking advantage of its cheap labor or lax environmental standards, the core exploits the periphery. The semiperiphery acts as a buffer between the core and periphery, preventing the polarization of the world into two extremes.

Political geographers, economic geographers, and other academics continue to debate world-systems theory. The major concerns are that it overemphasizes economic factors in political development and that it is very state-centric. Nonetheless, Wallerstein's work has encouraged many to see the world political map as a system of interlinking parts that need to be understood in relation to one another and as a whole. As such, the impact of world-systems theory has been considerable in political geography, and it is increasingly commonplace for geographers to refer to the kinds of core–periphery distinctions suggested by world-systems theory.

World-systems theory helps explain how colonial powers were able to amass great concentrations of wealth. During the first wave of colonialism (which happened during mercantilism), colonizers extracted goods from the Americas and the Caribbean and exploited Africa for slave labor, amassing wealth through sugar, coffee, fruit, and cotton production. During the second wave of colonialism (which happened after the Industrial Revolution), colonizers set their sights on cheap industrial labor, cheap raw materials, and large-scale agricultural plantations.

Not all core countries in the world today were colonial powers, however. Countries such as Switzerland, Singapore, and Australia have significant global clout even though they were never classic colonial powers, and that clout is tied in significant part to their positions in the global economy. These positions were gained through these countries' access to the networks of production, consumption, and exchange in the wealthiest parts of the world and their ability to take advantage of that access.

World-Systems and Political Power

Are economic power and political power one and the same? No, but certainly economic power can bring political power. In the current system, economic power means wealth, and political power means the ability to influence

Figure 8.10
The World Economy. The three-tier structure of the world economy: the core, periphery, and semi-periphery. *Adapted with permission from*: Michael Bradshaw, *World Regional Geography*, McGraw-Hill.

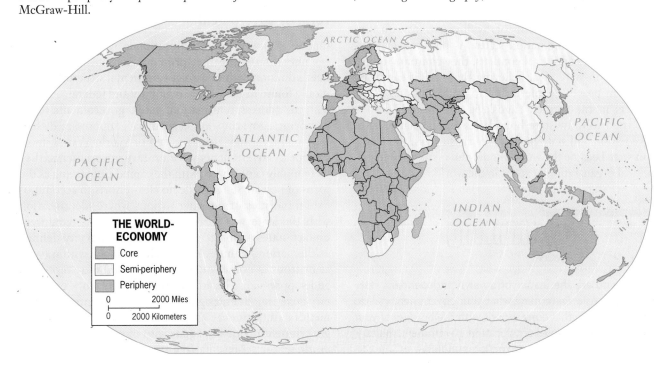

THE WORLD-ECONOMY
Core
Semi-periphery
Periphery
0   2000 Miles
0   2000 Kilometers

others to achieve your goals. Political power is not defined by sovereignty. Each state is sovereign, but not all states have the same **ability** to influence others or achieve their political goals. Having wealth helps leaders amass political power. For instance, a wealthy country can establish a mighty military. But political influence is not simply a function of hard power; it is also diplomatic. Switzerland's declared neutrality, combined with its economic might, aids the country's diplomatic efforts.

World-systems theory helps us understand how Europe politically reorganized the world during colonialism. When colonialism ended in Africa and Asia, the newly independent people continued to follow the European model of political organization. The arbitrarily drawn colonies of Africa from the Berlin Conference became the boundaries of the newly independent states. On the map, former colonies became new states; administrative borders transformed into international boundaries; and, in most cases, colonial administrative towns became capitals. The greatest political challenge facing the states of Africa since independence has been building nation-states out of incredibly divergent (even antagonistic) peoples. The leaders of the newly independent states continually work to build nation-states in the hope of quelling division among the people, securing their territory, and developing their economic (as well as other) systems of organization.

The Enduring Impact of the Nation-State Idea

The idea of meshing the nation and state into a nation-state was not confined to nineteenth-century Europe or twentieth-century Africa. Major players in international relations still see the validity of dividing nations with state borders—of creating nation-states. As players seek solutions to complex political conflicts, they continue to turn to the nation-state idea, believing that only it can bring long-term peace. People trying to find solutions to the conflicts in the former Yugoslavia and Israel/Palestine have tried to draw state boundaries around nations—to make nation and state fit. In all of these ways, the European state became the world model and is still shaping the political organization of space in the world.

Imagine you are the leader of a newly independent state in Africa or Asia. Determine what your government can do to build a nation that corresponds with the borders of your state. Consider the roles of education, government, military, and culture in your exercise in nation-building.

HOW DO STATES SPATIALLY ORGANIZE THEIR GOVERNMENTS?

In the 1950s, a famous political geographer, Richard Hartshorne, described the forces within the state that unify the people as **centripetal** and the forces that divide them as **centrifugal**. Whether a nation (or a state) continues to exist, according to Hartshorne, depends on the balance between centripetal and centrifugal forces. Many political geographers have thought about Hartshorne's theory, and most have concluded that we cannot take a given event or process and declare it as centrifugal or centripetal in isolation from the context in which it is situated. An event, such as a war, can pull the state together for a short time and then divide the state over the long term. Timing, scale, interaction, and perspective factor into unification and division in a state at any given point.

Instead of creating a balance sheet of centripetal and centrifugal forces, governments attempt to unify the state through nation-building, through structuring the government in a way that melds the nations within, through defining and defending boundaries, and through expressing control over all of the territory within those boundaries.

By looking at how different governments have attempted to unify their states, we are reminded how important geography is. Governance does not take place in a vacuum. The uniqueness of place factors in and shapes whether any possible governmental "solution" solves or exacerbates matters.

Form of Government

One way states promote unification is by choosing a governmental structure that promotes nation-building and quells division within. Two governmental structures commonly found in the world are unitary and federal.

To address multination states, governments, even democratic governments, can and have suppressed dissent by forceful means. Until the end of World War II, most European governments were **unitary** governments: they were highly centralized, with the capital city serving as the focus of power. States made no clear efforts to accommodate minorities or outlying regions where identification with the state was weaker. Europe's nation-states were unitary states, with the culture of the capital city defined as the nation's culture. Any smaller nations within (such as Brittons in France or Basques in Spain) were repressed and suppressed. The administrative framework of a unitary government is designed to ensure the central government's authority over all parts of the state. The French government divided the state into more than 90 *départements*, whose representatives came to Paris not to express

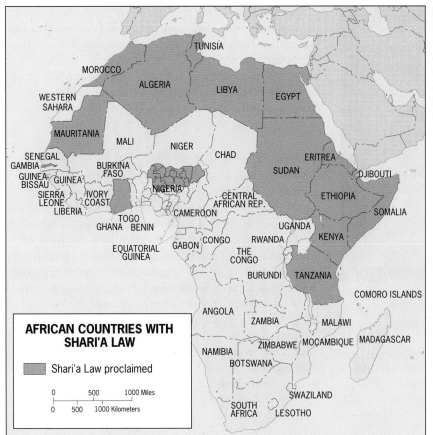

■■■■ **Figure 8.11**
Countries in Africa with Shari'a Laws (Either Civil or Criminal). *Data from a variety of sources, including*: The United States Department of State, the CIA World Factbook, University of Pittsburgh Law School, Emory University School of Law, and All Africa.

regional concerns but to implement governmental decisions back home.

Another way to govern a mulitnational state is to construct a **federal** system, organizing state territory into regions, substates (States), provinces, or cantons. In a strong federal system, the regions have much control over government policies and funds, and in a weak federal system, the regions have little control over government policies and funds. Most federal systems are somewhere in between, with governments at the state scale and at the substate scale each having control over certain revenues and certain policy areas. By giving control over certain policies (especially culturally relative policies) to smaller-scale entities, a government can keep the state as a whole together.

Federalism functions differently depending on the context. In Nigeria, the 36 States choose their own judicial system. In the Muslim north, the States have Shari'a laws (legal systems based on traditional Islamic laws), and in the Christian and animist south, the States do not (Fig. 8.11). In the United States, States take different approaches to matters such as the death penalty, access to alcohol, and the right to carry concealed weapons (Fig. 8.12), but many of the fundamentals of the legal system do not differ among States.

Federalism accommodates regional interests by vesting primary power in provinces, States, or other regional units over all matters except those explicitly given to the central government. The Australian geographer K. W. Robinson described a federation as "the most geographically expressive of all political systems, based as it is on the existence and accommodation of regional differences... federation does not create unity out of diversity; rather, it enables the two to coexist."

Choosing a federal system does not always quell nationalist sentiment. After all, the multinational states of the Soviet Union, Yugoslavia, and Czechoslovakia fell apart, despite their federalist systems, and the future of Belgium as a single state is increasingly in doubt.

Devolution

Devolution is the movement of power from the central government to regional governments within the state. Sometimes, devolution is achieved by reworking a constitution to establish a federal system that recognizes the permanency of the regional governments, as Spain has done. In other places, governments devolve power without

Figure 8.12
St. Paul, Minnesota.   A sign hanging on the front door of the Minnesota Children's Museum cautions visitors that the museum "bans guns in these premises." Under Minnesota's concealed weapons law, businesses that do not want concealed weapons on the premises must post signs of a certain size, font, and color at each entrance to the establishment.   © Erin H. Fouberg.

altering constitutions, almost as an experiment. In the United Kingdom, the Northern Ireland Assembly (a parliamentary body) resulted from devolution, but the British government suspended its activities in 2002 and then reinstated the Northern Ireland Assembly in 2007. Devolutionary forces can emerge in all kinds of states, old and young, mature and emergent. These forces arise from several sources: ethnocultural, economic, and spatial.

Ethnocultural Devolutionary Movements

Many of Europe's devolutionary movements came from nations within a state that define themselves as being ethnically, linguistically, or religiously distinct.

The capacity of ethnocultural forces to stimulate devolutionary processes has been evident, for example, in eastern Europe. Parts of the eastern European map have changed quite drastically over the past two decades, and two countries—Czechoslovakia and Yugoslavia—succumbed to devolutionary pressures. In the case of Czechoslovakia, the process was peaceful: Czechs and Slovaks divided their country along a new international border. As Figure 8.13 shows, however, one of the two new states, Slovakia, is not homogeneous: about 11 percent of the population is Hungarian, and that minority is concentrated along the border

Figure 8.13
Ethnic Mosaic of Eastern Europe.
© Adapted (in part) with permission from George Huffman, ed., *Europe in the 1990s: A Geographical Analysis*, 6 rev. ed., p. 551.

between Slovakia and Hungary. The Hungarian minority, facing discriminatory policies involving language and other aspects of its culture, has at times demanded greater autonomy (self-governance) to protect its heritage in the new state of Slovakia.

Compared to the constituent units of the former Yugoslavia (discussed in detail in Chapter 7), other countries shown in Figure 8.14 have dealt with devolutionary pressures more peacefully. Among these are Lithuania and

Ukraine. Elsewhere in the world, however, ethnocultural fragmentation has produced costly wars. Ethnocultural differences lie at the heart of the decades-long conflict between the Muslim North and the non-Muslim South in Sudan, Africa. Similar forces have given rise to a seemingly endless civil war in Sri Lanka (South Asia), where the Sinhalese (Buddhist) majority has been unable to suppress or to accommodate the demands of the Tamil (Hindu) minority for an independent state. Moreover, devolutionary

Figure 8.14
Europe: Foci of Devolutionary Pressures, 2009. © H. J. de Blij, P. O. Muller, and John Wiley & Sons.

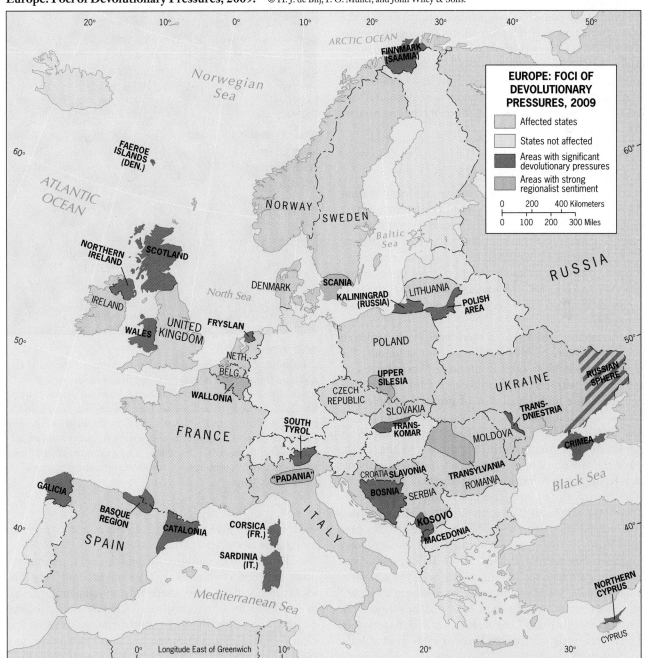

forces are gaining momentum in places that have long looked stable from the outside. China's far west is a case in point, where Tibetan and Uyghur separatist movements are gaining momentum. The point is that ethnocultural differences are weakening the fabric of many states in today's global political framework, and, if anything, the trend is in the direction of more, rather than fewer, calls for autonomy, or even independence.

Devolution does not necessarily fuel greater calls for independence. In the United Kingdom, Scotland managed to secure the right to establish its own parliament, but then the parliament came in for its share of criticism—raising doubts among some about whether Scotland would truly be better off as an independent entity. And in the wake of the European Union's efforts to provide greater recognition and support of regions, some Scottish nationalists now see less of a need to separate themselves from London. What all of this shows is just how complicated devolution can be. At the heart of most devolutionary movements, however, is a strong sense of ethnocultural or economic difference.

Economic Devolutionary Forces

Devolutionary pressures often arise from a combination of sources. In Catalonia, ethnocultural differences play a significant role, but Catalonians also cite economics; with about 6 percent of Spain's territory and just 17 percent of its population, Catalonia produces some 25 percent of all Spanish exports by value and 40 percent of its industrial exports (Fig. 8.15). Such economic strength lends weight to devolutionary demands based on Catalonian nationalism.

Economic forces play an even more prominent role in Italy and France. In Italy, demands for autonomy for Sardinia are deeply rooted in the island's economic circumstances, with accusations of neglect by the government in Rome high on the list of grievances. Italy also faces serious devolutionary forces on its mainland peninsula. One is rooted in regional disparities between north and south. The Mezzogiorno region lies to the south, below the Ancona Line (an imaginary border extending from Rome to the Adriatic coast at Ancona). The wealthier north stands in sharp contrast to the poorer south. Despite the large subsidies granted to the Mezzogiorno, the development gap between the north, very much a part of the European core, and the south, part of the European periphery, has been widening. Some Italian politicians have exploited widespread impatience with the situation by forming organizations to promote northern interests, including devolution. The most recent of these organizations was the Northern League, which raised the prospect of an independent state called Padania in the part of Italy lying north of the Po River. After a surge of enthusiasm, the Padania campaign faltered. But it did push the Italian

Figure 8.15

Catalonia, Spain. Barcelona's long-standing economic and political significance is indelibly imprinted in the urban landscape. Once the heart of a far-flung Mediterranean empire, Barcelona went on to become a center of commerce and banking as the Iberian Peninsula industrialized. In the process, the city became a center of architectural innovation that is not just evident in the major public buildings. The major streets are lined with impressive buildings—many with intricate stone façades. © Alexander B. Murphy.

government to give more rights to the country's regions, moving it toward a more federal system.

Brazil provides another example of the interconnections between devolutionary movements and economics. As in northern Italy, a separatist movement emerged in the 1990s in a better-off, well-defined region of the country, the south (the three southernmost States of Rio Grande do Sul, Santa Catarina, and Parana). Southerners complained that the government was misspending their tax money on assistance to Amazonia (in northern Brazil).

The southerners found a leader, manufactured a flag, and demanded independence for their Republic of the Pampas. The Brazilian government responded by outlawing the separatists' political party, but the economic differences between north and south continue, and devolution pressures will certainly arise again.

Spatial Influences on Devolution

We have seen how political decisions and cultural and economic forces can generate devolutionary processes in states. Devolutionary events have at least one feature in common: they most often occur on the margins of states. Note that every one of the devolution-affected areas shown in Figure 8.14 lies on a coast or on a border. Distance, remoteness, and marginal location are allies of devolution. The regions most likely to seek devolution are those far from the national capital. Many are separated by water, desert, or mountains from the center of power and adjoin neighbors that may support separatist objectives.

Note also that many islands are subject to devolutionary processes: Corsica (France), Sardinia (Italy), Taiwan (China), Singapore (Malaysia), Zanzibar (Tanzania), Jolo (Philippines), Puerto Rico (United States), Mayotte (Comoros), and East Timor (Indonesia) are notable examples. As this list indicates, some of these islands became independent states, while others were divided during devolution. Insularity clearly has advantages for separatist movements.

Not surprisingly, the United States faces its most serious devolutionary pressures on the islands of Hawai'i (Fig. 8.16). The year 1993 marked the hundred-year anniversary of the United States' annexation of Hawai'i, and in that year, a vocal minority of native Hawai'ians and their sympathizers demanded the return of rights lost during the "occupation." These demands included the right to reestablish an independent state called Hawai'i (before its annexation Hawai'i was a Polynesian kingdom) on several of the smaller islands. Their hope is that ultimately the island of Kauai, or at least a significant part of that island, which is considered ancestral land, will become a component of the independent Hawai'ian state.

At present, the native Hawai'ians do not have the numbers, resources, or influence to achieve their separatist aims. The potential for some form of separation between Hawai'i and the mainland United States does exist, however. The political geographer Saul Cohen theorized in 1991 that political entities situated in border zones

Field Note

"As I drove along a main road through a Honolulu suburb I noticed that numerous houses had the Hawai'i State flag flying upside down. I knocked on the door of this house and asked the homeowner why he was treating the State flag this way. He invited me in and we talked for more than an hour. 'This is 1993,' he said, 'and we native Hawai'ians are letting the State government and the country know that we haven't forgotten the annexation by the United States of our kingdom. I don't accept it, and we want our territory to plant our flag and keep the traditions alive. Why don't you drive past the royal palace, and you'll see that we mean it.' He was right. The Iolani Palace, where the Hawai'ians' last monarch, Queen Liliuokalani, reigned until she was deposed by a group of American businessmen in 1893, was draped in black for all of Honolulu to see. Here was devolutionary stress on American soil."

Figure 8.16
Honolulu, Hawai'i. © H. J. de Blij.

between geopolitical powers may become gateway states, absorbing and assimilating diverse cultures and traditions and emerging as new entities, no longer dominated by one or the other. Hawai'i, he suggests, is a candidate for this status.

Spatial influences can play a significant role in starting and sustaining devolutionary processes. Spatial distance can be compounded by differences in physical geography—a feeling of remoteness can be fueled by being isolated in a valley or separated by mountains or a river. Basic physical-geographic and locational factors can thus be key ingredients in the devolutionary process.

Electoral Geography

The partitioning of state territory into electoral districts represents a final key component of a state's internal political geography. Electoral geographers examine how the spatial configuration of electoral districts and the voting patterns that emerge in particular elections reflect and influence social and political affairs. Various countries use different voting systems to elect their governments. For example, in the 1994 South African election, the leaders of the country formulated a system to provide majority rule while awarding some power to each of nine newly formed regions. The overall effect was to protect, to an extent, the rights of minorities in those regions.

The geographic study of voting behavior is especially interesting because it shows how the way people vote may be influenced by their geographic situation. Maps of voting patterns often produce surprises that can be explained by other maps, and Geographic Information Systems have raised this kind of analysis to new levels. Political geographers study church affiliation, income level, ethnic background, education attainment, and numerous other social and economic factors to learn why voters in a certain region voted the way they did.

The domain in which electoral geographers can have the most concrete influence is in the drawing of electoral districts. In a democracy with representatives elected by district, spatial organization of the districts determines whose voice is heard in a given place—with impacts on who is elected. A voter's most direct and important contact with government is at the local level. The United States Constitution establishes a system of **territorial representation** in the House of Representatives, where each representative is elected from a territorially defined district.

The Constitution also establishes a census every ten years in order to enumerate the population and reapportion the representatives accordingly. **Reapportionment** is the process by which districts are moved according to population shifts, so that each district encompasses approxi-

mately the same number of people. For example, after the 2000 census, the State of New York lost two representatives and the State of Georgia gained two representatives.

In the United States once reapportionment is complete, individual States go through redistricting, each following its own system. The criteria involved in redistricting are numerous, but the most important is equal representation, achieved by ensuring that districts are equally populated. In addition, the Supreme Court prefers compact and contiguous districts that keep political units (such as counties) intact. Finally, the courts have repeatedly called for representational equality of racial and linguistic minorities.

Even after the civil rights movement of the 1950s and 1960s in the United States, minorities were refused voting rights in a multitude of districts and States around the country. County registrars would close their doors when African Americans came to register to vote, and intimidation kept many away from voting at the polls. Even in places where minorities were allowed to register and vote, the parties drawing the voting districts or choosing the electoral system would make it nearly impossible for the election of a minority to occur. For example, if a government has to draw ten districts in a State that is 60 percent white, 30 percent African American, and 10 percent Hispanic, it can easily dilute the minority voters by **splitting** them among the ten districts, ensuring that the white population holds the majority in each district.

In 1982, the United States Congress amended the 1965 Voting Rights Act by outlawing districts that have the effect of weakening minority voting power. In a series of decisions, the courts interpreted this amendment to mean States needed to redistrict in a way that would maximize minority representation. Using this criterion in the redistricting that followed the 1990 census, States increased the number of majority-minority districts in the House of Representatives from 27 to 52. **Majority-minority districts** are packed districts in which a majority of the population is from the minority. In the hypothetical State described above, a redistricting following this criterion could have the goal of creating at least three majority-minority districts and a fourth where minorities had a sizable enough population to influence the outcome of the election.

Ideally, majority-minority districts would be compact and contiguous and follow existing political units. Both political geographers Jonathan Leib and Gerald Webster have researched the court cases that have resulted from trying to balance these often-conflicting criteria. To pack minorities who do not live compactly and contiguously, States have drawn crazy-shaped districts, connecting minority populations with meandering corridors and following Interstates to connect urban areas that have large minority populations (Fig. 8.17).

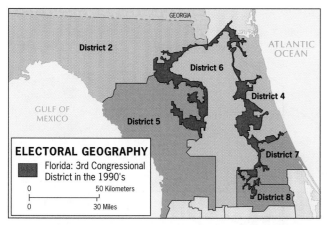

■■■ Figure 8.17
Electoral Geography. Florida's Third Congressional District during the 1990s was an example of the spatial manipulation used to create majority-minority districts after the 1990 census. In 1990, District 3 had about 310,000 African American residents, 240,000 whites, and 16,000 Hispanics. In places, District 3 was no wider than U.S. Highway 90. *Adapted with permission from*: Tanya de Blij, Geographer/Analyst for the Florida House of Representatives.

Strange-looking districts that have been constructed to attain certain political ends are nothing new in American politics. In 1812, Governor Elbridge Gerry of Massachusetts signed into law a district designed to give an advantage to his party—a district that looked so odd to artist Gilbert Stuart that he drew it with a head, wings, and claws. Stuart called it the "salamander district," but a colleague immortalized it by naming it a gerrymander. Ever since, the term **gerrymandering** has been used to describe "redistricting for advantage." Certainly, many of the districts now on the United States electoral map may be seen as gerrymanders, but for an important purpose: to provide representation to minorities who, without it, would not be represented as effectively in the House of Representatives. Despite this well-intended goal, others argue that the packing of minorities into majority-minority districts simply concentrates minority votes, creating a countrywide government that is less responsive to minority concerns.

The larger point is that the spatial organization of voting districts is a fundamentally geographical phenomenon, and it can have profound impacts on who is represented and who is not—as well as peoples' notions of fairness. And that is only the beginning. The voting patterns that emerge from particular elections can help reinforce a sense of regionalism and can shape a government's response to issues in the future. Small wonder, then, that many individuals who have little general understanding of geography at least appreciate the importance of its electoral geography component.

Choose an example of a devolutionary movement and determine whether autonomy (self-governance) for that region would benefit the autonomous region, the country in which it is located, or both.

HOW ARE BOUNDARIES ESTABLISHED, AND WHY DO BOUNDARY DISPUTES OCCUR?

The territories of individual states are separated by international boundaries (borders). Boundaries may appear on maps as straight lines or may twist and turn to conform to the bends of rivers and the curves of hills and valleys. But a boundary is more than a line, far more than a fence or wall on the ground. A **boundary** between states is actually a vertical plane that cuts through the rocks below (called the subsoil) and the airspace above, dividing one state territory from another (Fig. 8.18). Only where the vertical plane intersects the Earth's surface (on land or at sea) does it form the line we see on a map.

Many boundaries were established on the world map before the extent or significance of subsoil resources was known. As a result, coal seams stretch over boundaries, and oil and gas reserves are split between states. Europe's coal reserves, for example, extend from Belgium underneath the Netherlands and on into the Ruhr area of Germany. Soon after mining began in the mid-nineteenth century, these three neighbors began to accuse each other of mining coal that did not lie directly below their own national territories. The underground surveys available at the time were too inaccurate to pinpoint the ownership of each coal seam.

During the 1950s–1960s, Germany and the Netherlands argued over a gas reserve that lies in the subsoil across their boundary. The Germans claimed that the Dutch were withdrawing so much natural gas that the gas was flowing from beneath German land to the Dutch side of the boundary. The Germans wanted compensation for their "lost" gas. A major issue between Iraq and Kuwait, which in part led to Iraq's invasion of Kuwait in 1990, was the oil in the Rumaylah reserve that lies underneath the desert and crosses the boundary between the two states. The Iraqis asserted that the Kuwaitis were drilling too many wells and draining the reserve too quickly; they also alleged that the Kuwaitis were drilling oblique boreholes to penetrate the vertical plane extending downward along the boundary. At the time the Iraq-Kuwait boundary was established, however, no one knew this giant oil reserve lay in the subsoil or that it would help create an international crisis (Fig. 8.19).

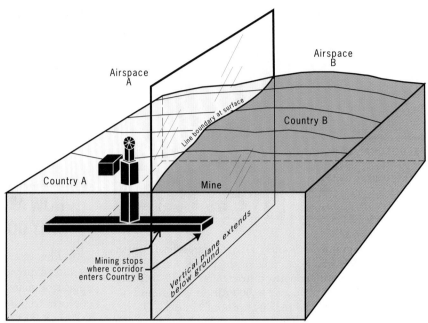

Figure 8.18
The Vertical Plane of a Political Boundary. © E. H. Fouberg, A. B. Murphy, H. J. de Blij, and John Wiley & Sons, Inc.

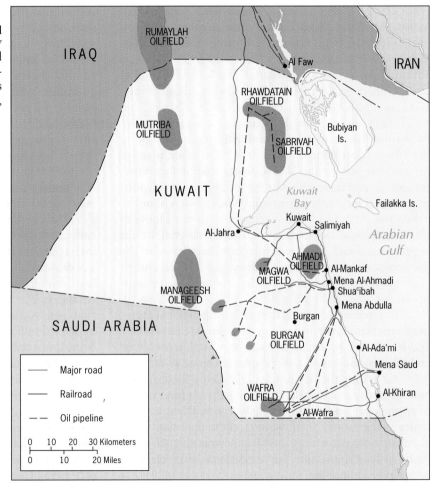

Figure 8.19
The International Boundary between Iraq and Kuwait. Kuwait's northern boundary was redefined and delimited by a United Nations boundary commission; it was demarcated by a series of concrete pillars 1.24 miles (2 kilometers) apart. © E. H. Fouberg, A. B. Murphy, H. J. de Blij, and John Wiley & Sons, Inc.

Above the ground, too, the interpretation of boundaries as vertical planes has serious implications. A state's "airspace" is defined by the atmosphere above its land area as marked by its boundaries, as well as by what lies beyond, at higher altitudes. But how high does the airspace extend? Most states insist on controlling the airline traffic over their territories, but states do not yet control the paths of satellite orbits.

Establishing Boundaries

Establishing a boundary between two states typically involves four steps. First, states *define* the boundary through a treaty-like legal document in which actual points in the landscape or points of latitude and longitude are described. Next, cartographers *delimit* the boundary by drawing on a map. Third, if either or both of the states so desire, they can *demarcate* the boundary by using steel posts, concrete pillars, fences, walls, or some other visible means to mark the boundary on the ground. By no means are all boundaries on the world map demarcated. Demarcating a lengthy boundary is expensive, and it is hardly worth the effort in high mountains, vast deserts, frigid polar lands, or other places with few permanent settlements. The final step is to *administrate* the boundary—to determine how the boundary will be maintained and how goods and people will cross the boundary.

Types of Boundaries

When boundaries are drawn using grid systems such as latitude and longitude or township and range, political geographers refer to these boundaries as **geometric boundaries**. In North America, the United States and Canada used a single line of latitude west of the Great Lakes to define their boundary. During the Berlin Conference, colonial powers used arbitrary reference points and drew straight lines to establish the boundaries in much of Africa.

At different times, political geographers and other academics have advocated "natural" boundaries over geometric boundaries because they are visible on the landscape as physical geographic features. **Physical-political** (also called natural-political) **boundaries** are boundaries that follow an agreed-upon feature in the physical geographic landscape, such as the center point of a river or the crest of a mountain range. The Rio Grande is an important physical-political boundary between the United States and Mexico; an older boundary follows crest lines of the Pyrenees between Spain and France. Lakes sometimes serve as boundaries as well; for example, four of the five Great Lakes of North America (between the United States and Canada) and several of the Great Lakes of East Africa (between Congo and its eastern neighbors) serve as boundaries.

Physical features sometimes make convenient political boundaries, but topographic features are not static. Rivers change course, volcanoes erupt, and slowly, mountains erode. People perceive physical-political boundaries as more stable, but many states have entered territorial conflicts over physical-political boundaries (notably Chile and Argentina). Similarly, physical boundaries do not necessarily stop the flow of people or goods across boundaries, leading some states to reinforce physical boundaries with human-built obstacles (the United States on the Rio Grande). The stability of boundaries has more to do with local historical and geographical circumstances than with the character of the boundary itself.

Boundary Disputes

The boundary we see as a line on an atlas map is the product of a complex series of legal steps that begins with a written description of the boundary. Sometimes that legal description is old and imprecise. Sometimes it was dictated by a stronger power that is now less dominant, giving the weaker neighbor a reason to argue for change. At other times the geography of the borderland has actually changed; the river that marked the boundary may have changed course, or a portion of it has been cut off. Resources lying across a boundary can lead to conflict. In short, states often argue about their boundaries. These boundary disputes take four principal forms: definitional, locational, operational, and allocational.

Definitional boundary disputes focus on the legal language of the boundary agreement. For example, a boundary definition may stipulate that the median line of a river will mark the boundary. That would seem clear enough, but the water levels of rivers vary. If the valley is asymmetrical, the median line will move back and forth between low-water and high-water stages of the stream. This may involve hundreds of meters of movement—not very much, it would seem, but enough to cause serious argument, especially if there are resources in the river. The solution is to refine the definition to suit both parties.

Locational boundary disputes center on the delimitation and possibly the demarcation of the boundary. The definition is not in dispute, but its interpretation is. Sometimes the language of boundary treaties is vague enough to allow mapmakers to delimit the line in various ways. For example, when the colonial powers defined their empires in Africa and Asia, they specified their international boundaries rather carefully. But internal administrative boundaries often were not strictly defined. When those internal boundaries became the boundaries of independent states, there was plenty of room for argument.

In a few instances, locational disputes arise because no definition of the boundary exists at all. An important case involves Saudi Arabia and Yemen, whose potentially oil-rich boundary area is not covered by a treaty.

Operational boundary disputes involve neighbors who differ over the way their border should function. When two adjoining countries agree on how cross-border migration should be controlled, the border functions satisfactorily. However, if one state wants to limit migration while the other does not, a dispute may arise. Similarly, efforts to prevent smuggling across borders sometimes lead to operational disputes when one state's efforts are not matched (or are possibly even sabotaged) by its neighbor's. And in areas where nomadic lifeways still prevail, the movement of people and their livestock across international borders can lead to conflict.

Allocational boundary disputes of the kind described earlier, involving the Netherlands and Germany over natural gas and Iraq and Kuwait over oil, are becoming more common as the search for resources intensifies. Today many such disputes involve international boundaries at sea. Oil reserves under the seafloor below coastal waters sometimes lie in areas where exact boundary delimitation may be difficult or subject to debate. Another growing area of allocational dispute has to do with water supplies: the Tigris, Nile, Colorado, and other rivers are subject to such disputes. When a river crosses an international boundary, the rights of the upstream and downstream users of the river often come into conflict.

People used to think physical-political boundaries were more stable than geometric boundaries. Through studies of many places, political geographers have confirmed that this idea is false. Construct your own argument explaining why physical-political boundaries can create just as much instability as geometric boundaries.

HOW DO GEOPOLITICS AND CRITICAL GEOPOLITICS HELP US UNDERSTAND THE WORLD?

Geopolitics is the interplay among geography, power, politics, and international relations. Political science and international relations tend to focus on governmental institutions, systems, and interactions. Geopolitics brings locational considerations, environmental contexts, territorial perspectives, and spatial assumptions

to the fore. Geopolitics helps us understand the arrangements and forces that are transforming the map of the world.

Classical Geopolitics

Classical geopoliticians of the late nineteenth and early twentieth centuries generally fit into one of two camps: the German school, which sought to explain why certain states are powerful and how to become powerful, and the British/American school, which sought to offer strategic advice for states and explain why countries interact at the global scale the way they do. A few gepoliticians tried to bridge the gap, blending the two schools, but for the most part classical geopoliticians who are still writing today are in the British/American school, offering geostrategic perspectives on the world.

The German School

Why are certain states powerful, and how do states become powerful? The first political geographer who studied these issues was the German professor Friedrich Ratzel (1844–1904). Influenced by the writings of Charles Darwin, Ratzel postulated that the state resembles a biological organism whose life cycle extends from birth through maturity and, ultimately, decline and death. To prolong its existence, the state requires nourishment, just as an organism needs food. Such nourishment is provided by the acquisition of territories belonging to less powerful competitors (what Ratzel deemed *lebensraum*) and by the people who live there. If a state is confined within permanent and static boundaries and deprived of overseas domains, Ratzel argued, it will atrophy. Territory is the state's essential, life-giving force.

Ratzel's theory was based on an effort to describe the experience of states in the nineteenth century, including the United States. It was so speculative that it might have been forgotten if some of Ratzel's German followers in the 1930s had not translated his abstract writings into policy recommendations that ultimately led to Nazi expansionism.

The British/American School

Not long after the publication of Ratzel's initial ideas, other geographers began looking at the overall organization of power in the world, studying the physical geographic map of the world with a view toward determining where the most strategic places on Earth were located. Prominent among them was the Oxford University geographer Sir Halford J. Mackinder (1861–1947). In 1904, he published an article titled "The Geographical Pivot of History" in the Royal Geographical Society's *Geographical Journal*. That article became one of the most intensely debated geographic publications of all time.

Mackinder was concerned with power relationships at a time when Britain had acquired a global empire through its strong navy. To many of his contemporaries, the oceans—the paths to colonies and trade—were the key to world domination, but Mackinder disagreed. He concluded that a land-based power, not a sea power, would ultimately rule the world. His famous article contained a lengthy appraisal of the largest and most populous landmass on Earth—Eurasia (Europe and Asia together). At the heart of Eurasia, he argued, lay an impregnable, resource-rich "pivot area" extending from eastern Europe to eastern Siberia (Fig. 8.20). Mackinder issued a warning: if this pivot area became influential in Europe, a great empire could be formed.

Mackinder later renamed his pivot area the heartland, and his warning became known as the heartland theory. In his book *Democratic Ideals and Reality* (1919), Mackinder (calling Eurasia "the World Island") issued a stronger warning to the winners of World War I, stating:

> *Who rules East Europe commands the Heartland*
>
> *Who rules the Heartland commands the World Island*
>
> *Who rules the World Island commands the World*

When Mackinder proposed his **heartland theory**, there was little to foretell the rise of a superpower in the heartland. Russia was in disarray, having recently lost a war against Japan (1905), and was facing revolution. Eastern Europe was fractured. Germany, not Russia, was gaining power. But when the Soviet Union emerged and World War II gave Moscow control over much of Eastern Europe, the heartland theory attracted renewed attention.

▬▬ **Figure 8.20**

The Heartland Theory. The Pivot Area/Heartland, the Inner Crescent/Rimland, and the World Island, following the descriptions of Halford Mackinder.

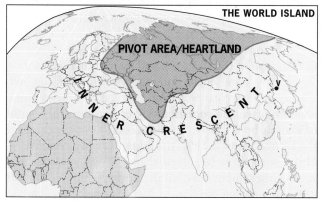

In 1943, Mackinder wrote a final paper shortly before he died. He was concerned about Stalin's power in the Soviet Union—Mackinder worried the Soviet Union could exert control over the states of Eastern Europe. He offered strategies for keeping the Soviets in check, including avoiding the expansion of the Heartland into the Inner Crescent (Fig. 8.20) and creating an alliance around the North Atlantic to join the forces of land and sea powers against the Heartland. Within the next ten years, the United States began its containment policy (to stop the expansion of the Soviet Union), and the United States, Canada, and Western Europe formed an alliance called the North Atlantic Treaty Organization (NATO).

Influence of Geopoliticians on Politics

Ratzel and Mackinder are only two of many geopoliticians who influenced international relations. Their writings, grounded in history, current events, and physical geography, sounded logical and influenced many politicians, and in some ways still do. NATO still exists and has not invited Russia to join the military alliance, but it has extended membership to eastern European states and is working in partnerships with former republics of the Soviet Union.

Despite the staying power of geopolitical theories, geopolitics dropped from the map after World War II. Because of the influence Ratzel's theory had on Hitler and because another geopolitician, Karl Haushofer, also influenced Hitler, the term *geopolitics* acquired a very negative connotation. For some decades after World War II, the term was in such disrepute that few political geographers, even those studying power relationships, would identify themselves as students of geopolitics. Time, along with more balanced perspectives, has reinstated geopolitics as an appropriate name for the study of the spatial and territorial dimensions of power relationships past, present, and future.

Critical Geopolitics

Today, geopoliticians do much less predicting and prescribing. Rather, most geographers focus on revealing and explaining the underlying spatial assumptions and territorial perspectives of politicians. Political geographers Gearoid O'Tuathail and John Agnew refer to the politicians in the most powerful states, the core states, as "intellectuals of statecraft." The basic concept behind **critical geopolitics** is that intellectuals of statecraft construct ideas about places, these ideas influence and reinforce their political behaviors and policy choices, and these ideas affect how we, the people, process our own notions of places and politics.

In a number of publications, O'Tuathail has studied American geopolitical reasoning by examining speeches and statements by U.S. intellectuals of statecraft regarding certain wars, certain places, and certain times. He has highlighted how American intellectuals of statecraft have spatialized politics into a world of "us" versus "them." In American politics, the president has an incredible influence on Americans, shaping how they see places and organize international space in their minds. By drawing on American cultural logic and certain representations of America, presidents have repeatedly defined an "us" that is pro-democracy, independent, self-sufficient, and free and a "them" that is in some way against all of these things.

During the Cold War, President Ronald Reagan coined the term *Evil Empire* for the Soviet Union and represented the United States as "the shining city on a hill." Over the last two presidencies, terrorism has replaced the Soviet Union as the "they." Sounding remarkably similar, Democratic President William J. Clinton and Republican President George W. Bush justified military actions against terrorists. In 1998, President Clinton explained American military action in Sudan and Afghanistan as a response to terrorist plans by Osama bin Laden by stating that the terrorists "come from diverse places but share a hatred for democracy, a fanatical glorification of violence, and a horrible distortion of their religion, to justify the murder of innocents. They have made the United States their adversary precisely because of what we stand for and what we stand against." Immediately after September 11, President George W. Bush exclaimed to the world, "They [the terrorists] stand against us because we stand in their way." In 2002, President Bush again explained, "I've said in the past that nations are either with us or against us in the war on terror."

Statements such as these are rooted in a particular geopolitical perspective on the world—one that divides the globe into opposing political camps. That much may seem obvious, as there are clear ideological fault lines between an organization such as al-Qaida and a state such as the United States. But critical geopolitics seeks to move beyond such differences to explore the spatial ideas and understandings that undergird particular political perspectives and that shape policy approaches. Consider the following 2006 statement from then-Secretary of Defense Donald Rumsfeld before the Senate Arms Services Committee:

> *If we left Iraq prematurely—as the terrorists demand—the enemy would tell us to leave Afghanistan and then withdraw from the Middle East. And if we left the Middle East, they'd order us and all those who don't share their militant ideology to leave what they call the occupied Muslim lands from Spain to the Philippines.*

This type of statement reflects a particular perspective on the ability of a group of terrorists to exert control over a large geographical area. It also suggests, at least implicitly, that there is, or can be, a degree of unity in the "Muslim lands." Both of these contentions are highly debatable. Terrorist groups have not demonstrated the kind of mili-

tary capability that would allow them to fulfill Rumsfeld's vision, and cultural and political tensions among Muslims in the Middle East suggest that the region stretching "from Spain to the Philippines" is far from a monolithic geopolitical node. The Middle East region has had more conflict than almost any other in recent times (the Iran-Iraq War, the Gulf War, the Afghanistan-Soviet Union War, as well as the civil war in the Sudan). Whether realistic or not, if such geopolitical formulations are believed—and they clearly were in the case cited above—they shape the policies that are pursued and affect what happens on the ground. The goal of critical geopoliticians is to understand the ideological roots and implications of geopolitical reasoning by intellectuals of statecraft.

Geopolitical World Order

Political geographers study the geopolitical world order—the temporary periods of stability in the way international politics is conducted. For example, during the Cold War, the geopolitical world order was bipolar—the Soviet Union versus the United States (and its close ally the United Kingdom). After a stable geopolitical world order breaks down, the world goes through a transition, eventually settling into a new geopolitical world order. Noted political geographers Peter J. Taylor and Colin Flint argue that at the end of World War II, five possible orders could have emerged among the three major powers, the United Kingdom, the United States, and the Soviet Union. Each could have created its own bloc with its own allies; the three could have come together under the United Nations; or three possible alliances could have occurred—the US and USSR against the UK, the US and UK against the USSR, or the UK and USSR against the US. What emerged was the bipolar world order of the Cold War: the US and UK against the USSR.

After the USSR collapsed in 1991, the world entered a transition period, and during the transition any range of possible world orders was possible. Politicians spoke optimistically about a new geopolitical world order—one in which a standoff of nuclear terror between two superpowers would no longer determine the destinies of states. Supposedly this new geopolitical order would be shaped by forces that connect nations and states, by supranational unions like the European Union (discussed in the next section of this chapter), and by multinational action should any state violate international rules of conduct. The risks of nuclear war would recede, and negotiation would replace confrontation. When Iraq was driven out of Kuwait by a United Nations coalition of states led by the United States in 1991, the framework of a New World Order seemed to be taking shape. Russia, which a few years earlier might have led the Soviet Union in support of Iraq, endorsed the United Nations operation. Arab as well as non-Arab forces helped repel the invaders.

Soon, however, doubts and uncertainties began to cloud hopes for a mutually cooperative geopolitical world order. Although states were more closely linked to each other than ever before, national self-interest still acted as a powerful force. For all its faults and changed circumstances, the state continued to function as a central building block in the new global framework. Nations wanted to become states, and many did, as the number of United Nations members increased from 159 in 1990 to 184 by 1993 and 192 as of 2006. At the same time, a variety of organizations not tied to specific territories posed a new challenge to the territorially defined state. The number and power of economic and social networks that extend across state borders increased. The new world order includes nonstate organizations with political agendas that are not channeled through states (such as al-Qaida)—and are often spread across the world.

Some see the new geopolitical world order as one of **unilateralism**, with the United States in a position of hard-power dominance and with allies of the United States following rather than joining the political decision-making process. But in the early 2000s the United States' unabashed unilateralism, its abandonment of traditional diplomatic practices, and its controversial invasion of Iraq significantly undermined its influence in many parts of the globe. Southeast Asian states that had long been oriented toward the United States began to turn away. A significant rift developed across the Atlantic between the United States and some European countries, and anti-Americanism surged around the world. Challenges to American unilateralism also came from the processes of globalization, the diffusion of nuclear weapons, the emergence of China and India as global powers, the growth of terrorist groups, and the economic strength of the European Union.

When geopolitical strategists and intellectuals of statecraft predict future geopolitical orders, they often assume that individual states will continue to be the dominant actors in the international arena. Yet with the traditional powers of the state under increasing strain, other geopolitical arrangements may emerge. A new multipolar order may arise with states clustering together as regional forces, or as we discussed in Chapter 9, global cities may gain increasing power over issues typically addressed by states. In the final section of this chapter, we consider several other challenges to the state that may influence the next geopolitical order.

Read a major newspaper (in print or online) and look for a recent statement by a world political leader regarding international politics. Using the concept of critical geopolitics, determine what geopolitical view of the world the leader has—how does he or she define the world spatially?

WHAT ARE SUPRANATIONAL ORGANIZATIONS, AND WHAT IS THE FUTURE OF THE STATE?

Ours is a world of contradictions. Over the past couple of decades some Quebecois have demanded independence from Canada even as Canada joined the United States and Mexico in NAFTA (the North American Free Trade Agreement). At soccer games in Scotland, fans drown out "God Save the Queen" with a thunderous rendition of "Flower of Scotland," while in London, Parliament debates Britain's position on the European Monetary Union. At every turn we are reminded of the interconnectedness of nations, states, and regions, yet separatism and calls for autonomy are rampant. In the early years of the twenty-first century, we appear to be caught between the forces of division and those of unification.

Despite the conflicts arising from these contradictory forces, today hardly a country exists that is not involved in some supranational organization. A **supranational organization** is an entity composed of three or more states that forge an association and form an administrative structure for mutual benefit and in pursuit of shared goals. The twentieth century witnessed the establishment of numerous supranational associations in political, economic, cultural, and military spheres.

Today, states have formed over 60 major supranational organizations (such as NATO and NAFTA), many of which have subsidiaries that bring the total to more than 100. The more states participate in such multilateral associations, the less likely they are to act alone in pursuit of a self-interest that might put them at odds with neighbors. Ample research establishes that participation in a supranational entity is advantageous to the partners and that being left out can have serious negative effects on states and nations.

From League of Nations to United Nations

The modern beginnings of the supranational movement can be traced to conferences following World War I. Woodrow Wilson, president of the United States, proposed an international organization that would include all the states of the world (fewer than 75 states existed at that point), leading to the creation of the League of Nations in 1919. Even though it was the idea of an American president, the United States was among the countries that did not join this organization because isolationists in the U.S. Senate opposed joining. In all, 63 states participated in the League, although the total membership at any single time never reached that number. Costa Rica and Brazil left the League even before 1930; Germany departed in 1933, shortly before the Soviet Union joined in 1934. The

League was born of a worldwide desire to prevent future aggression, but the failure of the United States to join dealt the organization a severe blow. In the mid-1930s, the League had a major opportunity when Ethiopia's Haile Selassie made a dramatic appeal for help in the face of an invasion by Italy, a member state until 1937. However, the League failed to take action, and in the chaos of the beginning of World War II the organization collapsed.

Even though the League of Nations collapsed, it did spawn other international organizations. Between World War I and World War II, states created the Permanent Court of International Justice to adjudicate legal issues between states, such as boundary disputes and fishing

rights. The League of Nations also initiated international negotiations on maritime boundaries and related aspects of the law of the sea. The conferences organized by the League laid the groundwork for the final resolution of the size of territorial seas decades later.

After World War II, states formed a new organization to foster international security and cooperation: the United Nations (UN). Membership in the UN has grown significantly since its 1947 inception (Fig. 8.21). A handful of states still do not belong to the United Nations, but with the most recent additions in 2006, it now has 192 member states. The United Nations Security Council, the United Nations General Assembly, and their work are frequently in the news. The

Figure 8.21
Member States of the United Nations.   This map shows charter members, members after 1945 (with dates of entry), and nonmembers of the United Nations. *Data from*: the United Nations, www.un.org

THE UNITED NATIONS

Charter members, 1945

Members after 1945 with dates of entry

Nonmembers

United Nations organization includes numerous less visible but enormously productive subsidiaries, including the FAO (Food and Agriculture Organization), UNESCO (United Nations Educational, Scientific and Cultural Organization), and WHO (World Health Organization). Not all United Nations members participate in every United Nations subsidiary, but their work has benefited all humanity.

We can find evidence of the important work of the United Nations in the "world" section of any major newspaper. UN peacekeeping troops have helped maintain stability in some of the most contentious regions of the world. The United Nations High Commissioner on Refugees is called upon to aid refugees in crises throughout the world. UN

documents on human rights standards, such as the Universal Declaration on Human Rights, the Covenant on Civil and Political Rights, and the Covenant on Economic and Social Rights, set a precedent and laid the groundwork for countless human rights groups working in the world today.

By participating in the United Nations, states commit to internationally approved standards of behavior. Many states still violate the standards, embodied in the United Nations Charter, but such violations can lead to collective action (economic sanctions or Security Council-supported military action). Scholars of international relations and political geography point to United Nations actions in South Africa (Apartheid), Iraq (the

Gulf War), and North Korea (nuclear proliferation) as examples of UN success.

Regional Supranational Organizations

The League of Nations and the United Nations are global manifestations of a phenomenon that is expressed even more strongly at the regional level. States organize supra-

national organizations at the regional scale to position themselves more strongly economically, politically, and even militaristically.

Belgium, the Netherlands, and Luxembourg undertook the first major modern experiment in regional economic cooperation. The three countries have much in common, culturally and economically. Dutch farm products are sold on Belgian markets, and Belgian industrial goods go to the Netherlands and Luxembourg. During

Figure 8.22
European Supranationalism.   Members of the European Union and their dates of entry. *Data from*: the European Union, www.europa.eu.int   ©H. J. de Blij, P. O. Muller, and John Wiley & Sons, Inc.

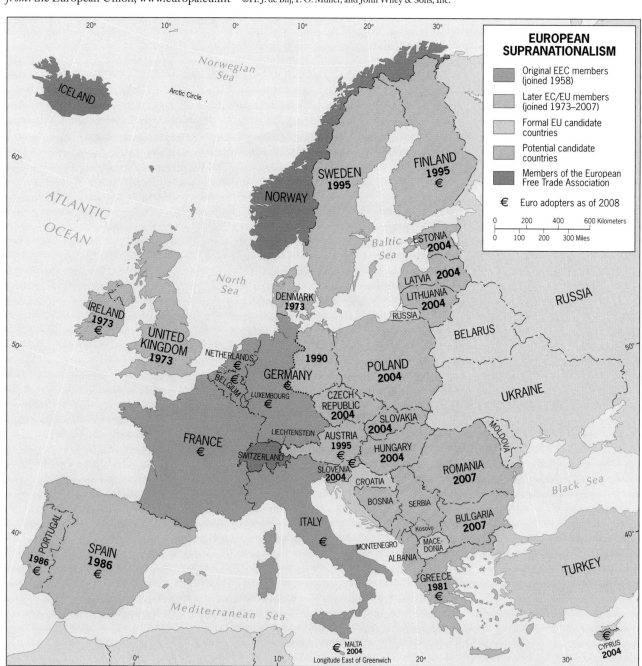

World War II, representatives of the three countries decided to create common tariffs and eliminate import licenses and quotas. In 1944, even before the end of the war, the governments of the three states met in London to sign an agreement of cooperation, creating the *Benelux* (*Bel*gium, the *Ne*therlands, and *Lux*embourg) region.

Following World War II, U.S. Secretary of State George Marshall proposed that the United States finance a European recovery program. A committee representing 16 Western European states plus (then) West Germany presented the United States Congress with a joint program for economic rehabilitation, and Congress approved it. From 1948 to 1952, the United States gave Europe about $12 billion under the Marshall Plan. This investment revived European national economies and also spurred a movement toward cooperation among European states.

The European Union

From the European states' involvement in the Marshall Plan came the Organization for European Economic Cooperation (OEEC), and this body in turn gave rise to other cooperative organizations. Soon after Europe established the OEEC, France proposed the creation of a European Coal and Steel Community (ECSC) with the goal of lifting the restrictions and obstacles that impeded the flow of coal, iron ore, and steel among the mainland's six primary producers: France, West Germany, Italy, and the three Benelux countries. The six states entered the ECSC, and gradually, through negotiations and agreement, enlarged their sphere of cooperation to include reductions and even eliminations of certain tariffs and a freer flow of labor, capital, and nonsteel commodities. This led, in 1958, to the creation of the European Economic Community (EEC).

The success of the EEC induced other countries to apply for membership. Denmark, Ireland, and the United Kingdom joined in 1973, Greece in 1981, and Spain and Portugal in 1986. The organization became known as the European Community (EC) because it began to address issues beyond economics. By the late 1980s, the EC had 12 members: the three giants (Germany, France, and the United Kingdom); the four southern countries (Italy, Spain, Portugal, and Greece); and the five small states (the Netherlands, Belgium, Luxembourg, Denmark, and Ireland). These 12 members initiated a program of cooperation and unification that led to the formal establishment of a European Union (EU) in 1992. In the mid-1990s, Austria, Sweden, and Finland joined the EU, bringing the total number of members to 15 (Fig. 8.22).

In the late 1990s, the EU began preparing for the establishment of a single currency—the euro (Fig. 8.23).

Figure 8.23
Hesdin, France. A market in northern France advertises the price of mushrooms in euros. © Marie-Louise Avery/Alamy Images.

First, all electronic financial transactions were denominated in euros, and on January 1, 2002, the EU introduced euro coins and notes. Not all EU member states are currently a part of the euro-zone, but others may join soon as the euro begins to creep into their economies anyway and the strength of the euro against other global currencies gains.

The integration of ten eastern European and Mediterranean island states into the European Union in 2004, and two more in 2007, is a significant development. Integration is a difficult process and often requires painful adjustments because of the diversity of the European states. For example, agricultural practices and policies have always varied widely. Yet some general policy must govern agriculture throughout the European Union. Individual states have found these adjustments difficult at times, and the EU has had to devise policies to accommodate regional contrasts and delays in implementation. In addition, integration requires significant expenditures. Under the rules of the EU, the richer countries must subsidize (provide financial support to) the poorer ones; therefore, the entry of eastern European states adds to the financial burden on the wealthier western and northern European members.

Another concern is the loss of traditional state powers. The Union is a patchwork of states with many different ethnic traditions and histories of conflict and competition. Economic success and growing well-being tend to submerge such differences, but in the face of difficult economic or social times, divisive forces can, and have, reasserted themselves. Moreover, as the EU gets bigger, it becomes increasingly difficult for individual states to exert significant influence. This, in turn, leads to concerns that the interests of Ireland, Austria, and Sweden could get lost in the mix.

Another difficult problem involves Turkey. Some western Europeans would like to see Turkey join the EU, thereby widening the organization's reach into the Muslim world. The government of Turkey has a strong interest in joining, but many Greeks are hesitant to support Turkish integration because of the long-standing dispute between Greece and Turkey over Cyprus (among other matters). Other EU members have expressed concern over Turkey's human rights record, specifically its treatment of the Kurdish minority, which would not meet the standards set by the European Union. Behind these claims lies an unspoken sense among many that Turkey is not "European" enough to warrant membership. Moreover, the debate within the EU about Turkey has alienated many Turkish people, causing them to question their support for EU membership.

European Union member states will determine future policies of the European Union. Since 2000, member states have rejected a constitution for the European Union, while at the same time the European Union has become more activist in international affairs.

How Does Supranationalism Affect the State?

Supranational is a worldwide phenomenon. Other economic associations, such as the North American Free Trade Agreement (NAFTA), the Association of Caribbean States (ACS), the Central American Common Market, the Andean Group, the Southern Cone Community Market (MERCOSUR), the Economic Community of West African States (ECOWAS), the Asia-Pacific Economic Council (APEC), and the Commonwealth of Independent States (CIS), have drawn up treaties to reduce tariffs and import restrictions in order to ease the flow of commerce in their regions. Not all of these alliances are successful, but economic supranationalism is a sign of the times, a grand experiment still in progress.

Yet, when we turn back to the European Union, we are looking at a supranational organization that is unlike any other. In simple terms, it is a beast we have never seen before. It is not a state, nor is it simply an organization of states. The European Union is remarkable in that it has taken on a life of its own—with a multifaceted government structure, three capital cities, and billions of euros flowing through its coffers. The European Union is extending into foreign relations, domestic policies, and military policies, with sovereignty over certain issues moving from the states to the European Union. Alexander Murphy has studied how Europeans in some regions are feeling a greater attachment to their region and to the European Union than to their own state (Fig. 8.24). Identifying with the European Union (over the state) is strong in the Benelux countries (the first members) and in regions where people have been disempowered by their state governments. With the European Union, we may be witnessing a transformation in the political organization of space similar to the transformation to the modern state system in Europe in the seventeenth century.

Other movements in addition to the European Union are posing major challenges to the state as we know it—all raising questions as to whether the spatial organization of the world into states is logical, effective, or even necessary. Among these challenges are the demand of nations within states for independence (discussed earlier), the proliferation of nuclear weapons, economic globalization, and increasing connectedness among people and cultures.

Nuclear weapons give even small states the ability to inflict massive damage on larger and distant adversaries.

Combined with missile technology, this may be the most serious danger the world faces, which is why the United Nations insisted on dismantling Iraq's nuclear capacity after the 1991 Gulf War and why North Korea's progress in the nuclear arms arena caused President Clinton to threaten military action and President Bush to push so hard for nuclear nonproliferation in North Korea. Some states publicize their nuclear weapons programs, and others keep their nuclear abilities a carefully guarded secret. Reports of nuclear proliferation by enemies led to military actions in the last 30 years. In 1981, when reports of Iraq's nuclear program reached Israel, the Israelis attacked Iraq. During the apartheid period, South Africa built nuclear weapons; adversaries India and Pakistan both possess nuclear weapons, and Iran may well be building itself up as a nuclear power. As nuclear weapons have become smaller and "tactical" nuclear arms have been developed, the threat of nuclear weapons sales has to be taken seriously. It is now possible for a hostile state or group to purchase the power with which to threaten the world.

Although states provide the territorial foundation from which producers and consumers still operate and they continue to exert considerable regulatory powers, economic globalization makes it ever more difficult for states to control economic relations. States are responding to this situation in a variety of ways, with some giving up traditional regulatory powers and others seeking to insulate themselves from the international economy. Still others are working to build supranational economic blocs that they hope will help them cope with an increasingly globalized world. The impacts of many of these developments are as yet uncertain, but it is increasingly clear that states now compete with a variety of other forces in the international arena.

The state's traditional position is being further eroded by the globalization of social and cultural relations. Networks of interaction are being constructed in ways that do not correspond to the map of states. When unrest breaks out in southern Mexico, for example, activists use the Internet to contact interested people throughout the world. Scholars and researchers in different countries work together in teams. Increased mobility has brought individuals from far-flung places into much closer contact than before. Paralleling all this change is the spread of popular culture in ways that make national borders virtually meaningless. Justin Timberlake is listened to from Iceland to Australia; fashions developed in northern Italy are hot items among Japanese tourists visiting Hawai'i; Thai restaurants are found in towns and cities across the

United States; Russians hurry home to watch the next episode of soap operas made in Mexico; and movies produced in Hollywood are seen on screens from Mumbai to Santiago.

Another global phenomenon with major implications for a future world order is the role of religion as a force in global affairs. In Chapter 6, we noted that extremist religious movements commit violent acts in the name of their faith. Whether at the local scale, with an individual acting alone, or at the global scale, with an entire network operating, violence by extremists challenges the state. The state's mission to defeat extremism often produces support for the state government in the short term, but the state's inability to defeat extremist attacks may weaken the state in the long term. Bolstered by a sense of righteousness rooted in Christian fundamentalist ideas, Timothy McVeigh wreaked havoc in Oklahoma City in the late 1900s. A wave of international terrorism toward western states began in the 1980s, with events such as the bombing of an airplane in Lockerbie, Scotland, in 1988. Terrorism came to dominate the international scene on September 11, 2001, with the attacks on the World Trade Center and the Pentagon and the downing of Flight 93 in Pennsylvania.

Some speculate that the divisions emerging in the wake of recent events could lead to a new bipolar international system pitting the Islamic world against the Judeo-Christian world. This is the scenario posited in a controversial book, *The Clash of Civilizations and the Remaking of World Order*, by Harvard political scientist Samuel Huntington. Many academics have strenuously challenged Huntington's thesis for its failure to recognize the extraordinary diversity within the Islamic and the Judeo-Christian realms and for its role in promoting stereotypes that do not represent the diversity within religious traditions.

Globalization has produced economic, social, and cultural geographies that look less and less like the map of states (Fig. 8.3). At the same time, nationalism continues to be a fundamental social force in the world today. The state system is unlikely to disappear anytime soon, but we are headed for a world in which the spatial distribution of power is more complex than the traditional map of states would suggest. Describing that spatial distribution will be a challenge for geographers for generations to come.

In 2004, the European Union welcomed ten additional states, and in 2007, it welcomed two more. Examine the European Union website (listed below in the Learn More Online section). Read about the European Union's expansion and what is going on in the European Union right now. Assess how complicated it is for the European Union to bring together these many divergent members into one supranational organization.

Summary

We tend to take the state for granted. Although the modern state idea is less than 400 years old, the idea and ideal of the nation-state have diffused around the globe, primarily through colonialism and international organizations.

The state may seem natural and permanent, but it is not. New states are being recognized, and existing states are vulnerable to destructive forces. From organizing governments to defining and defending boundaries, to nation-building, to terrorism, to sharing or splitting sovereignty with supranational organizations, political geographers wonder what the future of the state is. How long can this way of politically organizing space last?

As we look to political organization beyond the state, we can turn to the global scale and consider what places the global world economy most affects, shapes, and benefits. In the next chapter, we study global cities—places where major links in the world economy connect and places that in many ways transcend the state.

Geographic Concepts

political geography
state
territoriality
sovereignty
territorial integrity
mercantilism
Peace of Westphalia
nation
nation-state
democracy
multinational state
multistate nation
stateless nation
colonialism

scale
capitalism
commodification
core
periphery
semiperiphery
ability
centripetal
centrifugal
unitary
federal
devolution
territorial representation
reapportionment

splitting
majority-minority
   districts
gerrymandering
boundary
geometric boundary
physical-political
   boundary
heartland theory
critical geopolitics
unilateralism
supranational
   organization

Learn More Online

About Country Studies Published by the United States Library of Congress
http://lcweb2.loc.gov/frd/cs/cshome.html

About the European Union
http://europa/

About Nationalism
www.nationalismproject.org/

About Political Geography
www.politicalgeography.org

Watch It Online

Devolution

Slovakia: New Sovereignty. Click on Video on Demand.
www.learner.org/resources/series180.html#program_descriptions

International Boundaries

Boundaries and Borderlands. Click on Video on Demand.
http://www.learner.org/resources/series180.html#program_descriptions

Supranationalism and the European Union

Strasbourg: Symbol of a United Europe. Click on Video on Demand
http://www.learner.org/resources/series180.html#program_descriptions

CHAPTER 9

Urban Geography

Field Note Straddling the Wall

Figure 9.1
West Berlin, West Germany.   The Berlin Wall as it stood when the city was divided. This photo was taken in West Berlin, looking across the wall to East Berlin.   © Alexander B. Murphy.

As a child, I stood in West Berlin, facing the Berlin Wall. I looked at the gray wall and gray city of East Berlin (Fig. 9.1) and turned around to see the more vibrant city of West Berlin. Why, I wondered, why is this city divided this way? Why is the East German government working so hard to keep their citizens in East Berlin? My mother interrupted my thought, saying, "Look! Look at the guards. Their guns are pointing EAST!" The East German guards along the wall were watching the East Germans to make sure they did not escape to the West.

In 1989, the people of East Berlin and West Berlin took control of the streets, the guard towers, and the wall itself. Berliners occupied the buffer spaces that had divided East Berlin and West Berlin, and they stood on the wall. The guards stood down. As hundreds of millions of people throughout Europe and the rest of the world watched the events unfold live on television, they knew the people who occupied these previously forbidden spaces were not only crushing the wall, but were fundamentally changing the space and the city, starting it down the path of reunification. No one knew what reunification would feel like or look like, and certainly no one knew with any certainty what problems would manifest themselves as a result of reunification, but everyone knew on that fateful night in December that Berlin had fundamentally changed.

In the summer of 2001, I took my own children to the place in Berlin where I had stood with my parents 40 years earlier. Instead of looking at the guards, my family looked for the wall. We tried to find traces of the old wall. Along the relict boundary (one that no longer functions) between the cities, we could see differences in architecture, differences in streets, and even a few remnants of the wall itself. It was a difficult task, as seemingly everything was under construction. New buildings had sprung up, city planners were changing street patterns, and cars were traveling freely across what used to be a fervently defended boundary.

Walking past Potsdamer Platz, we spotted a remnant of the old order that no one could miss: an old East German guard tower looming over a cultural landscape being remade before our eyes (Fig. 9.2). My son was the first to point out that on the street next to the guard tower was a heavy machine, helping to re-create and recast the cultural landscape of Berlin.

Berlin is no longer a divided city, and the German government is altering the cultural landscape and the urban morphology of the city to prove it. The **urban morphology** of a city is the layout of the city, its physical form and structure.

▬▬▬ Figure 9.2
Berlin, Germany. An East German guard tower stands among old buildings torn down to make room for new construction in the Potsdamer Platz area of Berlin. © Alexander B. Murphy.

When Berlin was divided, a study of its urban morphology showed how many roads ended at checkpoints, how buffers of little development traced the outline of the wall, and how each city had its own focal point where the roads led to particular buildings that were larger than others. The urban morphology of Berlin today reveals how street patterns have changed, how new buildings stand astride the old wall, and how the layout of the eastern and western parts of the cities reflects their different histories.

Urban geographers use concepts such as urban morphology to study cities. Urban geographers also study how states build and rebuild cities, and work to understand the interlinkages between political geography and urban geography. When West Germany and East Germany reunified in 1990, Germans debated the choice of a new capital. Many favored Bonn, which served as the capital of West Germany and is located near the country's western border—symbolizing Germany's prominence in western Europe. Many others preferred a return to Berlin, which had served as the capital since Bismarck united the country and formed the first German state in 1870. Still other Germans wanted to put the past and both cities behind them; they argued for a totally new choice, such as Hanover, near the center of the country. In the end, the German government selected Berlin and began a giant construction program to transform Berlin, to symbolize a new era.

In this chapter, we trace the evolution of urbanization in geographic context, identify the factors that influenced the location and growth of cities, investigate the internal structure of cities in various cultural settings, and examine the way cities are organized and how they function. Finally, we study how people make cities and the roles cities play in globalization.

Key Questions For Chapter 9

1. When and why did people start living in cities?
2. Where are cities located and why?
3. How are cities organized, and how do they function?
4. How do people make cities?
5. What role do cities play in globalization?

WHEN AND WHY DID PEOPLE START LIVING IN CITIES?

Cities are centers of political power and industrial might, higher education and technological innovation, artistic achievement and medical advances. They are the great markets, centers of specialization and interaction, sources of news and information, suppliers of services, and providers of sports and entertainment. Cities are the anchors of modern culture; urban systems and their spokes form the structural skeleton of society. A **city** is a conglomeration of people and buildings clustered together to serve as a center of politics, culture, and economics.

Virtually everywhere in the world, people are moving from the countryside to urbanized areas, to towns, cities, and suburbs. Globally, more people live in towns and cities than in rural areas, making the global population predominantly **urban**, a term we use to describe the buildup of the central city and the suburban realm—the city and the surrounding environs connected to the city. An urban place is distinctively nonrural and nonagricultural. The move of people from rural to urban areas reflects the changing global economy and the increasing ease of movement in our globalized world. Urbanization is happening everywhere; however, the distribution of urbanization across the globe is not even (Fig. 9.3). In western Europe, the United States, Canada, and Japan, four out of five people live in cities or towns. In India and China, the figure is closer to four out of ten.

In the modern world, urbanization can happen quite quickly. A rural area or a small town can be transformed quickly into a major metropolitian area. During the later part of the twentieth century, the Chinese government announced a major economic development project in Guangdong, a province in southern China (Fig. 9.4). The Chinese government established a special economic zone (SEZ) in Guangdong Province, and business and industry mushroomed. The small fishing village of Shenzhen in Guangdong Province is adjacent to Hong Kong. Hundreds of industries moved from Hong Kong to Shenzhen to take advantage of lower labor costs. The small fishing village of Shenzhen experienced extraordinary growth as its population, rushing to the area to find work, swelled from 20,000 to 3.1 million in just three decades. Shenzhen was quickly transformed: skyscrapers now tower where thatch houses, rice paddies, and duck ponds once stood (Fig. 9.5).

The urbanization that can happen so quickly today took thousands of years to develop originally; indeed, the rise of the city is a very recent phenomenon in human history. Human communities have existed for over 100,000 years, but more than 90,000 years passed before people began to cluster in towns. Archaeological evidence indicates that people established the first cities about 8000 years ago. However, only in the last 200 years did cities begin to resemble their modern size and structure.

The Hearths of Urbanization

Before people could live in cities, they had to switch from hunting and gathering to agriculture. After agriculture began between 10,000 and 12,000 years ago, people became more sedentary, staying in one place to tend their fields. People clustered in small agricultural villages and towns, living there year round.

Agricultural villages were relatively small in size and in population. Everyone living in an **agricultural village** was involved in agriculture, and the people lived at near-subsistence levels, producing just enough to get by. The dwellings in ancient agricultural villages were about the same size and contained about the same number of possessions, reflecting the egalitarian nature (sharing of goods in common among the people) of the societies living in these early villages. The populations were permanent, reflected in the dwelling units where people moved rocks in, built permanent structures, and laid out floors made of plaster. Egalitarian societies persisted long after agriculture began.

Scholars are fairly certain that these descriptors accurately depict the agricultural villages in the first agricultural hearth, the area of Southwest Asia called the Fertile Crescent. Additional archaeological evidence portrays agricultural villages in the later hearths of agricultural innovation, the Indus River Valley and Mesoamerica, as also fitting these descriptors. When people establish cities, however, these descriptors become inaccurate. In cities, people generate personal material wealth, trade over long distances, live in stratified classes that are usually reflected in the housing, and engage in a diversity of economic activities—not just agriculture.

Two components enable the formation of cities: **agricultural surplus** and **social stratification**. Archaeologists, anthropologists, and geographers have studied the remains and records of the first cities, creating numerous theories as to how cities came about. Most agree that some series of events led to the formation of an agricultural surplus and a leadership class; which came first varies by theory. The series of events spurring these two components also varies by theory. One theory maintains that advances in technology such as irrigation generated an agricultural surplus, and a leadership class formed to control the surplus and the technology that produced it. Another theory holds that a king or priest-king centralized political power and then demanded more labor to generate an agricultural surplus, which would help the ruler retain political power.

Regardless of how the leadership class was established, we do know that once established, it helped generate the surplus and facilitated that control of its distribution. The link between the surplus and the leadership class is clear in early cities, where the home of the leaders was often positioned close to the grain storage. The **leadership class**, or urban elite, consisted of a group of decision makers and organizers who controlled the resources, and often the lives, of others. The urban elite controlled the food supply, including its production, storage, and distribution. Generating an agricultural surplus enabled some people to devote their efforts to pursuits besides agriculture. The Urban elite, for instance, did not work the fields. Rather, they

URBAN POPULATION AS A PERCENTAGE OF THE TOTAL POPULATION

- 90% and above
- 70–89%
- 55–69%
- 40–54%
- 25–39%
- 24% and below
- Data not available

0   1000   2000   3000 Kilometers
0   1000   2000 Miles

Figure 9.3

Urban Population as a Percentage of the Total Population, by State. *Data from*: United Nations, Department of Economic and Social Affairs, Population Division, 2003.

devoted time to other pursuits such as religion and philosophy. Out of such pursuits came the concepts of writing and recordkeeping. Writing made possible the codification of laws and the preservation of traditions. Urban elites defended themselves by constructing walls on the outskirts of the city. However, the leadership class collected taxes and tribute from people within their control beyond the city walls.

Some cities grew out of agricultural villages, and others grew in places previously unoccupied by sedentary people. The innovation of the city is called the **first urban revolution**, and it occurred independently in five separate hearths, a case of independent invention[1] (Fig. 9.6).

---

[1]Some scholars argue that there are fewer than five hearths and attribute more urbanization to diffusion.

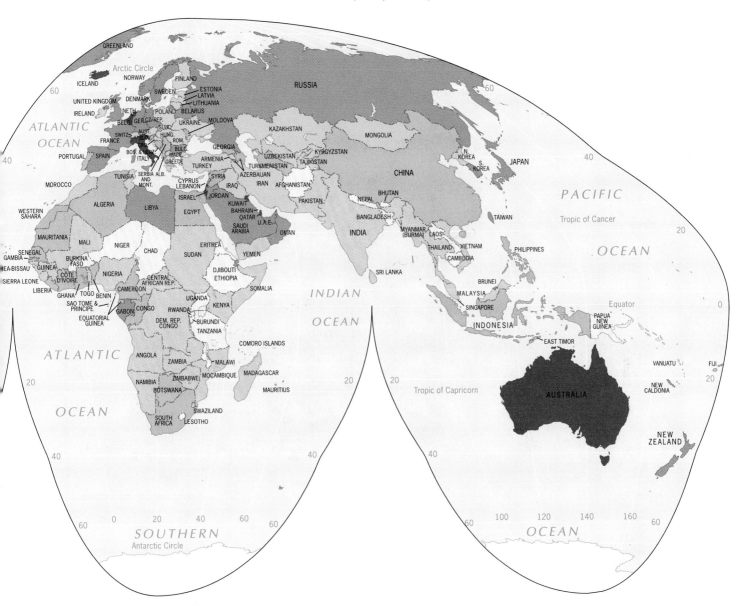

In each of the urbanization hearths, something triggered the establishment of a leadership class and an agricultural surplus. People became engaged in economic activities beyond agriculture, including specialty crafts, the military, trade, and government.

Not surprisingly, the five urban hearths are tied closely to the hearths of agriculture. The first hearth of agriculture, the Fertile Crescent, is the first place we see cities, in about 3500 BCE. This urban hearth is called **Mesopotamia**, referring to the region of great cities (such as Ur and Babylon) located between the Tigris and Euphrates rivers. Studies of the cultural landscape and urban morphology of Mesopotamian cities have found signs of social inequality in the varying sizes and ornamentation of houses. Urban elite erected palaces, protected themselves with walls, and employed countless artisans to

Figure 9.4
Hong Kong and Shenzhen, China. © H. J. de Blij, P. O. Muller, and John Wiley & Sons, Inc.

Figure 9.5
Shenzhen, China. Shenzhen changed from a fishing village to a major metropolitan area in just 25 years. Everything you see in this photograph is less than 25 years old; all of this stands where duck ponds and paddies lay less than three decades ago. © H. J. de Blij.

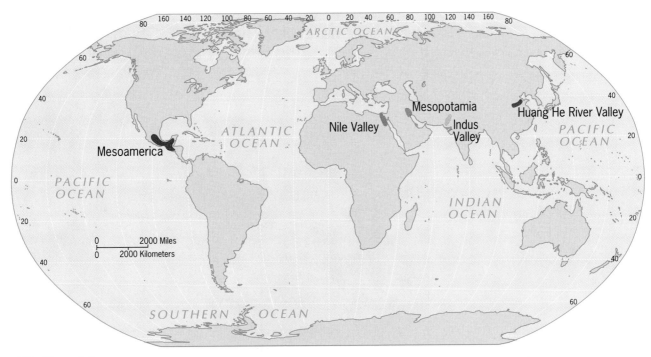

Figure 9.6
Five hearths of Urbanization.   © E. H. Fouberg, A. B. Murphy, H. J. de Blij, and John Wiley & Sons, Inc.

beautify their spaces. They also established a priest-king class and developed a religious-political ideology to support the priest-kings. Rulers in the cities were both priests and kings, and they levied taxes and demanded tribute from the harvest brought by the agricultural laborers.

Archaeologists, often teaming up with anthropologists and geographers, have learned much about the ways ancient Mesopotamian cities functioned by studying the urban morphology of the cities. The ancient Mesopotamian city was usually protected by a mud wall surrounding the entire community, or sometimes a cluster of temples and shrines at its center. Temples dominated the urban landscape, not only because they were the largest structures in town but also because they were built on artificial mounds often over 100 feet (30 meters) high.

In Mesopotamia, priests and other authorities resided in substantial buildings, many of which might be called palaces. Ordinary citizens lived in mud-walled houses packed closely together and separated only by narrow lanes. Lining the narrow lanes, craftspeople set up their workshops. The poorest inhabitants lived in tiny huts, often with mud-smeared reed walls, on the outskirts of the city. The leadership class held slaves in prison-like accommodations, sometimes outside the city wall.

Lacking waste-disposal or sewage facilities, ancient cities were far from sanitary. Mesopotamians threw their garbage and refuse into the streets and other open spaces, and in some places layers of this waste accumulated to a depth of several yards. As a result, disease kept the population of ancient cities small. Although many died from the unsanitary conditions, archaeologists have been able to sift through the garbage for clues to life in the ancient city.

The second hearth of urbanization is the **Nile River Valley**, dating back to 3200 BCE. Some scholars contend that this region is not a hearth, but rather a case of diffusion from Mesopotamia. Many argue that agriculture diffused to this region from the Fertile Crescent, but evidence supports the independent invention of urbanization in the Nile River Valley. At the very least, the interrelationship between urbanization and irrigation in this region distinguishes it from other urban hearths. Unlike other early cities, the people of the Nile River Valley did not build walls around their cities. From early on, power along the river was concentrated in the hands of the people who controlled the irrigation systems. The absence of walls around individual cities reflects the singular control of the region. The might of the rulers of the Nile River Valley is reflected in the feats of architecture such as the great pyramids, tombs, and sphinx that were built by thousands of slaves.

The third urban hearth, dating to 2200 BCE, is the **Indus River Valley**, another place where agriculture likely diffused from the Fertile Crescent. Unable to decipher ancient Indus writing, scholars are puzzled by Harappa and Mohenjo-Daro, the first cities of the Indus River Valley (Fig. 9.7). The intricate planning of the cities points to the existence of a leadership class, but the houses continued to be equal in size, with no palaces or monuments appearing

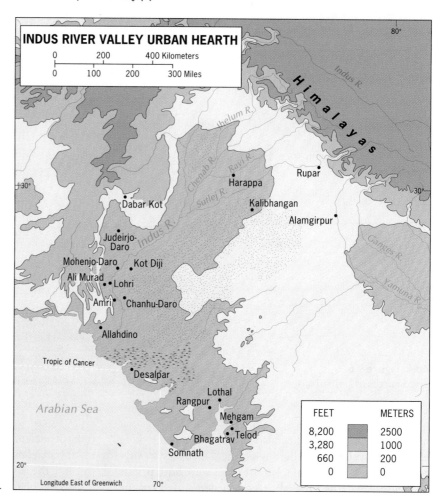

Figure 9.7
Indus River Valley Urban Hearth.
© H. J. de Blij, P. O. Muller, and John Wiley & Sons, Inc.

in the cities. In addition, all the dwellings in the cities had access to the same infrastructure—including wastewater drains and carefully maintained stonelined wells. The cities had thick walls, and the discovery of coins from as far away as the Mediterranean found at the gateways to these walls points to significant trade over long distances.

The fourth urban hearth arose around the confluence of the **Huang He** (Yellow) and **Wei** (Yangtzi) **River Valleys** of present-day China, dating to 1500 BCE. The Chinese purposefully planned their ancient cities to center on a vertical structure in the middle of the city and then built an inner wall around it. Within the inner wall, the people of this hearth typically placed temples and palaces for the leadership class. The urban elite of the Huang He and Wei region, like the urban elite of the Nile River Valley, demonstrated their power by building enormous, elaborate structures. Around 200 BCE, the Emperor Qin Xi Huang directed the building of the Great Wall of China. Like the Egyptians, he also had an elaborate mausoleum built for himself. An estimated 700,000 slaves worked for over 40 years to craft the intricate faces and weapons, horses, and chariots of an army of over 7000 terracotta warriors who stand guard over his burial place (Fig. 9.8).

Chronologically, the fifth urban hearth is **Mesoamerica**, dating to 200 BCE. The ancient cities of Mesoamerica were religious centers. The urban elite in Mesoamerica augmented their authority with priests, temples, and shrines. Many ancient cities were theocratic centers where rulers were deemed to have divine authority and were, in effect, god-kings. Examples include the great structures of Yucatan, Guatemala, and Honduras built by the Maya Indians (including Tikal, Chichén-Itzá, Uxmal, and Copán in Fig. 9.9).

The Role of the Ancient City in Society

Ancient cities not only were centers of religion and power, but also served as economic nodes. Cities were the chief marketplaces and bases from which wealthy merchants, land and livestock owners, and traders operated. As educational centers, residents of cities included teachers and philosophers. They also had handicraft industries that attracted the best craftspeople and inventors. In all of these roles, ancient cities were the anchors of culture and society, the focal points of power, authority, and change.

Figure 9.8
Terracotta Warriors guarding the tomb of the Chinese Emperor Qin Xi Huang. An estimated 700,000 slaves worked for over 40 years, around 200 BCE, to craft more than 7000 terracotta warriors who stand guard over the emperor's tomb. © O. Louis Mazzatenta/National Geographic Society/Getty Images.

Figure 9.9
Mayan and Aztec Civilizations. © E. H. Fouberg, A. B. Murphy, H. J. de Blij, and John Wiley & Sons, Inc.

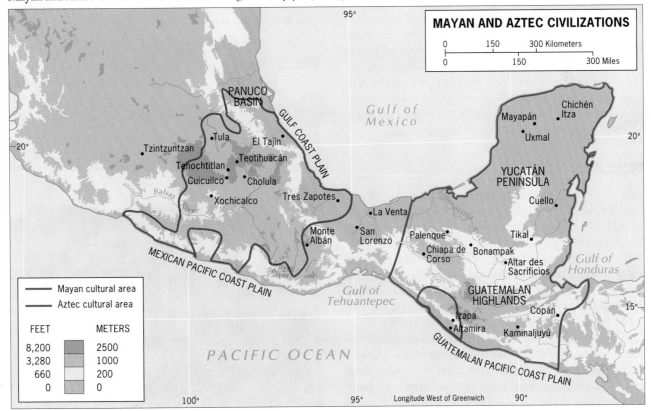

As the principal centers, crossroads, markets, places of authority, and religious headquarters, the earliest towns drew talent, trade, and travelers from far distances. Where else would metallurgy have developed? Where would a traveler, tradesman, priest, or pilgrim rest before continuing the journey? Towns had to have facilities that would not be found in farm villages: buildings to entertain visitors, package food, process raw materials, provide a place for worship, and house those who defended the town.

How large were the ancient cities? We have only estimates because it is impossible to judge from excavated ruins the dimensions of a city at its height or the number of people who might have occupied each residential unit. By modern standards, the ancient cities were not large. The cities of Mesopotamia and the Nile Valley may have had between 10,000 and 15,000 inhabitants after nearly 2000 years of growth and development. That, scholars conclude, is about the maximum sustainable size based on existing systems of food production, gathering, distribution, and social organization, These urban places were geographical exceptions in an overwhelmingly rural world. The modern city we know today did not emerge until several thousand years later.

Diffusion of Urbanization

Urbanization diffused from Mesopotamia in several directions. Populations in Mesopotamia grew with the steady food supply and a sedentary lifestyle. People migrated out from the hearth, diffusing their knowledge of agriculture and urbanization. Diffusion from Mesopotamia happened early, even before agriculture developed independently in some other hearths. In fact, urbanization diffused to the Mediterranean from Mesopotamia (and perhaps the Nile River Valley) more than 3500 years ago, at about the same time cities were developing in the hearth of the Huang He and long before cities originated in Mesoamerica.

Greek Cities

More than 3500 years ago, the city of Knossos on the island of Crete was the cornerstone of a system of towns in the Minoan civilization. By 500 BCE, Greece had become one of the most highly urbanized areas on Earth. The urbanization of Ancient Greece ushered in a new stage in the evolution of cities. At its height, Ancient Greece encompassed a network of more than 500 cities and towns, not only on the mainland but also on the many Greek islands. Seafarers connected these urban places with trade routes and carried the notion of urban life throughout the Mediterranean region. Athens and Sparta, often vying with each other for power, soon became Greece's leading cities. Athens may have been the largest city in the world at the time, with an estimated 250,000 inhabitants.

With the hilly topography of Greece, the people had no need to build earthen mounds on which to perch temples; these were provided by nature. Every city had its **acropolis** (acro=highpoint, polis=city), on which the people built the most impressive structures—usually religious buildings. The Parthenon of Athens remains the most famous of all, surviving to this day despite nearly 2500 years of war, earth tremors, vandalism, and environmental impact (Fig. 9.10). Building this magnificent columned structure, designed by the Athenian architect-engineer Phidias, began in 447 BCE, and its rows of tapering columns have inspired architects ever since.

Like the older Southwest Asian cities, Greece's cities also had public places. In the Southwest Asian towns these seem to have been rather cramped, crowded, and bustling with activity, but in Ancient Greece they were open, spacious squares, often in a low part of town with steps leading down to them (Fig. 9.11). On these steps the Greeks debated, lectured, judged each other, planned military campaigns, and socialized. As time went on, this public space called the **agora** (meaning market) also became the focus of commercial activity.

Greece's cities also had excellent theaters. The aristocracy attended plays and listened to philosophical discourses, but for many people life in a Greek city was miserable. Housing was no better than it had been in the Mesopotamian cities thousands of years earlier. Sanitation and health conditions were poor. And much of the grandeur designed by Greece's urban planners was the work of hundreds of thousands of slaves.

Figure 9.10

Athens, Greece. The rocky hilltop of Athens is home to the Acropolis (acro means high point). The Athens Acropolis is still crowned by the great Parthenon, standing after nearly 25 centuries. © H. J. de Blij.

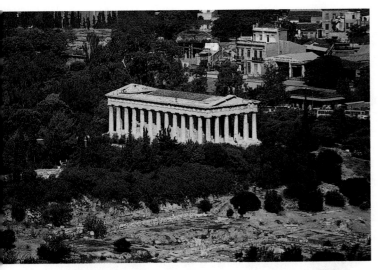

Figure 9.11

Athens, Greece. Looking down from the Acropolis, you can see the agora, the ancient trade and market area, which is surrounded by new urban buildings. © H. J. de Blij.

Although Greece was not a hearth of urbanization, the Greek city had global, rather than regional, impact. Urbanization diffused from Greece to the Roman Empire. Roman urbanization and urban culture diffused through Western Europe. The city declined in Europe for a time after the fall of the Roman Empire, but Europeans eventually carried Western concepts of city life around the world through colonialism and capitalism. From Washington, D.C. to Canberra, Australia, the urban landscape shows the imprints of Greco-Roman urban culture.

Roman Cities

The great majority of Greece's cities and towns were located near the Mediterranean Sea on peninsulas and islands and linked by sea routes. When the Romans succeeded the Greeks (and Etruscans) as rulers of the region, their empire incorporated not only the Mediterranean shores but also a large part of interior Europe and North Africa (Fig. 9.12). The Roman urban system was the

Figure 9.12

Roman Empire c. 117 CE. The Romans established a system of cities linked by a network of land and sea routes. Many of the Roman cities have grown into modern metropolises. © E. H. Fouberg, A. B. Murphy, H. J. de Blij, and John Wiley & Sons, Inc.

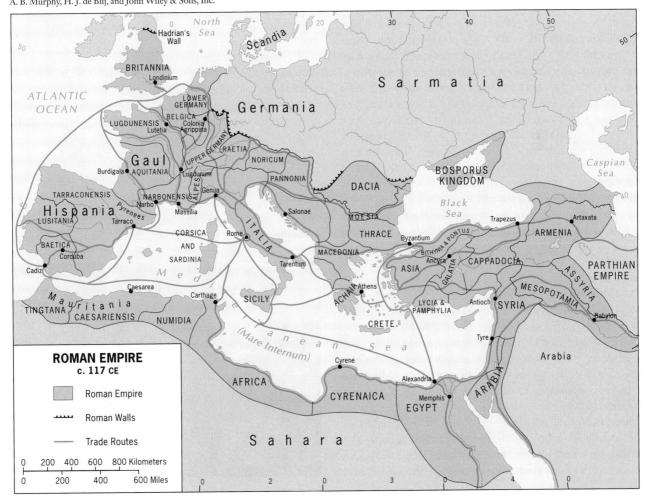

Field Note

"There can be few spaces of greater significance to the development of Western civilization than the Roman Forum. This was the nerve center of a vast empire that transformed the face of western Europe, Southwest Asia, and North Africa. It was also the place where the decisions were made that carried forward Greek ideas about governance, art, urban design, and technology. The very organization of space found in the Roman Forum is still with us: rectilinear street patterns; distinct buildings for legislative, executive, and judicial functions; and public spaces adorned with statues and fountains."

Figure 9.13
Rome, Italy.   © Alexander B. Murphy.

largest yet—much larger than Greece's domain. The capital, Rome, served as the apex of a hierarchy of settlements ranging from small villages to large cities. The Romans linked these places with an extensive transportation network that included hundreds of miles of roads, well-established sea routes, and trading ports along the roads, sea, and rivers. Roman regional planners displayed a remarkable capacity for choosing the **site** of cities, for identifying suitable locales for settlements. The site of a city is its absolute location, often chosen for its trade location, defensive advantages, or because it was seen as an appropriate religious location.

Romans were greatly influenced by the Greeks, as is evident in Roman mythology and visible in the cultural landscape and urban morphology of Roman cities. Greeks planned their colonial cities in a rectangular grid pattern, and Romans adopted this plan wherever surface conditions made it possible. Romans took the Greek acropolis and agora and combined them into one zone, the **Forum**, the focal point of Roman public life (Fig. 9.13). In Rome, the forum includes the world's first great stadium, the Colosseum, which was a much grander version of the Greek theater. Before crowds of thousands of onlookers, Roman gladiators fought each other or killed wild animals imported from Africa in the Colosseum. After Christianity diffused to Rome, but before the Roman Empire adopted Christianity, Romans even forced Christians into the Colosseum where hungry lions attacked and ate them. All Roman cities of any size had an arena like the Colosseum

where competitions, war games, ceremonies, and other public events took place.

Throughout the Roman Empire, cities were places of cultural contrasts. What still stands in ruins in many places around the Mediterranean are monumental buildings, impressive villas, spacious avenues, ingenious aqueducts and baths, and sewage systems built of stone and pipe (Fig. 9.14). What we can no longer see in the ruins of the empire are the thousands of slaves who built these structures (estimates are

Figure 9.14
Nimes, France.   Aqueducts outside of Nimes, France were built during the Roman Empire, about 2000 years ago.   © Alexander B. Murphy.

between one-third and two-thirds of the population of the empire was enslaved) and the wretchedly poor who were crammed into overcrowded tenements and lived in filth. The city of the Roman Empire, like the city of today, was home to both rich and poor and reflected both the greatest achievements and the worst failings of civilization.

Urban Growth after Greece and Rome

After the Roman Empire fell in 495 CE, Europe entered an era historians called the Middle Ages, which spans from about 500 to 1300 (or later in parts of Europe). During the first two-thirds of this period in Europe, little urban growth occurred, and in some parts of the continent, urbanism went into sharp decline. The urban growth that did take place during this time occurred on sites of oases and resting places along the Silk Route between Europe and Asia. Many of these places grew into towns, and some, such as Bukhara and Samarqand, became major cities. In Asia, Chinese styles of city-building diffused into Korea and Japan, with Seoul becoming a full-fledged city by 1200 and Kyoto, Japan's historic capital, growing rapidly after the turn of the ninth century.

During Europe's Middle Ages, urbanization continued vigorously outside of Europe. In West Africa, trading cities developed along the southern margin of the Sahara. By 1350, Timbuktu (part of Mali today) was a major city—a seat of government, a university town, a market, and a religious center. The Americas also experienced significant urban growth during Europe's Middle Ages, especially within the Mayan and Aztec empires (Fig. 9.15).

Figure 9.15

Altun Ha, Belize. Between 300 and 900 CE, Altun Ha served as a thriving trade and distribution center for the Caribbean merchant canoe traffic. Some of the trails in Altun Ha led all the way to Teotihuacan. © H. J. de Blij.

The largest pre-Columbian city in the Americas was in the Aztec Empire on the Mexican Plateau. The Aztec capital of Tenochtitlán had nearly 100,000 inhabitants when many European cities lay in ruins.

Site and Situation during European Exploration

Early Eurasian urban areas extended in a crescent-shaped zone across Eurasia from England in the west to Japan in the east, including the cities of London, Paris, Venice, Constantinople (Istanbul today), and Tabriz, Samarqand, Kabul, Lahore, Amra, Jaunpur, Xian, Anyang, Kyoto and Osaka. Before European exploration, most cities in the world were sited in the interiors of continents, not just in Eurasia, but also in West Africa and indigenous America. Interior trade routes such as the Silk Route and the caravan routes of West Africa sustained these inland cities and, in many cases, helped them prosper.

The relative importance of the interior trade routes changed, however, when European maritime exploration and overseas colonization ushered in an era of oceanic, worldwide trade. With this shift, the situation of cities like Paris and Xian changed from being crucial in an interior trading route to being left out of an oceanic trade. The **situation** of a city is its relative location, its place in the region and world around it.

After European exploration took off during the 1400s, the dominance of interior cities declined. Other cities, sited on coasts, gained prominence as their situations changed. In Asia, coastal cities such as Bombay (now Mumbai, India), Madras (Chennai, India), Malacca (Malaysia), Batavia (Jakarta, Indonesia), and Tokyo (Japan) came to the fore. Exploration and oceanic trade refocused the situations of cities in West Africa as well. Before 1500, urbanization in West Africa was concentrated in a belt extending along the southern margin of the Sahara, including such cities as Timbuktu (Mali), Niani (Guinea), Gao (Mali), Zaria (Nigeria), Kano (Nigeria), and Maiduguri (Nigeria). Here, cross-desert caravan traffic met boat traffic on the River Niger (where "camel met canoe"), and people exchanged goods from northern deserts for goods from coastal forests. Maritime trade disrupted this pattern of trade: coastal ports became the leading markets and centers of power, and the African cities of the interior began a long decline.

Coastal cities remained crucial after exploration led to colonialism. During the colonial period key cities in international trade networks included the coastal cities of Cape Town (South Africa), Lima-Callao (Peru), and New York City.

The trade networks European powers commanded (including the slave trade) brought unprecedented riches to Europe's burgeoning medieval cities, such as Amsterdam (the Netherlands), London (England), Lisbon (Portugal),

Field Note

"The contemporary landscape of Genoa stands as a reminder of the city's historic importance. Long before Europe became divided up into states, a number of cities in northern Italy freed themselves from the strictures of feudalism and began to function autonomously. Genoa and Venice were two of these, and they became the foci of significant Mediterranean maritime trading empires. In the process, they also became magnificent, wealthy cities. Although most buildings in Genoa's urban core date from a more recent era, the layout of streets and public squares harkens back to the city's imperial days. Is it a surprise that the city gave birth to one of the most famous explorers of all time: Christopher Columbus?"

Figure 9.16
Genoa, Italy.   © Alexander B. Murphy.

Liverpool (England), and Seville (Spain). Successful merchants built ornate mansions, patronized the arts, participated in city governance, and supported the reconstruction of city centers. As a result, cities that thrived during mercantilism took on similar properties whether it was Antwerp (Belgium), Copenhagen (Denmark), Lisbon (Portugal), or Genoa (Italy). A central square became the focus of the city, fronted by royal, religious, public, and private buildings evincing wealth and prosperity, power and influence (Fig. 9.16). Streets leading to these central squares formed arteries of commerce, and the beginnings of "downtowns" emerged.

During the sixteenth and seventeenth centuries, European mercantile cities became the nodes of a widening network of national, regional, and global commerce. So wealthy and powerful were the merchants that, supported by their rulers, they were able to found and expand settlements in distant lands. Cities such as Dakar (Senegal), Lourenco Marques (now Maputo, Moçambique), and Saigon (now Ho Chi Minh City, Vietnam) were endowed with the ornate trappings of the mercantile cities of Europe, including elaborately inlaid sidewalks, tree-lined avenues, and neo-Gothic architecture.

The Second Urban Revolution

During the last decades of the eighteenth century, the Industrial Revolution began in Great Britain. None of Europe's cities was prepared for what lay ahead: an avalanche of changes that ripped the fabric of urban life. Around 1800, western Europe was still overwhelmingly rural. As thousands migrated to the cities with industrialization, cities had to adapt to the mushrooming population, the proliferation of factories and supply facilities, the expansion of transport systems, and the construction of tenements for the growing labor force.

Before the second urban revolution could take place, a second revolution in agriculture was necessary. In order for people to move from the fields to the cities to work in manufacturing, food production had to increase. During the late seventeenth century and into the eighteenth century, Europeans invented a series of important improvements in agriculture, including the seed drill, hybrid seeds, and improved breeding practices for livestock. Freed from the fields, laborers were able to migrate to cities in hopes of a job. Manufacturers tapped into this labor force for the burgeoning industries (for a further discussion of industrialization, see Chapter 12).

Not all mercantile cities turned into industrial cities. Many industrial cities grew from small villages or along canal and river routes. The primary determinant in the location of early industrial cities was proximity to a power source. For textile manufacturing, industrial cities had to be sited near fresh water sources to power the water loom. In Great Britain, industrial cities involved in textile manufacturing were located in the Pennines, where fresh water flowed down the hillsides. Industrial cities involved in iron manufacturing were located around Birmingham and Coalbrookdale, easily accessible to Britain's coal and iron ore fields.

When industrialization diffused from Great Britain to the European mainland, the places most ready for industrialization had undergone their own second agricultural revolution, had surplus capital from mercantilism and colonialism, and were located near coal fields (Fig. 9.17).

With industrialization, cities became unregulated jumbles of activity. Factories engulfed private homes. Open spaces became garbage dumps. Urban dwellers converted elegant housing into overcrowded slums. Sanitation systems failed, and water supplies were inadequate and often polluted. By the late 1800s, the Industrial Revolution had changed transportation significantly. The steam engine, powered by coal, not only pumped water from mines for coal mining but also powered the railroad and steamship. The diffusion of the railroad gave cities that were not near coal fields the chance to industrialize. The central parts of cities like London, Paris, and Amsterdam retained their preindustrial shape. But with the diffusion of the railroad, railroad tracks knifed through long-stable neighborhoods.

Living conditions were dreadful for workers in cities, and working conditions were shocking. Children worked 12-hour shifts in textile mills, typically six days a week. In industrial cities, health conditions were worse than they had been in medieval times; the air was polluted and the water contaminated. The grimy, soot-covered cities of the British Midlands were appropriately deemed the "black towns." Few if any safety mechanisms protected the laborers, and injuries were common.

In the mid-1800s, as Karl Marx and Frederick Engels (writing in Germany, Belgium, and England) encouraged "workers of the world" to unite, conditions in European manufacturing cities gradually improved. Industries began to recognize workers' rights, and governments intervened by legislating workers' rights and introducing city planning and zoning. Many manufacturing cities in North America never suffered as much as their European predecessors, although living and working conditions for factory workers (and "blue-collar" workers generally) were

Figure 9.17

Industrialized Regions of Europe, 1914. *Adapted with permission from*: Geoffrey Barraclough, ed. *The Times Concise Atlas of World History*, 5th edition, Hammond Incorporated, 1998.

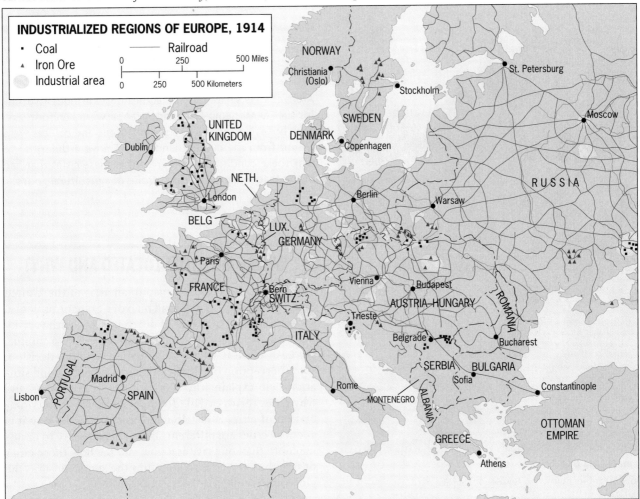

Field Note

"The Ruhr Valley long functioned as the incubator of Germany's industrial economy. Largely destroyed during World War II, the Ruhr rose again to help Germany back to recovery. But as declining transportation costs and rising labor costs prompted heavy industries to move their operations to other parts of the world, factories such as this iron and steel mill on the edge of Duisburg fell silent. Unemployment soared, and the area became depressed. In an effort to rebound, local authorities are now trying to turn a few of these relics into tourist destinations. They are unlikely to compete with the great churches or medieval palaces found elsewhere in Germany, but for the geographer they provide fascinating insights into the urban and economic arrangements that made modern Europe what it is today."

Figure 9.18
Duisburg, Germany.   © Alexander B. Murphy.

far from satisfactory. American manufacturing cities did not altogether escape the problems of the European industrial cities. During the late nineteenth and early twentieth centuries, the American manufacturing city grew rapidly, often with inadequate planning and rapid immigration leading to the development of slums and ghettoes.

During the second half of the twentieth century, the nature of manufacturing changed, as did its location: cities repositioned many factories away from congested, overcrowded, expensive urban areas. Companies simply abandoned large manufacturing plants, making "rust belts" out of once-thriving industrial districts. Many of these plants still stand today, overgrown by weeds, with broken windows and cracking walls (Fig. 9.18).

Although factories and factory jobs are not permanent, the urbanization that went along with industrialization is still apparent. Today, western Europe is about 80 percent urban. The statistics on urbanization vary by source, as some define urban areas as being over 2500 people and others over 5000 people; still others use employment (percent nonagricultural) as the major criterion. By whatever definition, urbanization has become a global phenomenon, with the majority of the world's people living in cities today.

Archaeologists have found that the houses in Indus River cities, such as Mohenjo-Daro and Harappa, were a uniform size: each house had access to a sewer system, and palaces were absent from the cultural landscape. Derive a theory as to why these conditions were present in these cities that had both a leadership class and a surplus of agricultural goods.

WHERE ARE CITIES LOCATED AND WHY?

When you look at a map in an atlas of the United States or Canada, or at a road map of a State or province, you see an array of places of different sizes, with varying distances between them. The map looks like a jumble, yet each place is where it is because of some decision, some perception of the site or its situation. Site and situation help explain why certain cities were planned and why cities thrive or fail. To understand why a conglomeration of cities is distributed across space the way it is and why cities are different sizes, it is necessary to examine more than one city at a time and see how those cities fit together, into the region, into the state, and into the globe as a whole.

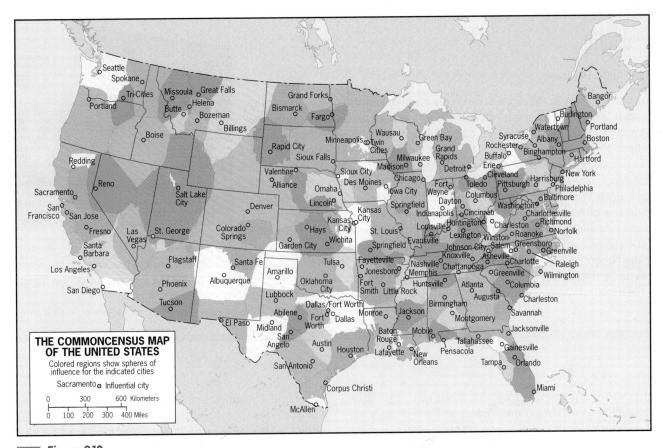

THE COMMONCENSUS MAP
OF THE UNITED STATES
Colored regions show spheres of
influence for the indicated cities

Sacramento ○ Influential city

0   300   600 Kilometers
0 100 200 300 400 Miles

Figure 9.19

Regions of Influence for cities in the contiguous United States. This map is based on
survey data from over 45,000 voters on commoncensus.org who answered the question, "On
the Level of North America as a whole, what major city do you feel has the most cultural and
economic influence on your area overall?" Adapted with permission from: www.commoncensus.
org, last accessed August 2008.

Urban geographers studied the distribution of cities
in Europe and the Americas during the 1900s, using quantitative techniques to determine how many cities and what
size cities are needed within a certain space. In studying
the size of cities and distances between them, urban geographers explored the trade areas of different size cities.
Every city and town has a **trade area**, an adjacent region
within which its influence is dominant. Customers from
smaller towns and villages come to the city to shop and
to conduct other business. An online survey of approximately 50,000 people helped one armchair geographer
create a map of trade areas for the contiguous United
States (Fig. 9.19). The city's newspapers are read, and its
television stations are watched in the surrounding region
(Fig. 9.20).

Across the multitude of quantitative studies in urban
geography, three key components arose frequently: population, trade area, and distance. The simplest way to think
through the relationship among these three variables is
to consider your State or province map. On the map, you
will see many villages with unfamiliar names, a number
of small towns sited on highways, several medium-sized

cities where transportation routes converge, and likely
one familiar, dominant city. The largest city has the largest trade area, and as a result fewer places rival it as the
major trade area: the several medium-sized cities trade in
smaller areas of commerce and are scattered apart from
the major city, small towns house the grocery stores and
other necessities, and finally villages may still have a café
or a gas station. The trade areas and population combine
to give us a hierarchy of urban places, following a pattern
commonly called the rank-size rule.

The **rank-size rule** holds that in a model urban hierarchy, the population of a city or town will be inversely
proportional to its rank in the hierarchy. Thus, if the largest city has 12 million people, the second largest will have
about 6 million (that is, half the population of the largest city); the third city will have 4 million (one-third); the
fourth city 3 million; and so on. Note that the size differences between city levels become smaller at lower levels of
the hierarchy, so that the tenth-largest city would have 1.2
million inhabitants.

The rank-size rule does not apply in all countries,
especially countries with one supremely dominant city

Many trade areas in the United States are named, and their names typically coincide with the vernacular region, the region people perceive themselves as living in. In promoting a trade area, companies often adopt, name, or shape the name of the vernacular region. In Oklahoma, the label Green Country refers to the northeastern quarter of the state, the trade area served by Tulsa. Tourism promoters derived the label in the 1970s, and the Tulsa media have used the name since. Promoters see the label as positive, implying Green Country is a landscape of forests, lakes, rivers, hills, and wealth—a perception that challenges popular notions of Dust Bowl Oklahoma as a treeless, dry, flat, windy, and impoverished region of the 1930s. Green Country's popularity is confirmed

■ **Figure 9.20**

by the hundreds of businesses, organizations, and agencies that have adopted the name. In turn, the presence of the trade area name throughout the cultural landscape reinforces the vernacular region, strengthening the importance of the region in the minds of the people.

Credit: Brad Bays, Oklahoma State University

(often called a primate city because it is much larger than all other cities within a country), such as Paris (France) or Mexico City (Mexico), but it does seem to apply in a number of countries with a multitude of large cities, such as the United States (see final section of this chapter). The rank-size rule is an impressive trick when it works. However, it does not explain where cities will be located or distributed across the hierarchy.

Central Place Theory

Walter Christaller wrote the classic urban geography study to explain where cities, towns, and villages are likely to be located. In his book, *The Central Places in Southern Germany* (1933), Christaller laid the groundwork for **central place theory**. He attempted to develop a model to predict how and where central places in the urban hierarchy (hamlets, villages, towns, and cities) would be functionally and spatially distributed. Christaller began his theory development with a set of assumptions: first, the surface of the ideal region would be flat and have no physical barriers; second, soil fertility would be the same everywhere; third, population and purchasing power would be evenly distributed; next, the region would have a uniform transportation network to permit direct travel from each settlement to the other; and, finally, from any given place, a good or service could be sold in all directions out to a certain distance.

Through his studies, Christaller calculated the ideal central place system and then compared his model to real-world situations and tried to explain the variations and exceptions. In the urban hierarchy, the central places would be nested, so the largest central place provides the greatest number of functions to most of the region. Within the trade area of the largest central place, a series of larger towns would provide functions to several smaller places. The smaller places would then provide fewer central functions to a smaller-yet service area.

To determine the locations of each central place, Christaller needed to define the goods and services provided. He studied the sale of goods and services and calculated the distance people would willingly travel to acquire them. Cities, he postulated, would be regularly spaced, with central places where the same product was sold at the same price located a standard distance apart. He reasoned that a person would not be expected to travel 11 miles to one place to buy an item if it were possible to go only 9 miles to purchase it at another place. Central place theory maintains that each central place has a surrounding complementary region, an exclusive trade area within which the town has a monopoly on the sale of certain goods, because it alone can provide such goods at a given price and within a certain range of travel.

Hexagonal Hinterlands

Based on this description of Christaller's theory, you may expect the shape of each central place's trade area to be circular (bullseye shapes surrounding each place). But circles either have to overlap or leave certain areas unserved.

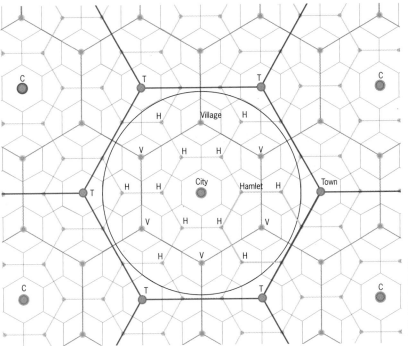

Figure 9.21
Christaller's Hierarchy of Settlements and Their Service Areas. Christaller's interlocking model of a hierarchy of settlements and their service areas include: C = city, T = town, V = village, H = hamlet.

Hence, Christaller chose perfectly fitted hexagonal regions as the shape of each trade area (Fig. 9.21).

Urban geographers were divided on the relevance of his model. Some saw hexagonal systems everywhere; others saw none at all. Christaller received support from geographers, who applied his ideas to regions in Europe, North America, and elsewhere. In China, both the North China Plain and the Sichuan Basin display the seemingly uninterrupted flatness assumed by Christaller's model. When G. William Skinner examined the distribution of villages, towns, and cities there in 1964, he found a spatial pattern closely resembling the one predicted by Christaller's model. Studies in the U.S. Midwest suggested that while the square layout of the township-and-range system imposed a different kind of regularity on the landscape, the economic forces at work there tended to confirm Christaller's theory.

Christaller recognized that not all his assumptions would be met in reality; physical barriers, uneven resource distributions, and other factors all modify Christaller's hexagons. Nonetheless, his model yielded a number of practical insights. His studies pointed to a hierarchy of urban places that are spatially balanced and also established that larger cities would be spaced farther from each other than smaller towns or villages. Although Christaller's model of perfectly fit hexagons is not often realized, his studies confirm that the distribution of cities, towns, and villages in a region is not an accident but is tied to trade areas, population size, and distance.

Central Places Today

When Christaller worked on his spatial model and projected central place theory to help explain the distribution of urban areas, the world was a simpler and much less populated place than it is today. As many urban geographers have pointed out during the debate that followed Christaller's publications, new factors, forces, and conditions not anticipated by his models and theories (including the Internet and the interstate system) make them less relevant today.

Geographer Larry Ford stresses that central place notions still have a role in explaining current developments. Take, for example, the **Sunbelt phenomenon** of the past four decades—the movement of millions of Americans from northern and northeastern States to the South and Southwest. This is not just an internal, voluntary migration made possible by social security funds and retirement plans; it also results from deliberate governmental economic and social polices that favor "Sunbelt" cities through federal spending on military, space, and research facilities. And even as Northerners moved southward, millions of Middle and South American migrants moved northward—into the same urban centers already growing for domestic reasons.

The overall effect of all this movement was to create a changed urban hierarchy in the Sunbelt region. Central place theory would predict that some existing cities would respond by increasing their production of higher-order (technological) goods and services, increasing their economic reach and bypassing others. And this is what happened: Atlanta, Dallas, and Phoenix became headquarters cities for large regions, moving up in the urban hierarchy. Charlotte, Tampa, San Antonio, and Tucson also rose, but took secondary status. Other centers participated less in the new spatial economy and remained where they were in the urban hierarchy.

As Ford emphasized, central place theory can still add "analytical power to the understanding of patterns of urban growth, even in this era of fast and long-distance transportation, suburbanization, and multiple urban functions."

Sketch a map of your city or town and the cities or towns nearby. Make a list of the kinds of goods and services available in each of these towns. Do the ideas about central places presented in this section of the chapter apply to your region?

HOW ARE CITIES ORGANIZED, AND HOW DO THEY FUNCTION?

For a number of years, urban geographers have studied, charted, and mapped cities to create models that describe how different parts of cities come together in different regions of the world. In this section of the chapter, we discuss a number of models that urban geographers have drawn for North American, South American, and other cities. In the next section of this chapter, we discuss the people and institutions that organize and create cities.

Across cities, you can see certain spaces defined for certain functions. The various parts of a city may be designated residential, industrial, or parkland. Or a group of people may take over an area of a city and redefine it to function for them. Cities are not simply random collections of buildings and people. Cities exhibit functional structure: they are spatially organized to perform their functions as places of commerce, production, education, and much more.

Models of the City

Each model of the city, regardless of the region, is a study in **functional zonation**—the division of the city into certain regions (zones) for certain purposes (functions). For example, cities typically have residential zones that are separate from industrial zones, which are separate from garbage dumps. By studying the kinds of zones cities have and by examining where the zones are located with respect to one another, urban geographers draw models of cities.

Before examining the models of urban spaces, we must define some terms commonly used in referring to parts of the city (especially cities in North America). The term **zone** is typically preceded by a descriptor that conveys the purpose of that area of the city. The models describe zones as areas with a relatively uniform land use, for example, an industrial zone or a residential zone. Most models define the key economic zone of the city (if there is such) as the **central business district** (CBD). The CBD is a concentration of business and commerce in the city's downtown. The American CBD typically has high land values, tall buildings, busy traffic, converging highways, and mass transit systems.

The term **central city** describes the urban area that is not suburban. In effect, central city refers to the older city as opposed to the newer suburbs. A **suburb** is an outlying, functionally uniform part of an urban area, and is often (but not always) adjacent to the central city. Most suburbs are residential, but some have other land uses, including schools, shopping malls, and office parks.

Suburbanization is the process by which lands that were previously outside of the urban environment become urbanized, as people and businesses from the city move to these spaces. The process of suburbanization holds special interest for human geographers because it involves the transformation of large areas of land from rural to urban uses and affects large numbers of people who can afford to move to larger and more expensive suburban homes. The aesthetic of the suburb reveals the occupants' idealized living patterns because their layout can be planned in response to choice and demand. Elsewhere in the metropolis, constraints imposed by preexisting land-use arrangements make it difficult to build now houses with large lawns, multiple garages, and fenced-in yards.

In *Contemporary Suburban America* (1981), urban geographer P. O. Muller offers a thorough analysis of suburbanization, describing how suburbia "evolved into a self-sufficient urban entity, containing its own major economic and cultural activities, that is no longer an appendage to the central city." Muller found suburban cities ready to compete with the central city for leading urban economic activities such as telecommunications, high-technology industries, and corporate headquarters. In addition to expanding of residential zones, the process of suburbanization rapidly creates distinct urban regions complete with industrial, commercial, and educational components.

The overall importance of suburban life in the United States is underscored by the results of the 2000 census, which indicated that no less than 50 percent of the entire American population resided in the suburbs (up from 37 percent in 1970); the remaining 50 percent were divided between the central cities (30.3 percent) and nonmetropolitan or rural areas (19.7 percent). Of the population living in metropolitan areas, 62.2 percent resided in the suburbs, which in 2000 had 141 million residents. Thus, the suburbs have become the essence of the modern American city.

Just by using such terms as *residential area* and *central business district*, people acknowledge the existence of a regional structure within cities. When you refer to downtown, or to the airport, or to the city zoo, you are in fact referring to urban regions where certain functions prevail (business activity, transportation, and recreation, in the three just mentioned). All of these urban regions or zones lie near or adjacent to each other and together make up the metropolis. But how are they arranged? Is there any regularity or recurrent pattern in the location of the various zones, perhaps reflecting certain prevailing growth processes? In other words, can we create a model of the zones of a city that can then be recognized in every city, perhaps with modifications related to a city's particular site, size, shape, and relief?

Modeling the North American City

Urban geographers have constructed a succession of models, which reflect change and growth in the geographic layout of North American cities. The first model, the **concentric zone model** (Fig. 9.22 A), resulted from sociologist Ernest Burgess's study of Chicago in the 1920s. Burgess's model divides the city into five concentric zones, defined by their function. As the city grew, land was converted in zones around the outside of the city, and the concentric zone model emerged. At the center is the CBD (1), itself subdivided into several subdistricts (financial, retail, theater).

The zone of transition (2) is characterized by residential deterioration and encroachment by business and light manufacturing. Zone 3 is a ring of closely spaced but adequate homes occupied by the blue-collar labor force. Zone 4 consists of middle-class residences, and zone 5 is the suburban ring. Burgess described his model as dynamic: as the city grew, inner zones encroached on outer ones, so that CBD functions invaded zone 2 and the problems of zone 2 affected the inner margins of zone 3.

In the late 1930s, Homer Hoyt published his sector model (Fig. 9.22B), partly as an answer to the limitations of the Burgess model. Hoyt focused on residential patterns explaining where the wealthy in a city chose to live. Hoyt argued that the city grows outward from the center, so a low-rent area could extend all the way from the CBD

Figure 9.22

The Three Classical Models of Urban Structure.   The three classical models of urban structure are the concentric zone model, the sector model, and the multiple nuclei model.   © E. H. Fouberg, A. B. Murphy, H. J. de Blij, and John Wiley & Sons, Inc.

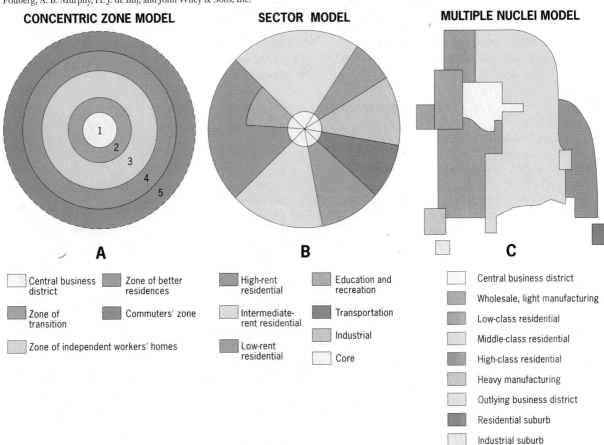

CONCENTRIC ZONE MODEL

SECTOR MODEL

MULTIPLE NUCLEI MODEL

A

B

C

Central business district

Zone of transition

Zone of independent workers' homes

Zone of better residences

Commuters' zone

High-rent residential

Intermediate-rent residential

Low-rent residential

Education and recreation

Transportation

Industrial

Core

Central business district

Wholesale, light manufacturing

Low-class residential

Middle-class residential

High-class residential

Heavy manufacturing

Outlying business district

Residential suburb

Industrial suburb

to the city's outer edge, creating zones that are shaped like a piece of pie. Hoyt found that the pie-shaped pieces describe the high-rent residential, intermediate rent residential, low-rent residential, education and recreation, transportation, and industrial sectors.

Researchers studied both theories, and Chauncy Harris and Edward Ullman argued that neither the concentric rings nor the sector model adequately reflected city structure by the mid-twentieth century. In the 1940s, Harris and Ullman proposed the multiple nuclei model (Fig. 9.22 C). Their model recognizes that the CBD is losing its dominant position as the single nucleus of the urban area. Several of the urban regions shown in the figure have their own nuclei.

Most urban geographers think these models are too simplistic to describe the modern city. With the availability of personal automobiles and the construction of ring roads and other arteries around cities in the 1970s and 1980s, suburbanization exploded around the new transportation corridors. The outer city grew rapidly and became more functionally independent of the central city, and new suburban downtowns emerged to serve their new local economies. Often located near key freeway intersections, these suburban downtowns developed mainly around big regional shopping centers and attracted industrial parks, office complexes, hotels, restaurants, entertainment facilities, and even sports stadiums. They became **edge cities**. Edge cities such as Tysons Corner, Virginia (outside Washington, D.C.) and Irvine, California (outside Los Angeles) flourished. They attracted tens of thousands of nearby suburbanites—offering workplaces, shopping,

leisure activities, and all the other elements of a complete urban environment—thereby loosening remaining ties not only to the central city but to other suburban areas as well (Fig. 9.23). As early as 1973, American suburbs surpassed the central cities in total employment. By the mid-1980s, in some metropolises in the Sunbelt, the majority of jobs in the metropolis were in the suburbs.

Geographers use the term **urban realm** to describe the spatial components of the modern metropolis, where each realm is a separate economic, social, and political entity that is linked together to form the larger metropolitan framework (Fig. 9.24). The urban realms model takes the latest step forward in interpreting the American urban structure. It clearly demonstrates that today's outer cities are not satellites of the central city; they too are shaping the metropolis.

Modeling the Cities of the Global Periphery and Semiperiphery

The number of cities in the world with millions of inhabitants can now be counted in the hundreds; it therefore becomes increasingly difficult to model, classify, or typify urban centers. In the 1960s, researchers classified "colonial" cities as urban areas where European transplants dominated the form of the city, laying it out with Western styles. They also drew models of "indigenous" cities that remained remote from globalizing influences and various forms of the Western city. Today, the "colonial" cities that served as the colonial headquarters (and have since

Figure 9.23
Tysons Corner, Virginia. In the suburbs of Washington, D.C., on Interstate 495 (the beltway), Tysons Corner has developed as a major edge city, with offices, retail, and commercial services.   © Rob Crandall/The Image Works.

URBAN REALMS MODEL

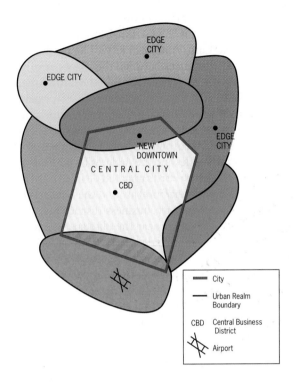

Figure 9.24
Urban Realms Model. The Urban Realms Model includes a central business district, central city, new downtown, and suburban downtown. *Adapted with permission from*: T. Hartshorn and P. O. Muller, "Suburban Downtowns and the Transformation of Metropolitan Atlanta's Business Landscape," *Urban Geography* 10 (1989); p. 375.

grown through massive migration) defy generalization. Even indigenous cities deep in continental interiors (such as those in West Africa's Sahel and in Central Asia) have been swept by the forces of globalization and immigration, and in the process they have been transformed.

In Middle and South America, Mexico City (Mexico) and São Paulo (Brazil) are now the kinds of megacities that make analysis difficult. But South American cities have been endowed with strong Iberian cultural imprints that define a certain common social-spatial geography. In Subsaharan Africa, some former colonial cities have retained the spatial components lost in enormous cities like Lagos (Nigeria) and Kinshasa (The Congo). And in Southeast Asia some middle-sized cities continue to exhibit a fairly consistent pattern.

The Latin American City

In 1980, geographers Ernst Griffin and Larry Ford studied Latin American cities and derived a model of the Latin American city referred to as the **Griffin-Ford model**. Griffin and Ford found that Latin American cities blend traditional elements of Latin American culture with the forces of globalization that are reshaping the urban scene, combining radial sectors and concentric zones.

Anchoring the model is the thriving CBD, which remains the city's primary business, employment, and

entertainment focus. The CBD is divided into a traditional market sector and a more modern high-rise sector. Adequate public transit systems and nearby affluent residential areas assure the dominance of the CBD. Emanating outward from the urban core along the city's most prestigious axis is the commercial spine, which is surrounded by the elite residential sector. This widening corridor is essentially an extension of the CBD. It features offices, shopping, high-quality housing for the upper and upper-middle classes, restaurants, theaters, and such amenities as parks, zoos, and golf courses. At the end of the elite spine sector lies an incipient edge city shown as "mall" on the model and flanked by high-priced residences. This reflects the emergence of suburban nodes from the North American model in South America's cities.

In the Griffin-Ford model, the remaining concentric zones are home to less well-off residents, who compose the great majority of the urban population. Socioeconomic levels and housing quality decrease markedly with greater distance from the city center (Fig. 9.25). The zone of maturity in the inner city contains the best housing outside the spine sector, attracting the middle classes, who invest sufficiently to keep their solidly built but aging dwellings from deteriorating. The adjacent zone is one of much more modest housing. Interspersed with the more modest areas are densely populated unkempt areas, which represent a transition from inner-ring affluence to outer-ring poverty. The outermost zone

A NEW AND IMPROVED MODEL
OF LATIN AMERICAN CITY STRUCTURE

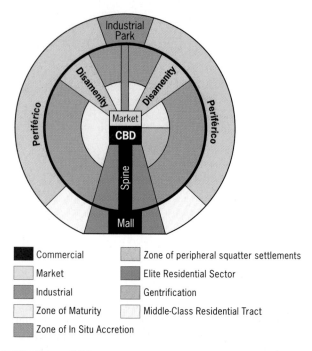

Commercial | Zone of peripheral squatter settlements

Market | Elite Residential Sector

Industrial | Gentrification

Zone of Maturity | Middle-Class Residential Tract

Zone of In Situ Accretion

Figure 9.25

**A New and Improved Model of the Latin American City
Structure.** This model includes both the zones created in the
original Griffin-Ford model and the new Ford model of the
Latin American city. *Adapted with permission from:* L. Ford, "A
New and Improved Model of Latin American City Structure,"
The Geographical Review 86 (1996), p. 438.

of peripheral squatter settlements is home to the impoverished and recent migrants. Although this ring consists
mainly of teeming, high-density shantytowns, residents
here are surprisingly optimistic about finding work and
improving their living conditions.

A structural element of many Latin American cities
is the **disamenity sector**, the very poorest parts of cities
that in extreme cases are not connected to regular city
services and are controlled by gangs and drug lords. The
disamenity sectors in Latin American cities contain relatively unchanging slums known as *barrios* or *favelas*. The
worst of these poverty-stricken areas often include large
numbers of people who are so poor that they are forced
to live in the streets (Fig. 9.26). There is little in the way
of regular law enforcement within such communities,
and drug lords often run the show—or battle with other
drug lords for dominance. Such conditions also prevail in
places beyond the ring highway or *periférico*, which is now
a feature of most South American cities.

Finally, the Griffin-Ford model displays two smaller
sectors: an industrial park, reflecting the ongoing concentration of industrial activity in the city, and a gentrification

zone, where historic buildings are preserved. Gentrification
remains much less common in South American cities than
in North America, but it is an emerging phenomenon.

To what extent is the Griffin-Ford model a realistic
portrayal of the Latin American city? The model reflects
the enormous differences between the spaces of privilege
and the spaces of abject poverty within the Latin American
city. The model also describes elements of sector development evident in many large South American cities, but the
concentricity suggested by the model seems to be breaking
down. Figure 9.25 incorporates both the original zones of
the Griffin-Ford model and the updates Larry Ford added
in a 1996 article. Larry Ford's updated Griffin-Ford model
adds a ring highway (*periférico*) around the outskirts of the
city, divides the downtown business district into a CBD
and a market, adds a mall near the elite space, and leaves
space for suburban industrial parks.

The African City

At the beginning of this century, Subsaharan Africa
included countries with some of the world's lowest levels of
urbanization. In the tropical region of Africa, the majority
of the people are farmers, and most countries in the tropics
remain under 40 percent urbanized. Outside the tropics,
the region is about 57 percent urban. Despite the region's
lower levels of overall urbanization than much of the rest
of the world, Africa now has the world's fastest growing
cities, followed by those in South Asia and mainland East
Asia and South and Middle America. In contrast, the cities
of North America, southern South America, and Australia
are growing more slowly, and those of western Europe are
barely growing at all.

The imprint of European colonialism can be seen
in many African cities. During colonialism, Europeans
laid out prominent urban centers such as Kinshasa (The
Congo), Nairobi (Kenya), and Harare (Zimbabwe) in
the interior, and Dakar (Senegal), Abidjan (Ivory Coast),
Luanda (Angola), Maputo (Mozambique), and other ports
along the coast. Africa even has cities that are neither
traditional nor colonial. South Africa's major urban
centers (Johannesburg, Cape Town, and Durban) are
essentially Western, with elements of European as well
as American models, including high-rise CBDs and
sprawling suburbs.

As a result of this diversity, it is difficult to formulate
a model African city. Studies of African cities indicate that
the central city often consists of not one but three CBDs
(Fig. 9.27): a remnant of the colonial CBD, an informal
and sometimes periodic market zone, and a transitional
business center where commerce is conducted from curb-
side, stalls, or storefronts. Vertical development occurs
mainly in the former colonial CBD; the traditional business center is usually a zone of single-story buildings with

Field Note

"February 1, 2003. A long-held hope came true today: thanks to a Brazilian intermediary I was allowed to enter and spend a day in two of Rio de Janeiro's hillslope *favelas*, an eight-hour walk through one into the other. Here live millions of the city's poor, in areas often ruled by drug lords and their gangs, with minimal or no public services, amid squalor and stench, in discomfort and danger. And yet life in the older *favelas* has become more comfortable as shacks are replaced by more permanent structures, electricity is sometimes available, water supply, however haphazard, is improved, and an informal economy brings goods and services to the residents. I stood in the doorway of a resident's single-room dwelling for this overview of an urban landscape in transition: satellite-television disks symbolize the change going on here. The often blue cisterns catch rainwater; walls are made of rough brick and roofs of corrugated iron or asbestos sheeting. No roads or

Figure 9.26
Rio de Janeiro, Brazil.   © H. J. de Blij.

automobile access, so people walk to the nearest road at the bottom of the hill. Locals told me of their hope that they will some day have legal rights to the space they occupy. During his campaign for president of Brazil, Lula de Silva suggested that long-term inhabitants should be awarded title, and in 2003 his government approved the notion. It will be complicated: as the photo shows, people live quite literally on top of one another, and mapping the chaos will not be simple (but will be made possible with geographic information systems). This would allow the government to tax residents, but it would also allow residents to obtain loans based on the value of their *favela* properties, and bring millions of Brazilians into the formal economy. The hardships I saw on this excursion were often dreadful, but you could sense the hope for and anticipation of a better future. In 2007, President de Silva's government pledged $3.6 billion to bring water, sewage, roads, and improved housing to the 20 percent of the city of Rio de Janeiro who live in the favelas."

some traditional architecture; and the market zone tends to be open-air, informal, yet still important. Sector development marks the encircling zone of ethnic and mixed neighborhoods (often characterized by strong ethnic identities); manufacturing or mining operations are found next to some parts of this zone. Finally, many African cities are ringed by satellite townships that are squatter settlements.

The Southeast Asian City

Some of the most populated cities in the world are in Southeast Asia. The city of Kuala Lumpur, Malaysia, is a complex of high-rise development, including the 1483-foot-tall Petronas Towers, which until recently was the world's tallest building. The city of Jakarta, Indonesia, called Jabotabek by the locals, is an enormous conurbation of Bogor, Tangerang, and Bekasi.

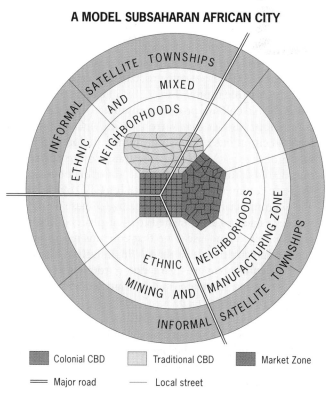

A MODEL SUBSAHARAN AFRICAN CITY

Colonial CBD   Traditional CBD   Market Zone
Major road   Local street

Figure 9.27
Model of the Subsaharan African City.   One model of the African city includes a colonial CBD, traditional CBD, and market zone.   © E. H. Fouberg, A. B. Murphy, H. J. de Blij, and John Wiley & Sons, Inc.

**A GENERALIZED MODEL OF
LAND USE AREAS IN THE LARGE
SOUTHEAST ASIAN CITY**

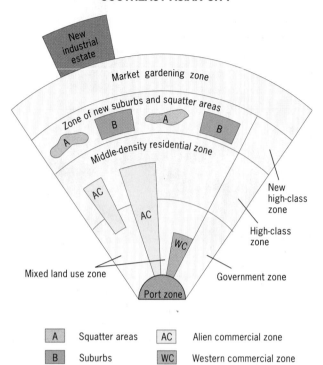

	A	Squatter areas		AC	Alien commercial zone
	B	Suburbs		WC	Western commercial zone

Figure 9.28

Model of the Large Southeast Asian City. A model of land use in the medium-sized Southeast Asian city includes sectors and zones within each sector. *Adapted with permission from*: T. G. McGee, *The Southeast Asian City*, London: Bell, 1967, p. 128.

In 1967, urban geographer T. G. McGee studied the medium-sized cities of Southeast Asia and found that they exhibit similar land-use patterns, creating a model referred to as the **McGee model** (Fig. 9.28). The focal point of the city is the old colonial port zone combined with the largely commercial district that surrounds it. McGee found no formal central business district; rather, he found the elements of the CBD present as separate clusters surrounding the old colonial port zone: the government zone; the Western commercial zone (practically a CBD by itself); the alien commercial zone, dominated by Chinese merchants whose residences are attached to their places of business; and the mixed land-use zone that contains miscellaneous economic activities, including light industry. The other nonresidential areas are the market-gardening zone at the outskirts of the urban area and, still farther from the city, a recently built industrial park or "estate."

The residential zones in McGee's model are similar to those in the Griffin-Ford model of the Latin American city. Other similarities between the McGee and Griffin-Ford model are the hybrid structure of sectors and zones, an elite residential sector that includes new suburbs, an

inner-city zone of middle-income housing, and peripheral low-income squatter settlements. One main difference is that the McGee model includes middle-income housing in a suburban zone, reflecting the larger middle class in these cities of the global semiperiphery and the small middle class in Latin American cities.

Regardless of the region or city, we recognize that models do not explain how or why cities are organized the way they are. A model of a city shows us an end product, whether planned or not and suggests the forces that created that end product.

Employing the concepts defined in this section of the chapter, draw a model of the city with which you are most familiar. Label each section of the city accordingly. After reading through the models described in this section, determine which model best corresponds to the model you drew and hypothesize as to why it is so.

HOW DO PEOPLE MAKE CITIES?

People and institutions make places, and the city is no exception to this rule. The roles individual people, governments, corporations, developers, financial lenders, and realtors play in making places varies across the world. For example, in some parts of the world, governments pass strict laws on urban structures and enforce them, and in other parts of the world governments either do not pass laws or do not enforce them.

Powerful social and cultural preferences shape the character of particular parts of the city and influence who lives where. Wander through the residential neighborhoods of any city, keep your eyes open, and study the cultural landscape. You will find yourself surrounded by landscape indicators of social and cultural preferences. You can see differences in the existence of single-family or multifamily homes, in particular styles of construction and building materials, in the distance between houses, in the nature and style of vegetation around houses, in the distance between the houses and the streets, and even in the amount of space devoted to automobile movement and storage.

Comparing and contrasting the urban cultural landscapes of two cities helps us understand the different social and cultural forces at play. Compare Figure 9.29 with Figure 9.30. Analyze each picture and guess which city is located in a wealthy country in the world and which is located in a poor country. What factors can

you consider? You may look at the presence or absence of high-rise buildings, the aesthetics of the buildings, the transportation, and the distance between houses, and after doing so, you may guess that Figure 9.29 is in the wealthy country. Look again. This time, look for whether the cars are operable, the presence of telephone and electrical wires, and the building materials. Figure 9.29 is actually in a poorer country; it is the city of Luanda, Angola, in Subsaharan Africa. Figure 9.30 is part of a suburb of Tokyo, Japan. Japanese houses in this middle-class neighborhood are on top of each other because the city is so densely populated that land is at a premium. In Luanda, the high rises are part of the central business district, and they and the houses immediately surrounding

Guest Field Note

Manila, the Philippines

I passed through cargo shipping piers in Manila, the Philippines, and encountered row after row of hand-built squatter houses. I was struck by the scale of the settlements and the sheer number of people who inhabit them. I was shocked at the level of squalor in people's living conditions. The garbage scavengers in this picture wore cotton gloves and held prods to dig through the trash for items they can use, trade, or sell. The city of Manila is hoping to clear the city of squatters by 2010 and create more permanent structures (such as the buildings in the background of this photo). The task will not be easy -- the poor and destitute live throughout the city because housing stocks are inadequate, underlying poverty persists, and still thousands flock to Manila daily recognizing that petty services and even trash picking often offer more opportunity than life in the rural provinces.

Figure 9.31

Credit: Johnathan Walker, James Madison University

them are where the wealthy live. The houses in the foreground are where the poor live. Here the roofs are tin or cardboard, the houses are makeshift, many of the cars do not run, and the one utility pole is connected to nothing. Notice that in this picture of Luanda, we see no evidence of a middle class; this is common in cities of the periphery where there are the "haves" and the "have-nots" and little in between.

Making Cities in the Global Periphery and Semiperiphery

Many of the world's most populous cities are located in the less prosperous parts of the world, including São Paulo (Brazil), Mexico City (Mexico), Mumbai (India), Dhaka (Bangladesh), and Delhi (India). Across the world, people continue to migrate to cities in response to "pull" factors that are often more imaginary than real; their expectations of a better life mostly fail to materialize.

Particularly in the economic periphery, new arrivals (and many long-term residents, too) are crowded together in overpopulated apartment buildings, dismal tenements, and teeming slums (Fig. 9.31). New arrivals come from other cities and towns and from the rural countryside, often as large families; they add to the cities' rate of natural growth. Housing cannot keep up with this massive inflow. Almost overnight huge **shantytowns**, unplanned developments of crude dwellings and shelters made mostly of scrap wood, iron, and pieces of cardboard, develop around these cities. The overcrowding and dismal conditions do not deter additional urban migration, and as a result millions of people spend their entire lives in urban housing of wretched quality.

Cities in poorer parts of the world generally lack enforceable **zoning laws**, which, over the last century, most city governments in North America drew up to ensure use of space in ways that the society at large would deem culturally and environmentally acceptable. Under a city's zoning laws, a fast-food franchise could not occupy a corner lot in a residential American suburb if the city zoned all the lots in that suburban block exclusively for single-family homes. Zoning laws do not exist, nor are they equally enforced everywhere in the core. In Europe, for example, few cities have zoning laws, but most have looser land-use plans. In the United States, Houston, Texas is the only large city that does not have zoning laws on the books, with citizens in the city voting against the creation of zoning laws three different times (as recently as 1993).

Without zoning laws, cities in the periphery will have mixed land use throughout the city. For example, in cities such as Madras, India (and in other cities in India), open space between high-rise buildings is often occupied by squatter settlements (Fig. 9.32). In Bangkok, Thailand, elementary schools and noisy, polluting factories stand side by side. In Nairobi, Kenya, hillside villas overlook some of Africa's worst slums. Over time, such incongruities may disappear, as is happening in many cities in East Asia. Rising land values and greater demand for enforced zoning regulations are transforming the central cities of East Asia. But in South Asia, Subsaharan Africa, Southwest Asia, North Africa, and Middle and South America, unregulated, helter-skelter growth continues.

Across the global periphery, the one trait all major cities display is the stark contrast between the wealthy and poor. Sharp contrasts between wealthy and poor areas can be found in major cities all over the world—for example, homeless people sleeping on heating grates half a block from the White House in Washington, D.C. Yet the intensity and scale of the contrast are greater in cities of the periphery. If you stand in the central area of Cairo, Egypt, you see what appears to be a modern, Mediterranean metropolis (Fig. 9.33). But if you get on a bus and ride it toward the city's outskirts, that impression fades almost immediately as paved streets give way to dusty alleys, apartment buildings to harsh tenements, and sidewalk coffee shops to broken doors and windows (Fig. 9.34). Traffic-choked, garbage-strewn, polluted

Figure 9.32
Hyderabad, India.   Temporary shelters, built to withstand the summer monsoon, protect the migrants who work to build the new construction in the background.   © Enn H. Fouberg

Cairo is home to an estimated 12.5 million people, more than one-fifth of Egypt's population; the city is bursting at the seams. And still people continue to arrive, seeking the better life that pulls countless migrants from the countryside year after year.

Field Note

"Central Cairo is full of the multistory buildings, transportation arteries, and commercial signs that characterize most contemporary big cities. Outside of a number of mosques, few remnants of the old medieval city remain. The first blow came in the nineteenth century, when a French-educated ruler was determined to recast Cairo as a world-class city. Inspired by the planning ideas of Paris's Baron von Hausman, he transformed the urban core into a zone of broad, straight streets. In more recent years the forces of modern international capitalism have had the upper hand. There is little sense of an overall vision for central Cairo. Instead, it seems to be a hodge-podge of buildings and streets devoted to commerce, administration, and a variety of producer and consumer services."

Figure 9.33
Cairo, Egypt.   © Alexander B. Murphy.

Field Note

"Moving out from central Cairo, evidence of the city's rapid growth is all around you. These hastily built housing units are part of the (often losing) effort to keep up with the city's exploding growth. From a city of just one million people in 1930, Cairo's population expanded to six million by 1986. And then high growth rates really kicked in. Although no one knows the exact size of the contemporary city, most estimates suggest that Cairo's population has doubled in the last 20 years. This growth has placed a tremendous strain on city services. Housing has been a particularly critical problem—leading to a landscape outside the urban core dominated by hastily built, minimally functional, and aesthetically non-descript housing projects."

Figure 9.34
Cairo, Egypt.   © Alexander B. Murphy.

Making Cities in the Global Core

The goals people have in making cities have changed over time. One way people make cities is by remaking them, reinventing neighborhoods, or changing layouts to reflect current goals and aesthetics. During the segregation era in the United States, realtors, financial lenders, and city governments defined and segregated spaces in urban environments. For example, before the civil rights movement of the 1960s, financial institutions in the business of lending money could engage in a practice known as **redlining**. They would identify what they considered to be risky neighborhoods in cities–often predominately Black neighborhoods–and refuse to offer loans to those in the districts (marked by red lines on a map). This practice, which is now illegal, worked against those living in poorer neighborhoods and helped to precipitate a downward spiral in which poor neighborhoods became increasingly rundown because funds were not available for upkeep.

Before the civil rights movement, realtors could purposefully sell a house in a white neighborhood at a very low price to a member of the African American community. In a practice called **blockbusting**, the realtors would solicit other white residents of the neighborhood to sell their homes under the guise that the neighborhood was going downhill because an African American person or family had moved in. This produced what urban geographers and sociologists call *white flight*—movement of whites from the city and adjacent neighborhoods to the outlying suburbs. Blockbusting led to significant turnover in housing, which of course benefited real estate agents through the commissions they earned. Blockbusting also prompted landowners to sell their properties at low prices (to get out of the neighborhood quickly), which in turn allowed developers to subdivide lots and build tenements. Typically, the developers did not maintain the tenements well, dropping the property values even further.

Developers and governments are also important actors in the making of cities. In cities of the global core that have experienced high levels of suburbanization, people have left the central city for the suburbs for a number of reasons, among them single-family homes, yards, better schools, and safety. With suburbanization, city governments lose tax revenue, as middle- and upper-class taxpayers leave the central city and pay taxes in the suburbs instead. In order to counter the suburbanization trend, city governments are encouraging commercialization of the central city and gentrification of the central city's neighborhoods.

The plans that city governments draft to revive central cities usually involve cleaning streets, sidewalks, and buildings; tearing down old, abandoned buildings; and building up commercial offerings and residences. In the downtowns, city governments have often created programs to encourage **commercialization**, which entails transforming the central city into an area attractive to residents and tourists alike. Several cities, including Miami, New York, and Baltimore, have created waterfront "theme" areas to attract visitors. These areas include festival marketplaces, parks with exotic sculptures and play

Field Note

"In 2008, downtown Fort Worth, Texas looked quite different than it did when I first visited in 1997. In that eleven year period, business leaders in the City of Fort Worth gentrified the downtown. The Bass family, who has a great deal of wealth from oil holdings and who now owns about 40 blocks of downtown Fort Worth, was instrumental in the city's gentrification. In the 1970s and 1980s, members of the Bass family looked at the empty, stark, downtown Fort Worth, and sought a way to revitalize the downtown. They worked with the Tandy family to build and revitalize the spaces of the city, which took off in the late 1990s and into the present century. The crown jewel in the gentrified Fort Worth is the beautiful cultural center called the Bass Performance Hall, named for Nancy Lee and Perry R. Bass (Fig. 9.24), which opened in 1998."

Figure 9.35
Fort Worth, Texas.   © Erin H. Fouberg.

areas, and amusement zones occupying former industrial sites. Such ventures have been successful in attracting tourists and in generating business, but they alone cannot revive downtowns because they cannot attract what the core of the city needs most: permanent residents with a stake in its future. The newly commercialized downtowns often stand apart from the rest of the central city.

Since the 1960s, some people have moved back into central cities—often in conjunction with a process known as **gentrification**. Gentrification occurs when individuals buy up and rehabilitate the houses, raising the housing value in the neighborhood and changing the neighborhood itself.

Gentrification began in cities with a tight housing market and defined central city neighborhoods, such as San Francisco, Portland, and Chicago. Gentrification slowed in the 1990s but is growing again, as governments are encouraging gentrification through beautification programs and significant tax breaks to people who buy up abandoned or dilapidated housing. The growing interest in central city housing has resulted in part from the changing character of American society: the proportion of childless couples (heterosexual and homosexual) and single people in the

population is growing, and for these urbanites, the suburbs do not look so attractive. Living within walking distance of the workplace, and very near the cultural and recreational amenities (Fig. 9.35) the central city still attracts more residents every year. For them, the gentrified neighborhood is a good choice. In many cities, gentrification has displaced lower income residents, however, and for those displaced by gentrification, the consequences can be serious. Rising housing costs associated with gentrification have played a key role in the growing problem of homelessness.

The suburb is not immune to gentrification. Rampant in many American suburbs (especially those close to the city) are **tear-downs**, houses that new owners bought with the intention of tearing them down and building a much larger home. The new homes, sometimes referred to as **McMansions** (because of their super size and their similar look), often stretch to the outer limits of the lot (Fig. 9.36). Like gentrification in the city, the tear-down phenomenon changes the landscape and increases average housing values, tax revenue for the city, and the average household income of the neighborhood. Unlike gentrification, with tear-downs, the original houses are

Figure 9.36
Hinsdale, Illinois. In this upscale suburb of Chicago, a new McMansion stands in the place where a smaller house (similar in size to the one still standing in the left of the photo) used to stand. In the last 20 years, about 25 percent of Hinsdale's houses have been torn down to make room for much larger houses.   © Dennis Light/ Light Photographic.

destroyed instead of preserved. Also unlike gentrification, teardowns often occur in wealthy suburbs, such as Greenwich, Connecticut, and Hinsdale, Illinois. In Greenwich (just outside of New York City), the city issued 138 permits for tear-downs in 2004 (56 more than it did the year before). In Hinsdale (just outside Chicago), in the last 20 years, about one-quarter of the suburb's 1100 house have been torn down. Those in favor of tear-downs argue that the phenomenon slows urban sprawl by replacing existing homes with new homes, rather than converting farmland to residential lots. Those opposed to teardowns see the houses as too large for their lots, dwarfing the neighboring houses, and destroying the character of the place by demolishing the older homes.

Urban Sprawl and New Urbanism

As populations have grown in certain areas of the United States, such as the Sunbelt and the West, urban areas have experienced **urban sprawl**, unrestricted growth of housing, commercial developments, and roads over large expanses of land, with little concern for urban planning. Urban sprawl is easy to spot as you drive down major roadways in any urbanized part of the country. You will see strip malls, big box stores, chain restaurants, huge intersections, and numerous housing developments, all spread out over many acres (Fig. 9.36). Sprawl is a phenomenon of the automobile era. Cities that grew before the automobile typically grew "up" instead of "out." For instance, Boston

Figure 9.37
Henderson, Nevada. Henderson is the largest suburb of Las Vegas, and it was also the fastest-growing urban settlement in the United States between 1990 and 2000.
© Mike Yamashita/Woodfin Camp & Associates.

grew around the marketplace and port, but it grew before the automobile, resulting in development over smaller areas. If you walk through the central city of Boston today, you can walk where you need to go or take the T (metro). Places are built up vertically, and curving, narrow streets and commercial developments with a flavor of the old city (Quincy Market) give the city a cozy, intimate feel.

Does population growth explain which cities experience the most urban sprawl? In a study of sprawl from 1960 through the 1990s, Leon Kolankiewicz and Roy Beck (two antisprawl writers) used United States Census data on urbanized areas and found that urban sprawl happened even in urban areas without significant population growth. In the United States, urban sprawl is more rampant in the Sunbelt of the South (Atlanta) and in the West (Houston) in urban areas whose population is rapidly growing (Table 9.1). Yet, even in cities such as Detroit and Pittsburgh, where urban populations fell during the study period—by 7 percent in Detroit and 9 percent in Pittsburgh—urban sprawl increased the urbanized areas of the cities by 28 percent and 30 percent, respectively. For urban sprawl to happen, farmlands and old industrial sites are razed, and roads are built or widened, strip malls are erected, and housing developments monopolize the horizon.

To counter urban sprawl, a group of architects, urban planners, and developers (now numbering over 2000 in more than 20 countries) outlined an urban design vision they call new urbanism. Forming the Congress for the New Urbanism in 1993, the group defines **new urbanism** as development, urban revitalization, and suburban reforms that create walkable neighborhoods with a diversity of housing and jobs. On their website, the Congress for the New Urbanism explains that "New Urbanists support regional planning for open space, appropriate architecture and planning, and the balanced development of jobs and housing. They believe these strategies are the best way to reduce how long people spend in traffic, to increase the supply of affordable housing, and to rein in urban sprawl." New urbanists want to create neighborhoods that promote a sense of community and a sense of place.

The most famous new urbanist projects are cities that new urbanists designed from the ground up, including Seaside, Florida (featured in the movie *The Truman Show*), West Laguna, California, and Kentlands, Maryland.

TABLE 9.1

Top 20 Urban Sprawl Cities in the United States. Several different ways to measure sprawl exist. This index measures residential density, neighborhood mixture of homes, jobs and services, strength of downtowns, and accessibility to the street network.

TOP 20 URBAN SPRAWL CITIES IN THE UNITED STATES	
Metropolitan Area	**State**
1. Riverside–San Bernardino	CA
2. Greensboro–Winston Salem–High Point	NC
3. Raleigh–Durham	NC
4. Atlanta	GA
5. Greenville–Spartanburg	SC
6. West Palm Beach–Boca Raton–Delray Beach	FL
7. Bridgeport–Stamford–Norwalk–Danbury	CT
8. Knoxville	TN
9. Oxnard–Ventura	CA
10. Fort Worth–Arlington	TX
11. Gary–Hammond	IN
12. Rochester	NY
13. Dallas	TX
14. Vallejo–Fairfield–Napa	CA
15. Detroit	MI
16. Syracuse	NY
17. Newark	NJ
18. Little Rock–North Little Rock	AR
19. Albany–Schenectady–Troy	NY
20. Hartford–New Britain–Middletown–Bristol	CT

Source: Smart Growth.org, http://www.smartgrowthamerica.org/sprawlindex/measuringsprawl.pdf last accessed July 2005.

When new urbanists build a town, the design is reminiscent of Christaller over a much smaller area. The planners choose the central shopping areas and open spaces and develop the neighborhoods around them, with housing clustered around the central space, so that people can walk to the shopping area within five minutes. One goal of new urbanist designs is to build housing more densely, to take up less space. Along with that, making shopping and other amenities walkable decreases dependency on the automobile, in the process helping the environment.

Although some see new urbanist designs as manufactured communities and feel disconnected in a new urbanist space, others see new urbanist designs as superior to sprawl. Celebration, Florida, is a remarkable new urbanist space: it is adjacent to Walt Disney's theme parks, was envisioned by Walt Disney himself, and is owned by the Disney Company (Fig. 9.38). Built in 1994, Celebration is centered on Market Street, a shopping district with restaurants (including a 1950s-style diner and a pizza place), a town hall, banks, a post office, and a movie theater with a nostalgic marquee (Fig. 9.39). The town includes schools, a health center, a fitness center, and a church. The Disney Company chose certain architectural styles for the houses in Celebration, and builders offer homes and townhouses in a price range from $300,000 to over $1 million. To meet the new urbanist goal of incorporating diverse people in a community, Celebration includes apartments for rent and condominiums for sale.

For geographers, new urbanism is seen as a redefinition of space in the city. Public spaces become privatized for the enjoyment of the few (the residents of the neighborhood). Geographers Stuart Aitken, Don Mitchell, and Lynn Staeheli note that as new urbanism strives to turn neighborhoods back in time, "spaces and social functions historically deemed public (such as parks, neighborhood centers, shopping districts)" are privatized. The houses with porches that encourage neighbors to talk and the parks that are within walking distance for the residents create "mythic landscapes that are ingratiating for those who can afford them and exclusionary for those who cannot."

Noted geographer David Harvey offers one of the strongest critiques of new urbanism, explaining first that most new urbanist designs are "greenfield" projects designed for the affluent to make the suburbs more livable. This fact is evidence, Harvey argues, that the new urbanism movement is a kind of "spatial determinism" that does not recognize that "the fundamental difficulty with modernism was its persistent habit of privileging spatial forms over social processes." Harvey, and others who critique new urbanism, claim that new urbanism does nothing to break down the social conditions that privilege some white disadvantaging others; that new urbanist projects take away much of the grittiness and character of the city; and that the "communities" that new urbanists form through their projects are exclusionary communities that further the racial segregation of cities.

Despite the critiques against new urbanism, developments in the new urbanist tradition are attracting a growing number of people, and when they are situated within cities, they can work against urban sprawl.

Gated Communities

As you drive through urban spaces, suburban and central city alike, you will note more and more neighborhoods being developed or redesigned to align with new urbanist principles. In your inventory of landscapes, even more overwhelming will be the proliferation of gated communities. **Gated communities** are fenced-in neighborhoods with controlled access gates for people and automobiles. Often, gated communities have security cameras and security forces (privatized police) keeping watch over the community, as the main objective of a gated community is to create a space of safety within the uncertain urban world. A secondary objective is to maintain or increase housing values in the neighborhood through enforcement of the neighborhood association's bylaws that control everything from the color of a house to the character and size of additions.

During the late 1980s and early 1990s, developers in the United States began building gated communities in urban areas around the country. In a 2001 census of housing, the United States government reported that 16 million people, or about 6 percent of Americans, live in gated communities. The urban design of gating communities has diffused around the globe at record speed, with gated communities in Europe, Asia, Africa, and Latin America.

In poorer countries, where cities are divided between wealthy and poor, gated communities provide another layer of comfort for the city's wealthy. In the large cities of Latin America and Africa, you commonly see walls around individual houses, walling in yards and pools and keeping out crime. During the last ten years, many neighborhoods in these cities have added gates around the neighborhoods in addition to the walls. Walled houses and gated communities in the wealthy northern suburbs of Johannesburg, South Africa are threatening the desegregation of the post-Apartheid city. White, wealthy residents fear crime in the city with a murder rate, along with neighboring Pretoria, of 5000 per year (in an area with about 5 million people). In response to their fear of crime, people in the suburbs of Johannesburg blocked off over 2500 streets and posted guards to control access to these streets by 2004. Many fear that the gated communities are a new form of segregation. Since the vast majority of the crimes in the city occur in poor black townships or in the central city, the concern is that these developments only worsen the plight of less well-off segments of society.

In China, gated communities have taken off, now crossing socioeconomic classes and creating a ubiquitous feature

Field Note

"When I visited Celebration, Florida in 1997, I felt like I was walking onto a movie or television set. The architecture in the Walt Disney-designed new urbanist development looked like the quintessential New England town. Each house has a porch, but on the day I was there, the porches sat empty—waiting to welcome the arrival of their owners at the end of the work day. We walked through town, past the 50s-style movie marquee, and ate lunch at a 50s-style diner. At that point, Celebration was still growing. Across the street from the 'Bank of Celebration' stood a sign marking the future home of the 'Church in Celebration.'"

Figure 9.38
Celebration, Florida. © Erin H. Fouberg.

Figure 9.39
Celebration, Florida. © Erin H. Fouberg.

Figure 9.40
Gated Housing Community in Beijing, China. © Liu Liqun/China Stock Photo Library.

on the urban landscape (Fig. 9.40). Like the gated communities in Europe and North America, the gated communities of China privatize spaces and exclude outsiders with gates, security cameras, and restricted access. However, the gated communities in China are five to ten times more densely populated than gated communities in Europe and North America. Geographer Youqin Huang has found other differences between gated communities in China and those in North America and Europe. China has a long history of gated communities, dating back to the first Chinese cities and persisting since. Huang argues that the "collectivism-oriented culture and tight political control" in China explain why the Chinese government built gated communities during the socialist period and why a proliferation of gated communities has occurred by private developers since China's housing reform in 1998 promoted individual home ownership.

In Europe and North America, gated communities are not only for the wealthy and privileged. Especially since September 11, people have a growing desire to feel safe at home, and this is just as true of middle and lower classes as it is of the rich. Some urban planners have encouraged governments to recast low-income housing as small communities, gated from each other, in order to reduce the flowthrough traffic and crime associated with it. Cities have torn down the enormous high rises, typically ridden with crime and referred to as "the projects" such as Cabrini Green in Chicago and Pruitt-Igoe in St. Louis, in effort to remake the spaces of the poor into "defensible" spaces (Fig. 9.41).

Urban planners want to gate middle-income and low-income neighborhoods in order to create a sense of community and to make the spaces "defensible" from undesired activities such as drug dealing and prostitution. One of the best-documented cases of gating a middle-income community is the Five Oaks district of Dayton, Ohio, a neighborhood that is about 50 percent African American and 50 percent white and has a high rate of rentals. Urban planner Oscar Newman encouraged planners in Dayton to divide the 2000 households in the Five Oaks district into ten smaller, gated communities with restricted access. The city turned most of the residential streets in each of these mini-neighborhoods into cul-de-sacs. They have experienced a serious reduction in crime, along with an increase in housing sales and housing values.

Ethnic Neighborhoods in the European City

Ethnic neighborhoods in European cities are typically affiliated with migrants from former colonies. For example, Algeria was a colony of France, and now Paris and other French cities have distinct Algerian neighborhoods. Similarly, London (the United Kingdom) has a Jamaican neighborhood, and Madrid (Spain) has a distinct Moroccan neighborhood, reflecting their colonial ties with these now sovereign countries. Other European countries cultivated relationships with countries outside of Europe after the colonial era. For example, after World War II, Germany

Figure 9.41

St. Louis, Missouri. This photo taken in 1971 captured a view of the massive Pruitt-Igoe housing project, before it was demolished in 1972. Pruitt-Igoe was designed in 1951, and by 1972 the rampant crime in the project's 33 apartment buildings solidified the image of this public housing project as a failure. © Corbis-Bettmann.

invited young men from Turkey to migrate to Germany as guest workers (see Chapter 3). Cities in Germany, such as Frankfurt, have distinct Turkish neighborhoods. Current immigration to countries in Europe typically focuses on the cities. And most of the migrants to European cities come from the global periphery or from eastern Europe, not from other countries in western Europe.

Migration to Europe is constrained by government policies and laws. Many western European cities have public housing zones that were built after World War II following the devastation of the war years. Governments in Europe are typically much more involved in the social rights of people, such as health care and housing than the United States government. European cities are also much older than American cities, and when the cities were laid out they were designed for foot and horse traffic, not automobiles. Thus, European cities are typically more compact, densely populated, and walkable than American cities. European cities also have historic city centers where much of the city's history took place and is preserved and to which tourists are attracted today. Rather than the skyscrapers that are typically the focal point of downtown in American cities, a historic city center is the focal point of downtown in European cities and skyscrapers are reserved for developments on the outskirts of town. Housing in the European city is often combined with places of work, with work spaces on the bottom floors of buildings and housing above. Large zones of housing in Europe typically begin in a ring around the outside of the city center, in what Ernest Burgess called the zone of transition. After the war, many European governments built public housing structures in the spaces leveled by bombing *around* the city center.

Immigration is changing the spatial-cultural geography of European cities. As immigrants have settled in large numbers in the zone of transition, locals have moved out. Walking from the city center of Paris out through immigrant neighborhoods, one can see the cultural landscape change to reflect the significant number of immigrants from the "Maghreb" of Africa, the region of North Africa around Algeria and Morocco. Maghrebis are by far the most numerous inhabitants in the tough, hardscrabble immigrant neighborhoods around Paris, where unemployment is high, crime is widespread, resentment festers. Many Maghrebis provides solace in Islam. Walk along the tenement-lined, littered streets here, and the elegant avenues of historic Paris seem remote indeed—but they are not. A short subway ride takes you from one world to another.

Whether a public housing zone is divided into ethnic neighborhoods in a European city depends in large part on government policy. Urban geographers Christian Kesteloot and Cees Cortie studied housing policies and zones in Brussels, Belgium, and Amsterdam, the Netherlands. They found that Brussels has very little public housing and that immigrants live in privately owned rentals throughout the city. Kesteloot and Cortie also found that immigrant groups in Brussels who came from a distinct region of their home country (especially rural regions), such as the Turks in Brussels, tend to cluster in ethnic neighborhoods. In contrast, the researchers reported that immigrant groups who came from cities, such as the Moroccans in Brussels, chose rental units scattered throughout the city and therefore did not establish ethnic neighborhoods in Brussels.

Amsterdam is quite different from Brussels: Amsterdam has a great deal of public housing and few ethnic neighborhoods within the public housing units. When immigration to Amsterdam from former colonies (Indonesia, Surinam) and noncolonies (Morocco and Turkey) increased in the 1960s, Amsterdammers moved from the transition zone of public housing to neighboring towns such as Almere. The Dutch government then implemented a policy in the public housing zone that slowed the creation of ethnic neighborhoods. The Dutch government allots public housing to legal immigrants by assigning homes on a sequential basis in the city's zone of transition, where some 80 percent of the housing stock is public housing. As a result of government assignment of housing, if you walk through the public housing zone of Amsterdam, you will find a family from Suriname living next to an Indonesian family and a Moroccan family, not just other Surinamese. The housing and neighborhoods are multicultural. The ethnic groups maintain their local cultures through religious and cultural organizations rather than through residential segregation. In Amsterdam, the call to Friday prayer for Muslims rings out all over the immigrant areas, as Muslims from various countries are spread throughout the city.

Ethnic Neighborhoods in the Global Periphery and Semiperiphery City

In cities of the periphery and semiperiphery, a sea of slum development typically begins where the permanent buildings end, in some cases engulfing and dwarfing the central city. If you stand on a hill outside Lima (Peru) or overlooking the Cape Flats near Cape Town (South Africa), you see an unchanging panorama of makeshift shacks built of every conceivable material, vying for every foot of space, extending to the horizon. You will notice few, if any, trees, and you will see narrow footpaths leading to a few unpaved streets that go into the central city.

Millions of migrants travel to such ominous environments every year. The total number of people living in these types of slum developments is uncertain because government control is impossible and enumeration impractical. In Rio de Janeiro (Brazil), the migrants build their dwellings on dangerous, landslide-prone slopes; in Port Moresby (Papua New Guinea), the migrants sink stilts in the mud and build out over the water, risking wind and waves. In Calcutta (India), thousands of migrants do not even try to erect shelters: there and in many other cities they live in the streets, under bridges, even in storm drains. City governments do not have the resources to adequately educate, medicate, or police the burgeoning populations, let alone to provide even minimal housing for most.

Even the people living in the squalid conditions of shanty settlements are not really squatters—they pay rent. When the settlements expand outward from the central city, they occupy land owned by previous residents, families who farmed what were once the rural areas beyond the city's edge. Some of the farming families were favored by the former colonial administration; they moved into the cities but continued to own the lands their farms were on. As shanty developments encroached on their lands, the landowners began to charge people rent for living on the dilapidated housing the new residents built on the land. After establishing an owner-tenant relationship, the landowners steadily raise rents, threatening to destroy the flimsy shacks if residents fail to pay. In this way, powerful long-term inhabitants of the city exploit the weaker, more recent arrivals.

The vast slums of cities in poorer parts of the world are typically ethnically delineated, with new arrivals precariously accommodated. For example, Nairobi, Kenya, has a large slum area, one of the worst in Subsaharan Africa in terms of amenities, called Kibera. Much of the land where Kibera is located is owned by Nubians, who are of Sudanese descent. The Sudanese Nubians settled in the area of Kibera during the colonial era. Many of the Nubians have become businesspeople in the city of Nairobi. The modern tenants of the shanty settlements in Kibera are largely Luo from western Kenya and Luhya from northwestern Kenya. During the fall of 2001, some of the Kiberian tenants were unable to pay the latest increase in rents. The Nubian landowners came to evict them, and in the fighting that followed, a number of people were killed. Groups of Luo, Luhya, and others even took to fighting among themselves. The government intervened to stabilize the situation. The latest rent increases were withdrawn, but the fundamental problems—crowding, unemployment, unsanitary conditions, hunger, and lack of education—remain, and the ethnic groups living in the neighborhoods of Kibera will likely experience fighting again.

Geography plays a major role in the relationships among ethnic components of a former colonial city. The settlement patterns of cities developed during the colonial period often persist long after. In a study of the city of Mombasa, Kenya, during the 1960s, H. J. de Blij found that the central city, in effect the island on which Mombasa was built, was informally partitioned among major ethnic groups. Apart from the Swahili who occupied the Old Town and adjacent historic portions of the built-up area, the spatial pattern of occupance by ethnic groups in the city of Mombasa mirrored the status of the ethnic groups in the country of Kenya as a whole. The port of Mombasa, the country's largest, was the city's major employer. The Kikuyu, whose historic homeland lies far away from Mombasa to the north of Nairobi, were privileged by the British during colonial times. Because of their important position during colonialism, Kikuyu workers and their families living in Mombasa resided closest to the port and to the center of economic power. Although the most powerful workers lived closest to the central commercial district, the Asians (often from India and thus referred to as Indians in Mombasa) who controlled the city's commerce were concentrated on the opposite side of the island, away from the port. Another powerful ethnic group, the Kamba, occupied a zone farther outward from the port. The Mijikenda, a less powerful African ethnic group, migrated from off-island villages to work in Mombasa and lived farther from the commercial center.

In recent times, as the city's population has grown seven times larger than it was in the 1960s, the spatial pattern of Mombasa still reflects the power of ethnic groups. The most recent immigrants, desperate for jobs, crowd the outer zone of the city, off of the island, and in the shanty settlements.

How do the many millions of urban immigrants living in the slum-ridden rings and pockets of the cities of the global periphery and semiperiphery survive? Extended families share and stretch every dollar they manage to earn; when one member of the family has a salaried job, his or her income saves the day for a dozen or more relatives. When a member of the family (or several members of a larger community) manages to emigrate to a core country or an island of development and makes good money there, part of that income is sent back home and becomes the mainstay for those left behind. Hundreds of millions of dollars are transferred this way every year; *remittances* make a critical difference in the poorer countries of the world (see Chapter 3).

In the vast slums, barrios, and favelas, those who are jobless or unsalaried are not idle. Everywhere you look people are at work, inside or in front of their modest habitats, fixing things, repairing broken items for sale, sorting through small piles of waste for salvageable items, trading and selling

goods from makeshift stands. What prevails here is referred to as the **informal economy**—the economy that is not taxed and is not counted toward a country's gross national income. What is generated in the informal economy can add up to a huge total in unrecorded monetary value. The informal economy worries governments because it is essentially a recordless economy and no taxes are paid. Remittances are usually delivered in cash, not via Western Union or a bank. Typically, a trusted community member (who might pay a comparatively small bribe at the airport when passing through immigration) carries remittances to family members.

Even as the informal economy thrives among the millions in the shantytowns, the new era of globalization is making a major impact in the major cities founded or fostered by the colonial powers. In 2002, geographers Richard Grant and Jan Nijman documented this transformation in former colonial port cities, including Mumbai, India. In this city, formerly called Bombay, colonial rule produced an urban landscape marked by strong segregation of foreign and local activities, commercial as well as residential (Fig. 9.42), and

Figure 9.42
The Changing Character of Mumbai, India. *Adapted with permission from*: Richard Grant and Jan Nijman, "Globalization and the Corporate Geography of Cities in the Less-Developed World," *Annals of the Association of American Geographers*, 92, 2 (2002).

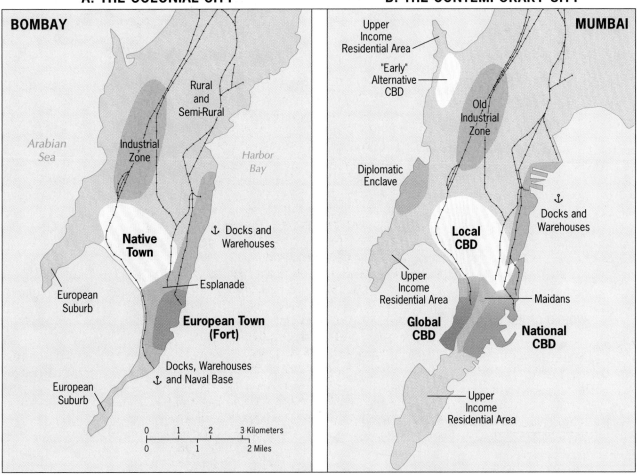

high levels of functional specialization and concentration. Adjacent to the port area was a well-demarcated European business district containing foreign (mostly British) companies. Most economic activities in this European commercial area involved trade, transport, banking, distribution, and insurance. Zoning and building codes were strictly enforced. Physically separated from this European district were the traditional markets and bazaars of the so-called Native Town, a densely populated mix of commercial and residential land uses.

In this era of globalization, a new spatially demarcated foreign presence has arisen. The city now has a global CBD at the heart of the original colonial city, housing mostly foreign corporations and multinational companies and linked mainly to the global economy. The former European Town has a large presence of big domestic companies and a pronounced orientation to the national (Indian) economy. And the Native Town now has a high concentration of small domestic company headquarters and the strongest orientation to the immediate urban area.

Using the city you sketched in the last "Thinking Geographically" question, consider the concepts and processes introduced in this section of the chapter and explain how people and institutions created this city and the model you sketched.

Figure 9.43
World Cities: Alpha, Beta, and Gamma. *Data from*: J. V. Beaverstock, R. G. Smith, and P. J. Taylor, "A Roster of World Cities," *Cities*, 16, 6 (1999): 445–458.

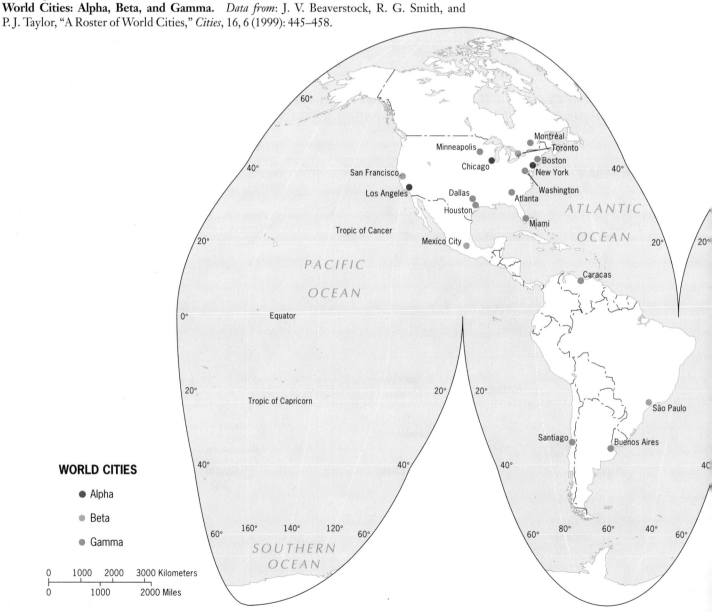

WHAT ROLE DO CITIES PLAY IN GLOBALIZATION?

Globalization, as we defined the term in the first chapter, is a set of processes and outcomes that occur on the global scale, circumventing and leaping over state boundaries to affect the world. In the processes of globalization, cities are taking over in ways we barely understand. Most statistics about economic activity at the global scale are gathered and disseminated by states. Nonetheless, many of the most important processes occur among and between cities, not states as a whole, masking the integral role world cities play in globalization. **World cities** function at the global scale, beyond the reach of the state borders, functioning as the service centers of the world economy.

Contending that models of cities and hierarchies of cities within states (such as Christaller) no longer represent what is happening with the city, Taylor and Lang maintain that the city has become "something else" than a simple CBD tied into a hierarchy of other cities within the state. The world city is a node in globalization, reflecting processes that have "redrawn the limits on spatial interaction," according to Felsenstein, Schamp, and Shachar. A node is a place through which action and interaction occur. As a node, a world city is connected to other cities, and the forces shaping globalization pulse across these connections and through the cities.

Most lists of world cities provide a hierarchy of the most important nodes, the most important world cities, then

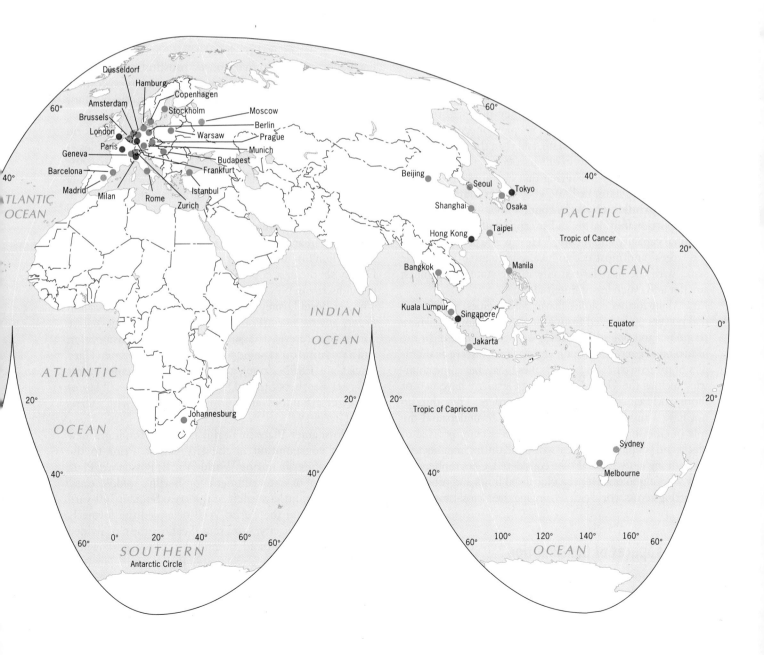

the next most important, and so forth. Virtually all agree that New York, London, and Tokyo are the most important world cities, but beyond that point, the definition of what makes a world city and the list of world cities changes depending on the perspective of the researcher. Geographers Jon Beaverstock and Peter J. Taylor and their Globalization and World Cities Study Group and Network have produced nearly 200 research papers, chapters, and books on the geography of world cities over the past few years. By studying which cities provide producer services (integral to the processes of globalization) in the areas of banking, law, advertising, and accounting, these geographers have produced an inventory of world cities mapped in Figure 9.43. They delineate 10 Alpha, 10 Beta, and 35 Gamma world cities. The Alpha cities (London, Paris, New York, Tokyo, Chicago, Frankfurt, Hong Kong, Los Angeles, Milan, and Singapore) have a global capacity to provide services in the world-economy.

World cities do not exist merely to service players in the global economy. Major world cities such as London and Paris are also capital cities. States concentrate development and encourage interconnectedness between certain cities and the rest of the world. Even though London and Paris are a short distance apart, both function as world cities in part because of the role they play within their respective states: each became a magnet for economic and political activity within its state, and then the globe. States often focus development in one particular city, such as the capital city, thereby bolstering that city above the rest of the cities in the state. In 1939, geographer Mark Jefferson defined a **primate city** as "a country's leading city, always disproportionately large and exceptionally expressive of national capacity and feeling." He saw the primate city as the largest and most economically influential within the state, with the next largest city in the state being much smaller and much less influential.

Many former colonies have primate cities, as the colonial powers often ruled from a single dominant city, where economic and political activities were concentrated. In the noncolonial context, London and Paris each serve as examples of primate cities and world cities today, but some countries such as the United States and Germany have two or more world cities within their state borders. They thus do not have a single, distinct primate city. To understand the role of cities in globalization, the services cities provide to places and peoples around the world and the interconnectedness among cities must also be considered. Geographers are now working to uncover the globalized flows and processes occurring across world cities, bringing them closer together.

Cities as Spaces of Consumption

In addition to being nodes in globalization, cities are also products of globalization. Major changes in cities, such as the redevelopment of New York's Times Square and

the remaking of Berlin's Potsdamer Platz, are the result of global processes. Frank Roost has found that "the global media industry is becoming the driving force in the reshaping of cities" such as New York and Berlin, turning city centers into **spaces of consumption**. Global media giants such as Time Warner, Viacom, and Walt Disney use cross promotion to encourage the consumption of their products. It is no accident that characters on television sit-coms produced and aired on ABC (a television channel owned by Walt Disney) visit Disney theme parks or host Disney Princess-themed birthday parties on a given episode. These same media companies are investing heavily in urban centers in order to create entertainment spaces, places where tourists can go to consume their products. Media corporations are helping transform urban centers into major entertainment districts ("variations on a theme park") where items are *consumed*.

For example, in New York City, government entities began to try to redevelop Times Square in the early 1980s. At that time, this area of the city was known for its neon lights, pornography movie houses, prostitution, and other illicit economic activities. The city sought to push these businesses out of Times Square and return the business district to a conglomeration of restaurants, hotels, bars, and entertainment spaces (as it had been before World War II). Over the decade of the 1980s, the city closed hundreds of small businesses in Times Square. In 1995, Mayor Rudolph Giuliani reached a deal with Michael Eisner, CEO of Walt Disney. The mayor promised to remove the remaining sex shops, and Eisner committed to renovating the New Amsterdam Theater, a focal point in Times Square (Fig. 9.44 left and right). Secured with a $26 million low-interest loan from the State of New York, Disney set the new course for a family-friendly entertainment district in New York. The restored New Amsterdam Theater hosts Disney musicals such as *The Lion King* and *Beauty and the Beast* (both based on Disney movies). The Times Square area is assuredly a space of consumption and a variation on a theme park: themed restaurants (Hard Rock Café, ESPN Zone), cross-promoting themed stores (Warner Brothers Store, Disney Store), and retail stores that cater to families (an enormous Toys R Us with a ferris wheel inside).

Potsdamer Platz in Berlin is also becoming a new space of consumption in the city center. Prior to the bombing of Berlin during World War II, Potsdamer Platz was a center of entertainment for Berlin's middle class. After the war, little was left of the area. Soon, a 500-yard border zone and the Berlin Wall occupied the formerly vibrant area of the city. After reunification, the city divided Potsdamer Platz and sold the land. The two largest owners are the German company Daimler-Benz and the Japanese company Sony. Sony built a huge entertainment structure called the Sony Center for cross promotion. According to Roost, much of the Daimler-Benz structure, Daimler

Figure 9.44, left and right
New York, New York. (left) The New Amsterdam Theater in Times Square as it stood in 1947. Note the signs around the building, advertising arcade games and a flea circus. (right) During the 1980s and 1990s, Times Square was "cleaned up" and reinvigorated. The Walt Disney Company renovated the New Amsterdam Theater and now shows productions of musicals such as *Beauty and the Beast* and *The Lion King*. © Corbis-Bettmann.

City, is a space of consumption, with entertainment venues, restaurants, bars, and hotels.

Although the tourist will be focused on the theme park atmosphere of these spaces of consumption, the renovations of the districts in both of these cities have also brought spaces of media production to the cities. Sony has placed its European headquarters in Berlin, Warner Brothers moved its offices to Times Square, and new office towers around Times Square house many other media companies.

thinking *geographically*

Thinking through the challenges to the state presented in Chapter 8, predict whether and under what circumstances world cities could replace states as the basic and most powerful form of political organization in the world.

Summary

The city is an ever changing cultural landscape, its layers reflecting grand plans by governments, impassioned pursuits by individuals, economic decisions by corporations, and processes of globalization. Geographers who study cities have a multitude of topics to examine. From gentrification to tear-downs, from favelas to McMansions, from spaces of production to spaces of consumption, from ancient walls to gated communities, cities have so much in common and yet each has its own pulse, its own feel, its own spatial structure, its own set of realities. The pulse of the city is undoubtedly created by the peoples and cultures who live there. For it is the people, whether working independently or as part of global institutions, who continuously create and re-create the city and its geography.

Geographic Concepts

urban morphology	Forum	McGee model
city	situation	shantytowns
urban	trade area	zoning laws
agricultural village	rank-size rule	redlining
agricultural surplus	central place theory	blockbusting
social stratification	Sunbelt phenomenon	commercialization
leadership class	functional zonation	gentrification
first urban revolution	zone	tear-downs
Mesopotamia	central business district	McMansions
Nile River Valley	central city	urban sprawl
Indus River Valley	suburb	new urbanism
Huang He and Wei	suburbanization	gated communities
River Valleys	concentric zone model	informal economy
Mesoamerica	edge cities	world city
acropolis	urban realm	primate city
agora	Griffin-Ford model	spaces of consumption
site	disamenity sector	

Learn More Online

About Celebration, Florida
http://www.celebration.fl.us/

About the Congress for the New Urbanism
http://www.cnu.org/

About Globalization and World Cities
http://www.lut.ac.uk/gawc/index.html

About Opposition to Urban Sprawl
http://www.sierraclub.org/sprawl/

About Seaside, Florida
http://www.seasidefl.com/

Watch It Online

About Berlin
http://www.learner.org/resources/series180.html#program_descriptions
Click on Video On Demand for "Berlin: United
We Stand"
http://www.learner.org/resources/series85.html#program_descriptions"
Click on Video On Demand for "Berlin: Changing Center of a Changing Europe"
About Sprawl in Chicago
http://www.learner.org/resources/series180.html
Click on Video On Demand for "Chicago: Farming on the Edge"

CHAPTER 10

Development

Field Note   Geography, Trade, and Development

Figure 10.1
Timbuktu, Mali. The dirt streets found throughout much of the town reflect the impoverishment of this once celebrated place.   © Alexander B. Murphy.

Walking down one of the major streets of Timbuktu, Mali (Fig. 10.1), I could hardly believe I was in the renowned intellectual, spiritual, and economic center of the thirteenth to sixteenth centuries—a place with such a great reputation for wealth that it spurred the first European explorations along the African coast. What survives is a relatively impoverished town of some 35,000 people providing central place functions for the surrounding area and seeking to attract some tourist business based on its legendary name.

What happened to Timbuktu? The city's wealth many centuries ago derived from its ability to control the trans-Sahara trade in gold, salt, ivory, kola nuts, and slaves. But when trade patterns shifted with the development of maritime routes along the west coast of Africa, Timbuktu lost its strategic position and a long period of decline set in.

Timbuktu's story serves as a reminder that where a place is located in relation to patterns of economic development and exchange can be as important as, or even more important than, the commodities found in that place. Indeed, there are many examples of places where the presence of a valuable commodity does not translate into improved economic lives for those living nearby. The people working on the oil booms in Gabon or workers chopping down rare hardwood trees in Thailand, for example, are not the ones who benefit from most of the wealth associated with demand for the goods they help produce. Instead, international corporations or the wealthiest families in a place, those who own the industry, are the principal beneficiaries.

To understand how the production of a building material (or any product) creates wealth for some and not for others, we must understand the concept of a commodity chain. A **commodity chain** is a series of links connecting the many places of production and distribution and resulting in a commodity that is then exchanged on the market. The generation of wealth differs along the commodity chain. Each link along the chain adds a certain value to the commodity, producing differing levels of wealth for the place and the people where production occurs.

What Timbuktu had to offer was the ability to coordinate and facilitate an overland trade based on its geographic situation near the Niger River—the last major water source for those crossing the Sahara from south to north across what is now Mali and Algeria. When the trade that was essential to the commodity chain shifted westward, Timbuktu's economic foundation crumbled. In modern times, commodity chains include miners and agriculturalists, manufacturers, exporters and importers, wholesalers and retailers, advertisers and designers, and of course consumers. Places positioned strategically along a commodity change can benefit, but they benefit in different ways, and the commodity chain can always shift.

How much wealth is generated along each step of production (each link in the commodity chain) depends on how production occurs at that step. In Chapter 8, we introduced the concepts of core and periphery. Sophisticated technology, high skill levels, extensive research and development, and high salaries tend to be associated with the segment of global commodity chains located in the core. The segment centered in the periphery, by contrast, tends to be associated with low technology, less education, little research and development, and lower wages. Since the people with the highest salaries own the businesses or work in advertising, and the people with the lowest salaries work in the mines or fields, global commodity chains often reinforce divisions between periphery and core.

One challenge of development is transforming peripheral processes into core ones, or redirecting the profit generated through core processes to improve peripheral processes. As the twenty-first century unfolds, countless governments, academics, nongovernmental organizations, and international financial institutions offer ideas about how to lift up the peripheral and semi-peripheral parts of the world. The theories, methods, and recommendations vary, but they are all focused on the illusive concept of development.

In this chapter, we review how development is defined and measured and some of the theories of development. We also examine how geography affects development, considering the structures of the world-economy. We also look at the barriers to and costs of development within countries, and we ask why uneven development occurs within the state.

Key Questions For Chapter 10

1. How do you define and measure development?
2. How does geographical situation affect development?
3. What are the barriers to and the costs of development?
4. How do political and economic institutions influence uneven development within states?

HOW DO YOU DEFINE AND MEASURE DEVELOPMENT?

The economic and social geography of the contemporary world is a patchwork of almost inconceivable contrasts. On the simple fields of shifting cultivators in equatorial American and African forests, farmers grow root crops using ancient methods and rudimentary tools. On the Great Plains of North America, in Ukraine, and in eastern Australia, farmers use expensive, modern machines to plow the land, seed the grain, and harvest the wheat. Toolmakers in the villages of Papua New Guinea still fashion their implements by hand, as they did many centuries ago, whereas the factory workers in Japan produce automobiles by the shipload for distribution to markets thousands of miles away. Between these extremes, the range and variety of productive activities are virtually endless.

These contrasts point to a major issue in understanding development: wealth does not depend solely on *what is produced*; it depends in large part on *how and where it is produced*. People can grow agricultural commodities with rudimentary tools or with expensive combines. Is one or the other necessary for development to occur? The idea of development is everywhere, but rarely do we pause to ask exactly what development means or how we can measure it (Fig. 10.2).

Development implies progress, and in the modern world, progress means improvements in technology and production as well as improvements in the social and economic welfare of people. To say a country is **developing**, then, is to say progress is being made in technology, production, and socioeconomic welfare. Our modern notion of development is related to the Industrial Revolution and the idea that technology can improve the lot of humans. Through advances in technology, people can produce more food, create new products, and accrue material wealth. But these things do not necessarily bring happiness, social stability, or environmental sustainability—making development a narrow, and sometimes controversial, indicator of the human condition.

Gross National Income

Ways of measuring development fit into three major areas of concern: development in economic welfare, development in technology and production, and development in social welfare. Over the past five decades, the most common way of comparing development in economic welfare was to use the index economists created to compare countries, the gross national product. **Gross national product (GNP)** is a measure of the total value of the officially recorded goods and services produced by the citizens and corporations of a country in a given year. It includes things produced both inside and outside the country's territory, and it is therefore broader than **gross domestic product (GDP)**, which encompasses only goods and services produced within a country during a given year.

In recent years, economists have turned to **gross national income (GNI)**, which calculates the monetary worth of what is produced within a country plus income received from investments outside the country, as a more accurate way of measuring a country's wealth in the context of a global economy. In order to compare GNI across countries, economists must standardize the data. The most common way to standardize GNI data is to divide it by the population of the country, yielding the **per capita GNI**. In Japan the per capita gross national income in U.S. dollars in 2008 was $31,410. In the United States it was $41,950. In Luxembourg it was $65,340. But in India it was $3460, in Nigeria it was $1040, and in Indonesia, the world's fourth most populous country, it was $3720. This enormous range across the globe in per capita GNI reflects the often-searing contrasts between rich and poor.

Although the map of per capita GNI (Fig. 1.3) clearly shows the startling contrasts between rich and poor in the world, the statistic has several shortcomings. GNI is a limited measure because it includes transactions in the **formal economy**, the legal economy that governments tax and monitor. Quite a few countries have per capita GNI of less than $1000 per year—a figure so low it seems impossible that people could survive on it. A key component of survival in these countries is the **informal**

Guest Field Note

Sukabumi, West Java

My own research is based on fieldwork in Indonesia as well as ongoing engagement with students in the United States. The women pictured here collaborated with me on a research/activism project for migrant women workers in Indonesia. The woman on the left ("Rina") had returned from working in Saudi Arabia as a domestic worker for two years. She wanted to return to Saudi Arabia for another contract to earn more money for herself and her family, but she was concerned about her rights and her safety. She had been employed by a person she considered fair and reasonable, but she had heard from friends and neighbors that many migrants had expe-

Figure 10.2

rienced serious abuses while abroad. The woman pictured on the right ("Sorani") is an Indonesian activist who works in support of migrant rights. She discussed with Rina and me her strategies for mobilizing political change, and she helped us to see possibilities for building transnational alliances among American and Indonesian workers, students, and activists. Based on these interviews, as well as many years of working with migrant women working in factories in Indonesia, my own research has increasingly sought to understand the ways in which we in the United States, as scholars, students, workers, and consumers can better serve global justice.

Credit: Rachel Silvey, University of Toronto

---

economy, the illegal or uncounted economy that governments do not tax and keep track of, including everything from a garden plot in a yard to the black market to the illegal drug trade. The informal economy is a significant element in the economies of many countries, but GNI statistics omit the informal economy entirely.

GNI per capita also masks the extremes in the distribution of wealth within a country. In Figure 1.3, the Middle Eastern oil countries of Kuwait and the United Arab Emirates (UAE) have per capita GNIs over $24,000, a level higher than that of several European countries. These figures give us no hint of the degree of overall participation in the country's economy, the average citizen's material standard of living, or gaps between genders or among regions. For example, economic production and the wealth it generates are not distributed evenly across the seven emirates that make up the United Arab Emirates. Abu Dhabi, the emirate that dominates the petroleum industry, generated over half of the country's GDP in 2007. Dubai, the next largest emirate, generated about a quarter of the GDP, and the Qaywayn emirate generated less than 1 percent of the country's gross GDP.

Another limitation of GNI per capita is that it measures only outputs (i.e., production). It does not take into account the costs of production, which take a toll on the environment through resource depletion and pollution of air and water. Per capita GNI may even treat such externalities as a plus. For example, the sale of cigarettes augments GNI—and if the cigarettes cause sickness and hospitalization is required, the GNI figure is boosted further. Conversely, the use of energy-efficient devices can actually lower GNI.

To measure development, some analysts now focus on development of technology and improvements in productivity or on the development of social welfare, instead of simply focusing on the GNI. The limitations of GNI have prompted some analysts to look for alternative measures of economic development, ways of measuring the roles technology, production, transportation, and communications play in an economy.

To gain a sense of the role of technology in the economy, the *Occupational Structure of the Labor Force* can be measured using the percentage of workers employed in various sectors of the economy. A high percentage of laborers engaged in the production of food staples signals a low overall level of development, as conventionally defined, and a high percentage of workers involved in high-tech industries and services signals a high level of

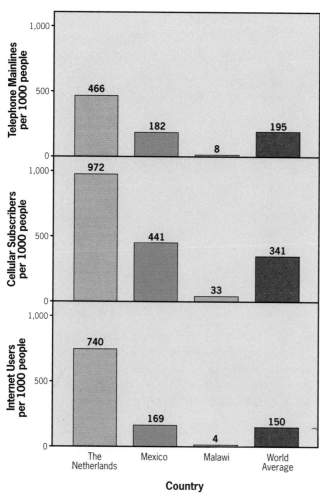

Figure 10.3

Differences in Communications Connectivity, 2005. *Data from:* Earthtrends, World Resources Institute.

development. *Productivity per Worker* is examined by summing production over the course of a year and dividing it by the total number of persons in the labor force. A more productive workforce points to a higher level of mechanization in production. To measure access to technology, some analysts use *Transportation and Communications Facilities per Person*, which reduces railway, road, airline connections, telephone, radio, television, and so forth to a per capita index—and reflects the amount of infrastructure that exists to facilitate economic activity. Figure 10.3 highlights some of the extraordinary disparities in communications access around the world.

Other analysts focus on social welfare to measure development. One way to measure social welfare is the *Dependency Ratio*, a measure of the number of dependents, young and old, that each 100 employed people must support (Fig. 10.4). A high dependency ratio can result in significant economic and social strain. Yet, as we saw in Chapter 2, the aging countries of Europe have high depen-

dency ratios and also very high per capita GNIs. We can employ countless other statistics to measure social welfare, including literacy rates, infant mortality, life expectancy, caloric intake per person, percentage of family income spent on food, and amount of savings per capita.

Looking through all of the maps that measure development, we gain a sense that many countries come out in approximately the same position no matter which of these measures is used. Each map and each statistic shares one limit with per capita GNI: they do not capture differences in development within countries, a question we consider at the end of this chapter.

Development Models

This discussion of ways of measuring development takes us back to the problem with terminology. The word *developing* suggests that all countries are improving their place in each of these indicators, increasing literacy, improving communications, or increasing productivity per worker. Beyond the problem of terminology, the very effort to classify countries in terms of levels of development has come under increasing attack during the last three decades. The central concern is that development suggests a scale or ladder, whereby all countries have moved or will move through the same process of development. The development model does not take geographical differences very seriously. Just because Japan moved from a rural, agrarian state to an urbanized, industrial one does not mean that Sudan will, or that it will do so in the same way. Another criticism of the development model is that the conceptualization of development has a Western bias. Critics argue that some of the measures taken in poorer countries that the West views as progress, such as attracting industry and mechanizing agriculture, can lead to worsened social and environmental conditions for many people in the poorer countries. Still others criticize the development model because it does not consider geography or interrelations across scales. The actions at one scale influence socioeconomic changes at other scales. Instead, the development model treats countries as autonomous units moving through a process of development at different speeds.

The classic development model, one that is subject to each of these criticisms, is economist Walt Rostow's **modernization model**. Many theories of development grew out of the major decolonization movements of the 1960s. Concerned with how the dozens of newly independent countries in Africa and Asia would survive economically, economists like Rostow looked to how the economically powerful countries had gotten where they were.

Rostow's model assumes that all countries follow a similar path to development or modernization, advancing through five stages of development. In the first stage, the society is *traditional*, and the dominant activity is subsistence

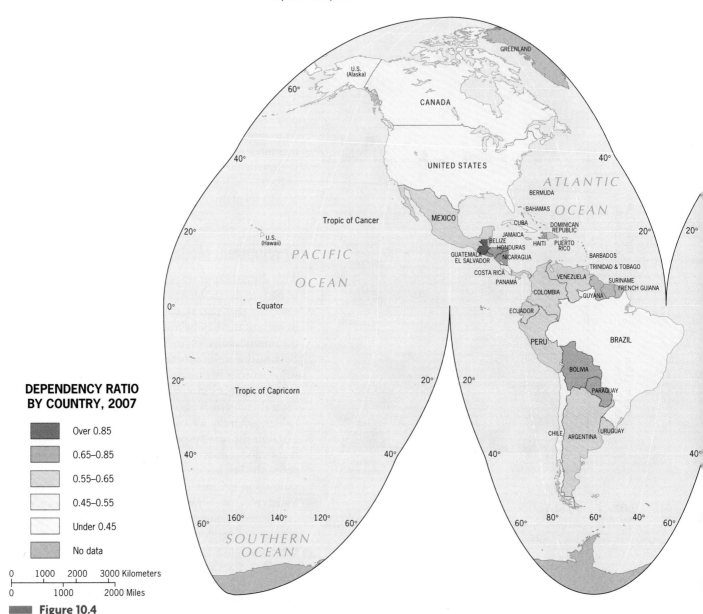

**DEPENDENCY RATIO
BY COUNTRY, 2007**

- Over 0.85
- 0.65–0.85
- 0.55–0.65
- 0.45–0.55
- Under 0.45
- No data

0   1000   2000   3000 Kilometers

0   1000   2000 Miles

Figure 10.4
Dependency Ratio.   The dependency ratio is a measure of the number of people under the age of 15 and over the age of 65 that depends on each working-age adult. The working-age adults in the formal economy contribute to a country's tax base, thereby supporting the young and old in the country.   *Data from:* World Health Organization, 2006.

farming. The social structure is rigid, and technology is slow to change. The second stage brings the *preconditions of takeoff*. New leadership moves the country toward greater flexibility, openness, and diversification. This, in turn, will lead to the third stage, *takeoff*. Now the country experiences something akin to an industrial revolution, and sustained growth takes hold. Urbanization increases, industrialization proceeds, and technological and mass-production breakthroughs occur. Next, the economy enters the fourth stage, the *drive to maturity*. Technologies diffuse, industrial specialization occurs, and international trade expands. Modernization is evident in key areas of the country, and population growth slows. In Rostow's model, some countries reach the final stage, *high mass consumption*, which is marked by high incomes and widespread production of many goods and services. During this stage, a majority of workers enter the service sector of the economy.

Another name for Rostow's model (and other models derived from it) is the *ladder of development*. Visually, we can see his five stages of development as rungs on a ladder (Fig. 10.5), where each country climbs the ladder

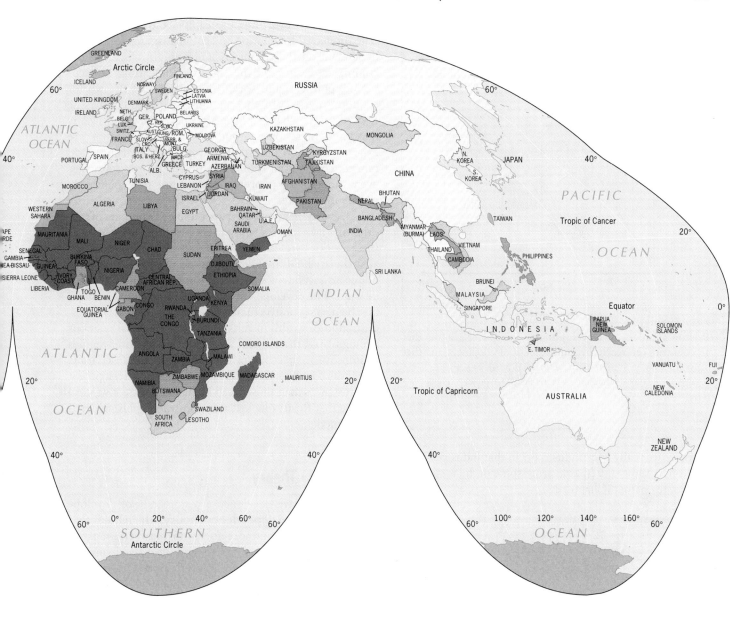

one rung at a time. In addition to the general criticisms of development models, the major problem with Rostow's model is that it provides no larger context to development. Is a climb up the ladder truly dependent on what happens within one country? Or do we need to take into account all of the other countries, their places on the ladder, and how their actions as well as global forces affect an individual country's movement on the ladder? The theory also misses the context within an individual country, leaving us to wonder where cultural differences fit into the picture?

Because it is descriptive of the experiences of some countries, Rostow's model is still influential, despite all of these criticisms. Even the notion of calling wealthy countries "industrialized" and saying poor countries need to "industrialize" implies that economic development can be achieved only by climbing the same ladder of development the wealthy countries have already climbed. Yet if a poor country quickly industrialized today through foreign investment, it might not reap much economic benefit, but it could experience severe environmental damage. It is also interesting to note that the "industrial" countries

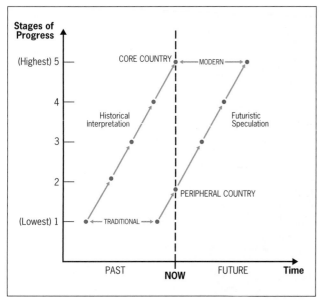

Figure 10.5

Rostow's Ladder of Development. This ladder assumes that all countries can reach the same level of development and that all will follow a similar path. *Adapted with permission from:* P. J. Taylor. "Understanding Global Inequalities: A World-Systems Approach," *Geography,* 77 (1992): 10–21.

of today are really "postindustrial," in that industrial production has now shifted away from some of the wealthiest parts of the planet (Chapter 12).

Is the idea of economic development inherently Western? If the West (North America and Europe) were not encouraging the "developing world" to "develop," how would people in the regions of the "developing world" think about their own economies?

HOW DOES GEOGRAPHICAL SITUATION AFFECT DEVELOPMENT?

Development happens in **context**: it reflects what is happening in a place as a result of forces operating concurrently at multiple scales. To understand why some countries are poor and others are wealthy, we need to consider the context not only at the state scale, but also at the local, regional, and global scales.

At the global scale, the European idea of the state diffused throughout the world via colonialism, bringing much of the world into the capitalist world-economy. The Industrial Revolution and colonialism made colonies dependent on the colonizers and brought wealth to the colonizers. Even after the end of colonization, the economic, political, and social interlinkages of the world-economy persist. In the capitalist world-economy, the flow of capital changed little after decolonization. Many development scholars argue that, today, the poor are experiencing **neo-colonialism**, whereby the major world powers control the economies of the poorer countries, even though the poorer countries are now politically independent states.

Development scholars have produced a number of theories that take into account the context of neo-colonialism; these theories are called structuralist theories. A **structuralist theory** holds that difficult-to-change, large-scale economic arrangements shape what can happen in fundamental ways. The development of the global economy brought into being a set of structural circumstances, such as the concentration of wealth in certain areas and unequal relations among places, that make it very difficult for poorer regions to improve their economic situation. Structuralists argue that these countries face a very different set of development circumstances than those faced by the countries of western Europe that Rostow looked at in constructing his modernization model.

Dependency Theory

Structuralists have developed a major body of development theory called **dependency theory**, which holds that the political and economic relationships between countries and regions of the world control and limit the economic development possibilities of poorer areas. Dependency theorists note, for example, that colonialism created political and economic structures that caused the colonies to become dependent on the colonial powers. They further argue that such dependency helps sustain the prosperity of dominant regions and the poverty of other regions, even after decolonization occurs.

Many poorer countries tie their currency into a wealthy country's currency, either by tying the value of their currency to the wealthy country's currency or by completely adopting the wealthy country's currency as their own, creating a significant link between the poor and wealthy countries' economies. For example, El Salvador has gone through a process of **dollarization**, through which the country's currency, the colon, was abandoned in favor of the dollar (Fig. 10.6). For the people of El Salvador, dollarization made sense because the economies of the two countries were tied long before dollarization occurred. Over 2 million Salvadorians live in the United States and send more than $2 billion in remittances to El Salvador annually. With this flow of American dollars to

Figure 10.6
A woman sells fruit juice at a stand in San Salvador, El Salvador. Note that the prices are in dollars, a reflection of the dollarization of the country in 2001.   ©Victor Ruiz Caballero/©AP/Wide World Photos.

El Salvador, many transactions occurred in dollars long before the official switch. In addition, over two-thirds of El Salvador's exports go to the United States. When the Federal Reserve Board in the United States controls the supply of dollars by altering the interest rates, the ramifications are felt directly in El Salvador.

Dependency theory sees little hope for economic prosperity in regions and countries that have traditionally been dominated by external powers. This aspect of dependency theory has been criticized, since some traditionally "dependent" regions have made economic gains. Indeed, like modernization theory, dependency theory is based on generalizations about economic change that pay relatively little attention to geographical differences in culture, politics, and society. Although both models provide some insights into the development process, neither is greatly concerned with the spatial and cultural situation of places—central elements of geographical analysis.

Geography and Context

As geographers, economists, and other social scientists came to realize that studying economic development divorced from political and social context did not reflect reality, geographers began to search for a development theory that encompassed geography, scale, place, and culture. Immanuel Wallerstein's **world-systems theory** provided a useful framework for many. We discussed world-systems theory in Chapter 8, focusing on how the theory provides insights into the political organization of space.

In this chapter, we focus on how world-systems theory helps us understand the geography of development.

Many geographers are drawn to world-systems theory because it is sensitive to geographical differences and the relationships among development processes that occur in different places. Specifically, Wallerstein's division of the world into a **three-tier structure**—the core, periphery, and semiperiphery—helps explain the interconnections between places in the global economy. As discussed in more detail in Chapter 8, core processes generate wealth in a place because they require higher levels of education, more sophisticated technologies, and higher wages and benefits. When core processes are embedded in a place (such as the Telecom corridor in Richardson-Plano, Texas), wealth is generated for the people in that place. Peripheral processes, on the other hand, require little education, lower technologies, and lower wages and benefits. Core regions are those that have achieved high levels of socioeconomic prosperity and are dominant players in the global economic game. When peripheral processes are embedded in a place (such as banana growers in Ecuador), the processes often generate little wealth for the people in that place. Periphery regions are poor regions that are dependent in significant ways on the core and do not have as much control over their own affairs, economically or politically. The semiperiphery exhibits both core and peripheral processes, and semiperipheral places serve as a buffer between the core and periphery in the world-economy. Countries of the semiperiphery exert more power than peripheral regions but remain heavily influenced by core regions.

Dividing the world into cores, semiperipheries, and peripheries might seem to do little more than replace developed—developing—underdeveloped with a new set of terms. But the core-periphery model is fundamentally different from the modernization model because it holds that not all places can be equally wealthy in the capitalist world-economy. World-systems theory also makes the power relations among places explicit and does not assume that socioeconomic change will occur in the same way in all places. It is thus sensitive to geographical context—at least in economic terms.

Geographer Peter J. Taylor uses the analogy of a school of tadpoles to demonstrate these ideas. He envisions different places in the world as the tadpoles and explains that not all tadpoles can survive to develop into toads. Rather, those who dominate survive, and the others perish. World-systems theorists see domination (exploitation) as a function of the capitalist drive for profit in the global economy. Thus, capitalists can move production quickly from one place to another around the globe to enhance profits, but places that lose a production facility can suffer. Moreover, their coping capacity can be small if, as is often the case, they earlier abandoned traditional ways and shifted to an export economy when external investment first came in.

World-systems theory is applicable at scales beyond the state. A core-periphery relationship can exist within a region, a state (country), or a local area. For example, Los Angeles can be described as the core of the Southern California region; the Johannesburg area can be described as the core of the South African state; or the Central Business District can be described as the core of São Paulo, Brazil.

Compare and contrast Rostow's ladder of development with Wallerstein's three-tier structure of the world-economy as models for understanding a significant economic shift that has occurred in the place where you grew up. What are the advantages and disadvantages of the two models?

WHAT ARE THE BARRIERS TO AND THE COSTS OF ECONOMIC DEVELOPMENT?

International organizations and governments measure development and then create programs to help improve the condition of humans around the world, espe-cially in the poorest countries of the world. By measuring human development, organizations and governments hope to discern how to break down barriers to development and improve the human condition globally.

One of the most widely referenced measurements of development today is the United Nations Human Development Index (Fig. 10.7). According to the United Nations, the Human Development Index goes beyond economics and incorporates the "three basic dimensions of human development: a long and healthy life, knowledge and a decent standard of living." Several statistics, including per capita GDP, literacy rates, school enrollment rates, and life expectancy at birth, factor into the calculation of the Human Development Index.

In 2000, the United Nations held a high-profile summit, during which 189 world leaders adopted the United Nations Millennium Declaration, with the goal of improving the condition of the people in the countries with the lowest standards of human development. At the summit, the world leaders recognized the principal barriers to economic development and identified eight key development goals to be achieved by the year 2015. They were:

1. Eradicate extreme poverty and hunger.
2. Achieve universal primary education.
3. Promote gender equality and empower women.
4. Reduce child mortality.
5. Improve maternal health.
6. Combat HIV/AIDS, malaria, and other diseases.
7. Ensure environmental sustainability.
8. Develop a global partnership for development.

These **Millennium Development Goals** represent a fairly high degree of consensus about the key conditions that need to be changed if economic development is to be achieved.

Barriers to Economic Development

As described in the last section of this chapter, the structures and geography of the world-economy inhibit economic development in the periphery. Numerous factors serve as barriers to the economic development of the periphery. In Chapter 1, we discussed the causes of malnutrition, and in Chapter 2, we examined how AIDS has ravaged Subsaharan Africa. In Chapter 13, we discuss the natural hazards found in many peripheral countries and the lack of infrastructure to cope with those hazards. It is clear that the world economic system often works to the disadvantage of the periphery but that the system is not the only obstacle that peripheral countries face.

Conditions within the periphery, such as high population growth rates, lack of education, foreign debt, political instability, and widespread disease, hamper development. It is possible to get into the chicken-or-the-egg debate here: did the structures of the world-economy create these conditions, or do these conditions help to create the structures of the world-economy? Many think that neither argument can stand alone, but understanding both the structures and the conditions is important if you are to form your own opinion.

Regardless of which came first, numerous people throughout the periphery are burdened with familial, economic, cultural, and political upheavals. In this section of the chapter, we discuss several of the conditions that affect the economic development prospects of people in the poorest countries of the world, including many factors outlined in the United Nations Millennium Development Goals.

Social Conditions

Countries in the periphery face numerous demographic, economic, and social problems. Most of the less well-off countries have high birth rates, with a relatively low life expectancy at birth (see Chapter 2). Across the global periphery, as much as half the population is 15 years old or younger, making the supply of adult, taxpaying laborers low relative to the number of dependents. Low life expectancies and high infant and child mortality rates stem from inadequate nutrition (protein deficiency is a common problem). Many in the global economic periphery also lack public sewage systems, clean drinking water, and access to health care, making economic development all the more difficult.

Lack of access to education is also a major problem in the periphery. In some places, even the poorest families pay for their children to attend school. As a result, large numbers of school-age children do not go to school, and illiteracy rates are high. Moreover, access to education in the periphery is often gendered, with boys attending school longer than girls. Girls often stop attending school and instead work in the city to pay for school fees for their brothers.

Lack of education for girls is founded on and compounded by the widespread assumption (not just in the periphery but in most of the world) that girls will leave their homes (and communities) when they marry, no longer bringing income to the family. In parts of the periphery, trafficking in children, especially girls, is common. Mike Dottridge, a modern antislavery activist, explains that **trafficking** happens when "adults and children fleeing poverty or seeking better prospects are manipulated, deceived, and bullied into working in conditions that they would not choose." This phenomenon is not considered slavery because the family does not sell a child; instead the child is sent away with a recruiter in the hopes that the recruiter will send money and the child will earn money to send home. The trafficked children are often taken to neighboring or nearby countries that are wealthier and in demand of domestic servants. Others are trafficked across the world, again typically to work as domestic servants. Dottridge explains that the majority of trafficked children are girls and that the majority of girls are "employed as domestic servants or street vendors," although some girls are "trafficked into prostitution." The assumption that girls will leave the house when they marry and will no longer contribute financially to the family dissuades families in poorer areas from sending their daughters to school. Instead, many families are persuaded (financially or by recruiters) to send their girls (and sometimes their boys) to work in the city, in another country, or across the world.

Some countries are working to change access to primary education in order to make education universally available. In 2000, the Millennium Development Report prompted the government of Rwanda to improve access to education. In 2003, fees for primary education were eliminated, and two years later schools started receiving revenues based on the number of students they were educating. Rwanda's goal is to make primary education available to all by 2010. But access and completion are two different things; of the 1.85 million children currently in primary schools, only half reach the sixth year of school. Moreover, without adequate funding to support the growing student population, Rwanda's students meet under trees and in swelling classrooms. Aid is flowing in from outside, but sustaining support for the country's educational sector remains an ongoing challenge.

Foreign Debt

Complicating the picture further is the foreign debt crisis that many periphery and semi-periphery countries face. Shortly after the decolonization wave of the 1960s, banks and other international financial institutions began lending large sums of money to the newly independent states, money earmarked for development projects. By the 1980s and 1990s, the World Bank and the International Monetary Fund (IMF) were lending massive amounts of money to peripheral and semi-peripheral countries, but with strings attached. To secure the loans, countries had to agree to implement economic or governmental reforms, such as privatizing government entities, opening the country to foreign trade, reducing tariffs, and

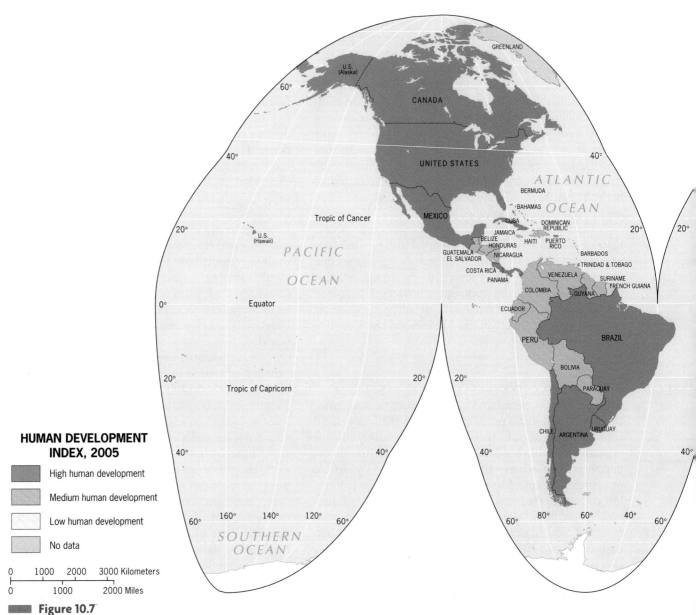

**HUMAN DEVELOPMENT
INDEX, 2005**

High human development

Medium human development

Low human development

No data

0   1000   2000   3000 Kilometers

0   1000   2000 Miles

Figure 10.7

Human Development Index **The data are available at:** http://hdr.undp.org/en/media/
HDR_20072008_Table_1.pdf

encouraging foreign direct investment. These loans are
known as **structural adjustment loans**. The IMF, whose
manager is by tradition a European, lends money to
peripheral countries in an effort to head off major economic problems.

Once peripheral countries owe money to the IMF,
the World Bank, and private banks and lending institutions, they need to repay their debts. Spending a large part
of the country's budget on debt repayment makes it difficult for a country to invest in more development projects.

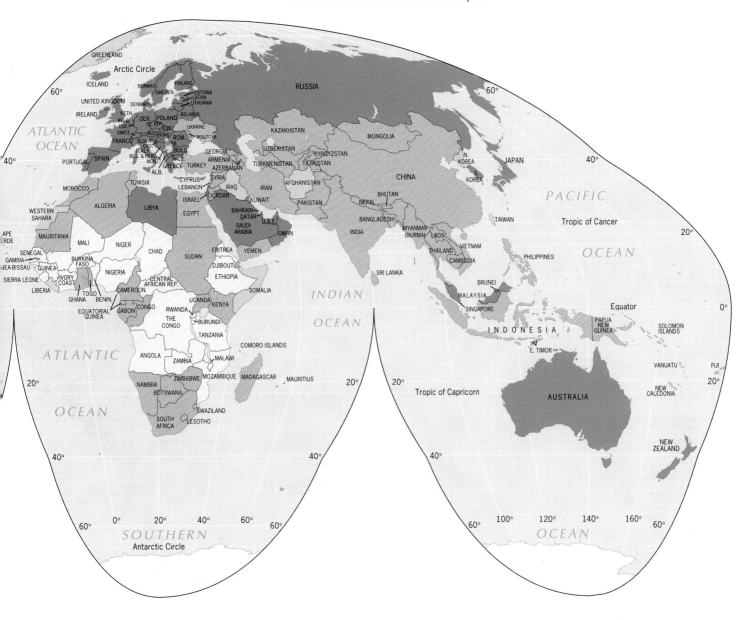

For many countries the cost of servicing their debts (that is, the cost of repayments plus interest) has exceeded revenues from the export of goods and services (Fig. 10.8). Meanwhile, in many countries, the returns on development projects have been much lower than anticipated.

These factors have created a global debt crisis for the poorest countries in the world.

Structural adjustment loans were part of a larger trend toward **neoliberalism** in the late twentieth century. Neoliberalism derives from the neo-classical economic

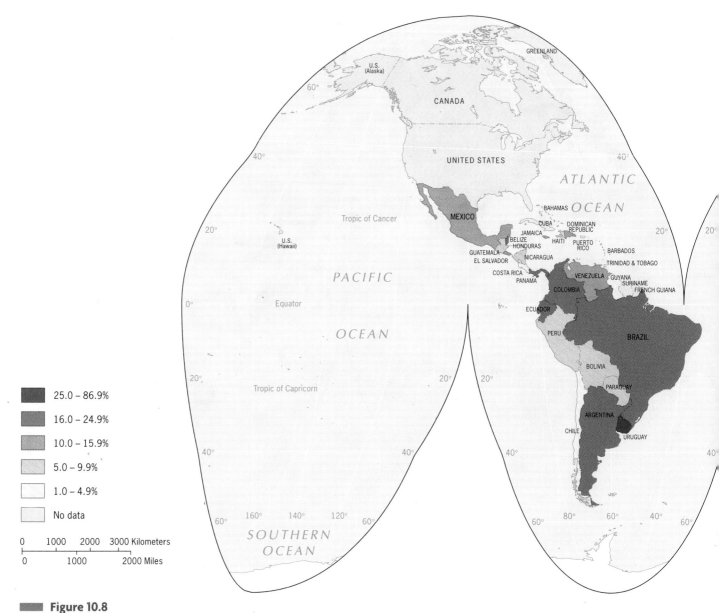

Figure 10.8
External debt service as a percentage of exports of goods and services for low-and middle-income economies, 2006.   *Data from:* The World Bank. *Millennium Development Goals Atlas*. Washington, D.C.: The World Bank, 2008. Online at http://devdata.worldbank.org/atlas-mdg/.

idea that government intervention into markets is inefficient and undesirable, and should be resisted wherever possible. These ideas were at the heart of the conditions that were attached to loans and refinancing programs, but neoliberal ideas spurred a general turn toward the transfer of economic control from states to the private sector. This, in turn, fostered economic globalization while shrinking the size of the public sector in a number of countries. The trade-off, however, was the expansion of corporate control and the erosion of

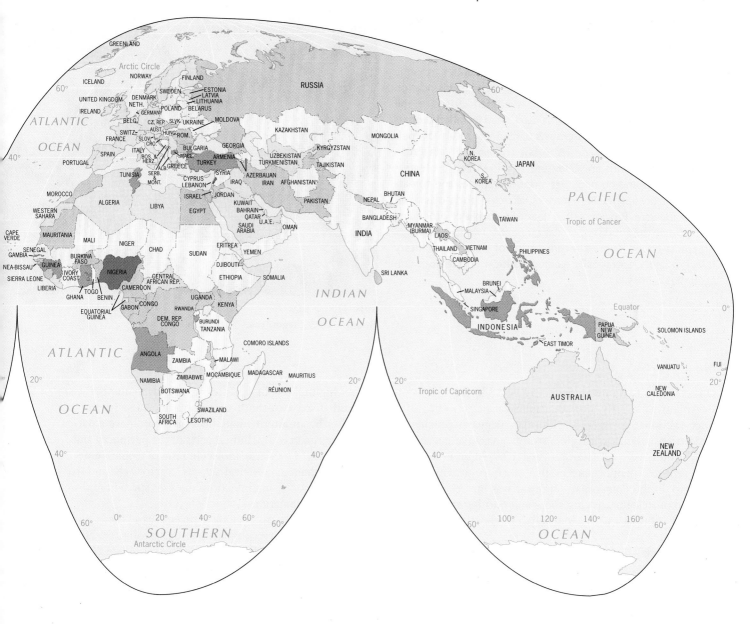

the ability of regions and states to control their economic destinies. Hence, the neoliberal turn has been highly contentious.

High debt obligations and related neoliberal reforms arguably contributed to the economic and political crisis in Argentina at the end of 2001—leading to overreliance on a privatized export sector that left the country vulnerable when shifts in the global economy weakened the competitiveness of Argentinian exports. But government spending also was also unsustainably high, and

Field Note

"Arriving in Argentina during the political and economic upheavals that had begun in 2001, I saw signs of dislocation and trouble everywhere. Beggars pursued pedestrians on the once-fashionable Avenida Florida. Banks had installed protective shutters against angry crowds demanding return of their frozen and devalued deposits. A bus trip on the Patagonian Highway turned into an adventure when masked protesters carrying rocks and burning rags stopped vehicles and threatened their occupants. Newspapers carried reports of starvation in Tucumán Province—in a country capable of producing seven times the food its population needs. Twenty years ago, Argentina ended its most recent period of disastrous military rule, but its democratically elected politicians have not managed the country well."

Figure 10.9
Buenos Aires, Argentina. © H. J. de Blij.

corruption was rampant. In 2001, H. J. de Blij arrived in Argentina shortly after the upheaval began. On the once-fashionable Avenida Florida, beggars pursued pedestrians. Banks with glass storefronts were covered with protective steel shutters (Fig. 10.9). The newspapers reported people starving in a northern province. A bus trip on the Patagonian Highway was interrupted by masked protesters carrying rocks and burning rags, who stopped vehicles on the highway and threatened their occupants.

By 2005, internal economic growth and aid from Venezuela put Argentina in a position to work out a complex debt restructuring plan that has pulled the country back from the brink. But in cases where countries are facing imminent economic, political, and social meltdown, the only alternative may be to default on loans. Defaulting countries then find themselves in a severely disadvantaged position when it comes to attracting future external investment. And if a substantial number of countries were to default at the same time, a global economic crisis could ensue that would work to the disadvantage of almost everyone.

Disease

Those living in the global economic periphery experience comparatively high rates of disease and a corresponding lack of adequate health care. These circumstances directly affect economic development, making survival difficult for many people, orphaning children, and weakening the labor force.

As highlighted in Chapters 1 and 2, a number of **vectored diseases**—those spread by one host (person) to another by an intermediate host or vector—are a particular scourge in warm, humid parts of the periphery and semiperiphery. The warm, moist climates of tropical environments enhance biological activity. Vectors abound in such environments, and infectious diseases spread rapidly through host populations.

Development experts look at malaria as a "silent tsunami" in the periphery, comparing its death toll to the tsunami that ravaged South and Southeast Asia in late 2004. That tsunami killed some 300,000 people (including children) *at once*. Malaria kills about *150,000 children* in the global periphery *each month*. **Malaria** is an infectious disease spread by mosquitoes that carry the parasite in their saliva. Scientists did not determine the role of mosquitoes in the diffusion of the disease until the late eighteenth century. Today, the sequence of the disease is well known. The mosquito stings an infected host and sucks up some of the disease agents. In the mosquito's stomach, the parasites reproduce and multiply, eventually reaching its saliva. When the mosquito stings the next person, some of the parasites are injected into that person's bloodstream. The person who has been stung develops malaria and becomes a host.

The disease manifests itself through recurrent fever and chills, with associated symptoms such as anemia and an enlarged spleen. More than one million people in the world die of the disease each year. Malaria is a major factor in infant and child mortality, as most of the victims are children age 5 or younger. If a person survives the disease, he or she will develop a certain degree of immunity. However, many infected by malaria are weak, lack energy, and face an increased risk of other diseases taking hold in their weakened body.

Malaria occurs throughout the world, except in higher latitudes and altitudes, and drier environments. Although people in the tropical portions of Africa suffer most from this disease, malaria also prevails in India, Southeast Asia, China, and the tropical Americas.

Several types of malaria spread throughout these regions, with some being more severe than others. In addition to humans, various species of monkeys, rats, birds, and even snakes can be affected by the disease. In Subsaharan Africa, malaria's virulence results from the effectiveness of its vectors—three African mosquitoes (*Anopheles gambiae*, *A. arabiensis*, and *A. funestus*). Whole populations are afflicted, and entire regions have been abandoned because of the prevalence of the disease.

Antimalarial drugs exist, but to defeat malaria, afflicted regions must eliminate the vector: the mosquito. During the 1940s, the government of Sri Lanka (then Ceylon) launched a massive attack on the mosquito with the aid of a pesticide called *dichloro diphenyl trichloroethane* (DDT). The results were dramatic. The mosquito was practically wiped out, and the rate of deaths attributable to malaria fell markedly. In 1945, Sri Lanka's death rate overall had been 22 per 1000; in 1972, it reported a death rate of only 8 per 1000. The figure was further reduced to 5 per 1000 by 2004, as reflected in Figure 10.10.

The conquest of malaria produced a new set of problems, however. DDT proved to be highly carcinogenic and to have negative health and environmental consequences of its own. Also, the lowered death rate through malaria eradication led to a substantial rise in the population growth rate, creating new problems for Sri Lanka. By the time the birth rate dropped (it is 19 per 1000 today), the island had experienced a population explosion.

Success in combating major vectored diseases often is only temporary. Following the Sri Lankan experiment, India initiated a massive assault against the malaria mosquito, and the number of new cases of malaria declined dramatically. But ten years after the program was introduced, India reported that 60 million people were infected with malaria, more than half the number who had the disease before the antimalaria campaign began. This example proved the mosquito population's ability to rebound quickly after even the most intensive application of pesticides.

Today the war against malaria is taking a new tack: genetic interference with the mosquito so that its capacity to transmit the malaria parasite, *Plasmodium*, is destroyed. By introducing "engineered" mosquitoes into the general population, health experts hope that the number of nonvirulent mosquitoes will rise significantly. A number of programs also focus on distributed insecticide-laden mosquito nets to surround sleeping quarters and protect people from the mosquitoes that are most active at night (Fig. 10.11).

These efforts are having some dramatic impacts in parts of Africa, but malaria remains a scourge of the poorer peoples of the world — and an impediment to economic development.

Political Instability

Although not addressed in the Millennium Development goals, political instability can greatly impede economic development as well. Establishing a government that can maintain control over and lead a low-income country can be a daunting task. In peripheral countries, a wide divide often exists between the very wealthy and the poorest of the poor. In Kenya, for example, the wealthiest 10 percent of the population controls over 40 percent of the country's income. The disenfranchisement of the poor and the competition among the rich for control of the government (and the potential spoils that go along with that) can lead to extreme political instability within a state—as Kenya experienced in 2007–2008. Add to these factors involvement from outside the country (especially by powerful countries), and the political instability escalates, yielding horrid conditions in which military dictators, selfish megalomaniacs, and corrupt governments can come to power.

Political stability is difficult to achieve and maintain in a poorer country. Countries of the core have established liberal democracies for themselves; since World War II, all of them have held regularly scheduled democratic elections. But countries in the periphery and semi-periphery have had a much harder time establishing and maintaining democracies. In the process of decolonization, the colonizing countries typically left governments that reflected political and social hierarchies during the colonial period. Some failed, some were overthrown by military coups, and some saw the consolidation of power around a dictatorial strongman. Many countries in the periphery and semi-periphery have alternated repeatedly between quasidemocratic and military governments. Some argue that without considerable wealth, maintaining a liberal democracy is all but impossible.

Opening the homepage of any major newspaper on any given day will reveal a story somewhere in the world that demonstrates the link between economic stability and political stability. In post-Taliban Afghanistan, economic woes represent one of the greatest threats to the stability of the United States—supported government in Kabul. More than half of the population is impoverished, and the government lacks the funds to invest in development. Foreign aid—much of it from the United States—has

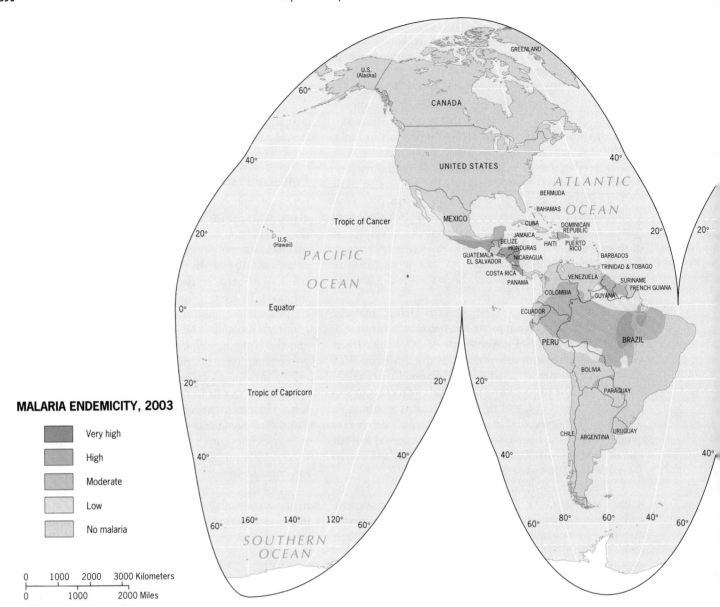

MALARIA ENDEMICITY, 2003

- Very high
- High
- Moderate
- Low
- No malaria

0   1000   2000   3000 Kilometers

0   1000   2000 Miles

Figure 10.10

Global Distribution of Malaria Transmission Risk, 2003. *Adapted with permission from:* World Health Organization, Roll Back Malaria Department and United Nations Children's Fund. World Malaria Report, 2005. http://rbm.who.int/wmr2005/html/map1.htm

provided some help, but the flow of aid has been variable and its amount insufficient to address the country's searing economic problems. Many analysts see this as a key impediment to achieving stability in Afghanistan. As the *Economist* put it in 2006, "poverty helps the Taliban."

In places where poverty is rampant, politicians often become corrupt, misusing aid and exacerbating the plight of the poor. In Zimbabwe, the year 2002 left many people starving, as poor weather conditions created a meager harvest. The country's ruling party,

ZANU-PF, headed by Robert Mugabe, demanded cards from Zimbabweans who registered for the "food for work" program—cards demonstrating membership in the ZANU-PF political party. As conditions worsened in subsequent years, the Mugabe government faced increasing resistance. A potential challenger emerged in 2008, but after members of his opposition party were killed and the challenger was harassed, he pulled out and Mugabe was once again elected on an uncontested ballot.

Figure 10.11
Tamolo, India. Tamolo is on the Car Nicobar islands off the coast of India. After the 2004 tsunami, the wetlands became breeding grounds for the mosquitoes that carry malaria. This baby sleeps under a mosquito net distributed to villagers by United Nations Children's Fund (UNICEF) workers.   © Pallava Bagla/Corbis.

The Zimbabwe case shows that in low-income countries, corrupt leaders can stay in power for decades because the people are afraid to rise up against the leader's extreme power or because those who have risen up have been killed or harmed by the leader's followers. Circumstances and timing need to work together to allow a new government to come to power. When governments become excessively corrupt, other countries and nongovernmental organizations sometimes cut off development aid to the country. Yet when this happens, everyday people often bear the brunt of hardship. Even when the global community cuts off the corrupt government's aid, core countries and nongovernmental organizations typically provide food aid to the people, but this is rarely sufficient to meet basic needs or reverse the trajectory of hardship in the country.

Costs of Economic Development

Economic development changes a place. To increase productivity, whether industrial or agricultural, people transform the environment. When a country goes through intensification of *industrial production*, air and surface water are often polluted. When a country goes through intensification of *agricultural production*, the introduction of pesticides and herbicides can have deleterious impacts on the soil and groundwater. *Tourism* can be just as difficult on the environment—taxing the existing infrastructure beyond its capacities. The costs of tourism often stretch far beyond the environment, affecting ways of life and fundamentally altering the cultural landscape.

Industrialization

In their efforts to attract new industries, the governments of many countries in the global periphery and semiperiphery have set up special manufacturing export zones called **export processing zones (EPZs),** which offer favorable tax, regulatory, and trade arrangements to foreign firms. By the early 2000s, more than 60 countries had established such zones, and many of these had become major manufacturing centers (Fig. 10.12). Two of the best known of these zones are the Mexican **maquiladoras** and the **special economic zones** of China (discussed in Chapter 9). Governments site such zones in places with easy access to export markets. Thus, the maquiladora zone in Mexico is located directly across the border from the United States, and the special economic zones of China are sited near major ports. These zones typically attract a mix of manufacturing operations, depending on the skill levels of the labor force and the available infrastructure.

The maquiladora started several decades ago when the Mexican government designated the region of northern Mexico as a maquiladora district, making it a place where manufactured products could be sent to the United States free of import tariffs. In response, many U.S. corporations established manufacturing plants where workers

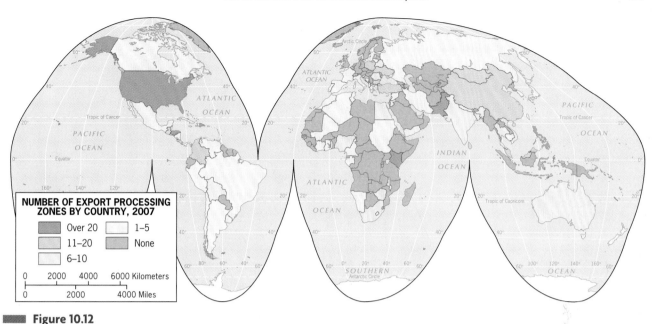

Figure 10.12

Export Processing Zones. Number of export processing zones by country, 2006.   *Data from:* International Labor Organization.

assembled a collection of components and raw materials into finished industrial products, tax free. The corporations then exported at least 80 percent of these goods to the United States.

Although the maquiladora phenomenon started during the 1960s, it did not really take off until the 1980s. During the 1980s, American companies recognized the expanding wage differences between the United States and Mexican worker and began relocating to the maquiladora district in northern Mexico. Although competition from other parts of the world has led to the closing of some plants, today some 3000 maquiladoras continue to function, employing 1 million workers and accounting for 45 percent of Mexico's exports. The maquiladora plants produce goods such as electronic equipment, electrical appliances, automobiles, textiles, plastics, and furniture. The plants are controversial both in Mexico and the United States, as corporations that have relocated there avoid the employment and environmental regulations that are in force just a few miles to the north. Many maquiladora factories hire young women and men for low pay and few if any benefits, putting them to work in repetitive jobs, often in environmentally questionable conditions.

In 1992, the United States, Mexico, and Canada established the **North American Free Trade Agreement (NAFTA)**, which prompted further industrialization of the border region. NAFTA took effect January 1, 1994. In addition to manufacturing plants, NAFTA has facili-

tated the movement of service industries from the United States to Mexico, including data processing operations. Most of the new plants are located in two districts: Tijuana on the Pacific Coast—linked to San Diego across the border—and Ciudad Juarez on the Rio Grande across from El Paso, Texas.

Agriculture

In peripheral countries, agriculture typically focuses on personal consumption or on production for a large agricultural conglomerate. Where zones of larger-scale, modernized agriculture have developed in the periphery, foodstuffs are produced for the foreign market and often have minimal impact on the impoverished conditions of the surrounding lands. Little is produced for the local marketplace because distribution systems are poorly organized and because the local population is typically unable to pay for foodstuffs. If the local population owns land, their landholdings are usually fragmented, creating small plots of land that are difficult to farm in a manner that produces much income. Even on larger plots of land, most farmers are equipped with outdated, inefficient tools and equipment. The main crops tend to be grains and roots; farmers produce little protein because high-protein crops typically have lower yields than grain crops. On the farms in the periphery, yields per unit area are low, subsistence modes of life prevail, and many families are constantly in debt.

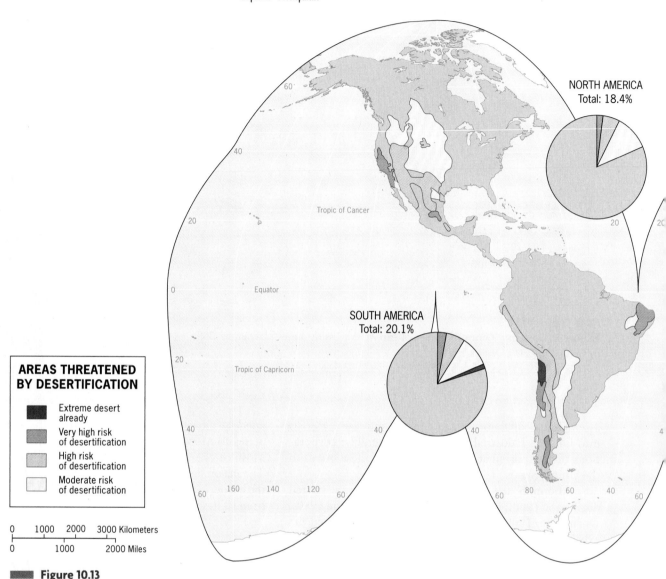

AREAS THREATENED BY DESERTIFICATION

- Extreme desert already
- Very high risk of desertification
- High risk of desertification
- Moderate risk of desertification

0   1000   2000   3000 Kilometers

0   1000   2000 Miles

NORTH AMERICA
Total: 18.4%

SOUTH AMERICA
Total: 20.1%

Tropic of Cancer

Equator

Tropic of Capricorn

Figure 10.13

Areas Threatened by Desertification. Deserts expand and contract cyclically, but nature's cycles can be distorted by human intervention. This map shows areas threatened or affected by desertification.   *Data from* several sources, including J. Turk et al., *Environmental Science*, Philadelphia: Saunders, 1984, p. 305.

Impoverished farmers can ill afford such luxuries as fertilizers, and educational levels are typically too low to achieve widespread soil conservation efforts. As a result, soil erosion is commonplace in most peripheral areas. Severe soil erosion in areas with dry or semidry climates around deserts results in extreme degradation of the land and the spread of the desert into these lands. Although the expansion and contraction of deserts can occur naturally and cyclically, the process of **desertification** is more often caused by humans destroying vegetation and eroding soils through the overuse of lands for livestock grazing or crop production.

Desertification has hit Africa harder than any of the other continents (Fig. 10.13). More than half of Africa is arid or semiarid, and many people farm the marginal, dry lands of the continent. Land ownership patterns, the need for crops and protein sources (both for local consumption and for export), and power differences among groups of people lead some farmers and ranchers to turn marginal, semiarid lands into farm and ranch lands. Lands that are available for farming or ranching may be used more intensively in order to increase agricultural production (see Chapter 13). In semiarid regions, the

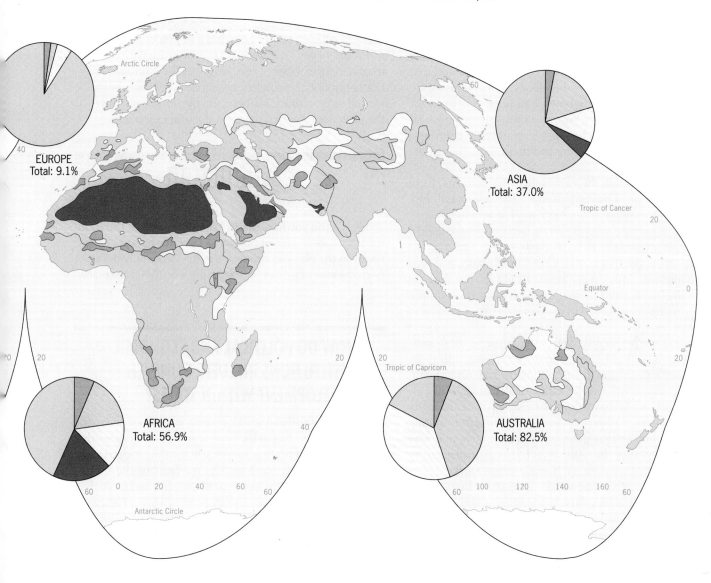

decision to farm more intensively and increase agricultural production has the unintended consequences of eroding the land, causing migration flows, and creating conflict.

In Subsaharan Africa over the last 50 years, more than 270,000 square miles (700,000 square kilometers) of farming and grazing land have become desert, extending the Sahara Desert to the south. Some of the African desertification may be caused by climatic fluctuations, but overgrazing, woodcutting, soil exhaustion, and misuse have undoubtedly accelerated the process.

Tourism

All development strategies have pros and cons, as is well illustrated by the case of tourism. Peripheral countries in the Caribbean region of Middle America and in other parts of the world have become leading destinations for millions of tourists from richer states. Tourism brings some wealth and employment to these countries (see Chapter 12), but the industry's contributions are often narrow in scope and time. Tourism may also have serious negative effects on cultures and environments in the periphery.

In economic terms, the "host" country must make a substantial investment. Sometimes imports of building materials and equipment strain the country's supply system, and funds are diverted to hotel construction that could have been spent on other needs such as housing for citizens. Moreover, many hotels and other tourist facilities are owned not by the host country but by large multinational corporations. These corporations earn enormous profits, most of which are sent back to headquarters in the home country.

Countries that do earn substantial income from tourism include Thailand, Kenya, Barbados, and Fiji. However, that income does not always benefit local economies. It is not uncommon for much of the income to flow to outside investors or to be reinvested in the construction of airports, cruise-ports, and other infrastructure that supports tourism. Tourism can create local jobs, but they are often low-paying and there is little job security. In tourist zones, many employees work two or three jobs in order to break even.

Tourism frequently strains the fabric of local communities as well. The invasion of poor communities by wealthier visitors can foster antipathy and resentment. Tourism can also have the effect of debasing local culture, which is adapted to suit the visitors' taste. In many instances tourism fosters a "demonstration effect" among locals that encourages them to behave in ways that may please or interest the visitors but that is disdained by the larger local community. Some tourism workers consider employment in the tourist industry dehumanizing because it demands displays of friendliness and servitude that locals find insulting.

A flood of affluent tourists may be appealing to the government of a poor country (whose elite may have a financial stake in the hotels where they can share the pleasures of the wealthy), but local entrepreneurs often take a different view. Indeed, powerful multinational corporations and national governments may intervene to limit the opportunities of local, small-scale operators in favor of mass, prearranged tourist destinations ("exclusive" resorts) that isolate the tourist from local society. Overreliance on tourism can also leave an economy vulnerable if shifting economic circumstances cause a sharp decline in the number of tourists or if natural disasters hit. Because many tourist destinations in poorer countries are beach attractions, natural hazards such as the 2004 tsunami in Southeast Asia can destroy the lynchpin of a country's economy (we discuss the tsunami and other natural hazards in detail in Chapter 13). Suffering the loss of thousands of people; dealing with the after-effects of sewage, homelessness, orphans, and the destitute; and coping with rebuilding the tourist destinations must occur while the flow of tourist-related income has stopped.

The cultural landscape of tourism is frequently a study in harsh contrasts: gleaming hotels tower over modest, often poor housing; luxury liners glide past poverty-stricken villages; opulent meals are served in hotels while, down the street, children suffer from malnutrition. If the tourist industry offered real prospects for economic progress in low-income countries, such circumstances might be viewed as temporary, unfortunate by-products. However, the evidence too often points in the other direction.

Think of a trip you have made to a poorer area of the country or a poorer region of the world. Describe how your experience in the place as a tourist was fundamentally different from the everyday lives of the people who live in the place.

HOW DO POLITICAL AND ECONOMIC INSTITUTIONS INFLUENCE UNEVEN DEVELOPMENT WITHIN STATES?

In our globalized world, poverty is not confined to the periphery. Core countries have regions and peoples that are markedly poorer than others. On the Pine Ridge Indian Reservation in the northern Great Plains of the United States, unemployment hovers at 80 percent, and more than 60 percent of the people live in poverty with a per capita income of just over $6000. Other countries of the core have similar regions where peoples' economic lives do not improve when the country's economy grows. In Europe, areas of isolation and stagnation persist—particularly in the east. At the same time, some places in peripheral countries are experiencing rapid economic growth. The local conditions in these places differ sharply from those prevailing in surrounding areas. Recent economic growth on the Pacific Rim of East Asia has created huge regional disparities in economic conditions between some coastal provinces of China and distant interior provinces. Such regional economic contrasts have significant political as well as social consequences.

As noted at the beginning of this chapter, regional contrasts in wealth are a reminder that per capita GNI does not accurately represent the economic development of individual places. Any statistic that is derived for an entire country or State hides the variety of economic situations within. Peripheral countries are notoriously marked by severe regional disparities. In Chapter 9 we discussed the stark contrasts between wealthy and poor within Latin American and African cities. When viewed at the scale of the State, however, major cities (particularly capitals) and their surroundings often look like islands of prosperity, with modern buildings, factories on the outskirts, and modern farms nearby. In some cases roads and rails lead to a bustling port, where luxury automobiles are unloaded for use by the privileged elite and raw materials or agricultural products from the country are exported to points around the world. In these core areas of countries, the rush of "progress" may be evident. If you travel a few miles into the countryside or into a different neighborhood in the city, however, you will likely see a very different picture. In this section of the chapter, we discuss how government policy affects development, how governments collaborate with corporations to create islands of development, and how people try to generate growth in the periphery of the periphery.

The Role of Governments

The actions of governments influence whether, how, and where wealth is produced. This is because the distribution of wealth is influenced by tariffs, trade agreements, taxation structures, land ownership rules, environmental regulations, and many other manifestations of governmental authority. Government policies play an important role at the interstate level, but they also shape patterns of

development within States—not just between urban and rural areas, but within each of these sectors.

Of course, governments alone do not determine patterns of wealth and poverty, but they are almost always part of the picture. Consider the case of the Ninth Ward in New Orleans, which was devastated by Hurricane Katrina in 2005. On its surface, what happened to the Ninth Ward was the result of a natural disaster. But the flooding of that part of New Orleans was also the result of government decisions decades ago to build levies and settle flood-prone areas. The concentration of people living there was also the product of innumerable policies affecting housing, the construction of businesses, and the like. Once the hurricane hit, many looked to government to rebuild the devastated section of the city. The limited nature of the governmental response is evident in the landscape today (Fig. 10.14).

At a somewhat larger scale, consider the contrasts between parts of rural Wisconsin and rural Appalachia in the United States. In rural Wisconsin, many of the surviving family farmers are educated at land-grant universities in plant and animal sciences and in agribusiness. They may well be running a highly mechanized dairy farm. On such farms, the farmer equips each cow with a barcode and keeps a range of data about that particular cow—data

Field Note

"Walking through New Orleans' Lower Ninth Ward more than two years after Hurricane Katrina, it seemed as if the natural disaster had just happened. Street after street of devastated, vacant buildings was all the eye could behold—many still bearing the markings of the emergency crews that had moved through the neighborhood in the wake of the hurricane, showing whether anyone had died inside. It struck me that reconstruction would require a public commitment on the order of what occurred in Europe after World War II, when cities reduced to rubble by bombing were rebuilt almost from scratch. It is an open question whether a comparable commitment exists to rebuild a poor part of New Orleans, or whether it even makes sense to rebuild in such a vulnerable location."

Figure 10.14
Destroyed House in the Lower Ninth Ward, New Orleans. © Alexander B. Murphy.

regarding any medical attention the cow has needed, how much milk the cow is producing, and when the cow last calfed. The farmer then feeds the cow a diet geared toward improving or maintaining milk production. When the cow ambles over to the trough to feed, a sensor reads the cow's barcode and automatically mixes the correct balance of proteins, carbohydrates, and nutrients for the cow, dispensing them into the trough for the cow to eat. If the cow has already eaten that day, the computer dispenses nothing into the trough, and the cow is left to amble away.

In parts of rural Appalachia, by contrast, hardscrabble farming is the norm. Farmers have limited education, and there is little mechanization. In short, life in some of the poorest parts of rural Appalachia is a world apart from life on a modern Wisconsin dairy farm. Some of those differences can be attributed to geographic situation and economic swings. But others are the product of government policies that influence educational opportunities, provide subsidies for particular agricultural pursuits, and promote the development of particular technologies. Every policy has a geographical expression, meaning that some regions are favored whereas others are disadvantaged as a result of the implementation of that policy. When policies come together to favor some regions over others, uneven development is the result. And uneven development can easily be exacerbated over time as the wealthy grow wealthier.

Government policy can also help alleviate uneven development. In the case of Appalachia, the U.S. Congress created an Appalachian Regional Commission in 1965 to address poverty in the region. The Commission has orchestrated a program of government investment in roads, schools, health-care facilities, and water and sewer systems that has fostered development throughout much of the region. Significant parts of Appalachia have benefited from these policies, although pockets of deep poverty remain.

Looking at commodity chains can also help us understand the role of governments in uneven development—both within and between states. In her 2005 book *The Travels of a T-Shirt in the Global Economy*, economist Pietra Rivoli described the significant influences governments have on the distribution of wealth between and within states. Rivoli grabs a T-shirt out of a bin at a Walgreens in Florida, buys it, and then traces its production back through the commodity chain to see how it ends up in her hands. The cotton for her T-shirt was grown in West Texas, where the cotton lobby (the political arm of America's cotton producers) has effectively politicked for governmental labor programs and price supports that help the lobby grow cotton and sell it at predictable prices.

From West Texas, the cotton bale reaches China by ship. There, it is spun into thread and woven into fabric. Women from rural China work in state-owned factories set up in regions that are slated for economic development—cutting and sewing T-shirts and keeping the textile machines in good repair. The women are considered cheap labor at the global scale, earning about $100 per month. Rivoli reports that over 40,000 garment factories operate in China alone.

The T-shirts are then shipped to the United States for sale. In an attempt to protect T-shirts produced in America with higher labor costs from those produced in China, the U.S. government has established quotas on how many items from various clothing categories can be imported into the United States from China and other countries. An unintended consequence of the quota system has been a "quota market," whereby countries buy and sell their U.S. quota numbers to producers in other countries (an illegal but a rampant practice). Instead of trading in quotas, some production facilities have moved to places where quotas and cheap labor are available—places such as Sri Lanka, Poland, and Lesotho. Rivoli describes how one producer of cotton shirts has moved around the world:

> *The Esquel Corporation, today the world's largest producer of cotton shirts, started in Hong Kong in the late 1970s, but, unable to obtain quota to sell to the United States, shifted production to mainland China. When the United States tightened Chinese shirt quotas in the early 1980s, Esquel moved production to Malaysia. When Malaysian quota also became difficult to obtain, Esquel moved yet again, this time to Sri Lanka. The globe hopping continued, with the Chinese shirt producer setting up operations in Mauritius and Maldives.*

The point is that quota laws, like other policies made by governments, regional trade organizations, and international political regimes (such as the World Trade Organization and the International Labor Organization) affect whether and how regions can produce and exchange goods on the world market.

Islands of Development

In both periphery and core, governments often prioritize the creation of wealth in the seat of governmental authority: the capital city. In most states, the capital city is the political nerve center of the country, its national headquarters and seat of government. Capital cities are home to government buildings and jobs, and often house universities, museums, heritage centers, convention centers, and the headquarters of large corporations. After gaining independence, many former colonial states spent lavishly on their capitals, not because this was essential to political or economic success but because the states wanted to showcase their independence, their futures, and create a national treasure. The European colonizers who focused their wealth and treasures on their capital cities, such as Great Britain's London, France's Paris, and the Netherlands' Amsterdam, served as models for the newly independent states (just as the state system itself did).

In many countries of the global economic periphery, the capital cities are by far the largest and most economically influential cities in the state (i.e., primate cities). Some newly independent states have built new capital cities, away from the colonial headquarters. Their goals in doing so are to separate themselves from their colonizers, to bring together diverse groups into one state with a city built to reflect their common culture, or to extend economic development into the interior of the state.

Nigeria, for example, moved its capital from Yoruba-dominated Lagos along the coast to an ethnically neutral territory in the center of the state: Abuja. Malawi moved its capital from Zomba, deep in the south, to more central Lilongwe. Pakistan moved the capital from the colonial headquarters of Karachi to Islamabad in the far north to symbolize the country's reorientation toward its historically important interior and north. Brazil moved its capital from coastal Rio de Janeiro to centrally located Brasilia in order to direct attention to the huge, sparsely populated, yet poorly integrated interior. More recently, Malaysia has moved its capital from the colonial capital of Kuala Lumpur to a completely new center called Putrajaya, about 25 miles (40 kilometers) to the south. The Malaysian government decided to build a new, ultramodern seat of government to symbolize the country's rapid economic growth (Fig. 10.15).

Corporations can also make cities focal points of development by concentrating corporate activities in a particular place. Often, corporations build up the cities near the resources they are extracting or near manufacturing centers they have built. Multinational oil companies create subsidiaries in periphery and semi-periphery countries, creating or expanding cities near oil reserves. For example in Gabon, Elf and Shell, two oil companies based in Europe, run ElfGabon and ShellGabon in the Central African country. The oil companies took the small colonial town of Port Gentile in Gabon and turned it into a city that the locals call "oil city." The oil companies built housing, roads, and stores, and provide much of the employment in the town (Fig. 10.16).

When a government or corporation builds up and concentrates economic development in a certain city or small region, geographers call that place an **island of development**. In Chapter 3, we identified islands of development in the periphery and semiperiphery and discussed why people migrate to these cities from rural areas and other poorer cities. The hope for a job drives many migrants to move to these islands of comparative prosperity.

Creating Growth in the Periphery of the Periphery

One of the greatest challenges to development is creating development opportunities outside of islands of development. In the most rural, impoverished regions of

Figure 10.15
Putrajaya, Malaysia. Putrajaya is the newly built capital of Malaysia, replacing Kuala Lumpur.
© Bazuki Muhammad/Reuters/Corbis.

Field Note

"Before the 1970s, Gabon's principal exports were manganese, hardwoods, and uranium ores. The discovery of oil off the Gabonese coast changed all that. This oil storage tank at the edge of Port Gentil is but one reminder of a development that has transformed Gabon's major port city—and the economy of the country as a whole. Oil now accounts for 80% of Gabon's export earnings, and that figure is climbing as oil prices rise and new discoveries are made. But how much the average citizen of Gabon is benefiting from the oil economy remains an open question. Even as health care and infrastructure needs remain unmet, the French publication *L'Autre Afrique* lists Gabon's ruler as the African leader with the largest real estate holdings in Paris."

Figure 10.16
Port Gentile, Gabon.   © Alexander B. Murphy.

developing countries, some nongovernmental organizations try to improve the plight of the people. **Nongovernmental organizations (NGOs)** are not run by state or local governments. Rather, NGOs operate independently, and the term is usually reserved for entities that operate as nonprofits. Thousands of NGOs operate in the world today, from churches to charities such as Heifer International. Each NGO has its own set of goals, depending on the primary concerns outlined by its founders.

Some countries have so many NGOs operating within them that they serve as what the *Economist* calls "a parallel state, financed by foreigners and accountable to nobody." For example, more than 20,000 NGOs operate within the country of Bangladesh at any time, focusing mainly on the rural areas and villages of the state. One particular kind of program by NGOs that has found success in South Asia and South America is the microcredit program. The idea behind a **microcredit program** is simple: give loans to poor people, particularly women, to encourage development of small businesses. Programs either have the women in the village guarantee each other's credit, or they make future lending to others contingent on repayment by the first borrowers. With repayment rates hovering at 98 percent, microcredit programs can finance themselves, and many NGOs offer the programs (Fig. 10.17).

By providing microcredit to women, NGOs can alter the gender balance in a region, giving more fiscal power to women. Some microcredit programs are credited with lowering birth rates in parts of developing countries and altering the social fabric of cultures by diminishing men's positions of power. Successful microcredit programs also help alleviate malnourishment, as women with income can feed themselves and their children.

Microcredit programs have been less successful in places with high mortality rates from diseases such as AIDS. If the borrower is unable to work or if the family has medical and funeral bills, the borrower is much more likely to default on the microcredit loan. When people in the periphery of the periphery (the poorest regions of peripheral countries) experience a multitude of problems, such as disease, corrupt governments, high mortality rates, high fertility rates, and disruptions from natural hazards, the goal of economic development takes a backseat to daily survival.

Take an item of clothing out of your closet and, using the Internet, try to trace the commodity chain of production. What steps did the item go through before reaching you? Consider the types of economic processes that were operating at each step and consider the roles governments and international political regimes played along the way.

Figure 10.17
Bwindi, Uganda. Women walk by a microcredit agency that has facilitated economic development in the town. © Alexander B. Murphy.

Summary

The idea of economic development is relatively new; it implies a sense of progressively improving a country's economic situation. The idea took hold in the wake of the Industrial Revolution. Geographers focus on the spatial structure of the economy, assessing how that structure influences the ability of states and regions to reach the same level of economic development. Geographers also recognize that economic development in a single place is based on a multitude of factors, including the situation within the global economy, the link the place plays in commodity chains, the efficacy of government, the presence of disease, the lack of nutrition, the presence and amount of foreign debt, the success or failure of government policies, and the influence of nongovernmental programs. Geographers also realize that all of these processes are operating concurrently across scales, making a country's journey toward economic development much more complicated than climbing a ladder.

Geographic Concepts

commodity chain
developing
gross national product
    (GNP)
gross domestic product
    (GDP)
gross national income
    (GNI)
per capita GNI
formal economy
informal economy
modernization model
context

neo-colonialism
structuralist theory
dependency theory
dollarization
world-systems theory
three-tier structure
Millennium
    Development Goals
trafficking
structural adjustment
    loans
neoliberalism
vectored diseases

malaria
export processing zones
maquiladoras
special economic zones
North American Free
    Trade Agreement
    (NAFTA)
desertification
island of development
nongovernmental
    organizations (NGOs)
microcredit program

Learn More Online

About Global Poverty
http://www.worldbank.org/poverty

Watch It Online

About Gabon
http://www.learner.org/resources/series180.html#program_descriptions
Click on Video On Demand for Gabon: Sustainable Resources?

CHAPTER 11

Agriculture

Field Notes Changing Greens

Figure 11.1
Presho, South Dakota. Soybeans growing in the semiarid ranchlands of western South Dakota. © Erin H. Fouberg.

Driving across the semiarid ranchlands of western South Dakota, I noticed the presence of a crop in the landscape that was recently found only in the eastern, moister region of the state: soybeans (Fig. 11.1).

I called a colleague who works in agriculture at South Dakota State University to ask, "When did the cattle ranchers of western South Dakota start growing soybeans?" He replied, "When the soy biodiesel plants started popping up in Nebraska and Kansas and when genetically modified soybeans made it possible to grow the crop here." He explained the development of Roundup Ready soybeans, a particular genetically modified soybean that can grow in more arid regions of the country.

First, you plant the soybean; then you use an airplane to spray Roundup, a common weed killer that is manufactured by the company that produces the Roundup Ready soybeans, over the field. The application of Roundup over the entire field saves a lot of time and energy for the farmers because the genetically modified soybeans are resistant to the Roundup, but the weeds are killed. Monsanto, the company that produces Roundup, has developed soybeans, corn, cotton, and other crops that are resistant to Roundup.

Counter to the genetically modified Roundup Ready crops, **organic agriculture**—the production of crops without the use of synthetic or industrially produced pesticides and fertilizers—is also on the rise in North America. In wealthier parts of the world, the demand for organic products has risen exponentially in recent years. Sales of organic food in the United States, for example, went from under $200 million in 1980 to $1.5 billion by the early 1990s to over $10 billion by 2003 and $17.8 billion in 2007. Organic foods are now about 3 percent of all food sales in the country. The growth rate is so strong that some predict organic sales will approach 10 percent of total U.S. food sales within a decade. Parts of western Europe are already approaching that figure—notably Denmark, Sweden, Finland, and parts of Germany.

Agricultural fields are devoted to organic agriculture in the core, semiperiphery, and periphery. Fields devoted to organic agriculture produce all kinds of foodstuffs, including fruits, vegetables, coffee, tea, grains, nuts, and spices. Compared to all land devoted to agriculture, the organic segment is still quite small and relatively scattered, but a farmer who can gain organic certification from a government or an internationally recognized third party has some prospect of developing a lucrative business (Fig. 11.2).

Although organic crops are grown everywhere, most organic foods are sold in the global economic core: in the United States, Canada, Japan, and Europe. The best-selling organic crops in the United States are fruits and vegetables, accounting for 42 percent of organic food sales, followed by nondairy beverages at 15 percent and dairy at 13 percent. Organic products typically cost more than conventional products in the grocery store. Nonetheless, a 2002 report issued by the United States Department of Agriculture explains that in 2000 organic foods crossed a threshold, moving out of health food stores and into supermarkets: "for the first time, more organic food was purchased in conventional supermarkets than in any other venue." Organic foods are sold in 73 percent of conventional grocery stores in the United States, with increasing demands for organic animal products such as meats and dairy.

Organic agriculture, then, has a very specific geography. It is an increasingly important part of agricultural production and consumption in wealthier countries. In the core, organic farming has helped some farmers extract themselves to a degree from the control of large, external corporate interests by tapping a niche market. The position of organic agriculture in the periphery and semiperiphery is similar to that of other major cash crops: production is almost entirely for export to the global economic core. Yet, in the periphery and semiperiphery, when organic agriculture bears a fair trade certification, more wealth can go directly to the producers (see the discussion of fair trade coffee in the last section of this chapter).

The organic movement has some clear environmental benefits, particularly in reducing levels of synthetic chemicals in soil and water. The health and taste advantages of organic produce will ensure the continued growth of the organic movement. The continually increasing demand for organic products has led the United States Department of Agriculture to certify organic products in the country, giving some standardization to claims of organic production. Yet, we are a long way from being able to grow enough crops organically to feed the mass of humanity.

ACRES USED TO RAISE CERTIFIED ORGANICALLY PRODUCED CROPS, 2002

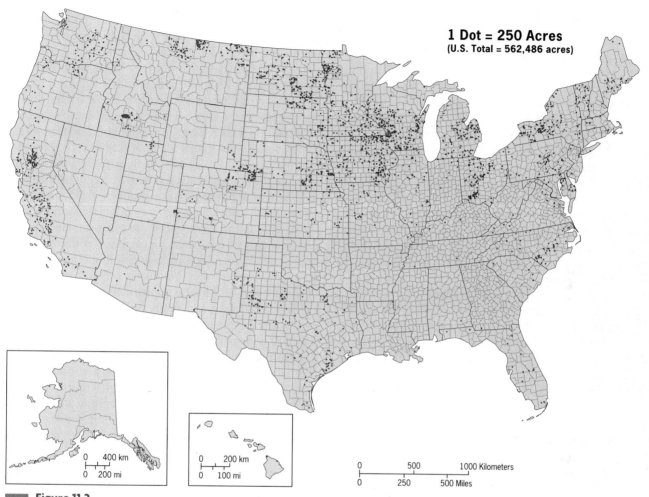

1 Dot = 250 Acres
(U.S. Total = 562,486 acres)

Figure 11.2
Acres of land certified for organic agricultural production in the United States, 2002.
Courtesy of: United States Census of Agriculture, 2002.

In this chapter, we examine the origins of agriculture and trace the geography of change in agriculture across time to the latest movements in agricultural production: genetic modification and organic production. In the process, we describe the early hearths of agriculture, the geography of technological changes in agriculture, the global pattern of agricultural production, and the imprint of agriculture on the cultural landscape.

Key Questions For Chapter 11

1. What is agriculture, and where did agriculture begin?
2. How did agriculture change with industrialization?
3. What imprint does agriculture make on the cultural landscape?
4. What is the global pattern of agriculture and agribusiness?

WHAT IS AGRICULTURE, AND WHERE DID AGRICULTURE BEGIN?

Agriculture is the deliberate tending of crops and livestock to produce food, feed, and fiber. When we think about agriculture, we tend to think about production of foodstuffs for humans. Only about half of all the staple grains grown in the United States are consumed directly by people; the other half are used for *feed*, grains fed directly to livestock. Raising livestock for their milk, eggs, or meat makes up a large segment of U.S. agriculture.

Whether talking about the growing of food or feed, or livestock raising, agricultural activity is classified as a primary industry. A common way of classifying economic activities is to focus on what is being produced. **Primary economic activities** involve those products closest to the ground, such as agriculture, ranching, hunting and gathering, fishing, forestry, mining, and quarrying. **Secondary economic activities** are those activities that take a primary product and manufacture it—that is, change it into something else such as toys, ships, processed foods, chemicals, and buildings. **Tertiary economic activities** are part of the service industry, connecting producers to consumers and facilitating commerce and trade. People who work as bankers, lawyers, doctors, teachers, nurses, salespeople, clerks, and secretaries are working in the tertiary sector. Some analysts separate specialized services into **quaternary** and **quinary economic activities**, dividing economic activities into those concerned with information or the exchange of money or goods (quaternary) and those tied into research or higher education (quinary). In this chapter, we use primary, secondary, and a broad classification of tertiary sectors for our analysis.

By classifying economic activities into sectors and analyzing the percentage of the population employed in each sector, we can gain insight into how goods are produced, as well as the employment structures of different societies. As we explained in our discussions of world-systems theory in Chapters 8 and 10, any product (such as wheat or rice) can be produced in core ways or in periphery ways. The generation of wealth across the globe is *better illuminated by focusing on how goods are produced (the kinds of technology, research, wages, and education that go into production), and not simply on what is produced.* Examining the proportion of people employed in a given sector in an economy gives us a basic idea of how the good is produced. For example, in Guatemala the agriculture sector accounts for 22.7 percent of the country's gross domestic product (GDP), yet 50 percent of the labor force is employed in agriculture. Contrast that with Canada, where the agriculture sector accounts for 2.3 percent of the GDP and only 3 percent of the labor force is employed in agriculture. The tertiary sector in Canada accounts for 75 percent of the labor force

and over 71 percent of the GDP, and the tertiary sector in Guatemala accounts for 35 percent of the labor force and 57.9 percent of the country's GDP.

These data do not tell us exactly how goods are produced, but they are revealing. The high proportion of the labor force involved in agriculture in Guatemala (relative to the role of agriculture in the GDP) tells us that agriculture is still quite labor dependent in Guatemala, implying a lack of mechanization. In Canada, the United States, and the rest of the core, agriculture is produced with core processes on a large scale for commercial consumption. When agricultural goods are produced in core ways, the number of people involved directly with the field is quite small. In the United States, less than 2 percent of the workforce is involved in agricultural production. Thousands of others participate in supporting agricultural production by working in the tertiary sector as research scientists for universities, seed companies, or chemical (antibiotics, pesticides, and herbicides) producers; as lobbyists for industry groups such as wheat producers or cattle ranchers; as engineers who design farm implements; as the people who sell and repair the implements; and as owners and clerks at retail establishments where farmers buy other farm and nonfarm goods.

In the United States, where most agricultural products are produced with core processes, the total agricultural production is at an all-time high, but the proportion of the labor force in agriculture is at an all-time low. Mechanization and efficiencies created by new technologies have led to a significant decrease in the number of workers needed in agricultural production. In 1950, one farmer in the United States produced enough to feed 27 people; today, one farmer in the United States produces enough to feed 135 people. The mechanization of agriculture goes beyond machinery such as combines and harvesters. New technologies bring hybrid seeds and genetically engineered crops, pesticides, and herbicides, all of which are designed to increase yields. To gain economic efficiencies, the average size of farms (acres in production) in the United States is growing, regardless of the kind of agricultural good produced. The U.S. Department of Agriculture keeps data sharring the dollar value of agricultural production. The farms with the highest total production have at least $500,000 in 2002 dollars. These high-producing farms accounted for 43.9 percent of agricultural goods produced in 2002 (compared with 28.9 percent in 1989).

Agriculture in the United States has changed enormously in the last 50 years, but this is just the last episode in a human activity that has been going on for thousands of years. In the next section of the chapter, we discuss how people lived before the origins of agriculture and the circumstances that gave rise to the invention of agriculture many millennia ago.

Hunting, Gathering, and Fishing

Before agriculture, hunting, gathering, and fishing occurred anywhere in the world where people lived. What people hunted or gathered depended on the region. North America provides a good example of the diversity of regional specializations among hunter-gatherers. The oak forests of parts of North America provided an abundant harvest of nuts, sometimes enough to last more than a full year; American Indian communities living in and around these forests therefore collected and stored this food source. Other American Indians living near the Pacific Ocean became adept at salmon fishing. The bison herds of the Great Plains provided sustenance, and so bison served as a focal point for many plains cultures. In more northerly regions of North America, people followed the migrations of the caribou herds. In the north, in the coastal zone stretching from present-day Alaska to Russia, the Aleut developed specialized techniques for fishing and for sea mammal hunting.

The size of hunting and gathering clans varied according to climate and resource availability. Hunting and gathering communities in areas of abundance could support larger populations. For example, people living on the margins of forests could gather food in the forest when hunting yielded poor results and then return to hunting when the opportunities improved.

Terrain and Tools

Before developing agriculture, hunter-gatherers worked on perfecting tools, controlling fires, and adapting environments to their needs. The first tools used in hunting were simple clubs—tree limbs that were thin at one end and thick and heavy at the other. The use of bone and stone and the development of spears made hunting far more effective. The fashioning of stone into hand axes and, later, handle axes was a crucial innovation that enabled hunters to skin their prey and cut the meat; it also made it possible to cut down trees and build better shelters and tools.

The controlled use of fire was another important early achievement of human communities. The first opportunities to control fire were offered by natural conditions (lightning, spontaneous combustion of surface-heated coal). Archaeological digs of ancient settlement sites suggest that people would capture a fire caused accidentally (by lightening, for instance) and would work to keep the fire burning continuously. Later, people learned that fire could be generated by rapid hand rotation of a wooden stick in a small hole surrounded by dry tinder. Fire became the focal point of settlements, and the camp-fire became a symbol of the community. It was a means of making foods digestible and was used to drive animals into traps or over cliffs.

In addition to hunting game on land, humans harvested shellfish, trapped fish by cutting small patches of standing water off from the open sea, and invented tools to catch fish, including harpoons for spearing large fish, hooks for catching fish, and baskets to catch fish in streams that had fish runs.

Through tools and fire, human communities altered their environments, establishing more reliable food supplies by combining hunting and fishing with some gathering and by making use of the migration cycles of fish and animal life. American Indians along the Pacific Coast and on Arctic shores, the Ainu of Japan and coastal East Asia, and communities in coastal western Europe caught salmon as they swam up rivers and negotiated rapids and falls. Archaeologists have found huge accumulations of fish bones at prehistoric sites near salmon runs.

Hunter-gatherers migrated to take advantage of cyclical movements of animals and to avoid exhausting the supply of edible plants in any one area. After the summer salmon runs, people hunted deer during the fall and again in the spring, taking advantage of seasonal movements to trap deer where they crossed rivers or in narrow valleys. During the winter, people lived off dried meat and other stored foods.

The First Agricultural Revolution

Out of areas of plenty came agriculture, the deliberate tending of crops and livestock to produce food, feed, and fiber. Geographer Carl Sauer believed the experiments necessary to establish agriculture and settle in one place would occur in lands of plenty. Only in a place of plenty could people afford to experiment with raising plants or take the time to capture animals and breed them for domestication. Sauer studied the geography of the First Agricultural Revolution, focusing on the location of the agriculture hearths and what kinds of agricultural innovations took place in those hearths.

Where did **plant domestication** begin? Sauer, who spent a lifetime studying cultural origins and diffusion, suggested that *Southeast and South Asia* may have been the scene, more than 14,000 years ago, of the first domestication of tropical plants. There, he believed, the combination of human settlements, forest margins, and fresh water streams may have given rise to the earliest planned cultivation of **root crops**—crops that are reproduced by cultivating either the roots or cuttings from the plants (such as tubers, including manioc or cassava, yams, and sweet potatoes in the tropics). A similar but later development may have taken place in northwestern South America.

The planned cultivation of **seed crops**, plants that are reproduced by cultivating seeds, is a more complex process, involving seed selection, sowing, watering, and well-timed harvesting. Again, the practice seems to have developed in more than one area and at different times. Some scholars believe that the first domestication of seed plants may have occurred in the Nile River Valley in North Africa, but the majority view is that this crucial development took place in a region of *Southwest Asia* (also called the *Fertile Crescent*), through which flow the two major rivers of present-day Iraq: the Tigris and the Euphrates (Fig. 11.3). This marked the beginning of what has been called the **First Agricultural Revolution**.

Archaeologists note that a number of changes occurred in Southwest Asia along with plant domestica-

tion. First, the plants themselves changed because people would choose seeds from the largest, heartiest plants to save for planting, yielding domesticated plants that grew *larger* over time than their counterparts in the wild. Archaeologists in Southwest Asia have found preserved seeds, which tell them what plants were being domesticated when. The grain crops wheat and barley grew well in the warming Southwest Asian climate. Soon, people found that the river-inundated plains of Mesopotamia provided alternate irrigable fields for farming. Agriculture provided a reliable food source, and grain surpluses enabled people to store grain for long-term distribution and use and to settle permanently in one place. With a reliable food source and a permanent settlement, the population of settlements began to increase.

Figure 11.3
The Fertile Crescent. The Fertile Crescent and ancient states (in different colors) of Mesopotamia and adjacent areas, and of the Nile Valley. Modern political boundaries are shown for reference.   © E. H. Fouberg, A. B. Murphy, H. J. de Blij, and John Wiley & Sons, Inc.

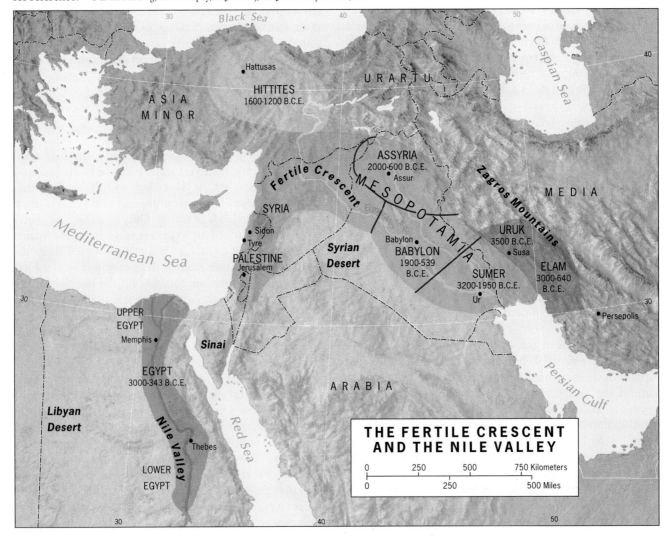

Figure 11.4 depicts the truly global distribution of plant domestication hearths. In Southeast Asia (Region 1), taro, yams, and bananas were the leading food plants. In Southwest Asia (Region 4), plant domestication centered on wheat, barley, and other grains. In the Mesoamerican region (Region 6), the basic plants were maize (corn), squashes, and several kinds of beans.

Archaeologists continually find new sites to excavate, and as places are analyzed further, academics revise their assumptions about the timing of the hearths of agriculture. The Central China hearth (Region 7) has recently attracted greater attention because new evidence supports a much earlier development of agriculture in this region—so early, in fact, that Chinese farmers may have been among the world's first. Another agricultural source region lies in West Africa (Region 9). Archaeological research on agriculture in this area is relatively recent, and analysts are not certain whether agriculture developed independently there, but they are certain secondary domestication took place in West Africa.

Table 11.1 may be overwhelming at first glance, but it is worth careful attention. It reveals the enormous range of crops that were cultivated around the world, as well as how at various times and in different locales, particular groups of crops became the mainstays of life. Soon the knowledge needed to farm such crops diffused outward from these agricultural hearths. For example, both millet and sorghum diffused from the West African region—millet to India and sorghum to China.

In many cases, what we now think of as centers of production of particular crops are not the places where those crops were originally domesticated. The corn (maize) we associate with the American Corn Belt diffused from Central America and Southern Mexico into North America. Later, the Portuguese brought it across the Atlantic, and corn became a staple in much of Africa. The white potato we associate with Ireland and Idaho came originally from the Andean highlands but was brought to Europe in the 1600s where it became a staple from Ireland to the eastern expanses of the North European Plain. The banana we associate with Central America came from Southeast Asia, as did a variety of yams. Diffusion of crops and seeds was greatly accelerated by worldwide trade and communications networks established with mercantilism and colonialism.

Domestication of Animals

Some scholars believe that animal domestication began earlier than plant cultivation, but others argue that animal domestication began as recently as 8000 years ago—well after crop agriculture. In any case, goats, pigs, and sheep became part of a rapidly growing array of domestic animals, and in captivity they changed considerably from their wild state. As with the growing of root crops, the notion of **animal domestication** must have emerged over time, in stages.

▬▬ **Figure 11.4**
World Areas of Agricultural Innovations. Cultural geographer Carl Sauer identified 11 areas where agricultural innovations occurred.   *Adapted with permission from:* C. O. Sauer, *Agricultural Origins and Dispersals.* New York: American Geographical Society, 1952, p. 24.

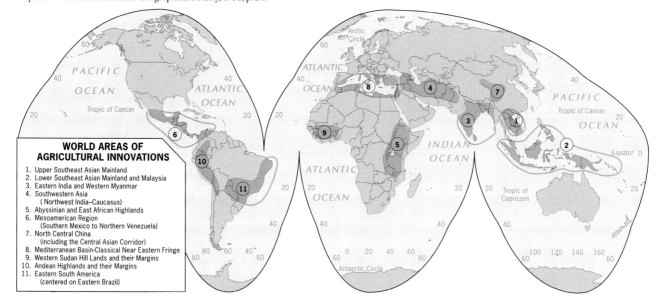

WORLD AREAS OF
AGRICULTURAL INNOVATIONS
1. Upper Southeast Asian Mainland
2. Lower Southeast Asian Mainland and Malaysia
3. Eastern India and Western Myanmar
4. Southwestern Asia
   (Northwest India–Caucasus)
5. Abyssinian and East African Highlands
6. Mesoamerican Region
   (Southern Mexico to Northern Venezuela)
7. North Central China
   (including the Central Asian Corridor)
8. Mediterranean Basin-Classical Near Eastern Fringe
9. Western Sudan Hill Lands and their Margins
10. Andean Highlands and their Margins
11. Eastern South America
    (centered on Eastern Brazil)

TABLE 11.1

Chief Source Regions of Important Crop Plant Domestications. *Adapted with permission*

from: J. E. Spencer and W. L. Thomas, *Introducing Cultural Geography*, 1978, John Wiley & Sons, Inc.

A. Primary Regions of Domestications

1. The Upper Southeast Asian Mainlands

Citrus Fruits*	Bamboos*	Yams*	Rices*	Eugenias*	Lichi	Teas	Ramie
Bananas*	Taros*	Cabbages*	Beans*	Job's tears	Longan	Tung oils	Water chestnut

2. Lower Southeast Asian Mainland and Malaysia (including New Guinea)

Citrus fruits*	Taros*	Pandanuses	Breadfruits	Lanzones	Vine peppers*	Nutmeg	Areca
Bananas*	Yams*	Cucumbers*	Jackfruits	Durian	Gingers*	Clove	Abaca
Bamboos*	Almonds*	Sugarcanes	Coconuts	Rambutan	Brinjals*	Cardamom	

3. Eastern India and Western Burma

Bananas*	Beans*	Millets*	Grams	Vine peppers*	Mangoes	Safflower	Lotus
Yams*	Rices*	Sorghums*	Eggplants	Gingers*	Kapok*	Jute	Turmeric
Taros*	Amaranths*	Peas*	Brinjals*	Palms*	Indigo	Sunn	Hemp

4. Southwestern Asia (Northwest India-Caucasus)

Soft wheats*	Peas*	Rye*	Beets*	Hemp	Soft Pears*	Pomegranates	Walnuts
Barleys*	Oil seeds*	Onions	Spinach	Apples	Cherries*	Grapes*	Melons
Lentils*	Poppies	Carrots*	Sesames	Almonds*	Plums*	Jujubes*	Tamarind
Beans*	Oats*	Turnips	Flax	Peaches*	Figs	Pistachio	Alfalfa

5. Ethiopian and East African Highlands

Hard wheats*	Sorghums*	Barleys	Beans*	Oil seeds*	Melons*	Coffees	Okras
Millets*	Rices*	Peas*	Vetches	Cucumbers*	Gourds*	Castor beans	Cottons*

6. Meso-American Region (Southern Mexico to Northern Venezuela)

Maizes	Taros*	Tomatoes*	Avocados	Muskmelons	Cottons*	
Amaranths*	Sweet potatoes	Chili peppers	Sapotes	Palms*	Agaves	
Beans*	Squashes	Custard apples	Plums*	Manioc	Kapok	

B. Secondary Regions of Domestications

7. North-Central China (including the Central Asian corridor)

Millets*	Soybeans	Naked oat*	Mulberries	Bush cherries*	Peaches*
Barleys*	Cabbages*	Mustards	Persimmons	Hard pears*	Jujubes*
Buckwheats	Radishes*	Rhubarb	Plums*	Apricots	

8. Mediterranean Basin—Classical Near Eastern Fringe

Barleys*	Lentils*	Grapes*	Dates	Parsnips	Lettuces	Carrots*	Sugar beet
Oats*	Peas*	Olives	Carobs	Asparagus	Celeries	Garlic	Leek

9. Western Sudan Hill Lands and Their Margins

Sorghums*	Rices*	Yams*	Peas*	Melons*	Oil palms	Kola nut
Millets*	Fonio	Beans*	Oil seeds*	Gourds*	Tamarind*	

10. Andean Highlands and Their Margins

White potatoes	Tomatoes*	Beans*	Quinoa	Cubio	Ulluco
Pumpkins	Strawberries	Papayas	Oca	Arrocacha	

11. Eastern South America (centered on eastern Brazil)

Taros*	Peanuts	Cashew nut	Cacao	Cottons*
Beans*	Pineapples	Brazil nut	Passion fruits	Tobaccos

Source: J. E. Spencer and W. L. Thomas, *Introducing Cultural Geography*: 1978. Reproduced by permission from John Wiley & Sons.

*The asterisk indicates domestication of related species or hybridized development of new species during domestication in some other region or regions. Some of these secondary domestications were later than in the original region, but evidence of chronologic priority seldom is clear-cut.

The plural rendering of the crop name indicates that several different varieties/species either were involved in initial domestication or followed thereafter,

The term *oil seeds* indicates several varieties or species of small-seeded crop plants grown for the production of edible oils, without further breakdown.

In regions 2 and 3 the brinjals refer to the spicy members of the eggplant group used in curries, whereas in region 3 the eggplants refer to the sweet vegetable members.

None of the regional lists attempts a complete listing of all crop plants/species domesticated within the region.

The table has been compiled from a wide variety of sources.

The process of animal domestication began when people became more sedentary. Animals were kept as pets or for other reasons, such as for ceremonial purposes. Quite possibly, animals attached themselves to human settlements as scavengers (foraging through garbage near human settlements) and even for protection against predators, thus reinforcing the idea that they might be tamed and kept. Orphaned young probably were adopted as pets; some wild animals were docile and easily penned up. Goats were domesticated in the Zagros Mountains (in the Fertile Crescent) as long as 10,000 years ago; sheep some 9500 years ago in Anatolia (Turkey); and pigs and cattle shortly thereafter. The advantages of animal domestication—their use as beasts of burden, as a source of meat, and as providers of milk—stimulated the rapid diffusion of this idea among interlinked places and gave the sedentary farmers of Southwest Asia and elsewhere a new measure of security.

Archaeological research indicates that when animals such as wild cattle are penned in a corral, they undergo physical changes over time. In a pen, animals are protected from predators, allowing the survival of animals that would have been killed in the wild. Our domestic versions of the goat, the pig, the cow, and the horse differ considerably from those first kept by our ancestors. In early animal domestication, people chose the more docile, often smaller animals to breed, in order to protect themselves from the animals. Archaeologists discern the beginnings of animal domestication in a region by inspecting the bones of excavated animals. They look for places where bones get smaller over time, as this usually indicates early domestication.

As with plant domestication, archaeologists can use the combination of bone fragments and tools to identify general areas where the domestication of particular animals occurred. In Southwest Asia and adjacent parts of Northeast Africa, people domesticated the goat, sheep, and camel. Southeast Asians domesticated several kinds of pigs, the water buffalo, chickens, and some water fowl (ducks, geese). In South Asia, people domesticated cattle, and cattle came to occupy an important place in the regional culture. In Central Asia, people domesticated the yak, horse, some species of goats, and sheep. In the Mesoamerican region (including the Andes from Peru northward and Middle America north to central Mexico), early Americans domesticated the llama and alpaca, along with a species of pig and the turkey.

Some species of animals may have been domesticated almost simultaneously in different places. The water buffalo, for example, was probably domesticated in both Southeast and South Asia during the same period. Camels may have been domesticated in Central Asia as well as in Southwest Asia. The pig was domesticated in numerous areas. Different species of cattle were domesticated in regions other than South Asia. Dogs and cats attached

themselves to human settlements very early (they may have been the first animals to be domesticated) and in widely separated regions. Single, specific hearths can be pinpointed for only a few animals, including the llama and the alpaca, the yak, the turkey, and the reindeer.

Efforts to domesticate animals continue today. In Africa, people are attempting to domesticate the eland, to serve as a source of meat in a region where a stable protein source is greatly needed. Several experiment stations in the savannalands are trying to find ways to breed Africa's wildlife. They have had some success with a species of eland, but less so with various species of gazelles, and they have been unable to domesticate the buffalo (Fig. 11.5). In fact, throughout the world only about 40 species of higher animals have been domesticated—and most of these were domesticated long ago. Jared Diamond, author of *Guns, Germs, and Steel*, explains that only five domesticated mammals are important throughout the world: the cow, sheep, goat, pig, and horse. According to Diamond, if we select only the big (over 100 pounds), herbivorous, terrestrial animals, we have 148 species that meet these criteria in the "wild." Only 14 of those 148 have been domesticated successfully, and each of these 14 was domesticated at least 4500 years ago. Modern attempts at animal domestication, even those driven by knowledgeable geneticists, have failed because of problems with the breed of animal's diet, growth rate, breeding, disposition, or social structure.

Thus, the process of animal domestication, set in motion more than 8000 (and perhaps as long as 14,000) years ago, continues. The integrated use of domesticated plants and domesticated animals eased the work burden for early farmers. Animal waste fertilized crops, animals pulled plows, and crops fed animals. The first place that successfully integrated domesticated plants and animals was Southwest Asia (the Fertile Crescent).

Hunter-Gatherers in the Modern World

In the modern world, hunter-gatherers live in the context of a globalized economy and experience pressures to change their livelihoods. In many cases, the state places pressures on hunter-gatherers to settle in one place and farm. Cyclical migration by hunter-gatherers does not mesh well with bounded, territorial states. Some nongovernmental organizations encourage settlement by digging wells or building medical buildings, permanent houses, or schools for hunter-gatherers. Even hunter-gatherers who continue to use their knowledge of seeds, roots, fruits, berries, insects, and animals to gather and trap the goods they need for survival do so in the context of the world-economy. The San of Southern Africa, the Aboriginals of Australia, the indigenous peoples of Brazil, and several other groups in the Americas, Africa, and Asia have been

Field Note

"Attempts to tame wildlife started in ancient times, and still continue. At Hunter's Lodge on the Nairobi-Mombasa road, we met an agricultural officer who reported that an animal domestication experiment station was located not far into the bush, about 10 miles south. On his invitation, we spent the next day observing this work. In some herds, domestic animals (goats) were combined with wild gazelles, all penned together in a large enclosure. This was not working well; all day the gazelles seek to escape. By comparison, these eland were docile, manageable, and in good health. Importantly, they also were reproducing in captivity. Here, our host describes the program."

Figure 11.5
Nairobi, Kenya.   © H. J. de Blij.

studied, mapped, recorded, photographed, donated to, defended, and in many cases exploited.

Subsistence Agriculture in the Modern World

Hundreds of millions of farmers are involved in **subsistence agriculture**, growing only enough food to survive. The term *subsistence* can be used in the strictest sense of the word—that is, to refer to farmers who grow food only to sustain themselves and their families, and find building materials and firewood in the natural environment, and who do not enter into the cash economy at all. This definition fits farmers in remote areas of South and Middle America, Africa, and South and Southeast Asia (Fig. 11.6). Yet many farm families living at the subsistence level

sometimes sell a small quantity of produce (perhaps to pay taxes). They are not subsistence farmers in the strict sense, but the term *subsistence* is surely applicable to societies where farmers with small plots sometimes sell a few pounds of grain on the market but where poverty, indebtedness, and tenancy are ways of life. For the indigenous peoples in the Amazon Basin, the sedentary farmers of Africa's savanna areas, villagers in much of India, and peasants in Indonesia, subsistence is not only a way of life but a state of mind. Experience has taught farmers and their families that subsistence farming is often precarious and that times of comparative plenty will be followed by times of scarcity.

Subsistence farmers often hold land in common; surpluses are shared by all the members of the community; accumulation of personal wealth is restricted; and

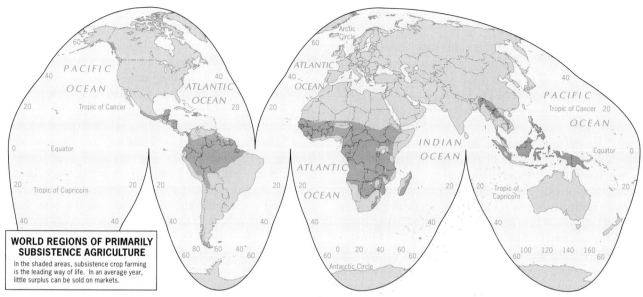

WORLD REGIONS OF PRIMARILY SUBSISTENCE AGRICULTURE

In the shaded areas, subsistence crop farming is the leading way of life. In an average year, little surplus can be sold on markets.

▬▬ **Figure 11.6**

World Regions of Primarily Subsistence Agriculture. Definitions of subsistence farming vary. On this map, India and China are not shaded because farmers sell some produce at markets; in Equatorial Africa and South America, subsistence farming allows little excess, and thus little produce is sold at markets.   © E. H. Fouberg, A. B. Murphy, H. J. de Blij, and John Wiley & Sons, Inc.

individual advancement at the cost of the group as a whole is limited. As A. H. Bunting wrote in *Change in Agriculture* (1970):

> *To allocate the land or manage the seasonal migrations, and to survive through hardship and calamity these societies have to be cohesive, communal and relatively little differentiated socially and economically: the chiefs, elders or elected headmen may be little richer than their fellows—to many of whom they are in addition linked by ties of relationship within the extended family. Mutual dependence, imposed by the environment and the state of the agricultural art, is maintained and reinforced by genetic relationships. The community is enclosed socially and may even tend to be isolated culturally. Landlords and feudal rulers are unknown; the cultivators are poor but free.*

Although much has changed for subsistence farmers since Bunting wrote these words in 1970, a strong sense of community remains important to the social fabric of the people.

Some subsistence farmers are sedentary, living in one place throughout the year, but many others move from place to place in search of better land. The latter engage in a form of agriculture known as **shifting cultivation**. This agriculture is found primarily in tropical and subtropical zones, where traditional farmers had to abandon plots of land after the soil became infertile. Once stripped of their natural vegetative cover and deprived of the constant input of nutrients from decaying vegetative matter

on the forest floor, soils in these regions can quickly lose their nutrients as rain water leaches out organic matter. Faced with these circumstances, farmers move to another parcel of land, clear the vegetation, turn the soil, and try again. This practice of shifting cultivation, like hunting and gathering, still goes on today.

In tropical areas, a plot of cleared soil will carry a good crop at least once and perhaps two or three times. After that, the land is best left alone to regenerate its natural vegetative cover and replenish the soil with nutrients lost during cultivation. Several years later, the plot may yield a good harvest once again.

Today, shifting cultivation is a way of life for many more people than hunting and gathering. Between 150 million and 200 million people still sustain themselves through shifting cultivation in Africa, Middle America, tropical South America, and parts of Southeast Asia. The system of cultivation has changed little over thousands of years.

With shifting cultivation, people usually live in a central village surrounded by parcels of land that are worked successively. The farmers first clear vegetation from a parcel of land. Next they plant crops that are native to the region: tubers in the humid, warm tropical areas, grains in the more humid subtropics, and vegetables and fruits in cooler zones. When the village grows too large and the distance to usable land becomes too great, part of the village's population may establish a new settlement some distance away. Population densities in areas of shifting agriculture cannot be very high; therefore, shifting cultivation continues only in areas where population densities are low.

One specific kind of shifting cultivation is **slash-and-burn agriculture** (also called milpa agriculture and patch agriculture), reflecting the central role of the controlled use of fire in places where this technique is used. Trees are cut down and all existing vegetation is burned off. In slash-and-burn, farmers use tools (machetes and knives) to slash down trees and tall vegetation, and then burn the vegetation on the ground. A layer of ash from the fire settles on the ground and contributes to the soil's fertility.

Used to seeing enormous fields of grain farmed by gigantic machines, we may look at shifting cultivation as wasteful and disorganized. Regions with shifting cultivation do not have neat rows of plants, carefully turned soil, or precisely laid-out fields. Nonetheless, shifting cultivation conserves both forest and soil; its harvests are substantial given the environmental limitations; and it requires better organization than one might assume. It also requires substantially less energy than more modern techniques of farming. Shifting cultivation and specifically slash-and-burn agriculture have been a sustained method of farming for thousands of years. Shifting cultivation gave ancient farmers opportunities to experiment with various plants, to learn the effects of weeding and crop care, to cope with environmental vagaries, and to discern the decreased fertility of soil after sustained farming.

Marginalization of Subsistence Farming

During colonialism (1500 to 1950), European powers sought to "modernize" the economies of the colonies by ending subsistence and integrating farmers into colonial systems of production and exchange. Sometimes their methods were harsh: by demanding that farmers pay some taxes, they forced subsistence farmers to begin selling some of their produce to raise the necessary cash. They also compelled many subsistence farmers to devote some land to a cash crop such as cotton, thus bringing them into the commercial economy. The colonial powers encouraged commercial farming by conducting soil surveys, building irrigation systems, and establishing lending agencies that provided loans to farmers. In addition, the colonial powers sought to make profits, yet it was difficult to squeeze very much from subsistence-farming areas. Forced cropping schemes were designed to solve this problem. If farmers in a subsistence area cultivated a certain acreage of, say, corn, they were required to grow a specified acreage of a cash crop, such as cotton, as well. Whether this crop would be grown on old land that was formerly used for grain or on newly cleared land was the farmers' decision. If no new lands were available, the farmers would have to give up food crops for the compulsory cash crops. In many areas, severe famines resulted and local economies were disrupted.

Many scholars have considered the question of how "to tempt [subsistence farmers] into wanting cash by the availability of suitable consumer goods," as A. N. Duckham and G. B. Masefield wrote in *Farming Systems of the World* in 1970. In the interests of "progress" and "modernization," subsistence farmers have been pushed away from their traditional modes of livelihood. Yet many aspects of subsistence farming may be worth preserving.

Subsistence land use is giving way to more intensive farming and cash cropping—even to mechanized farming in which equipment does much of the actual work. In the process, societies from South America to Southeast Asia are being profoundly affected. Land that was once held communally is being parceled out to individuals for cash cropping. The system that ensured an equitable distribution of resources is breaking down. And the distribution of wealth has become stratified, with poor people at the bottom and rich landowners at the top.

Settling down in one place, a rising population, and the switch to agriculture are interrelated occurrences in human history. Hypothesize which of these three happened first, second, and third and explain why.

HOW DID AGRICULTURE CHANGE WITH INDUSTRIALIZATION?

For the Industrial Revolution (see Chapter 12) to take root, a **Second Agricultural Revolution** had to take place—one that would move agriculture beyond subsistence to generate the kinds of surpluses needed to feed thousands of people working in factories instead of in agricultural fields. Like the Industrial Revolution, the Second Agricultural Revolution was composed of a series of innovations, improvements, and techniques, in this case, in Great Britain, the Netherlands, Denmark, and other neighboring countries.

By the seventeenth and eighteenth centuries, European farming underwent significant changes. New crops came into Europe from trade with the Americas, including corn and potatoes. Many of the new crops were well suited for the climate and soils of western Europe, bringing new lands (previously defined as marginal) into cultivation. The governments of Europe played a role in spurring on the Second Agricultural Revolution by passing laws such as Great Britain's Enclosure Act, which encouraged consolidation of fields into large, single-owner holdings. Farmers increased the size of their farms, pieced together more contiguous parcels of land, fenced in their land, and instituted field rotation. Methods of soil preparation, fertilization, crop care, and harvesting improved.

New technologies improved production as well. The seed drill enabled farmers to avoid wasting seeds and to plant in rows, making it simpler to distinguish weeds from crops. Advances in breeding livestock enabled farmers to develop new breeds that were either strong milk producers or good for beef. By the 1830s, farmers were using new fertilizers on crops and feeding artificial feeds to livestock. Increased agricultural output made it possible to feed much larger urban populations, enabling the growth of a secondary (industrial) economy.

Innovations in machinery that occurred with the Industrial Revolution in the late 1800s and early 1900s helped sustain the Second Agricultural Revolution. The railroad helped move agriculture into new regions, such as the United States' Great Plains. Geographer John Hudson traced the major role railroads and agriculture played in changing the landscape of that region from open prairie to individual farmsteads. The railroad companies advertised in Europe to attract immigrants to the Great Plains region, and the railroads took the new migrants to their new towns, where they would transform lands from prairie grass to agricultural fields.

Later, the internal combustible engine made possible the invention of tractors, combines, and a multitude of large farm equipment. New banking and lending practices helped farmers afford the new equipment.

Understanding the Spatial Layout of Agriculture

When commercial agriculture is geared to producing food for people who live in a nearby town or city, a clear geography based on perishability of products and cost of transportation emerges. In the 1800s, Johann Heinrich von Thünen (1783–1850) experienced the Second Agricultural Revolution firsthand: he farmed an estate not far from the town of Rostock, in northeast Germany. Studying the spatial patterns of farming around towns such as Rostock, von Thünen noted that one commodity or crop gave way to another in succession, as one moved away from Rostock. He also noted that this process occurred without any visible change in soil, climate, or terrain. When he mapped this pattern, he found that each town or market center was surrounded by a set of more-or-less concentric rings within which particular commodities or crops dominated.

Nearest the town, farmers produced commodities that were perishable and commanded high prices, such as dairy products and strawberries. In this zone, von Thünen believed agriculture would be produced with a high level of intensity, and much effort would go into production in part because of the value of the land closer to the city. In von Thünen's time, the town was still surrounded by a belt of forest that provided wood for fuel and building; but immediately beyond the forest the ring-like pattern of agriculture continued. In the next ring the crops were less perishable and bulkier, including wheat and other grains. Still farther out, livestock raising began to replace field crops.

Von Thünen used these observations to build a model of the spatial distribution of agricultural activities. As with all models, he had to make certain assumptions. For example, he assumed that the terrain was flat, that soils and other environmental conditions were the same everywhere, and that there were no barriers to transportation to market. Under such circumstances, he reasoned, transport costs would govern the use of land. He reasoned that the greater the distance to market, the higher the transport costs that had to be added to the cost of producing a crop or commodity. At a given distance to market, then, it would become unprofitable to produce high-cost, perishable commodities—and market gardens would give way to field crops such as grains and potatoes. Still farther away, livestock raising would replace field agriculture.

The **Von Thünen model** (including the ring of forest) is often described as the first effort to analyze the spatial character of economic activity (Fig. 11.7). The

Figure 11.7
Von Thünen's Model. © H. J. de Blij, P. O. Muller, and John Wiley & Sons, Inc.

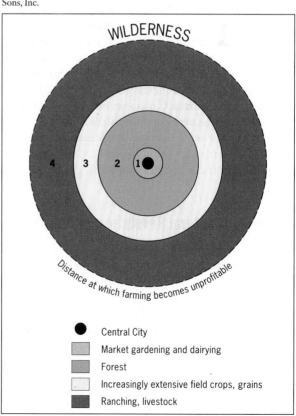

Thünian patterns discerned in many parts of the world are not solely the result of the forces modeled by von Thünen. Differences in climate type and soil quality weigh heavily on the kinds of goods produced in a place. If you drive east out of Denver, heading for Nebraska, you cannot miss a certain concentric zonation that puts dairying and market gardening nearest the city, cash grains such as corn (plus soybeans) in the next "ring," more extensive grain farming and livestock raising beyond, and cattle ranching in the outermost zone.

Geographer Lee Liu studied the spatial pattern of agricultural production in one province of China, giving careful consideration to the intensity of the production methods and the amount of land degradation. Liu found that the farmers living in a village would farm lands close to the village and lands far away from the village with high levels of intensity. However, the methods used varied spatially, resulting in land improvements close to the village and land degradation farther from the village. In lands close to the village, farmers improved lands through "decades of intensive care," in particular putting organic material onto the fields, which made the grasslands close to the village "fertile and productive." In lands more remote from the village, farmers tended to use more "chemical fertilizer, pesticides, and herbicides" and fewer conservation tactics, resulting in land degradation, whereby "the originally fertile remote land became degraded." Liu argued that this pattern in modern China occurs in large part because the farmers live in the village, not in the remote fields, and therefore put most of their time and energy into the fields closest to them.

Even when agricultural production does not conform to the concentric rings of von Thünen's model, his underlying concern with the interplay of land use and transportation costs is frequently still determinative. The fresh flowers grown in the Caribbean for sale in New York City could be viewed as the application of the von Thünen model on a larger scale, for it is less expensive to grow flowers in the Caribbean and ship them to New York City than it is to grow them in other locations.

The Third Agricultural Revolution

The **Third Agricultural Revolution**, also called the **Green Revolution**, dates as far back as the 1930s, when agricultural scientists in the American Midwest began experimenting with technologically manipulated seed varieties to increase crop yields. In the 1940s, American philanthropists funded research on maize (corn) production in Mexico, trying to find a hybrid seed that would grow better. They did, and by 1960 Mexico was no longer importing corn because production within the country was high enough to meet demand. In the 1960s, the focal point of the Green Revolution shifted to India, when scientists at a research institution in the Philippines crossed a dwarf Chinese variety of rice with an Indonesian variety and produced IR8. This new rice plant had a number of desirable properties: it developed a bigger head of grain, and it had a stronger stem that did not collapse under the added weight of the bigger head. IR8 produced much better yields than either of its parents, but the researchers were not satisfied. In 1982 they produced IR36, bred from 13 parents to achieve genetic resistance against 15 pests and a growing cycle of 110 days under warm conditions, thus making possible three crops per year in some places. By 1992, IR36 was the most widely grown crop on Earth, and in September 1994, scientists developed a strain of rice that was even more productive than IR36. In addition to improving the production of rice, the Green Revolution brought new high-yield varieties of wheat and corn from the United States to other parts of the world, particularly South and Southeast Asia.

Coming at a time of growing concern about global hunger, the successes of the Green Revolution were truly extraordinary. Today, most famines result from political instability rather than failure in production. India became self-sufficient in grain production by the 1980s, and Asia saw a two-thirds increase in rice production between 1970 and 1995. These drastic increases in production stemmed not only from new seed varieties but also from the use of fertilizers, pesticides, irrigation in some places, and significant capital improvements.

The geographical impact of the Green Revolution is highly variable, however. Its traditional focus on rice, wheat, and corn means that it has had only limited impact throughout much of Africa, where agriculture is based on different crops and where lower soil fertility makes agriculture less attractive to foreign investment. Researchers at the International Rice Research Institute, for example, are working to breed a genetically modified "super rice" that will not have to be transplanted as seedlings but can be seeded directly in the paddy soil. It may yield nearly twice as much rice per acre than the average for strains in current use. The charting of the genome of rice (the 12 chromosomes that carry all of the plant's characteristics) is under way, so it may also be possible to transform rice genetically so that it will continuously acquire more desirable properties. Not only could yields improve; so could resistance to diseases and pests.

Increasingly, researchers are turning their attention to new agricultural products, and this could expand the geographical impact of the Green Revolution. Research has already led to methods for producing high-yield cassava and sorghum—both of which are grown in Africa. And beyond Africa, research on fattening livestock faster and improving the appearance of fruits is having an impact in North and South America.

The promise of increasing food production in a world in which almost a billion people are malnourished has led many people to support genetically engineered foods. However, many other people question whether gene manipulation could create health risks and produce environmental hazards. Environmentalists have speculated about the impacts of pollen dispersal from genetically modified plants and the potential for disease-resistant plants to spur the evolution of super-pests. Vocal opponent of the Green Revolution in India, Vandana Shiva, argues that

[t]he Green Revolution has been a failure. It has led to reduced genetic diversity, increased vulnerability to pests, soil erosion, water shortages, reduced soil fertility, micronutrient deficiencies, soil contamination, reduced availability of nutritious food crops for the local population, the displacement of vast numbers of small farmers from their land, rural impoverishment and increased tensions and conflicts. The beneficiaries have been the agrochemical industry, large petrochemical companies, manufacturers of agricultural machinery, dam builders and large landowners.

One difficulty of assessing the situation at present is that developments are occurring so fast that it is not easy to keep up with them.

The Green Revolution today has a large number of detractors concerned that the higher inputs of chemical fertilizers and pesticides can lead to reduced organic matter in the soil and to groundwater pollution. Moreover, many small-scale farmers lack the resources to acquire genetically enhanced seeds and the necessary fertilizers and pesticides. In most of the world that is affected by the Green Revolution, farmers produce on very small acreages. A 2005 report in *Scientific American* explains that in these cases, the Green Revolution has done little to alleviate poverty: "The supply-driven strategies of the Green Revolution, however, may not help subsistence farmers, who must play to their strengths to compete in the global marketplace. The average size of a family farm is less than four acres in India, 1.8 acres in Bangladesh and about half an acre in China." Smaller farmers are in a poor competitive position, and some are being driven off their lands. In addition, the need for capital from the West to implement Green Revolution technologies has led to a shift away from production for local consumers toward export agriculture. In the process, local places become subject to the vicissitudes of the global economy, where a downward fluctuation in the price of a given crop can create enormous problems for places dependent on the sale of that crop.

New Genetically Modified Foods

An entire field of biotechnology has sprung up in conjunction with the Third Agricultural Revolution, and the development of genetically engineered crops (GE) or **genetically modified organisms (GMOs)** is its principal orientation. Since the origin of agriculture, people have experimented with hybrid crops and cross-breeding of animals. Today, according to the Grocery Manufacturers of America, genetically modified organisms are found in 75 percent of all processed foods in the United States. The United States leads the world in production of genetically engineered crops, with 38 percent of all acres in corn and 80 percent of all acres in soybeans in the United States sown with genetically engineered seeds.

Some regions have embraced genetically engineered crops, and others have banned them. Many of the poorer countries of the world do not have access to the necessary capital and technology. Moreover, ideological resistance to genetically engineered foods is strong in some places—particularly in western Europe. Agricultural officials in most west European countries have declared genetically modified foods to be safe, but in many places, the public has a strong reaction against them based on combined concerns about health and taste. Such concerns have spread to less affluent parts of the world as well. In many poorer regions, seeds are a cultural commodity, reflecting agricultural lessons learned over generations. In these regions, many resist the invasion of foreign, genetically engineered crops.

Regional and Local Change

Recent shifts from subsistence agriculture to commercial agriculture have had dramatic impacts on rural life. Land-use patterns, land ownership arrangements, and agricultural labor conditions have all changed as rural residents cope with shifting economic, political, and environmental conditions. In Latin America, dramatic increases in the production of export crops (or *cash crops* such as fruits and coffee) have occurred at the expense of crop production for local consumption. In the process, subsistence farming has been pushed to ever more marginal lands. In Asia, where the Green Revolution has had the greatest impact, the production of cereal crops (grains such as rice and wheat) has increased for both foreign and domestic markets. Agricultural production in this region remains relatively small in scale and quite dependent on manual labor. In Subsaharan Africa, total commercialized agriculture has increased, but overall agricultural exports have decreased. As in Asia, farm units in Subsaharan Africa have remained relatively small and dependent on intensified manual labor.

What this regional-scale analysis does not tell us is how these changes have affected local rural communities. These changes can be environmental, economic, and social. A recent study in the small country of Gambia (West Africa) by Judith Carney has shown how changing agricultural practices have altered not only the rural

Guest Field Note

Gambia

I am interested in women and rural development in Subsaharan Africa. In 1983, I went to Gambia to study an irrigated rice project that was being implemented to improve the availability of rice, the dietary staple. What grabbed my attention? The donors' assurance that the project would benefit women, the country's traditional rice growers. Imagine my surprise a few months after project implementation when I encountered hundreds of angry women refusing to work because they received nothing for their labor from the first harvest.

In registering women's traditional rice plots as "family" land, project officials effectively sabotaged the equity objectives of the donors. Control now was concentrated under male heads

Figure 11.8
Gambia.

of household who reaped the income produced by female labor. Contemporary economic strategies for Africa depend increasingly upon labor intensification. But whose labor? Human geography provides a way of seeing the significance of gender in the power relations that mediate culture, environment, and economic development.

Credit: Judith Carney, University of California, Los Angeles

environment and economy, but also relations between men and women (Fig. 11.8). Over the last 30 years, international developmental assistance of Gambia has led to ambitious projects designed to convert wetlands to irrigated agricultural lands, making possible production of rice year-round. By the late 1980s, virtually all of the country's suitable wetlands had been converted to year-round rice production. This transformation created tensions within rural households by converting lands women traditionally used for family subsistence into commercialized farming plots. In addition, when rice production was turned into a year-round occupation, women found themselves with less time for other activities crucial for household maintenance.

This situation underscores the fact that in Africa, as in much of the rest of the less industrialized world, agricultural work is overwhelmingly carried out by women. In Subsaharan Africa over 85 percent of all women in the labor force work in agriculture, while in China the number is close to 75 percent and in India 70 percent. A geographical perspective that is sensitive to scale helps to shed light on how changes in agricultural practices throughout the world not only alter rural landscapes but also affect family and community relationships.

Genetically engineered crops are yielding some ethical problems. In the semi-periphery and periphery, farmers typically keep seeds from crops so that they can plant the seeds the next year. Companies that produce genetically engineered seeds do not approve of this process; generally, they want farmers to purchase new seeds each year. Using the concepts of scale and jumping scale, determine the ethical questions in this debate.

WHAT IMPRINT DOES AGRICULTURE MAKE ON THE CULTURAL LANDSCAPE?

Flying from the West Coast of the United States to the East Coast, if you have a window seat, you will see the major imprint agriculture makes on the American cultural landscape. The green circles standing out in arid regions of the country are places where center-pivot irrigation systems circle around a pivot, providing irrigation to a circle of crops. The checkerboard pattern on the landscape reflects the pattern of land ownership in much of the country.

The pattern of land ownership seen in the landscape reflects the cadastral system—the method of land survey through which land ownership and property lines are defined. Cadastral systems were adopted in places where settlement could be regulated by law, and land surveys were crucial to their implementation. The prevailing survey system throughout much of the United States, the one that appears as checkerboards across agricultural fields, is the **rectangular survey system**. The U.S. government adopted the rectangular survey system after the American Revolution as part of a cadastral system known as the **township-and-range system**. Designed to facilitate the movement of non-Indians evenly across farmlands of the United States interior, the system imposed a rigid gridlike pattern on the land (Fig. 11.9). The basic unit was the 1 square mile *section*—and land was bought and sold in whole, half, or quarter sections. The section's lines were drawn without reference to the terrain, and they thus imposed a remarkable uniformity across the land. Under the Homestead Act, a homesteader received one section of land (160 acres) after living on the land for five years and making improvements to it. The pattern of farms on the landscape in the interior of the United States reflects the township-and-range system, with farms spaced by sections, half sections, or quarter sections.

The imprint of the rectangular survey system is evident in Canada as well, where the government adopted a similar cadastral system as it sought to allocate land in the Prairie Provinces. In portions of the United States and Canada different cadastral patterns predominate, how-

ever (Fig. 11.10). These patterns reflect particular notions of how land should be divided and used. Among the most significant are the **metes and bounds survey** approach adopted along the eastern seaboard, in which natural features were used to demarcate irregular parcels of land. One of the most distinct regional approaches to land division can be found in the Canadian Maritimes and in parts of Quebec, Louisiana, and Texas where a **long-lot survey system** was implemented. This system divided land into narrow parcels stretching back from rivers, roads, or canals. It reflects a particular approach to surveying that was common in French America.

In addition to the influence of the cadastral system of the landscape, a society's norms for property ownership are reflected in the landscape. Property ownership is symbolized by landscapes where parcels of land are divided into neat, clearly demarcated segments. The size and order of those parcels are heavily influenced by rules about property inheritance. In systems where one child inherits all of the land—such as the Germanic system of **primogeniture** in which all land passes to the eldest son—parcels tend to be larger and farmers work a single plot of land. This is the norm in Northern Europe and in the principal areas of Northern European colonization—the Americas, South Africa, Australia, and New Zealand.

In areas where land is divided among heirs, however, considerable fragmentation can occur over time. The latter is the norm throughout much of Asia, Africa, and Southern Europe and most of the allotted Indian reservations in the United States, meaning that farmers living in villages tend a variety of scattered small plots of land. In some places, land reform initiatives have consolidated landholdings to some degree, but fragmentation is still common in many parts of the world.

■■■ **Figure 11.9**

Garden City, Iowa. The township-and-range system has left its imprint on the landscape of Garden City, Iowa, where the grid pattern of 6 mile by 6 mile townships and the sections of 1 square mile each are marked by property lines and roads.   © Craig Aurne/ Corbis Images.

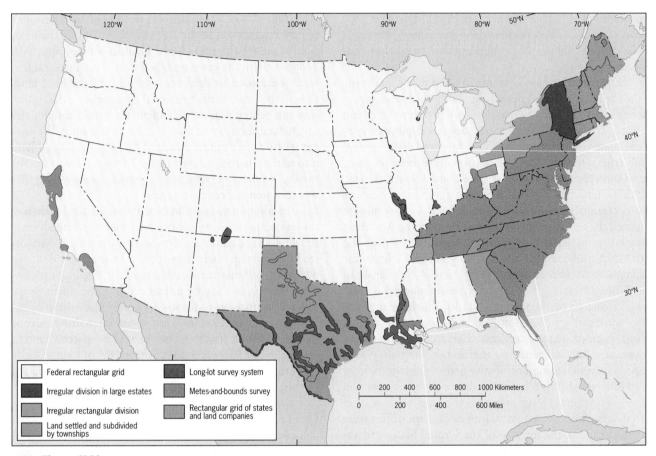

Figure 11.10
Dominant Land Survey Patterns in the United States. *Data from: Dividing the Land: Early American Beginnings of Our Private Property Mosaic.* Chicago: University of Chicago Press, 1995, p. 8 and several other sources.

Villages

Throughout this book we take note of various core-periphery contrasts our world presents. Such contrasts are prominent in rural as well as urban areas. Traditional farm-village life is still common in India, Subsaharan Africa, China, and Southeast Asia. In India, farming, much of it subsistence farming, still occupies nearly 70 percent of the population. In the world's core areas, however, agriculture has taken on a very different form, and true farm villages, in which farming or providing services for farmers are the dominant activities, are disappearing. In the United States, where farming once was the leading economic activity, only some 2 percent of the labor force remains engaged in agriculture.

Traditionally, the people who lived in villages either farmed the surrounding land or provided services to those who do the farming. Thus, they were closely connected to the land, and most of their livelihoods depended, directly or indirectly, on the cultivation of nearby farmland. As such, they tended to reflect historical and environmental conditions. Houses in Japanese farming villages, for example, are so tightly packed together that only the narrowest

passageways remain between them. This reflects the need to allocate every possible square foot of land to farming; villages must not use land where crops could grow.

Unlike Japan, in the United States Midwest, individual farmhouses lie quite far apart in what we call a *dispersed settlement* pattern: the land is intensively cultivated but by machine rather than by hand. In the populous Indonesian island of Java, villages are located every half-mile or so along a rural road, and settlement there is defined as nucleated. Land use is just as intense, but the work is done by people and animals. Hence, when we consider the density of human settlement as it relates to the intensity of land use, we should keep in mind the way the land is cultivated. *Nucleated settlement* is by far the most prevalent rural residential pattern in agricultural areas (Fig. 11.11). When houses are grouped together in tiny clusters or hamlets, or in slightly larger clusters we call villages, their spatial arrangement also has significance.

In the hilly regions of Europe, villages frequently are clustered on hillslopes, leaving the level land for farming. Often an old castle sits atop the hill, so in earlier times the site offered protection as well as land conservation.

Figure 11.11

Burgundy, France. The agricultural landscape of Burgundy demonstrates three features of rural France: people living in nucleated villages, a highly fragmented land ownership pattern, and land divided according to the French long-lot system.   © Barbara A. Weightman.

In many low-lying areas of western Europe, villages are located on dikes and levees, so that they often take on linear characteristics (Fig. 11.12 A). Where there is space, a house and outbuildings may be surrounded by a small garden; the farms and pasturelands lie just beyond. In other cases, a village may take on the characteristics of a cluster (Fig. 11.12 B). It may have begun as a small hamlet at the intersection of two roads and then developed by accretion. The European version of the East African circular village, with its central cattle corral, is the round village or *rundling* (Fig. 11.12 C). This layout was first used by Slavic farmer-herdsmen in eastern Europe and was later modified by Germanic settlers.

In many parts of the world, farm villages were fortified to protect their inhabitants against marauders. Ten thousand years ago, the first farmers in the Fertile Crescent faced attacks from the horsemen of Asia's steppes and clustered together to ward off this danger. In Nigeria's Yorubaland, the farmers would go out into the surrounding fields by day but retreat to the protection of walled villages at night. Villages, as well as larger towns and cities in Europe, were frequently walled and surrounded by moats. When the population became so large that people had to build houses outside the original wall, a new wall would be built to protect them as well. *Walled villages* (Fig. 11.12 D) still exist in rural areas of many countries, reminders of a turbulent past.

More modern villages, notably planned rural settlements, may be arranged on a grid pattern (Fig. 11.12 E). This is not, however, a twentieth-century novelty.

Centuries ago the Spanish invaders of Middle America laid out *grid villages* and towns, as did other colonial powers elsewhere in the world. In urban Africa, such imprints of colonization are pervasive.

Although the twentieth century has witnessed unprecedented urban growth throughout the world, half of the world's people still reside in villages and rural areas. As total world population increases, total population in rural areas is increasing in many parts of the world (even though the proportion of the total population in rural areas may be stagnant or declining). In China alone, some 60 percent of the more than 1.3 billion people inhabit villages and hamlets. In India, with a population over 1 billion, about 70 percent of the people live in places the government defines as nonurban. Small rural settlements are home to most of the inhabitants of Indonesia, Bangladesh, Pakistan, and other countries of the periphery, including those in Africa. The agrarian village remains one of the most common forms of settlement on Earth.

In some places, rural villages have changed as the global economy has changed. For example, Mexico has experienced rapid economic change since passage of the North American Free Trade Act (NAFTA) in 1992. Along with major changes in industrial production (see Chapter 12), major changes in agricultural production have occurred in Mexico. Daniel Klooster studied changes in Mexican agriculture and found that since NAFTA, U.S. exports of maize (corn) to Mexico have tripled and "now supply a third of Mexican domestic demand." Agricultural production in Mexico has decreased since NAFTA, but

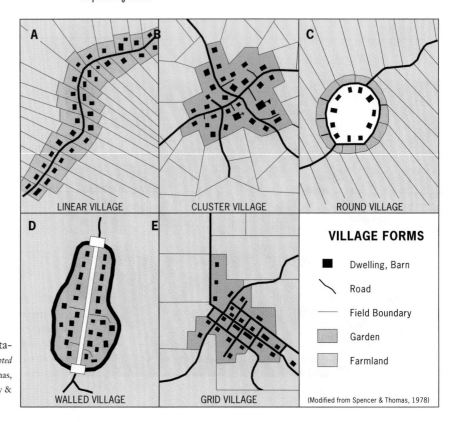

Figure 11.12
Village Forms. Five different representative village layouts are shown here. *Adapted with permission from:* J. E. Spencer and W. H. Thomas, *Introducing Cultural Geography.* New York: John Wiley & Sons, Inc., 1978, p. 154.

LINEAR VILLAGE

CLUSTER VILLAGE

ROUND VILLAGE

WALLED VILLAGE

GRID VILLAGE

VILLAGE FORMS

■   Dwelling, Barn

╲   Road

─   Field Boundary

Garden

Farmland

(Modified from Spencer & Thomas, 1978)

the total rural population in Mexico is growing (along with the total population of the country). How, then, are people in rural areas making a living? Klooster found that "as agriculture declined, off-farm income from activities such as construction work, petty commerce and craft production increased" and that for rural families in Mexico (as in much of the rural United States), off-farm income accounts for "more than half of family income." Decreasing agricultural production has increased the rate of migration of Mexicans to the United States, with many people from rural areas without jobs coming to the United States for work and sending remittances home.

Functional Differentiation Within Villages

Villages everywhere display certain common qualities, including evidence of social stratification and differentiation of buildings. The range in size and quality of houses, representing their owners' wealth and standing in the community, reflects social stratification. Material well-being is the chief determinant of stratification in Western commercial agricultural regions, where it translates into more elaborate homes. In Africa, a higher social position in the community is associated with a more impressive house. The house of the chief or headman may not only be more elaborate than others but may also be in a more prominent location. In India, caste still strongly influences daily life, including village housing; the manors of landlords, often

comprising large walled compounds, stand in striking contrast to the modest houses of domestic servants, farm workers, carpenters, and craftspeople. The poorest people of the lowest castes live in small one-room, wattle-and-thatch dwellings. In Cambodia, the buildings in the stilt villages built throughout the Mekong Basin look similar (Fig. 11.13). The building along the pond in the left foreground of Figure 11.13 has a different function—it is an outhouse. Its location on the pond accounts for a major part of the pollution problem in this village: waste from the outhouses drains directly into the pond, which has become mosquito-infested and severely polluted.

The functional differentiation (like the functional zonation of cities whereby different areas of the village play different roles and function differently) of buildings within farm villages is more elaborate in some societies than in others. Protection of livestock and storage of harvested crops are primary functions of farm villages, and in many villages where subsistence farming is the prevailing way of life, the storage place for grains and other food is constructed with as much care as the best-built house. Moisture and vermin must be kept away from stored food; containers of grain often stand on stilts under a carefully thatched roof or behind walls made of carefully maintained sun-dried mud. In India's villages, the paddy-bin made of mud (in which rice is stored) often stands inside the house. Similarly, livestock pens are often attached to houses, or, as in Africa, dwellings are built in a circle surrounding the corral.

Figure 11.13
Siem Reap, Cambodia. A stilt village in the Mekong Basin of Cambodia. © Barbara A. Weightman.

The functional differentiation of buildings is greatest in Western cultures, where a single farmstead may contain as many buildings as an entire hamlet elsewhere in the world. A prosperous North American farm is likely to include a two-story farmhouse, a stable, a barn, and various outbuildings, including a garage for motorized equipment, a workshop, a shed for tools, and a silo for grain storage (Fig. 11.14). The space these structures occupy often exceeds that used by entire villages in Japan, China, and other agrarian regions where space must be conserved.

Figure 11.14
Winthrop, Minnesota. The modern American farm typically has a two-story farm house surrounded by several outbuildings. © Erin H. Fouberg.

Think of an agricultural region you have either visited or seen from an airplane. Describe the imprint of agriculture on the landscape and consider what the cultural landscape tells you about how agriculture is produced in this region and how production has changed over time.

WHAT IS THE GLOBAL PATTERN OF AGRICULTURE AND AGRIBUSINESS?

When looking at patterns of agriculture at the global scale, it is important to recognize that von Thünen's concerns with the interplay of market location, land use, and transportation costs can reveal only one part of the picture. We must also consider the effects of different climate and soil conditions, variations in farming methods and technology, involvement by governments, and the lasting impacts of history. Decisions made by colonial powers in Europe led to the establishment of plantations from Middle America to Malaysia. The plantations grew crops not for local markets but for consumers in Europe; similarly, U.S. companies founded huge plantations in the Americas. Over the past few centuries, the impact of this plantation system transformed the map of world agriculture. The end of colonial rule did not merely signal the end of the agricultural practices and systems that had been imposed on the former colonial areas. Even food-poor countries must continue to grow commercial crops for export on some of their best soils where their own food should be harvested. Long-entrenched agricultural systems and patterns are not quickly or easily transformed.

Commercial farming has come to dominate in the world's economic core, as well as some of the places in the semiperiphery and periphery. Commercial farming is the agriculture of large-scale grain producers and cattle ranches, mechanized equipment and factory-type labor forces, plantations and profit. As we will see, it is a world apart from the traditional farms of Asia and Africa.

The roots of modern **commercial agriculture** can be traced to the vast colonial empires established by European powers in the eighteenth and nineteenth centuries. Europe became a market for agricultural products from around the world but with an added dimension: European countries manufactured and sold in their colonies the finished products made from imported raw materials. Thus, cotton grown in Egypt, Sudan, India, and other countries colonized by Europe was bought cheaply, imported to European factories, and made into clothes—many of which were then exported and sold, often in the very colonies where the cotton had been grown in the first place.

Major changes in transportation and food storage, especially refrigeration, have further intertwined agricultural production and food processing regions around the world (Fig. 11.15). The beef industry of Argentina, for example, secured a world market when the invention of

Field Note

"The technology of refrigeration has kept pace with the containerization of seaborne freight traffic. When we sailed into the port of Dunedin, New Zealand, I was unsure of just what those red boxes were. Closer inspection revealed that they are refrigeration units, to which incoming containers are attached. Meats and other perishables can thus be kept frozen until they are transferred to a refrigerator ship."

Figure 11.15
Dunedin, New Zealand. © H. J. de Blij.

refrigerated ships made it possible to transport a highly perishable commodity over long distances. European colonial powers required farmers in their colonies to cultivate specific crops. One major impact of colonial agriculture was the establishment of **monoculture** (dependence on a single agricultural commodity), throughout much of the colonial world. Colonies became known for certain crops, and colonizers came to rely on those crops. Ghanaians still raise cacao; Moçambiquans still grow cotton; and Sri Lankans still produce tea. The production of cash crops by poorer countries today is often perpetuated by loan and aid requirements from lending countries, the World Trade Organization, the International Monetary Fund, and the World Bank (see Chapter 10).

The World Map of Climates

Before we can study the distribution of agriculture in the world today, we need to examine Figure 11.16, the distribution of climate zones in the world today. All of the elements of weather, absorption of the sun's energy, rotation of the Earth, circulation of the oceans, movement of weather systems, and the jet stream produce a pattern of climates represented in the map. We owe this remarkable map to Wladimir Köppen (1846–1940), who devised a scheme called the **Köppen climate classification system** for classifying the world's climates on the basis of temperature and precipitation.

Köppen's map provides one means of understanding the distribution of **climatic regions** (areas with similar climatic characteristics) across the planet. The legend looks complicated, but it really is not; here is one of those maps worth spending some time on. For present purposes, it is enough to get a sense of the distribution of the major types of climate. The letter categories in the legend give a clear indication of the conditions they represent.

The (A) climates are hot or very warm and generally humid. The "no dry season" (Af) regions are *equatorial rainforest* regions. The "short dry season" (Am) climate is known as the *monsoon climate*. And if you can envisage an African savanna, you know what the (Aw, *savanna*) designation means.

Once you realize that the yellow and light brown colors on the map represent dry climates (BW, *desert* and BS, *steppe*), it becomes clear how much of the world has limited water availability. Nonetheless, some very large population clusters have developed in these water-deficient regions, especially at lower (and warmer) latitudes. The world faces a long-term water crisis, and the Köppen map helps show why.

The (C) climates also have familiar names. The (Cf) climate, represented by dark green, prevails over the southeastern United States. If you know the local climate in Atlanta or Nashville or Jacksonville, you understand why this climate is often called "humid temperate." It is moist, and it does not get as cold as it does in Canada or as warm (continuously, anyway) as in the Amazon Basin. If you have experienced this kind of climate, the map gives you a good idea of what it's like in much of eastern China, southeastern Australia, and a large part of southeastern South America.

The "dry summer" (C) climates are known as *Mediterranean* climates (the small s in Cs means that summers are dry). This mild climate occurs not only around the Mediterranean Sea, and thus in the famous wine countries of France, Italy, and Spain, but also in California, Chile, South Africa's Cape, and southern parts of Australia. So you know what kind of climate to expect in Rome, San Francisco, Santiago, Cape Town, and Adelaide.

Farther toward the poles, the planet gets rather cold. Note that the (D) climates dominate in the United States' upper Midwest and Canada, but it gets even colder in Siberia. The "milder" (Da) climates (here the key is the small a, which denotes a warm summer) are found only in limited parts of Eurasia. Winters are very cold in all the (D) climates and downright frigid (and long) in the (Dfb) and (Dfc) regions. The latter merge into the *polar* climates, where tundra and ice prevail.

The World Map of Agriculture

When comparing the world map of agriculture (Fig. 11.17) with the distribution of climate types across the world (Fig. 11.16), we can see the correlation between climate and agriculture. Drier lands rely on livestock ranching, where moister climates are marked with grain production. In this section of the chapter, we examine climatic patterns and other influences on the distribution of agriculture.

Cash Crops and Plantation Agriculture

Nonsubsistence farming in many poorer countries is a leftover from colonial times. Colonial powers implemented agriculture systems to benefit their needs, a practice that has tended to lock poorer countries into production of one or two "cash" crops. Cash farming continues to provide badly needed money, even if the conditions of sale to the urban-industrial world are unfavorable. In the Caribbean region, for example, whole national economies depend on sugar exports (sugar having been introduced by the European colonists in the 1600s). These island countries wish to sell the sugar at the highest possible price, but they are not in a position to dictate prices. Sugar is produced by many countries in various parts of the world, as well as by farmers in the core (Fig. 11.17). Governments in the core place quotas on imports of agricultural products and subsidize domestic production of the same commodities.

WORLD CLIMATES
After Köppen–Geiger

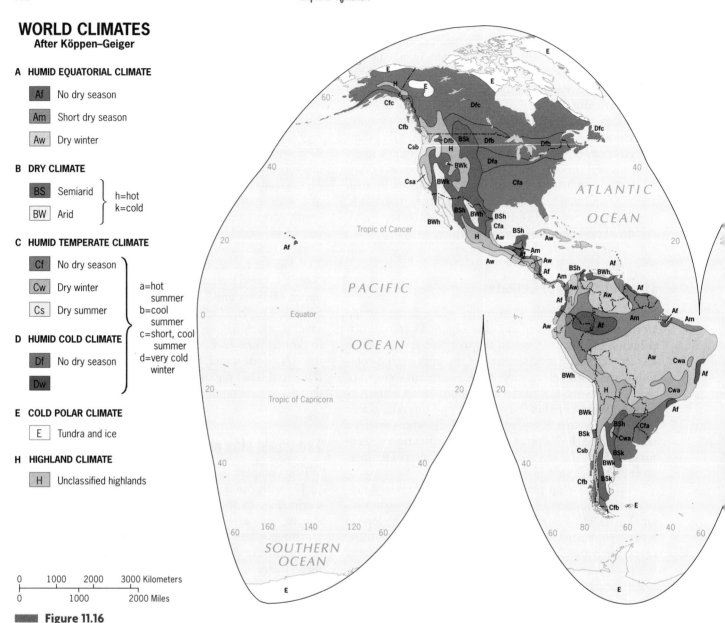

A HUMID EQUATORIAL CLIMATE

- **Af** No dry season
- **Am** Short dry season
- **Aw** Dry winter

B DRY CLIMATE

- **BS** Semiarid
- **BW** Arid

    h=hot
    k=cold

C HUMID TEMPERATE CLIMATE

- **Cf** No dry season
- **Cw** Dry winter
- **Cs** Dry summer

    a=hot summer
    b=cool summer
    c=short, cool summer
    d=very cold winter

D HUMID COLD CLIMATE

- **Df** No dry season
- **Dw**

E COLD POLAR CLIMATE

- **E** Tundra and ice

H HIGHLAND CLIMATE

- **H** Unclassified highlands

0   1000   2000   3000 Kilometers
0   1000   2000 Miles

Figure 11.16
World Climates. The Köppen map of world climates, as modified by R. Geiger. These are macroclimatic regions; microclimates are set within these but cannot be shown at this scale.

Occasionally, producing countries consider forming a cartel in order to present a united front to the importing countries and to gain a better price, as oil-producing states did during the 1970s. Such collective action is difficult, as the wealthy importing countries can buy products from countries that are not members of the cartel. Also, the withholding of produce by exporting countries may stimulate domestic production among importers. For example, although cane sugar accounts for more than 70 percent of the commercial world sugar crop each year, farmers in the United States, Europe, and Russia produce sugar from sugar beets. In Europe and Russia, these beets already yield 25 percent of the annual world sugar harvest.

Collective action by countries producing sugarcane could easily cause that percentage to increase.

When cash crops are grown on large estates, we use the term **plantation agriculture** to describe the production system. Plantations are colonial legacies that persist in poorer, primarily tropical, countries along with subsistence farming. Figure 11.17 shows that plantation agriculture (7 in the legend) continues in Middle and South America, Africa, and South Asia. Laid out to produce bananas, sugar, coffee, and cocoa in Middle and South America, rubber, cocoa, and tea in West and East Africa, tea in South Asia, and rubber in Southeast Asia, these plantations have outlasted the period of decolonization and

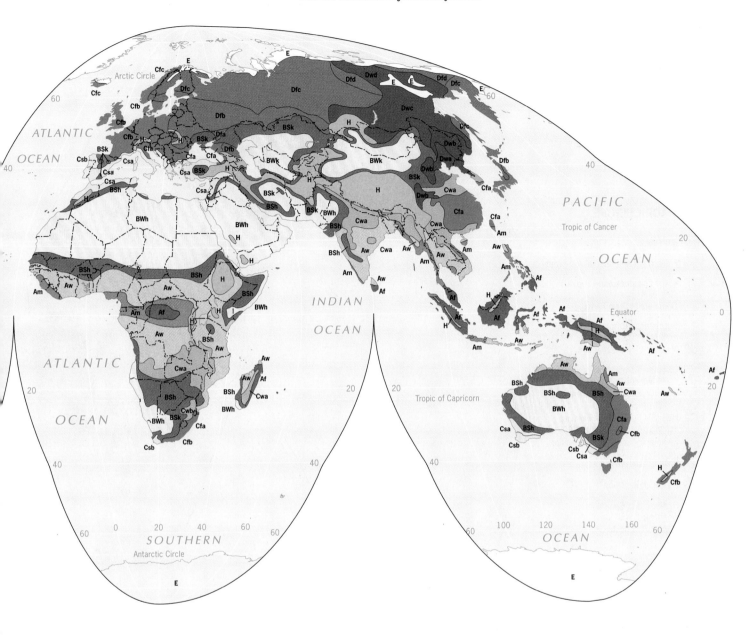

continue to provide specialized crops to wealthier markets. Many of the most productive plantations are owned by European or American individuals or corporations.

Multinational corporations have tenaciously protected their economic interests in plantations. In the 1940s and 1950s, the Guatemalan government began an agrarian reform program. In part, the plan entailed renting unused land from foreign corporations to landless citizens at a low appraised value. The United Fruit Company, an American firm with extensive holdings in the country, was greatly concerned by this turn of events. The company had close ties to powerful individuals in the American government, including Secretary of State John Foster Dulles, CIA director Allen

Dulles (the two were brothers), and Assistant Secretary of State for Inter-American Affairs John Moors Cabot. In 1954, the United States supported the overthrow of the government of Guatemala because of stated concerns about the spread of communism. This ended all land reform initiatives, however, leading many commentators to question the degree to which the United Fruit Company was behind the coup. Indeed, with the exception of President Dwight Eisenhower, every individual involved in the decision to help topple Guatemala's government had ties to the company. This example illustrates the inextricable links between economics and political motivations—and it raises questions about the degree to which multinational corporations based in wealthy

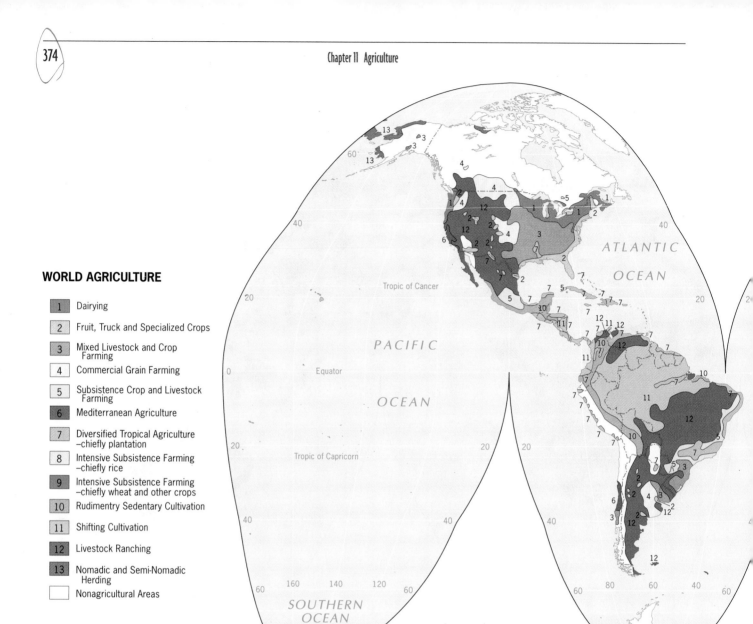

WORLD AGRICULTURE

1 Dairying

2 Fruit, Truck and Specialized Crops

3 Mixed Livestock and Crop Farming

4 Commercial Grain Farming

5 Subsistence Crop and Livestock Farming

6 Mediterranean Agriculture

7 Diversified Tropical Agriculture –chiefly plantation

8 Intensive Subsistence Farming –chiefly rice

9 Intensive Subsistence Farming –chiefly wheat and other crops

10 Rudimentry Sedentary Cultivation

11 Shifting Cultivation

12 Livestock Ranching

13 Nomadic and Semi-Nomadic Herding

Nonagricultural Areas

0 1000 2000 3000 Kilometers

0 1000 2000 Miles

Figure 11.17

World Agriculture. Different kinds of agricultural areas are shown throughout the world. *Adapted with permission from*: Hammond, Inc., 1977.

countries influence decisions about politics, agriculture, and land reform in the semiperiphery and periphery.

Cotton and Rubber

Two of the most significant contemporary cash crops are cotton and rubber. Colonialism encouraged the production of plantation-scale cotton in many regions of the world. India, for example, began producing cotton on a large scale under British colonialism.

Cotton cultivation expanded greatly during the nineteenth century, when the Industrial Revolution produced machines for cotton ginning, spinning, and weaving that

increased productive capacity, brought prices down, and put cotton goods within the reach of mass markets. As with sugar, the colonial powers laid out large-scale cotton plantations, sometimes under irrigation. Cotton cultivation was also promoted on a smaller scale in numerous other countries: in Egypt's Nile Delta, in the Punjab region shared by Pakistan and India, and in Sudan, Uganda, Mexico, and Brazil. The colonial producers received low prices for their cotton, and the European industries prospered as cheap raw materials were converted into large quantities of items for sale at home and abroad.

Wealthier countries continue to buy cotton, and cotton sales remain important for some former colo-

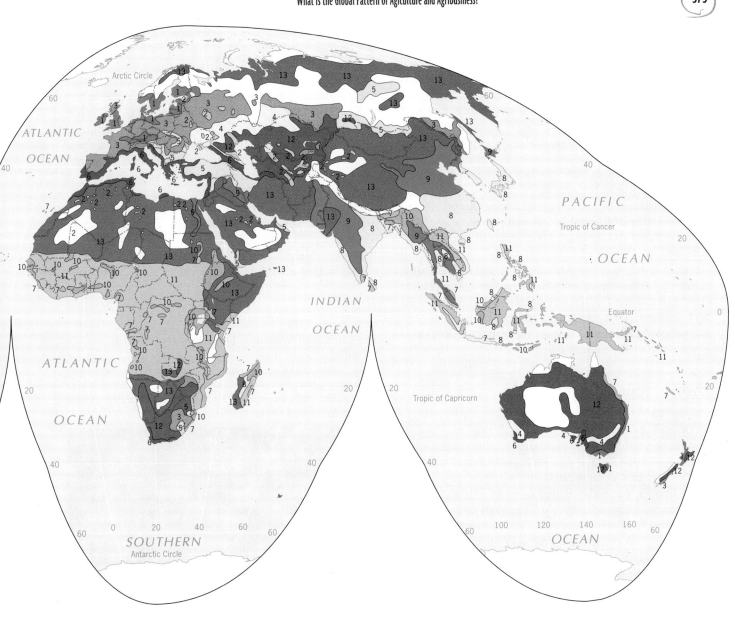

nies. But they compete with cotton being grown in the United States, Northeast China, and Central Asia. Much of the cotton purchased by Japan, the United Kingdom, and western Europe, for example, comes from the United States. Cotton is also a major product in northeastern China and in several Central Asian Republics.

Cotton is in competition today with synthetic fibers such as nylon and rayon, and rubber is in competition with synthetic rubber. Before synthetic rubber was developed, rubber was collected from rubber-producing trees in equatorial rainforests, mainly in the Amazon Basin in northern South America. Around 1900, the town of Manaus on the Amazon River experienced a rubber boom.

Rubber companies in the Congo Basin in Africa experienced a similar period of prosperity. The boom in wild rubber was short-lived, however. Rubber-tree plantations were created to make rubber collection easier and more efficient. Seedlings of Brazilian rubber trees were planted elsewhere, and they did especially well in Southeast Asia. Within two decades nearly 90 percent of the world's rubber came from new plantations in colonial territories in Malaysia, the Netherlands East Indies (now Indonesia), and neighboring colonies.

As time went on, more and more uses for rubber were found, and consumer demand grew continuously. The advent of the automobile was an enormous boost for the industry, and most of the rubber now produced is used to manufacture vehicle tires. World War II created a need for alternative sources of rubber, since Japan had occupied much of Southeast Asia. This stimulated the production of synthetic rubber. In 2007, world rubber production totaled approximately 23.4 million tons, more than 13.5 million of it synthetic; of the remainder, natural rubber, almost 70 percent was produced on the plantations of Southeast Asia.

The development of rubber plantations in Southeast Asia, rather than in sections of the Amazon Basin or the Congo Basin, is due less to environmental factors than to the availability of labor. The colonial powers were aware that Southeast Asia combined conditions of tropical environment and labor availability that neither Amazon South America nor Equatorial Africa could match. Eventually, a large-scale rubber industry developed in Liberia (West Africa), but in the 1990s it was destroyed during the country's disastrous civil war. Lately, efforts have been made to introduce the plantation system along the Amazon River in the heart of northern Brazil.

Luxury Crops

Similar conditions—a combination of suitable environment and available labor—led the European colonial powers to establish huge plantations for the cultivation of **luxury crops** such as tea, cacao, coffee, and tobacco. Coffee was first domesticated in the region of present-day Ethiopia, but today it thrives in Middle and South America, where approximately 70 percent of the world's annual production is harvested. The United States buys more than half of all the coffee sold on world markets annually, and western Europe imports most of the rest.

Coffee is one of the best examples of the colonial legacy's impact on present-day agricultural practices. In the early eighteenth century, coffee was virtually unknown in most of the world. After petroleum, coffee is now the second most valuable traded commodity in the world. The best-known image of coffee production in North America is probably that of Juan Valdez, who is portrayed as a simple yet proud Colombian peasant who handpicks beans by day and enjoys a cup of his own coffee by night. This image is quite contrary to the reality of much coffee production in Latin America. In most cases coffee is produced on enormous, foreign-owned plantations, where it is picked by local laborers who are hired at very low wage rates. Most coffee is sent abroad; and if the coffee pickers drink coffee, it is probably of the imported and instant variety.

Coffee production is undergoing changes as more consumers demand fair trade coffee and more coffee producers seek fair trade certification. CNN reports that "Retailers who are certified Fair Traders return up to 40 percent of the retail price of an item to the producer." Once a producer meets the requirements of organic coffee production and a few other criteria, that producer can be registered on the International Fair Trade Coffee Register. Coffee importers then purchase the fair trade coffee directly from the registered producers. Being registered guarantees coffee producers a "fair trade price" of $1.26 per pound of coffee (plus bonuses of $0.20 per pound for organic). Over 500,000 farmers in 20 countries in the periphery and semi-periphery are on the fair trade register (Fig. 11.18). The fair trade campaign pressured Starbucks into selling fair trade coffee, and Starbucks now purchases more than 10 percent of the global production of fair trade coffee. Other retailers have followed suit; for example, all espresso sold at Dunkin' Donuts in North America and Europe is fair trade certified. Fair trade coffee is available at large retail outlets and under corporate brands at Target, Wal-Mart, and Sam's Club.

Figure 11.18
Las Colinas Cooperative, Department of Ahuachapan, El Salvador. This fair trade coffee farmer in El Salvador grows his coffee beans in the shade, under the canopy of the rainforest. His coffee is fair trade certified, allowing him to get a much better price for his beans in exchange for producing shade-grown, organic coffee beans.   © Equal Exchange.

Fair trade production goes beyond coffee today. Dozens of commodities and products from tea, bananas, fresh cut flowers, and chocolate to soccer balls can be certified fair trade. According to Fair Trade Labeling Organizations International, consumers spent more than $2.2 billion on fair trade certified products in 2006, representing an increase by 42 percent over 2005 consumption levels.

Tea production, both the fair trade and the traditionally traded varieties, is on the rise globally to meet the increasing consumption of the luxury crop. Compared to coffee, tea is consumed in greater quantities in areas where it is grown: India, China, Sri Lanka, and Japan. Whereas coffee is cultivated and consumed mainly in the Americas, tea is the dominant beverage in significant parts of Eurasia. It goes from the Asian-producing areas to the United Kingdom and the rest of Europe and North America. Tea is a rather recent addition to the Western diet. It was grown in China perhaps 2000 years ago, but it became popular in Europe only during the nineteenth century. The colonial powers (mainly the British) established enormous tea plantations in Asia and thus began the full-scale flow of tea into European markets.

Commercial Livestock, Fruit, and Grain Agriculture

By far the largest areas of commercial agriculture (1 through 4 in the legend) lie outside the tropics. Dairying (1) is widespread at the northern margins of the midlatitudes—particularly in the northeastern United States and in northwestern Europe. Fruit, truck, and specialized crops (2), including the market gardens von Thünen observed around Rostock, are found in the eastern and southeastern United States and in widely dispersed small areas where environments are favorable. (Major oases can be seen in the Sahara and in Central Asia.)

Mixed livestock and crop farming (3) is widespread in the more humid parts of the midlatitudes, including much of the eastern United States, western Europe, and western Russia, but it is also found in smaller areas in Uruguay, Brazil, and South Africa. Commercial grain farming (4) prevails in the drier parts of the midlatitudes, including the southern Prairie Provinces of Canada, in the Dakotas and Montana in the United States, as well as in Nebraska, Kansas, and adjacent areas. Spring wheat (planted in the spring and harvested in the summer) grows in the northern zone, and winter wheat (planted in the autumn and harvested in the spring of the following year) is used in the southern area. An even larger belt of wheat farming extends from Ukraine through Russia into Kazakhstan. The Argentinean and Australian wheat zones are smaller in area, but their exports are an important component of world trade.

Even a cursory glance at Figure 11.17 reveals the wide distribution of **livestock ranching** (12), the raising

of domesticated animals for the production of meat and by-products, such as leather and wool. In addition to the large cattle-ranching areas in the United States, Canada, and Mexico, much of eastern Brazil and Argentina are devoted to ranching, along with large tracts of Australia and New Zealand, as well as South Africa. You may see a Thünian pattern here: livestock ranching on the periphery and consumers in the cities. Refrigeration has overcome the problem of perishability, and high volume has lowered the unit cost of transporting beef, lamb, and other animal products.

Subsistence Agriculture

The map of world agriculture labels three types of subsistence agriculture: subsistence crop and livestock farming; intensively subsistence farming (chiefly rice); and intensively subsistence farming (chiefly wheat and other crops). In some regions that are labeled as subsistence, that label does not tell the whole story. For example. in Southeast Asia, rice is grown on small plots and is labor-intensive, so that subsistence and export production occur side by side. Despite the region's significant rice exports, most Southeast Asian farmers are subsistence farmers. Thus, Southeast Asia appears on the map as primarily a subsistence grain-growing area.

Mediterranean Agriculture

Only one form of agriculture mentioned in the legend of Figure 11.17 refers to a particular climatic zone: **Mediterranean agriculture** (6). As the map shows, this kind of specialized farming occurs only in areas where the dry summer Mediterranean climate prevails (Fig. 11.16): along the shores of the Mediterranean Sea, in parts of California and Oregon, in central Chile, at South Africa's Cape, and in parts of southwestern and southern Australia. Farmers here grow a special combination of crops: grapes, olives, citrus fruits, figs, certain vegetables, dates, and others. From these areas come many wines; these and other commodities are exported to distant markets because Mediterranean products tend to be popular and command high prices.

Illegal Drugs

Important cash crops that cannot be easily mapped and do not appear in Figure 11.17 are those that are turned into illegal drugs. Because of the high demand for drugs—particularly in the core—farmers in the periphery often find it more profitable to cultivate poppy, coca, or marijuana plants than to grow standard food crops. Cultivation of these plants increased steadily through the 1980s and 1990s, and they now constitute an important source of revenue for parts of the global economic periphery. Coca, the source plant of cocaine, is grown widely in Colombia, Peru, and Bolivia. Over half of the world's cultivation of coca occurs in Colombia alone.

Heroin and opium are derived from opium poppy plants, grown predominantly in Southeast and Southwest Asia, especially in Afghanistan and Myanmar. In the 2008 World Drug Report, the United Nations reported that 92 percent of the world's opium production took place in Afghanistan. The United States-led overthrow of the Taliban in Afghanistan in 2001 created a power vacuum in the country and an opportunity for illegal drug production to quickly rebound (the austere Taliban government had virtually eradicated opium production in Afghanistan by 2001). Most opium production in Afghanistan today occurs in the five unstable southern provinces. The World Drug Report also reports an overall decline in illegal drug use in the United States in the last five years.

United States government policies have also affected production of illegal drugs in Latin America. During the 1980s and 1990s, the United States government cracked down on coca production in Colombia. With this crackdown, much of the drug production and trafficking moved north to northern Mexico. In June 2005, the *Economist* quoted one American official as reporting that "Mexican criminal gangs 'exert more influence over drug trafficking in the U.S. than any other group.' Mexicans now control 11 of the 13 largest drug markets in the United States." In 2003, Mexico's marijuana production rose 70 percent and in recent years, Mexico's methamphetamine production rose 74 percent. The United States government estimates that in 2004, 92 percent of the cocaine entering the country came through Mexico.

Environmental Impacts of Commercial Agriculture

Commercial agriculture creates significant environmental change. The growing demand for protein-rich foods and more efficient technologies are leading to overfishing in many regions of the world. Fish stocks are declining rapidly. From mid-century to the late 1980s, the fish harvest from oceans and seas increased fivefold, and there seemed to be no limit to it. Countries quarreled over fishing rights, poorer countries leased fishing grounds to richer ones, and fleets of trawlers plied the oceans. International attempts to regulate fishing industries failed. Then in the 1970s and 1980s, overfishing began destroying fish stocks. The cod fisheries on Canada's Grand Banks off Newfoundland collapsed. In 1975 biologists estimated the Atlantic bluefin tuna population at 250,000; today the western stock is listed as critically endangered, and the stock in the Mediterranean is listed as endangered. From ocean perch and king crabs off Alaska to rock lobsters and roughies off New Zealand, fish and shellfish populations are depleted. The total annual catch is also declining and may already

be beyond the point of recovery. Much of the damage has been done, and fishing industries in many parts of the world report dwindling harvests and missing species.

Travel to Mediterranean Europe today and you will see a landscape that reflects the clearing of forests in ancient times to facilitate agriculture and trade. Look carefully at many hillslopes and you will see evidence of terraces cut into the hills many centuries ago. The industrialization and commercialization of agriculture has accelerated the pace and extent of agriculture's impact on the environment. More land has been cleared, and the land that is under cultivation is ever more intensively used.

Significant changes in environment go far beyond the simple clearing of land. They range from soil erosion to changes in the organic content of soils to the presence of chemicals (herbicides, pesticides, even antibiotics and growth hormones from livestock feces) in soils and groundwater. In places where large commercial crop farms dominate, the greatest concerns often center around the introduction of chemical fertilizers and pesticides into the environment—as well as soil erosion. And, as we have seen, the movement toward genetically modified crops carries with it another set of environmental concerns.

The environmental impacts can be particularly severe when commercial agriculture expands into marginal environments. This has happened, for example, with the expansion of livestock herding into arid or semiarid areas (see the map of world climate, Fig. 11.16). The natural vegetation in these areas cannot always sustain the herds, especially during prolonged droughts. This can lead to ecological damage and, in some areas, to desertification (see Chapter 10).

In recent years, the popularity of fast-food chains that serve hamburgers has led to the deforestation of wooded areas in order to open up additional pastures for beef cattle, notably in Central and South America. Livestock ranching is an extremely land-, water-, and energy-intensive process. Significant land must be turned over to the cultivation of cattle feed, and the animals themselves need extensive grazing areas. By stripping away vegetation, the animals can promote the erosion of river banks, with implications for everything from water quality to wildlife habitat.

Agribusiness and the Changing Geography of Agriculture

The commercialization of crop production and the associated development of new agricultural technologies have changed how agricultural goods are grown and have sparked the rapid growth of agribusiness. **Agribusiness** is an encompassing term for the businesses that provide a vast array of goods and services to support the agricultural industry. Agribusiness serves to connect local farms to a spatially extensive web of production and exchange. At the same time, it fosters the spatial concentration of agricultural activities. Both of these trends are revealed in the development of the poultry industry in the United States.

Early in the twentieth century, poultry production in the United States was highly disaggregated, with many farmers raising a few chickens as part of a multifaceted farming operation. Over the past 50 years, however, poultry production has fundamentally changed. In an article on modern agriculture, David Lanegran summarized the impact of this transformation as follows:

> Today, chickens are produced by large agribusiness companies operating hatcheries, feed mills, and processing plants. They supply chicks and feed to the farmers. The farmers are responsible for building a house and maintaining proper temperature and water supply. Once a week the companies fill the feed bins for the farmers, and guarantee them a price for the birds. The companies even collect market-ready birds and take them away for processing and marketing. Most of the nation's poultry supply is handled by a half dozen very large corporations that control the process from chicks to chicken pieces in stores.

Lanegran goes on to show how selective breeding has produced faster growing, bigger chickens, which are housed in enormous broiler houses that are largely mechanized. These are concentrated in northwestern Arkansas, northern Georgia, the Delmarva Peninsula (Delaware, Maryland, and Virginia) east of Washington, D.C., the Piedmont areas of North Carolina, and the Shenandoah Valley of Virginia. He shows that in many respects the "farmers" who manage these operations are involved in manufacturing as much or more than farming. They are as likely to spend their time talking to bank officers, overseeing the repair of equipment, and negotiating with vendors as they are tending their animals. As such, they symbolize the breakdown between the rural and the urban in some parts of the world—as well as the interconnections between rural places and distant markets.

Not only poultry is produced in an industrial fashion. During the 1990s, hog production on the Oklahoma and Texas panhandles increased rapidly with the arrival of corporate hog farms. John Fraser Hart and Chris Mayda described the quick change with statistics. In 1992, the U.S. Census of Agriculture counted just over 31,000 hogs marketed in Texas County, Oklahoma, and just four years later "the panhandle was plastered with proliferating pork places, and Texas County alone produced 2 million hogs. It was the epicenter of an area that produced 4 million hogs, 4 percent of the national total and one-seventh as many finished hogs as the entire state of Iowa." The availability of both inexpensive water and natural gas on the Oklahoma panhandle was enticing for corporate hog farms, which require both. Hart and Mayda explain that the "reasonable" price of land and the accessibility to "growing metropolitan markets of the South and the West" also made the region attractive for hog production. Similar to poultry production, a corporation built a processing plant, and production (both by farms owned by the corporation and those owned privately) increased to meet the demand.

Agribusiness is shaping the world distribution of commercial agricultural systems and their relationship to subsistence agriculture. Through time, many factors have affected that relationship. History and tradition have played important roles, as have environment and technology. At times governments have encouraged their citizens to limit family size in an attempt to lift the population above the subsistence level. Some governments have sought to maintain the privileges of large landowners, whereas others have initiated bold land reform programs. Communist governments, notably those of the former Soviet Union and Maoist China, have tried to control agricultural output by creating collective farms and agricultural communes—a giant experiment that resulted in significant displacement of rural peoples and mixed results in terms of output. (Today farming reprivatization is under way in both Russia and China.)

Most of all, the map of global agricultural regions reveals the capacity of markets to influence the activities of farmers. The range and variety of products on the shelves of urban supermarkets in the United States is a world away from the constant quest for sufficient, nutritionally balanced food that exists in some places. A global network of farm production is oriented to the one-fifth of the world's population that is highly urbanized, wealthy, and powerful. Few farmers in distant lands have real control over land-use decisions, for the better off people in the global economic core continue to decide what will be bought at what price. The colonial era may have come to an end, but, as the map of agricultural regions reminds us, its imprint remains strong.

Loss of Productive Farmland

As cities expand outward, converting agricultural land into suburbs, some of the most fertile, productive farmlands are lost to housing and retail developments (Fig. 11.19). Many cities were established amid productive farmlands that could supply the needs of their inhabitants. Now the cities are absorbing the productive farmlands as they expand. The American Farmland Trust, for example, reported in the 1990s that 12 U.S. areas are severely affected, including California's Central Valley, South Florida, California's coastal zone, North Carolina's Piedmont, and the Chicago–Milwaukee–Madison triangle in Illinois–Wisconsin. These 12 areas represent only 5 percent of U.S. farmland, but they produce 17 percent of total agricultural sales, 67 percent of all fruit, 55 percent of all vegetables, and one-quarter of all dairy products. Figures for other countries in the richer

HIGH QUALITY FARMLAND IN THE PATH OF DEVELOPMENT

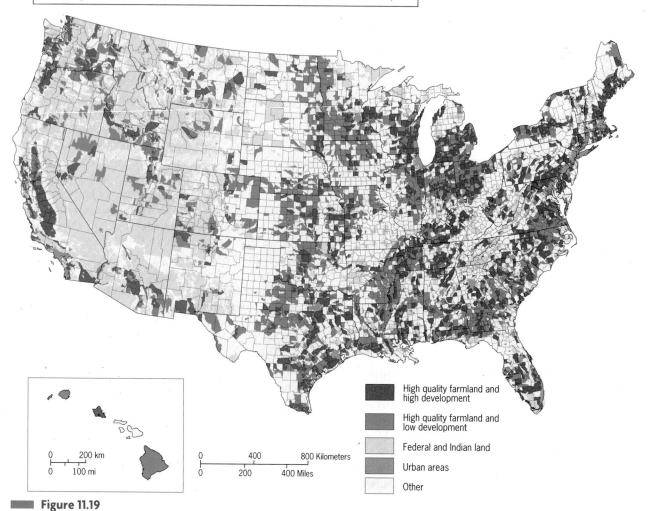

High quality farmland and
high development

High quality farmland and
low development

Federal and Indian land

Urban areas

Other

Figure 11.19

Farming on the Edge: High-Quality Farmland in the Path of Development, 2002. This
map from American Farmland Trust, whose charge is to preserve farmland, highlights farmland
that is endangered of being suburbanized as cities expand into neighboring farmlands.   *Courtesy of:*
American Farm Trust, http://www.farmland.org/farmingontheedge/maps.htm, last accessed November 2005.

parts of the world (such as Japan) as well as for poorer countries (such as Egypt) prove that this is a global problem with
serious implications for the future.

The conversion of farmlands into housing developments is not confined to areas close to major cities that
could become suburbs. Expendable wealth and the desire
to have a place to "get away from it all" have led highly
productive commercial agricultural areas to be converted
into regions for second homes. One of the most intensive
commercial agricultural areas in the United States is the
Delmarva Peninsula, where the broiler chicken industry
began in the 1920s. Four major poultry companies provide chickens to local farmers who produce 8 percent
of the poultry produced in the United States, using the
industrialized poultry production methods described
above. The price of land is rising on the peninsula, as

urbanites from Pennsylvania, Maryland, and New York
buy land on the eastern shore to build second homes.
Many of the new residents on the peninsula are demanding higher environmental standards, and in turn are
placing a squeeze in costs on chicken production. Tyson
Foods closed its production facility in spring 2004, and
the *Washington Times* reported 650 lost jobs. As urban
population continues to grow and expendable wealth
increases for the wealthiest of the population, more
agricultural lands will be converted to housing developments, especially lands in beautiful areas with recreational amenities, like the eastern shore of Maryland and
its Chesapeake Bay. The Maryland State government and
other State governments are balancing preservation of
agricultural lands and open spaces with demand for housing and retail developments.

Summary

Agricultural production has changed drastically since the First Agricultural Revolution. Today, agricultural products, even perishable ones, are shipped around the world, and agriculture has industrialized and spurred the growth of agribusiness. A major commonality between ancient agriculture and modern agriculture remains: the need to change. Trial and error were the norms of early plant and animal domestication. And today, trial and error are still the norm, as agriculture in the globalized economy is complicated by new technologies, genetically engineered crops, cultural change, government involvement, and the lasting impacts of history.

Geographic Concepts

organic agriculture
agriculture
primary economic
    activity
secondary economic
    activity
tertiary economic activity
quaternary economic
    activity
quinary economic activity
plant domestication
root crops
seed crops
First Agricultural
    Revolution

animal domestication
subsistence agriculture
shifting cultivation
slash-and-burn
    agriculture
Second Agricultural
    Revolution
von Thünen model
Third Agricultural
    Revolution
Green Revolution
genetically modified
    organisms (GMOs)
rectangular survey
    system

township- and range-
    system
metes and bounds system
long-lot survey system
primogeniture
commercial agriculture
monoculture
Köppen climatic
    classification system
climatic regions
plantation agriculture
luxury crops
livestock ranching
Mediterranean agriculture
agribusiness

Learn More Online

About food production and development
http://www.foodfirst.org/media/opeds/2000/4-greenrev.html

About the preservation of agricultural lands
http://www.farmland.org/

Watch It Online

Guns, Germs, and Steel
http://www.pbs.org/gunsgermssteel/

Loss of agricultural land to suburbanization in Chicago
http://www.learner.org/resources/series180.html#program_descriptions

click on video on demand for program 24

Russia's Farming Revolution
http://www.learner.org/resources/series180.html#program_descriptions

click on video on demand for program 7

Sustainable agriculture in India
http://www.learner.org/resources/series180.html#program_descriptions

click on video on demand for program 17

CHAPTER 12

Industry and Services

Field Note Branding the Backboard

■■■ **Figure 12.1**
Skopje, Macedonia. The Nike "swoosh" is everywhere—even on the backboard of a basketball hoop in this relatively poor neighborhood of Skopje, Macedonia.   © Alexander B. Murphy.

Walking through a relatively poor neighborhood in Skopje, Macedonia, with the midday Muslim call to prayer ringing in my ears, the last thing I expected to see was something from my home State of Oregon (Fig. 12.1). But there it was—the unmistakable Nike swoosh on the backboard of a basketball hoop where the local kids play pick-up games!

As ubiquitous as the Nike brand of athletic shoes and its trademark swoosh are on the landscape, it is difficult to examine the cultural landscape and pinpoint where Nikes are produced. Nike was founded in Oregon in 1961 by a former competitive runner (its first year of sales was $8000), and it has grown to be one of the giants of the shoe and apparel business (with sales of $16.3 billion in 2007). With headquarters in Beaverton, Oregon, a suburb of Portland, the company is far more than a Beaverton concern. Despite a Beaverton, Oregon workforce of over 6000 people, not a single individual in Oregon is directly involved in the process of putting a shoe together. Worldwide, 30,000 people work directly for Nike today, and according to Nike, upwards of 800,000 workers are employed by Nike's almost 700 contract factories in 52 countries. Nike began production in the 1960s by contracting with an Asian firm to manufacture its shoes. In 1974, Nike set up its first domestic shoe manufacturing facility in the small town of Exeter, New Hampshire. By the end of that year, Nike's workforce was still modest in number, but the Oregon contingent focused on running the company and expanding sales, whereas the New Hampshire and the Asian contingents focused primarily on the production of athletic shoes.

As Nike grew to become the world's leading manufacturer of athletic shoes (with almost a 40 percent share of the world's athletic shoe market), its employment numbers skyrocketed and many new manufacturing plants were established in Asia and beyond. This transformation did not translate into manufacturing jobs in Beaverton, Oregon, however. The employment opportunities now provided by Nike at its world headquarters are for the financial administrators, marketing and sales specialists, information technology directors, computer technicians, lawyers, and support personnel needed to run an international company with over $9 billion in annual revenues. The local social and economic geography of Beaverton bears little resemblance to what one might have expected in a town housing an important shoe company 80 years ago.

Eighty years ago, economic geographer J. Russel Smith reported that "three hundred shoe factories have sales offices located within a few blocks of each other in Boston." In a leather district close to the city, hides were imported from around the world, and tanneries prepared the hides. In a ring of suburbs around Boston, great shoe towns like Haverhill, Brockton, and Lynn had factories specializing in men's or women's shoes. Writing in 1925, Smith described the process of shoe production in the shoe factory town of Lynn:

> Walking the streets of Lynn one realizes what concentration an industry can have; the signs upon the places of business read—heels, welts, insoles, uppers, eyelets, thread, etc., etc. It is an astonishing proof of the degree to which even a simple commodity like a shoe, so long made by one man, can be subdivided and become the work of scores of industries and thousands of people.

Shoe salespeople periodically flocked to the shoe company headquarters in Boston to learn about the company's newest offerings and fill their sample suitcases with shoes to show their clients as they made the rounds of their sales territories.

Today, the production and marketing of Nike shoes and apparel involves an elaborate global network of international manufacturing and sales. The global processes have local outcomes and realities, as each node of the Nike network is functionally specialized, dependent on other nodes, and influenced by the niche it occupies in the network.

In this chapter, we examine the origins of the Industrial Revolution in Great Britain and its diffusion into mainland Europe. In addition, we look at the first manufacturing belts in Europe, Asia, and North America. The conditions of industrialization have changed since its beginnings; thus, we also examine how industrialization has changed, focusing on the global labor force and the post-Fordist concepts of just-in-time manufacturing and global division of labor. Changes in the world-economy have spurred new manufacturing belts, considerably changing places in the semiperiphery. We also study how the expanding service economy is changing the nature of employment and the economic bases of many countries.

Key Questions For Chapter 12

1. Where did the Industrial Revolution begin, and how did it diffuse?

2. How do location theories explain historical patterns of industrialization?

3. How has industrial production changed, and with what geographic consequences?

4. Where are the major industrial belts in the world today and why?

5. What is the service economy, and where are services concentrated?

WHERE DID THE INDUSTRIAL REVOLUTION BEGIN, AND HOW DID IT DIFFUSE?

Industrial production began long before the Industrial Revolution. Cottage industries and community workshops were located throughout the world, and trade in these industrial products was widespread. For example, in the towns and villages of India, workshops produced goods made of iron, gold, silver, and brass. India's carpenters were artists as well as artisans, and their work was in demand wherever it could be bought. India's textiles, made on individual spinning wheels and hand looms, were considered the best in the world. These industries were sustained both by local aristocrats and by international trade. Textiles in Great Britain were produced in rural villages within individual homes where, during the winter months, rural residents would spin thread or weave fabric. The quality of production varied according to place. India's textiles were so finely produced that British textile makers rioted in 1721, demanding legislative protection against imports from India.

China and Japan possessed a substantial industrial base long before the Industrial Revolution. Even European industries, from the textile makers of Flanders and Britain to the iron smelters of Thüringen, had developed considerably, but in price and quality Europe's products could not match those of other parts of the world.

What Europe's products lacked in quality, its merchants more than made up for in aggressiveness. Commercial companies, such as the Dutch and British East India Companies, laid the groundwork for Europe's colonial expansion. They gained control over local industries in India, Indonesia, and elsewhere, profited from political chaos, and played off allies against enemies. British merchants imported tons of raw fiber for their expanding textile industries. With the eventual development of technologies that allowed for mass-production, the British were able to bury local industries in Asia and Africa by flooding the market with inexpensive products.

The Industrial Revolution

During the eighteenth century, markets for European goods were growing, especially in the colonies. Better machines were urgently needed, especially improved spinning and weaving machines. The first steps in the **Industrial Revolution** did not use a revolutionary energy source: the new spinning wheels were still powered by foot pedals, and the new water looms were driven by water running downslope.

The eighteenth century was marked with a series of inventions that brought new uses for known energy sources (coal) and new machines to improve efficiencies (steam engines) and enable other new inventions (water pumps and railroads). Funding inventions and supporting inventors and inventions required money. The eighteenth century was marked by a flow of capital from the colonies and from global trade to western Europe (Fig. 12.2). The flow of capital into western Europe enabled investors to fund inventors and to perfect inventions. For example, James Watt is credited with improving the steam engine by creating a separate chamber to house the steam and by perfecting the pistons and getting them to perform correctly. The invention did not happen overnight: a series of attempts over a few decades finally worked when Watt partnered with toymaker and metal worker Matthew Boulton (who inherited great wealth from his wife). Boulton financed the final trials and errors that made Watt's steam engine functional and reliable.

During the Industrial Revolution, innovations in iron manufacturing enabled the production of the steam engine and other products made of iron. In Coalbrookdale, England, in 1709, iron worker Abraham Darby found a way to *smelt* iron. By burning coal in a vacuum-like environment, the English already knew they could cook off the impurities, leaving behind coke, the high-carbon portion of coal. Carbon is found in all life forms, and all fossil fuels are carbon based. In 1709, Darby put iron ore and coke in a blast furnace, and then pushed air into the furnace, a combination that allowed the furnace to burn at a much higher temperature than wood charcoal or coal allowed. Mixing the iron ore with limestone (to attract impurities) and water and

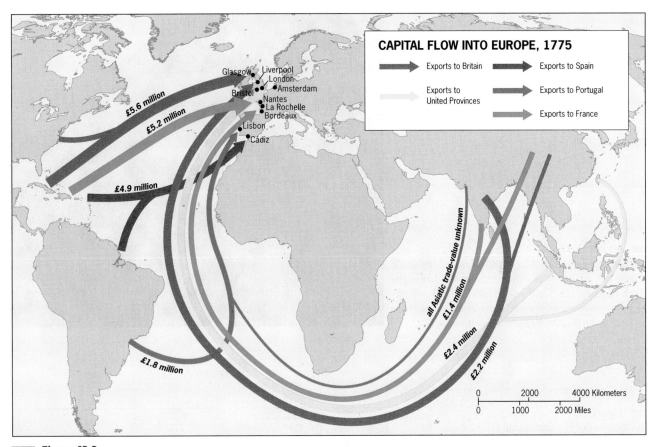

CAPITAL FLOW INTO EUROPE, 1775

Exports to Britain | Exports to Spain
Exports to United Provinces | Exports to Portugal
Exports to France

£5.6 million
£5.2 million
£4.9 million
£1.8 million
all Asiatic trade-value unknown
£1.4 million
£2.4 million
£2.2 million

Glasgow, Liverpool, London, Amsterdam, Bristol, Nantes, La Rochelle, Bordeaux, Lisbon, Cádiz

0   2000   4000 Kilometers
0   1000   2000 Miles

▭ Figure 12.2
Capital Flows into Europe during Colonialism. This map shows the major flows of capital into Europe from Europe's colonies. The capital helped fuel Europe's Industrial Revolution at the end of the 1700s and into the 1800s.   *Adapted with permission from: Geoffrey Barraclough, ed. The Times Concise Atlas of World History, 5th edition, Hammond Incorporated, 1998.*

smelting it with coke enabled iron workers to pour melted iron ore into molds (instead of shaping it with anvils) making *cast iron*. The use of molds allowed more consistency in iron parts and increased production of iron components. The residents of Ironbridge, a town neighboring Coalbrookdale, still take pride in their town's bridge, the first in the world made entirely from cast iron in 1779 (Fig. 12.3).

The steam engine alone had dramatic effects. It was used to pump water out of coal mines, enabling coal workers to reach deeper coal seams; to power spinning wheels that spun 100 plus spools of thread at a time; to power dozens of looms in a factory all at once; and to create a new mode of transportation, the railroad. The first railroad in England was opened in 1825. In 1830, Manchester (a center of textile manufacturing) was connected by rail to the nearby port of Liverpool (a westward-facing port that linked Britain with the colonies), and in the next several decades thousands of miles of iron and then steel track were laid. Ocean shipping also entered a new age when the first steam-powered vessel crossed the Atlantic in 1819.

With the advent of the railroad and steam ship, Britain enjoyed even greater advantages than it did at the beginning of the Industrial Revolution. Not only did it hold a monopoly over products that were in demand around the world, but it alone possessed the skills necessary to make the machines that manufactured them. Europe and America wanted railroads and locomotives; England had the know-how, the experience, and the capital to supply them. Soon British influence around the world was reaching its peak.

Meanwhile, the spatial pattern of modern Europe's industrial activity began to take shape. In the early part of the Industrial Revolution, before the railroad connected places and reduced the transportation costs of coal, manufacturing needed to be located close to coal fields. Manufacturing plants also needed to be connected to ports where raw materials could arrive and finished products could depart. In the first decades of the Industrial Revolution, plants were usually connected to ports by a broad canal or river system. In Britain, densely populated

■ **Figure 12.3**
Ironbridge, England. The world's first bridge made entirely of cast iron was constructed in the late eighteenth century near Coalbrookdale, England, reflecting the resources, technology, and available skills in this area at the time.   © John Robertson/Alamy.

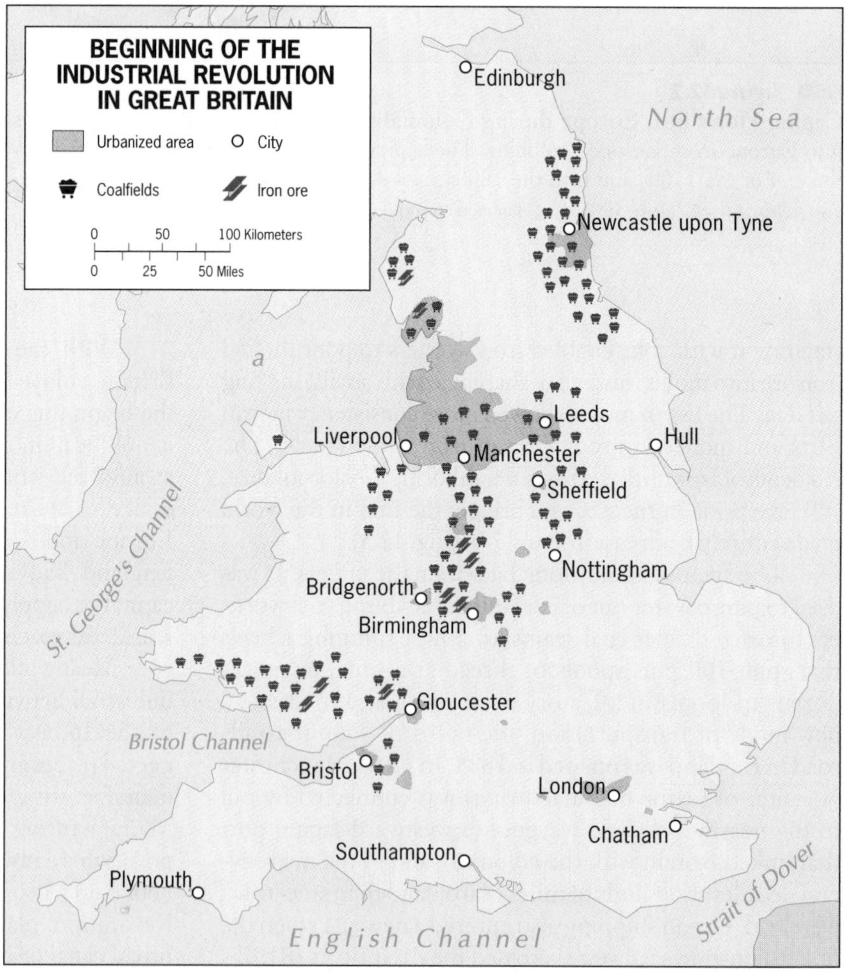

■ **Figure 12.4**
The Origins of the Industrial Revolution. The areas of Great Britain that industrialized earliest were those closest to the resources needed for industrialization: coal, iron ore, and capital. Large areas of urbanization grew near industrial zones and in the port cities where materials came in and from which industrialized products went out. *Adapted with permission from*: Geoffrey Barraclough, ed. *The Times Concise Atlas of World History*, 5th edition, Hammond Incorporated, 1998.

BEGINNING OF THE INDUSTRIAL REVOLUTION IN GREAT BRITAIN

Urbanized area   ○ City

Coalfields   Iron ore

0   50   100 Kilometers
0   25   50 Miles

Edinburgh

North Sea

Newcastle upon Tyne

Liverpool
Leeds
Hull
Manchester
Sheffield
Nottingham

Bridgenorth
Birmingham

Gloucester
Bristol
London
Chatham
Southampton
Plymouth

St. George's Channel

Bristol Channel

English Channel

Strait of Dover

and heavily urbanized industrial regions developed near the coal fields (Fig. 12.4). The largest such region was the Midlands of northcentral England.

Diffusion to Mainland Europe

In the early 1800s, as the innovations of Britain's Industrial Revolution diffused into mainland Europe, the same set of locational criteria for industrial zones applied: proximity to coal fields and connection via water to a port. A belt of major coal fields extends from west to east through mainland Europe, roughly along the southern margins of the North European Lowland—across northern France and southern Belgium, the Netherlands, the German Rühr, western Bohemia in the Czech Republic, and Silesia in Poland. Iron ore is dispersed along a similar belt, and the map showing the pattern of diffusion of the Industrial Revolution into Europe reflects the resulting concentrations of economic activity (Fig. 12.5). Industrial developments in one area,

Figure 12.5
Diffusion of the Industrial Revolution. The eastward diffusion of the Industrial Revolution occurred during the second half of the nineteenth century. © H. J. de Blij, P. O. Muller, and John Wiley & Sons, Inc.

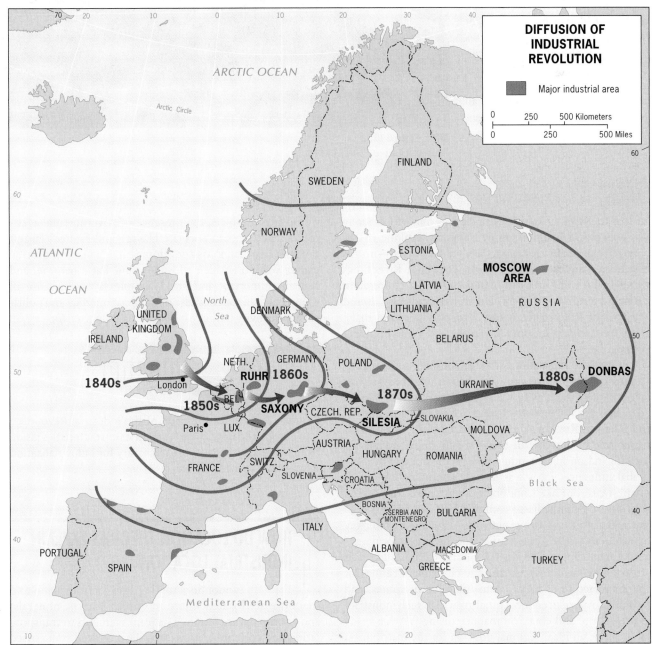

Field Note

"Paris and the Paris Basin form the industrial as well as agricultural heart of France. The city and region are served by the Seine River, along which lies a string of ports from Le Havre at the mouth to Rouen at the head of navigation for oceangoing ships. Rouen has become a vital center on France's industrial map. As we approached on the river, you could see the famous cathedral and the city's historic cultural landscape to the left (north), but on the right bank lay a major industrial complex including coal-fired power facilities (although France leads Europe in nuclear energy), petrochemical plants, and oil installations. It is all part of the industrial region centered on Paris."

Figure 12.6
Rouen, France.   © H. J. de Blij.

such as the Rühr area of present-day Germany (Germany was not consolidated into a single country until the 1870s) changed the port cities to which they are linked—in this case Rotterdam in the Netherlands. The Rhine River flows through the Rühr area and enters the sea at Rotterdam. Over the last 200 years, the Dutch have radically altered the port of Rotterdam to ease transportation and make it the most important port in Europe and a hub of global commerce.

Once the railroad was well established, some manufacturing moved to or grew in existing urban areas with large markets, such as London and Paris. London was an attractive site for industry because of its port location on the Thames River and more importantly because of its major role in the flow of regional and global capital. By locating in London, an industry was at the pulse of Britain's global influence. Paris was already continental Europe's greatest city, but like London, it did not have coal or iron deposits in its immediate vicinity. When a railroad system was added to the existing network of road and waterway connections to Paris, the city became the largest local market for manufactured products for hundreds of miles. Paris attracted major industries, and the city, long a center for the manufacture of luxury items (jewelry, perfumes, and fashions), experienced substantial growth in such industries as metallurgy and chemical manufacturing. With a ready labor force, an ideal regional position for the distribution

of finished products, the presence of governmental agencies, a nearby ocean port (Le Havre), and France's largest domestic market, Paris's development as a major industrial center was no accident. London and Paris became, and remain, important industrial complexes not because of their coal fields but because of their commercial and political connectivity to the rest of the world (Fig. 12.6).

Examine the map of diffusion of the Industrial Revolution into Europe and determine what other characteristics (aside from presence of coal) were necessary for industrialization to take hold in these regions.

HOW DO LOCATION THEORIES EXPLAIN INDUSTRIAL LOCATION?

Primary economic activities draw from the land and therefore are located where resources (forests, minerals, and good soils) are found. The improvements in transportation and communications that have created time–space compression (see Chapter 4) in our globalized world make secondary industries much less dependent on resource location. Raw materials can be transported to distant locations to be converted into manufactured products—if the resulting profits outweigh the costs. A large body of work in economic geography focuses on **location theory**, predicting where businesses will or should be located.

Any attempt to establish a model for the location of secondary industry runs into complications much greater than those confronting von Thünen, who dealt only with primary industries. The location of secondary industries depends to an important extent on human behavior and decision making, on cultural, political, and economic factors, and even on intuition or whim. Since models must be based on assumptions, economic geographers have to assume that decision makers are trying to maximize their advantages over competitors, that they want to make as much profit as possible, and that they will take into account **variable costs** such as energy supply, transport expenses, labor costs, and other needs when choosing an industrial location.

In calculating efforts to maximize advantages, a key issue is the **friction of distance**, the increase in time and cost that usually comes with increasing distance. If a raw material has to be shipped hundreds of miles to a factory, rather than being manufactured right next door, the friction of distance increases. A corollary to the concept of the friction of distance is what geographers call distance decay (see Chapter 4), which assumes that the impact of a function or an activity will decline as one moves away from its point of origin. Distance decay suggests that manufacturing plants will be more concerned with serving the markets of nearby places than more distant places. This basic principle is important in efforts to understand the locational dynamics of a variety of phenomena—including manufacturing.

Weber's Model

The German economic geographer Alfred Weber (1868–1958) did for the secondary industries what von Thünen had done for agriculture: he developed a basic model for the location of manufacturing plants. Weber drew from the research of other economic geographers and began with a set of assumptions that enabled him to create his model. In *Theory of the Location of Industries* (1909), Weber eliminated labor mobility and varying wage rates and calculated the "pulls" exerted on each point of manufacturing in his hypothetical region of analysis.

Weber's **least cost theory** accounted for the location of a manufacturing plant in terms of the owner's desire to minimize three categories of costs. The first and most important of these categories was *transportation*: the site chosen must entail the lowest possible cost of moving raw

materials to the factory and finished products to the market. Weber suggested that the site where transportation costs are lowest is the place where it would be least expensive to bring raw materials to the point of production and to distribute finished products to consumers. The second cost was that of *labor*. Higher labor costs reduce the margin of profit, so a factory might do better farther from raw materials and markets if cheap labor made up for the added transport costs.

The third factor in Weber's model was what he called **agglomeration**: when a substantial number of enterprises cluster in the same area, as happens in a large industrial city, they can provide assistance to each other through shared talents, services, and facilities. All manufacturers need office furniture and equipment; the presence of one or more producers in a large city satisfies this need for all. Thus, agglomeration makes a big-city location more attractive, perhaps overcoming some increase in transport and labor costs. Excessive agglomeration, however, leads to high rents, rising wages, circulation problems (resulting in increased transport costs and loss of efficiency), and other problems. These problems may eventually negate the advantages of agglomeration. Such factors have led many industries to leave the crowded urban centers of the U.S. eastern megalopolis and move to other locations—a process known as **deglomeration**.

Hotelling's Model

Similar to Weber through his theory of agglomeration, an economist by the name of Harold Hotelling (1895–1973) sought to understand the issue of **locational interdependence** by posing the question of where two ice cream vendors might stand on a beach occupied by people distributed evenly along its stretch. In choosing a simple, one-dimensional space, Hotelling was able to simplify the analysis. He concluded that the two vendors might start at locations somewhat distant from one another so that they could each be as close to as many customers as possible. As the two vendors seek to maximize sales, however, Hotelling argued that they would seek to constrain each other's sales territory as much as possible. This would lead them to move ever closer to the center of the beach, until they were standing back-to-back. And once they reached those positions, they were likely to stay there because a decision by one of them to move could only hurt profitability.

The point of Hotelling's analysis is to show that the location of an industry cannot be understood without reference to the location of other industries of like kind. But in the example of the ice cream vendors, only one variable is considered: the effort to maximize the number of sales. The costs for some of the consumers will be greater if the two sellers cluster at the center of the beach—for those at the edges will have to walk farther to buy ice cream than if the two vendors were each located close to the center of each half of the beach. Moreover, more consumers may be aware of the ice cream vendors if they are spread out.

Lösch's Model

August Lösch (1967) worked to determine the locations manufacturing plants could choose to maximize profit. He added the spatial influence of consumer demand and production costs to his calculations. Determining the point of maximum profit is often difficult, but as Figure 12.7 suggests, firms will usually try to identify a zone in which some kind of profit can be expected. To the left and right of the zone, distance decay will make sales unprofitable. Firms will try to situate themselves away from the margins of that zone. However, other businesses can always come along and change the configuration of that zone—and this is one element that can easily cause a locational change in production in a capitalist system.

Major Industrial Regions of the World before 1950

Each of these models helps explain where industries are located, but before 1960, the main locational costs for industries were transportation of raw materials and shipping of finished products. Thus, the first manufacturing belts, regions of major manufacturing concentration, tended to be close to raw materials and accessible to transportation routes. Yet, at the global scale, several major areas of raw materials did not industrialize early. The world map of major regional-industrial development reveals that before 1950, only a small minority of countries were major industrial economies. Beyond raw mate-

rials, many factors help explain this pattern, including relative location in relation to flows of goods and capital, political circumstances, economic leadership, labor costs, and levels of education and training.

The four **primary industrial regions** that stand out on the world map are Western and Central Europe, Eastern North America, Russia and Ukraine, and Eastern Asia. Each of these regions consists of one or more core areas of industrial development with subsidiary clusters.

Western and Central Europe

The manufacturing regions of western Europe are largely the regions that experienced industrialization between the late eighteenth and early twentieth centuries. From this region of Europe came the European Coal and Steel Community (ECSC), which initiated the experiment with European integration (see Chapter 8). Europe's principal coal deposits lie in a belt across northern France, Belgium, northcentral Germany, the northwestern Czech Republic, and southern Poland—and it was along this zone that industrialization expanded in mainland Europe. Colonial empires gave France, Britain, Belgium, and the Netherlands, and later Germany, access to the capital necessary to fuel industrialization and in some cases the raw materials necessary for production. Three manufacturing districts lay in Germany: the Rühr, based on the Westphalian coal field; the Saxony district, near the border of the former Czechoslovakia; and Silesia (now part of Poland). Germany still ranks among the world's leading producers of both coal and steel and remains Europe's leading industrial power (Table 12.1). By the early twentieth century, industry began to diffuse far from the original European hearth to such places as northern Italy (now one of Europe's major industrial regions), Catalonia (anchored by Barcelona) and northern Spain, southern Sweden, and southern Finland.

The Manufacturing Belts of Germany

The Rühr (in present-day Germany) became Europe's greatest industrial complex. Named after a small tributary of the Rhine River, the Rühr had the combined advantages of high-quality resources, good accessibility, and proximity to large markets. When local iron ore reserves became depleted, ores could be brought in from overseas. The Rühr was already undergoing industrialization in the closing decades of the nineteenth century, and by the 1930s the river basin had become one of the most important industrial regions in the world, pouring forth the products of heavy industry, including tanks and other weapons for Hitler's armies.

Saxony (also in present-day Germany), on the other hand, was always oriented toward specialized lighter manufactures. Anchored by Leipzig and Dresden, it became known for such products as optical equipment and cam-

■■■ **Figure 12.7**
Economic Influences on Business Location. This diagram shows the connections among price, space, income, and costs.
© E. H. Fouberg, A. B. Murphy, H. J. de Blij, and John Wiley & Sons, Inc.

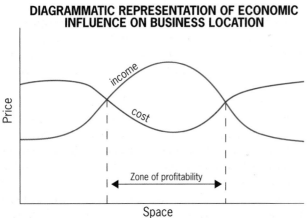

DIAGRAMMATIC REPRESENTATION OF ECONOMIC INFLUENCE ON BUSINESS LOCATION

TABLE 12.1

Top 20 Crude Steel Producers.

TOP STEEL-PRODUCING COUNTRIES OF THE WORLD, 2005		
Country	Rank	Tonnage
China	1	349.4
Japan	2	112.5
United States	3	94.9
Russia	4	66.1
South Korea	5	47.8
Germany	6	44.5
Ukraine	7	38.6
India	8	38.1
Brazil	9	31.6
Italy	10	29.3
Turkey	11	21
France	12	19.5
Taiwan	13	18.6
Spain	14	17.8
Mexico	15	16.2
Canada	16	15.3
United Kingdom	17	13.2
Belgium	18	10.4
South Africa	19	9.5
Iran	20	9.4

Data from: International Iron and Steel Institute, "World Steel in Figures," 2006. http://www.worldsteel.org/pictures/publicationfiles/WSIF06%20Final.pdf, last accessed August 2008.

eras, refined textiles, and ceramics. Farther east, the industrial district of Silesia was originally part of Germany but now lies in Poland and extends into the Czech Republic (Fig. 12.8). The development of the Silesian district was based on high-quality coal resources and lesser iron ores that were later supplemented by imports from Ukraine.

The sophistication of European industry ensured that World War II would be the most destructive conflict ever fought, but the war ended up destroying much of the continent's industrial infrastructure in the process. This outcome created considerable challenges in the decade following the war, but from an industrial standpoint it was not altogether a minus. German industry had been reduced to rubble, but with American aid new factories sprang up that incorporated the latest technology. In time, such factories had a competitive edge over older industrial establishments in North America and less-hard-hit parts of Europe.

North America

By the beginning of the twentieth century, the only serious rival to Europe was a realm heavily settled by Europeans with particularly close links to Britain (and links to the capital and innovations that fueled industrialization there): North America. Manufacturing in North America began in New England as early as late colonial times, but the northeastern States are not especially rich in mineral resources.

North America benefited from the capacity of its companies to acquire needed raw materials from overseas sources. It did not need to go overseas for the raw materials to produce energy, however. Coal was the chief fuel for industries at the time, and there was never any threat of a coal shortage. U.S. coal reserves are among the world's largest and are widely distributed—from Appalachian Pennsylvania to the northwestern Great Plains (Fig. 12.9). The United States still vies with China as the world's largest coal producer.

The steel plants along the northeastern seaboard of the United States were built there largely because they used iron ore shipped from Venezuela, Labrador (Canada), Liberia, and other overseas sources. Instead of transferring the iron ore from oceangoing ships onto trains and transporting them inland, the plants used them right where they arrived—practically at the point of unloading at such huge steel-mill complexes as Sparrows Point, near Baltimore, and Fairless, near Philadelphia. So in this case distant ore deposits affected the location of industry in the United States.

In the decades after World War I, the United States emerged as the world's preeminent industrial power.

Figure 12.8
Major Industrial Regions of Europe. This maps shows the major industrial districts of
Europe.   © E. H. Fouberg, A. B. Murphy, H. J. de Blij, and John Wiley & Sons, Inc.

Having escaped the destruction that World War I brought
to much of western Europe, the United States capitalized
on its newfound global political stature, its developed
infrastructure, and its highly trained workforce to build an
industrial economy that was second to none. The Great
Depression that began in 1929 was an enormous setback, of course, but only in absolute terms. The effects
of the depression were felt worldwide, and if anything,
the United States came out of it with an expanded industrial dominance. That dominance grew even greater after
World War II, when once again the United States avoided
destruction within its own boundaries and yet received a

Figure 12.9
Major Deposits of Fossil Fuels in North America. North America is the world's largest energy consumer, and the realm is also endowed with substantial energy sources. © H. J. de Blij, P. O. Muller and John Wiley & Sons, Inc.

major industrial boost from the wartime effort. Canada, too, was in a strong position, and a major American Manufacturing Belt emerged in the rectangular region shown in Figure 12.10.

The American Manufacturing Belt

The American Manufacturing Belt extends from the northeastern seaboard to Iowa and from the St. Lawrence Valley to the confluence of the Ohio and Mississippi riv-

ers. At the belt's northeastern edge, the light industries of New England and New York give way to heavier manufacturing. Here lies the Southeast Pennsylvania district, centered on metropolitan Philadelphia and encompassing the Baltimore area. Throughout much of the twentieth century, iron ores were smelted right on the waterfront in tidewater steel mills. Major chemical industries (notably in northern Delaware), pharmaceutical industries, and lighter manufacturing plants were established there as well.

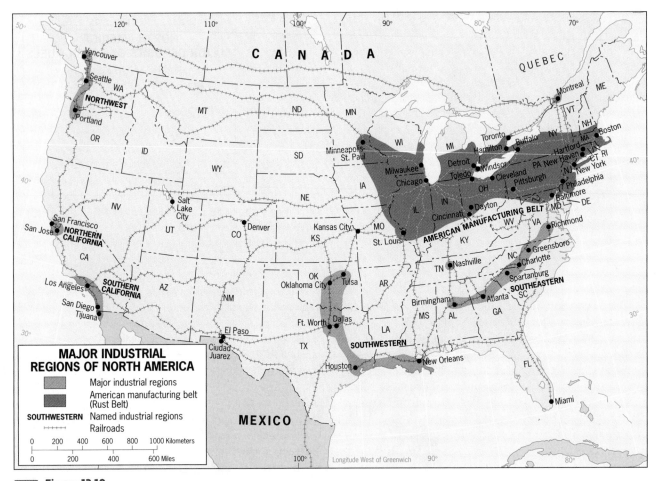

Figure 12.10

Major Manufacturing Regions of North America. North American manufacturing has dispersed westward and southward, but the eastern core area remains dominant. © E. H. Fouberg, A. B. Murphy, H. J. de Blij, and John Wiley & Sons, Inc.

Industrialization began early in New York, which today is at the heart of the American megalopolis and home to tens of thousands of industrial establishments. An early start, large urban growth, and agglomeration played roles in this development. The New York area is not especially endowed with mineral resources, but, like Paris and London, it is a large market. It also has a huge skilled and semiskilled labor force, is the focus of an intensive transport network, and has long been one of the world's great ports. The port serves as a major **break-of-bulk point**, where cargo is transported from one mode of transportation (for example, a ship) to another mode of transportation (truck or train). Such transfers generate employment, activity, and wealth.

Farther west lies the well-defined upstate New York district, extending from Albany, on the Hudson River, to Buffalo, on the shore of Lake Erie. Growth there was originally stimulated by the Erie Canal, which was dug in the early nineteenth century to connect the East Coast to the Great Lakes. During the mid-twentieth century, spe-

cialty manufactures developed in this region. Rochester came to be known for cameras and optical products, Schenectady for electrical appliances, and Buffalo for steel.

Canada's Southern Ontario district extends from the western end of Lake Ontario to the industrial zone at the western end of Lake Erie. As Figure 12.10 shows, this district links two parts of the U.S. Manufacturing Belt anchored by Buffalo and Detroit; the most direct route between these two industrial cities is through Ontario.

Canadian and U.S. manufacturing complexes meet in two great horseshoe-shaped zones around the western ends of Lakes Ontario and Erie. In the Northeast is a horseshoe-shaped cluster of industries, which curls from Oshawa through Toronto and Hamilton to Buffalo. Westward, around the western end of Lake Erie, is another horseshoe-shaped cluster of industries, which extends from Windsor in Ontario through Detroit and Toledo to Cleveland. The first of these zones is mainly Canadian, and the second is largely American.

The Montreal area along the upper St. Lawrence River also forms part of the Canadian industrial zone. This area is no match for the Ontario district, but it has one big advantage: cheap hydroelectric power. Aluminum-refining and papermaking industries therefore are located there.

Westward lies the remainder of the U.S. industrial heartland. This comprises the interior industrial district, with nodes such as the Pittsburgh–Cleveland area, the Detroit–Southeast Michigan area, Chicago–Gary–Milwaukee, and smaller areas centered on Minneapolis, St. Louis, Cincinnati, and other areas. There industrial power truly transformed the landscape during the twentieth century as Appalachian coal and Mesabi iron ore were converted into autos, bulldozers, harvesters, armored cars, and tanks.

The Former Soviet Union

The Soviet effort to industrialize focused on manufacturing in the western part of Russia, the region of the Soviet Union that was the base of the Russian culture and the location of the country's capital, Moscow. In Moscow, the city and its surrounding area offered an important local market, converging transport routes, a large labor force, and strong centrality—just like Paris, London, and New York. Light manufacturing could already be found in this district during Tsarist times, but under communist rule heavy industries were added. Nizhni Novgorod (southeast of Moscow), with its huge automobile factories, became the "Soviet Detroit."

The Soviet Union had an enormous expanse of resources and raw materials within its borders. East of Moscow, the Ural Mountains yield an incredible variety of metallic ores, including iron, copper, nickel, chromite, bauxite, and many more. In the first decades of the 1900s, Russia tapped a large supply of coal and iron ore in Siberia. Russia's eastern region afforded a great deal of resources and raw materials for the industrialization of Russia's west. Between the Kuzbas and Lake Baykal lies the Krasnoyarsk–Baykal Corridors region. Served by the Trans-Siberian Railroad and several important rivers, this 1600-kilometer-long (1000-mile-long) region contains impressive resources, including coal, timber, and water.

The St. Petersburg area is one of Russia's oldest manufacturing centers. It was chosen by Tsar Peter the Great not only to serve as Russia's capital but also to become the country's modern industrial focus. The skills and specializations that Peter the Great nurtured with the help of western European artisans still mark the area's key industries: high-quality machine building, optical products, and medical equipment. Industries such as shipbuilding, chemical production, food processing, and textile making were also located there.

The Volga experienced major development beginning in the mid-1930s, where the combination of accessible raw materials and ease of transport facilitated its development. When the Ukraine and Moscow areas were threatened by the German armies in World War II, whole industrial plants were dismantled and reassembled in Volga cities—protected from the war by distance. Samara (formerly Kuibyshev) even served as the Soviet capital for a time during World War II. This was part of a more general eastward shift of industry that occurred during World War II, when Russia was invaded from the west.

After the war, the industrialization program continued. A series of dams, constructed on the Volga River, made electrical power plentiful. Known oil and natural gas reserves were larger there than anywhere else in the former USSR. Canals linked the Volga to both Moscow and the Don River, making it easy to import raw materials. The cities lining the Volga, spaced at remarkably regular intervals, were assigned particular industrial functions in the state-planned economy of the Soviet Union. Samara became an oil refinery center, Saratov acquired a chemical industry, and Volgograd became known for its metallurgical industries. The Volga was set on a course that has allowed it to remain one of Russia's dominant industrial regions to this day (Fig. 12.11).

The Ukraine Manufacturing Belt

Before its incorporation into the Soviet Empire, in the last decades of the nineteenth century, Ukraine and other western portions of the former Soviet Union started to industrialize. After World War I, the Soviet Union annexed Ukraine (the people of the Ukraine fought annexation every step of the way and suffered greatly under Stalin's purges) and used the rich resources and industrial potential of Ukraine to become an industrial power. Ukraine produced as much as 90 percent of all the coal mined in the then Soviet Union, and, with iron ores from the Krivoy Rog reserve (in Ukraine) and later from Russia's Kursk Magnetic Anomaly, the Soviet Union grew into one of the world's largest manufacturing complexes during the mid-twentieth century.

Eastern Asia

Japan and China were the most significant areas of East Asia that avoided direct European colonization—and these are the Asian countries where large-scale industrialization first took root. Of the two, Japan was clearly the early dominant player. China's industrialization came later, and we discuss China as one of the newly industrialized countries later in this chapter.

In less than a century after the beginning of the Industrial Revolution, Japan became one of the world's leading industrial countries. This accomplishment is all the more remarkable when one realizes that Japan has limited natural resources. Much of what Japan manufactures is made from raw materials imported from all over

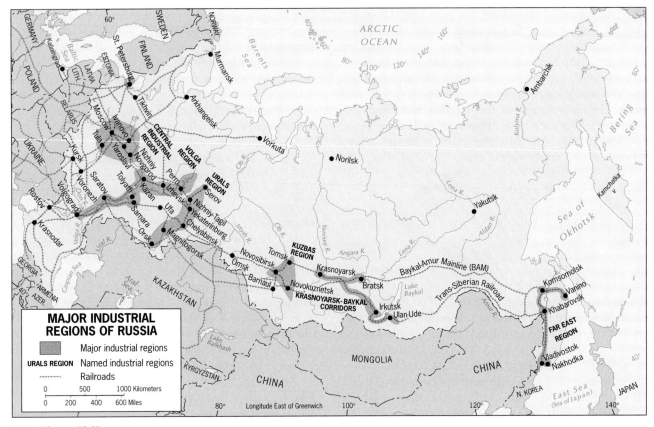

Figure 12.11

Major Manufacturing Regions of Russia. The major manufacturing regions of Russia reflect the dominance of the west in the country's economic geography.   © H. J. de Blij, P. O. Muller and John Wiley & Sons, Inc.

the world. Japan's national territory is just one twenty-fifth the size of the United States, and its population is less than half the U.S. total. Its transformation into the world's second-largest economy has often been described as a miracle.

Yet, Japan's economic development was not a miracle; like Europe's, it was built on capital from colonization and on government policies that had the specific goal of industrialization. Japan's economic development began during the second half of the nineteenth century, when it embarked on a campaign of industrialization and colonization. Between 1866 and 1869, under the banner of the Meiji Restoration, reformers mechanized Japan's domestic industries, moved the capital from the interior to the coast, organized its armed forces, and obtained advice from British experts on issues ranging from education to transportation (which is why the Japanese drive on the left side of the road). The Japanese also established colonies, and soon raw materials and capital were flowing to Japan from an expanding colonial empire in Korea, Taiwan, and mainland China.

The 1930s and early 1940s brought triumph and disaster: triumph in the form of a military campaign that included vast conquests in the Pacific, East Asia, and Southeast Asia and a surprise attack on Pearl Harbor in Hawaii, and disaster when Japanese forces were driven back with great loss of life. The war ended with the utter destruction of two Japanese cities by American atomic bombs. When U.S. forces took control of Japan in 1945, the nation's economy was in shambles. Yet a few decades later Japan had not only recovered but had become a global economic power.

The Japanese Manufacturing Belt

Japan's dominant region of industrialization and urbanization is the *Kanto Plain* (Fig. 12.12), which contains about one-third of the nation's population and includes the Tokyo–Yokohama–Kawasaki metropolitan area. This gigantic cluster of cities and suburbs forms the eastern anchor of the country's core area. The Kanto Plain possesses a fine natural harbor at Yokohama and is centrally located with respect to the country as a whole. It has also benefited from Tokyo's designation as the country's capital. When Japan embarked on its planned course of economic development, many industries and businesses chose Tokyo as their headquarters in order to be near

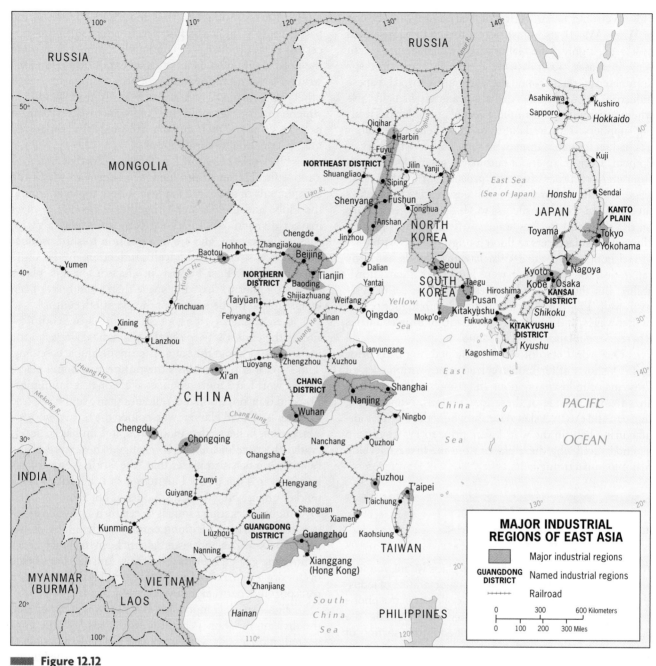

Figure 12.12
Major Manufacturing Regions of East Asia. In China, the Northeast district was the first to take off. The Chang district followed, and most recently, the Guangdong district has been growing.
© E. H. Fouberg, A. B. Murphy, H. J. de Blij, and John Wiley & Sons, Inc.

government decision makers. During the mid-twentieth century, the Tokyo–Yokohama–Kawasaki metropolitan area became Japan's leading manufacturing complex, producing more than 20 percent of the country's annual output.

Japan's second largest industrial complex extends from the eastern end of the Seto Inland Sea to the Nagoya area and includes the Kobe–Kyoto–Osaka triangle. This, the *Kansai district*, comes close to rivaling the Kanto area:

it is a vast industrial region with steel mills, a major chemical industry, automobile manufacturing, shipbuilding, textile factories, and many other types of production. The Kansai district lies on the eastern edge of the Seto Inland Sea, Japan's pivotal waterway. During the nineteenth century, raw materials from Korea and later from northeast China moved in large quantities along the Seto Inland Sea, bringing a stream of raw materials into the Kansai district.

Even after Japan lost its colonial empire with the end of World War II, its industries continued to be sustained by a large, highly skilled labor force (which, before recent wage increases, was relatively cheap). Japanese products dominated markets around the world and allowed Japanese industries to purchase needed raw materials virtually anywhere. Australia, for example, became one of Japan's leading suppliers. The availability of cheap semiskilled labor has had an immense impact on regional industrial development. Even in an era of automated assembly lines and computerized processing, the prospect of a large, low-wage, trainable labor force continues to attract manufacturers. Japan's postwar success was based in large measure on the skills and the low wages of its labor force, which allowed manufacturers to flood foreign markets with low-priced goods. Into the 1950s, Japanese goods had little reputation for quality but were known for their affordability. But then Japan's factories began to excel in quality as well. This development in turn led to higher prices, higher wages, and, inevitably, competition from countries where cheaper labor could be found.

Our world map of major manufacturing belts prior to 1950 shows other industrialized zones within each of these major industrial regions and some smaller industrialized zones outside of these four regions. Nonetheless, the map and this overview describe where the largest manufacturing belts in the world were prior to 1950 and help us understand why these places were the first to develop major manufacturing belts.

Think of an industrial area near the place where you live, either an industrial park or a major conglomeration of industries. Drive through the area or look online or in the phone book to see what industries are located there. Consider the models of industrial location described in this section of the chapter and determine whether any of the models help explain the mix of industries present in this place.

HOW HAS INDUSTRIAL PRODUCTION CHANGED?

The manufacturing boom of the twentieth century can be traced to early innovations in the production process. Perhaps the most significant of these innovations was the mass-production assembly line pioneered by Henry Ford, which allowed for the inexpensive production of consumer goods at a single site on a previously unknown scale. So significant was Ford's idea that the dominant mode of mass production that endured for much of the past century is known as **Fordist**. In addition to the process of mass production, economic geographers also see the Fordist system as including a set of political-economic structures (corporations and countries supporting each other) and financial orders (such as Bretton Woods in which countries adopted the gold standard, agreeing to peg the values of their currency to gold) that supported mass production by corporations.

The world-economy is now a **post-Fordist** system—a more flexible set of production practices in which the components of goods are made in different places around the globe and then brought together is needed to meet market demand. Multinational companies play a major role in this system, and are in a position to shift production to new sites when a given production site becomes uncompetitive. Post-Fordist production brings places closer together in time and space than would have been imaginable at the beginning of the twentieth century.

Geographically, the concept of time–space compression is the easiest way to see the dramatic changes in the ways we think about time and space in the global economy. Time–space compression is the notion that some places in the world are more connected through communication and transportation technologies than ever before (see Chapter 4). David Harvey, who coined the term *time–space compression*, believes that modern capitalism has so accelerated the pace of life and so changed the nature of the relationship between places that "the world seems to collapse inwards upon us." Fluctuations in the Tokyo stock market impact New York just hours, if not minutes, later. Overnight, marketing campaigns can turn a product innovation into a fad in far-flung corners of the globe. Kiwis picked in New Zealand yesterday can be in the lunch boxes of boys and girls in Canada tomorrow. And decisions made in London can make or break a fast-developing deal over a transport link between Kenya and Tanzania.

Time–space compression has fundamentally altered the division of labor. When the world was less interconnected, most goods were produced close to the point of consumption. Thus, the major industrial belt in the United States was in the Northeast both because of the readily available coal and other raw materials and because of the major concentration of the North American population there. With **just-in-time delivery** (rather than keeping a large inventory of components or products, companies keep just what they need for short-term production and new parts are shipped quickly when needed), corporations can draw from labor around the globe for different components of production, creating a **global division of labor**.

The major global economic players, such as General Motors, Philips, Union Carbide, and Exxon, take advantage of low transportation costs, favorable governmental regulations, and expanding information technology to construct vast economic networks in which different facets of production are carried out in different places in order to benefit from the advantages of specific locations. Publicly traded companies (companies whose stock you can buy or sell publicly on the stock exchange) are pressured by shareholders to grow their profits annually. One way to grow profits is to cut costs, and labor (wages, benefits, insurance) makes up a sizable proportion of production costs. Most multinational corporations have moved the labor-intensive manufacturing, particularly assembly activities, to peripheral countries where labor is cheap, regulations are few, and tax rates are low. The manufacturing that remains in the core is usually highly mechanized. Technologically sophisticated manufacturing also tends to be sited in the core because both the expertise and the infrastructure are there.

Research and development activities tend to be concentrated in the core, where high levels of education and access to technology are the norm. The global division of labor has reshaped the role different economic sectors play within countries. With mechanized, highly efficient agriculture (see Chapter 11) and with the move of manufacturing jobs to the semiperiphery and periphery, core countries now have large labor forces employed in the tertiary sector of the economy.

Supporting the global division of labor are elaborate trading networks and financial relations. Trade itself is a tertiary economic activity of considerable importance to the global economy. Regardless of where goods are produced, consumption still takes place in the core and increasingly among the wealthy and middle classes of the semiperiphery. The newly industrializing countries of the semiperiphery send manufactured goods to the core (thus the "made in China" labels found on goods throughout the United States). Trade flows among countries in the periphery are typically low because, for peripheral countries, the dominant flow of goods is exports to the core.

Televisions—the Core, the Semiperiphery, and the Periphery

Following the production of televisions around the globe gives us insight into the workings of the global division of labor and the shifts in production that occur as goods become standard commodities of trade. Commercial production of television sets began after World War II, with a variety of small and medium-sized firms in Europe, Asia, and North America involved in production. Firms in the United States, such as Zenith, were the dominant producers of televisions until the 1970s. During the 1970s and 1980s a dramatic shift occurred, with a small number of large Asian producers—particularly in Japan—seizing a much larger percentage of the market and with a few European firms increasing their position as well. By 1990, ten large firms were responsible for 80 percent of the

world's color television sets; eight of them were Japanese and two European. Only one firm in the United States, Zenith, remained, and its share of the global market was relatively small.

The television production industry has three key elements: research and design; manufacture of components; and assembly. Research and design was and continues to be located in the home countries of the major television manufacturers. During the 1970s, the major firms began to move the manufacture of components and assembly out of the country. U.S. firms moved these functions to the *maquiladora* of Mexico (discussed in Chapter 10) and the special economic zones of China (described in Chapter 9); Japanese firms moved component manufacturing and assembly to Taiwan, Singapore, Malaysia, and South Korea. Because the assembly stage was the most labor intensive, television manufacturers tapped into labor pools around the world, locating assembly plants not just in Mexico, China, and Southeast Asia, but also in India and Brazil. By the 1990s, television manufacturing methods had changed to employ greater mechanization in the production and assembly process. Starting in the 1980s, the major television producers in Japan (by then dominating the market) moved a number of their offshore production sites to Europe and the United States, regions with suitable infrastructure, skilled labor, and accessible markets. Recently, the process began again, with research and development in high-definition and plasma televisions leading to production of these high-end televisions in Japan. Production is expanding into China and South Korea today.

Tracing the production of televisions throughout the world over time helps us see how the global division of labor currently works. (Similarly, the production of textiles described in Chapter 10 is shaped by the global division of labor.) Labor is moved to the periphery and semiperiphery to take advantage of lower labor costs. And as methods of assembly and the product itself change, the production may be moved again to take advantage of infrastructure, skilled labor, and accessible markets.

New Influences on the Geography of Manufacturing

Any multinational company (whether producing televisions or anything else) is involved in designing products and finding buyers for the products. Many multinationals hire out the other steps in manufacturing, including extraction of raw materials, manufacturing products, marketing, and distribution, to outside companies or subsidiaries. In the post-Fordist era, the major influences on industrial location include the low wages we have already discussed, along with intermodal transportation, regional and world trade agreements, and availability of energy.

Importance of Transportation in Industrial Location

One factor we can map is transportation. Efficient transportation systems enable manufacturers to purchase raw materials from distant sources and to distribute finished products to a widely dispersed population of consumers. Manufacturers desire maximum transport effectiveness at the lowest possible cost. They will also consider the availability of alternative systems in the event of emergencies (e.g., truck routes when rail service is interrupted). Since World War II, major developments in transportation have focused on improving **intermodal connections**, places where two or more modes of transportation meet (including air, road, rail, barge, and ship), in order to ease the flow of goods and reduce the costs of transportation.

The current volume of resources and goods shipped around the globe daily could not be supported without the invention of the container system, whereby goods are packed in containers that are picked up by special, mechanized cranes from a container ship at an intermodal connection and placed on the back of a semi-trailer truck, on a barge, or on a railroad car. This innovation lowered costs and increased flexibility, permitting many manufacturers to pay less attention to transportation in their location decisions. Refrigerated containers also ease the shipment of perishable goods around the globe.

Jacques Charlier has studied the major changes to the Benelux (Belgium, the Netherlands, and Luxembourg) seaport system and the role containerization played in these changes. Charlier stressed the importance of containerization to the growth of sea trade in the Benelux ports and explained the locational advantage of Rotterdam, which is no more than six hours by rail or truck from 85 percent of the population of western Europe.

The container system and the growth in shipping at Rotterdam and other Benelux ports have promoted the growth of other industries in the region, helping to make the Netherlands, in Charlier's words, a warehouse for Europe. The Netherlands is now home to more than 1800 U.S. firms, including call centers, distribution centers, and production centers, especially for food. In 2003, over 50 percent of all goods entering the European Union went through Rotterdam or Amsterdam (also in the Netherlands).

Importance of Regional and Global Trade Agreements

Regional trade organizations such as the North American Free Trade Agreement (NAFTA) and the European Union (EU) have trade agreements that influence where imported goods (and components of goods) are produced. Similarly, governments have individual agreements with each other about production and imports, and most governments (153 states in 2008) are part of the World Trade Organization (WTO), which works to negotiate rules of trade among the member states.

The WTO promotes freer trade by negotiating agreements among member states, agreements that push the world in the direction of free trade, typically dismissing import quota systems and discouraging protection by a country of its domestically produced goods. Agreements negotiated under the WTO are typically enacted in steps in order to avoid a major shock to any state's economy. In 2001 when Europe and the United States agreed to allow China to become a member of the WTO, they also agreed to remove the quota system that restricts the importation of Chinese goods into Europe and the United States (discussed in Chapter 10). Soon after these quotas were eliminated, both the United States and the European Union issued "safeguard quotas" against Chinese imports. The safeguard quotas were part of the agreement that permitted the admission of China to the WTO, and the United States and the European Union will not be able to use them in a few years. In the meantime, the safeguards are slowing the importation of Chinese textiles once again, buffering their impact on domestic textile producers.

In addition to the growth of the purview of the WTO, the proliferation of regional trade associations in the last two decades is unprecedented. The list of acronyms for regional trade associations is almost overwhelming: EU, NAFTA, MERCOSUR, SAFTA, CARICOM, ANDEAN AFTA, COMESA, to name but a few. The World Trade Organization estimates that close to 300 regional trade organizations are in existence. Regional trade organizations are similar to bilateral agreements on trade between two countries, although they involve more than two countries. Most regional trade agreements encourage movement of production within the trade region and promote trade by diminishing (or deleting) trade quotas and tariffs among member countries. A regional trade agreement sets up a special free trade agreement among parties to the association, leaving nonmember countries to trade through the rules of the WTO or an existing bilateral agreement. Whether regional or global, trade agreements directly affect the location of production and even what is produced in a place.

Importance of Energy in Industrial Location

During the mid-twentieth century, the use of coal as an energy source in industry increasingly gave way to oil and gas. Dependence on external fuel supplies affects three of the four world industrial regions that were the principal regions of industrial development during the mid-twentieth century. Despite discoveries of oil and gas in the North Sea, Europe still depends on foreign shipments of petroleum. The United States has two neighbors with substantial fossil fuel reserves (Mexico's oil and gas may rank among the world's largest), but its own supplies remain rather limited. Japan is almost totally dependent on oil from distant sources.

The role of energy supply as a factor in industrial location decisions has changed over time. During the Industrial Revolution, manufacturing plants were often established on or near coal fields; today major industrial complexes are not found near oil fields. Instead, a huge system of pipelines and tankers delivers oil and natural gas to manufacturing regions throughout the world. For some time during and after the global oil supply crises of the 1970s, fears of future rises in oil costs led some industries that require large amounts of electricity to move to sites where the environment is moderate and heating and air-conditioning costs are low. When the crisis waned, national energy-conservation goals were modified, and in the early 2000s the United States' reliance on foreign energy resources was even greater than it had been in the 1970s. Energy supply has become a less significant factor in industrial location, but securing an energy supply is an increasingly important national priority.

Nowhere was this more true than in the United States. U.S. consumption of petroleum and natural gas today is about 27 percent and 37 percent, respectively, of the annual world total. By 2007, the United States required more than 20.6 million barrels of petroleum per day to keep its power plants, machinery, vehicles, aircraft, and ships functioning. However, U.S. production of oil in recent years has averaged about 10 percent of the world total, and even including the known Alaskan potential,

U.S. oil reserves are estimated to amount to only about 4 percent of the world total. The United States taps its oil resources, and in 2006, the country was the third largest oil producer in the world (Table 12.2). Even with this level of production, the United States remains heavily dependent on foreign oil supplies, with all the uncertainties that involves.

Petroleum is not the only energy source for which the United States leads world demand and consumption. As Figure 12.9 shows, natural gas often occurs in association with oil deposits. The use of natural gas has increased enormously since World War II. One result of the increased use of natural gas is the proliferation of pipelines shown on the map. In North America in 2006, there were over 4 million kilometers (2.5 million miles) of pipelines, including parts of a new pipeline designed to carry Alaskan natural gas across Canada to the U.S. market.

On the other side of the coin, countries with large reserves of oil and natural gas—Saudi Arabia, Kuwait, Iraq, Russia, and others—occupy a special position in the global economic picture. None of these countries except Russia is a major industrial power, but they all played a key role in the industrial boom of the twentieth century. And while oil has brought wealth to some in the Middle East, it has also ensured that outside powers such as the United States and Great Britain are involved and invested in what happens in the region. This has often produced an uneasy relationship at best between countries in the Middle East and the major industrial powers of the "West."

TABLE 12.2
World's Largest Oil Producers.

Country	Rank	Total Oil Production (million barrels per day)
Saudi Arabia	1	10.66
Russia	2	9.67
United States	3	8.33
Iran	4	4.14
China	5	3.84
Mexico	6	3.7
Canada	7	3.29
United Arab Emirates	8	2.95
Venezuela	9	2.80
Norway	10	2.79
Kuwait	11	2.68
Nigeria	12	2.44
Brazil	13	2.17
Algeria	14	2.12
Iraq	15	2.01

Data from: http://tonto.eia.doe.gov/country/index.cfm?view=production, last accessed August 2008.

The sensation of a shrinking world is so strong that a few commentators have proposed that we are entering an era characterized by the "end of geography." Alvin Toffler first suggested this idea in his *Future Shock* (1970). More recently, Richard O'Brien dealt with similar concepts in *Global Financial Integration: The End of Geography* (1992) and Thomas Friedman suggested *The World Is Flat* (2005). Each author argues that a combination of technological changes and developments in the global economy have reduced the significance of location and place to the point where they matter little. Geographers who study industrial production recognize that the nature and meaning of location and place have changed greatly in recent times, but they also note that these changes do not create an undifferentiated world. New production methods have reshaped the economic geography of the planet profoundly and rapidly. We need a greater understanding of how places have changed as a result of new production methods and new corporate structures, as well as an examination of the interplay between global processes and local places.

Think about a cutting-edge, high-technology product that is still quite expensive to purchase and not yet broadly used (perhaps something you have read about but not even seen). Using the Internet, determine where this product is manufactured and assess why the product is manufactured there. Hypothesize which countries production will shift to and how long it will take for production costs (and the price of the product) to decrease substantially.

WHERE ARE THE MAJOR INDUSTRIAL BELTS IN THE WORLD TODAY AND WHY?

Over the last 20 years, many manufacturing regions have experienced **deindustrialization**, a process by which companies move industrial jobs to other regions with cheaper labor, leaving the newly deindustrialized region to switch to a service economy and to work through a period of high unemployment and, if possible, switch to a service economy. At the same time, the places with lower labor costs and the right mix of laws attractive to businesses (often weak environmental laws and pro-free trade laws) become newly industrial regions. The new industrial regions emerge as shifts in politics, laws, capital flow, and labor availability occur.

Both Europe and the United States have large deindustrialized regions. In the United Kingdom, for example, the major industrial zones of Newcastle and Liverpool and Manchester lost much of their industrial bases during the 1960s and 1970s. Similarly, the industrial zone of the northeastern United States (around the Great Lakes) lost much of its industrial base in the same time period with the loss of steel manufacturing jobs to areas of the world with lower wages. This region of the United States, which used to be called the Manufacturing Belt, is now commonly called the Rust Belt, evoking the image of long-abandoned, rusted-out steel factories.

The economic processes leading to deindustrialization in some parts of the world have led to industrialization in other parts of the world. In this section of the chapter, we look at the major manufacturing belts that have developed since World War II. More than two centuries after the onset of the Industrial Revolution, East Asia has become the cauldron of industrialization. Some of the economic policies we discussed in Chapter 10, such as structural adjustments and import quotas, help encourage foreign direct investment in a country, and many draw industrial developers seeking to take advantage of economic breaks and inexpensive labor. From Japan to Guangdong and from South Korea to Singapore, the islands, countries, provinces, and cities fronting the Pacific Ocean are caught up in a frenzy of industrialization that has made the geographic term *Pacific Rim* synonymous with manufacturing. In this section of the chapter, we examine one newly industrialized region of the Pacific Rim, eastern China.

Eastern China

Although some industrial growth occurred in China during the period of European colonial influence, and later during the Japanese occupation, China's major industrial expansion occurred during the communist period. When the communist planners took over in 1949, one of their leading priorities was to develop China's resources and industries as rapidly as possible.

China is a vast country and has a substantial resource base. The quality of its coal is good, the quantity enormous, and many of the deposits are near the surface and easily extracted. China's iron ores are not as productive and are generally of rather low grade, but new finds are regularly being made.

Until the early 1960s, Soviet planners helped promote China's communist-era industrial development. China was spatially constrained by the location of raw materials, the developments that had taken place before the 1949 communist takeover, the pattern of long-term urbanization in the country, the existing transport network, and the eastern clustering of the population. Like their then-Soviet allies, China's rulers were determined to speed up the industrialization of the economy, and their decisions created several major and lesser industrial districts.

Under state planning rules, the *Northeast district* (formerly known as Manchuria and called Dongbei in China today) became China's industrial heartland, a complex of heavy industries based on the region's coal and iron deposits located in the basin of the Liao River. Shenyang became the "Chinese Pittsburgh," with metallurgical, machine-making, engineering, and other large factories. Anshan, to the south, emerged as China's leading iron- and steel-producing center. Harbin to the north (China's northernmost large city, with more than 5.4 million inhabitants) produced textiles, farm equipment, and light manufactures of many kinds (Fig. 12.12).

The second largest industrial region in China, the *Shanghai and the Chang Jiang district*, developed in and around the country's biggest city, Shanghai. The communist planners never allowed Shanghai to attain its full potential, often favoring the Beijing–Tianjin complex. The Chang Jiang district, containing both Shanghai and Wuhan, rose to prominence and, by some measures, exceeded the Northeast as a contributor to the national economy. As Figure 12.12 shows, still another industrial complex developed farther upstream along the Chang Jiang River focused on the city of Chongqing. Whether we view the Chang Jiang district as one industrial zone or more, it became a pacesetter for Chinese industrial growth, if not in terms of iron and steel production, then in terms of its diversified production and local specializations. Railroad cars, ships, books, foods, chemicals—an endless variety of products—come from the thriving Chang Jiang district.

China's large labor force could attract hundreds of companies in the world-economy's global division of labor. Add to the enormous labor force a low daily wage, and it becomes clear why thousands of companies have moved their manufacturing to China. Rather than move entire companies to China, typically production of component parts is moved to China to lower the cost of the product. Thousands of companies take advantage of the lower wages and favorable tax regulations in China's special economic zones, which have transformed cities and towns in the region.

In Chinese cities such as Dalian, Shanghai, Zhuhai, Xiamen, and Shenzhen, pollution-belching smokestacks rise above a smog-choked urban landscape. Streets are jammed with traffic ranging from animal-drawn carts and overloaded bicycles to trucks and buses. Bulldozers are sweeping away vestiges of the old China; cottages with porches and tile roofs on the outskirts of the expanding city must make way for often faceless tenements (Fig. 12.13). Decaying vestiges of the old city stand amid glass-encased towers that symbolize the new economic order.

At the same time, the Northeast has become China's Rust Belt. Many of its state-run factories have been sold or closed, or are operating below capacity. Unemployment is high, and economic growth has stopped. Eventually, the Northeast is likely to recover because of its resources and its favorable geographic site. But under the new economic policies the dynamic eastern and southern provinces have

Field Note

"Beijing, Shanghai, and other Chinese cities are being transformed as the old is swept away in favor of the new. Locals, powerless to stop the process, complain that their neighborhoods are being destroyed and that their relocation to remote apartment complexes is a hardship. Urban planners argue that the 'historic' neighborhoods are often dilapidated, decaying, and beyond renovation. The housing shown in Figure 12-13 top was demolished to make room for what is going up in Figure 12-13 bottom, a scene repeated countless times throughout urbanizing China."

Figure 12.13 top
Beijing, China. © H. J. de Blij.

Figure 12.13 bottom
Beijing, China. © H. J. de Blij.

grown into major manufacturing belts and have changed the map of this part of the Pacific Rim.

Today, China is pushing industrialization into the interior of the country. A fall 2004 issue of *The Economist* highlighted the growth of China's industrial economy and the push to spread the wealth into the interior of the country, rather than just the coastal export-oriented zones. On the coast, Shanghai recently trumped the Netherlands' Rotterdam as the world's busiest port. The Chinese government's new focus is on generating greater economic activity in the interior. *The Economist* reported that

> [t]hough China's seaboard is still far richer than its interior, the coast has a mighty and growing hinterland, extending back hundreds of miles. The economic dynamo that is Shanghai has lit up a corridor running much of the length of the Yangtze. And, as we report, Guangdong province in the south, long one of the world's great workshops, now aspires to extend its reach a thousand miles inland, almost to the border with India. Its party secretary is promoting a plan he calls "9 + 2"; the creation of an integrated free-trade area as populous as the European Union, including nine provinces and the special administrative regions of Hong Kong and Macau. It is home to nearly a third of China's population.

China is a major recipient of industrial work that is **outsourced** or moved **offshore**. Each of the steps in commodity production that used to take place within the confines of a single factory is now often outsourced to suppliers, which focus their production and offer cost savings. When outsourced work is located outside of the country, it is called *offshore*. The movement of industry into China's interior will likely occur through the outsourcing of production from China's coasts to the interior.

How does a place change when deindustrialization occurs? Consider a place that has experienced deindustrialization, and research recent news articles on the Internet to find out how the economy of the place has changed since the loss of industry. What has happened to the place and its economy?

WHAT IS THE SERVICE ECONOMY, AND WHERE ARE SERVICES CONCENTRATED?

By the end of World War II, the increasing saturation of consumer markets, the tremendous growth in governmental activity, rising labor activism, and declines in the

cost of transportation and communication began to challenge the Fordist order. The challenge shifted into high gear in the early 1970s, when a sharp rise in oil prices during a period of international financial instability and inflation produced a dramatic downturn in the global economy. Under these circumstances, it became increasingly difficult for the core industrial regions to sustain their competitive advantage without significant readjustment. The direction that readjustment would take was toward mechanization and the development of service and information industries. These changes worked together with the need for new markets and the growth of multinational concerns to bring about a postindustrial or post-Fordist economic order in many of the core economies.

Service industries (tertiary industries) do not generate an actual, tangible product; instead, they encompass the range of services that are found in modern societies. So many different types of activities can be thought of as service activities that, as we saw in Chapter 11, specialized aspects of the service economy were given their own designations: *quaternary industries* for the collection, processing, and manipulation of information and capital (finance, administration, insurance, legal services, computer services) and *quinary industries* for activities that facilitate complex decision making and the advancement of human capacities (scientific research, higher education, high-level management).

Distinguishing among types of services is useful, given the extraordinary growth in the size and complexity of the service sector. In the global economic core, service industries employ more workers than the primary and secondary industries combined, yet these service industries range from small-scale retailing to tourism services to research on the causes of cancer. Placing all of these activities in a single category seems unwarranted.

Specificity in terminology is also useful in highlighting different phases in the development of the service sector. In the early decades of the twentieth century, the domestic and quasidomestic tertiary industries were experiencing rapid growth in the industrialized world. With the approach of World War II, the quaternary sector began expanding rapidly, and this expansion continued after the war. During the last three decades, both the quaternary and quinary sectors have experienced very rapid growth, giving greater meaning to the term *postindustrial*.

The expanding service sector in the core economies is only one aspect of the changing global economy. Accompanying, and in some cases driving, this expansion are several other developments that have already been mentioned: the increasing mechanization of production, particularly in manufacturing enterprises operating in the core; the growth of large multinational corporations; and the dispersal of the production process, with components for complex products such as automobiles and consumer electronics coming from factories in many different countries.

Geographical Dimensions of the Service Economy

Deindustrialization and the growth of the service economy unfolded in the context of a world-economy that was already characterized by wide socioeconomic disparities. Only areas that had industry could deindustrialize, of course, and at the global scale the wealthier industrial regions were the most successful in establishing a postindustrial service economy. We should not be surprised that deindustrialization did little to change the basic disparities between core and periphery that have long characterized the global economy. Indeed, even in the manufacturing realm, mechanization and innovative production strategies have allowed the core industrial regions to retain their dominance. In the first decade of the twenty-first century, eastern Asia, western Russia and Ukraine, western Europe, and North America still account for well over 75 percent of the world's total output of manufactured goods.

Despite its continued dominance in the manufacturing arena, the core has experienced some wrenching changes associated with the economic shifts of the past three decades. Anyone who has ever spent time in northern Indiana, the British Midlands, or Silesia (southern Poland and northeastern Czech Republic) knows that there are pockets of significant hardship within the core (Fig. 12.14). These examples serve to remind us that not all deindustrialized regions (even in the core) are finding their way into the tertiary sector. Location, albeit often defined in new ways, affects where and what kinds of service economies are developed.

Some secondary industrial regions have made the transition to a service economy while retaining the manufacturing base. The **Sunbelt** is the southern region of the United States, stretching through the Southeast to the Southwest. The population and economy of the Sunbelt region have grown over the last few decades, as companies from the service sector have chosen to locate in areas such as Atlanta and Phoenix where the climate is warm and the local laws welcome their presence. The eastern part of the Sunbelt served as a secondary industrial region, with Birmingham developing an iron and steel economy and Atlanta an industrial economy around cotton, tobacco, and furniture. In recent decades, high-tech and financial industries changed the economy and landscape of the Sunbelt, as can be seen in the toponyms of stadiums in the region, such as Alltel Stadium in Jacksonville, Florida, Bank of America Stadium in Charlotte, North Carolina, and Bank One Ballpark in Phoenix, Arizona.

New Influences on Location

With the striking growth of the service sector and information technologies, new factors have come into play that are affecting patterns of economic activity. Most service industries are not tied to raw materials and do not need large amounts of energy. Hence, those factors of production are markedly less important for service industries than for traditional manufacturing concerns. Market accessibility is more relevant for the service sector, but advances in telecommunications have rendered even that factor less important for some types of service industries.

Figure 12.14
Liverpool, England, United Kingdom. With the deindustrialization of the Liverpool region, the city has lost thousands of jobs and the city's population has decreased by one-third. Abandoned streets, such as this one, are a reflection of the city's industrial decline.
© Philip Wolmuth/Panos Pictures.

For most geographers the simple act of daily observation of the world around them becomes a profoundly satisfying habit. For the last 14 years my daily observations have been of the rapidly changing urban/economic landscape of northwest Arkansas, one of the fastest growing metropolitan areas in the United States. Wal-Mart originated in Bentonville, Arkansas and as it became increasingly successful it remained committed to its home in this affordable, rural corner of the Mid-South. By the early 1990s the company's growth had fueled the growth of other service industries and had contributed to the retention of several other major corporations. A recent decision to require Wal-Mart suppliers to locate offices in the region has similarly boosted growth

Figure 12.15
Fayetteville, Arkansas.

in the area. Procter & Gamble put its office in Fayetteville, only 25 miles from Wal-Mart's home in Bentonville. Dozens of other major corporations have a presence in the region, as well. The results have been both positive and negative. Property prices have risen, with rising tax revenues and better public service provision, and the corporations have proven to be generous philanthropists. However, sprawl, congestion, overcrowded schools, and serious waste disposal issues have also followed. This once-rural corner of America has become a metropolitan growth pole, complete with national coffee shops, rush hour congestion, and sprawling golf-course subdivisions of 6000 square foot "European" mansions.

Credit: Fiona M. Davidson, University of Arkansas

To understand these new influences on the location of services, it is useful to go back to our distinction among tertiary, quaternary, and quinary industries. Tertiary services related to transportation and communication are closely tied to population patterns and to the location of primary and secondary industries. As the basic facilitators of interaction, they are strongly linked to the basic geography of production and consumption. Other tertiary services—restaurants, hotels, and retail establishments—are influenced mainly by market considerations. If they are located far from their consumers, they are unlikely to succeed.

Economic geographers working for corporations use these location theories. Employing technologies such as Geographic Information Systems (GIS) and Remote Sensing (see Chapter 1), geographers model the best locations for new businesses, office complexes, government centers, or transportation connections. Major retailers not only shape the landscapes of the places where they choose to put stores, but they also change the landscapes of their hometowns, the location of their headquarters.

An extreme example of this is Wal-Mart's headquarters in Bentonville, Arkansas. If producers of consumer products want to sell their goods in Wal-Mart stores, they must travel to Bentonville, Arkansas to negotiate deals with Wal-Mart. In order to provide low prices to consumers, Wal-Mart negotiates very low prices with major producers. To create lower-priced products, companies have moved production abroad, and to create good relationships with the world's number one retailer (with sales of $374.526 billion in fiscal year 2008), companies have moved into Bentonville, Arkansas (Fig. 12.15).

The locational influences on quaternary services—high-level services aimed at the collection, processing, and manipulation of information and capital—are more diverse. Some of these services are strongly tied geographically to a particular locus of economic activity. Retail banking and various types of administrative services require a high level of interpersonal contact and therefore tend to be located near the businesses they are serving. Other types of quaternary services, however, can operate almost anywhere as long as they have access to digital processing equipment and telecommunications. When you send in your credit card bill, it is unlikely to go to the city where the headquarters of the issuing bank is located. Instead, it is likely to go to North Dakota, South Dakota, Nebraska, or Colorado. Similarly, many "back-office" tasks related to insurance are performed in places such as Des Moines, Iowa, not Chicago or Hartford. Many of the call centers for technical help for computers and related industries (software, hardware) are located in India and the Philippines. With relatively high levels of college attainment, vast numbers of English-speakers, and phones routed through the Internet, "help desks" need not be located down the hall or even down the street. These location curiosities occur because technological advances in the telecommunications sector have made it possible for all sorts of quaternary industries to be located far away from either producers or consumers. What matters most is infrastructure, a workforce that is sufficiently skilled but not too expensive, and favorable tax rates.

Those who work in the quinary sector tend to be concentrated around nodes of quinary activity—governmental seats, universities, and corporate headquarters. Corporate headquarters tend to be located in large metropolitan areas, whereas seats of government and universities can be found in places that were chosen long ago as appropriate sites for administrative or educational activities based on cultural values or political compromises. The American ideal of the university town (which originated in Germany) led to the establishment of many universities at a distance from major commercial and population centers, in such towns as Champaign-Urbana, Illinois; Norman, Oklahoma; and Eugene, Oregon. Political compromises led to the establishment of major seats of government in small towns. Ottawa, Canada, and Canberra, Australia, are examples of this phenomenon. The point is that historical location decisions influence the geography of the quinary sector. And it is not just university professors and government officials who are affected. All sorts of high-level research and development activities are located on the fringes of universities, and a host of specialized consultants are concentrated around governmental centers. These then become major nodes of quinary activity.

High-Technology Corridors

A high-technology corridor is an area designated by local or state government to benefit from lower taxes and high-technology infrastructure with the goal of providing high-technology jobs to the local population. The goal of a high-technology corridor is to attract designers of: computers, semiconductors, telecommunications, sophisticated medical equipment, and the like.

California's Silicon Valley is a well-known example of a high-technology corridor. Several decades ago a number of innovative technology companies located their research and development activities in the area around the University of California, Berkeley, and Stanford University near San Francisco, California. They were attracted by the prospect of developing links with existing research communities and the availability of a highly educated workforce. Once some high-technology businesses located in the Silicon Valley, others were attracted as well. Today, the Silicon Valley is home to dozens of computer companies, many of which are familiar to the computer literate (such as Cisco Systems, Adobe, Hewlett-Packard, Intel, IBM, and Netscape). The resulting collection of high-technology industries produced what Manuel Castells, Peter Hall, and John Hutriyk call a **technopole**, an area planned for high technology where agglomeration built on a synergy among technological companies occurs. A similar sort of technopole developed outside Boston, where the concentration of technology-based businesses close to Harvard and the Massachusetts Institute of Technology gave rise to what is called the Route 128 high-technology corridor. The Route 128 corridor has been largely supported by the federal government rather than the local government, which supports many other technopoles.

Technopoles can be found in a number of countries in western Europe, eastern Asia, North America, and Australia. Few are on the scale of Silicon Valley, but they are noticeable elements of the economic landscape. Many of them have sprung up on the edges of good-sized cities, particularly near airports. In Brussels (Belgium), for example, the route into the city from the airport passes an array of buildings occupied by computer, communication, and electronics firms. In Washington, D.C., the route from Dulles International Airport (located in the Virginia suburbs) to the city passes the headquarter buildings of companies such as AOL, MCI, and Orbital Sciences (the Dulles Corridor). In the Telecom Corridor of Plano-Richardson (just outside of Dallas, Texas), telecom companies such as Nortel and Ericsson have taken root, but so too have numerous high-technology companies that are not telecom related (Fig. 12.16). In each of these technopoloes, the presence of the major multinational companies attracts other startup companies hoping to become major companies, provide services to major companies, or be bought by major companies.

Many of the technology firms are multinationals, and like their counterparts in other countries, they function in an information environment and market their products all over the world. Being near raw materials or even a particular market is unimportant for these firms; what matters to them is proximity to major networks of transportation and communication. High-technology industries have become such an important symbol of the postindustrial

Figure 12.16
Plano-Richardson, Texas. The Plano-Richardson Telecom Corridor is located just north of Dallas and is home to telecom corporate headquarters, such as Electronic Data Systems Corporation's headquarters in this photograph. © EDS/AP/Wide World Photos.

world that local, regional, and national governments often pursue aggressive policies to attract firms in this sector. These industries are thought to be pollution free and to offer positive benefits for the communities in which they are located. Bidding wars sometimes develop between localities seeking to attract such industries. Although high-technology industries do indeed bring a variety of economic benefits, they have some drawbacks as well. Communities that have attracted production facilities find that the manufacture of computer chips, semiconductors, and the like requires toxic chemicals and large quantities of water. And even more research-oriented establishments sometimes have negative environmental impacts in that land must be cleared and buildings constructed to house them. Despite these drawbacks, the high-technology sec-

tor is clearly here to stay, and areas that can tap into it are likely to find themselves in an advantageous economic position in the coming years.

What majors are most popular at your college or university? Consider what service/high-technology corridors may already exist near your college or university. Propose a new service/high-technology corridor for your region based on what your college/university has to offer the industry. Where might it be located? What are the advantages and disadvantages of different possible locations?

Summary

The Industrial Revolution transformed the world economically, politically, and socially. Many of the places where industrialization first took hold have since become deindustrialized, both with the relocation of manufacturing plants and with the outsourcing of steps of the production process domestically and offshore. With changing economics, places change. Some now look like ghost towns, serving merely as a reminder that industrialization took place there. Others have booming economies and are thriving, having kept industry or successfully cultivated a service economy. Other places are still redefining themselves. In the next chapter, we consider another lasting effect of industrialization and deindustrialization: environmental change.

Geographic Concepts

Industrial Revolution
location theory
variable costs
friction of distance
distance decay
least cost theory
agglomeration
deglomeration

locational
    interdependence
primary industrial
    regions
break-of-bulk point
Fordist
post-Fordist
just-in-time delivery

global division of labor
intermodal connections
deindustrialization
outsourced
offshore
Sunbelt
Technopole

Learn More Online

About the port of Rotterdam:
http://www.portofrotterdam.com

About Nike
http://www.nikebiz.com/company_overview/

Watch It Online

About Wal-Mart's influence on Bentonville, Arkansas
http://www.pbs.org/wgbh/pages/frontline/shows/walmart/

CHAPTER 13

Human Environment

Field Note Disaster along Indian Ocean Shores

▬ **Figure 13.1**
Galle, Sri Lanka. The December 26, 2004 Indian Ocean Tsunami destroyed this passenger train in Sri Lanka, ripping apart tracks and killing more than a thousand people.   ©AP/Wide World Photos.

Watching the horrors of the tsunami of December 26, 2004 unfold on screen (Fig. 13.1), I found it quite eerie to see such devastation in places where earlier I walked and drove and rode—like that Sri Lankan train on which I took a group of students in 1978 including my own children—now smashed by the waves, the carriages toppled, killing more than a thousand passengers, some of them tourists. And the beaches near Phuket in Thailand, so serene and beautiful in memory, now proved a fatal attraction leading to disaster for thousands more, tourists and workers alike.

I went online to follow the events of that day and those that followed, horrified by the rising death toll and by the images of destruction and devastation. The in-box of my e-mail began to include messages from former students who remembered my in-field assessment of the tsunami risks in Southeast Asia. But I had not been especially prescient. Just like people farming the fertile soils on the slopes of an active volcano, people living at or near sea level near an earthquake zone live with risk.

A few weeks later I began to hear and read stories about an English girl named Tilly Smith, who had been vacationing with her parents at a hotel on the beach at Phuket and was on Maikhao Beach when she saw the water suddenly recede into the distance. Tilly had just taken a geography class in her school not far from London, and her teacher, Mr. Andrew Kearney, had told the class what happens when a tsunami strikes: the huge approaching wave first sucks the water off the beaches and then the sea foams, rises and returns as a massive, breaking wall that crashes over and inundates the whole shoreline. Tilly saw what was happening and alerted her parents, her father told hotel security, and they ran back and forth, screaming at beachgoers to seek shelter on higher ground in the hotel behind them. About a hundred people followed the Smith family into the building, and they all survived. Of those who stayed behind, none did. Being aware of some of the basics of physical geography has its advantages, and Mr. Kearney clearly had the attention of his students.

Newspaper editors could use some of this awareness. Many headlines referred to the tsunami as a tidal wave, but a tsunami has nothing to do with the tides that affect all oceans and seas. A tsunami results from an undersea earthquake involving a large displacement of the Earth's crust. Most submarine earthquakes do not generate tsunamis, but in some cases, fortunately relatively rarely, a large piece of crust is pushed up or pulled under (or both), and this causes the water overhead to pile up and start rolling away in all directions. If you were on a cruise ship somewhere in the middle of the ocean, nothing catastrophic would mark the passing of this tsunami wave; your ship would be lifted up and then lowered, but it would not overturn. But when such a huge wave reaches a beach, it does what all waves do: it breaks. Most of us have seen this happen with waves several feet (or even tens of feet) high. But imagine a wave over 200 feet high approaching a beach. As it begins to break, it pulls the water away, exposing wide swaths of muddy bottom. Then it comes crashing into the shore, pushing deep inland.

Tsunamis of the magnitude of 2004 occur rarely, but the hazard is continuous. As the Earth's human population has grown, so have the numbers of people vulnerable to such a calamity. As we learn more about the submarine zones where earthquakes are most likely to occur, we can begin to determine where the hazards are greatest. Here we combine two major fields of study in geography, physical geography and human geography. Geographers who work in this arena study human-environmental relationships—the reciprocal relationships between human societies and natural environments. Both, clearly, are dynamic. The environment is not a passive stage, and environmental change affects human societies. At the same time, humans have an impact on their natural environments. The study of hazards, not just from tsunamis but also from volcanic eruptions, terrestrial earthquakes, landslides, floods, avalanches, and other threats, is a key part of this research.

The tsunami that struck coasts along the Indian Ocean from Indonesia to Somalia and from Thailand to the Maldives resulted from a violent earthquake measuring more than 9.0 on the (10-point) Richter scale off the west coast of the island of Sumatra (Indonesia).

There, two of the planet's tectonic plates are colliding, forcing one beneath the other (Fig. 13.2). A continuous tremble of tremors and quakes affects the crust

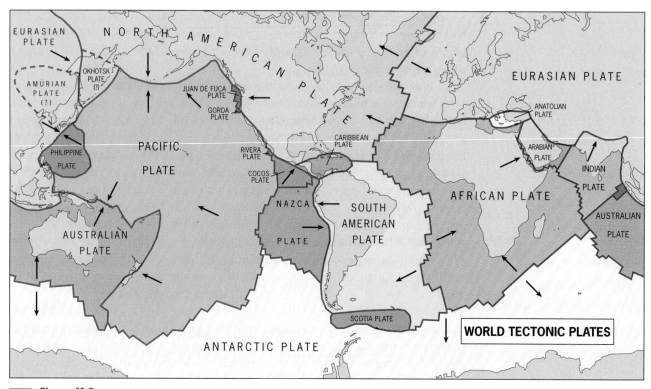

Figure 13.2
World Tectonic Plates.   © H. J. de Blij, P. O. Muller, and John Wiley & Sons, Inc.

in such subduction zones, but sometimes a major shock occurs. In this case, the towering wave generated by the December 26 earthquake had but a short distance to travel to reach northern Sumatra, where it struck in full force. By the time it had done its damage in remote Somalia (in Africa), it had claimed approximately 300,000 lives and ruined the livelihoods of millions more. It illustrated the consequences of our planet's crowding and the impact of a global industry—the tourist industry—in drawing millions of tourists and workers to the very shores where vulnerability is highest.

Geography is a discipline in which the relationship between humans and the environment is a primary concern. One of the most influential nineteenth-century texts on this relationship, *Man and Nature* (1865), was written by the geographer George Perkins Marsh. In 1955, geographers were centrally involved in an international interdisciplinary symposium on "Man's Role in Changing the Face of the Earth." This symposium, like Marsh's earlier book, focused primarily on local and regional changes. More recently, a symposium led by geographers on "The Earth as Transformed by Human Action" picked up where the 1955 discussion left off, addressing global environmental changes. The geographer's concern with how things are organized on the Earth and how they are connected in space provides an analytical platform from which to consider human-induced environmental change.

As the study of environmental change has moved forward, one of the most important lessons we have learned is that global environmental systems are interconnected at numerous temporal and spatial scales. For example, the release of **chlorofluorocarbons** (CFCs) in Japan contributes to a growing hole in the Earth's ozone layer that is centered over Antarctica. Industrial production in the Netherlands and Germany contributes to acid rain in Scandinavia. The use of water from the Rio Grande for irrigation in northern New Mexico affects the amount and quality of the river's water that flows along the Texas-Mexico border. Human actions—the activities we undertake individually and collectively—are increasingly important factors in all sorts of global environmental changes. To confront these changes, we must consider the complex relationship between humans and the environment.

Key Questions For Chapter 13

1. How has the Earth environment changed over time?
2. How have humans impacted Earth's environment?
3. What are the major factors contributing to environmental change today?
4. How are humans responding to environmental change?

HOW HAS THE EARTH ENVIRONMENT CHANGED OVER TIME?

Environmental variation, spatial as well as temporal, is one of the Earth's crucial characteristics. Temperatures rise and fall, precipitation waxes and wanes. Forests flourish and wither, deserts expand and contract. Humanity has evolved during a series of alternatively warm and cold phases of an ice age that is still in progress. But today humanity itself is part of the process. The Earth has been warming, and we are probably contributing to this warmup. The world's governments are trying to find ways to combat industrial pollution and the release of greenhouse gases, gases that in the atmosphere cause warming.

Modern *Homo sapiens* emerged less than 200,000 years ago (and possibly not much more than 100,000 years ago). Virtually everything you have read about in this book—plant and animal domestication, state formation, urbanization, industrialization, and the diffusion of major world religions—has occurred over the past 10,000 years. This raises the question: how representative is the short-term present of the long-term past? Over the past century, geographers and other scientists have been engaged in a joint mission to reconstruct our planet's history on the basis of current evidence. One of them, the climatologist-geographer Alfred Wegener, used his spatial view of the world to make a key contribution. Viewing the increasingly accurate maps of the opposite coastlines of the North and South Atlantic oceans, he proposed a hypothesis that would account for the close "fit" of the shapes of the facing continents, which, he argued, would be unlikely to be a matter of chance. His continental drift hypothesis required the preexistence of a supercontinent, which he called **Pangaea**, that broke apart into the fragments we now know as Africa, the Americas, Eurasia, and Australia (Fig. 13.3). Wegener's hypothesis engendered the later theory of plate tectonics and crustal spreading, and scientists now know that Pangaea and its fragmentation were only the latest episodes in a cycle of continental coalescence and splintering that spans billions of years. This latest Pangaean breakup, however, began only 180 million years ago and continues to this day. Earthquakes and volcanic eruptions we hear about on the news usually take place along the boundaries of the crust's rocky plates.

During our brief presence on this planet, humans have had a powerful impact on environments ranging from rainforests to tundras. Long before we became technologically proficient we exterminated wildlife by the millions and burned grasslands and forests by the hundreds of thousands of square miles. The twentieth-century population explosion, combined with a rapid escalation in human consumption, magnifies humanity's impact on the Earth in unprecedented ways. Adjectives such as "calamitous" and "catastrophic" are often used to describe this impact, yet our planet has been the scene of calamities and catastrophes throughout its existence. *Homo sapiens* has not dominated this world long enough to have much experience with such events, but the environments with which we are familiar today result from long histories—and are temporary. Environmental change is a hallmark of Earth, and understanding long-term change helps us put the present in context and prepare for the future.

Ocean and Atmosphere

Earth today is often called the Blue Planet because more than 70 percent of its surface is covered by water and views from space are dominated by blue hues and swirls of white

CONTINENTAL DRIFT

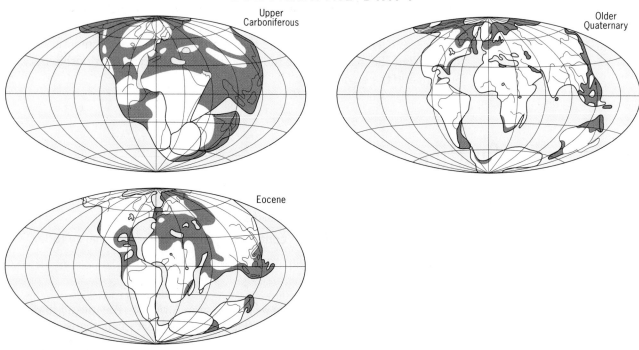

Figure 13.3
Wegener's Hypothesis of Continental Drift. Wegener's dates have been revised but were
remarkably prescient.   *Adapted with permission from:* Wegener, *The Origin of the Continents and Oceans,* 1914.

clouds. We do not know with any certainty how the Earth acquired its watery cloak or exactly when. Some scientists hypothesize that the water was originally trapped inside the Earth during its formation and rose to the surface during the time when heavier constituents sank to form the core. Others calculate that most of the water that did reach the surface in this way would have been evaporated into space by the searing heat then prevailing, suggesting that another source must be identified. This has led to the comet hypothesis, which proposes that icy comets bombarded the Earth for more than a billion years while its atmosphere was still thin, accumulating fresh water from space that filled the basins in the formative crust.

Neither do we know precisely how the atmosphere formed. Originally, the atmosphere was loaded with the gas carbon dioxide (CO_2), and if you could have looked up at the sky it would have been bright red because CO_2 scatters red light. Eventually, however, the primitive ocean, still heated from below, began to absorb CO_2 in huge quantities, depositing limestone and other carbonate rocks and turning the sky a familiar blue. Yet it was to be a very long time before oxygen became a substantial gas in the atmosphere. Around 1500 million years ago, green algae started to spread across the Earth's ocean surfaces, and as their colonies grew, their **photosynthesis** (the conversion of carbon dioxide and water into carbohydrates

and oxygen through the absorption of sunlight) raised the atmosphere's oxygen content. About 800 million years ago, the oxygen content in the atmosphere was about one-twentieth of its present strength, or just 1 percent of the total. But that was enough to support the emergence of the first single-celled animals, the protozoa.

Fire and Ice

Today a major volcanic eruption is rare enough to make the news. Krakatoa (1883), Mount St. Helens (1980), Pinatubo (1991), and Etna (2001) took lives, damaged property, and, in the case of Pinatubo, even changed global climate slightly. One billion years ago, however, the Earth's crust was still immature and subject to huge bursts of volcanic activity. Such episodes poured incalculable volumes of gases and ash into the atmosphere, causing **mass depletions** (loss of diversity through a failure to produce new species) and contributing to the three **mass extinctions** (mass destruction of most species) known to have occurred over the past 500 million years.

The Earth's most recent experience with mass volcanism took place between 180 and 160 million years ago, when the supercontinent Pangaea began to fracture. Lava poured from fissures and vents as South America separated from Africa and India moved northeast. Skies were blackened, the atmosphere choked with ash. Animals responded as they always have in time of crisis: by migrating, fragmenting into smaller groups, and speeding up their adaptive, evolutionary response. Physical geographers hypothesize that the earliest phase of Pangaea's fragmentation was also the most violent, that the plate separations that started it all were driven by built-up, extreme heat below the supercontinent, but that the motion of the plates has since slowed down. The **Pacific Ring of Fire**—an ocean-girdling zone of crustal instability, volcanism, and earthquakes—is but a trace of the paroxysm that marked the onset of Pangaea's breakup (Fig. 13.4). Yet, as we saw with the tsunami in December 2004, tectonic events have cost millions of humans their lives and altered the course of history.

When Pangaea still was a supercontinent, an Ice Age cooled the Earth and may have contributed to, if not caused, the greatest known extinction crisis in the history of life on Earth. Ice Ages are not uniform cooling events: surges of coldness and advances of glaciers are interrupted by temporary warming spells long enough to reverse much of the glacial impact. By the time the **Pleistocene** epoch opened, less than 2 million years ago, the planet was in a deep freeze.

The Pleistocene was an epoch marked by long **glaciations** and short, warm **interglaciations**. When the Pleistocene glaciations were most severe, permanent ice advanced deep into the landmasses of the Northern Hemisphere. Plants, animals, and hominids saw their liv-

ing space diminished, their refuges shrunk, their niches unusable. Such glaciations could last as long as 100,000 years, but eventually a warming spell would arrive, the ice would recede, and space as well as opportunity expanded again. A warming phase of this kind occurred between about 120,000 and 100,000 years ago, and some scientists suggest that this is the time when *Homo sapiens* appeared on the Earth.

The most recent glaciation of the Pleistocene, the **Wisconsin Glaciation**, left its mark on much of the Northern Hemisphere (Fig. 13.5). But resourceful humans managed to survive where their predecessors could not, and there is ample evidence of human occupation in Europe ranging from cave art to tool kits. Even during a glacial advance brief periods of milder climate emerge. Thus, Figure 13.5 represents a glacial extreme, not the whole picture. So human communities—fishing, hunting and gathering, and using increasingly sophisticated tools (and probably means of verbal communication)—exploited the milder times by expanding their frontiers.

About 73,500 years ago, something happened that came close to exterminating humanity altogether. A volcano, Mount Toba, erupted on the Indonesian island of Sumatra. This was not just an eruption: the entire mountain exploded, sending millions of tons of debris into orbit, obscuring the sun, creating long-term darkness, and altering global climate. Mount Toba's detonation could hardly have come at a worse time. The Earth's habitable zone was already constricted because of glaciation. Anthropologists refer to this event as humanity's "evolutionary bottleneck,"

Figure 13.4
Recent Earthquakes and Volcanic Eruptions.   © H. J. de Blij, P. O. Muller, and John Wiley & Sons, Inc.

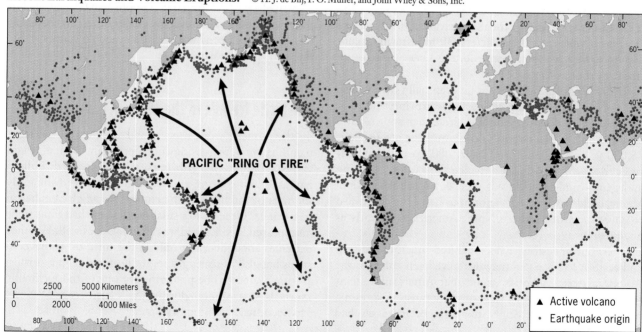

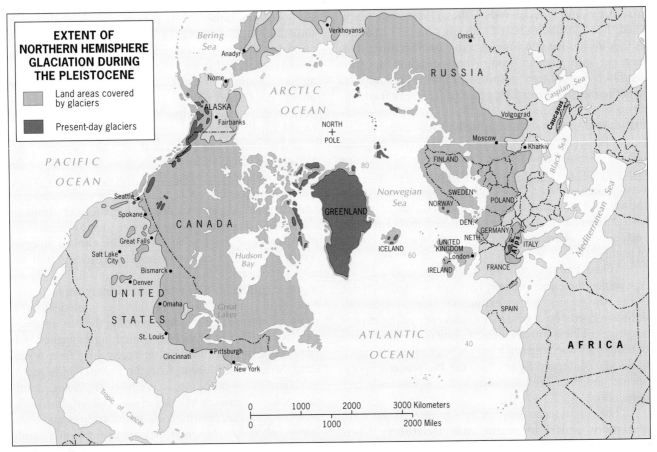

Figure 13.5
Extent of Northern Hemisphere Glaciation During the Late Pleistocene's Wisconsinan Glaciation. The evidence on which this map is based includes glacial deposits and the marks of glaciers' erosion on bedrock.   © H. J. de Blij, P. O. Muller, and John Wiley & Sons, Inc.

suggesting that much genetic diversity was lost. Today, the filled-in caldera marking Toba's cataclysm is 90 kilometers (55 miles) long and 50 kilometers (30 miles) wide, silent witness to the greatest threat to our existence ever to come from any source (Fig. 13.6).

The Wisconsinan Glaciation eventually gave way to a full-scale interglaciation, the current warm interlude that has been given its own (and not altogether appropriate) designation, the **Holocene**. Global warming began about 18,000 years ago, and for the next 6000 years, temperatures rose rapidly. Although the ice sheets were thinning and giant, mud-laden floods sped down the Mississippi Valley, building the river's enormous delta; ice continued to cover most of northern North America as recently as 13,000 years ago.

To our ancestors, who inhabited much of western and eastern Eurasia and may just have been entering the Americas (some scholars argue that American Indians were here much earlier), this warming must have been a welcome experience. Slight temperature increases had

happened earlier, during the Wisconsinan Glaciation, but these were quickly followed by colder times. So persistent was this most recent warming that people ventured farther and farther poleward.

The Little Ice Age in the Modern Era

To the farmers, winegrowers, and seafarers of the fourteenth century, increasing cold, decreasing rainfall, frigid winds, and shortened growing seasons made for dwindling harvests, failing farms, and seas too stormy for fishing. By the turn of the fourteenth century, alpine glaciers began to advance. Greenland's small settlement had long since disappeared, and Iceland was abandoned as well. Weather extremes abounded, not only in the form of record cold snaps but also as searing summer heat and raging storms. Nature seemed to be preparing for one of those climatic reversals so common during the Pleistocene. Was the Holocene itself coming to an end?

Figure 13.6
Mount Toba, Indonesia. The lake in this photo fills in the gigantic caldera left from the eruption of Mount Toba on the island of Sumatera in Indonesia. © A. M. & K. D. Hollitzer/Asiafoto.

Famines struck all over Europe, just at a time when more people were clustered in towns than ever before. The climatic record, pieced together from farmers' diaries (winegrowers' diaries are especially useful), tree ring research (dendochronology), ice cores, contemporary writings, illustrative paintings, and surviving sketches and drawings, justify the designation of the post–1300 period as a shift in the direction of reglaciation. We now know that this return to colder times, marked by advancing mountain glaciers and thickening Subarctic ice, would end in the mid-nineteenth century and that even the worst of it, starting in the late 1600s, did not lead to full-scale Pleistocene glaciation. Whatever was happening precipitated serious social disruptions in Europe and in other parts of the world as well, but of course those who experienced it were unaware of the long-term implications. Only when new methods of analysis became available did scientists realize what had happened—and then they gave the episode an inappropriate name. This temporary cooling was no ice age: it was a minor glaciation and not the first over the past 6000 years. But the name **Little Ice Age** certainly was more dramatic than "Minor Glaciation," and it stuck.

To those affected, it was anything but little or minor. Europe's climate fluctuated wildly, often over relatively short periods of time, so that recovery would be followed by renewed famine; populations mushroomed and then fell back again. In the fourteenth century, the human geography of eastern and western Eurasia became fatally interlocked. The salubrious conditions that enabled Mongol peoples to thrive and expand, leading to a Mongol dynasty in China, also facilitated their penetration westward. In the process, Mongol migrants and their horse caravans picked up the strain of bacteria that brings on the bubonic plague, and its vector, the flea, rode into Europe. The Black Death swept over an already weakened Europe in waves that often killed half the population or more. Recovery, medical as well as environmental, did not start until the last quarter of the fifteenth century.

In China, meanwhile, the full impact of the Little Ice Age occurred after the end of the Mongol (Yuan) dynasty (1368). The early Ming rulers inherited a populous state sustained by wheat in the north and rice in the center, linked by the Grand Canal and other busy waterways. Late in the fourteenth century the Ming rulers, exhorted by the legendary admiral Chung Ho, authorized the construction of an oceangoing fleet that would stake China's claim and enhance its reputation in the Indian Ocean and beyond. The fleet eventually numbered more than 6000 ships, the largest carrying as many as 500 people; these were 400 feet long, had four decks and nine masts, and carried sufficient fresh water and supplies to sail for 20 days. Nothing built in Europe even began to approach these vessels in terms of technology or capacity—the first expedition, in 1405, involved 315 ships and 27,000 people. Later voyages reached the Persian Gulf and the Red Sea as well as East Africa, possibly as far south as Sofala. The Chinese seemed poised to round the Cape of Good Hope and enter the Atlantic.

But then disaster struck at home. The first onslaught of the Little Ice Age came later than it did in Europe, but it was no less severe. Interior rains failed, rivers dried up, the wheat crop shrank, famines broke out, and social disorder and epidemics raged. The Ming rulers ordered an end to the maritime expeditions, dictated the burning of all oceangoing vessels, and instructed the Nanjing shipyard, then by far the largest in the world, to build only barges that could navigate the Grand Canal with cargoes of rice, thus alleviating the plight of the colder, drier north. Environments do not determine the capacities of humans, but environmental events can certainly influence the course of history.

In his book *The Little Ice Age* (2000), archaeologist Brian Fagan describes how the Franz Josef Glacier on New Zealand's South Island "thrust downslope into the valley below, smashing into the great rainforests…felling giant trees like matchsticks." In North America, our growing understanding of the Little Ice Age helps explain why the Jamestown colony collapsed so fast, a failure attributed by historians to ineptitude and lack of preparation. The chief cause may well have been environmental. Geographer David Stahle (1998) and his team, studying tree ring records that go back eight centuries, found that the Jamestown area experienced a seven-year drought between 1606 (the year before the colony's founding) through 1612, the worst in nearly eight centuries. European colonists and American Indians were in the same situation, and their relations worsened as they were forced to compete for dwindling food and falling water tables. The high rate of starvation was not unique to the colonists. They, and their American Indian neighbors, faced the rigors of the Little Ice Age as well.

As the Little Ice Age continued into the 1800s, a large-scale volcano had a major impact on human society. On April 5, 1815, the Tambora Volcano on the island of Sumatera in what was then the Dutch East Indies, located not far East of Bali, rumbled to life. Less than a week later it was pulverized in a series of explosions that could be heard a thousand miles away, killing all but 26 of the island's population of 12,000. When it was over, the top 4000 feet of the volcano were gone, and much of what is now Indonesia was covered by debris. Darkness enveloped most of the colony for weeks, and tens of thousands died of famine in the months that followed. Colonial reports describe fields covered by poisonous ash and powder, waters clogged by trees and cinders, and air rendered unbreathable by a fog of acid chemicals.

Tambora's explosions rocketed tens of millions of tons of ash into orbit, darkening skies around the world. What began as a narrow equatorial band of ash and dust gradually widened into a globe-girdling membrane that blocked part of the sun's radiation. By the middle of 1816, it was clear to farmers everywhere that this would be a year without summer, a growing season without growth. In Europe, food shortages were acute and grain prices rose rapidly, forcing governments to close their borders to prevent speculation. Food riots nevertheless broke out in the towns, and in the countryside armed gangs raided farms and stores. In the United States, the "year without summer" was especially difficult on the farms of New England, where corn would not ripen, grain prices escalated, and the livestock market collapsed. We can only guess at the impact of Tambora's eruption in other parts of the world, but there can be no doubt that 1816 was a desperate year—a crisis that reminds us of the risks under which all of humanity lives.

Since the 1850s, when the Little Ice Age waned and a slow but nearly persistent warming phase began, climatologists and other scientists have learned much about the workings of our planet, but they do not yet know enough to be able to make reliable predictions about what will happen.

Take time to search the Internet and read about what has happened to Phuket, Thailand, since the Indian Ocean tsunami hit in December 2004. Look for before and after images of Phuket—how did it look before the tsunami hit and after? Research how Phuket has been rebuilt and determine why Phuket has been rebuilt the way it has.

HOW HAVE HUMANS IMPACTED EARTH'S ENVIRONMENT?

Biologists estimate that there may be as many as 25 million types of organisms on Earth, perhaps even more; most have not yet been identified, classified, or studied. *Homo sapiens* is only one of these, yet in ten millennia our species has developed a complex culture that is transmitted from one generation to the next through learning and is also to some degree encoded in our genes. Humans are not unique in possessing a culture: gorillas, orangutans, chimpanzees, and dolphins have cultures too. Ours is the only species, however, with a vast and complex array of artifacts, technologies, laws, and belief systems.

No species, not even the powerful dinosaurs, ever affected their environment as strongly as humans do today. A cometary impact probably made the dinosaurs and many other species extinct. Some biogeographers suggest that the next great extinction may be caused not by asteroids but by humans, whose numbers and demands are destroying millions of species.

Alteration of Ecosystems

Destructiveness is not just a matter of modern technology and its capacity to do unprecedented damage, whether by wartime forest defoliation, peacetime oil spills, or other means. Humans altered their environment from the beginning, when they set fires to kill herds of reindeer and bison, or hunted entire species of large mammals to extinction. The Maori, who arrived in New Zealand not much more than 1000 years ago, greatly altered native species of animals and plants long before the advent of modern technology. Elsewhere in the Pacific realm, Polynesians reduced the forest cover to brush and, with their penchant for wearing bird-feather robes, had exterminated more than 80 percent of the regional bird species by the time the first Europeans arrived. The Europeans ravaged species ranging from Galapagos turtles to Antarctic seals. European fashions had a disastrous impact on African species ranging from snakes to leopards. Traditional as well as modern societies have had devastating impacts on their ecosystems (ecological units consisting of self-regulating associations of living and nonliving natural elements) as well as on those of areas into which they migrated.

Human alteration of the environment continues in many forms today. For the first time in history, however, the combined impact of humanity's destructive and exploitative actions is capable of producing environmental changes at the global scale. Consider for a moment the history of human life on Earth. Early human societies had relatively small populations, and their impacts on the physical environment were limited in both duration and intensity. With the development of agrarian and preindustrial societies, human alterations of the physical environment increased, yet the effects of these early activities were still limited in scale. Even the onset of urbanization and the development of urban centers, which concentrated large numbers of people in particular places, had relatively limited effects. Over the last 500 years, however, both the rate and the scale at which humans modify the Earth have increased dramatically. Particularly during the last half-century, every place on earth has been transformed, either directly or indirectly, by humans.

Environmental Stress

The natural environment is being modified and stressed by human activity in many obvious and some less obvious ways. Among the more obvious actions (obvious because they take place around human habitats) causing **environmental stress** are the cutting of forests and the emission of pollutants into the atmosphere. Less obvious actions include the burying of toxic wastes that foul groundwater supplies, the dumping of vast amounts of garbage into the oceans, and the use of pesticides in farming. Humans have built seawalls, terraced hillslopes, dammed rivers, cut canals, and modified the environment in many constructive as well as destructive ways. All of these activities have an impact on the environment and have given rise to a number of key concerns. Among these are the future of water supplies, the state of the atmosphere, climate change, desertification, deforestation, soil degradation, and the disposal of industrial wastes.

Water

Resources that are replenished even as they are being used are **renewable resources**, and resources that are present in finite quantities are nonrenewable. Water, the essence of life, is a renewable resource. But the available supply of fresh water is not distributed evenly across the globe. Figure 1.10 shows the world distribution of precipitation, with the largest totals recorded in equatorial and tropical areas of Southeast Asia, South Asia, Central and coastal West Africa, and Middle and South America. That distribution is sustained through the **hydrologic cycle**, which brings rain and snow from the oceans to the landmasses (Fig. 13.7). The volume of precipitation in the world as a whole is enormous; spread out evenly, it would cover the land area of the planet with about 83 centimeters (33 inches) of water each year. Much of that water is lost through runoff and evaporation, but enough of it seeps downward into porous, water-holding rocks called **aquifers** to provide millions of wells with steady flows. In the United States alone, it is estimated that there is 50 times as much water stored in aquifers as there is precipitation falling on the land surface every year.

Despite such favorable data, the supply of water is anything but plentiful (Fig. 13.8). Chronic water shortages afflict tens of millions of farmers in Africa and hundreds of thousands of city dwellers in Southern California; water rationing has been imposed in rainy South Florida and in Spain, which faces the Mediterranean Sea.

In many areas of the world, people have congregated in places where water supplies are insufficient, undependable, or both. In California, people are sometimes not allowed to wash their cars or refill their swimming pools; these are minor inconveniences compared to the fate faced by millions of Sudanese trying to escape their country's civil war by fleeing to parched pans of the Sahara. In Florida, where the urban population depends on the Biscayne Aquifer for most of its water, the long-term prospect is troubled: whenever seasonal rainfalls do not reach their projected averages, Floridians overuse the Biscayne Aquifer, and saltwater enters the aquifer from the nearby Atlantic Ocean. The invasion of saltwater over time can permanently destroy a fresh water aquifer.

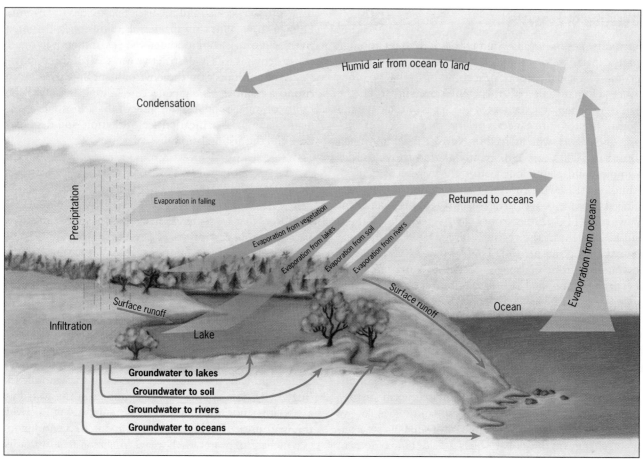

Figure 13.7

The Hydrologic Cycle. The hydrologic cycle carries moisture from the oceans and from other water bodies over the land, where precipitation, runoff, and evapotranspiration sustain the system.   © E. H. Fouberg, A. B. Murphy, H. J. de Blij, and John Wiley & Sons, Inc.

Field Note

"We drove north on Route 89 from Tucson, Arizona, across the desert. Drought rules the countryside here, and dams conserve what water there is. Snaking through the landscape are lifelines such as this, linking Coolidge Dam to distant farms and towns. In the vast, arid landscape, this narrow ribbon of water seems little more than an artificial brook—but to hundreds of thousands of people, this is what makes life possible in the Southwest."

Figure 13.8
Tucson, Arizona.   © H. J. de Blij.

Hundreds of millions of people still cluster along several of the Earth's great rivers. Indeed, nearly three-quarters of all the fresh water used annually is consumed in farming, not in cities. In California, where about 80 percent of available water is used for irrigation, this has led to an intense debate: should cities be provided with ample water at the expense of Central Valley farms, and should fruits and vegetables be bought from elsewhere, even overseas, rather than be grown locally?

Industries use another 20 percent of the world's water supply, contributing heavily to pollution when the used water is returned to streams, lakes, and aquifers. When communist rule ended in Eastern Europe, tests indicated that the region's rivers and groundwater were among the most severely polluted in the world because industries there had not been adequately regulated.

As human populations have expanded, people have increasingly settled in arid regions. One of the great ecological disasters of the twentieth century occurred in Kazakhstan and Uzbekistan, whose common boundary runs through the Aral Sea. Streams that fed this large body of water were diverted to irrigate the surrounding desert (mainly for commercial cotton production). Heavy use of chemical pesticide ruined the groundwater below, causing a health crisis that some observers describe as an "ecological Chernobyl" (referring to the 1986 nuclear reactor meltdown in the Ukraine). In the meantime the Aral Sea began to dry up, and by the mid-1990s it had lost more than three-quarters of its total surface area (Fig. 13.9).

Throughout the world, people have come to depend on water sources whose future capacity is uncertain. Rocky Mountain and Sierra Nevada snows feed the Colorado River and the aquifers that irrigate the California Central Valley. Aqueducts snake their way across the desert to urban communities. None of this slows the population's move to the Sunbelt (see Chapter 12), and the water situation there is becoming problematic. In coastal eastern Spain, low water pressures in city pipes often deprive the upper floors of high-rise buildings of water. In Southwest Asia and the Arabian Peninsula, growing populations strain ancient water supply systems and desalinization plants are a necessity. Regional conflicts in places such as Sudan (especially the Darfur region of Sudan) are fueled by conflicts over water.

Water and Politics in the Middle East

When relations between countries and peoples are problematic, disputes over water can make them even worse. As populations grow and as demand for water rises, fears of future shortages intensify.

Water supply is a particularly difficult problem affecting relations among Israel and its neighbors. With under 6 million people, Israel annually consumes nearly three times as much water as Jordan, the West Bank Palestinian areas, and Gaza combined (total population: over 7 million). As much as half of Israel's water comes from sources outside the Israeli state.

Figure 13.9

The Dying Aral Sea. Affected by climatic cycles and afflicted by human interference, the Aral Sea on the border of Kazakhstan and Uzbekistan is dying. In a quarter of a century, it lost three-quarters of its surface area.   © E. H. Fouberg, A. B. Murphy, H. J. de Blij, and John Wiley & Sons, Inc.

A   Aral Sea, mid-1960s

B   Aral Sea, early 2000s

The key sources of water for the entire area are the Jordan River and an aquifer beneath the West Bank. When Israel captured the Golan Heights from Syria and the West Bank from Jordan during the 1967 war, it gained control over both of these sources, including the Jordan River's important tributary, the Yarmuk (Fig. 13.10). As the map shows, the Sea of Galilee forms a large fresh water reservoir in the Jordan River Valley. This is the source of most of Israel's water (desalinization facilities do not yet contribute significantly).

The water supply complicates the relationships between Israel and its Palestinian neighbors in the West Bank and Gaza. The aquifer beneath the West Bank yields about 625 million cubic meters through hundreds of wells linked together by a system of pipelines. Of this, some 450 million cubic meters go directly to Israel; another 35 million are consumed by Israeli settlers on the West Bank, and only some 140 million are allotted to the West Bank's nearly 2 million Arabs.

This is unfair, say the Palestinian Arabs: if the West Bank is to become independent Palestinian territory, the water below the surface should belong to the Palestinians.

▬▬ Figure 13.10
Key Water Resources in the Middle East. © E. H. Fouberg, A. B. Murphy, H. J. de Blij, and John Wiley & Sons, Inc.

But the Israeli cities of Tel Aviv and Jerusalem depend heavily on water from the West Bank, and Israel cannot survive without this source.

The water issue will complicate any hoped-for settlement of territorial disputes among Israel and its neighbors. Israel might contemplate the return of most of the Golan Heights to Syria, but about 30 percent of all water reaching the Sea of Galilee comes from the Golan Heights. Israel might support the establishment of an independent state in the West Bank, but approximately 30 percent of Israel's water supply comes from the West Bank aquifer. Any effort to negotiate a lasting peace in the region will have to take these geographical circumstances into account.

Atmosphere

The Earth's **atmosphere** is a thin layer of air lying directly above the lands and oceans. We depend on the atmosphere for our survival: we breathe its oxygen; it shields us from the destructive rays of the sun; it moderates temperatures; and it carries moisture from the oceans over the land, sustaining crops and forests and replenishing soils and wells.

The atmosphere has a truly amazing capacity to cleanse itself. In 1883 the Indonesian volcano Krakatau erupted catastrophically, throwing 10 cubic kilometers (2.5 cubic miles) of rock and ash into the atmosphere. Total darkness prevailed in the area for nearly three days; dust from the explosion encircled the Earth and created vividly colored sunsets for years afterward. However, eventually the atmosphere cleared, and all traces of the eruption disappeared. In 1980 the eruption of Mount St. Helens in the northwestern United States caused a similar, though much smaller, globe-encircling cloud of volcanic dust in the upper atmosphere. Again, the atmosphere soon cleansed itself.

Human pollution of the atmosphere, however, will likely result in longer lasting, possibly permanent, damage. True, the air disperses even the densest smoke and most acrid chemical gases. However, some of the waste pouring into the atmosphere may be producing irreversible change. The nature of the change is still being debated, but two centuries of industrial expansion have caused an enormous increase in the pollution. The rapid industrialization of China, India, Brazil, and other places is compounding global atmospheric pollution. Although global concern and action to limit atmospheric pollution are much in evidence, the problem remains.

Global Warming

Most scientists argue that tropospheric pollution (pollution in the lowest layer of the atmosphere), particularly the release of "greenhouse" gases, causes the Earth to retain more heat (hence the term *greenhouse*) and that its full effect will not be felt until well into the twenty-first century. Estimates of **global warming** differ: in the early 2000s computer models still predicted a warming of 2.7°C to 3.7°C (about 3.57°F to 5.57°F) over the next 50 years. This might be enough to melt some glacial ice and raise sea levels as much as 15 centimeters (6 inches). Indeed, this is already happening, as evidenced by the disappearance of two uninhabited Islands in the pacific atoll state of Kirinati.

Moreover, changes in climate involve changes in the hydrologic cycle, affecting patterns of precipitation. These changes in turn can affect where certain types of vegetation can grow, which can alter everything from agricultural patterns to the location of animal habitats.

Although there is some debate about how much the earth will warm, there is no question that growing populations and increased human activity, ranging from the burning of tropical forests to pollution of the atmosphere by industry and automobiles, are having an unprecedented impact on the atmosphere. The amounts of key "greenhouse" gases, carbon dioxide (CO_2), methane, and nitrous oxides in the atmosphere have been increasing at a rate of about 2 percent per decade; automobiles, steel mills, refineries, and chemical plants account for a large part of this increase. Without doubt there will be consequences; all that remains uncertain is exactly what those consequences will be.

Acid Rain

A by-product of the enormous volume of pollutants spewed into the atmosphere is **acid rain**. Acid rain forms when sulfur dioxide and nitrogen oxides are released into the atmosphere by the burning of fossil fuels (coal, oil, and natural gas). These pollutants combine with water vapor in the air to form dilute solutions of sulfuric and nitric acids, which then are washed out of the atmosphere by rain or other types of precipitation, such as fog and snow.

Although acid rain usually consists of relatively mild acids, it is caustic enough to harm certain natural ecosystems (the mutual interactions between groups of plant and animal organisms and their environment). Already we know that acid rain is causing acidification of lakes and streams (with resultant fish kills), stunted growth of forests, and loss of crops in affected areas. In cities, corrosion of buildings and monuments has accelerated.

The geography of acid rain is most closely associated with patterns of industrial concentration and middle- to long-distance wind flows. The highest densities of coal and oil burning are associated with large concentrations of heavy manufacturing, such as those in western and eastern Europe, the United States, and Eastern China. As these industrial areas began to experience increasingly severe air pollution problems in the second half of the twentieth century, many countries (including the United States in 1970) enacted legislation establishing minimal clean-air standards.

In the United States and western Europe, compliance with legislated emission reductions is having positive results. In Canada as well as in Scandinavia, where acid rain from neighboring industrial regions damaged forests and acidified lakes, recovery came faster than scientists had predicted. This evidence is now encouraging other countries to impose stricter controls over factory emissions.

The Land

Over the centuries, human population growth has put increasing pressure on the land surface. More land is cleared and placed under cultivation, trees are cut down, and cities expand. The effects can be seen almost everywhere and are so extensive that it is often difficult even to reconstruct what an area might be like in the absence of humans. The human impact on the Earth's land surface has several key aspects, of which the most significant are deforestation, soil erosion, waste disposal (discussed here) and biodiversity less.

Deforestation

From the tropical Amazon Basin to high-latitude North America and Eurasia, humans have cut down forests and whittled away woodlands.

The world's forests, especially those of lower and middle latitudes, play a critical role in what biogeographers call the **oxygen cycle**. Atmospheric oxygen is consumed by natural processes as well as by human activities. Forests counteract this loss through photosynthesis and related processes, which release oxygen into the atmosphere. The destruction of vast tracts of forest alarms ecologists and others, who warn of unforeseeable and incalculable effects—not only for the affected areas but for the planet as a whole.

In the early 1980s, the Food and Agriculture Organization (FAO) of the United Nations undertook a study of the rate at which forests were being depleted. This analysis showed that 44 percent of the tropical rainforest had already been affected by cutting and that more than 1 percent was being logged every year (Fig. 13.11). In 1990, the FAO predicted that if this rate of cutting were to continue, the entire equatorial rainforest would be gone in less than 90 years.

In 2005, the FAO released a comprehensive, ten-year study of the world's forests. It found that the annual net loss of forests globally was 7.3 million hectares/year between 2000 and 2005—a rate that was lower than the 8.9 million hectares/year between 1990 and 2000.

Field Note

"This was one of the most depressing days of this long South American field trip. We had been briefed and had seen the satellite pictures of the destruction of the rainforest, with ugly gashes of bare ground pointing like rows of arrows into the woods. But walking to the temporary endpoints of some of these new roads made a lot more impact. From the remaining forest around came the calls of monkeys and other wildlife, their habitat retreating under the human onslaught. Next week this road would push ahead another mile, the logs carted away and burned, the first steps in a process that would clear this land, ending billions of years of nature's dominance."

Figure 13.11
Para, Brazil. © H. J. de Blij.

Deforestation is not a singular process: it has been going on for centuries, and the motivations for deforestation vary vastly. Forests are cut and reforested for wood and paper products; forests are preserved for the maintenance of biodiversity; and other forests are cleared for new agricultural production.

The effects of **deforestation** are not clearly understood. The reforestation (and harvesting) of deforested areas is not the whole answer, even if it could be done on a large scale. Forests in the United States, for example, consist mainly of second-growth trees, which replaced the original forest after it was logged. However, the controlled second-growth forest does not (as the natural forest did) have many trees dying of old age after their trunks and limbs become soft from rot. As a result, many animal species that depend on holes in trunks and hollows in tree limbs cannot find places to nest (thus, the spotted owl dispute in the Pacific Northwest of the United States). For them the forest has ceased to be a favorable habitat.

Soil Erosion

The loss of potentially productive soil to erosion has been described as a "quiet crisis" of global proportions. Ecologists Lester Brown and Edward Wolf point out that the increasing rate of this loss over the past generation is not the result of a decline in the skills of farmers but rather of the pressures on farmers to produce more. In an integrated world food economy, the pressures on land resources are not confined to particular countries; they permeate the entire world.

Why has **soil erosion** increased so much? Part of the answer lies in population pressure: world population is moving toward 7 billion. Associated with population growth is the cultivation of ever-steeper slopes, with hastily constructed terraces or without any terraces at all (Fig. 13.12). As the pressure on land increases, farmers are less able to leave part of their soil fallow (unused) to allow it to recover its nutrients. Shifting cultivators (see Chapter 11) must shorten their field rotation cycle, and as a result their soil, too, is less able to recover. Altogether 99.7 percent of all human food is grown in soil (some is grown in water), and annual soil erosion shrinks the cropland available for agriculture. A 2006 study reported that globally about 37,000 square miles (10 million hectares) of cropland are lost to soil erosion each year.

Soil erosion is caused by a variety of factors: livestock are allowed to graze in areas where they destroy the natural vegetation; lands too dry to sustain farming are plowed, and wind erosion follows. Soil is a renewable resource because with proper care it can recover. However, it is being "mined" as if it were a nonrenewable resource. International cooperation in food distribution, education of farmers and governments, and worldwide dissemination of soil conservation methods are urgently needed to solve this "quiet crisis."

Waste Disposal

If anything has grown faster than population itself, it is the waste generated by households, communities, and industries—much of it a matter of bulk, some of it a source of danger.

The United States, the world's largest consumer of resources, is also the largest producer of **solid waste**, debris, and garbage discarded by those living in cities, industries, mines, and farms. According to current estimates, the United States produces about 1.7 kilograms

Figure 13.12
Guangxi-Zhuang, China. Overuse of land in this area of China was leading to the collapse of formerly sound terracing systems.   © H. J. de Blij.

(3.7 pounds) of solid waste per person per day, which adds up to well over 160 million metric tons (just under 180 million tons) per year. But the United States is not alone. Other high-technology economies with a high ratio of disposable materials (containers, packaging) face the same problems.

Disposal of these wastes is a major worldwide problem. The growing volume of waste must be put somewhere, but space for it is no longer easy to find. In poorer countries waste is thrown onto open dumps where vermin multiply, decomposition sends methane gas into the air, rain and waste liquids carry contaminants into the groundwater below, and fires pollute the surrounding atmosphere. In countries that can afford it, such open dumps have been replaced by **sanitary landfills**. The waste is put in a hole that has been dug and prepared for the purpose, including a floor of materials to treat seeping liquids and soil to cover each load as it is compacted and deposited in the fill.

The number of suitable sites for sanitary landfills is decreasing, however, and it is increasingly difficult to design new sites. In the United States landfill capacity has been reached or will soon be reached in about a dozen States, most of them in the Northeast and Mid-Atlantic regions, and those States must now buy space from other States for this purpose. Trucking or sending garbage by rail to distant landfills is very expensive, but there are few alternatives.

Similar problems arise on a global scale. The United States, the European Union, and Japan export solid (including hazardous) wastes to countries in Africa, Middle and South America, and East Asia. While these countries are paid for accepting the waste, they do not always have the capacity to treat it properly. So the waste often is dumped in open landfills, where it creates the very hazards that the exporters want to avoid. In the late 1980s, the richer countries' practice of "managing" waste by exporting it became a controversial issue, and in 1989 a treaty was drawn up to control it. The treaty did not (as many poorer countries wished) prohibit the exporting of hazardous waste, although it did place some restrictions on trade in hazardons materials.

It is useful to differentiate between **toxic wastes**, in which the danger is caused by chemicals, infectious materials, and the like, and **radioactive wastes**, which are of two types: low-level radioactive wastes, which give off small amounts of radiation and are produced by industry, hospitals, research facilities, and nuclear power plants; and high-level radioactive wastes, which emit strong radiation and are produced by nuclear power plants and nuclear weapons factories. In the United States, low-level radioactive wastes have for many years been disposed of in steel drums placed in six special government-run landfills, three of which are now closed.

High-level radioactive waste is extremely dangerous and difficult to get rid of. Fuel rods from nuclear reactors will remain radioactive for thousands of years and must be stored in remote places where they will not contaminate water, air, or any other part of the environment. In fact, no satisfactory means or place for the disposal of high-level radioactive waste has been found. Among many suggested disposal sites are deep shafts in the bedrock, chambers dug in salt deposits (salt effectively blocks radiation), ice chambers in Antarctica, sediments beneath the ocean floor, and volcanically active midocean trenches. Meanwhile, spent fuel rods (which last only about three years in the reactor) are put in specially designed drums and stored in one of about 100 sites, all of them potentially dangerous. In the early 2000s the U.S. government developed two major disposal sites—one at Yucca Mountain in southern Nevada, for waste from commercial nuclear power plants, and the other near Carlsbad in southern New Mexico, for military waste.

There is a related problem: transportation of waste. Even if secure and safe storage can be found for high-level radioactive waste, the waste has to be transported from its source to the disposal site. Such transportation presents an additional hazard; a truck or train accident could have disastrous consequences.

The dimensions of the waste-disposal problem are growing and globalizing. The threat to the planet's environment is not just over the short term but can exist for centuries, indeed millennia.

Biodiversity

A significant change that is related to all of the developments discussed so far is the accelerating loss of **biodiversity**. An abbreviation of "biological diversity," biodiversity refers to the diversity of all aspects of life found on the Earth. Although the term is commonly used when referring to the diversity of species, it encompasses the entire range of biological diversity, from the genetic variability within individuals of a species to the diversity of ecosystems on the planet.

How many species are there? Estimates range from 10 million to 100 million, and no one is quite sure how many. So far only some 1.75 million species have been identified, and new species, particularly new species of insects, are being discovered regularly. Yet species are also becoming extinct at a rapid rate. It is difficult to say exactly how quickly extinctions are occurring, since we do not know how many species there are. What is clear, however, is that although extinction is a natural process, humans have dramatically increased rates of extinction, particularly over the last few hundred years. Estimates from the United Nations Environment Program's Global Biodiversity Assessment indicate that 8 percent of plants, 5 percent of fish, 11 percent of birds, and 18 percent of the world's mammal species are currently threatened.

Where is biodiversity most threatened? Whether a species is threatened with extinction depends on the range of the species, its scarcity, and its geographic concentra-

tion. If a species with a small range, a high degree of scarcity, and a small geographic concentration has its habitat threatened, extinction can follow. Because most species have small ranges, change in a small area can affect a species. A 2005 report in *Scientific American* explained that "Clearing a forest, draining a wetland, damming a river or dynamiting a coral reef to kill its fish can more readily eliminate species with small ranges than more widespread species."

Human impacts on biodiversity have increased over time. The domestication of animals, followed by the agricultural domestication of plant life, caused significant changes in our relationship with other species. Large vertebrates have always been particularly hard hit by human activities. Many birds and mammals have been hunted not only for food but also for their skins, feathers, and so forth. During the eighteenth and nineteenth centuries, beaver populations in North America were drastically reduced as the beavers were trapped and skinned for their pelts; many bird species were hunted for their feathers, which were sold to decorate fashionable hats. Elephants and walruses continue to be hunted for their ivory tusks. From historical records we know that over 650 species of plants and over 480 animal species have become extinct in just the last 400 years. These represent only the documented extinctions. The actual number of extinctions that occurred during this period is almost certainly much higher.

Humans have also indirectly contributed to extinctions. Human travel, for instance, introduced new species to areas around the globe—rats are among the more destructive of these; they have had devastating effects on oceanic islands. Introduced species may cause extinctions by preying upon native species or competing with them for resources. A famous example is the dodo bird (*Raphus cuculatus*), which was hunted to extinction by humans, dogs, and rats on the island of Mauritius. Introduced species may also carry new diseases, leading to the decimation and extinction of local populations. Species on islands are particularly susceptible to extinction because of the more insular ecosystems found on islands. An estimated 2000 species of birds on tropical Pacific Islands became extinct following human settlement.

Identifying the nature and extent of environmental changes is only a first step toward understanding the extent of human alteration of the planet. A second, and more complicated step is to consider the forces driving these changes.

What is the greatest environmental concern facing the region where you live, and in what other regions of the world is this a major concern?

WHAT ARE THE MAJOR FACTORS CONTRIBUTING TO ENVIRONMENTAL CHANGE TODAY?

Global environmental changes express themselves at all scales, from local to global. For example, deforestation can have a local effect by reducing the diversity of species in a particular area. It can have regional impacts by increasing sediment runoff into rivers. Finally, at a global scale, deforestation is associated with the release of carbon dioxide into the atmosphere and may affect global climate by altering processes that occur at the land surface. To fully understand deforestation, we must keep all of these scales in mind.

Several interrelated factors are responsible for the expanding impact of humans on the environment over the past two centuries. One of these factors is the dramatic growth of the human population. Even considering the minimal needs for human survival, there can be little doubt that the fourfold increase in the human population in the twentieth century had significant environmental impacts. Another factor is consumption, which has increased dramatically in the modern world. Yet another is technology, which has both expanded the human capacity to alter the environment and brought with it increasing energy demands. Each of these interrelated factors that contribute to environmental change can be studied broadly, focusing on the general impacts of each factor on the global environment. Yet, when we shift scales to the local and regional, and we consider the context of human actions at these scales, we often find that the causes of environmental change vary depending on the local and regional context.

Political Ecology

Leslie Gray and William Moseley describe the field of political ecology, beginning in the 1960s and 1970s, as a way of considering the roles of "political economy, power and history in shaping human-environmental interactions." Political ecologists use scale to consider how attempts to affect environmental change, such as deforestation, differ across scales. Following an environmental problem from its location of outcome (e.g., a cleared patch of forest) backward to the "cause" of the problem is made difficult due to the many players, scales, and power relationships involved. In concerning ourselves only with the global scale, we miss the local. As Gray and Moseley observe, "The spatial distribution of environmental degradation and resource access is unequal both within localities and globally".

At the local scale, Moseley has studied the conservation behaviors of farmers in southern Mali (Fig 13.13).

He found that one view that is widely held at the global scale—that poorer people degrade the land more than wealthier people—was not true at the local scale. In fact, through extensive fieldwork, interviews, and soil surveying, moseley, found that poorer farmers in southern Mali were more likely to use organic materials to preserve topsoil and that wealthier farmers were more likely to use inorganic fertilizers and pesticides. Aside from being able to afford inorganic fertilizers, wealthier farmers did so in order to produce cotton more easily. Policies and power relationships at the local, national, and global scales help explain why wealthier farmers in southern Mali produce cotton. For example, the government of Mali's agricultural extension service singled out the wealthiest households for cotton farming, which "helped these households become even wealthier in the short term."

Population

Because humans across the world do not consume or pollute in exactly the same ways, we cannot make a simple chart showing that each additional human born on Earth results in a certain amount of consumption or pollution. We can, however, recognize that humans impact the environment and that a greater number of people on Earth translates into a greater capacity for environmental change.

Similarly, environmental change impacts humans differently, depending in part on who they are and where they live. To underscore the spatial differences in environmental impact on humans, we can consider two maps of natural disaster hot spots published by the Earth Institute at Columbia University and the World Bank in a 2005 report. The maps highlight the places in the world most susceptible to natural disasters, whether caused by drought, tectonic activity (earthquakes and volcanoes), or hydrological hazards (floods, cyclones, and landslides) (Fig. 13.14). Comparing the map of mortality risk with the map of total economic loss risk demonstrates that when a natural disaster hits a wealthier area of the world, the place will more likely be hit financially, whereas, in a poorer area of the world, the place will likely be hit by both financial loss and the loss of lives.

To understand better the differences in mortality and financial risks shown on these maps, we need to focus attention on the spatial differences in human impacts on environment. A clear difference emerges when we consider varying spatial patterns of consumption, transportation, and energy use in the world.

Patterns of Consumption

Humans rely on the Earth's resources for our very survival. At the most basic level, we consume water, oxygen, and organic and mineral materials. Over time we have

Try, Mali

In this photo, a young man brings home the cotton harvest in the village of Try in southern Mali. Prior to my graduate studies in geography, I spent a number of years as an international development worker concerned with tropical agriculture—both on the ground in Africa and as a policy wonk in Washington, D.C. I drew at least two important lessons from these experiences. First, well intentioned work at the grassroots level would always be limited if it were not supported by broader scale policies and economics. Second, the people making the policies were often out of touch with the real impacts their decisions were having in the field. As such, geography, and the subfield of political ecology, were appealing to me because of its explicit attention to processes operating at multiple scales, its tradition of fieldwork, and its long, standing attention to human–environment interactions. I employed a political ecology approach during fieldwork for my dissertation in 1999–2000. Here, I sought to test the notion that poor farmers are more likely to degrade soils than their wealthier counterparts (a concept widely proclaimed in the development policy literature of the 1990s). Not only did I interview rich and poor farmers about their management practices, but I tested their soils and questioned policymakers at the provincial, national, and international levels. My findings (and those of others) have led to a questioning of the poverty-environmental degradation paradigm.

Credit: William Moseley, Macalester College

Figure 13.13
Try, Mali

developed increasingly complex ways of using resources by such means as intensive agriculture and industrial production. Consequently, many societies now consume resources at a level and rate that far exceed basic subsistence needs. In a 1996 article on "Humanity's Resources" in *The Companion Encyclopedia of Geography: The Environment and Humankind*, I. G. Simmons notes that a hunter-gatherer could subsist on the resources found within an area of about 26 square kilometers, whereas today many people living in urban centers in the global economic core have access to resources from all over the planet.

Generally, the smaller numbers of people in the core parts of the world make far greater demands on the Earth's resources than do the much larger numbers in the poorer countries. It has been estimated that a baby born in the United States during the first decade of the twenty-first century, at current rates, consumes about 250 times as much energy over a lifetime as a baby born in Bangladesh over the same lifetime. In terms of food, housing, and its components, metals, paper (and thus trees), and many other materials, the consumption of individuals in affluent countries far exceeds that of people in poorer countries. Thus, rapid population growth in the periphery tends to have local or regional environmental impacts. Population growth in the core is also a matter of concern, one whose impact is not just local or regional but global.

All of this underscores the importance of thinking geographically about human impacts on the natural world. People living in the global economic periphery tend to affect their immediate environment, putting pressure on soil, natural vegetation, and water supplies, and polluting the local air with the smoke from their fires. The reach of affluent societies is much greater. The demand for low-cost meat for hamburgers in the United States has led to deforestation in Central and South America to make way for pastures and cattle herds. This, in turn, has greatly increased water demand in such areas (Table 13.1). Thus, the American (and European, Japanese, and Australian) consumer has an impact on distant environments.

MORTALITY RISKS

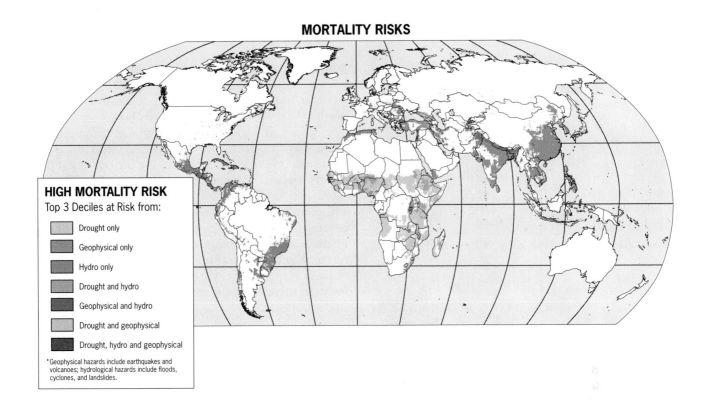

HIGH MORTALITY RISK

Top 3 Deciles at Risk from:

- Drought only
- Geophysical only
- Hydro only
- Drought and hydro
- Geophysical and hydro
- Drought and geophysical
- Drought, hydro and geophysical

*Geophysical hazards include earthquakes and volcanoes; hydrological hazards include floods, cyclones, and landslides.

ECONOMIC LOSS RISKS

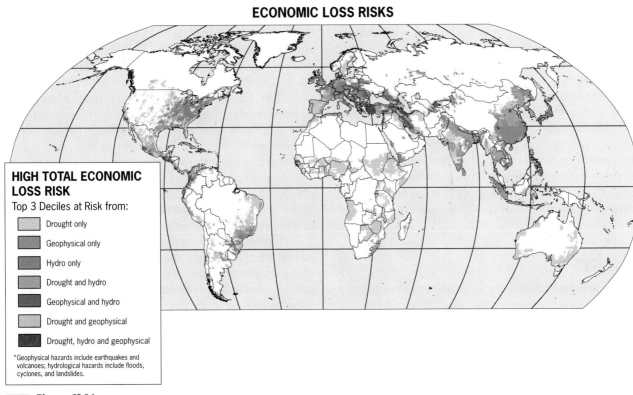

HIGH TOTAL ECONOMIC LOSS RISK

Top 3 Deciles at Risk from:

- Drought only
- Geophysical only
- Hydro only
- Drought and hydro
- Geophysical and hydro
- Drought and geophysical
- Drought, hydro and geophysical

*Geophysical hazards include earthquakes and volcanoes; hydrological hazards include floods, cyclones, and landslides.

Figure 13.14

Natural Disaster Hot Spots. The top map shows the potential mortality risks if major natural disasters occur in global natural disaster hot spots, and the bottom map shows the potential economic risks if major natural disasters occur in natural disaster hot spots.   *Courtesy of:* Center for Hazards and Risk Research at Columbia University and the World Bank, "Natural Disaster Hotspots—A Global Risk Analysis," March 29, 2005.

TABLE 13.1

Estimated Liters of Water Required to Produce 1 Kilogram of Food

Crop	Liters/Kg
Potatoes	500
Wheat	900
Corn	1400
Rice	1912
Chicken	3500
Beef	100,000

Source: D. Pimentel et al., *Bioscience*, vol. 47, no. 2, February 1997, p. 98.

Globally, consumption is tied to technology, for (as we saw in Chapter 12) the industrialized core has access to a vast array of transportation and communication technologies that allow advertisers to stimulate demand for particular goods around the world and allow manufacturers to bring those goods from distant places. The growth of wealth over the last ten years in the semiperiphery, including India and China, and their growing middle and upper classes, have increased the global consumption of consumer goods. For example, in 2008, the Indian company Tata (which we talked about at the beginning of Chapter 4) created the Nano, an automobile for the Indian market that is priced below $2500. Tata plans to produce 250,000 Nano cars a year.

Technological developments have expanded the production of consumer goods for consumption, and technological developments have also allowed humans to manipulate atmospheric, land, oceanic, and biological systems in profound ways. Understanding the complex ties between technology and environmental change requires consideration of several different facets of the technology picture.

Technology

Technological advances have increased rapidly since the Industrial Revolution and today affect all aspects of our lives. We are continually developing technologies that we hope will improve our standard of living, protect us against disease, and allow us to work more efficiently. These technologies have not come without a cost. Resource extraction practices such as mining and logging, which provide the materials to produce technologies, have created severe environmental problems. Energy is required not only to develop new technologies but to use them as well; fossil fuel consumption has contributed to many types of pollution and is a factor in climate change. Technological innovations have produced hazardous and toxic by-products, creating pollution and health problems that we are only

now beginning to recognize. Most significant for our discussion of global environmental change, however, is the fact that technology has enabled humans to alter large portions of the planet in a short space of time.

There are many dramatic examples of the role of technology in environmental change. Great open-pit mines exist where huge machines have carved away at the Earth's surface. The enormous clear-cuts of the Pacific Northwest forests are made possible by chainsaws, trucks, and even helicopters. The heavy blanket of smog that envelops cities such as Taipei (Taiwan) is a product of the internal combustion engine and mechanized manufacturing. Key elements of the technologies that contribute to these examples of environmental change are developments in two critical sectors of the economy: transportation and energy.

Transportation

Modes of transportation represent some of the most important technological advances in human history. Each innovation in transportation has required increased resource use, not only to make the vehicles that move people and goods, but also to build and maintain the related infrastructure—roads, railroad tracks, airports, parking structures, repair facilities, and the like. With each innovation the impacts seem to widen. As David Headrick points out in a study discussed in the *Companion Encyclopedia of Geography*, Chicago's O'Hare Airport covers a larger area (approximately 28 square kilometers or 17 square miles) than Chicago's central business district (which covers approximately 8 square kilometers or 5 square miles). Moreover, transportation innovations offer access to remote areas of the planet. There are vehicles that allow people to travel through extreme climates, to the bottoms of the ocean, and across the polar ice caps. These places, in turn, have been altered by human activity.

Transportation is also implicated in global environmental change—albeit sometimes indirectly. Advances in transportation have produced significant pollution, as seen, for example, in the extent of oil spills along major shipping lanes (Fig. 13.15).

Transportation facilitates the types of global networks necessary to sustain the patterns of consumption outlined earlier. Many of the products available in stores—be they electronics or clothing or food—come from distant places. Resources are required to produce and ship them, and except those that meet basic subsistence needs, they all contribute to the greater strains placed on the environment that come from those living in the wealthier parts of the world. This realization has led some individuals to reduce their levels of consumption or to consume more environmentally friendly, locally produced products. These changes have had some effect, but so far their

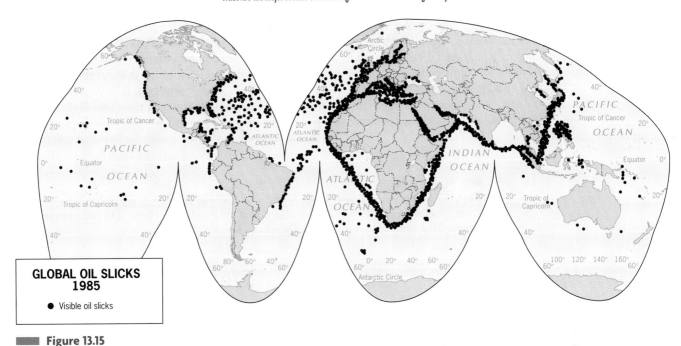

**GLOBAL OIL SLICKS
1985**

● Visible oil slicks

▰▰ **Figure 13.15**

Locations of Visible Oil Slicks.   Oil slicks are a problem around the globe, as this map shows.   *Adapted with permission from:* Organization for Economic Co-operation and Development, *The State of the Environment*, 1985, p. 76.

impact on the geography of global consumption has been marginal.

Energy

Consumption of material goods is closely linked to the consumption of energy. It takes energy to produce material goods, energy to deliver them to markets, and, for many products (such as appliances and automobiles), energy to keep them running. The resulting demands for energy are a factor in environmental change. Much of our energy supply comes from nonrenewable fossil fuels, such as coal, oil, and natural gas. Moreover, the evolution of tertiary, quaternary, and quinary economic activities has not reduced the consumption of nonrenewable resources. As populations grow, so does the demand for energy, and we can expect that over the coming decades energy production will expand to meet the increased demand. In developing countries in particular, demands for more energy are met by increasing the development of fossilfuel sources. This helps explain why, according to the United States Energy Information Administration, global oil production increased from 45.89 million barrels per day in 1970 to 73.27 million barrels per day in 2007.

Oil is a finite resource. It is not a question of *if* the world's oil supply will run out but *when*. Because discoveries of new reserves continue to be made, and because the extraction of fossil fuels is becoming ever more efficient, it is difficult to predict exactly how much longer oil

will remain a viable energy source. Many suggest that the current level of oil consumption can be sustained for up to 100 years, although some argue for much shorter or much longer time frames. Despite the range of opinion, the majority of scientists believe that, by the middle of this century, alternative sources will have to be developed.

When one considers that oil could become an increasingly scarce commodity within the lifetimes of many college students today, the importance of finding alternative energy sources becomes apparent. Adding further urgency to the quest are the pollution problems associated with the burning of fossil fuels and the geopolitical tensions that arise from global dependence on a resource concentrated in one part of the world. Moving away from a dependence on oil carries with it some clear positives, but it could lead to wrenching socioeconomic adjustments as well.

The effects of a shift away from oil will certainly be felt to some degree in the industrial and postindustrial countries, where considerable retooling of the economic infrastructure will be necessary. It is the oil-producing countries, however, that will face the greatest adjustments. More than half of the world's oil supply is found in the Middle Eastern countries of Saudi Arabia, Iraq, Kuwait, the United Arab Emirates (UAE), and Iran. In each of these countries, the extraction and exportation of oil account for at least 75 percent of total revenue and 90 percent of export-generated income. What will happen to these countries when their oil reserves run dry?

Consider the case of Kuwait—a country in which the incomes of 80 percent of the wage earners is tied to oil. Kuwait's citizens are currently guaranteed housing, education, and health care, and each adult couple receives a one-time stipend when a child is born. All of these programs are provided tax free, and when workers retire, their pensions are close to the salaries they earned as active members of the workforce.

Concerns over the long-term implications of a decline in oil revenue in Kuwait have led to efforts to find an alternative source of wealth: potable water. In a part of the world that can go for months without rain, water is a most precious resource. Some people in Kuwait joke that for each million dollars spent in the quest for sources of fresh water, all that is found is a billion dollars worth of oil! But where fresh water cannot be found, it can poten-

Figure 13.16

World Distribution of Fossil Fuels Sources of Carbon Dioxide. Geographical distribution of fossil fuel sources of carbon dioxide (CO_2) as of 1990 is depicted here. The basic pattern has remained the same.   *Adapted with permission from: Science, July 25, 1997.*

GLOBAL DISTRIBUTION OF FOSSIL FUEL SOURCES OF CO₂ AS OF 1990

tially be made, and Kuwait has begun to position itself to become one of the world's leaders in the field of desalinization (the conversion of saltwater to fresh water). This is currently a very expensive process, but Kuwait is able to devote some of its oil revenues to research and development on the desalinization process. Absent a major technological breakthrough, in the short term income generated by desalinization will amount to only a tiny frac-

tion of the income provided by oil production. The long term may be a different story, however. If not, Kuwait—and other countries in its position—will be facing a socio-economic adjustment of enormous proportions.

If we look at the global distribution of fossil fuel sources of CO_2 (Fig. 13.16), we can see that production is concentrated in the highly industrialized part of the global economic core. Pollution associated with this

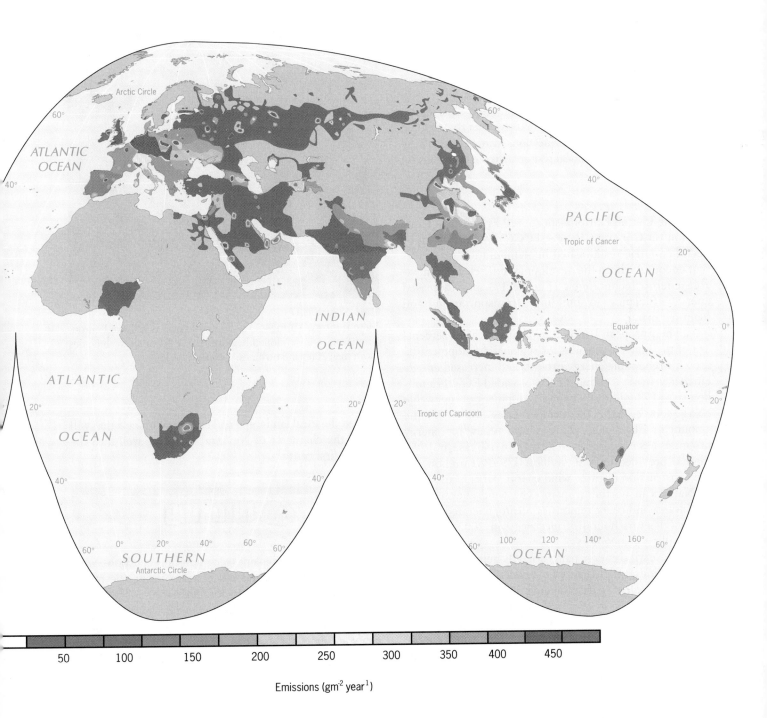

Emissions (gm^{-2} year^{-1})

energy production creates acid rain. The damming of rivers for hydropower alters fresh water systems. Nuclear power is being experimented with throughout the world, but the highly volatile byproducts of this form of energy production and the potential for accidents have limited the expansion of nuclear energy.

Technology has played a key role in amplifying human-induced environmental change. At the same time, technologies are being developed to identify and solve environmental problems. Some of these offer alternative approaches to local energy production.

The growing number of international environmental agreements signed in recent years reflects mounting international concern over the state of the global environment. The scope of these international agreements is primarily global in the sense that members of the international community agree to a global blueprint for action. How do these international agreements translate into regional or local action? What actual steps have signatory countries taken in their attempts to meet these global goals? Insights into these questions can be gained by looking at regional and local responses to conventions on climate change.

Alternative Energy

Since the United Nations-sponsored Framework Convention on Climate Change (FCCC) in 1992, a number of countries established implementation programs that encourage both the development of "clean" renewable energy technologies (Fig. 13.17) and increased energy efficiency in buildings, transportation, and manufacturing.

The European Union has mandated that a percentage of the funds it provides for regional development be used for renewable energy projects and increased energy efficiency. In 1994 alone, the EU provided ECU 175 million (US$159 million) for the development of renewable energy sources within the member states. Since 1994, the amount of EU money going toward renewable energy programs has increased even further. In one case, in 1997, the EU provided ECU 43 million (US$39.1 million) for the construction of three wind energy parks in the State of Navarra in northern Spain. The wind energy parks in Navarra and other regions of Spain generated a 9120 GWh (gigawatt hours) of electricity in 2002, creating €695 million in income.

These wind energy parks not only help the EU meet its obligations under the FCCC; they also help Navarra achieve a goal of self-sufficiency in energy. Navarra's wind energy parks now provide over 50 percent of the region's electric energy needs. More has changed in Navarra than its energy situation. The wind energy parks, located in the Guerinda Mountains 30 kilometers (18.6 miles) southeast of the city of Pamplona have

Figure 13.17
Lake Benton, Minnesota.   The wind park near Lake Benton, Minnesota was developed beginning in 1994 and now includes more than 200 wind turbines.   © Erin H. Fouberg.

altered the local landscape and economy in ways that will shape the character of Navarra as a place well into the twenty-first century.

Go back to the last Thinking Geographically question—what is the greatest environmental concern facing the region where you live? Now, add to your answer by concentrating on how people in the community (leaders, students, locals, businesses) discuss this environmental concern. Read newspaper accounts of the debate over this environmental concern. Are the actors in this debate thinking and operating at different scales?

HOW ARE HUMANS RESPONDING TO ENVIRONMENTAL CHANGE?

Technology is only one part of the picture of the human response to environmental change. The extent and rapidity of that change have led to numerous policies aimed at protecting the environment or reversing the negative impacts of pollution. These policies range from local ordinances that restrict urban development in environmentally sensitive areas to global accords on topics such as biodiversity and climate change.

A major challenge in confronting environmental problems is that many of those problems do not lie within a single jurisdiction. Many environmental problems cross political boundaries, and people sometimes move across those boundaries in response to environmental pressures. Designing policy responses is thus complicated by the fact that the political map does not reflect the geography of environmental issues. The problem is particularly acute when environmental problems cross international boundaries, for there are few international policymaking bodies with significant authority over multinational environmental spaces. Moreover, those that do exist—the European Union, for example—often have limited authority and must heed the concerns of member states. Those concerns, in turn, may not coincide with the interests of the environment. Within democracies, politicians with an eye to the next election may hesitate to tackle long-term problems that require short-term sacrifices. Most authoritarian regimes have an even worse record, as can be seen in the policies of the Soviet-dominated governments of Eastern Europe during the communist era. Moreover, governmental leaders in peripheral countries find it very difficult to take action when, as is often the case, action requires reductions in already marginal standards of living and even greater difficulties in meeting the kinds of debt payments discussed in Chapter 10.

Despite these obstacles, the growing extent and urgency of global environmental changes have led to a number of international agreements to address some of the most severe problems. Some of these have been spearheaded by nongovernmental organizations (NGOs) that operate outside of the formal political arena. They tend to focus on specific issues and problems, often in particular places. With the 1972 *United Nations Conference on the Human Environment* in Stockholm, international governmental organizations began playing a major role in environmental policy.

The framework that currently guides international governmental activity in the environmental arena evolved from the United Nations Conference on Environment and Development (UNCED) held in Rio de Janeiro in June 1992. The delegates to UNCED gave the Global Environment Facility (GEF)—a joint project of the United Nations and the World Bank—significant authority over environmental action on a global scale. The GEF funds projects related to six issues: loss of biodiversity, climate change, protection of international waters, depletion of the ozone layer, land degradation, and persistent organic pollutants. The delegates to UNCED believed that significant progress could be made through these funded projects, along with bilateral (that is, government-to-government) aid. They also made it easier for NGOs to participate in international environmental policymaking.

These actions hold the promise of a more coherent approach to environmental problem solving than is possible when decisions are made on a state-by-state basis. Yet individual states continue to influence decision making in all sorts of ways. Take the case of the GEF. Even though the GEF is charged with protecting key elements of the global environment, it still functions in a state-based world, as suggested by Figure 13.18—a map from a 1994 World Bank technical report on the forest sector in Subsaharan Africa that divides the realm into "major regions" that cut across forest zones. In addition to often limiting its perceptions of environmental issues to state boundaries, the GEF depends on states for funding projects. Between 1991 and 2004, the GEF provided $4.5 billion in grants. Although the GEF is often limited by state boundaries, it nonetheless serves the important role of providing financial resources to four major international conventions on the environment: the Convention on Biological Diversity, the United Nations Framework Convention on Climate Change, the United Nations Convention to Combat Desertification, and the Stockholm Convention on Persistent Organic Pollutants.

A few global environmental issues are so pressing that efforts are being made to draw up guidelines for action in the form of international conventions or treaties. The most prominent examples are in the areas of biological diversity, protection of the ozone layer, and global climate change.

Biological Diversity

International concern over the loss of species led to calls for a global convention (agreement) as early as 1981. By the beginning of the 1990s, a group working under the auspices of the United Nations Environment Program reached agreement on the wording of the convention, and it was submitted to UNCED for approval. It went into effect in late 1993; by 2001, 168 countries had signed it. The convention calls for the establishment of a system of protected areas and for a coordinated set of national and international regulations on activities that can have significant negative impacts on biodiversity. It also provides

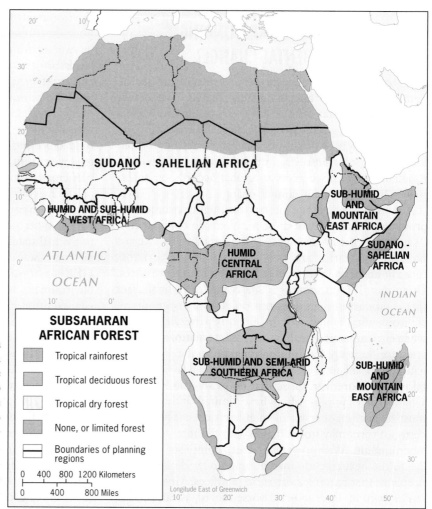

Figure 13.18

Major Regions and Forest Zones in Subsaharan Africa. This map is based on a figure in a World Bank technical paper on the forest sector in Subsaharan Africa. The map shows major forest regions crossing state boundaries, but planning regions adhere to state boundaries. *Adapted with permission from: N. P. Sharma, S. Rietbergen, C. R. Heimo, and J. Patel. A Strategy for the Forest Sector in Sub-Saharan Africa, World Bank Technical Paper No. 251, Africa Technical Department Series (Washington, D.C.: The World Bank, 1994).*

funding for developing countries that are trying to meet the terms of the convention.

The biodiversity convention is a step forward in that it both affirms the vital significance of preserving biological diversity and provides a framework for cooperation toward that end. However, the agreement has proved difficult to implement. In particular, there is an ongoing struggle to find a balance between the need of poorer countries to promote local economic development and the need to preserve biodiversity, which happens to be richest in parts of the global economic periphery. Also, there has been controversy over the sharing of costs for conservation programs, which has led to heated debates over ratification of the convention in some countries. Nevertheless, this convention, along with a host of voluntary efforts, has helped to focus attention on the biodiversity issue and to promote the expansion of protected areas. Whether those areas will succeed in providing long-term species protec-

tion is an open question that will occupy geographers and biologists for years to come.

Protection of the Ozone Layer

When found in the troposphere (0 to 16 kilometer or 1.0 to 10 mile altitude), ozone (O_3) gas is a harmful pollutant closely associated with the creation of smog. However, a naturally occurring **ozone layer** exists in the upper levels of the stratosphere (between 30 and 45 kilometer altitude). The ozone layer is of vital importance, because since it protects the Earth's surface from the sun's harmful ultraviolet rays. In 1985, a group of British scientists working in Antarctica discovered that the thickness of the ozone layer above the South Pole had been dramatically reduced, from 300 Dobson units (DUs) in the 1960s to almost 200 DUs by 1985. Studies revealed that the main culprits in ozone depletion were a group of human-made gases collectively known as CFCs (chlorofluorocarbons). These gases, used mainly as refrigerants in fire extinguishers and in aerosol cans, had only been in use since the 1950s and were thought to be completely harmless to humans. The strength of the scientific evidence pointing to a rapid reduction of the ozone layer led to an unusually rapid and united international response.

International cooperation began in 1985 with the negotiation of the **Vienna Convention for the Protection of the Ozone Layer**. Specific targets and timetables for the phase-out of production and consumption of CFCs were defined and agreed upon as part of the international agreement known as the **Montreal Protocol**, which was signed in September 1987 by 105 countries and the European Community. The original agreement called for a 50 percent reduction in the production and consumption of CFCs by 1999. At a meeting in London in 1990, scientific data showing that ozone depletion would continue for many years after a phase-out of CFCs led the signators of the Montreal Protocol to agree to halt CFC production entirely by the year 2000. Finally, at a meeting in Copenhagen in 1992, the timetable for CFC phaseout was accelerated; participants agreed to eliminate CFC production by 1996 and to accelerate the phaseout of other ozone-depleting chemicals such as halons, hydrochlorofluorocarbons, carbon tetrachloride, methyl chloroform, and methyl bromide. This response is an encouraging example of international cooperation in the face of a significant, albeit clearly defined, problem. Unfortunately, the long residence time of CFCs in the atmosphere will mean that their effects will be felt for a long time to come.

Global Climate Change

Beginning in the late 1980s, growing concern about climate change led to a series of intergovernmental conferences on the nature and extent of human impacts on the climate system. The second of these conferences, held in Geneva in 1990, was sponsored by the World Meteorological Organization, the United Nations Environment Program, and other international organizations. It brought together representatives from 137 states and the European Community. The delegates concluded that there was enough evidence of human impacts on climate to justify efforts to draw up a treaty on climate change. The final declaration, adopted after hard bargaining, did not specify any international targets for reducing emissions. Instead, it proclaimed climate change as a "common concern of humankind," while noting that "common but differentiated responsibilities" existed between the industrialized core and the less industrialized periphery.

In December 1990, the United Nations General Assembly approved the start of treaty negotiations. A draft convention was prepared and submitted to UNCED for consideration. The convention was presented in general terms, but it called on the developed countries to take measures aimed at reducing their emissions to 1990 levels by the year 2000 and to provide technical and financial support for emission-reduction efforts in the developing countries. The convention was signed by 154 states and the European Community in Rio de Janeiro.

For several years after UNCED, various committees met to discuss matters relating to the convention. By 1995, mounting concerns about the nature of long-term commitments under the convention led the participants in these discussions to call for a revised treaty that would cover the post–2000 period. They appointed a group to draft an agreement to be considered at a 1997 meeting in Kyoto, Japan. Different proposals were made in the months before this meeting, including one by the Association of Small Island States for a 20 percent cut in CO_2 by the year 2005 and one by the European Union for cuts of 7.5 percent by 2005 and 15 percent by 2010. The United States, however, was concerned about the economic effects of such cuts and the extent to which the burden of reducing emissions fell on the developed countries. It made a more modest proposal to return to 1990 CO_2 levels by 2012 and to reduce CO_2 levels below the 1990 benchmark thereafter.

After ten days of tough negotiations, an agreement was reached that involved compromises for practically every participating country. The agreement set a target period of 2008–2012 for the United States, the European Union, and Japan to cut their greenhouse gas emissions by 7, 8, and 6 percent, respectively, below 1990 levels. In addition, the agreement reached in Kyoto did not obligate less developed countries to adhere to specific reduction goals; instead it called for voluntary emission reduction plans to be implemented individually by those countries with financial assistance from industrialized countries. These plans have been revisited in successive climate change summits in The Hague (November 2000), Bonn (July 2001), and Marrakech (November 2001). The Hague summit collapsed without any agreement, and a further setback occurred in March 2001 when a new presidential administration in the United States suddenly announced its intention to abandon unilaterally the Kyoto Protocol. The Bonn summit thus opened amidst serious differences among countries, but by the end of the summit countries other than the United States signed a statement calling for the Kyoto Protocol to be salvaged. This paved the way for the Marrakech summit, where most countries agreed to a set of general rules for international implementation of the Kyoto Protocol. Without the participation of the United States, however, the impact of this and future agreements will be limited given that the United

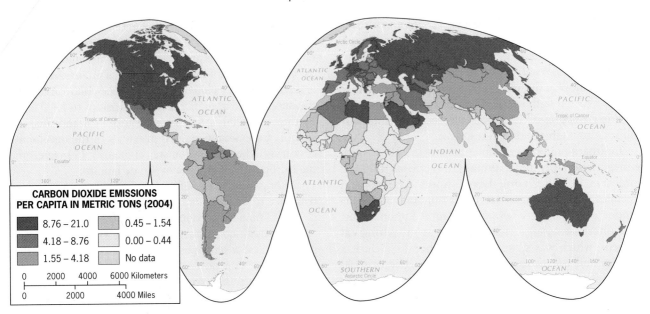

■ Figure 13.19

Carbon Dioxide Emissions per Capita, 2004. Recently, China's total Carbon Dioxide emissions have increased to the level of the United States. However, in per capita emissions of Carbon Dioxide, mapped here, the US, Canada, and the United Arab Emirates are the highest.

Data from: United Nations Development Programme, Hum Development Report, 2007/2008.

States produces approximately 24 percent of global CO_2 emissions in 2004.

The United States continues to be the largest producer of carbon dioxide emissions, per person, in the world. The United States emitted 19.4 tons of carbon dioxide per capita in 2007, and it was followed by the European Union with 8.6 tons, China with 5.1 tons, and India with 1.8 tons (Fig. 13.19). However, in 2006, China took the lead as the world's single largest total emitter of carbon dioxide, pushing the United States out of the top spot. The Beijing Olympics in 2008 opened the world's eyes to the incredibly high emissions level in China (Fig. 13.20).

■ Figure 13.20

Beijing, China. Smog covers the traffic on a motorway in the Central Business Districts of Beijing just a few months before the opening of the 2008 Olympics in Beijing. © David G. McIntyre/ epa/Corbis.

Neither the United States nor China, the world's two largest emitters of carbon dioxide, signed the Kyoto Protocol, which is slated to expire in 2012. By the end of 2009, the Copenhagen climate change agreement will be established. The pressure is high for the United States to play a role in this agreement and in affected climate change. Ongoing discussions of climate change will invariably concentrate on China.

One way individuals, corporations, and governments are working to abate their carbon output (or carbon footprint) is by purchasing carbon offsets. Corporations, including concert promoters, such as Reverb, which we discussed in Chapter 4, encourage recycling, the consumption of local produce, car pooling, and other practices that help people reduce their carbon footprints. Corporations and individuals also purchase carbon offsets (many are available online), and in turn trees are planted, wind turbines are built, and other carbon-reducing actions take place.

Globally, governments are considering a carbon market through which countries could exchange carbon dioxide emissions for preservation of carbon-absorbing forests. A global carbon market would include countries of the periphery and semiperiphery, and would provide these countries with incentive to maintain their forests, which absorb carbon dioxide, rather than clear them. A global carbon market may also provide countries such as the United States an opportunity to continue to emit carbon dioxide at high rates, simply by paying for the rights to do so.

Examine the map of global carbon dioxide emissions and explain the pattern you see. What other geographic patterns are correlated with those shown in the map?

Summary

What will the future be like? Many would agree with geographer Robert Kates, who foresees a "warmer, more crowded, more connected but more diverse world." As we consider this prospect, we must acknowledge that global environmental changes illustrate the limits of our knowledge of the Earth. Many of today's global environmental changes were not anticipated. Moreover, many global changes are nonlinear, and some are "chaotic" in the sense that future conditions cannot be reliably predicted. Nonlinearity means that small actions in certain situations may result in large impacts and may be more important than larger actions in causing change. Thresholds also exist in many systems, which, once past, are irreversible. This occurs, for example, when the habitat for a species is diminished to the point where the species quickly dies off. Unfortunately, we may not be able to identify these thresholds until we pass them. This leaves open the possibility of "surprises"—unanticipated responses by physical systems.

The complexity and urgency of the environmental challenge will tax the energies of the scientific and policy communities for some time to come. Geography must be an essential part of any serious effort to grapple with these challenges. The major changes that are taking place have different origins and spatial expressions, and each results from a unique combination of physical and social processes. We cannot simply focus on system dynamics and generalized causal relationships. We must also consider emerging patterns of environmental change and the impacts of differences from place to place on the operation of general processes. Geography is not the backdrop to the changes taking place; it is at the very heart of the changes themselves.

Geographic Concepts

chlorofluorocarbons
Pangaea
photosynthesis
mass depletions
mass extinctions
Pacific Ring of Fire
Pleistocene
glaciation
interglaciation
Wisonconsinian
    Glaciation

Holocene
Little Ice Age
environmental stress
renewable resources
hydrologic cycle
aquifers
atmosphere
global warming
acid rain
oxygen cycle
deforestation

soil erosion
solid waste
sanitary landfills
toxic waste
radioactive waste
biodiversity
ozone layer
Vienna Convention for
    the Protection of the
    Ozone Layer
Montreal Protocol

Learn More Online

About geography and environmental hazards
http://www.bbc.co.uk/scotland/education/int/geog/envhaz/index.shtml

CHAPTER 14

Globalization and the Geography of Networks

Field Note Global Consumption

Walking into a Gap store in the Mall of America, my eyes were immediately drawn to a display of t-shirts on a circular table at the store's entrance. Each t-shirt had a special tag identifying it as (Gap) RED, which explained that a portion of the shirt's sale price would go directly to the Global Fund to combat AIDS in Subsaharan Africa. (PRODUCT) RED is a business model that creates partnerships with corporations, such as the Gap and Motorola (Figure 14.1), to establish a network of private sector funding for designated AIDS projects in Africa supported by the Global Fund.

Economic geographers have studied the geographies of consumption, focusing on spaces of consumption (discussed in Chapter 8), like the Mall of America, as well as consumer choices – how consumers make choices and whether social concerns, such as AIDS in Subsaharan Africa, factor into their purchases. According to geographer Jon Goss, economic geographers have observed an "attitude-behavior gap," meaning that "consumers are not willing to pay higher prices for 'cause-related products,' lack adequate information to make effective choices, suffer from 'care fatigue,' respond more to short-term negative campaigns" and at the same time are concerned over "exploitation of labor and environment."

▬▬ **Figure 14.1**
(PRODUCT) RED offerings include items from the Gap, Converse, and Motorola.   ©Tony Cenicola/The New York Times/Redux.

(PRODUCT) RED works to overcome the attitude-behavior gap by keeping the prices of RED products the same as non-RED products, by sustaining a dynamic marketing campaign, and by advocating transparency and disseminating information about the projects supported through funds raised.

The success of (PRODUCT) RED and other goods with connections to social concerns is one of many processes creating and recreating globalization. In Chapter 1, we defined **globalization** as a set of processes that are increasing interactions, deepening relationships, and heightening interdependence without regard to country borders. We explained that globalization is also a set of outcomes that are felt from these global processes—outcomes that are unevenly distributed and differently manifested across the world.

In the media and in debates on campus, the topic of globalization is often too quickly reduced to black and white—either you are for it or you are against it. If this were true, your choices as a consumer would be equally black and white. Globalization is possible because of increasing interdependence throughout the globe, where communications across people and places are relatively easy and inexpensive.

Rarely does the consumption of a certain product have a clear outcome — whether positive or negative. Jobs created by industry in one place can cause environmental damage in another. Consumption, or purchasing an item, is the end point in a commodity chain (see Chapter 10). Economic geographers study commodity chains to trace a product to its origins and discover why production occurs where and how it does and to understand the impacts of production (including labor and environmental) at each step in the commodity chain.

Take, for example, the production of an iPod. Central to the iPod is the microchip that runs the iPod's wheel, stores your favorite songs and movies, and provides high-quality sound. The iPod's microchip is produced by PortalPlayer, a Californian company with offices in India. In his piece on PortalPlayer called "The World in an iPod," journalist Andrew Leonard explains that PortalPlayer has a 24-hour development cycle because engineers in California and in India can work around the clock (with time zones 12 hours apart) to design and redesign the microchip. The actual microchips are created in Taiwan, and the commodity chain for PortalPlayer (Figure 14.2) reveals how people and places around the world interconnect to design and create the company's microchip.

The act of consumption is an end point of a commodity chain, and it is also the beginning of the product's afterlife. What happens when you discard or donate the item, or what are the costs or benefits created by the funds (whether funds for a charity or profits for a corporation) generated by your purchase? Corporations such as Apple, which sells the iPod, work to reduce consumer waste by recycling iPods and computers, and by offering discounts to consumers who recycle their old iPods. Nonetheless, in many global cities in poorer parts of the world, adults and children work in garbage dumps to recover valuable copper wire and other components of computers and other electronics made by Apple and its competitors.

Your everyday acts as consumers happen in a global context and have global (though not always easy to see or track) ramifications. In this chapter, we recognize that understanding outcomes and impacts is not an easy task, and in so doing, we focus on the geography of globalization and the outcomes of globalization across scales. We describe how people and places are interconnected and the kinds of networks they have built both because of and in spite of globalization. Finally, we examine changing identities, looking at how people make sense of themselves in a globalized world.

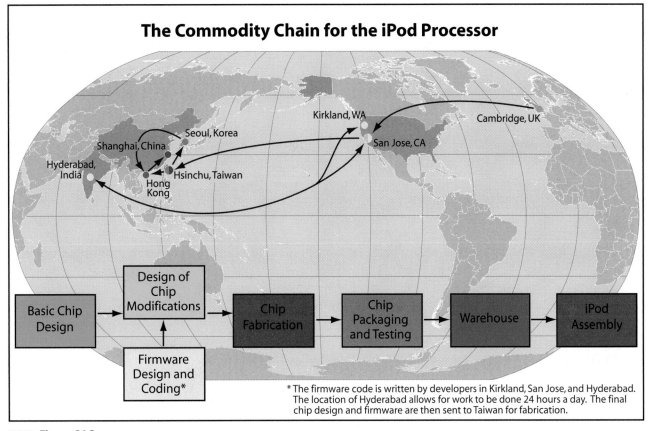

Figure 14.2

Inside an iPod: The PortalPlayer World. Map designed by Stephen P. Hanna, based on information from: Andrew Leonard, "The World in the iPod" Spiegel Online, 8 August 2005.

Key Questions   For Chapter 14

1. What is globalization, and what role do networks play in globalization?
2. At what scales do networks operate in the globalized world?
3. How have identities changed in a globalized world?

WHAT IS GLOBALIZATION, AND WHAT ROLE DO NETWORKS PLAY IN GLOBALIZATION?

Whether you are in favor of or opposed to globalization, we all must recognize that globalization is "neither an inevitable nor an irreversible set of processes," as John O'Loughlin, Lynn Staeheli, and Edward Greenberg put it. Andrew Kirby explains that globalization is "not proceeding according to any particular playbook. It is not a smoothly evolving state of capitalist development." Rather, it is fragmented, and its flows are "chaotic in terms of origins and destinations."

Globalization is a "chaotic" set of processes and outcomes created by people, be they corporate CEOs, university administrators, readers of blogs, or protesters at a trade meeting. The processes of globalization and the connectedness created through globalization are not limited to state-to-state interaction. Rather, the connectedness of globalization occurs across scales and across networks, regardless of state borders.

The backbone of globalization is trade; thus, debates over globalization typically focus on trade. To visualize how trade creates and maintains a globalized world, examine a

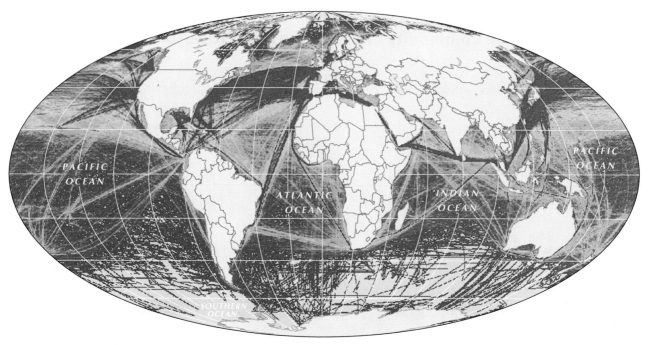

■■■ Figure 14.3
Global Shipping Lanes.   The map traces over 3,000 shipping routes used by commercial
and government vessels during 2006. The red lines mark the most frequently used shipping
lanes, globally. Map courtesy of: National Center for Ecological Analysis and Synthesis,
http://ebm.nceas.ucsb.edu/GlobalMarine/impacts/transformed/jpg/shipping.jpg, last
accessed August 2008.

map of shipping routes used around the world in one year
(Fig. 14.3). The arguments in favor of globalization, as
economist Keith Maskus states, are that "free trade raises
the well-being of all countries by inducing them to specialize their resources in those goods they produce relatively most efficiently" in order to lower production costs,
and that "competition through trade raises a country's
long-term growth rate by expanding access to global technologies and promoting innovation."

These fundamental principles of free trade (and
how to achieve it) are often described as the **Washington
Consensus**. Antiglobalizationists see the Washington
Consensus as a Western push for the rest of the world
to privatize state-owned entities, to open financial markets, to liberalize trade by removing restrictions on the
flow of goods, and to encourage foreign direct investment. Antiglobalizationists focus on the role of the World
Bank, International Monetary Fund, and World Trade
Organization as purveyors of the Washington Consensus,
often gathering at the meetings of these major global
organizations because they see the organizations as set
up to benefit the countries of the global economic core.
(Fig. 14.4) Antiglobalizationists argue that the countries
of the core continue to protect their own economies while

forcing the countries of the semi-periphery and periphery to open their economies to foreign direct investment
and to remove protections on their domestic production.
According to Maskus, the rules negotiated for the World
Trade Organization "inevitably reflect the economic
interest of powerful lobbyists" in states such as the United
States and the European Union. Antiglobalizationists
agree with Maskus and argue that free trade is not "free;"
rather, it builds up a global economic network that sends
most benefits to the core.

With globalization, we are living on an unprecedented scale. As Andrew Kirby perceptively describes it,
we are living "not so much in a world without boundaries,
or in a world without geography—*but more literally in a
world*, as opposed to a neighborhood or a region" (emphasis added). What does it mean to live "in a world?"

Networks

Manuel Castells defines **networks** as "a set of interconnected nodes" without a center. The idyllic network is
horizontally structured, with power shared among all participants and ideas flowing in all directions. The multitude

Field Note

"'You cannot come to southern Brazil without seeing our biggest city,' said the vintner who was showing me around the Cooperativa Aurora, the huge winery in Bento Gonçalves, in the State of Rio Grande do Sul. 'Besides, it's January, so they'll be having the big marches, it's almost like carnival time in Rio!'

So I headed for Porto Alegre, only to find that a hotel room was not to be had. Tens of thousands of demonstrators had converged on the State's capital, largest port, and leading industrial city—and what united them was opposition to globalization.

It was not quite a carnival, but the banners held aloft by the noisy, sometimes singing and dancing demonstrators left no doubt as to their common goals.

The World Social Forum has become an annual event held in cities around the world, with ever-larger marches and meetings to protest the actions of the world's dominant states, especially the United States. The World Social Forum is a network of antiglobalizationists—people who seek an alternative economic reality for the globe, one not centered on accumulation of capital. Socialist economic views, leftist political leanings, and support for minority causes combine each year at the World Social Forum in a show of strength."

Figure 14.4

Porto Alegre, Brazil. © Lima Agliberto/Gamma-Presse/Zuma Press.

of networks that exist in the world—financial, transportation, communication, kinship, corporate, nongovernmental, trade, government, media, education, and dozens of others—enable globalization to occur and create a higher degree of interaction and interdependence among people than ever before in human history.

While networks have always existed, Castells says that they have fundamentally changed over the last 20 years as a result of the diffusion of information technology that links places in a global, yet uneven, way. Through information technology networks, Castells argues that globalization has proceeded by "linking up all that, according to dominant interests, has value anywhere in the planet, and discarding anything (people, firms, territories, resources) which has no value or becomes devalued." Information technology networks link some places more than others, helping to create the spatial unevenness of globalization as well as the uneven outcomes of globalization.

Time–Space Compression

Access (or lack of access) to information technology networks creates time–space compression (Chapters 1 and 4). Time–space compression means that certain places, such

as global cities (especially in the core), are more interconnected than ever through communication and transportation networks, and that other places, such as those in the periphery, are farther removed than ever. According to Castells, the age of information technology networks has been more revolutionary than even the advent of the printing press or the Industrial Revolution. He claims that we are just at the beginning of this age "as the Internet becomes a universal tool of interactive communication, as we shift from computer-centered technologies to network-diffused technologies, as we make progress in nanotechnology (and thus in the diffusion capacity of information devices), and even more important, as we unleash the biology revolution, making possible for the first time, the design and manipulation of living organisms, including human parts."

A major divide in access to information technology between the core and periphery is both a hallmark of the current world and an example of the uneven outcomes of globalization. The United Nations Development Program's Human Development Report divides the world's states into high income, middle income, and low income (according to gross domestic product) and reports on accessibility to technology according to these classes. In 2005, the World Resources Institute reported that on average high-income states had 527 telephone mainlines, 849 cellular subscribers, and 571 Internet users per 1000 people. On average, middle-income states had 209 telephone mainlines, 382 cellular subscribers, and 111 Internet users per 1000 people. The states in the low-income class had an average of 35 telephone mainlines, 78 cellular subscriptions, and 43 Internet users per 1000 people.

The quickening pace of change in technology is another hallmark of the globalized world and magnifies the global technological divide. We may be shocked to see how quickly technology has changed and diffused. In 1992, the highest income states had on average only 10 cellular subscribers and 2.5 Internet users per 1000 people (contrasted with 849 and 571, respectively, in 2005).

Figure 14.5
World Cities Most Connected to New York City. This map shows the 30 world cities that are the most connected to New York City, as measured by flows in the service economy. *Data from*: P. J. Taylor and R. E. Lang, "U.S. Cities in the 'World City Network,'" The Brookings Institution, Survey Series, February 2005. *http://wwwe.brookings.edu/dybdocroot/metro/pubs/20050222_worldcities.pdf*, last accessed September 2005.

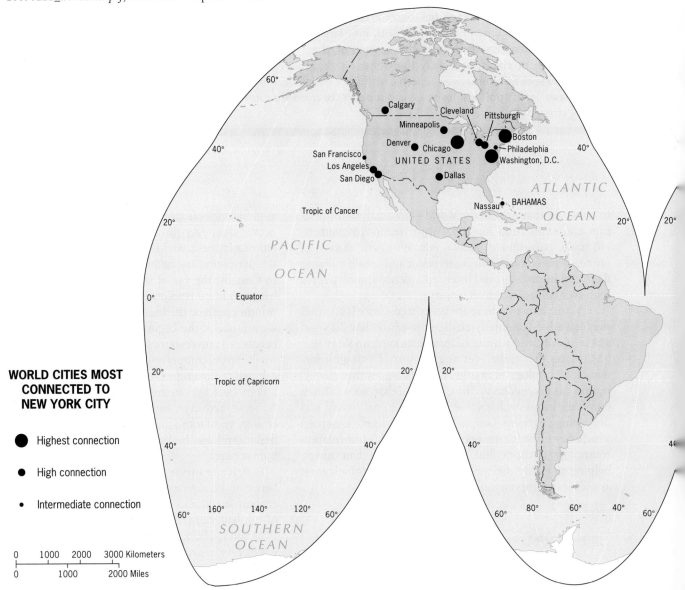

Global Cities

Time–space compression has helped both to create and reinforce a network of highly linked global cities. In Chapter 9, we discussed the growth of *global cities* in the core, semi-periphery, and periphery of the globe and the growth in their connectedness. We considered much of the research published by geographers in the Globalization and World Cities group based in the United Kingdom. The group of researchers who contribute to the Globalization and World Cities group use network analyses of global cities to examine levels of connectivity among cities for factors such as air travel between cities and global outreach of financial and advertising networks from global cities, and to generate data by individual cities rather than by countries.

The researchers generated data for 315 global cities, focusing on the interactions and connections among them. They measured the information technology flows among the cities by tracking the flow of advanced services among the cities, focusing on accounting, advertising, banking/finance, insurance, law, and management consulting. Figure 14.5 shows the 30 cities that are most connected to New York City, as measured by the flow of

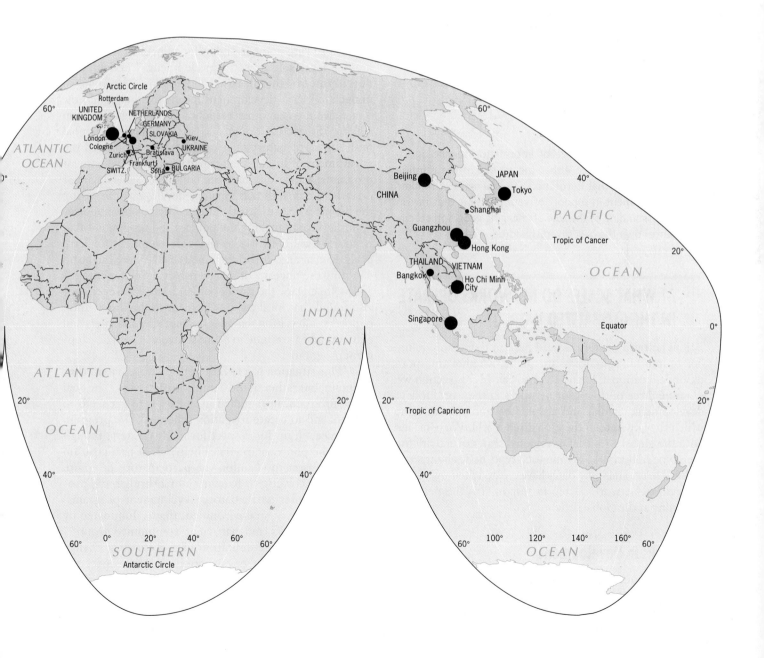

advanced services. By tracking flows, the authors found that Miami, not Los Angeles, is the U.S. city most closely linked to Latin America and New York is the second most *globally* linked city in the world (behind London and ahead of Tokyo). Chicago is also a highly ranked member of the global city network, coming in seventh. The researchers found that New York and Chicago stand apart from other world cities in that these American cities have greater domestic linkages than global cities in the Pacific Rim or the European Union.

The linkages among global cities provide insights into the spatial character of the networks that underlie globalized processes. A multitude of globalized processes such as financial transactions and flows (represented here by banking/finance and accounting) occur across the network of global cities. Similarly, this network reflects the flow of advertising and marketing consultation services, which in turn reflects the flow of ideas through the media across the globe.

Castells claims that the age of information technology is more revolutionary than either the advent of the printing press or the Industrial Revolution. Do you agree with him? Write an argument in support of your position, drawing on your understanding of the role of changing geographical circumstances over the past several hundred years.

AT WHAT SCALES DO NETWORKS OPERATE IN THE GLOBALIZED WORLD?

The term *network* is used here to define any number of interlinkages across the globe, whether transportation, educational, financial, or social. In this section we examine three of the major networks in the world today: development, media, and corporate—and the scales at which they operate in the globalized world. We consider both the global and local or regional scales of activity for each type of network. Within each type, nodes interact at a global scale, and individuals have created their own local or regional networks, often in response to the network operating at the global scale.

Networks in Development

Nongovernmental organizations (NGOs) have propagated a web of global development networks over the last 20 years in response to the top-down decision making (e.g., structural adjustment loans) coming from global organizations dominated by the core (e.g., the World Bank and the International Monetary Fund). Development networks are seen as counterhegemonic, serving as a response to the power of the major decision makers in the world. The goal of NGOs is to include the voices of the poor and those directly affected by development, permitting them to express their opinions and lifestyles. In development networks, northern NGOs and southern NGOs work together to reach a consensus on how to achieve economic development in a particular place.

Despite the goal of sharing power across a network, most development networks (like most other networks) have power differences within them. Indeed, Leroi Henry, Giles Mohan, and Helen Yanacopulos find that power relationships exist both within and between networks. Many networks have hierarchies of power within them, often privileging the views NGOs in the core, as opposed to those in the periphery.

A growing number of development entities are promoting local solutions to development. **Participatory development**—the idea that locals should be engaged in deciding what development means for them and how to achieve it—is another response to top-down decision making. Stuart Corbridge has studied how the global push for participatory development has encouraged the government of India to enact participatory development programs. Corbridge and his colleague Sanjay Kumar describe the goal of participatory development as giving the people who are directly affected by policies and programs a voice in making the policies and programs—that is, to use local networks to shape development for local goals. Kumar and Corbridge found that "[t]here can be no doubting the sincerity of" participatory development programs "to engage the rural poor" in India. However, they also found that local politics factor into the distribution of poverty alleviation schemes because richer farmers and elites in rural areas tend to be most involved with development program.

This situation is a failure not of development, they maintain, but rather of the definition of success. The goal of the program they studied in India was to get seeds to farmers and to create irrigation schemes. The program has succeeded in this respect for many farmers, though not for the poorest farmers. Their lack of participation is not a reason to abandon the participatory program, however. According to Kumar and Corbridge, the program (like other participatory development programs) has to "operate in an environment that is dominated by better off farmers and particular community groups." They argue that the definition of success must change because development organizations cannot expect the poorest to "participate in groups that have little meaning for them."

The World Bank, the International Monetary Fund, and even state governments are increasingly embracing the ideal of participatory development, loosening demands for trade liberalization in the periphery and semiperiphery. As Kumar and Corbridge explain, politics will enter participatory development, just as it enters the development networks and the global development organizations. The goal of participatory development is worthwhile, even if the short-term results do not mesh with Western concepts of success.

Local Currencies

Another way people in localities, whether in the core, semiperiphery, or periphery, shape local development is by establishing local currencies. Uneven development affects not just the periphery but also the core and semiperiphery. Economic downturns are a frequent occurrence in local places, and unemployment is a common result. As Michael Pacione explains, finding families and neighbors who can help in times of economic hardship can be quite difficult because globalization results in less connectedness:

> Social trends inherent in global capitalism, including decreasing household size, increasing distance between relatives, and attenuation of neighboring relations within cities, have served to inhibit the operation of informal relations in which disadvantaged households could exchange goods and services for partial or no payment within the "moral" economy of their own family or neighborhood.

During the 1980s, the people of Vancouver Island, Canada, established the first **local exchange trading system (LETS)**. When the two major employers in the area, a U.S. Air Force base and a lumber mill, closed, many of the island's 50,000 people faced severe economic hardship. The community began a local currency, LETS, through which members traded services or goods in a local network separated from the formal economy. People who needed services (such as plumbing) would pay others with their own services or goods (such as providing accounting services in exchange for the plumbing call).

LETS systems and other local currency systems are alternatives to global norms of development, serving as a local response to global or regional economic change affecting a locality (Fig. 14.6). Because the currency is local, it fuels the local economy: it can only be traded locally, thus keeping economic activity locally. The person who spends LETS for shoes, for example, can only spend them at the local shoe store, and not at an online store or in a catalog.

The number of local currencies in use in the world today total well over 1000. Many local currencies are used in rural areas, but local currencies have also found success in cities as diverse as Glasgow, Scotland and Berkeley,

Figure 14.6

Bernal Buenos Aires, Argentina. Since its economic crisis began, the number of local currencies in Argentina has proliferated, now hovering around 5000 different local currencies and barter clubs. In this suburb of Buenos Aires, girls sell clothing that is priced with "credits," a value system established in their local currency system. © Homer Sykes/Alamy.

California. In Berkeley, the local currency did not develop as a response to economic hardship. In Berkeley, the local currency developed from a desire to not support the global currency system.

Networks in Media

Global diffusion of products and ideas associated with popular culture depends largely on global media and retail store networks as well as the advertising practices in which both engage. The global media today encompass much more than print, radio, and television; they also include spaces of entertainment, such as the New Amsterdam Theater in Times Square in New York (owned by Disney); songs produced under record labels like RCA, Jive, and

BMG (all owned by Bertelsmann); games played on PlayStation (owned by Sony); information about a movie through MovieFone, and the directions to the movie theater through MapQuest (both owned by Time-Warner, as is the New Line Cinema movie you chose to see).

Through a series of mergers and consolidations occurring mostly in the post–Cold War era, global media are controlled largely by six global corporations: Time-Warner, Disney, Bertelsmann, Viacom, News Corporation, and Vivendi Universal. These six media corporations (along with other media corporations) are masters of **vertical integration**. A vertically integrated corporation is one that has ownership in a variety of points along the production and consumption of a commodity chain.

In a 2003 report, Miguel Mendes Pereira stated that media companies compete for three things: *content*, *delivery*, and *consumers*. Through consolidation and mergers, global media companies such as The Walt Disney Corporation (Fig. 14.7) are vertically integrated to gain content (production companies, radio shows, television programming, films, or books) and delivery (radio, television stations, magazines, and movies). Delivery of content also refers to the infrastructure of technology—the proprietary technologies used for creating and sharing digital media. Vertical integration also helps media giants attract and maintain customers through **synergy**, or the cross promotion of vertically integrated goods. For example, within the vertical integration of Disney, you can visit Disney's Hollywood studios at Walt Disney World, go to a High School Musical Pep Rally, and meet the muppets characters at Muppet vision 3-D. Then, you can hop over to Disney's Animal Kingdom to catch the Festival of the Lion King, based on the Disney Theatrical Production that was based on the Walt Disney Picture.

Vertical integration of media changes the geography of the flow of ideas globally by limiting the ultimate number of **gatekeepers**, that is, people or corporations that control access to information. A gatekeeper can choose not to tell a story and the story will not be heard. We can interpret the consolidation of media as resulting in fewer ultimate gatekeepers. In this vein, we would see the ultimate gatekeepers as the big media conglomerates. Or we can focus on the competition for customers and the proliferation of sources of delivery for media (the vast number of cable television channels, radio stations, Internet sources, and magazines) and argue that there are more gatekeepers in the world today. The diversity of media outlets supports this proposition, with television channels geared to specific segments (or markets) of the population. For example, both the globally reaching Al-Jazeera satellite television station and the new cable channels in the United States that are targeted toward the Muslim American population are geared to specific segments of the global or American population.

Figure 14.7

The Walt Disney Corporation. *Data from*: Columbia Journalism Review, Who Owns What. http://www.cjrarchives.org/tools/owners/disney.asp

Blogs

Historically, governments and journalists had the ability to be strong gatekeepers by choosing what stories to release or tell. Today, with the extraordinary growth of blogs on the Internet (upwards of 8 million in 2004 and over 100 million in 2008), tight gatekeeping is much more difficult. A blog is a free service provided on the Internet to post individual thoughts, photographs, and experiences, and to create links to websites or other blogs. Blogs are in many ways an individual way of creating local, regional, or global networks that respond to (and exist separate from) the global network of media.

Anyone with access to the Internet can read a blogger's postings and comment on them. Blogger, the original blog site created by the small company Pyra Labs in 1999, was sold to Google. Media giants are finding their way into the blogosphere (as the blog space of the Internet is called) with sites such as MSN spaces and AOL journals. The blog site hosts your blog for free and provides a format for your blog, so that you need know nothing about website publishing. Blogs influenced the U.S. elections in 2004 and 2008. They also help with cross promotion by linking other websites, and they spur stories in the mainstream media.

Networks of Retail Corporations

Unlike major media corporations that are vertically integrated, major retail corporations are typically horizontally integrated. A horizontally integrated corporation is one that at first glance appears to be different retail companies in pursuit of different market shares; however, all of the retail companies are owned by the same parent corporation.

Horizontal integration means that when you shop for similar products in different places or across a mall, your dollars will often support the same parent corporation. If you go to the mall to buy a pair of jeans, your choice to shop at Banana Republic, the Gap, and Old Navy sends your dollars to the same parent company. And your choice to take a break at the food court to drink a Gatorade, eat a bag of Doritos, and buy a Quaker granola bar for later also sends your dollars to the same parent corporation (in this case, PepsiCo). You may look up and wonder when Taco Bell started selling Kentucky Fried Chicken and Pizza Hut pizza (all three are part of YUM! corporation, which also owns A&W, and Long John Silvers. YUM! is a spin-off of PepsiCo).

Neil Wrigley, Neil Coe, and Andrew Currah have studied the globalization of retail corporations, such as Wal-Mart (U.S.), Costco (U.S.), Ikea (Sweden), Metro (Germany), and Carrefour (France). In their comparison of manufacturing corporations and retail corporations, they found that global retailers are more spatially disaggregated, with stores in hundreds or thousands of locations, whereas global manufacturers are more spatially concentrated, especially at production sites. In addition, global retailers engage directly with consumers and have a local presence in a place that manufacturing corporations do not. Consumers who enter local stores interact directly with the global retailer at the local scale.

Also at the local scale, people have created numerous networks of protest against the building of global retail stores in their locality, wheres others have created networks to encourage and invite such stores into their community.

Analyzing the global consolidation of media, the global networks of development, and the global presence of retail corporations helps us see the diversity of global networks, with some increasingly centralized and others increasingly disaggregated. In each case, the global network does not change local places uniformly. People interact with the global network, shaping it, resisting it, embracing it, and responding to globalization in unique ways.

Think of a place you have been where the global media have worked to create a synergy. Describe the presence of the global media entity in the place and show how the global media have imprinted the cultural landscape of the place. How has that imprint affected your experience in (and your sense of) the place?

HOW HAVE IDENTITIES CHANGED IN A GLOBALIZED WORLD?

Gillian Rose defines identity as "how we make sense of ourselves" and explains that we have identities at different scales: we have local, national, regional, and global identities. At each scale, place factors into our identities. We infuse places with meaning and emotions based on our experiences in those places. Few people living in the globalized world today are world travelers. And many of those who have traveled the globe have missed out on the uniqueness of place by visiting only global cities, living the lives of businesspeople (visiting airports, office buildings, and hotels), or staying in luxurious resorts (separated from the "local") as tourists. How, then, can a person have a global identity if he or she has not experienced the globe?

Columbine, Colorado

I took this photo at the dedication ceremony for the memorial to the victims of the Columbine High School shooting of April 20, 1999. Columbine is located near Littleton, Colorado, in Denver's southern suburbs. The memorial, dedicated on September 21, 2007, provides a quiet place for meditation and reflection in a public park adjacent to the school. Hundreds came to the ceremony to honor those killed and wounded in the attack, one of the deadliest school shootings in U.S. history.

After tragedies like the Columbine shootings, creating a memorial often helps to rebuild a sense of community. Public ceremonies like this can set an example for survivors

Figure 14.8
Columbine, Colorado.　© Ken Foote.

who may otherwise have difficulty facing their loss in private. A group memorial helps to acknowledge the magnitude of the community's loss and, by so doing, helps assure families and survivors that the victims did not suffer alone—that their deaths and wounds are grieved by the entire community. Memorials are important too because they can serve as a focus for remembrance and commemoration long into the future, even after all other evidence of a tragedy has disappeared.

In my research for *Shadowed Ground* I have visited hundreds of such places in the United States and Europe. I am still surprised by the power of such places and the fact that shrines and memorials resulting from similar tragedies are tended lovingly for decades, generations, and centuries. They produce strong emotions and sometimes leave visitors—including me—in tears. But by allowing individuals to share loss, tragedy, and sorrow with others, they create a sense of common purpose.

Kenneth E. Foote, University of Colorado at Boulder

Globalization networks interlink us, and the flow of information technology is a daily way in which we are interlinked with the globe. A person may be overwhelmed by the flow of information and choose to ignore it, but even this person has a global identity. People identify themselves by identifying with or against at the local, regional, and global scales. As the flow of information continues, many people feel a need to make sense of the world by identifying with people and places. People personalize the flow of information, and in so doing they feel more connected to the globe and alter their local cultural landscapes to reflect their feeling of connectedness.

Personal Connectedness

The news in 1995 that Princess Diana had died traveled quickly from global media sources among friends, family, and even strangers. Many felt the need to mourn for a princess they had never met in a place they had never been. Some wanted to leave a token offering for the princess—a rose, a note, a candle, a photograph. Impromptu shrines to Princess Diana cropped up at the British embassy in Washington, D.C., and at British embassies and consulates around the world. People in Britain left countless flowers at the royal palace in London, where Princess Diana resided.

In an incredibly divided world, in which the rift between rich and poor is growing at the global scale, what made people feel connected to a woman who represented the royal family, an elite group of people of wealth and privilege? The idea that people around the world are linked and have shared experiences, such as death, tragedy, and sorrow, draws from Benedict Anderson's concept of the nation as an imagined community (see Chapter 8). When massive tragedies such as 9/11, the Indian Ocean tsunami, or Hurricane Katrina occur, people often talk about someone they knew who was in the place (or had been at some point), someone who died (even those they did not know but heard about in the news), or an act of bravery or triumph that occurred in the midst of tragedy. The desire to *personalize*, to *localize* a tragedy feeds off of the imagined global community in which we live. In the process of personalizing and localizing, a tragedy can be *globalized* in an effort to appeal to the humanity of all people in the hope that all feel or experience the loss tangentially.

When a death or a tragedy does happen, how do people choose a local space in which to express a personal and/or global sorrow? In a world were some academics argue that place and territory are unimportant because things like global superhighways of information transcend place, people continue to recognize territories and create places. In the case of Princess Diana's death, people created hundreds of spaces of sorrow to mourn the loss of a magnanimous person whose life was cut short. In the case of September 11, people transformed homes, schools, public spaces, and houses of worship into spaces of reflection by creating human chains, participating in moments of silence, or holding prayer vigils for the victims.

In his book *Shadowed Ground: America's Landscapes of Violence and Tragedy*, Kenneth Foote examines the "spontaneous shrines" created at the place of loss or at a place that represents loss and describes these spontaneous shrines as a "first stage in the commemoration of a disaster." Foote draws from extensive field research of landscapes of tragedy and violence in the United States to show how people mark or do not mark tragedy, both immediately with spontaneous shrines and in the longer term with permanent memorials (Fig. 14.8). He examines the struggles over whether and how to memorialize significant people or experienced tragedy. His research focuses on the United States, and after tracing and following the stories of hundreds of people and places, Foote concludes that "the debate over what, why, when, and where to build" a memorial for a person or event is "best considered a part of the grieving process."

Foote realized that the ways sites are memorialized or not vary over time and across a multitude of circumstances, depending on whether funding is available, the kind of structure to be built, who is being remembered (only those who died or also those injured?), whether the site represents a socially contested event (which often happens when racism is involved), and whether people want to remember the site. In recent American history, major terrorist attacks have been memorialized, often with the word "closure" evoked. Oklahoma City permanently memorialized the site of a terrorist attack at the Murrah Federal Building on the five-year anniversary of the tragedy. Other tragedies, such as that experienced at the World Trade Center in New York City on September 11, 2001 take longer to memorialize (Fig. 14.9). Millions of people have a personal connection to the World Trade

Figure 14.9

New York, New York.   The World Trade Center site is undergoing construction of a $3.2 billion transportation hub, slated to open in 2013. By 2011, a portion of the National September 11 Memorial and Museum is slated to open, with the rest opening by 2013. This photo was taken September 10, 2007 at the site where almost 3,000 people died on September 11, 2001.
© Newscom/Photoshot

Center site, and so consensus as to how the site should be memorialized and used has been elusive.

The din of information flowing our way each day is often overwhelming. As people filter through or ignore the flow of information, they may personalize the information and may differentiate themselves from particular people or places, but in the end many people's identities are shaped by the global scale. Living in a world, at a scale we have not experienced previously, changes us and profoundly changes places. Globalization, for good or for ill, has modified how we interact and has shaped how we make sense of ourselves in our world, our state, our region, our locality.

Think of a large-scale tragedy you can remember, such as September 11, the Indian Ocean tsunami, or Hurricane Katrina. In what ways have memorials of that tragedy reflected both globalization and localization at the same time?

Summary

Globalization has been compared to a runaway train blowing through stations leaving much of the world to stare at its caboose. Yet this description is not entirely accurate. Globalization is a series of processes, not all of which are headed in the same direction. Even those processes headed down the globalization track are often stopped, sent back to the previous station, or derailed. The globalization track is not inevitable or irreversible (in the words of O'Loughlin, Staeheli, and Greenberg). Many of the most important globalization processes take place within networks of global cities (see Chapter 9), of places linked by popular culture (see Chapter 4), of governments (see Chapter 8), of trade (see Chapter 12), and of development (see Chapter 10). People and places are found all along these networks, and just as globalization influences people and places, those same people and places influence globalization's trajectory and future.

Geographic Concepts

globalization
Washington Consensus
networks
participatory development

local exchange trading
    system (LETS)
vertical integration

synergy
gatekeepers
horizontal integration

Learn More Online

About media ownership

Columbia Journalism Review's Who Owns What Website
www.cjr.org/tools/owners/

About (PRODUCT) RED
www.joinred.com

About the GlobalFund
www.theglobalfund.org/EN/

About the Network of World Cities
http://www.brook.edu/metro/pubs/20050222_worldcities.pdf

About the World Social Forum
www.forumsocialmundial.org.br/

Maps

The geographer's greatest ally is the map. Maps can present enormous amounts of information very effectively, and can be used to establish theories and solve problems. Furthermore, maps often are fascinating, revealing things no other medium can. It has been said that if a picture is worth a thousand words, then a map is worth a million.

Maps can be fascinating, but they often do not get the attention they deserve. You may spend 20 minutes carefully reading a page of text, but how often have you spent 20 minutes with a page-size map, studying what it reveals? No caption and no paragraph of text can begin to summarize what a map may show; it is up to the reader to make the best use of it. For example, in the chapters on population issues we study several maps that depict the human condition by country, in terms of birth and death rates, infant mortality, calorie intake, life expectancy, and so on. In the text, we can refer only to highlights (and low points) on those maps. But make a point of looking beyond the main issue to get a sense of the global distributions these maps represent. It is part of an intangible but important process: to enhance your mental map of this world.

While on the topic of maps, we should remind ourselves that a map—any map—is an incomplete representation of reality. In the first place, the map is smaller than the real world it represents. Second, it must depict the curved surface of our world on a flat plane, for example, a page of this book. And third, it must contain symbols to convey the information that must be transmitted to the reader. These are the three fundamental properties of all maps: scale, projection, and symbols.

Understanding these basics helps us interpret maps while avoiding their pitfalls. Some maps look so convincing that we may not question them as we would a paragraph of text. Yet maps, by their very nature, to some extent distort reality. Most of the time, such distortion is necessary and does not invalidate the map's message. But some maps are drawn deliberately to mislead. Propaganda maps, for example, may exaggerate or distort reality to promote political aims. We should be alert to cartographic mistakes when we read maps. The proper use of scale, projection, and symbolization ensures that a map is as accurate as it can be made.

MAP SCALE

The scale of a map reveals how much the real world has been reduced to fit on the page or screen on which it appears. It is the ratio between an actual distance on the ground and the length given to that distance on the map, using the same units of measurement. This ratio is often represented as a fraction (e.g., 1:10,000 or 1/10,000). This means that one unit on the map represents 10,000 such units in the real world. If the unit is 1 inch, then an inch on the map represents 10,000 inches on the ground, or slightly more than 833 feet. (The metric system certainly makes things easier. One centimeter on the map would actually represent 10,000 cm or 100 meters.) Such a scale would be useful when mapping a city's downtown area, but it would be much too large for the map of an entire state. As the real-world area we want to map gets larger, we must make our map scale smaller. As small as the fraction 1/10,000 seems, it still is 10 times as large as 1/100,000, and 100 times as large as 1/1,000,000. If the world maps in this book had fractional scales, they would be even smaller. A large-scale map can contain much more detail and be far more representative of the real world than a small-scale map. Look at it this way: when we devote almost a full page of this book to a map of a major city (Fig. A.1), we are able to represent the layout of that city in considerable detail. But if the entire continental realm in which that city is located must be represented on a single page, the city becomes just a large dot on that small-scale map, and the detail is lost in favor of larger-area coverage (Fig. A.2). So the selection of scale depends on the objective of the map.

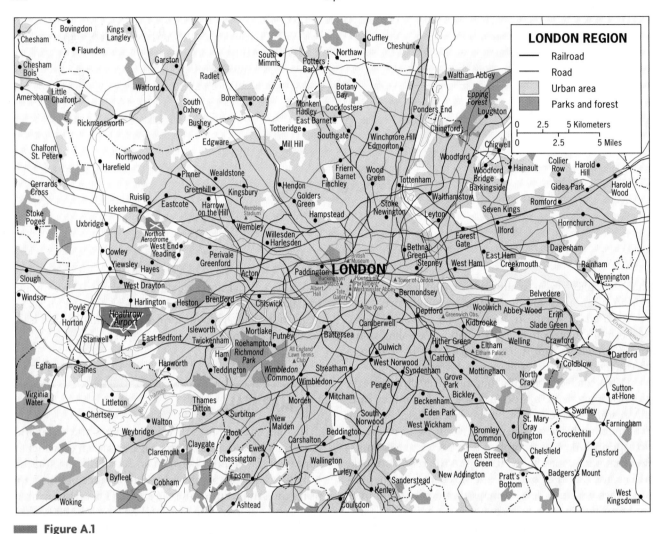

Figure A.1

The layout of a major city can be shown in considerable detail at this **large scale.**

MAP PROJECTIONS

For centuries cartographers have faced the challenge of map projection—the representation of the spherical Earth, or part of it, on a flat surface. To get the job done, but when you examine the maps in this book, you will note that most, if not all, of them have scales that are not given as ratios or fractions, but in graphic form. This method of representing map scale is convenient from several viewpoints. Using the edge of a piece of paper and marking the scale bar's length, the map reader can quickly—without calculation—determine approximate distances. And if a map is enlarged or reduced in reproduction, the scale bar is enlarged or reduced with it and remains accurate. That, of course, is not true of a ratio or fractional scale. Graphic scales, therefore, are preferred in this book.

there had to be a frame of reference on the globe itself, a grid system that could be transferred to the flat page. Any modern globe shows that system: a set of horizontal lines, usually at 10-degree intervals north and south from the equator, called parallels, and another set of vertical lines, converging on the poles, often shown at 15-degree intervals and called meridians (see box, "Numbering the Grid Lines"). On the spherical globe, parallels and meridians intersect at right angles (Fig. A.3).

But what happens when these lines of latitude (parallels) and longitude (meridians) are drawn to intersect at right angles on a flat piece of paper? At the equator, the representation of the real world is relatively accurate. But go toward the poles, and distortion grows with every degree until, in the northern and southern higher latitudes, the continents appear not only stretched out but also misshaped (Fig. A.4). Because the meridians cannot be made to converge in the polar areas, this projection makes Antarctica look like a giant, globe-girdling landmass.

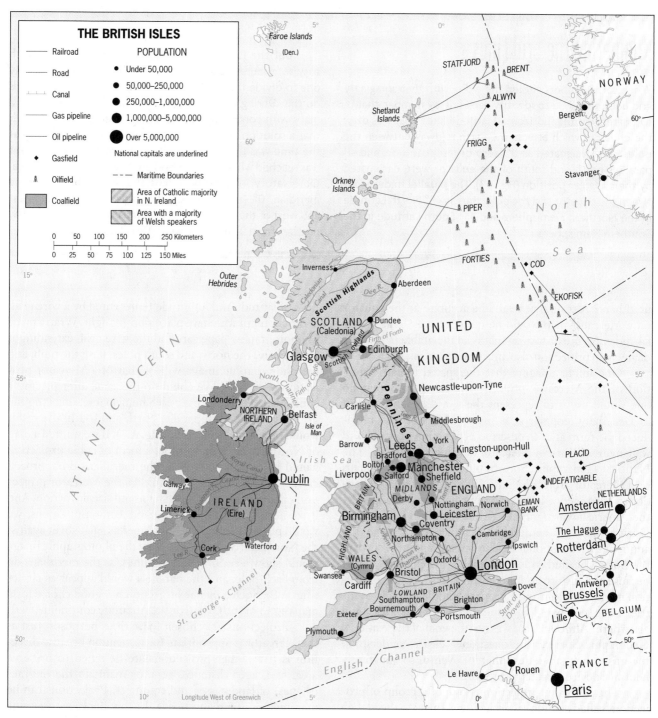

Figure A.2

Smaller scale allows display of larger area, but with less local detail.

Looking at this representation of the world, you might believe that it could serve no useful purpose. But in fact, the Mercator projection, invented in 1569 by Gerardus Mercator, a Flemish cartographer, had (and has) a very particular function. Because parallels and meridians cross (as they do on the spherical globe's grid) at right angles, direction is true everywhere on this map. Thus the Mercator projection enabled navigators to maintain an accurate course at sea simply by adhering to compass directions and plotting straight lines. It is used for that purpose to this day.

The spatial distortion of the Mercator projection serves to remind us that scale and projection are interconnected. What scale fraction or graphic scale bar could be

Numbering the Grid Lines

When cartographers girdled the globe with their imaginary grid lines, they had to identify each line by number, that is, by degree. For the (horizontal) latitude lines, that was easy: the equator, which bisects the Earth midway between the poles, was designated as 0° (zero degree) Latitude, and all parallels north and south of the equator were designated by their angular position (Fig. A.3). The parallel midway between the equator and the pole, thus, is 45° North Latitude in the Northern Hemisphere and 45° South Latitude in the Southern Hemisphere.

But the (vertical) longitude lines presented no such easy solution. Among the parallels, the equator is the only one to divide the Earth into equal halves, but all meridians do this. During the second half of the nineteenth century, maps with conflicting numbers multiplied, and it was clear that a solution was needed. The most powerful country at the time was Britain, and in 1884, international agreement was reached whereby the meridian drawn through the Royal Observatory in Greenwich, England, would be the prime meridian, 0° (zero degree) Longitude. All meridians east and west of the prime meridian could now be designated by number, from 0° to 180° East and West Longitude.

used here? A scale that would be accurate at the equator on a Mercator map would be quite inaccurate at higher latitudes. So the distortion that is an inevitable byproduct of any map projection also affects map scales.

One might imagine that the spatial (areal) distortion of the Mercator projection is so obvious that no one would use it to represent the world's countries. But in fact, many popular atlas maps (Mercator also introduced the term atlas to describe a collection of maps) and wall maps still use a Mercator for such purposes. The National Geographic Society published its world maps on a Mercator projection until 1988, when it finally abandoned the practice in favor of a projection developed by the American cartographer Arthur Robinson (Fig. A.5). During the news conference at which the change was announced, a questioner rose to pursue a point: Why had the Society waited so long to make this change? Was it because the distortion inherent in the Mercator projection made American and European middle-latitude countries large, compared to tropical countries in Africa and elsewhere? Although that was not the goal of the National Geographic Society, the questioner clearly understood the misleading subtleties inherent even in so apparently neutral a device as a map projection.

The Mercator projection is one of a group of projections called cylindrical projections. Imagine the globe's

lines of latitude and longitude represented by a wire grid, at the center of which we place a bright light. Wrap a piece of photographic paper around the wire grid, extending it well beyond the north and south poles, flash the bulb, and the photographic image will be that of a Mercator projection (Fig. A.6). We could do the same after placing a cone-shaped of paper over each hemisphere, touching the grid, say, at the 40th parallel north and south; the result would be a conic projection (Fig. A.7). If we wanted a map of North America or Europe, a form of conic projection would be appropriate. Now the meridians do approach each other toward the poles (unlike the Mercator projection), and there is much less shape and size distortion. And if we needed a map of Arctic and Antarctic regions, we would place the photographic paper as a flat sheet against the North and South Poles. Now the photographic image would show a set of diverging lines, as the meridians do from each pole, and the parallels would appear as circles (Fig. A.8). Such a planar projection is a good choice for a map of the Arctic Ocean or the Antarctic continent.

Projections are chosen for various purposes. Just as the Mercator is appropriate for navigation because direction is true, other projections are designed to preserve areal size, keep distances real, or maintain the outlines (shapes) of landmasses and countries. Projections can be manipulated for many needs. In this book, we examine

Figure A.3
Numbering of **grid lines.**
© H. J. de Blij, P. O. Muller, and John Wiley & Sons, Inc.

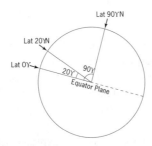
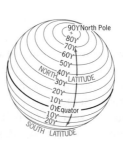
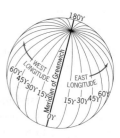

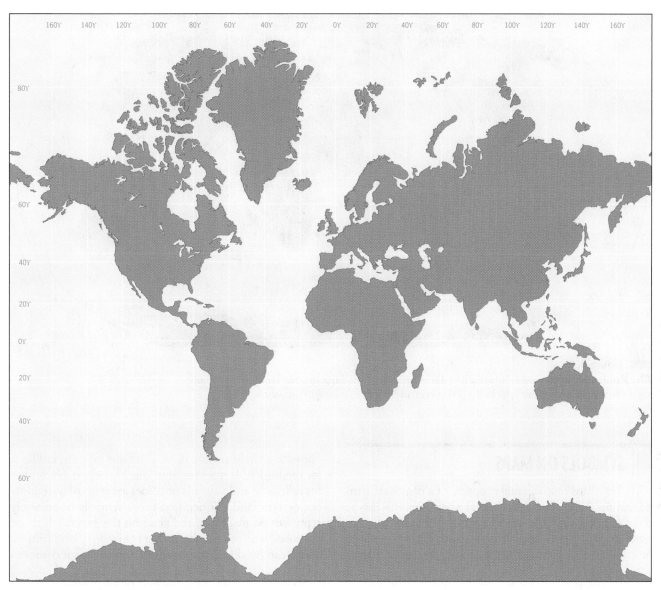

■ **Figure A.4**

Mercator's Projection greatly exaggerates the size and shape of higher-latitude landmasses, but direction is true everywhere on this map.

global distributions of various phenomena. The world map that forms the base for these displays is one that is designed to give prominence to land areas at the expense of the oceans. This is achieved by "interrupting" the projection where loss of territory (in this case water area) is not problematic.

When a map is planned, therefore, the choice of projection is an important part of the process. An inappropriate selection may weaken the effectiveness of a map and may lead to erroneous interpretations. Of course, the problem diminishes when the area to be mapped is smaller and the scale larger. We may consider various alternatives when it comes to a map of all of North America, but a map of a single State presents far fewer potential problems of distortion. And for a city map—even of a large city such as Chicago—the projection problem virtually disappears.

The old problem of how to represent the round Earth on a flat surface has been attacked for centuries, and there is no single best solution. What has been learned in the process, however, will be useful in fields of endeavor other than Earthly geography. As the age of planetary exploration dawns, and our space probes send back images of the surfaces of the Moon, Mars, Jupiter, and other components of our solar system, we will have to agree once again on grids, equators, and prime meridians. What has been learned in our efforts to map and represent the Earth will be useful in depicting the universe beyond.

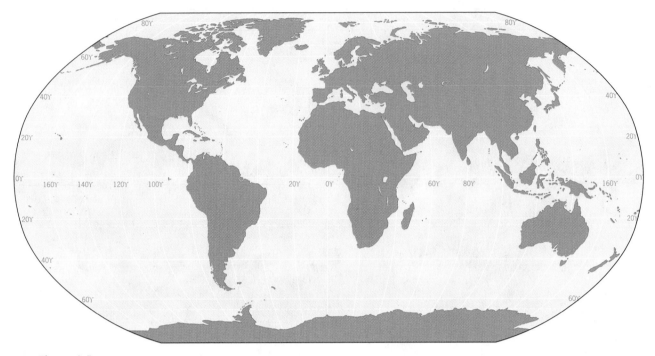

Figure A.5
The Robinson projection substantially reduces the exaggerated size of polar landmasses. It better approximates shape, but it lacks the directional utility of the mercator projection.

SYMBOLS ON MAPS

The third fundamental property of a map is its symbolization. Maps represent the real world, and this can be done only through the use of symbols. Anyone who has used an atlas map is familiar with some of these symbols: prominent dots (perhaps black or red) for cities; a large dot with a circle around it, or a star, for capitals; red lines for roads (double lines for four-lane highways), black lines for railroads; and patterns or colors for areas of water, forest, or farmland. Notice that these symbols respectively represent points, lines, and areas on the ground. For our purposes, we need not go further into map symbolization, which can become a very complex topic when it comes to

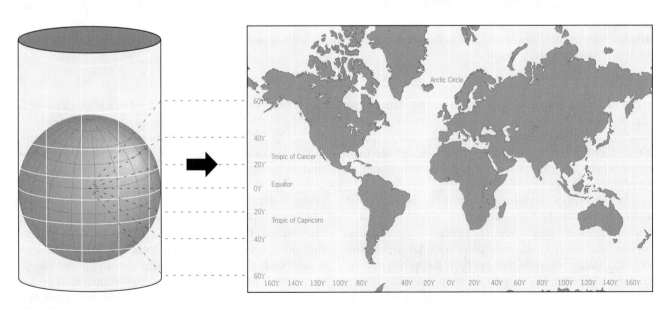

Figure A.6
Shadows of the globe's grid lines on wraparound paper: a **cylindrical projection** results.

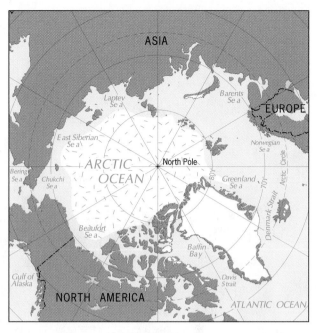

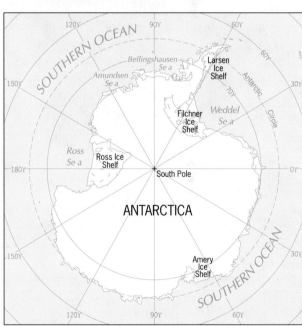

Figure A.8
Planar projection: now the light a the center of the globe projects diverging longitude lines on a flat sheet of paper placed over the North Pole (top) and the South Pole (bottom).
© H. J. de Blij, P. O. Muller, and John Wiley & Sons, Inc.

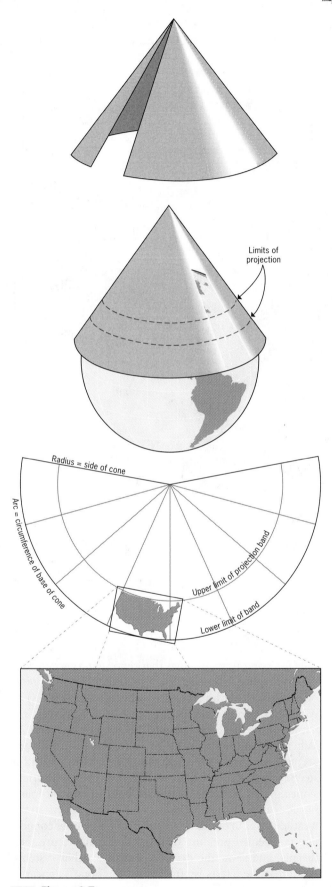

Figure A.7
Construction of a **conic projection.**

highly specialized cartography in such fields as geology and meteorology. Nevertheless, it is useful to know why symbols such as those used on the maps in this book were chosen.

Point symbols, as we noted, are used to show individual features or places. On a large-scale map of a city block, dots can represent individual houses. But on a small-scale map, a dot has to represent an entire "city." Still, cities have various sizes, and those size differences can be put

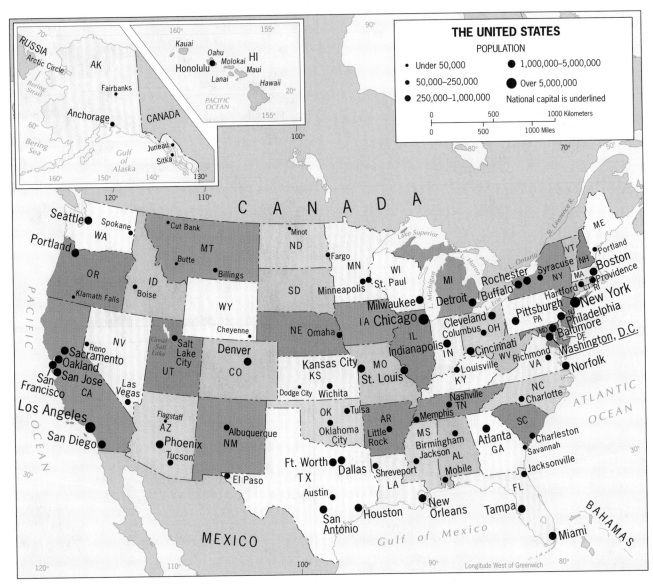

Figure A.9

This map uses **dot symbols** to indicate size categories of cities in the United States.

in categories and mapped accordingly (Fig. A.9). Thus New York, Chicago, and Los Angeles still appear as dots on the map, but their dots are larger than those representing Tucson, Milwaukee, or Denver. A dimensional scale is added to the map's graphic scale, and at a glance we can see the relative sizes of major cities in the United States and Canada.

Line symbols include not only roads and railroads, but also political and administrative boundaries, rivers, and other linear features. Again scale plays its crucial role: on a large-scale map, it is possible to represent the fenced boundaries of a single farm, but on a small-scale map, such detail cannot be shown.

Some lines on maps do not actually exist on the ground. When physical geographers do their field work

they use contour maps, lines that represent a certain consistent height above mean sea level (Fig. A.10). All points on such a contour line thus are at the same elevation. The spacing between contour lines immediately reveals the nature of the local topography (the natural land surface). When the contour lines at a given interval (e.g., 100 feet) are spaced closely together, the slope of the ground is steep. When they are widely separated, the land surface slopes gently. Of course contour lines cannot be found in the real world, and neither can the lines drawn on the weather maps in our daily newspaper. These lines connect points of equal pressure (isobars) and temperature (isotherms) and show the development of weather systems. Note that the letters iso (meaning "the same") appear in these terms. Invisible lines of this kind are collectively

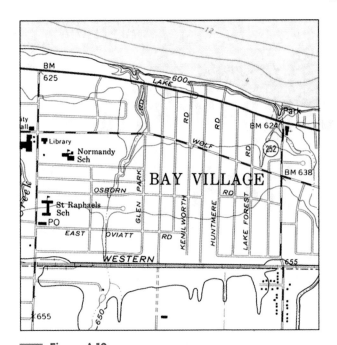

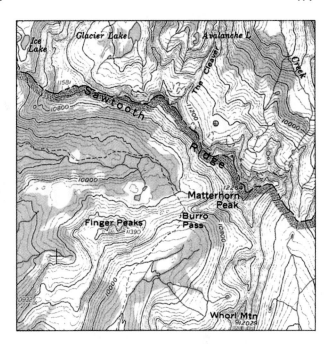

Figure A.10
Contour lines reflecting low relief (left) and high relief (right). The map at left is part of the U.S.G.S. North Olmstead Quadrangle, Ohio; the map at right is part of the U.S.G.S. Matterhorn Peak Quadrangle, California.

known as isolines, lines of equal or constant value. These are abstract constructions, but they can be of great value in geographic research and representation.

Area symbols take many forms, and we will see some of them on the maps in this book. Area symbols are used in various ways to represent distributions and magnitudes. Maps showing distributions (of such phenomena as regionally dominant languages or religions in human geography, and climates or soils in physical geography) show the world, or parts of it, divided into areas shaded or colored in contrasting hues. But be careful: those sharp dividing lines are likely to be transition zones in the real world, and a dominant language or religion does not imply the exclusion of all others. So distribution maps, and there are many in this book, tend to be small-scale generalizations of much more complex patterns than they can reveal. Again, maps showing magnitudes also must be read with care. Here the

objective is to reveal how much of a phenomenon prevails in one unit (e.g., country) on the map, compared to others. The maps on population in Part Two are examples of such maps. The important cartographic decision has to do with color (or, in black and white, graytones). Darker should mean more, and lighter implies less. That is relatively easily done when the dominant color is the same. But on a multicolored map, the use of reds, greens, and yellows can be confusing, and first impressions may have to be revised upon examination of the key.

Some students who are first drawn to the discipline of geography go on to become professional cartographers, and their work is seen in atlases, foldout magazine maps, books, and many other venues. Although cartographic technology is changing, the world's great atlases and maps still are designed and produced by researchers, compilers, draughtspeople, and other specialists.

Area and Demographic Data for the World's States

TABLE B-1

Area and Demographic Data for the World's States. ©H.J. de Blij, P. O. Muller, and John Wiley & Sons, Inc.

	Land Area Sq km	Land Area Sq mi	Population 2008 (Millions)	Population 2025 (Millions)	Pop. Density Arithmetic	Pop. Density Physiologic	Birth Rate	Death Rate	Natural Increase %	Infant Mortality per 1,000	Child Mortality per 1,000	Life Expectancy Male (years)	Life Expectancy Female (years)	Percent Urban Pop.	Literacy Male %	Literacy Female %	Corruption Index	Big Mac Price ($US)	Per Capita GNI ($US)
WORLD	134,134,451	51,789,601	6707.4	7940.0	50	432	21	9	1.2	52	76	65	69	50	83.4	69.9			$9,190
Europe	5,919,355	2,284,950	590.1	587.9	32	254	10	12	0.1	9	11	71	79	75	99.3	98.0			$21,120
Albania	28,749	11,100	3.3	3.5	113	452	14	6	0.8	16	18	72	79	45	95.5	88.0	2.6		$5,420
Austria	83,859	32,378	8.3	8.7	99	550	9	9	0.0	4	5	76	82	66	100.0	100.0	8.6		$33,140
Belarus	207,598	80,154	9.6	9.4	46	149	9	15	0.6	10	12	63	75	72	99.7	99.2	2.1		$7,890
Belgium	30,528	11,787	10.5	10.8	345	1,379	11	10	0.1	4	5	76	82	97	100.0	100.0	7.3		$32,640
Bosnia	51,129	19,741	3.9	3.7	76	587	9	9	0.1	13	15	71	77	43	96.5	76.6	2.9		$7,790
Bulgaria	110,908	42,822	7.6	6.6	69	167	9	15	0.5	12	15	69	76	70	99.1	98.0	4.0		$8,630
Croatia	56,539	21,830	4.4	4.3	78	298	9	11	0.2	6	7	71	78	60	99.4	97.3	3.4		$12,750
Cyprus	9,249	3,571	1.0	1.1	109	681	11	7	0.4	4	5	75	80	66	98.7	95.0	5.6		$22,230
Czech Republic	78,860	30,448	10.3	10.2	130	303	10	11	0.1	3	4	73	79	74	100.0	100.0	4.8	2.51	$20,140
Denmark	43,090	16,637	5.4	5.6	126	225	12	10	0.2	4	5	76	80	85	100.0	100.0	9.5	5.08	$33,570
Estonia	45,099	17,413	1.3	1.2	29	106	11	13	0.2	6	7	66	78	71	99.9	99.6	6.7		$15,420
Finland	338,149	130,560	5.3	5.4	16	225	11	9	0.2	3	4	75	82	62	100.0	100.0	9.6		$31,170
France	551,497	212,934	61.7	63.4	112	320	13	9	0.4	4	5	77	84	76	98.9	98.7	7.4		$30,540
Germany	356,978	137,830	82.1	82.0	230	657	8	10	0.2	4	5	76	82	88	100.0	100.0	8.0		$29,210
Greece	131,960	50,950	11.1	11.4	84	280	10	10	0.0	4	5	77	81	61	98.6	96.0	4.4		$23,620
Hungary	93,030	35,919	10.0	9.6	108	196	10	13	0.3	7	8	69	77	65	99.5	99.3	5.2	3.33	$16,940
Iceland	102,999	39,768	0.3	0.3	3	296	14	6	0.8	2	3	79	83	93	100.0	100.0	9.6	7.44	$34,760
Ireland	70,279	27,135	4.3	4.5	61	304	15	7	0.8	5	6	75	80	60	100.0	100.0	7.4		$34,720
Italy	301,267	116,320	59.0	58.7	196	529	10	10	0.0	4	4	78	83	90	98.9	98.1	4.9		$28,840
Latvia	64,599	24,942	2.3	2.2	35	122	9	14	0.5	9	11	67	77	68	99.8	99.6	4.7	2.52	$13,480
Liechtenstein	161	62	0.1	0.1	252	1,006	11	6	0.5	3	4	79	82	21	100.0	100.0	—		—
Lithuania	65,200	25,174	3.4	3.1	52	112	9	13	0.4	7	9	66	78	67	99.7	99.4	4.8	2.45	$14,220
Luxembourg	2,587	999	0.5	0.5	195	779	12	8	0.4	4	5	75	81	91	100.0	100.0	8.6		$65,340
Macedonia	25,711	9,927	2.0	2.1	78	300	11	9	0.2	15	17	71	76	59	94.2	83.8	2.7		$7,080
Malta	321	124	0.4	0.4	1,250	3,678	9	7	0.2	5	6	77	81	91	91.4	92.8	6.4		$18,960
Moldova	33,701	13,012	4.0	3.8	118	179	11	12	0.2	14	16	65	72	45	99.6	98.3	3.2		$2,150

	Land Area		Population		Population Density		Birth Rate	Death Rate	Natural Increase %	Infant Mortality per 1,000	Child Mortality per 1,000	Life Expectancy Male (years)	Life Expectancy Female (years)	Percent Urban Pop.	Literacy Male %	Literacy Female %	Corruption Index	Big Mac Price ($US)	Per Capita GNI ($US)
	Sq km	Sq mi	2008 (Millions)	2025 (Millions)	Arithmetic	Physiologic													
Montenegro	13,812	5,333	0.6	0.6	44	156	13	9	0.3	12	15	—	—	—	100.0	100.0	—	—	$32,480
Netherlands	40,839	15,768	16.5	16.9	405	1,499	12	8	0.3	4	5	77	81	90	100.0	100.0	8.7	—	$40,420
Norway	323,878	125,050	4.7	5.2	15	487	12	9	0.3	3	4	78	83	78	100.0	100.0	8.8	$6.63	$13,490
Poland	323,249	124,807	38.1	36.7	118	251	10	10	0.0	6	7	71	79	62	99.8	99.8	3.7	$2.51	$19,730
Portugal	91,981	35,514	10.6	10.4	115	397	10	10	0.1	4	5	75	81	55	94.8	90.0	6.6		$8,940
Romania	238,388	92,042	21.5	18.1	90	205	10	12	0.2	16	19	68	75	55	99.1	97.3	3.1		—
Serbia	88,357	34,115	9.5	9.2	108	284	13	12	0.1	12	15	69	75	52	100.0	100.0	3.0	$2.13	$15,760
Slovakia	49,010	18,923	5.4	5.2	110	324	10	10	0.0	7	8	70	78	56	100.0	100.0	4.7		$22,160
Slovenia	20,251	7,819	2.0	2.0	99	705	9	9	0.0	3	4	74	81	49	100.0	100.0	6.4		$25,820
Spain	505,988	195,363	45.7	46.2	90	231	11	9	0.2	4	5	77	84	78	100.0	100.0	6.8	$4.86	$31,420
Sweden	449,959	173,730	9.1	9.9	20	289	11	10	0.1	3	4	78	83	84	100.0	100.0	9.2	$5.20	$37,080
Switzerland	41,290	15,942	7.5	7.4	182	1,520	10	8	0.2	4	5	79	84	68	99.5	97.4	9.1	—	—
Ukraine	603,698	233,089	46.1	41.7	76	129	9	17	0.8	13	17	63	74	68	100.0	100.0	2.8	—	$6,720
United Kingdom	244,878	94,548	60.7	65.8	248	954	12	10	0.2	5	6	76	81	89	99.0	99.0	8.6	$4.01	$32,690
Russia	**17,075,323**	**6,592,819**	**140.6**	**130.0**	**8**	**137**	**10**	**16**	**0.6**	**14**	**18**	**59**	**72**	**73**	**99.8**	**99.2**	**2.5**	**$2.03**	**$10,640**
Armenia	29,800	11,506	3.0	3.4	101	507	13	9	0.4	26	29	67	75	65	99.4	98.1	2.9		$5,060
Azerbaijan	86,599	33,436	8.7	9.7	100	456	17	6	1.1	74	89	70	75	52	98.9	95.9	2.4		$4,890
Georgia	69,699	26,911	4.4	3.9	63	422	12	11	0.1	41	45	69	75	52	99.7	99.4	2.8		$3,270
North America	**19,599,647**	**7,567,466**	**335.6**	**387.0**	**17**	**138**	**14**	**8**	**0.6**	**6**	**7**	**75**	**81**	**79**	**95.7**	**95.3**	—	—	**$40,980**
Canada	9,970,600	3,849,670	32.9	37.6	3	66	11	7	0.3	5	6	77	82	80	95.7	95.3	8.5	$3.68	$32,220
United States	**9,629,047**	**3,717,796**	**302.7**	**349.4**	**31**	**157**	**14**	**8**	**0.6**	**6**	**7**	**75**	**80**	**79**	**95.7**	**95.3**	**7.3**	**$3.41**	**$41,950**
Middle America	**2,712,660**	**1,047,364**	**194.8**	**234.2**	**72**	**444**	**23**	**6**	**1.7**	**24**	**31**	**70**	**75**	**68**	**81.9**	**83.8**	—	—	**$7,475**
Antigua and Barbuda	440	170	0.1	0.1	233	1,292	18	6	1.3	11	12	69	74	37	—	—	—		$11,700
Bahamas	13,880	5,359	0.3	0.3	22	2,205	19	9	1.0	13	15	67	73	89	95.4	96.8	—		$15,800
Barbados	430	166	0.3	0.3	706	1,811	14	8	0.6	11	12	70	74	50	98.0	96.8	6.7		—
Belize	22,960	8,865	0.3	0.4	14	341	27	5	2.3	15	17	67	74	50	76.7	77.1	3.5		$6,740
Costa Rica	51,100	19,730	4.4	5.6	86	959	17	4	1.3	11	12	77	81	61	95.5	95.7	4.1	$2.18	$9,680
Cuba	110,859	42,803	11.4	11.8	103	251	11	7	0.4	6	7	75	79	76	96.5	96.4	3.5		—
Dominica	751	290	0.1	0.1	135	676	15	7	0.8	13	15	71	77	71	—	—	4.5		$5,560

Country	Land Area		Population		Population Density		Birth Rate	Death Rate	Natural Increase %	Infant Mortality per 1,000	Child Mortality per 1,000	Life Expectancy		Percent Urban Pop.	Literacy		Corruption Index	Big Mac Price ($US)	Per Capita GNI ($US)
	Sq km	Sq mi	2008 (Millions)	2025 (Millions)	Arithmetic	Physiologic						Male (years)	Female (years)		Male %	Female %			
Dominican Republic	48,731	18,815	9.3	11.6	191	616	23	6	1.7	26	31	66	69	64	84.0	83.7	2.8		$7,150
El Salvador	21,041	8,124	7.3	9.1	346	887	26	6	2.0	23	27	67	73	59	81.6	76.1	4.0		$5,120
Grenada	339	131	0.1	0.1	302	943	19	7	1.2	17	21	—	—	39	—	—	3.5		$7,260
Guadeloupe	1,709	660	0.5	0.5	298	1,989	16	6	1.0	—	—	75	82	100	89.7	90.5	—		—
Guatemala	108,888	42,042	13.7	20.0	126	701	34	6	2.8	32	43	63	71	44	76.2	61.1	2.6		$4,410
Haiti	27,749	10,714	8.9	13.0	321	971	36	13	2.3	84	120	51	54	36	51.0	46.5	1.8		$1,840
Honduras	112,090	43,278	7.8	10.7	69	385	31	6	2.5	31	40	67	74	47	72.5	72.0	2.5		$2,900
Jamaica	10,989	4,243	2.8	3.0	252	1,008	19	6	1.3	17	20	69	73	52	82.5	90.7	3.7		$4,110
Martinique	1,101	425	0.4	0.4	368	1,842	14	7	0.7	—	—	76	82	95	96.0	97.1	—		—
Mexico	1,958,192	756,062	112.0	129.4	57	409	22	5	1.7	22	27	73	78	75	93.1	89.1	3.3	$2.69	$10,030
Netherlands Antilles	800	309	0.2	0.2	252	2,524	13	8	0.5	—	—	72	79	69	96.6	96.6	—		—
Nicaragua	129,999	50,193	5.9	7.7	45	205	29	5	2.4	30	37	66	70	59	64.2	64.4	2.6		$3,650
Panama	75,519	29,158	3.4	4.2	45	502	22	5	1.7	19	24	73	78	62	92.6	91.3	3.1		$7,310
Puerto Rico	8,951	3,456	3.9	4.1	441	4,899	13	7	0.6	—	—	73	81	94	93.7	94.0	—		—
Saint Lucia	619	239	0.2	0.2	333	1,189	20	5	1.5	12	14	72	77	28	89.5	90.6	—		$5,980
St. Vincent & the Grenadines	391	151	0.1	0.1	261	933	18	7	1.1	17	20	68	74	45	—	—	—		$6,460
Trinidad and Tobago	5,131	1,981	1.3	1.3	256	1,068	14	8	0.6	17	19	67	73	74	99.0	97.5	3.2		$13,170
South America	**17,855,070**	**6,893,881**	**389.0**	**465.2**	**22**	**348**	**21**	**6**	**1.4**	**25**	**28**	**69**	**76**	**80**	**89.9**	**88.6**			**$8,210**
Argentina	2,780,388	1,073,514	39.8	46.4	14	143	18	8	1.1	15	18	71	78	90	96.9	96.9	2.9	$2.67	$13,920
Bolivia	1,098,575	424,162	9.5	12.1	9	433	31	8	2.2	52	65	62	66	63	92.1	79.4	2.7		$2,740
Brazil	8,547,360	3,300,154	192.4	228.9	23	322	21	6	1.4	31	33	68	76	83	85.5	85.4	3.3	$3.61	$8,230
Chile	756,626	292,135	16.8	19.1	22	738	16	5	1.0	8	10	75	81	87	95.9	95.5	7.3	$2.97	$11,470
Colombia	1,138,906	439,734	48.2	58.3	42	1,058	20	5	1.5	17	21	69	75	77	91.8	91.8	3.9	$3.06	$7,420
Ecuador	283,560	109,483	13.9	17.5	49	444	27	6	2.1	22	25	71	77	61	93.6	90.2	2.3		$4,070
French Guiana	89,999	34,749	0.2	0.3	2	234	31	4	2.7	—	—	72	79	75	83.6	82.3	—		—
Guyana	214,969	83,000	0.7	0.7	3	167	22	9	1.3	47	63	72	80	36	99.0	98.1	2.5		$4,230
Paraguay	406,747	157,046	6.5	8.6	16	267	22	5	1.7	20	23	69	73	57	94.4	92.2	2.6	$1.90	$4,970
Peru	1,285,214	496,224	29.1	34.1	23	756	19	6	1.3	23	27	67	72	74	94.7	85.4	3.3	$3.00	$5,830

| | Land Area | | Population | | Population Density | | Birth Rate | Death Rate | Natural Increase % | Infant Mortality per 1,000 | Child Mortality per 1,000 | Life Expectancy | | Percent Urban Pop. | Literacy | | Corruption Index | Big Mac Price ($US) | Per Capita GNI ($US) |
	Sq km	Sq mi	2008 (Millions)	2025 (Millions)	Arithmetic	Physiologic						Male (years)	Female (years)		Male %	Female %			
Suriname	163,270	63,039	0.5	0.5	3	315	21	7	1.4	30	39	66	73	74	95.9	92.6	3.0		—
Uruguay	177,409	68,498	3.3	3.5	19	268	15	10	0.5	14	15	71	79	93	97.4	98.2	6.4	$2.17	$9,810
Venezuela	912,046	352,143	27.9	35.2	31	765	22	5	1.7	18	21	70	76	88	93.3	92.7	2.3	$3.45	$6,440
Subsaharan Africa	**21,786,509**	**8,411,818**	**761.1**	**1,090.2**	**35**	**464**	**40**	**16**	**2.4**	**98**	**164**	**47**	**49**	**34**	**72.7**	**55.2**			**$1,970**
Angola	1,246,693	481,351	16.7	25.9	13	446	49	22	2.6	154	260	39	42	35	55.6	28.5	2.2		$2,210
Benin	112,620	43,483	9.2	14.3	82	511	41	12	2.9	89	150	53	55	40	47.8	23.6	2.5		$1,110
Botswana	581,727	224,606	1.8	1.7	3	309	26	27	-0.1	87	120	35	33	54	74.4	79.8	5.6		$10,250
Burkina Faso	274,000	105,792	14.3	23.2	52	435	44	19	2.5	96	191	48	49	18	31.2	13.1	3.2		$1,220
Burundi	27,829	10,745	8.2	14.0	296	689	46	18	2.7	114	190	44	45	10	56.3	40.5	2.4		$640
Cameroon	475,439	183,568	18.1	24.3	38	238	37	14	2.3	87	149	50	52	52	81.8	69.2	2.3		$2,150
Cape Verde Islands	4,030	1,556	0.5	0.7	130	1,185	30	5	2.5	26	35	68	74	55	84.3	65.3	—		$6,000
Central African Republic	622,978	240,533	4.5	5.5	7	238	37	19	1.7	115	193	43	44	43	59.6	34.5	2.4		$1,140
Chad	1,283,994	495,753	10.6	17.2	8	274	48	20	2.8	124	208	43	45	25	66.9	40.8	2.0		$1,470
Comoros	2,230	861	0.7	1.0	333	628	37	7	2.9	53	71	62	66	33	63.5	49.1	—		$2,000
Congo	341,998	132,046	3.9	5.9	11	1,139	40	14	2.6	81	108	50	52	51	87.5	74.4	2.2		$810
Congo, The	2,344,848	905,351	66.6	108.0	28	711	45	14	3.1	129	205	49	52	35	86.6	67.7	2.0		$720
Djibouti	23,201	8,958	0.8	1.1	36	3,580	31	12	1.9	88	133	52	54	82	65.0	38.4	—		$2,240
Equatorial Guinea	28,050	10,830	0.5	0.8	19	207	43	20	2.3	123	205	43	44	39	92.5	74.5	2.1		$7,580
Eritrea	117,598	45,405	4.9	7.4	41	1,033	39	11	2.8	50	78	53	57	19	43.9	33.4	2.9		$1,010
Ethiopia	1,104,296	426,371	78.4	107.8	71	646	39	15	2.4	109	164	48	50	15	83.7	70.0	2.4		$1,000
Gabon	267,668	103,347	1.5	1.8	5	272	33	13	2.0	60	91	53	55	81	79.8	62.2	3.0		$5,890
Gambia	11,300	4,363	1.6	2.4	140	665	38	12	2.7	97	137	52	55	50	43.8	29.6	2.5		$1,920
Ghana	238,538	92,100	23.7	32.7	99	431	33	10	2.3	68	112	57	58	45	79.5	61.2	3.3		$2,370
Guinea	245,860	94,927	10.4	15.2	42	702	41	13	2.8	98	150	54	54	30	55.1	27.0	1.9		$2,240
Guinea-Bissau	36,120	13,946	1.5	2.4	41	316	50	20	3.0	124	200	44	46	48	53.0	21.4	—		$700
Ivory Coast	322,459	124,502	20.7	27.1	64	279	39	14	2.5	118	195	49	53	48	54.6	38.5	2.1		$1,490

	Land Area Sq km	Sq mi	Population 2008 (Millions)	2025 (Millions)	Population Density Arithmetic	Physiologic	Birth Rate	Death Rate	Natural Increase %	Infant Mortality per 1,000	Child Mortality per 1,000	Life Expectancy Male (years)	Female (years)	Percent Urban Pop.	Literacy Male %	Female %	Corruption Index	Big Mac Price ($US)	Per Capita GNI ($US)
Kenya	580,367	224,081	36.5	49.4	63	785	40	15	2.5	79	120	49	47	40	89.0	76.0	2.2		$1,170
Lesotho	30,349	11,718	1.8	1.7	60	542	28	25	0.3	102	132	35	36	13	73.6	93.6	3.2		$3,410
Liberia	111,369	43,000	3.6	5.8	32	808	50	21	2.9	157	235	41	44	45	69.9	36.8	—		$130
Madagascar	587,036	226,656	18.8	28.2	32	641	40	12	2.7	74	119	53	57	30	87.7	72.9	3.1		$880
Malawi	118,479	45,745	13.5	23.8	114	542	44	18	2.6	79	125	44	47	17	74.5	46.7	2.7		$650
Mali	1,240,185	478,838	14.8	24.0	12	298	50	18	3.2	120	218	48	49	27	47.9	33.2	2.8		$1,000
Mauritania	1,025,516	395,954	3.4	5.0	3	330	42	14	2.8	78	125	53	55	51	50.6	29.5	3.1		$2,150
Mauritius	2,041	788	1.3	1.4	647	1,245	15	7	0.8	13	15	69	76	42	87.7	81.0	5.1		$12,450
Moçambique	801,586	309,494	20.7	27.6	26	647	41	20	2.0	100	145	41	42	34	59.9	28.4	2.8		$1,170
Namibia	824,287	318,259	2.2	2.5	3	262	29	15	1.4	46	62	47	47	33	82.9	81.2	4.1		$7,910
Niger	1,266,994	489,189	15.4	26.4	12	304	55	21	3.4	150	256	44	44	21	23.5	8.3	2.3		$800
Nigeria	923,766	356,668	141.0	199.5	153	449	43	19	2.4	100	194	43	44	43	72.3	56.2	2.2		$1,040
Réunion	2,510	969	0.8	1.0	328	2,185	19	5	1.4	—	—	72	80	89	84.8	89.2	—		—
Rwanda	26,340	10,170	9.6	13.8	364	866	43	17	2.7	118	203	46	48	17	73.7	60.6	2.5		$1,320
São Tomé and Príncipe	961	371	0.2	0.2	219	509	34	9	2.5	75	118	62	64	38	70.2	39.1	—		—
Senegal	196,720	75,954	12.6	17.3	64	534	39	10	2.9	77	136	55	58	50	47.2	27.6	3.3		$1,770
Seychelles	451	174	0.1	0.1	226	1,509	18	8	1.0	12	13	66	76	50	82.9	85.7	3.6		$15,940
Sierra Leone	71,740	27,699	6.0	8.7	83	1,039	46	23	2.3	165	282	39	42	36	50.7	22.6	2.2		$780
Somalia	637,658	246,201	9.4	14.9	15	739	46	17	2.9	133	225	46	50	34	85.8	84.5	—		—
South Africa	1,221,034	471,444	47.8	48.0	39	301	23	18	0.5	55	68	45	49	58	68.3	46.0	4.6	$2.22	$12,120
Swaziland	17,361	6,703	1.1	1.0	63	577	29	28	0.1	110	160	33	35	23	80.9	78.7	2.5		$5,190
Tanzania	945,087	364,900	39.8	53.6	42	843	42	17	2.5	76	122	44	45	32	84.1	66.6	2.9		$730
Togo	56,791	21,927	6.6	9.6	117	272	38	12	2.6	78	139	53	57	33	72.2	42.6	2.4		$1,550
Uganda	241,040	93,066	29.4	55.5	122	359	47	16	3.1	79	136	47	47	12	77.7	57.1	2.7		$1,500
Zambia	752,607	290,583	12.3	16.4	16	234	41	23	1.9	102	182	38	37	35	85.2	71.2	2.6		$950
Zimbabwe	390,759	150,873	13.3	14.4	34	378	30	23	0.7	81	132	37	34	34	95.5	89.9	2.4		$1,940

TABLE B-1 (Continued)

	Land Area		Population		Population Density		Birth Rate	Death Rate	Natural Increase %	Infant Mortality per 1,000	Child Mortality per 1,000	Life Expectancy		Percent Urban Pop.	Literacy		Corruption Index	Big Mac Price ($US)	Per Capita GNI ($US)
	Sq km	Sq mi	2008 (Millions)	2025 (Millions)	Arithmetic	Physiologic						Male (years)	Female (years)		Male %	Female %			
North Africa/ Southwest Asia	**19,318,887**	**7,459,064**	**581.0**	**754.1**	**30**	**328**	**26**	**7**	**1.8**	**47**	**51**	**66**	**70**	**55**	**76.2**	**56.9**	**—**		**$5,674**
Afghanistan	652,086	251,772	32.7	50.3	50	418	48	22	2.6	165	257	41	42	23	51.0	20.8	—		—
Algeria	2,381,730	919,591	34.6	43.1	15	485	21	4	1.7	34	39	74	76	81	75.1	51.3	3.1		$6,770
Bahrain	689	266	0.7	1.0	1,053	11,700	21	3	1.8	9	11	73	75	71	91.0	82.7	5.7		$21,290
Egypt	1,001,445	386,660	78.6	101.1	78	2,616	27	6	2.1	28	33	67	72	43	66.6	43.7	3.3	$1.68	$4,440
Iran	1,633,182	630,575	72.0	89.0	44	401	18	6	1.2	31	36	69	72	67	83.5	70.4	2.7		$8,050
Iraq	438,319	169,236	31.2	44.7	71	547	36	10	2.6	102	125	57	60	68	70.7	45.0	1.9		—
Israel	21,059	8,131	7.4	9.3	353	1,681	21	5	1.5	5	6	78	82	91	97.9	94.3	5.9		$25,280
Jordan	89,210	34,444	5.9	7.9	66	1,316	29	5	2.4	22	26	71	72	82	94.9	84.4	5.3		$5,280
Kazakhstan	2,717,289	1,049,151	15.5	16.0	6	48	18	10	0.8	63	73	61	72	57	99.1	96.1	2.6		$7,730
Kuwait	17,819	6,880	2.8	3.9	157	15,672	19	2	1.7	9	11	77	79	97	84.3	79.9	4.8		$24,010
Kyrgyzstan	198,499	76,641	5.3	6.6	27	385	21	7	1.4	58	67	64	72	35	98.6	95.5	2.2		$1,870
Lebanon	10,399	4,015	4.0	4.6	386	1,244	19	5	1.5	27	30	70	74	87	92.3	80.4	3.6		$5,740
Libya	1,759,532	679,359	6.2	8.3	4	351	27	4	2.4	18	19	74	78	86	90.9	67.6	2.7		$5,530
Morocco	446,548	172,413	32.7	38.8	73	332	21	6	1.6	36	40	68	72	55	61.9	36.0	3.2		$4,360
Oman	212,459	82,031	2.7	3.1	13	1,273	24	4	2.0	10	12	73	75	71	80.4	61.7	5.4		$14,680
Palestinian Territories	6,260	2,417	4.2	7.1	665	33,240	37	4	3.3	21	23	71	74	57	—	—	—		—
Qatar	11,000	4,247	0.8	1.2	75	7,508	18	2	1.6	18	21	71	76	100	80.5	83.2	6.0		—
Saudi Arabia	2,149,680	829,996	25.4	35.6	12	591	30	3	2.7	21	26	70	74	86	84.1	67.2	3.3	$2.40	$14,740
Sudan	2,505,798	967,494	43.5	61.3	17	248	36	9	2.6	62	90	57	59	37	36.0	14.0	2.0		$2,000
Syria	185,179	71,498	20.5	28.1	111	369	29	4	2.5	14	15	71	75	50	88.3	60.4	2.9		$3,740
Tajikistan	143,099	55,251	7.3	9.3	51	730	30	8	2.2	59	71	61	66	26	99.6	98.9	2.2		$1,260
Tunisia	163,610	63,170	10.3	11.6	63	197	17	6	1.1	20	24	71	75	65	81.4	60.1	4.6		$7,900
Turkey	774,816	299,158	75.6	86.0	98	257	19	6	1.3	26	29	69	74	62	93.6	76.7	3.8	$3.66	$8,420
Turkmenistan	488,099	188,456	5.5	6.6	11	281	25	8	1.6	81	104	58	67	47	98.8	96.6	2.2		—
United Arab Emirates	83,600	32,278	5.0	7.1	60	6,027	15	1	1.3	8	9	75	80	74	75.5	79.5	6.2	$2.72	$24,090
Uzbekistan	447,397	172,741	27.0	33.0	60	504	23	7	1.6	57	68	63	70	36	98.5	96.0	2.1		$2,020
Western Sahara	252,120	97,344	0.4	0.7	2	4	28	8	2.0	—	—	62	66	93	—	—	—		—

Country	Land Area Sq km	Land Area Sq mi	Population 2008 (Millions)	Population 2025 (Millions)	Population Density Arithmetic	Population Density Physiologic	Birth Rate	Death Rate	Natural Increase %	Infant Mortality per 1,000	Child Mortality per 1,000	Life Expectancy Male (years)	Life Expectancy Female (years)	Percent Urban Pop.	Literacy Male %	Literacy Female %	Corruption Index	Big Mac Price (US$)	Per Capita GNI (US$)
Yemen	527,966	203,849	23.0	38.8	44	1,452	41	9	3.2	76	102	59	62	26	67.4	25.0	2.6		$920
South Asia	**4,487,760**	**1,732,734**	**1,532.9**	**1,841.9**	**342**	**682**	**25**	**8**	**1.7**	**58**	**76**	**62**	**64**	**30**	**65.9**	**39.5**			**$3,330**
Bangladesh	143,998	55,598	152.2	190.0	1,057	1,678	27	8	1.9	54	73	61	62	23	51.7	29.5	2.0		$2,090
Bhutan	47,001	18,147	0.9	1.3	20	655	20	7	1.3	65	75	62	64	31	61.1	33.6	6.0		—
India	3,287,576	1,269,340	1,158.0	1,363.0	352	618	24	8	1.7	56	74	62	63	29	68.6	42.1	3.3		$3,460
Maldives	300	116	0.3	0.4	1,029	10,287	18	3	1.5	33	42	70	70	27	96.3	96.4	—		$4,635
Nepal	147,179	56,826	27.2	36.2	185	879	31	9	2.2	56	74	62	63	14	59.1	21.8	2.5		$1,530
Pakistan	796,098	307,375	173.9	228.8	218	753	33	9	2.4	79	99	61	63	38	57.6	27.8	2.2	$2.31	$2,350
Sri Lanka	65,610	25,332	20.4	22.2	311	1,073	19	6	1.3	12	14	71	77	20	94.5	88.9	3.1	$1.75	$4,520
East Asia	**11,773,125**	**4,545,629**	**1,550.6**	**1,699.4**	**132**	**1,068**	**12**	**7**	**0.5**	**21**	**24**	**71**	**75**	**43**	**93.3**	**80.4**			**$9,050**
China	9,572,855	3,696,100	1,324.5	1,476.0	138	988	12	7	0.6	23	27	70	74	37	92.3	77.4	3.3	$1.45	$6,600
Japan	377,799	145,869	128.1	121.1	339	2,607	9	8	0.0	3	4	79	86	79	100.0	100.0	7.6	$2.29	$31,410
Korea, North	120,541	46,541	23.5	25.8	195	1,219	16	7	0.9	42	55	68	73	60	99.0	99.0			—
Korea, South	99,259	38,324	48.9	49.8	493	2,592	9	5	0.4	5	5	74	81	82	99.2	96.4	5.1	$3.14	$21,850
Mongolia	1,566,492	604,826	2.7	3.1	2	170	18	6	1.2	39	49	64	68	57	99.2	99.3	2.8		$2,190
Taiwan	36,180	13,969	22.9	23.6	634	2,536	9	6	0.3	—	—	73	79	78	97.6	90.2	5.9	$2.28	$16,250
Southeast Asia	**4,494,792**	**1,735,449**	**581.7**	**682.0**	**129**	**621**	**21**	**6**	**1.4**	**30**	**39**	**66**	**71**	**39**	**92.8**	**85.7**			**$4,530**
Brunei	5,770	2,228	0.4	0.5	72	3,585	20	3	1.7	8	9	72	77	72	94.7	88.2	—		—
Cambodia	181,040	69,900	14.7	19.6	81	369	30	9	2.1	98	143	57	63	19	79.7	53.4	2.1		$2,490
East Timor	14,869	5,741	1.1	1.9	71	591	42	15	2.7	52	61	54	57	22	65.0	52.0	2.6		$600
Indonesia	1,904,561	735,355	231.9	263.7	122	716	20	6	1.4	28	36	67	72	42	91.9	82.1	2.4	$1.75	$3,720
Laos	236,800	91,429	6.4	8.7	27	899	36	13	2.3	62	79	53	56	21	73.6	50.5	2.6		$2,020
Malaysia	329,750	127,317	27.8	34.6	84	351	20	4	1.6	10	12	72	76	64	91.5	83.6	5.0	$1.60	$10,320
Myanmar/Burma	676,577	261,228	52.1	59.0	77	482	21	10	1.1	75	105	57	63	29	89.0	80.6	1.9		—
Philippines	299,998	115,830	90.1	115.7	300	910	27	5	2.1	25	33	67	72	59	95.5	95.2	2.5	$1.85	$5,300
Singapore	619	239	4.6	5.2	7,357	367,860	10	4	0.6	3	3	78	82	100	96.4	88.5	9.4	$2.59	$29,780
Thailand	513,118	198,116	66.1	70.2	129	322	14	7	0.7	18	21	68	75	34	97.2	94.0	3.6	$1.78	$8,440
Vietnam	331,689	128,066	86.6	102.9	261	1,186	19	5	1.3	16	19	70	73	27	95.7	91.0	2.6		$3,010
Austral Realm	**8,011,714**	**3,093,340**	**25.0**	**29.2**	**3**	**44**	**13**	**6**	**0.7**	**5**	**6**	**78**	**83**	**91**	**100.0**	**100.0**			**$29,352**
Australia	7,741,184	2,988,888	20.9	24.6	3	39	13	6	0.6	5	6	78	83	91	100.0	100.0	8.7	$2.95	$30,610

TABLE B-1 (Continued)

| | Land Area | | Population | | Population Density | | Birth Rate | Death Rate | Natural Increase % | Infant Mortality per 1,000 | Child Mortality per 1,000 | Life Expectancy | | Percent Urban Pop. | Literacy | | Corruption Index | Big Mac Price ($US) | Per Capita GNI ($US) |
	Sq km	Sq mi	2008 (Millions)	2025 (Millions)	Arithmetic	Physiologic						Male (years)	Female (years)		Male %	Female %			
New Zealand	270,529	104,452	4.2	4.6	15	128	14	7	0.7	5	6	77	81	86	100.0	100.0	9.6	$5.89	$23,030
Pacific Realm	975,341	376,804	9.0	11.4	24.5	757	30	9	2.0	44	58	59	61	22	69.1	59.0			$2,540
Federated States of Micronesia	699	270	0.1	0.1	149	286	26	6	2.0	34	42	67	67	22	67.0	87.2	—		—
Fiji	18,270	7,054	0.8	0.9	45	282	21	6	1.4	16	18	66	71	46	95.0	90.9	—		$5,960
French Polynesia	3,999	1,544	0.3	0.3	77	962	18	5	1.3	—	—	72	77	53	94.9	95.0	—		—
Guam	549	212	0.2	0.2	377	1,712	21	4	1.6	—	—	75	81	93	99.0	99.0	—		—
Marshall Islands	179	69	0.1	0.1	597	3,512	38	5	3.3	51	58	—	—	68	92.4	90.0	—		—
New Caledonia	18,581	7,174	0.2	0.3	11	1,102	17	5	1.2	—	—	71	77	71	57.4	58.3	—		—
Papua New Guinea	462,839	178,703	6.3	8.2	14	1,351	32	11	2.1	55	74	55	56	13	63.4	50.9	2.4		$2,370
Samoa	2,841	1,097	0.2	0.2	74	171	29	6	2.4	24	29	72	74	22	100.0	100.0	—		$6,480
Solomon Islands	28,899	11,158	0.5	0.7	18	607	34	8	2.6	24	29	62	63	16	62.4	44.9	—		$1,880
Vanuatu	12,191	4,707	0.2	0.4	17	172	31	6	2.5	31	38	66	69	21	57.3	47.8	—		$3,170

Glossary

Ability In the context of political power, the capacity of a state to influence other states or achieve its goals through diplomatic, economic, and militaristic means.

Absolute location The position or place of a certain item on the surface of the Earth as expressed in degrees, minutes, and seconds of **latitude**, 0° to 90° north or south of the equator, and **longitude**, 0° to 180° east or west of the **Prime Meridian** passing through Greenwich, England (a suburb of London).

Accessibility The degree of ease with which it is possible to reach a certain location from other locations. Accessibility varies from place to place and can be measured.

Acid rain A growing environmental peril whereby acidified rainwater severely damages plant and animal life; caused by the oxides of sulfur and nitrogen that are released into the atmosphere when coal, oil, and natural gas are burned, especially in major manufacturing zones.

Acropolis Literally "high point of the city." The upper fortified part of an ancient Greek city, usually devoted to religious purposes.

Activity (action) space The space within which daily activity occurs.

Agglomeration A process involving the clustering or concentrating of people or activities. The term often refers to manufacturing plants and businesses that benefit from close proximity because they share skilled-labor pools and technological and financial amenities.

Agora In ancient Greece, public spaces where citizens debated, lectured, judged each other, planned military campaigns, socialized, and traded.

Agribusiness General term for the businesses that provide the vast array of goods and services that support the agriculture industry.

Agricultural surplus One of two components, together with **social stratification**, that enable the formation of **cities**; agricultural production in excess of that which the producer needs for his or her own sustenance and that of his or her family and which is then sold for consumption by others.

Agricultural village A relatively small, egalitarian village, where most of the population was involved in agriculture. Starting over 10,000 years ago, people began to cluster in agricultural villages as they stayed in one place to tend their crops.

Agriculture The purposeful tending of crops and livestock in order to produce food and fiber.

AIDS (Acquired Immune Deficiency Syndrome) Immune system disease caused by the Human Immunodeficiency Virus (HIV) which over a period of years weakens the capacity of the immune system to fight off infection so that weight loss and weakness set in and other afflictions such as cancer or pneumonia may hasten an infected person's demise.

Animal domestication Genetic modification of an animal such that it is rendered more amenable to human control.

Animistic religion The belief that inanimate objects, such as hills, trees, rocks, rivers, and other elements of the natural landscape, possess souls and can help or hinder human efforts on Earth.

Aquifers Subterranean, porous, water-holding rocks that provide millions of wells with steady flows of water.

Arable Literally, cultivable; land fit for cultivation by one farming method or another.

Area A term that refers to a part of the Earth's surface with less specificity than **region**. For example, "urban area" alludes very generally to a place where urban development has taken place, whereas "urban region" requires certain specific criteria on which a delimitation is based (e.g., the spatial extent of commuting or the built townscape).

Arithmetic population density The population of a country or region expressed as an average per unit area. The figure is derived by dividing the population of the areal unit by the number of square kilometers or miles that make up the unit.

Assimilation The process through which people lose originally differentiating traits, such as dress, speech particularities or mannerisms, when they come into contact with another society or culture. Often used to describe immigrant adaptation to new places of residence.

Asylum Shelter and protection in one state for refugees from another state.

Atmosphere Blanket of gases surrounding the Earth and located some 350 miles above the Earth's surface.

Authenticity In the context of local cultures or customs, the accuracy with which a single stereotypical or typecast image or experience conveys an otherwise dynamic and complex local culture or its customs.

Backward reconstruction The tracking of **sound shifts** and hardening of consonants "backward" toward the original **language**.

Barrioization Defined by geographer James Curtis as the dramatic increase in Hispanic population in a given neighborhood; referring to *barrio*, the Spanish word for neighborhood.

Biodiversity The total variety of plant and animal species in a particular place; biological diversity.

Blockbusting Rapid change in the racial composition of residential blocks in American cities that occurs when real estate agents and others stir up fears of neighborhood decline after encouraging people of color to move to previously white neighborhoods. In the resulting outmigration, real estate agents profit through the turnover of properties.

Boundary   Vertical plane between states that cuts through the rocks below, and the airspace above the surface.

Break-of-bulk point   A **location** along a transport route where goods must be transferred from one carrier to another. In a port, the cargoes of oceangoing ships are unloaded and put on trains, trucks, or perhaps smaller riverboats for inland distribution.

Buddhism   **Religion** founded in the sixth century BCE and characterized by the belief that enlightenment would come through knowledge, especially self-knowledge; elimination of greed, craving, and desire; complete honesty; and never hurting another person or animal. Buddhism splintered from **Hinduism** as a reaction to the strict social hierarchy maintained by Hinduism.

Cadastral map   A large-scale map, usually created at the scale of 1:2500, depicting the value, extent, and ownership of land for purposes of taxation.

Capitalism   Economic model wherein people, corporations, and **states** produce goods and exchange them on the world market, with the goal of achieving profit.

Cartography   The art and science of making maps, including data compilation, layout, and design. Also concerned with the interpretation of mapped patterns.

Caste system   The strict social segregation of people—specifically in India's Hindu society—on the basis of ancestry and occupation.

Census   A periodic and official count of a country's population.

Central Business District (CBD)   The downtown heart of a **central city**, the CBD is marked by high land values, a concentration of business and commerce, and the clustering of the tallest buildings.

Central city   The urban area that is not suburban; generally, the older or original **city** that is surrounded by newer **suburbs**.

Central place   Any point or place in the urban hierarchy, such as a town or city, having a certain economic reach or hinterland.

Central Place Theory   Theory proposed by Walter Christaller that explains how and where **central places** in the **urban hierarchy** should be functionally and spatially distributed with respect to one another.

Centrality   The strength of an urban center in its capacity to attract producers and consumers to its facilities; a city's "reach" into the surrounding region.

Centrifugal   Forces that tend to divide a country—such as internal religious, linguistic, ethnic, or ideological differences.

Centripetal   Forces that tend to unify a country—such as widespread commitment to a national culture, shared ideological objectives, and a common faith.

Chain migration   Pattern of **migration** that develops when migrants move along and through kinship links (i.e. one migrant settles in a place and then writes, calls, or communicates through others to describe this place to family and friends who in turn then migrate there).

Child mortality rate   A figure that describes the number of children that die between the first and fifth years of their lives in a given population.

Chlorofluorocarbons (CFCs)   Synthetic organic compounds first created in the 1950s and used primarily as refrigerants and as propellants. The role of CFCs in the destruction of the ozone layer led to the signing of an international agreement (the **Montreal Protocol**).

Christianity   **Religion** based on the teachings of Jesus. According to Christian teaching, Jesus is the son of God, placed on Earth to teach people how to live according to God's plan.

Chronic (or degenerative) diseases   Generally long-lasting afflictions now more common because of higher life expectancies.

City   Conglomeration of people and buildings clustered together to serve as a center of politics, culture, and economics.

Climatic regions   Areas of the world with similar climatic characteristics.

Colonialism   Rule by an autonomous power over a subordinate and alien people and place. Although often established and maintained through political structures, colonialism also creates unequal cultural and economic relations. Because of the magnitude and impact of the European colonial project of the last few centuries, the term is generally understood to refer to that particular colonial endeavor.

Colonization   Physical process whereby the colonizer takes over another place, putting its own government in charge and either moving its own people into the place or bringing in indentured outsiders to gain control of the people and the land.

Commercial agriculture   Term used to describe large-scale farming and ranching operations that employ vast land bases, large mechanized equipment, factory-type labor forces, and the latest technology.

Commercialization   The transformation of an area of a **city** into an area attractive to residents and tourists alike in terms of economic activity.

Commodification   The process through which something is given monetary value. Commodification occurs when a good or idea that previously was not regarded as an object to be bought and sold is turned into something that has a particular price and that can be traded in a market economy.

Commodity chain   Series of links connecting the many places of production and distribution and resulting in a commodity that is then exchanged on the world market.

Complementarity   A condition that exists when two regions, through an exchange of raw materials and/or finished products, can specifically satisfy each other's demands.

Concentric zone model   A structural model of the American **central city** that suggests the existence of five concentric land-use rings arranged around a common center.

Confucianism   A philosophy of ethics, education, and public service based on the writings of Confucius and traditionally thought of as one of the core elements of Chinese culture.

Connectivity   The degree of direct linkage between one particular location and other locations in a transport network.

Conquest theory   One major theory of how **Proto-Indo-European** diffused into Europe which holds that the early speakers of Proto-Indo-European spread westward on horseback, overpowering earlier inhabitants and beginning the **diffusion** and differentiation of Indo-European tongues.

Contagious diffusion   The distance-controlled spreading of an idea, innovation, or some other item through a local population by contact from person to person—analogous to the communication of a contagious illness.

Context   The geographical situation in which something occurs; the combination of what is happening at a variety of **scales** concurrently.

Core   Processes that incorporate higher levels of education, higher salaries, and more technology; generate more wealth than **periphery** processes in the world-economy.

Core area   In geography, a term with several connotations. Core refers to the center, heart, or focus. The core area of a **nation-state** is constituted by the national heartland—the largest population cluster, the most productive region, the area with greatest **centrality** and **accessibility**, probably containing the capital city as well.

Creole language   A language that began as a **pidgin language** but was later adopted as the mother tongue by a people in place of the mother tongue.

Critical geopolitics Process by which geopoliticians deconstruct and focus on explaining the underlying spatial assumptions and territorial perspectives of politicians.

Crude Birth Rate (CBR) The number of live births yearly per thousand people in a population.

Crude Death Rate (CDR) The number of deaths yearly per thousand people in a population.

Cultural appropriation The process by which cultures adopt customs and knowledge from other cultures and use them for their own benefit.

Cultural barrier Prevailing cultural attitude rendering certain innovations, ideas or practices unacceptable or unadoptable in that particular **culture**.

Cultural complex A related set of **cultural traits**, such as prevailing dress codes and cooking and eating utensils.

Cultural diffusion The expansion and adoption of a cultural element, from its place of origin to a wider area.

Cultural ecology The multiple interactions and relationships between a culture and the natural environment.

Cultural hearth Heartland, source area, innovation center; place of origin of a major **culture**.

Cultural landscape The visible imprint of of human activity and culture on the landscape. The layers of buildings, forms, and artifacts sequentially imprinted on the landscape by the activities of various human occupants.

Cultural trait A single element of normal practice in a **culture**, such as the wearing of a turban.

Culture The sum total of the knowledge, attitudes, and habitual behavior patterns shared and transmitted by the members of a society. This is anthropologist Ralph Linton's definition; hundreds of others exist.

Custom Practice routinely followed by a group of people.

Cyclic movement Movement—for example, nomadic migration— that has a closed route and is repeated annually or seasonally.

Deep reconstruction Technique using the vocabulary of an **extinct language** to re-create the **language** that proceeded the extinct language.

Definition In political geography, the written legal description (in a treatylike document) of a boundary between two countries or territories. See also **delimitation**.

Deforestation The clearing and destruction of forests to harvest wood for consumption, clear land for agricultural uses, and make way for expanding settlement frontiers.

Deglomeration The process of industrial deconcentration in response to technological advances and/or increasing costs due to congestion and competition.

Deindustrialization Process by which companies move industrial jobs to other regions with cheaper labor, leaving the newly deindustrialized region to switch to a service economy and to work through a period of high unemployment.

Delimitation In political geography, the translation of the written terms of a boundary treaty (the **definition**) into an official cartographic representation.

Demarcation In political geography, the actual placing of a political boundary on the landscape by means of barriers, fences, walls, or other markers.

Democracy Government based on the principle that the people are the ultimate sovereign and have the final say over what happens within the state.

Demographic transition Multistage model, based on Western Europe's experience, of changes in population growth exhibited by countries undergoing industrialization. High birth rates and death rates are followed by plunging death rates, producing a huge net population gain; this is followed by the convergence of birth rates and death rates at a low overall level.

Dependency theory A structuralist theory that offers a critique of the **modernization model** of development. Based on the idea that certain types of political and economic relations (especially **colonialism**) between countries and regions of the world have created arrangements that both control and limit the extent to which regions can develop.

Deportation The act of a government sending a migrant out of its country and back to the migrant's home country.

Desertification The encroachment of desert conditions on moister zones along the desert margins, where plant cover and soils are threatened by desiccation—through overuse, in part by humans and their domestic animals, and, possibly, in part because of inexorable shifts in the Earth's environmental zones.

Developing With respect to a country, making progress in technology, production, and socioeconomic welfare.

Devolution The process whereby regions within a **state** demand and gain political strength and growing autonomy at the expense of the central government.

Dialect Local or regional characteristics of a **language**. While *accent* refers to the pronunciation differences of a standard language, a dialect, in addition to pronunciation variation, has distinctive grammar and vocabulary.

Dialect chains A set of contiguous dialects in which the dialects nearest to each other at any place in the chain are most closely related.

Diaspora From the Greek "to disperse," a term describing forceful or voluntary dispersal of a people from their homeland to a new place. Originally denoting the dispersal of Jews, it is increasingly applied to other population dispersals, such as the involuntary relocation of Black peoples during the slave trade or Chinese peoples outside of Mainland China, Taiwan and Hong Kong.

Diffusion The spatial spreading or dissemination of a culture element (such as a technological innovation) or some other phenomenon (e.g., a disease outbreak). See also **contagious, expansion, hierarchical, relocation**, and **stimulus diffusion**.

Diffusion routes The spatial trajectory through which **cultural traits** or other phenomena spread.

Disamenity sector The very poorest parts of **cities** that in extreme cases are not even connected to regular city services and are controlled by gangs or drug lords.

Dispersal hypothesis Hypothesis which holds that the Indo-European languages that arose from **Proto-Indo-European** were first carried eastward into Southwest Asia, next around the Caspian Sea, and then across the Russian-Ukrainian plains and on into the Balkans.

Distance Measurement of the physical space between two places.

Distance decay The effects of distance on interaction, generally the greater the distance the less interaction.

Dollarization When a poorer country ties the value of its currency to that of a wealthier country, or when it abandons its currency and adopts the wealthier country's currency as its own.

Dot map Maps where one dot represents a certain number of a phenomenon, such as a population.

Doubling time The time required for a population to double in size.

Dowry death In the context of arranged marriages in India, disputes over the price to be paid by the family of the bride to the father of the groom (the dowry) have, in some extreme cases, led to the death of the bride.

Eastern Orthodox Church One of three major branches of **Christianity**, the Eastern Orthodox Church, together with the **Roman**

Catholic Church, a second of the three major branches of Christianity, arose out of the division of the Roman Empire by Emperor Diocletian into four governmental regions: two western regions centered in Rome, and two eastern regions centered in Constantinople (now Istanbul, Turkey). In 1054 CE, Christianity was divided along that same line when the Eastern Orthodox Church, centered in Constantinople; and the Roman Catholic Church, centered in Rome, split.

Edge cities   A term introduced by American journalist Joel Garreau in order to describe the shifting focus of **urbanization** in the United States away from the **Central Business District (CBD)** toward new loci of economic activity at the urban fringe. These cities are characterized by extensive amounts of office and retail space, few residential areas, and modern buildings (less than 30 years old).

Emigrant   A person migrating away from a country or area; an out-migrant.

Endemic   A disease that is particular to a locality or region. See also **pandemic**.

Environmental determinism   The view that the natural environment has a controlling influence over various aspects of human life, including cultural development. Also referred to as environmentalism.

Environmental stress   The threat to environmental security by human activity such as atmospheric and groundwater pollution, deforestation, oil spills, and ocean dumping.

Epidemic   Regional outbreak of a disease.

Ethnic cleansing   The systematic killing or extermination of an entire people or **nation**.

Ethnic religion   A religion that is particular to one, culturally distinct, group of people. Unlike **universalizing religions**, adherents of ethnic religions do not actively seek converts through evangelism or missionary work.

Ethnic neighborhood   Neighborhood, typically situated in a larger metropolitan city and constructed by or comprised of a **local culture**, in which a local culture can practice its customs.

Ethnicity   Affiliation or identity within a group of people bound by common ancestry and culture.

Eugenic population policies   Government policies designed to favor one racial sector over others.

Expansion diffusion   The spread of an innovation or an idea through a population in an area in such a way that the number of those influenced grows continuously larger, resulting in an expanding area of dissemination.

Expansive population policies   Government policies that encourage large families and raise the rate of population growth.

Explorer   A person examining a region that is unknown to them.

Export Processing Zones (EPZs)   Zones established by many countries in the **periphery** and **semi-periphery** where they offer favorable tax, regulatory, and trade arrangements to attract foreign trade and investment.

Extinct language   **Language** without any native speakers.

Federal (state)   A political-territorial system wherein a central government represents the various entities within a **nation-state** where they have common interests—defense, foreign affairs, and the like—yet allows these various entities to retain their own identities and to have their own laws, policies, and customs in certain spheres.

Feng Shui   Literally "wind-water." The Chinese art and science of placement and orientation of tombs, dwellings, buildings, and cities. Structures and objects are positioned in an effort to channel flows of *sheng-chi* ("life-breath") in favorable ways.

Fertile Crescent   Crescent-shaped zone of productive lands extending from near the southeastern Mediterranean coast through Lebanon and Syria to the alluvial lowlands of Mesopotamia (in Iraq). Once more fertile than today, this is one of the world's great source areas of agricultural and other innovations.

Fieldwork   The study of geographic phenomena by visiting places and observing how people interact with and thereby change those places.

First Agricultural Revolution   Dating back 10,000 years, the First Agricultural Revolution achieved **plant domestication** and **animal domestication**.

First Urban Revolution   The innovation of the **city**, which occurred independently in five separate **hearths**.

Five themes (of geography)   Developed by the **Geography Educational National Implementation Project (GENIP)**, the five themes of geography are **location, human-environment, region, place**, and **movement**.

Folk culture   Cultural traits such as dress modes, dwellings, traditions, and institutions of usually small, **traditional** communities.

Folk-housing region   A region in which the housing stock predominantly reflects styles of building that are particular to the culture of the people who have long inhabited the area.

Forced migration   Human **migration** flows in which the movers have no choice but to relocate.

Fordist   A highly organized and specialized system for organizing industrial production and labor. Named after automobile producer Henry Ford, Fordist production features assembly-line production of standardized components for mass consumption.

Formal economy   The legal economy that is taxed and monitored by a government and is included in a government's **Gross National Product (GNP)**; as opposed to an **informal economy**.

Formal region   A type of **region** marked by a certain degree of homogeneity in one or more phenomena; also called uniform region or homogeneous region.

Forum   The focal point of ancient Roman life combining the functions of the ancient Greek *acropolis* and *agora*.

Friction of distance   The increase in time and cost that usually comes with increasing **distance**.

Functional region   A **region** defined by the particular set of activities or interactions that occur within it.

Functional zonation   The division of a **city** into different regions or **zones** (e.g. residential or industrial) for certain purposes or functions (e.g. housing or manufacturing).

Gated communities   Restricted neighborhoods or subdivisions, often literally fenced in, where entry is limited to residents and their guests. Although predominantly high-income based, in North America gated communities are increasingly a middle-class phenomenon.

Gatekeepers   People or corporations who control access to information.

Gender   Social differences between men and women, rather than the anatomical, biological differences between the sexes. Notions of gender differences—that is, what is considered "feminine" or "masculine"—vary greatly over time and space.

Gendered   In terms of a place, whether the place is designed for or claimed by men or women.

Genetic or inherited diseases   Diseases caused by variation or mutation of a gene or group of genes in a human.

Genetically Modified Oganisms (GMOs)   Crops that carry new traits that have been inserted through advanced genetic engineering methods.

Gentrification   The rehabilitation of deteriorated, often abandoned, housing of low-income inner-city residents.

Geocaching A hunt for a cache, the **Global Positioning System (GPS)** coordinates which are placed on the Internet by other geocachers.

Geographic concept Ways of seeing the world spatially that are used by geographers in answering research questions.

Geographic Information System (GIS) A collection of computer hardware and software that permits spatial data to be collected, recorded, stored, retrieved, manipulated, analyzed, and displayed to the user.

Geography From the Greek meaning "to write about the Earth." As a modern academic discipline, geography is concerned with the analysis of the physical and human characteristics of the Earth's surface from a **spatial** perspective. "Why are things located where they are?" and "What does it mean for things to be located in particular places?" are central questions that geographical scholarship seeks to answer.

Geography Educational National Implementation Project (GENIP) Joint effort undertaken in the 1980s by the American Geographical Society, the Association of American Geographers, the National Council for Geographic Education and the National Geographic Society designed to bring together the many subfields of human geography and to explain to nongeographers the discipline of geography; developed the **five themes** of geography: **location, human-environment, region, place**, and **movement.**

Geometric boundary Political boundary **defined** and **delimited** (and occasionally **demarcated**) as a straight line or an arc.

Germanic languages Languages (English, German, Danish, Norwegian, and Swedish) that reflect the expansion of peoples out of Northern Europe to the west and south.

Gerrymandering Redistricting for advantage, or the practice of dividing areas into electoral districts to give one political party an electoral majority in a large number of districts while concentrating the voting strength of the opposition in as few districts as possible.

Glaciation A period of global cooling during which continental ice sheets and mountain glaciers expand.

Global division of labor Phenomenon whereby corporations and others can draw from labor markets around the world, made possible by the compression of time and space through innovation in communication and transportation systems.

Global language The **language** used most commonly around the world; defined on the basis of either the number of speakers of the language, or prevalence of use in commerce and trade.

Global-local continuum The notion that what happens at the global scale has a direct effect on what happens at the local scale, and vice versa. This idea posits that the world is comprised of an interconnected series of relationships that extend across space.

Global Positioning System (GPS) Satellite-based system for determining the **absolute location** of **places** or geographic features.

Global scale Interactions occurring at the scale of the world, in a global setting.

Global warming Theory that the Earth is gradually warming as a result of an enhanced **greenhouse effect** in the Earth's **atmosphere** caused by ever-increasing amounts of carbon dioxide produced by various human activities.

Globalization The expansion of economic, political, and cultural processes to the point that they become global in scale and impact. The processes of globalization transcend state boundaries and have outcomes that vary across places and scales.

Glocalization The process by which people in a local place mediate and alter regional, national, and global processes.

Gondwana The southern portion of the primeval supercontinent, Pangaea.

Gravity model A mathematical prediction of the interaction of places, the interaction being a function of population size of the respective places and the distance between them.

Green Revolution The recently successful development of higher-yield, fast-growing varieties of rice and other cereals in certain developing countries, which led to increased production per unit area and a dramatic narrowing of the gap between population growth and food needs.

Greenhouse effect The widely used analogy describing the blanket-like effect of the atmosphere in the heating of the Earth's surface; shortwave insolation passes through the "glass" of the atmospheric "greenhouse," heats the surface, is converted to long-wave radiation that cannot penetrate the "glass," and thereby results in trapping heat, which raises the temperature inside the "greenhouse."

Griffin-Ford model Developed by geographers Ernst Griffin and Larry Ford, a model of the Latin American city showing a blend of traditional elements of Latin American culture with the forces of globalization that are reshaping the urban scene.

Gross Domestic Product (GDP) The total value of all goods and services produced within a country during a given year.

Gross National Product (GNP) The total value of all goods and services produced by a country's economy in a given year. It includes all goods and services produced by corporations and individuals of a country, whether or not they are located within the country.

Guest worker Legal **immigrant** who has a work visa, usually short term.

Hajj The Muslim **pilgrimage** to Mecca, the birthplace of Muhammad.

Hearth The area where an idea or cultural trait originates.

Heartland theory A geopolitical hypothesis, proposed by British geographer Halford Mackinder during the first two decades of the twentieth century, that any political power based in the heart of Eurasia could gain sufficient strength to eventually dominate the world. Mackinder further proposed that since Eastern Europe controlled access to the Eurasian interior, its ruler would command the vast "heartland" to the east.

Hierarchical diffusion A form of **diffusion** in which an idea or innovation spreads by passing first among the most connected places or peoples. An **urban hierarchy** is usually involved, encouraging the leap-frogging of innovations over wide areas, with geographic distance a less important influence.

High-technology corridors Areas along or near major transportation arteries that are devoted to the research, development, and sale of high-technology products. These areas develop because of the networking and synergistic advantages of concentrating high-technology enterprises in close proximity to one another. "Silicon Valley" is a prime example of a high-technology corridor in the United States.

Hinduism One of the oldest **religions** in the modern world, dating back over 4000 years, and originating in the Indus River Valley of what is today part of Pakistan. Hinduism is unique among the world's religions in that it does not have a single founder, a single theology, or agreement on its origins.

Hinterland Literally, "country behind," a term that applies to a surrounding area served by an urban center. That center is the focus of goods and services produced for its hinterland and is its dominant urban influence as well. In the case of a port city, the hinterland also includes the inland area whose trade flows through that port.

Holocene The current **interglaciation** period, extending from 10,000 years ago to the present on the geologic time scale.

Homo sapiens The only living species of the genus *Homo*; modern humans.

Horizontal integration Ownership by the same firm of a number of companies that exist at the same point on a **commodity chain**.

Huang He (Yellow) and Wei (Yangtzi) River Valleys Rivers in present-day China; it was at the confluence of the Huang He and Wei

Rivers where chronologically the fourth urban **hearth** was established around 1500 BCE.

Human-environment   The second theme of geography as defined by the **Geography Educational National Implementation Project**; reciprocal relationship between humans and environment.

Human geography   One of the two major divisions of **geography**; the spatial analysis of human population, its cultures, activities, and landscapes.

Human territoriality   A term associated with the work of Robert Sack that describes the efforts of human societies to influence events and achieve social goals by exerting, and attempting to enforce, control over specific geographical areas.

Hydrologic cycle   The system of exchange involving water in its various forms as it continually circulates among the atmosphere, the oceans, and above and below the land surface.

Identifying against   Constructing an **identity** by first defining the "other" and then defining ourselves as "not the other."

Identity   Defined by geographer Gillian Rose as "how we make sense of ourselves;" how people see themselves at different scales.

Imam   The political head of the Muslim community or the person who leads prayer services. In **Shiite** Islam the Imam is immune from sin or error.

Immigrant   A person migrating into a particular country or area; an in-migrant.

Immigration   The act of a person migrating into a new country or area.

Immigration laws   Laws and regulations of a state designed specifically to control immigration into that **state**.

Immigration wave   Phenomenon whereby different patterns of **chain migration** build upon one another to create a swell in **migration** from one origin to the same destination.

Independent invention   The term for a trait with many **cultural hearths** that developed independent of each other.

Indigenous religions   Belief systems and philosophies practiced and traditionally passed from generation to generation among peoples within an indigenous tribe or group.

Indus River Valley   Chronologically, the third urban **hearth**, dating to 2200 BCE.

Industrial Revolution   The term applied to the social and economic changes in agriculture, commerce and manufacturing that resulted from technological innovations and specialization in late-eighteenth-century Europe.

Infant Mortality Rate (IMR)   A figure that describes the number of babies that die within the first year of their lives in a given population.

Infectious diseases   Diseases that are spread by bacteria, viruses, or parasites. Infectious diseases diffuse directly or indirectly from human to human.

Informal economy   Economic activity that is neither taxed nor monitored by a government; and is not included in that government's **Gross National Product (GNP)**; as opposed to a formal economy.

Interfaith boundaries   Boundaries between the world's major faiths.

Interglaciation   Sustained warming phase between glaciations during an ice age.

Intermodal (connections)   Places where two or more modes of transportation meet (including air, road, rail, barge, and ship).

Internal migration   Human movement within a **nation-state**, such as ongoingly westward and southward movements in the United States.

Internal displaced person   People who have been displaced within their own countries and do not cross international borders as they flee.

International migration   Human movement involving movement across international boundaries.

Intervening opportunity   The presence of a nearer opportunity that greatly diminishes the attractiveness of sites farther away.

Intrafaith boundaries   Boundaries within a single major faith.

Islam   The youngest of the major world **religions**, Islam is based on the teachings of Muhammad, born in Mecca in 571 CE. According to Islamic teaching, Muhammad received the truth directly from Allah in a series of revelations during which Muhammad spoke the verses of the *Qu'ran (Koran)*, the Islamic holy book.

Island of development   Place built up by a government or corporation to attract foreign investment and which has relatively high concentrations of paying jobs and infrastructure.

Isogloss   A geographic **boundary** within which a particular linguistic feature occurs.

Isotherm   Line on a map connecting points of equal temperature values.

Jihad   A doctrine within **Islam**. Commonly translated as "Holy War," Jihad represents either a personal or collective struggle on the part of Muslims to live up to the religious standards set by the *Qu'ran*.

Judaism   Religion with its roots in the teachings of Abraham (from Ur), who is credited with uniting his people to worship only one god. According to Jewish teaching, Abraham and God have a covenant in which the Jews agree to worship only one God, and God agrees to protect his chosen people, the Jews.

Just-in-time delivery   Method of inventory management made possible by efficient transportation and communication systems, whereby companies keep on hand just what they need for near-term production, planning that what they need for longer-term production will arrive when needed.

Kinship links   Types of **push factors** or **pull factors** that influence a migrant's decision to go where family or friends have already found success.

Köppen climate classification system   Developed by Wladimir Köppen, a system for classifying the world's climates on the basis of temperature and precipitation.

Landscape   The overall appearance of an area. Most landscapes are comprised of a combination of natural and human-induced influences.

Language   A set of sounds, combination of sounds, and symbols that are used for communication.

Language convergence   The collapsing of two **languages** into one resulting from the consistent **spatial interaction** of peoples with different languages; the opposite of **language divergence**.

Language divergence   The opposite of **language convergence**; a process suggested by German linguist August Schleicher whereby new **languages** are formed when a language breaks into dialects due to a lack of **spatial interaction** among speakers of the language and continued isolation eventually causes the division of the language into discrete new languages.

Language family   Group of **languages** with a shared but fairly distant origin.

Latitude   An imaginary line running parallel to the equator that is used to measure distance in degrees north or south from the equator.

Laws of migration   Developed by British demographer Ernst Ravenstein, five laws that predict the flow of migrants.

Leadership class   Group of decision-makers and organizers in early **cities** who controlled the resources, and often the lives, of others.

Least Cost Theory   Model developed by Alfred Weber according to which the location of manufacturing establishments is determined by the minimization of three critical expenses: labor, transportation, and **agglomeration**.

Life expectancy A figure indicating how long, on average, a person may be expected to live. Normally expressed in the context of a particular state.

Lingua franca A term deriving from "Frankish language" and applying to a tongue spoken in ancient Mediterranean ports that consisted of a mixture of Italian, French, Greek, Spanish, and even some Arabic. Today it refers to a "common language," a language used among speakers of different languages for the purposes of trade and commerce.

Little Ice Age Temporary but significant cooling period between the fourteenth and the nineteenth centuries; accompanied by wide temperature fluctuations, droughts, and storms, causing famines and dislocation.

Livestock ranching The raising of domesticated animals for the production of meat and other byproducts such as leather and wool.

Local culture Group of people in a particular **place** who see themselves as a collective or a community, who share experiences, customs, and traits, and who work to preserve those traits and customs in order to claim uniqueness and to distinguish themselves from others.

Local Exchange Trading System (LETS) A barter system whereby a local currency is created through which members trade services or goods in a local **network** separated from the **formal economy**.

Location The first theme of geography as defined by the **Geography Educational National Implementation Project**; the geographical **situation** of people and things.

Location theory A logical attempt to explain the locational pattern of an economic activity and the manner in which its producing areas are interrelated. The agricultural location theory contained in the **von Thünen** model is a leading example.

Locational interdependence Theory developed by economist Harold Hotelling that suggests competitors, in trying to maximize sales, will seek to constrain each other's territory as much as possible which will therefore lead them to locate adjacent to one another in the middle of their collective customer base.

Longitude An imaginary line circling the Earth and running through the poles. Used to determine the location of things by measurement of the angular distance, in degrees east or west, from the **Prime Meridian**.

Long-lot survey system Distinct regional approach to land surveying found in the Canadian Maritimes, parts of Quebec, Louisiana, and Texas whereby land is divided into narrow parcels stretching back from rivers, roads, or canals.

Luxury crops Non-subsistence crops such as tea, cacao, coffee, and tobacco.

Majority-minority districts In the context of determining representative districts, the process by which a majority of the population is from the minority.

Malaria Vectored disease spread by mosquitoes that carry the malaria parasite in their saliva and which kills approximately 150,000 children in the global **periphery** each month.

Manufacturing export zones A feature of economic development in peripheral countries whereby the host country establishes areas with favorable tax, regulatory, and trade arrangements in order to attract foreign manufacturing operations. The goods manufactured in these export zones are primarily destined for the global market.

Maquiladora The term given to zones in northern Mexico with factories supplying manufactured goods to the U.S. market. The low-wage workers in the primarily foreign-owned factories assemble imported components and/or raw materials and then export finished goods.

Mass depletions Loss of diversity through a failure to produce new species.

Mass extinctions Mass destruction of most species.

Material culture The art, housing, clothing, sports, dances, foods, and other similar items constructed or created by a group of people.

McGee model Developed by geographer T.G. McGee, a model showing similar land-use patterns among the medium-sized cities of Southeast Asia.

McMansions Homes referred to as such because of their "super size" and similarity in appearance to other such homes; homes often built in place of **tear-downs** in American suburbs.

Medical geography The study of health and disease within a geographic context and from a geographical perspective. Among other things, medical geography looks at sources, diffusion routes, and distributions of diseases.

Mediterranean agriculture Specialized farming that occurs only in areas where the dry-summer Mediterranean climate prevails.

Megalopolis Term used to designate large coalescing supercities that are forming in diverse parts of the world; formerly used specifically with an uppercase "M" to refer to the Boston—Washington multimetropolitan corridor on the northeastern seaboard of the United States, but now used generically with a lower-case "m" as a synonym for conurbation.

Mental map Image or picture of the way space is organized as determined by an individual's perception, impression, and knowledge of that space.

Mercantilism In a general sense, associated with the promotion of commercialism and trade. More specifically, a protectionist policy of European **states** during the sixteenth to the eighteenth centuries that promoted a state's economic position in the contest with other countries. The acquisition of gold and silver and the maintenance of a favorable trade balance (more exports than imports) were central to the policy.

Mesoamerica Chronologically the fifth urban hearth, dating to 200 BCE.

Mesopotamia Region of great cities (e.g. Ur and Babylon) located between the Tigris and Euphrates Rivers; chronologically the first urban **hearth**, dating to 3500 BCE, and which was founded in the **Fertile Crescent**.

Metes and bounds system A system of land surveying east of the Appalachian Mountains. It is a system that relies on descriptions of land ownership and natural features such as streams or trees. Because of the imprecise nature of metes and bounds surveying, the U.S. Land Office Survey abandoned the technique in favor of the **rectangular survey system**.

Microcredit program Program that provides small loans to poor people, especially women, to encourage development of small businesses.

Migrant labor A common type of **periodic movement** involving millions of workers in the United States and tens of millions of workers worldwide who cross international borders in search of employment and become **immigrants**, in many instances.

Migration A change in residence intended to be permanent. See also **chain, forced, internal, international, step**, and **voluntary migration**.

Military service Another common form of **periodic movement** involving as many as 10 million United States citizens in a given year, including military personnel and their families, who are moved to new locations where they will spend tours of duty lasting up to several years.

Minaret Tower attached to a Muslim mosque, having one or more projecting balconies from which a crier calls Muslims to prayer.

Modernization model A model of economic development most closely associated with the work of economist Walter Rostow. The modernization model (sometimes referred to as modernization theory) maintains that all countries go through five interrelated stages of development, which culminate in an economic state of self-sustained economic growth and high levels of mass consumption.

Monoculture Dependence on a single agricultural commodity.

Monolingual states Countries in which only one **language** is spoken.

Monotheistic religion Belief system in which one supreme being is revered as creator and arbiter of all that exists in the universe.

Montreal Protocol   An international agreement signed in 1987 by 105 countries and the European Community (now European Union). The protocol called for a reduction in the production and consumption of chlorofluorocarbons (CFCs) of 50 percent by 2000. Subsequent meetings in London (1990) and Copenhagen (1992) accelerated the timing of CFC phaseout, and a worldwide complete ban has been in effect since 1996.

Movement   The fifth theme of geography as defined by the **Geography Educational National Implementation Project**; the mobility of people, goods and ideas across the surface of the planet

Multilingual states   Countries in which more than one **language** is spoken.

Multinational state   **State** with more than one nation within its borders.

Multistate nation   **Nation** that stretches across borders and across states.

Mutual intelligibility   The ability of two people to understand each other when speaking.

Nation   Legally, a term encompassing all the citizens of a state. Most definitions now tend to refer to a tightly knit group of people possessing bonds of language, ethnicity, religion, and other shared cultural attributes. Such homogeneity actually prevails within very few states.

Nation-state   Theoretically, a recognized member of the modern state system possessing formal **sovereignty** and occupied by a people who see themselves as a single, united **nation**. Most nations and states aspire to this form, but it is realized almost nowhere. Nonetheless, in common parlance, nation-state is used as a synonym for country or state.

Natural increase   Population growth measured as the excess of live births over deaths. Natural increase of a population does not reflect either **emigrant** or **immigrant** movements.

Natural resource   Any valued element of (or means to an end using) the environment; includes minerals, water, vegetation, and soil.

Neocolonialism   The entrenchment of the colonial order, such as trade and investment, under a new guise. See also **postcolonialism**.

Neolocalism   The seeking out of the regional culture and reinvigoration of it in response to the uncertainty of the modern world.

Networks   Defined by Manuel Castells as a set of interconnected nodes without a center.

Newborn mortality rate   The number of infants who die within the first month of life per 1,000 live births.

New urbanism   Outlined by a group of architects, urban planners, and developers from over 20 countries, an urban design that calls for development, urban revitalization, and suburban reforms that create walkable neighborhoods with a diversity of housing and jobs.

Nile River Valley   Chronologically the second urban **hearth**, dating to 3200 BCE.

Nomadism   Movement among a definite set of places—often **cyclic movement**.

Nongovernmental Organizations (NGOs)   International organizations that operate outside of the formal political arena but that are nevertheless influential in spearheading international initiatives on social, economic, and environmental issues.

Non-material culture   The beliefs, practices, aesthics, and values of a group of people.

North American Free Trade Agreement (NAFTA)   Agreement entered into by Canada, Mexico, and the United States in December, 1992 and which took effect on January 1, 1994, to eliminate the barriers to trade in, and facilitate the cross-border movement of goods and services between the countries.

Nostratic (language)   **Language** believed to be the ancestral language not only of **Proto-Indo-European**, but also of the Kartvelian languages of the of the southern Caucasus region, the Uralic-Altaic languages (including Hungarian, Finnish, Turkish, and Mongolian), the Dravadian languages of India, and the Afro-Asiatic language family.

Official language   In multilingual countries the **language** selected, often by the educated and politically powerful elite, to promote internal cohesion; usually the language of the courts and government.

Offshore   With reference to production, to **outsource** to a third party located outside of the country.

One-child policy   A program established by the Chinese government in 1979 to slow population growth in China.

Organic agriculture   Approach to farming and ranching that avoids the use of herbicides, pesticides, growth hormones, and other similar synthetic inputs.

Outsource   With reference to production, to turn over in part or in total to a third party.

Oxygen cycle   Cycle whereby natural processes and human activity consume atmoshperic oxygen and produce carbon dioxide and the Earth's forests and other flora, through **photosynthesis**, consume carbon dioxide and produce oxygen.

Ozone layer   The layer in the upper atmosphere located between 30 and 45 kilometers above the Earth's surface where stratospheric ozone is most densely concentrated. The ozone layer acts as a filter for the Sun's harmful ultraviolet rays.

Pacific Ring of Fire   Ocean-girdling zone of crustal instability, volcanism, and earthquakes resulting from the tectonic activity along plate boundaries in the region.

Pandemic   An outbreak of a disease that spreads worldwide. See also **endemic**.

Pangaea   The primeval supercontinent, hypothesized by Alfred Wegener, that broke apart and formed the continents and oceans as we know them today; consisted of two parts—a northern Laurasia and a southern **Gondwana**.

Participatory development   The notion that locals should be engaged in deciding what development means for them and how it should be achieved.

Pastoralist   Person involved in a form of agricultural activity that involves the raising of livestock. Many peoples described as herders actually pursue mixed agriculture, in that they may also fish, hunt, or even grow a few crops. But pastoral peoples' lives revolve around their animals.

Pattern   The design of a **spatial distribution** (e.g. scattered or concentrated).

Peace of Westphalia   Peace negotiated in 1648 to end the Thirty Years' War, Europe's most destructive internal struggle over religion. The treaties contained new language recognizing statehood and nationhood, clearly defined borders, and guarantees of security.

Per capita GNP   The **Gross National Product (GNP)** of a given country divided by its population.

Perception of place   Belief or "understanding" about a place developed through books, movies, stories or pictures.

Perceptual region   A **region** that only exists as a conceptualization or an idea and not as a physically demarcated entity. For example, in the United States, "the South" and "the Mid-Atlantic region" are perceptual regions.

Periphery   Processes that incorporate lower levels of education, lower salaries, and less technology; and generate less wealth than core processes in the world-economy.

Periodic Movement   Movement—for example, college attendence or military service—that involves temporary, recurrent relocation.

Photosynthesis   The formation of carbohydrates in living plants from water and carbon dioxide, through the action of sunlight on chlorophyll in those plants, including algae.

Physical geography One of the two major divisions of systematic geography; the spatial analysis of the structure, processes, and location of the Earth's natural phenomena such as climate, soil, plants, animals, and topography.

Physical-political (natural-political) boundary Political boundary **defined** and **delimited** (and occasionally **demarcated**) by a prominent physical feature in the natural landscape—such as a river or the crest ridges of a mountain range.

Physiologic population density The number of people per unit area of **arable** land.

Pidgin language When parts of two or more languages are combined in a simplified structure and vocabulary.

Pilgrimage Voluntary travel by an adherent to a **sacred site** to pay respects or participate in a ritual at the site.

Place The fourth theme of geography as defined by the **Geography Educational National Implementation Project**; uniqueness of a **location**.

Placelessness Defined by geographer Edward Relph as the loss of uniqueness of **place** in the **cultural landscape** so that one place looks like the next.

Plant domestication Genetic modification of a plant such that its reproductive success depends on human intervention.

Plantation agriculture Production system based on a large estate owned by an individual, family, or corporation and organized to produce a cash crop. Almost all plantations were established within the tropics; in recent decades, many have been divided into smaller holdings or reorganized as cooperatives.

Pleistocene The most recent epoch of the Late Cenozoic Ice Age, beginning about 1.8 million years ago and marked by as many as **20 glaciations** and **interglaciations** of which the current warm phase, the Holocene epoch, has witnessed the rise of human civilization.

Political ecology An approach to studying nature—society relations that is concerned with the ways in which environmental issues both reflect, and are the result of, the political and socioeconomic contexts in which they are situated.

Political geography A subdivision of **human geography** focused on the nature and implications of the evolving spatial organization of political governance and formal political practice on the Earth's surface. It is concerned with why political spaces emerge in the places that they do and with how the character of those spaces affects social, political, economic, and environmental understandings and practices.

Polytheistic religion Belief system in which multiple deities are revered as creators and arbiters of all that exists in the universe.

Popular culture **Cultural traits** such as dress, diet, and music that identify and are part of today's changeable, urban-based, media-influenced western societies.

Population composition Structure of a population in terms of age, sex and other properties such as marital status and education.

Population density A measurement of the number of people per given unit of land.

Population distribution Description of locations on the Earth's surface where populations live.

Population explosion The rapid growth of the world's human population during the past century, attended by ever-shorter **doubling times** and accelerating rates of increase.

Population pyramids Visual representations of the age and sex composition of a population whereby the percentage of each age group (generally five-year increments) is represented by a horizontal bar the length of which represents its relationship to the total population. The males in each age group are represented to the left of the center line of each horizontal bar; the females in each age group are represented to the right of the center line.

Possibilism Geographic viewpoint—a response to determinism—that holds that human decision making, not the environment, is the crucial factor in cultural development. Nonetheless, possibilists view the environment as providing a set of broad constraints that limits the possibilities of human choice.

Post-Fordist World economic system characterized by a more flexible set of production practices in which goods are not mass-produced; instead, production has been accelerated and dispersed around the globe by multinational companies that shift production, outsourcing it around the world and bringing places closer together in time and space than would have been imaginable at the beginning of the twentieth century.

Postcolonialism A recent intellectual movement concerned with examining the enduring impacts of **colonialism**, not just in economic and political relations (the focus of **neocolonialism**), but especially in cultural terms. Postcolonial studies examine the ways in which basic concepts of culture and forms of cultural interaction continue to be shaped by the hegemonic ideas and practices of colonialism.

Primary economic activity Economic activity concerned with the direct extraction of **natural resources** from the environment—such as mining, fishing, lumbering, and especially **agriculture**.

Primary industrial regions Western and Central Europe; Eastern North America; Russia and Ukraine; and Eastern Asia, each of which consists of one or more core areas of industrial development with subsidiary clusters.

Primate city A country's largest city—ranking atop the **urban hierarchy**—most expressive of the national culture and usually (but not always) the capital city as well.

Prime Meridian An imaginary north-south line of **longitude** on the Earth grid, passing through the Royal Observatory at Greenwich in London, defined as having a longitude of 0°.

Primogeniture System which the eldest son in a family—or, in exceptional cases, daughter—inherits all of a dying parent's land.

Protestant One of three major branches of **Christianity** (together with the **Eastern Orthodox Church** and the **Roman Catholic Church**). Following the widespread societal changes in Europe starting in the 1300s CE, many adherents to the Roman Catholic Church began to question the role of religion in their lives and opened the door to the Protestant Reformation wherein John Huss, Martin Luther, John Calvin, and others challenged many of the fundamental teachings of the Roman Catholic Church.

Proto-Indo-European (language) Linguistic hypothesis proposing the existence of an ancestral Indo-European **language** that is the **hearth** of the ancient Latin, Greek, and Sanskrit languages which hearth would link modern languages from Scandinavia to North Africa and from North America through parts of Asia to Australia.

Pull factor Positive conditions and perceptions that effectively attract people to new locales from other areas.

Push factor Negative conditions and perceptions that induce people to leave their abode and migrate to a new locale.

Quaternary economic activity Service sector industries concerned with the collection, processing, and manipulation of information and capital. Examples include finance, administration, insurance, and legal services.

Queer theory Theory defined by geographers Glen Elder, Lawrence Knopp, and Heidi Nast that highlights the contextual nature of opposition to the heteronormative and focuses on the political engagement of "queers" with the heteronormative.

Quinary economic activity Service sector industries that require a high level of specialized knowledge or technical skill. Examples include scientific research and high-level management.

Quotas   Established limits by governments on the number of immigrants who can enter a country each year.

Race   A categorization of humans based on skin color and other physical characteristics. Racial categories are social and political constructions because they are based on ideas that some biological differences (especially skin color) are more important than others (e.g., height, etc.), even though the latter might have more significance in terms of human activity. With its roots in sixteenth-century England, the term is closely associated with European **colonialism** because of the impact of that development on global understandings of racial differences.

Racism   Frequently referred to as a system or attitude toward visible differences in individuals, racism is an ideology of difference that ascribes (predominantly negative) significance and meaning to culturally, socially, and politically constructed ideas based on phenotypical features.

Radioactive waste   Hazardous-waste-emitting radiation from nuclear power plants, nuclear weapons factories, and nuclear equipment in hospitals and industry.

Rank-size rule   In a model urban hierarchy, the idea that the population of a **city** or town will be inversely proportional to its rank in the hierarchy.

Reapportionment   Process by which representative districts are switched according to population shifts, so that each district encompasses approximately the same number of people.

Rectangular survey system   Also called the Public Land Survey, the system was used by the U.S. Land Office Survey to parcel land west of the Appalachian Mountains. The system divides land into a series of rectangular parcels.

Redlining   A discriminatory real estate practice in North America in which members of minority groups are prevented from obtaining money to purchase homes or property in predominantly white neighborhoods. The practice derived its name from the red lines depicted on **cadastral maps** used by real estate agents and developers. Today, redlining is officially illegal.

Reference maps   Maps that show the absolute location of places and geographic features determined by a frame of reference, typically latitude and longitude.

Refugees   People who have fled their country because of political persecution and seek asylum in another country.

Region   The third theme of geography as defined by the **Geography Educational National Implementation Project**; an **area** on the Earth's surface marked by a degree of formal, functional, or perceptual homogeneity of some phenomenon.

Regional scale   Interactions occurring within a **region**, in a regional setting.

Relative location   The regional position or **situation** of a place relative to the position of other places. Distance, **accessibility**, and connectivity affect relative location.

Religion   Defined by geographers Robert Stoddard and Carolyn Prorak in the book *Geography in America* as "a system of beliefs and practices that attempts to order life in terms of culturally perceived ultimate priorities."

Religious extremism Religious fundamentalism carried to the point of violence.

Religious fundamentalism   Religious movement whose objectives are to return to the foundations of the faith and to influence state policy.

Relocation diffusion   Sequential **diffusion** process in which the items being diffused are transmitted by their carrier agents as they evacuate the old areas and relocate to new ones. The most common form of relocation diffusion involves the spreading of innovations by a migrating population.

Remittances   Money migrants send back to family and friends in their home countries, often in cash, forming an important part of the economy in many poorer countries.

Remote sensing   A method of collecting data or information through the use of instruments (e.g., satellites) that are physically distant from the area or object of study.

Renewable resources   Resources that can regenerate as they are exploited.

Renfrew hypothesis   Hypothesis developed by British scholar Colin Renfrew wherein he proposed that three areas in and near the first agricultural hearth, the **Fertile Crescent**, gave rise to three language families: Europe's Indo-European languages (from Anatolia [present-day Turkey]); North African and Arabian languages (from the western arc of the Fertile Crescent); and the languages in present-day Iran, Afghanistan, Pakistan, and India (from the eastern arc of the Fertile Crescent).

Repatriation   A refugee or group of refugees returning to their home country, usually with the assistance of government or a non-governmental organization.

Rescale   Involvement of players at other scales to generate support for a position or an initiative (e.g., use of the Internet to generate interest on a national or global scale for a local position or initiative).

Residential segregation   Defined by geographers Douglas Massey and Nancy Denton as the degree to which two or more groups live separately from one another, in different parts of an urban environment.

Restrictive population policies   Government policies designed to reduce the rate of natural increase.

Reterritorialization   With respect to popular culture, when people within a place start to produce an aspect of popular culture themselves, doing so in the context of their local culture and making it their own.

Roman Catholic Church   One of three major branches of **Christianity**, the Roman Catholic Church, together with the **Eastern Orthodox Church**, a second of the three major branches of Christianity, arose out of the division of the Roman Empire by Emperor Diocletian into four governmental regions: two western regions centered in Rome, and two eastern regions centered in Constantinople (now Istanbul, Turkey). In 1054 CE, Christianity was divided along that same line when the Eastern Orthodox Church, centered in Constantinople; and the Roman Catholic Church, centered in Rome, split.

Romance languages   Languages (French, Spanish, Italian, Romanian, and Portuguese) that lie in the areas that were once controlled by the Roman Empire but were not subsequently overwhelmed.

Root crop   Crop that is reproduced by cultivating the roots of or the cuttings from the plants.

Sacred site   **Place** or **space** people infuse with religious meaning.

Sanitary landfills   Disposal sites for non-hazardous solid waste that is spread in layers and compacted to the smallest practical volume. The sites are typically designed with floors made of materials to treat seeping liquids and are covered by soil as the wastes are compacted and deposited into the landfill.

Scale   Representation of a real-world phenomenon at a certain level of reduction or generalization. In **cartography**, the ratio of map distance to ground distance; indicated on a map as a bar graph, representative fraction, and/or verbal statement.

Second Agricultural Revolution   Dovetailing with and benefiting from the **Industrial Revolution**, the Second Agricultural Revolution witnessed improved methods of cultivation, harvesting, and storage of farm produce.

Secondary economic activity   Economic activity involving the processing of raw materials and their transformation into finished industrial products; the manufacturing sector.

Secularism   The idea that ethical and moral standards should be formulated and adhered to for life on Earth, not to accommodate the prescriptions of a deity and promises of a comfortable afterlife. A secular state is the opposite of a **theocracy**.

Seed crop Crop that is reproduced by cultivating the seeds of the plants.

Selective immigration Process to control immigration in which individuals with certain backgrounds (i.e. criminal records, poor health, or subversive activities) are barred from immigrating.

Semi-periphery Places where **core** and **periphery** processes are both occurring; places that are exploited by the core but in turn exploit the periphery.

Sense of place State of mind derived through the infusion of a place with meaning and emotion by remembering important events that occurred in that place or by labeling a place with a certain character.

Sequent occupance The notion that successive societies leave their cultural imprints on a place, each contributing to the cumulative **cultural landscape**.

Shamanism Community faith in traditional societies in which people follow their shaman—a religious leader, teacher, healer, and visionary. At times, an especially strong shaman might attract a regional following. However, most shamans remain local figures.

Shantytown Unplanned slum development on the margins of cities, dominated by crude dwellings and shelters made mostly of scrap wood, iron, and even pieces of cardboard.

Sharia law The system of Islamic law, sometimes called *Qu'ranic law*. Unlike most Western systems of law that are based on legal precedence, Sharia is based on varying degrees of interpretation of the *Qu'ran*.

Shifting cultivation Cultivation of crops in tropical forest clearings in which the forest vegetation has been removed by cutting and burning. These clearings are usually abandoned after a few years in favor of newly cleared forestland. Also known as **slash-and-burn agriculture**.

Shintoism Religion located in Japan and related to **Buddhism**. Shintoism focuses particularly on nature and ancestor worship.

Shiites Adherents of one of the two main divisions of Islam. Also known as Shiahs, the Shiites represent the Persian (Iranian) variation of Islam and believe in the infallibility and divine right to authority of the **Imams**, descendants of Ali.

Site The internal physical attributes of a **place**, including its absolute location, its spatial character and physical setting.

Situation The external locational attributes of a place; its **relative location** or regional position with reference to other nonlocal places.

Slash-and-burn agriculture See **shifting cultivation**.

Slavic languages Languages (Russian, Polish, Czech, Slovak, Ukrainian, Slovenian, Serbo-Croatian, and Bulgarian) that developed as Slavic people migrated from a base in present-day Ukraine close to 2000 years ago.

Social stratification One of two components, together with **agricultural surplus**, which enables the formation of **cities**; the differentiation of society into classes based on wealth, power, production, and prestige.

Soil erosion The wearing away of the land surface by wind and moving water.

Solid waste Non-liquid, non-soluble materials ranging from municipal garbage to sewage sludge; agricultural refuse; and mining residues.

Sound shift Slight change in a word across **languages** within a **subfamily** or through a language family from the present backward toward its origin.

Sovereignty A principle of international relations that holds that final authority over social, economic, and political matters should rest with the legitimate rulers of independent states.

Space Defined by Doreen Massey and Pat Jess as "social relations stretched out."

Spaces of consumption Areas of a **city**, the main purpose of which is to encourage people to consume goods and services; driven primarily by the global media industry.

Spatial Pertaining to space on the Earth's surface; sometimes used as a synonym for *geographic*.

Spatial distribution Physical location of geographic phenomena across **space**.

Spatial interaction See **complementarity** and **intervening opportunity**.

Spatial perspective Observing variations in geographic phenomena across **space**.

Special Economic Zone (SEZ) Specific **area** within a country in which tax incentives and less stringent environmental regulations are implemented to attract foreign business and investment.

Splitting In the context of determining representative districts, the process by which the majority and minority populations are spread evenly across each of the districts to be created therein ensuring control by the majority of each of the districts; as opposed to the result of **majority-minority districts**.

Standard language The variant of a **language** that a country's political and intellectual elite seek to promote as the norm for use in schools, government, the media, and other aspects of public life.

State A politically organized territory that is administered by a sovereign government and is recognized by a significant portion of the international community. A state has a defined territory, a permanent population, a government, and is recognized by other states.

Stateless nation Nation that does not have a state.

Stationary population level The level at which a national population ceases to grow.

Step migration Migration to a distant destination that occurs in stages, for example, from farm to nearby village and later to town and city.

Stimulus diffusion A form of diffusion in which a cultural adaptation is created as a result of the introduction of a **cultural trait** from another **place**.

Structural adjustment loans Loans granted by international financial institutions such as the World Bank and the International Monetary Fund to countries in the **periphery** and the **semi-periphery** in exchange for certain economic and governmental reforms in that country (e.g. privatization of certain government entities and opening the country to foreign trade and investment).

Structuralist theory A general term for a model of economic development that treats economic disparities among countries or regions as the result of historically derived power relations within the global economic system.

Subfamilies (language) Divisions within a **language** family where the commonalities are more definite and the origin is more recent.

Subsistence agriculture Self-sufficient **agriculture** that is small scale and low technology and emphasizes food production for local consumption, not for trade.

Suburb A subsidiary urban area surrounding and connected to the central city. Many are exclusively residential; others have their own commercial centers or shopping malls.

Suburban downtown Significant concentration of diversified economic activities around a highly **accessible** suburban location, including retailing, light industry, and a variety of major corporate and commercial operations. Late-twentieth-century coequal to the American central city's **Central Business District (CBD)**.

Suburbanization Movement of upper- and middle-class people from urban **core areas** to the surrounding outskirts to escape pollution as well as deteriorating social conditions (perceived and actual). In North America, the process began in the early nineteenth century and became a mass phenomenon by the second half of the twentieth century.

Succession   Process by which new **immigrants** to a **city** move to and dominate or take over areas or neighborhoods occupied by older immigrant groups. For example, in the early twentieth century, Puerto Ricans "invaded" the immigrant Jewish neighborhood of East Harlem and successfully took over the neighborhood or "succeeded" the immigrant Jewish population as the dominant immigrant group in the neighborhood.

Sunbelt   The South and Southwest regions of the United States

Sunbelt phenomenon   The movement of millions of Americans from northern and northeastern States to the South and Southwest regions (**Sunbelt**) of the United States.

Sunnis   Adherents to the largest branch of Islam, called the orthodox or traditionalist. They believe in the effectiveness of family and community in the solution of life's problems, and they differ from the **Shiites** in accepting the traditions (*sunna*) of Muhammad as authoritative.

Supranational organization   A venture involving three or more **nation-states** involving formal political, economic, and/or cultural cooperation to promote shared objectives. The European Union is one such organization.

Synergy   The cross-promotion of vertically-integrated goods.

Taoism Religion   believed to have been founded by Lao-Tsu and based upon his book entitled "Tao-te-ching," or "Book of the Way." Lao-Tsu focused on the proper form of political rule and on the oneness of humanity and nature.

Tear-downs   Homes bought in many American suburbs with the intent of tearing them down and replacing them with much larger homes often referred to as **McMansions**.

Technopole   Centers or nodes of high-technology research and activity around which a **high-technology corridor** is sometimes established.

Territorial integrity   The right of a **state** to defend sovereign territory against incursion from other states.

Territorial representation   System wherein each representative is elected from a territorially defined district.

Territoriality   In **political geography**, a country's or more local community's sense of property and attachment toward its territory, as expressed by its determination to keep it inviolable and strongly defended. See more generally **human territoriality**.

Tertiary economic activity   Economic activity associated with the provision of services—such as transportation, banking, retailing, education, and routine office-based jobs.

Thematic maps   Maps that tell stories, typically showing the degree of some attribute or the movement of a geographic phenomenon.

Theocracy   A **state** whose government is under the control of a ruler who is deemed to be divinely guided, or of a group of religious leaders, as in post-Khomeini Iran. The opposite of a theocracy is a secular state.

Third Agricultural Revolution   Currently in progress, the Third Agricultural Revolution has as its principal orientation the development of **Genetically Modified Organisms (GMOs)**.

Three-tier structure   With reference to Immanuel Wallerstein's **world-systems theory**, the division of the world into the **core**, the **periphery**, and the **semi-periphery** as a means to help explain the interconnections between places in the global economy.

Thunian pattern   See **Von Thunian Model**.

Time-Distance decay   The declining degree of acceptance of an idea or innovation with increasing time and distance from its point of origin or source.

Time-space compression   A term associated with the work of David Harvey that refers to the social and psychological effects of living in a world in which **time-space convergence** has rapidly reached a high level of intensity.

Time-space convergence   A term coined by Donald Janelle that refers to the greatly accelerated movement of goods, information, and ideas during the twentieth century made possible by technological innovations in transportation and communications.

Toponym   Place name.

Township-and-range system   A rectangular land division scheme designed by Thomas Jefferson to disperse settlers evenly across farmlands of the U.S. interior. See also **rectangular survey system**.

Toxic waste   Hazardous waste causing danger from chemicals and infectious organisms.

Trade area Region   adjacent to every town and **city** within which its influence is dominant.

Traditional   Term used in various contexts (e.g., traditional religion) to indicate originality within a culture or long-term part of an indigenous society. It is the opposite of modernized, superimposed, or changed; it denotes continuity and historic association.

Trafficking   When a family sends a child or an adult to a labor recruiter in hopes that the labor recruiter will send money, and the family member will earn money to send home.

Transhumance   A seasonal periodic movement of **pastoralists** and their livestock between highland and lowland pastures.

Unilateralism   World order in which one state is in a position of dominance with allies following rather than joining the political decision-making process.

Unitary (state)   A **nation-state** that has a centralized government and administration that exercises power equally over all parts of the state.

Universalizing religion   A belief system that espouses the idea that there is one true religion that is universal in scope. Adherents of universalizing religious systems often believe that their religion represents universal truths, and in some cases great effort is undertaken in evangelism and missionary work.

Urban (area)   The entire built-up, nonrural area and its population, including the most recently constructed suburban appendages. Provides a better picture of the dimensions and population of such an area than the delimited municipality (central city) that forms its heart.

Urban hierarchy   A ranking of settlements (hamlet, village, town, city, metropolis) according to their size and economic functions.

Urban morphology   The study of the physical form and structure of urban **places**.

Urban realm   A **spatial** generalization of the large, late-twentieth-century **city** in the United States. It is shown to be a widely dispersed, multicentered metropolis consisting of increasingly independent zones or realms, each focused on its own **suburban downtown**; the only exception is the shrunken central realm, which is focused on the **Central Business District (CBD)**.

Urban sprawl   Unrestricted growth in many American **urban** areas of housing, commercial development, and roads over large expanses of land, with little concern for urban planning.

Urbanization   A term with several connotations. The proportion of a country's population living in urban places is its level of urbanization. The process of urbanization involves the movement of people to, and the clustering of people in, towns and cities—a major force in every geographic realm today. Another kind of urbanization occurs when an expanding city absorbs the rural countryside and transforms it into suburbs; in the case of cities in the developing world, this also generates peripheral **shantytowns**.

Variable costs Costs that change directly with the amount of production (e.g. energy supply and labor costs).

Vectored disease A disease carried from one host to another by an intermediate host.

Vertical integration Ownership by the same firm of a number of companies that exist along a variety of points on a **commodity chain**.

Vienna Convention for the Protection of the Ozone Layer The first international convention aimed at addressing the issue of ozone depletion. Held in 1985, the Vienna Convention was the predecessor to the **Montreal Protocol**.

Voluntary migration Movement in which people relocate in response to perceived opportunity, not because they are forced to move.

Von Thünen Model A model that explains the location of agricultural activities in a commercial, profit-making economy. A process of spatial competition allocates various farming activities into rings around a central market city, with profit-earning capability the determining force in how far a crop locates from the market.

Washington Consensus Label used to refer to the following fundamnetal principles of free trade: 1) that free trade raises the well-being of all countries by inducing them to devote their resources to production of those goods they produce relatively most efficiently; and 2) that competition through trade raises a country's long-term growth rate by expanding access to global technologies and promoting innovation.

Wisconsinan Glaciation The most recent glacial period of the Pleistocene, enduring about 100,000 years and giving way, beginning about 18,000 years ago, to the current interglacial, the Holocene.

World city Dominant **city** in terms of its role in the global political economy. Not the world's biggest city in terms of population or industrial output, but rather centers of strategic control of the world economy.

World-systems theory Theory originated by Immanuel Wallerstein and illuminated by his **three-tier structure**, proposing that social change in the developing world is inextricably linked to the economic activities of the developed world.

Zionism The movement to unite the Jewish people of the **diaspora** and to establish a national homeland for them in the promised land.

Zone Area of a **city** with a relatively uniform land use (e.g. an industrial zone, or a residential zone).

Zoning laws Legal restrictions on land use that determine what types of building and economic activities are allowed to take place in certain areas. In the United States, areas are most commonly divided into separate zones of residential, retail, or industrial use.

References

Chapter 1

Abler, R., et al., eds. *Human Geography in a Shrinking World.* North Scituate, Mass.: Duxbury Press, 1975.

Allen, J., & Massey, D., eds. *Geographical Worlds.* Oxford: Oxford University Press, 1995.

Amedeo, D., & Golledge, R. *An Introduction to Scientific Reasoning in Geography.* New York: John Wiley & Sons, 1975.

Boyle, Peter. "The globalisation of cancer." *The Lancet.* 368, (19 August 2006), 629–630.

Brown, L. A. *Innovation Diffusion: A New Perspective.* New York: Methuen, 1981.

Buttimer, A. *Geography and the Human Spirit.* Baltimore, Md.: Johns Hopkins University Press, 1993.

Campbell, John. *Map Use and Analysis.* New York: McGraw-Hill, 2000.

Chrisman, N. R. *Exploring Geographic Information Systems.* New York: John Wiley & Sons, 2002.

Cloke, Paul, Crang, P., & Goodwin, M. *Introducing Human Geographies.* New York: Oxford University Press, 1999.

Crang, M. *Cultural Geography.* New York: Routledge, 1998.

de Blij, H. J., & Muller, P. O. *Geography: Realms, Regions and Concepts.* 10th rev. ed. New York: John Wiley & Sons, 2002.

Dent, Borden. *Cartography: Thematic Map Design.* 5th ed. Dubuque, Iowa: William C. Brown, 1998.

Dicken, Peter. *Geographies and Globalization: (yet) another missed boat?* Transactions of the Institute of British Geographers, 29 (2004): 5.

Dicken, Peter. *Global Shift,* 4th ed. New York: Guilford Press, 2003

Ember, C. R., & Ember, M. E. *Cultural Anthropology.* 6th rev. ed. Englewood Cliffs, N.J.: Prentice-Hall, 1990.

Gaile, G. L., & Willmott, C. J., eds. *Geography in America at the Dawn of the Twentieth Century,* New York: Oxford University Press, 2003.

Geertz, C. *The Interpretation of Cultures.* New York: Basic Books, 1973.

Gold, J. *An Introduction to Behavioral Geography.* New York: Oxford University Press, 1980.

Gould, P. *The Geographer at Work.* London: Routledge & Kegan Paul, 1985.

Gould, P., & White, R. *Mental Maps.* 2nd rev. ed. Boston: Allen & Unwin, 1992.

Gregory, D. *Ideology, Science and Human Geography.* London: Hutchinson, 1978.

Gregory, D., & Walford, R., eds. *Horizons in Human Geography.* Totowa, N.J.: Barnes & Noble Books, 1989.

Hägerstrand, Torsten. *What about People in Regional Science?* Papers, Regional Science Association, 24 (1970): 7-21.

Harris, C. D., ed. *A Geographical Bibliography for American Libraries.* Washington, D.C.: Association of American Geographers and the National Geographic Society, 1985.

Hartshorne, R. *The Nature of Geography.* Washington, D.C.: Association of American Geographers, 1939.

Hartshorne, R. *Perspective on the Nature of Geography.* Chicago: Rand McNally, 1959.

Hoebel, E. Adamson. *Anthropology: The Study of Man,* 4th ed. New York: McGraw-Hill, 1972.

Holz, R., ed. *The Surveillant Science: Remote Sensing of the Environment,* 2nd rev. ed. New York: John Wiley & Sons, 1985.

Houghton, J. T., Ding, Y., Griggs, D.J., Noguer, M., van der Linden P. J. & Xiaosu, D., eds. *Climate Change 2001: The Scientific Basis Contribution of Working Group I to the Third Assessment Report of the Intergovernmental Panel on Climate Change (IPCC).* Cambridge: Cambridge University Press, UK, 2001, p. 944.

Howat, D.D. *The "John Snow".* Anaesthesia 28, 4 (1973):430-4.

Huntington, E., and Cushing, S.W., *Principles of Human Geography,* 5th ed. New York: John Wiley & Sons, 1940.

Jackson, P. *Maps of Meaning.* London: Unwin Hyman, 1989.

James, P. E., & Jones, C. F., eds. *American Geography: Inventory and Prospect.* Syracuse, N.Y.: Syracuse University Press, 1954.

James, P. E., & Martin, G. *All Possible Worlds: A History of Geographical Ideas,* 3rd rev. ed. New York: John Wiley & Sons, 1993.

Johnston, R. J. *Geography and Geographers: Anglo-American Human Geography since 1945.* 5th ed. London; New York: Arnold, 1997.

Johnston, R. J. *On Human Geography.* Oxford, New York: Blackwell, 1986.

Johnston, R. J., et al., eds.; Smith, D. M., consultant editor. *The Dictionary of Human Geography.* 4th ed. Oxford, U.K.: Malden, Mass. Blackwell Publishers, 2000.

Johnston, R. J., Taylor, P., & Watts, M. J. *Geographies of Global Change: Remapping the World in the Late Twentieth Century,* 2nd ed. Oxford: Blackwell, 2002.

Kolivras, Korine. "Mosquito Habitat and Dengue Risk Potential in Hawaii: A Conceptual Framework and GIS Application." *The Professional Geographer,* 58 (2006) 139–154.

Lawson, Victoria. "The Geographical Advantage in Development Studies." Keynote Address. Annual Meeting of the Great Plains/Rocky Mountains Division of the Association of American Geographers. October 1, 2004.

Leib, Jonathan, Gerald Webster, and Roberta Webster "*Rebel with a Cause? Iconography and Public Memory in the Southern United States.*" Geojournal. 52 (2000):303–310.

Leib, Jonathan "*Heritage versus Hate: A Geographical Analysis of Georgia's Confederate Battle*

Flag Debate" Southeastern Geographer, 35, 1 (1995): 37–57.

Lewis, M. W., & Wigen, K. E. The Myth of Continents: A Critique of Metageography. Berkeley: University of California Press, 1997.

Lewis, Peirce. Axioms for Reading the Landscape: Some Guides to the American Scene. In The Interpretation of Ordinary Landscapes: Geographical Essays, Donald W. Meinig, ed. New York: Oxford University Press, 1979: 11–32.

Markham, S.F. Climate and the Energy of Nations. London: Oxford University Press, 1947.

Massey, D., & Allen, J., eds. Geography Matters! A Reader. New York: Cambridge University Press, 1985.

Michener, J. "The Mature Social Studies Teacher." Social Education, November 1970, pp. 760–766.

Monmonier, M. S. Computer-Assisted Cartography: Principles and Prospects. Englewood Cliffs, N.J.: Prentice-Hall, 1982.

Monmonier, M. S. How to Lie with Maps. Chicago: University of Chicago Press, 1990.

Monmonier, M. S. Mapping It Out: Expository Cartography for the Humanities and Social Sciences. Chicago: University of Chicago Press, 1993.

Monmonier, M. S. Maps with the News. Chicago: University of Chicago Press, 1989.

National Geographic Society, Maps, the Landscape, and Fundamental Themes in Geography. Washington, D.C., 1986.

National Geographic Society. Historical Atlas of the United States. Washington, D.C.: National Geographic Society, 1988.

National Research Council. Rediscovering Geography: New Relevance for Science and Society. Washington, D.C.: National Academy Press, 1997.

Pattison, W. "The Four Traditions of Geography." Journal of Geography 63 (1964): 211–216.

Peet, R. Modern Geographical Thought. Oxford: Malden, Mass.: Blackwell Publishers, 1998.

Robinson, A. H., et al. Elements of Cartography. 6th rev. ed. New York: John Wiley & Sons, 1995.

Sauer, Carl. "Recent Developments in Cultural Geography." In Recent Developments in the Social Sciences, Elwood, C. A., Wissler, C., and Gault, R. H., eds. Philadelphia: J. B. Lippincott, 1927, pp. 154–212.

Sauer, Carl. Agricultural Origins and Dispersals. American Geographical Society, 1952.

Wai-chung Yeung, Henry. "Globalization." In Student's Companion to Geography, 2nd ed. Alisdair Rogers and Heather Viles, eds. Oxford: Blackwell. 2002.

Whittlesey, Derwent. Sequent Occupance, Annals of the Association of American Geographers, 19, 2 (1929): 162–165.

Zelinsky, Wilbur. North America's Vernacular Regions. Annals of the Association of American Geographers, 70, 1 (1980): 1–16.

Chapter 2

Association for the Advancement of Science. Atlas of Population and Environment. Berkeley: University of California Press, 2000.

Boserup, E. Population and Technological Change. Chicago: University of Chicago Press, 1981.

Brown, L. et al. Beyond Malthus: Sixteen Dimensions of the Population Problem. Worldwatch Paper 143, 1998.

Brown, L. R., et al. State of the World. New York: W. W. Norton, Annual.

Ehrlich, P., & Ehrlich, A. Healing the Planet: Strategies for Resolving the Environmental Crisis. Reading, Mass.: Addison-Wesley, 1991.

Goldscheider, C., ed. Population, Ethnicity, and Nation-Building. Boulder, Colo.: Westview Press, 1995.

Gould, Peter. The Slow Plague: A Geography of the AIDS Pandemic. New York: Blackwell, 1993.

Heer, D. M., & Grigsby, J. S. Society and Population. 2nd ed. Englewood Cliffs, N.J.: Prentice-Hall, 1992).

Hornby, W., & Jones, M. An Introduction to Population Geography. 2nd ed. New York: Cambridge University Press, 1993).

Malthus, T. R. An Essay on the Principles of Population. Edited by A. Appelman. New York: W.W. Norton, 1976.

Mortimore, M. Adapting to Drought: Farmers, Famines, and Desertification in West Africa. Cambridge: Cambridge University Press, 1989.

Newman, J., & Matzke, G. Population: Patterns, Dynamics, and Prospects. Englewood Cliffs, N.J.: Prentice-Hall, 1984.

Oppong, Joseph R. "A Vulnerability interpretation of the geography of HIV/AIDS in Ghana, 1986–1995." The Professional Geographer, 50 (1998), 437–448.

Peters, G. L. & Larkin, R. P. Population Geography: Problems, Concepts, and Prospects. 6th ed. Dubuque, Iowa: Kendall/Hunt Publishing Company, 1998.

Plane, D. A. "Demographic Influences on Migration." Regional Studies, 27 (1993), 375–383.

Plane, D. A., & Rogerson, P. A. "Tracking the Baby Boom, the Baby Bust, and the Echo Generations: How Age Composition Regulates US Migration." The Professional Geographer. 43, no. 4 (1991), 416–430.

Population Reference Bureau. 1997 World Population Data Sheet. Washington, D.C., 1997.

Preston, S. H., ed. World Population: Approaching the Year 2000. Special edition of the Annals of the American Academy of Political and Social Science, July 1990, Vol. 510.

Roberts, G. Population Policy: Contemporary Issues. New York: Praeger, 1990.

Robson, E. "Hidden Child Workers: Young Carers in Zimbabwe." Antipode, 36, 5 (2004), 227–248.

Sharma, M. B. "Population in Advanced Placement Human Geography." Journal of Geography, 99, 3/4 (2000), 99–110.

Stanecki, K. "The AIDS Pandemic in the 21st Century." Washington, D.C.: United States Census Bureau, 2004.

Teitelbaum, M. S., & Winter, J. M., eds. Population and Resources in Western Intellectual Traditions. Cambridge: Cambridge University Press, 1989.

United Nations. The World at Six Billion. Table 1, "World Population from Year 0 to Stabilization," 1999, p. 5, http://www.un.org/esa/population/publications/sixbillion/sixbilpart1.pdf.

Wang, G. T. China's Population: Problems, Thoughts and Policies. London: Ashgate Publishing, 1999.

Watts, Jonathan. "Japan Ponders Economic Rescue by Immigration." The Guardian 5 August 1999.

Chapter 3

Agozino, B. Theoretical and Methodological Issues in Migration Research. London: Ashgate Publishing, 2000.

Appleyard, R. ed. Emigration Dynamics in Developing Countries (Series). London: Ashgate Publishing, 1999–2000.

Blaut, James. A Colonizer's Model of the World: Geographical Diffusionism and Eurocentric History. New York: Guilford Press, 1993.

Blavo, E. Q. The Problem of Refugees in Africa: Boundaries and Borders. London: Ashgate Publishing, 1999.

Blunt, Alison. "Cultural geographies of migration: mobility, transnationality and diaspora." Progress in Human Geography, 31 (2007), 684–694.

Boyle, Paul. "Population geography: transnational women on the move." Progress in Human Geography, 26 (2002), 531–543.

Chessum, L. From Immigrants to Ethnic Minority. London: Ashgate Publishing, 2000.

Clark, W.A.V. Human Migration. Beverly Hills, Calif.: Sage, 1986.

Clark, W.A.V. The California Cauldron: Immigration and the Fortunes of Local Communities. New York: Guilford Press, 1998.

Curtin, P. D. Death by Migration: Europe's Encounter with the Tropical World in the Nineteenth Century. New York: Cambridge University Press, 1989.

Davis, Benjamin and Paul Winters. "Gender, Networks and Mexico-U.S. Migration." *Journal of Developmental Studies*, Vol. 38(2), December 2001, 1–26.

Dittmer, Jason. "The Soufriere Hills Volcano and the Postmodern Landscapes of Montserrat" FOCUS on Geography, 2004, 1–7.

Gould, W.T.S., & Findlay, A. M., eds. *Population Migration and the Changing World Order*. New York: John Wiley & Sons, 1994.

Grossman, J. R. *Land of Hope: Black Southerners and the Great Migration*. Chicago: University of Chicago Press, 1989.

Hampton, J. *Internally Displaced People: A Global Survey*. London: Earthscan, 1998.

Hogan, Edward P., & Fouberg, Erin Hogan. *Ireland* in the Modern World Nations Series, Charles Gritzner, ed. Philadelphia: Chelsea House Publishers, 2003.

Kane, H. *The Hour of Departure: The Forces That Create Refugees and Migrants*. Washington, D.C.: Worldwatch Institute, 1995.

Kershen, A. J., ed. *Language, Labor and Migration*. London: Ashgate Publishing, 2000.

Lawson, Victoria. "Hierarchical Households and Gendered Migration in Latin America: Feminist Extensions to Migration Research." *Progress in Human Geography*. 22 (1998), 39–53.

Lewis, G. *Human Migration: A Geographical Perspective*. New York: St. Martin's Press, 1982.

Nyiri, P. *New Chinese Migrants in Europe*. London: Ashgate Publishing, 1999.

Ogden, P. E. *Migration and Geographical Change*. Cambridge: Cambridge University Press, 1984.

Pandit, K. & Davies Withers, S., eds. *Migration and Restructuring in the United States*. Lanham, Md.: Rowman & Littlefield, 1999.

Peters, G. L. & Larkin, R. P. *Population Geography: Problems, Concepts, and Prospects*. Dubuque 6th ed.: Kendall/Hunt Publishing Company, 1998.

Plane, D. A. "Demographic Influences on Migration." *Regional Studies*, 27 (1993), 375–383.

Plane, D. A., & Rogerson, P. A. "Tracking the Baby Boom, the Baby Bust, and the Echo Generations: How Age Composition Regulates US Migration." *The Professional Geographer*, 43, no. 4 (1991), 416–430.

Population Reference Bureau. *1997 World Population Data Sheet*. Washington, D.C., 1997.

Preston, S. H., ed. *World Population: Approaching the Year 2000*. Special edition of the *Annals of the American Acadamy of Political and Social Science*, July 1990, Vol. 510.

Pries, L., ed. *Migration and Transnational Social Spaces*. London: Ashgate Publishing, 1999.

Ravenstein, Ernst. "The Laws of Migration." *Journal of the Statistical Society*, 48 (1885): 167–235.

Roberts, G. *Population Policy: Contemporary Issues*. New York: Praeger, 1990.

Silvey, Rachel. "Power, difference and mobility: feminist advances in migration studies." *Progress in Human Geography*, 28 (2004) 490–506.

Silvey, Rachel, and Lawson, Victoria. "Placing the Migrant." *Annals of the Association of American Geographers*, 89 (1999), 121–132.

Simon, R., & Brettell, C., eds. *International Migration. The Female Experience*. Totowa, N.J.: Rowman & Allanheld, 1986.

Swann, M. M. *Migrants in the Mexican North: Mobility, Economy, and Society in a Colonial World*. Boulder, Colo.: Westview Press, 1989.

Teitelbaum, M. S., & Winter, J. M., eds. *Population and Resources in Western Intellectual Traditions*. Cambridge: Cambridge University Press, 1989.

United Nations High Commissioner for Refugees. *The State of the World's Refugees*. New York: Oxford, 2000.

Verhovek, S.H. "Tiny Stretch of Border, Big Test for Wall." *The New York Times*, 8 December 1997.

Wang, G. T. *China's Population: Problems, Thoughts and Policies*. London: Ashgate Publishing, 1999.

White, P., & Woods, R., eds. *The Geographical Impact of Migration*. London: Longman, 1980.

Wood, W. B. "Forced Migration: Local Conflicts and International Dilemmas." *Annals of the Association of American Geographers*, 84, no. 4 (1994), 607–635.

Chapter 4

Androutsopoulos, Jannis, and Scholz, Arno. "Spaghetti Funk: Appropriations of Hip-Hop Culture and Rap Music in Europe." *Popular Music and Society*, 26 (2003), 463–479.

Bascom, Johnathan. " 'Energizing' Rural Space: The Representation of Countryside Culture as an Economic Development Strategy." *Journal of Cultural Geography*, 19 (2001), 53–74.

Bell, Thomas. "Why Seattle? An Examination of an Alternative Rock Culture Hearth." *Journal of Cultural Geography*, 18, no. 1 (1998), 35–48.

Bertram, Dennison. "Czech Hip Republic Hop." *New Presence: The Prague Journal of Central European Affairs*, 5 (2003), 42–44.

Bowen, Dawn. "Lookin' for Margaritaville: Place and imagination in Jimmy Buffett's songs." *Journal of Cultural Geography*, 16, no. 2 (1997), 99–109.

Bowen, Dawn. "Agricultural Expansion in Northern Alberta." *Geographical Review*, 92 (2002), 503–526.

Burns, Mike. "The Pub Diaspora." *Europe*, 363 (1997), 44–46.

Carney, George O. "Music Geography." *Journal of Cultural Geography*, 18, no. 1 (1998), 1.

Colapinto, John. "The raging optimism and multiple personalities of Dave Matthews." *Rolling Stone*. December 12, 1996.

Connell, John, & Chris Gibson. *Sound Tracks: Popular Music, Identity and Place*. New York: Routledge, 2003.

Dave Matthews Band, www.drnband.com

Doan, Petra L. "Queers in the American city: Transgendered perceptions of urban space." *Gender, Place and Culture*, 14 (2007), 57–74.

Duncan, J. S., & Ley, D. *Place/Culture/Representation*. London and New York: Routledge, 1993.

The Economist. "No more pyrotechnics: taming the rock-concert industry's excesses," 2 June 2008.

Featherstone, M. "Global Culture: An Introduction." in Mike Featherstone, ed., *Global Culture: Nationalism, Globalization and Modernity*, 1–14. London: Sage, 1990.

Goreham, Gary A. "Community and Religion in a Post-Modern Global World: A Review Essay on Anabaptist Religious Groups." *Rural Sociology*, 67 (2002), 299–306.

Gumprecht, Blake. "Lubbock on Everything: The Evocation of Place in Popular Music (A West Texas Example)." *Journal of Cultural Geography*, 18, 1 (1998), 61.

Harrison, Simon. "Cultural Boundaries." *Anthropology Today*, 15, 5 (1999), 10–13.

Harvey, D. *The Condition of Postmodernity: An Enquiry into the Origins of Cultural Change*. Cambridge, Mass.: Blackwell, 1989.

Harvey, D. "The Art of Rent: Globalization, Monopoly and the Commodification of Culture." In Leo Panitch and Colin Leys, eds., *A World of Contradictions*. New York: Monthly Review Press, 2002.

Jameson, F., & Miyoshi, M., eds. *The Cultures of Globalization, Post-Contemporary Interventions*. Durham, N.C.: Duke University Press, 1998.

Kelly, P. *Landscapes of Globalization*. New York: Routledge, 2000.

Kniffen, F. B. "Folk Housing: Key to Diffusion." *Annals of the Association of American Geographers*, 55 (1965), 559–577.

Knox, P., & Taylor, P. J., eds. World Cities in a World-System. Cambridge: Cambridge University Press, 1995.

Kong, Lily. "Popular Music in a Transnational World: The Construction of Local Identities in Singapore." *Asia Pacific Viewpoint*, 38, no. 1 (1997), 19–36.

Kotler, P., et al. *Marketing Places: Attracting Investment, Industry, and Tourism to Cities, States, and Nations*. New York: Free Press, 1993.

Kraybill, Donald B., and Carl F. Bowman. *On the Backroad to Heaven: Old Order Hutterites, Mennonites, Amish, and Brethren*. Baltimore, Md.: Johns Hopkins University Press, 2001.

Layden, Tim. "Making Millions." *Sports Illustrated*, 96 (2002), 24, 80–89.

Massey, D. B. *Space, Place, and Gender*. Minneapolis: University of Minnesota Press, 1994.

Merchants of Cool. www.pbs.org/wgbh/pages/frontline/shows/cool/. Last accessed June 2005.

Mitchell, D. "There's No Such Thing as Culture: Towards a Reconceptualization of the Idea of Culture in Geography." *Transactions of the Institute of British Geographers*, 20 (1995), 102–116.

Myers, Garth A., Patrick McGreevy, George O. Carney, & Judith Kenny. "Cultural Geography." In Gary L. Gaile and Cort J. Willmott, eds., *Geography in America at the Dawn of the 21ˢᵗ Century*. Oxford: Oxford University Press, 2003, 81–96.

Pattacini, Melissa McCray. "Deadheads Yesterday and Today: An Audience Study." *Popular Music and Society*, 24 (2000), 1–14.

Relph, Edward C. *Place and Placelessness*. New York: Routledge, Kegan and Paul, 1976.

Reverb, www.reverbrock.org

Rooney, John F. *A Geography of American Sport: From Cabin Creek to Anaheim*. Reading, MA: Addison-Wesley, 1974.

Rosati, Clayton. "The Image Factory: MTV, Geography, and the Industrial Production of Culture." (Syracuse University, Ph.D. diss., 2005).

Rosati, Clayton. "MTV: 360 degrees of the industrial production of culture." *Transactions of the Institute of British Geographers*, 32 (2007), 556–575.

Roy, William G. "Aesthetic Identity, Race, and American Folk Music." *Qualitative Sociology*, 25, no. 3 (2002), 459–469.

Schnell, Steven M. "Creating Narratives of Place and Identity in 'Little Sweden, U.S.A.'" *Geographical Review*, 93 (2003), 1–29.

Schnell, Steven M., and Joseph F. Reese. "Microbreweries as Tools of Local Identity." *Journal of Cultural Geography*, 21, no. 1 (2003), 45–69.

Seidenberg, Robert. "The gospel according to Matthews." *Entertainment Weekly*. June 2, 1995.

Shapiro, Roberta. "The Aesthetics of Institutionalization: Breakdancing in France." *Journal of Arts Management, Law, and Society* 33 (2004), 316–335.

Shortridge, B. G., and James R. Shortridge, eds. *The Taste of American Place: A Reader on Regional and Ethnic Foods*. Lanham, MD: Rowman & Littlefield, 1998.

Shortridge, James R. "Keeping Tabs on Kansas: Reflections on Regionally Based Field Study." *Journal of Cultural Geography*, 16 (1996), 5–16.

Smith, Maureen Margaret and Becky Beal. "'So you can see how the other half lives': MTV 'Cribs' use of 'the Other' in framing successful athletic masculinities." *Journal of Sport and Social Issues*, 31 (2007), 103–127.

Storey, J. *Cultural Studies & the Study of Popular Culture*. Athens: University of Georgia, 1996.

Stump, Roger W. "Place and Innovation in Popular Music: The Bebop Revolution in Jazz." *Journal of Cultural Geography*. 18, no. 1(1998), 11–35.

Timmons Roberts, J., & Hite, A. *From Modernization to Globalization*. Oxford: Blackwell, 2000.

Toffler, A. *Future Shock*. New York: Random House, 1970.

Ultimate Fighting Championship, www.ufc.com

van Eeden, Jeanne. "The Colonial Gaze: Imperialism, Myths, and South African Popular Culture." *Design Issues*, 20 (2004), 18–33.

Waters, M. *Globalization, Key Ideas*. London: Routledge, 1995.

Chapter 5

Adepoju, A., & Oppong, C., eds. *Gender, Work & Population in Sub-Saharan Africa*. London: J. Currey, 1994.

Agarawal, B. *A Field of One's Own: Gender and Land Rights in South Asia*. Cambridge: Cambridge University Press, 1994.

Anderson, Benedict. *Imagined Communities*. New York: Verso, 1991.

Arreola, Daniel D., ed. *Hispanic Space, Latino Places: Community and Cultural Diversity in Contemporary America*. Austin: University of Texas Press, 2004.

Aslanbeigui, N., Pressman, S. & Summerfield, G., eds. *Women in the Age of Economic Transformation: Gender Impact of Reforms in Post-Socialist and Developing Countries*. London: Routledge, 1994.

Atkings, P. J., & Bowler, I. R. *Food in Society: Economy, Culture, Geography*. New York: Arnold, 2001.

Back, L., & Salomos, J. *Theories of Race and Racism: A Reader*. New York: Routledge, 2000.

Badran, M. *Feminists, Islam, and Nation: Gender and the Making of Modern Egypt*. Princeton, N.J.: Princeton University Press, 1995.

Bahvnani, K-K., ed. *Feminism and "Race."* New York: Oxford University Press, 2001.

Barnett, T., & Blaikie, P. *AIDS in Africa: Its Present and Future Impact*. New York: Guilford Press, 1992.

Beneria, L., & Feldman, S., eds. *Unequal Burden: Economic Crises, Persistent Poverty and Women's Work*. Boulder, Colo.: Westview Press, 1992.

Berry, Kate A. "Projecting the Voices of Others; Issues of Representation in Teaching Race and Ethnicity" *Journal of Geography in Higher Education*, 21, 2 (1997).

Biswas, M. R., & Gabr, M., eds. *Nutrition in the Nineties: Policy Issues*. New York: Oxford University Press, 1994.

Blaut, James. *The Colonizer's Model of the World: Geographical Diffusionism and Eurocentric History*. New York: Guilford Press, 1993.

Bradsher, Keith. "Bigger than Las Vegas? That's Macao's bet." *The New York Times*, August 28, 2007.

Brooks, G. *Nine Parts of Desire: The Hidden World of Islamic Women*. New York: Anchor Books/Doubleday, 1994.

Brown, B.J., & LaPrairie, L. A. *Shades of Opportunity and Access: Ethnic and Gender Minority Issues in America with Global Reflections*. Boulder, Colo.: Department of Geography, University of Colorado, 1991.

Brown, L. R. *The Changing World Food Prospects: The Nineties and Beyond*. Washington, D.C.: Worldwatch Institute, 1988.

Brown, L. R. *Full House: Reassessing the Earth's Population Carrying Capacity*. Washington, D.C.: Worldwatch Institute, 1994.

Chatty, D., & Rabo, A., eds. *Organizing Women: Formal and Informal Women's Groups in the Middle East*. New York: Berg, 1997.

Cho, David. "No Borders Between Them; Away From Conflict, Area Indians and Pakistanis Find Common Ground" *The Washington Post*. January 19, 2002, metro 1.

Clark, R. P. *Global Life Systems: Population, Food, and Disease in the Process of Globalization*. Lanham, Md.: Rowman & Littlefield, 2000.

Clarke, C., Ley, D., & Peach, C., eds. *Geography and Ethnic Pluralism*. London: George Allen & Unwin, 1984.

Cliff, A., & Haggett, P. *Atlas of Disease Distribution*. Oxford, UK: Basil Blackwell, 1989.

Cravey, A. J. *Women and Work in Mexico's Maquiladoras*. Lanham, Md.: Rowman & Littlefield, 1998.

Currey, B., & Hugo, G., eds. *Famines as a Geographical Phenomenon*. Boston: D. Reidel, 1984.

Currie, G., & Rothenberg, C., eds. *Feminist (Re)Visions of the Subject: Landscapes, Ethnoscapes, Theoryscapes*. Lanham, Md.: Rowman & Littlefield, 2001.

Curtis, James R. "Mexicali's Chinatown." *Geographical Review*, 85, no. 3 (1995), 335–348.

Curtis, James R. "Barrio Space and Place in Southeast Los Angeles, California." In Daniel D. Arreola, ed. *Hispanic Spaces, Latino Places: Community and Cultural Diversity in Contemporary America*. Austin: University of Texas Press, 2004.

Delaporte, F. *The History of Yellow Fever*. Trans. A. Goldhammer. Cambridge, Mass.: MIT Press, 1991.

DePalma, Anthony. "Canada's Indigenous Tribes receive formal apology." *The New York Times*. 8 January 1998.

Despommier, D. D. *Parasitic Diseases*. 4th ed. New York: Apple Trees Productions, 2000.

Devereux, S. *Famine in the Twentieth Century*. Brighton: Institute of Development Studies, 2000.

Domosh, M., & Seager, J. *Putting Women in Place: Feminist Geographers Make Sense of the World*. New York: Guilford Press, 2001.

Domosh, M., & Seager, J. *Putting Women in Place*. New York: Guilford Press, 2001.

Dyck, I., Lewis, N., & McLafferty, S., eds. *Geographies of Women's Health*. New York: Routledge, 2001.

Elder, G., Knopp, L., & Nast, H. "Sexuality and Space" in *Geography in America at the Dawn of the 21st Century*, Gary L. Gaile and Cort J. Willmott, eds. New York: Oxford University Press, 2003.

Flores, Rafael, & Gillespie, S. *Health and Nutrition: Emerging and Reemerging Issues in Developing Countries*. Washington, D.C.: International Food and Policy Research Institute, 2001.

Forest, B. "A New Geography of Identity? Race, Ethnicity and American Citizenship" in *American Space/American Place: Geographies of the United States on the Threshold of a New Century*, John Agnew and Jonathan Smith, eds. Edinburgh: University of Edinburgh Press, 2002, 231–263.

Frazier John W., Margai, Florence M., and Tettey-Fio, Eugene. 2003. *Race and Place: Equity Issues In Urban America*. Boulder, CO: Westview Press.

Gatrell, A. G., & Löytönen, M., eds. *GIS and Health*. Philadelphia: Taylor & Francis, 1998.

Gesler, W. *Health Care in Developing Countries*. Washington, D.C.: Association of American Geographers, Resource Publications in Geography, 1984.

Gordon, A. A. *Transforming Capitalism and Patriarchy: Gender and Developments in Africa*. Boulder, Colo.: Lynne Rienner, 1996.

Gould, P. R. *The Slow Plague: A Geography of the AIDS Pandemic*. Oxford: Basil Blackwell, 1993.

Haddad, Y. Y., & Esposito, J. L., eds. *Islam, Gender & Social Change*. New York: Oxford University Press, 1998.

Haggett, P. *The Geographical Structure of Epidemics*. New York: Clarendon Press, 2000.

Hall, S. "New Cultures for Old" in *A Place in the World? Places, Cultures, and Globalization*, Doreen Massey and Pat Jess, eds. New York: Oxford University Press, 1995.

Hall, S. Race: *The Floating Signifier [Videorecording]*. Media Education Foundation; Introduced by Sut Jhally, produced, directed & edited by Sut Jhally. Northampton, Mass., 1996.

Hancock, Peter. "The lived experience of female factory workers in rural West Java." *Labour and Management in Development Journal*, 1, 1 (2000), 1–18.

Hanson, S., & Pratt, G. *Gender, Work and Space*. New York: Routledge, 1995.

Hartl, D. L., & Clark, A.G. *Principles of Population Genetics*. 3rd ed. Sunderland, Mass.: Sinauer Associates, 1997.

Honari, M., & Boleyn, T., eds. *Health Ecology: Health, Culture, and Human-Environment Interaction*. New York: Routledge, 1999.

Howland, C. W. *Religious Fundamentalisms and the Human Rights of Women*. New York: Palgrave, 2001.

Hurrell, A., & Woods, N., eds. *Inequality, Globalization, and World Politics*. New York: Oxford University Press, 1999.

Iceland, John and Daniel H. Weinberg with Erika Steinmetz. *Racial and Ethnic Residential Segregation in the United States: 1980–2000*. Census 2000 Special Reports, August 2002. http://www.census.gov/hhes/www/housing/resseg/front-toc.html.

Jeffrey, R., & Jeffrey, P. *Population, Gender and Politics: Demographic Change in Rural North India*. Cambridge: Cambridge University Press, 1997.

Jeter, Lynne W. Columbus Brick Company Defies Industry Trend. *Mississippi Business Journal*, 23, 2, January 8, 2001: 1.

Jobin, W. *Dams and Disease: Ecological Design and Health Impacts of Large Dams, Canals, and Irrigation Systems*. New York: Routledge, 1999.

Johnson Jr. J. H., C. K. Jones, W. C. Farrell, and M. L. Oliver. "The Los Angeles Rebellion: A Retrospective in View" *Economic Development Quarterly*, 6, 4 (1992): 356–372.

Johnson, L., Huggins, J., & Jacobs, J. *Placebound: Australian Feminist Geographies*. New York: Oxford University Press, 2000.

Jones III, J. P., Nast, H. J., & Roberts, S. M., eds. *Thresholds in Feminist Geography: Difference, Methodology, Representation*. Totowa, N.J.: Rowman & Allanheld, 1997.

Kahne, H., & Giele, J. Z., eds. *Women's Work and Women's Lives: The Continuing Struggle Worldwide*. Boulder, Colo.: Westview Press, 1992.

Lieberson, S., & Waters, M. C. *From Many Strands: Ethnic and Racial Groups in Contemporary America*. New York: Russell Sage Foundation, 1990.

Lloyd, B. S., Rengert, A. C., & Monk, J. J. "Landscapes of the Home." In A. C. Rengert & J. J. Monk, eds., *Women and Spatial Change: Learning Resources for Social Science Courses*. Dubuque, Iowa: Kendall-Hunt, 1982.

Marchand, M. H., & Runyan, A. S., eds. *Gender and Global Restructuring: Sightings, Sites and Resistance*. New York: Routledge, 2000.

Marty, M. E., & Appleby, R. S., eds. *Religion, Ethnicity, and Self-Identity: Nations in Turmoil*. Hanover, N.H.: University Press of New England, 1997.

Massey, D. *Space, Place and Gender*. Minneapolis: University of Minnesota Press, 1994.

Massey, Doreen and Pat Jess. "Places and Cultures in an Uneven World" in *A Place in the World? Places, Cultures, and Globalization*, Doreen Massey and Pat Jess, eds. New York: Oxford University Press, 1995.

Massey, Douglas S., and Nancy A. Denton. "The Dimensions of Residential Segregation." *Social Forces*, 67 (1988): 281–315.

McCall, L. *Complex Inequality: Gender, Class and Race in the New Economy*. New York: Routledge, 2001.

McDowell, L., & Sharp, J. P., eds. *Space, Gender, Knowledge*. New York: Arnold, 1997.

McKee, J. O. *Ethnicity in Contemporary America*. Lanham, Md.: Rowman & Littlefield, 2000.

Meade, M. S., & Earickson, R. J. *Medical Geography: A Geographical Appraisal*. 2nd ed. New York: Guilford Press, 2000.

Mikesell, M. W., & Murphy, A. B. "A Framework for Comparative Study of Minority-Group Aspirations." *Annals of the Association of American Geographers*, 81 (1991). 581–604.

Miranne, K. B., & Young, A. H., eds. *Gendering the City*. Lanham, Md.: Rowman & Littlefield, 2000.

Miyares, Ines M. "Changing Latinization of New York City." In Daniel D. Arreola, ed. *Hispanic Spaces, Latino Places: Community and Cultural Diversity in Contemporary America*. Austin: University of Texas Press, 2004.

Momsen, J. H., & Kinnaird, V., eds. *Different Places, Different Voices: Gender and Development in Africa, Asia, and Latin America*. London: Routledge, 1993.

Momsen, J. H., & Townsend, J., eds. *Geography of Gender in the Third World*. Albany, N.Y.: SUNY Press, 1987.

Montagu, A. *Man's Most Dangerous Myth: The Fallacy of Race*. 5th rev. ed. Cleveland: World, 1975.

Oberhauser, Ann M., Donna Rubinoff, Karen De Bres, Susan Mains, and Cindy Pope. "Geographic Perspectives on Women" in *Geography in America at the Dawn of the 21st Century*, Gary L. Gaile and Cort J. Willmott, eds. New York: Oxford University Press, 2003.

Opdycke, S. *The Routledge Historical Atlas of Women in America*. New York: Routledge, 2000.

Oprah Winfrey Show. January 16, 2004. Harpo Productions, Inc. http://www.fistulafoundation.org/pdf/oprah%20transcript.pdf. Last accessed October 2005.

Ost, Jason and Gary Gales. *The Gay and Lesbian Atlas*. Washington, DC: Urban Institute Press, 2004.

Phillips, D. R. *Health and Health Care in the Third World*. Essex, UK: Longmans, 1990.

Pyle, G. *The Diffusion of Influenza: Patterns and Paradigms*. Totowa, N.J.: Rowman & Allanheld, 1986.

Roberts, L. "Disease and Death in the New World." *Science*, December 8, 1989, pp. 1245–1247.

Rose, Gillian. "Place and Identity: A Sense of Place" in *A Place in the World? Places, Cultures, and Globalization*, Doreen Massey and Pat Jess, eds. New York: Oxford University Press, 1995.

Rose, H. M., & McClain, P. D. *Race, Place and Risk: Black Homicide in Urban America*. Albany: State University of New York Press, 1990.

Roseman, C. C., Laux, H. D., & Thieme, G., eds. *EthniCity: Geographical Perspectives on Ethnic Change in Modern Cities*. Lanham, Md.: Rowman & Littlefield, 1996.

Sachs, C. *The Invisible Farmers: Women in Agricultural Production*. Totowa, N.J.: Rowman & Allanheld, 1983.

Said, Edward. *Orientalism*. London: Routledge, 1978.

Seager, J. *The State of Women in the World Atlas*. 2nd ed. New York: Penguin Group, 1997.

Shannon, G. W., Pyler, G., & Bashshur, R. *The Geography of AIDS*. New York: Guilford Press, 1991.

Sheldon, K., ed. *Courtyards, Markets, City Streets: Urban Women in Africa*. Boulder, Colo.: Westview Press, 1996.

Shinagawa, L. H., & Jang, M. *Atlas of American Diversity*. Walnut Creek, Ca.: AltaMira Press, 1998.

Shortridge, B. G. *Atlas on American Women*. New York: Macmillan, 1987.

Singer, M., & Berg, P. *Genes and Genomes: A Changing Perspective*. Mill Valley, Calif.: University Science Books, 1990.

Sivard, R. L. *Women: A World Survey*. Washington, D.C.: World Priorities, 1985.

Sowell, T. *Race and Culture: A World View*. New York: Basic Books, 1994.

Sperling, V. *Organizing Women in Contemporary Russia*. Cambridge: Cambridge University Press, 1999.

Staudt, K., ed. *Women, International Development and Politics*. Philadelphia: Temple University Press, 1997.

Stone, Brad. "Facebook expands into MySpace's territory." *The New York Times*. 25 May 2007.

UNICEF. *The Lesser Child: The Girl in India*. Geneva: United Nations, 1990.

UNICEF *The State of the World's Children 200*. New York: United Nations/Oxford University Press, 2001.

United Nations. *The World's Women, 1970–1990: Trends and Statistics*. New York: United Nations, 1991.

United Nations. *The World's Women, 2000: Trends and Statistics*. 3rd ed. New York: United Nations, 2000.

Zouev, A. ed. *Generation in Jeopardy: Children in Central and Eastern Europe and the Former Soviet Union*. UNICEF. Armonk, N.Y.: M. E. Sharpe, 1999.

Chapter 6

Alderman, Derek H. "A Street Fit for King: Naming Places and Commemoration in the American South." *Professional Geographer*, 52, no. 4 (2000), 672–684.

Alderman, Derek, H. "Street Names and the Scaling of Memory: The Politics of Commemorating Martin Luther King, Jr. within the African American Community." *Area*, 35, no. 2 (2003), 163–173.

Ammerman, Albert, and Cavalli-Sforza, Luigi. *The Neolithic Transition and the Genetics of Populations in Europe*. Princeton, NJ: Princeton University Press, 1984.

Baron, D. *The English Only Question*. New Haven, Conn.: Yale University Press, 1990.

Bellwood, P. "The Austronesian Dispersal and the Origin of Languages." *Scientific American*, July 1991, pp. 88–93.

Brenton, R. J. L. *Geolinguistics: Language Dynamics and Ethnolinguistic Geography*. Transl. H. F. Schiffman. Ottawa: University of Ottawa Press, 1991.

Cavalli-Sforza, L. L. "Genes, Peoples and Languages." *Scientific American*, November 1991, pp. 104–110.

Cormack, M. "Minority Language Media in Western Europe: Preliminary Considerations." *Journal of Communication*, 13, no.1, (March 1998) 759–763.

Crystal, D. *The Cambridge Encyclopedia of Language*. 2nd ed. New York: Cambridge University Press, 1997.

Crystal, D. *English as a Global Language*. New York: Cambridge University Press, 1997.

de Carvalho, C. "The Geography of Languages." In P. Wagner & M. Mikesell, eds. *Readings in Cultural Geography*. Chicago: University of Chicago Press, 1962, 75–93.

de Varennes, F. *Language, Minorities and Human Rights*. The Hague: Martinus Nijhoff Publishers, 1996.

Dixon, R. M. W. *Searching for Aboriginal Languages*. Chicago: University of Chicago Press, 1989.

Dolgopolsky, Aharon. *The Nostratic Macrofamily and Linguistic Palaeontology*. Cambridge: McDonald Institute for Archaeological Research, 1998.

Dwyer, Owen J. "Interpreting the Civil Rights Movement: Place, Memory and Conflict," Professional Geographer, 52 4 (2000), 660–671.

Frazer, T. C. *Geolinguistics: Language Dynamics and Ethnolinguistic Geography*. Concord, N.H.: Paul & Company Publishers Consortium, 1992.

Gamkrelidze, T. V., & Ivanov, V. V. "The Early History of Indo-European Languages." *Scientific American*, March 1990, pp. 110–116.

Gamkrelidze, T. V., & Ivanov, V. V. *Indo-European and the Indo-Europeans: A Reconstruction of a Proto-Language and a Proto-Culture: The Text (Trends I)*. Ed. W. Winter. Mouton De Gruyter, trans. 1995.

Greenberg, J. *The Languages of Africa*. Bloomington: Indiana University Press, 1963.

Greenberg, J. *Languages in the Americas*. Bloomington: Indiana University Press, 1987.

Holdon, C. "U.S. Dialects Persist by Both Religion and Race." *Science*, February 27, 1998, p. 1311.

Illich-Svitych, V.M. Translated in *Reconstructing Languages and Cultures*, Shevoroshkin, ed. Bochum, Germany: Brockmeyer Publishers, 1989.

Kaplan, D. H. "Population and Politics in a Plural Society: The Changing Geography of Canada's Linguistic Groups." *Annals of the Association of American Geographers*, 84, no. 1 (1994), 46–67.

Kirk, J., et al., eds. *Studies in Linguistic Geography*. Dover, N.J.: Longwood, 1985.

König, M. "Cultural Diversity and Language Policy." *International Social Science Journal*, no. 161 (1999), 401–408.

Kontra, M., Phillipson, R., & Skutnabb-Kangas, T. *Language: A Right and a Resource: Approaching Linguistic Human Rights*. Budapest: Central European University Press, 1999.

Krantz, G. S. *Geographical Development of European Languages.* New York: Peter Lang, 1988)

Kurath, Hans. *A Word Geography of the Eastern United States.* Ann Arbor: University of Michigan Press, 1949.

Laponce, J. A. *Languages and Their Territories.* Toronto: University of Toronto Press, 1987.

Lewin, R. "American Indian Language Dispute." *Science,* 23 (December 1988), 1632–1633.

Luo, Michael. "Now a Message From a Sponsor of the Subway?" *New York Times.* July 27 2004, p. 41.

Moseley, C., & Asher, R. E., eds. *Atlas of the World's Languages.* New York: Routledge, 1994.

Murphy, A. B. "European Languages." In T. Unwin, ed., *A European Geography.* London: Longman, 1998.

Murphy, A. B. *The Regional Dynamics of Language Differentiation in Belgium: A Study in Cultural-Political Geography.* Chicago: University of Chicago Geographical Research Paper No. 227, 1988.

Oppenheimer, Stephen. *The Real Eve: Modern Man's Journey Out of Africa.* New York: Carroll & Graf, 2004.

Pred, A. R. *Lost Words and Lost Worlds: Modernity and the Language of Everyday Life in Nineteenth-Century Stockholm.* Cambridge: Cambridge University Press, 1990.

Reid, T. R. "Dateline: Llanfairpwllgwyngyllgogerychwyrndrobwllllantysiliogogogoch: Wales Revives Its Language, Sending a Village's Name Tripping off Local Tongues." *Washington Post,* August 21, 2001.

Renfrew, C. *Archaeology and Language: The Puzzle of Indo-European Origins.* Cambridge: Cambridge University Press, 1988.

Renfrew, C. "The Origins of Indo-European Languages." *Scientific American,* October 1989, pp. 106–114.

Schleicher, August. *18ᵗʰ and 19ᵗʰ German Linguistics.* London: Routledge, 1995.

Schwartzberg, J. *An Historical Atlas of South Asia.* Chicago: University of Chicago Press, 1978.

Sopher, D., ed. *An Exploration of India: Geographical Perspectives on Society and Culture.* Ithaca, N.Y.: Cornell University Press, 1980.

Stewart, G. *Names on the Globe.* New York: Oxford University Press, 1975.

Stewart, G. *Names on the Land: A Historical Account of Place-Naming in the United States.* 4th rev. ed. San Francisco: Lexicos, 1982.

Swan, Clare. Quoted in "Alaska: the Last Frontier?" Annenberg CPB.

Tarantino, Quentin and Roger Avary. Pulp Fiction. http:///www.imsdb.com/scripts/Pulp-Fiction.html. last accessed September 2005.

Trudgill, P. "Linguistic Geography and Geographical Linguistics." In C. Board et al., eds. *Progress in Geography*, Vol. 7. New York: St. Martin's Press, 1975, 227–252.

Tuan, Yi-Fu. "Language and the Making of Place: A Narrative-Descriptive Approach." *Annals of the Association of American Geographers*, 81, no. 4 (1991), 684–696.

Vaux, Bert, Harvard Survey of North American Dialects. http://cfprod01.imt.uwm.edu/Dept/FLL/linguistics/dialect/ last accessed September 2005.

Williams, C. H., ed. *Language in Geographic Context.* Clevedon, Avon, England and Philadelphia: Multilingual Matters, 1988.

Wixman, R. *Language Aspects of Ethnic Patterns and Processes in the North Caucasus.* Chicago: University of Chicago Geographical Research Paper no. 191, 1980.

World Resources Institute in collaboration with United Nations Development Programme, United Nations Environment Programme, and World Bank. 2005. *World Resources 2005: The Wealth of the Poor – Managing Ecosystems to Fight Poverty.* Washington, DC: WRI.

Wurm, S., & Hattori, S., eds. *Linguistic Atlas of the Pacific Area.* Canberra, Australia: Australian Academy of the Humanities, 1982.

Chapter 7

al Faruqi, I., & Sopher, D., eds. *Historical Atlas of the Religions of the World.* New York: Macmillan, 1974.

Bearak, Barry. "When Hindus Brave a Big Crush for a Little Dip: Millions at Holy Festival Find Eternal Salvation Worth the Minor Discomforts." *The New York Times.* January 25, 2001.

Benevenisti, M. *Sacred Landscape: The Buried History of the Holy Land Since 1948.* Berkeley: University of California Press, 2000.

Bhardwaj, S. *Hindu Places of Pilgrimage in India: A Study in Cultural Geography.* Berkeley: University of California Press, 1973.

Bhardwaj, S. "Non-Hajj Pilgrimage in Islam: A Neglected Dimension of Religious Circulation." *Journal of Cultural Geography*, 17 (1998), 69–88.

Boal, Frederick W. "Territoriality on the Shankill-Falls Divide, Belfast." *Irish Geography*, 6 (1969), 30–50.

Boal, Frederick. "Integration and Division: Sharing and Segregating in Belfast." *Planning Practice and Research*, 11, no. 2 (1996).

Cooper, A. "New Directions in the Geography of Religion." *Area*, 24, no. 2 (1992), 123–129.

Curtis, J. "Miami's Little Havana: Yard Shrines, Cult Religion and Landscape." *Journal of Cultural Geography*, no. 1 (1980), 1–15.

de Blij, H. J. "Islam in South Africa." In J. Kritzeck & W. H. Lewis, eds., *Islam in Africa.* New York: van Nostrand, 1970.

"A bloody vacuum." *The Economist.* 30 September 2004.

"The barrier moves." *The Economist.* 24 February 2005.

"Will they sink or swim." *The Economist.* 22 September 2005.

Eliade, M. *The Sacred and the Profane: The Nature of Religion.* New York: Harcourt, Brace & World, 1959.

Emmet, C. F. *Beyond the Basilica: Christians and Muslims in Nazareth.* Chicago: University of Chicago Press, 1995.

Finegan, J. *An Archaeological History of Religions of Indian Asia.* New York: Paragon House, 1989.

Forbes-Boyte, Kari. "Fools Crow Versus Gullett: A Critical Analysis of the American Indian Religious Freedom Act." *Antipode*, 31, no. 3 (1999), 304–323.

Gaustad, E. *Historical Atlas of Religion in America.* New York: Harper & Row, 1962.

Griffith, J. S. *Beliefs and Holy Places: A Spiritual Geography of the Pimeria Alta.* Tucson: University of Arizona Press, 1992.

Halvorson, P., & Newman, W. *Atlas of Religious Change in America, 1952–1990.* Washington, D.C.: Glenmary Research Center, 1994.

Isaac, E. "The Act and the Covenant: The Impact of Religion on the Landscape." *Landscape*, no. 11 (1961), 12–17.

Khalidi, R. *Palestinian Identity: The Construction of Modern National Consciousness.* New York: Columbia University Press, 1997.

Kong, L. "Geography and Religion: Trends and Prospects." *Progress in Human Geography.* 14 (1990), 12–17.

Korp, M. *The Sacred Geography of the American Mound Builders.* Lewiston, N.Y.: E. Mellen Press, 1990.

Levine, G. J. "On the Geography of Religion." *Transactions of the Institute of British Geographers.* 11 (1987), 248–440.

Lewis, B., ed. *The World of Islam: Faith, People, Culture.* London, U.K.: Thames & Hudson, 1976.

Marty, M. E. *Pilgrims in Their Own Land: 500 Years of Religion in America.* Boston: Little, Brown, 1984.

Metcalf, B. D., ed. *Making Muslim Space in North America and Europe.* Berkeley: University of California Press, 1996.

Mitchell, G. *The Hindu Temple: An Introduction to Its Meaning and Forms.* New York: Harper & Row, 1977.

Noble, A. G., & Efrat E. "Geography of the Intifada." *The Geographical Review.* (July 1990), 288–307.

Nolan, Mary Lee. "Irish Pilgrimage: The Different Tradition." *Annals of the Association of American Geographers*. 73, 3 (1983), 421–438.

Park, C. *Sacred Worlds: An Introduction to Geography and Religion*. London: Routledge, 1994.

Peters, F. E. *The Hajj: The Muslim Pilgrimage to Mecca and the Holy Places*. Princeton, N.J.: Princeton University Press, 1994.

Pew Research Center. "Among Wealthy Nations…U.S. Stands Alone in its Embrace of Religion." December 19, 2002. http://people-press.org/reports/pdf/167.pdf last accessed September 2005.

Prorok, C. V. "The Hare Krishna's Transformation of Space in West Virginia." *Journal of Cultural Geography*. 7, no.1 (1986), 129–140.

Reid, T. R. "Hollow Halls in Europes Churches: Attendance by Christians Dwindles as Number of Faithful Decreases." *Washington Post*. May 6, 2001, A-1.

Romann, M., & Weingrod, A. *Living Together Separately: Arabs and Jews in Contemporary Jerusalem*. Princeton, N.J.: Princeton University Press, 1991.

Rowland, B. *The Art and Architecture of India: Buddhist, Hindu, Jain*. New York: Penguin, 1977.

Schwartberg, J. *An Historical Atlas of South Asis*. rev. ed., Chicago: University of Chicago Press, 1978.

Scott, J., & Simpson-Housley, P., eds. *Sacred Places and Profane Spaces: Essays in the Geographics of Judaism, Christianity, and Islam*. Westport, Conn.: Greenwood Press, 1991.

Sheskin, I. M. "Jewish Metropolitan Homelands." *Journal of Cultural Geography*. 13, no.2 (1993), 119–132.

Shortridge, J. R. "Patterns of Religion in the United States." *Geographical Review*, 66 (1976), 420–434.

Sidorov, Dmitri. "National Monumentalization and the Politics of Scale: The Resurrections of the Cathedral of Christ the Savior in Moscow." *Annals of the Association of American Geographers*, 90, no. 3 (2000), 548–573.

Sopher, D. E. *Geography of Religions*. Englewood Cliffs, N.J.: Prentice-Hall, 1967.

Sopher, D. E., ed. *An Exploration of India: Geographical Perspectives on Society and Culture*. Ithaca, N.Y.: Cornell University Press, 1980.

Stoddard, Robert and Carolyn Prorak "Geography of Religion and Belief Systems" In Gary L. Gaile and Cort J. Willmott, eds. *Geography in America at the Dawn of the 21st Century*. (New York: Oxford University Press, 2004.

Stump, R. *Boundaries of Faith: Geographical Perspectives on Religious Fundamentalism*. Lanham, Md.: Rowman & Littlefield Publishers, 2000.

Teather, Elizabeth K. "High-Rise Homes for the Ancestors: Cremation in Hong Kong." *Geographical Review*. 89 (1999), 409-431.

Weightman, B. A. "Changing Religious Landscapes in Los Angeles." *Journal of Cultural Geography*. 14, no.1 (1993), 1–20.

Zelinsky, W. "An Approach to the Religious Geography of the United States." *Annals of the Association of American Geographers*. 51 (1961), 139–167.

Zelinsky, W. *Cultural Geography of the United States*, rev.ed. Englewood Cliffs, N.J.: Prentice Hall, 1992.

Zelinsky, W. "The Uniqueness of the American Religious Landscape." *The Geographical Review*. 91, 3 (2001), p. 565–586.

Chapter 8

Agnew, J. A. *Place and Politics: The Geographical Mediation of State and Society*. Boston: Allen & Unwin, 1987.

Agnew, J. A. *Geopolitics: Re-visioning World Politics*. New York: Routledge, 1998.

Agnew, J. A., ed. *Political Geography: A Reader*. London: Arnold, 1997.

Anderson, Benedict. *Imagined Communities: Reflections on the Origin and Spread of Nationalism*. London: Verso, 1991.

Anderson, J., Brook, C., & Cochrane, A., eds. *A Global World?: Re-ordering Political Space*. Oxford: Oxford University Press, 1995.

Ardrey, R. *The Territorial Imperative*. New York: Antheneum, 1966.

Barakat, H. *The Arab World: Society, Culture, and State*. Berkeley: University of California Press, 1993.

Barton, J. R. *A Political Geography of Latin America*. London: Routledge, 1997.

Boateng, E. A. *A Political Geography of Africa*. Cambridge: Cambridge University Press, 1978.

Booth, J. A., & Walker, T. W. *Understanding Central America*. 3rd ed. Boulder, Colo.: Westview Press, 1999.

Boyd, A. *An Atlas of World Affairs*. 10th ed. New York: Routledge, 1998.

Bremmer, I., & Taras, R., ed. *New State, New Politics: Building the Post-Soviet Nations*. Cambridge: Cambridge University Press, 1997.

Bush, George W. *Address to the Joint Session of Congress*. September 20, 2001. http://www.september11news.com/PresidentBush-Speech.htm. Last accessed October 2005.

Bush, George W. *Rose Garden Address*. June 24, 2002. http://www.state.gov/p/nea/rls/rm/11408.htm

Clinton, William J. *Oval Office Remarks*. August 20, 1998. http://usinfo.state.gov/is/Archive_Index/President_Clintons_Oval_Office_Remarks_on_Antiterrorist_Attacks.htm. Last accessed October 2005.

Cohen, Saul B. "Global Geopolitical Change in the Post-Cold War Era." *Annals of the Association of American Geographers*, 81, 4, (1991): 551–580.

Connor, W. *Ethnonationalism: The Quest for Understanding*. Princeton, N.J.: Princeton University Press, 1994.

Crossette, B. *India: Facing the Twenty-first Century*. Bloomington: Indiana University Press, 1993.

Davidson, B. *The Black Man's Burden: Africa and the Curse of the Nation-State*. New York: Times Books/Random House, 1992.

Davidson, "Fiona. Integration and Disintegration: A Political Geography of the European Union." *Journal of Geography*, 96 (1997), 69–75.

Dawson, A. H. *The Geography of European Integration: A Common European Home?* New York: Belhaven, 1993.

Demko, G. J., & Wood, W. B. *Reordering the World: Geopolitical Perspectives on the 21st Century*. 2nd ed. Boulder, Colo.: Westview Press, 1999.

Dink, N., & Karatnycky, A. *New Nations Rising: The Fall of the Soviets and the Challenge of Independence*. New York: John Wiley & Sons, 1993.

Esposito, J. L. *The Islamic Threat: Myth or Reality?* New York: Oxford University Press, 1992.

Finkelstein, N. *The Separation of Quebec and the Constitution of Canada*. North York, Ontario: York University Centre for Public Law and Public Policy, 1992.

Fouberg, Erin Hogan. *Tribal Territory, Sovereignty and Governance: A Study of the Cheyenne River and Lake Traverse Indian Reservations*. New York: Garland Publishing, 2000.

Glassner, M. I. *Neptune's Domain: A Political Geography of the Sea*. Boston: Unwin Hyman, 1990.

Glassner, M. I. *Political Geography*. 2nd ed. New York: John Wiley & Sons, 1996.

Guéhenno, J. M. *The End of the Nation-State*. Trans. V. Elliott. Minneapolis: University of Minnesota Press, 1995.

Hancock, M. D., & Welsh, H., eds. *German Unification: Process and Outcomes*. Boulder, Colo.: Westview Press, 1993.

Hartshorne, Richard. The Functional Approach in Political Geography. *Annals of the Association of American Geographers*, 40, 2, (1950): 95–130.

Held, C. C. *Middle East Patterns: Places, Peoples, and Politics*. 3rd ed. Boulder, Colo.: Westview Press, 2000.

Herb, G., & Kaplan, H. D. *Nested Identities: Nationalism, Territory and Scale*. Lanham, Md.: Rowman & Littlefield Publishers, 1999.

Huntington, S. P. *The Clash of Civilizations and the Remaking of World Order*. New York: Simon & Schuster, 1996.

Jackson, P., & Penrose, J. *Constructions of Race, Place and Nation*. Minneapolis: University of Minnesota Press, 1994.

Johnston, R. J. *Geography and the State: An Essay in Political Geography*. New York: St., Martin's Press, 1983.

Johnston, R. J., Knight, D. B., & Kofman, E., eds. *Nationalism, Self-Determination, and Political Geography*. New York: Croom & Helm, 1988.

Johnston, R. J., Shelley, F. M., & Taylor, P. J. *Developments in Electoral Geography*. New York: Routledge, 1990.

Johnston, R. J., Taylor, P. J., and Watts, M. J., eds. *Geographies of Global Change: Remapping the World in the Late Twentieth Century*. Oxford: Blackwell, 1995.

Jones, Rhys. "Early State Formation in Native Medieval Wales." *Political Geography 17*, no. 6 (1998), 667–682.

Leib, Jonathan I. "Communities of Interest and Minority Districting after *Miller v. Johnson*." *Political Geography*, 17 (1998), 683–699.

Lewis, R. A., ed. *Geographic Perspectives on Soviet Central Asia*. New York: Routledge, 1992.

Mackinder, H. J. "The Geographical Pivot of History." *Geographical Journal*, 23 (1904), 421–444.

Mackinder, H. J., *Democratic Ideals and Reality: A Study in the Politics of Reconstruction*. New York: H. Holt & Company, 1919.

Mackinder, H. J. "The Round World and the Winning of the Peace." *Foreign Affairs* (1943).

Mikesell, M. A., & Murphy, A. B. "A Framework for Comparative Study of Minority-Group Aspirations." *Annals of the Association of American Geographers*, 81, no. 4 (1991), 581–604.

Muir, R. *Political Geography: A New Introduction*. New York: John Wiley & Sons, 1997.

Muni, S. D. *Pangs of Proximity: India and Sri Lanka's Ethnic Crisis*. Newbury Park, Calif.: Sage Publications, 1993.

Murphy, A. B. "The Sovereign State System as Political-Territorial Ideal: Historical and Contemporary Considerations." In T. Biersteker & C. Weber, eds., *State Sovereignty as Social Construct*. Cambridge: Cambridge University Press, 1996, 81–120.

Nahaylo, B., & Swoboda, V. *Soviet Disunion: A History of the Nationalities Problem in the USSR*. New York: Free Press, 1990.

Nijman, J. *The Geopolitics of Power and Conflict: Superpowers in the International System, 1945–1992*. London: Belhaven, 1993.

O'Loughlin, J. V., & Van der Wusten, H., eds. *The New Political Geography of Eastern Europe*. New York: Belhaven/Wiley, 1993.

O'Tuathail, G. *Critical Geopolitics: The Politics of Writing Global Space*. Minneapolis: University of Minneapolis Press, 1996.

O'Tuathail, G. & John Agnew, J. "Geopolitics and Discourse: Practical Geopolitical Reasoning and American Foreign Policy." *Political Geography*, 11 (1992), 155–175.

O'Tuathail, G., Dalby, S., & Paul Routledge, P., eds. *The Geopolitics Reader*. New York: Routledge, 1998.

Painter, J. *Politics, Geography, and "Political Geography": A Critical Perspective*. London: Arnold, 1995.

Prescott, J. R. V. *Political Frontiers and Boundaries*. London: Allen & Unwin, 1987.

Ratzel, F. "Laws of the Spatial Growth of States." In R. E. Kasperson & J. Minghi, eds., *The Structure of Political Geography*, trans. R. L. Bolin. Chicago: Aldine, 1969.

Robinson, K. W. "Sixty Years of Federation in Australia." *Geographical Review*, 51 (1961), 1–20.

Rumley, D., & Minghi, J. V., eds. *The Geography of Border Landscapes*. New York: Routledge, 1991.

Sack, R. D. *Human Territoriality: Its Theory and History*. Cambridge: Cambridge University Press, 1986.

Spykman, N. J. *The Geography of the Peace*. New York: Harcourt, Brace, 1944.

Stoessinger, J. *The Might of Nations*. New York: Random House, 1961.

Taylor, P. J. *The Way the World Works: World Hegemony to World Impasse*. New York: John Wiley & Sons, 1996.

Taylor, P. J., ed. *Political Geography of the Twentieth Century: A Global Analysis*. New York: Halsted Press, 1993.

Taylor, P., & Colin Flint, C. *Political Geography: World Economy, Nation-State, and Locality*. 4th ed. New York: Prentice Hall, 2000.

Van Dyke, J. M., et al. *Freedom for the Seas in the 21st Century: Ocean Governance and Environmental Harmony*. Washington, D.C.: Island Press, 1993.

Vasciannie, S. C. *Landlocked and Geographically Disadvantaged States in the International Law of the Sea*. New York: Oxford University Press, 1990.

Wallerstein, Immanuel. *Historical Capitalism*. London: Verso, 1983.

Wallerstein, Immanuel. *The Essential Wallerstein*. New York: New Press, 2001.

Webster, Gerald R. "Representation, Geographic Districting and Social Justice." *Journal of Geography*, 103, no. 2 (2004), 111–126.

Webster, Gerald R. (2000), "Playing a Game With Changing Rules: Geography, Politics and Redistricting in the 1990s," *Political Geography*, Vol. 19(2): 141–161.

White, G. *Nationalism and Territory: Constructing Group Identity in Southeastern Europe*. Lanham, Md.: Rowman & Littlefield, 2000.

William, C. H., ed. *The Political Geography of the New World Order*. New York: Halstead Press, 1993.

Chapter 9

Abu-Lughod, Janet L. *Changing Cities: Urban Sociology*. New York: HarperCollins, 1991.

Adams, J., ed. *Contemporary Metropolitan America*, 4 vols. Cambridge, Mass.: Ballinger, 1976.

Aiken, S., Mitchell, D., & Staeheli, L. "Urban Geography." In Gary L. Gaile and Cort J. Willmott, eds. *Geography in America at the Dawn of the 21st Century*. New York: Oxford University Press, 2004.

Al-Hindi, K. F. and Till, K. E. "(Re)Placing the New Urbanism Debates: Toward an Intedisciplinary Research Agenda." *Urban Geography*, 22, no. 3 (2001), 189–201.

Andersson, H., et al., eds. *Change and Stability in Urban Europe*. Burlington, Vt.: Ashgate, 2001.

Beaverstock, J. V., Smith, R.G. and Taylor, P. J. "A Roster of World Cities." *Cities*, 16, no. 6 (1999), 445–458.

Berry, B.J.L. *Comparative Urbanization: Divergent Paths in the Twentieth Century*. 2nd rev. ed. New York: St. Martin's Press, 1981.

Borchert, J. "American Metropolitan Evolution." *Geographical Review*, 57 (1967), 301–332.

Bourne, L. S., & Ley, D., eds. *The Changing Social Geography of Canadian Cities*. Montreal, Quebec: McGill-Queen's University Press, 1993.

Burgess, E. "The Growth of the City." in R. Park et al., eds. *The City*. Chicago: University of Chicago Press, 1925, pp. 47–62.

Burnett, J. A. *A Social History of Housing, 1815–1970*. North Pomfret, Vt.: David & Charles, 1978.

Carter, H. *The Study of Urban Geography*. 4th ed. New York: Edward Arnold, 1995.

Castells, M., & Hall, P. *Technopoles of the World: The Making of Twenty-First-Century Industrial Complexes* New York: Routledge, 1994.

Chant, C., & Goodman, D., eds. *Pre-Industrial Cities and Technology*. London: Routledge, 1999.

Christaller, W. "The Foundations of Spatial Organization in Europe." *Frankfurter Geographische Hefte*. 25 (1950).

Christaller, W. *The Central Places in Southern Germany*. Trans. C. Baskin (Englewood Cliffs, N.J.: Prentice-Hall, 1966 (originally published 1933).

Chudacoff, H. *The Evolution of American Urban Society*. 4th rev. ed. Englewood Cliffs, N.J.: Prentice-Hall, 1994.

Clay, G. *Close-Up: How to Read the American City.* Chicago: University of Chicago Press, 1980 (reprint of 1973 original).

Costa, F. J., et al. *Asian Urbanization: Problems and Processes.* Berlin: Gebruder Bomtraeger, 1988.

de Blij, H. J. *Mombasa: An African City.* Evanston: Northwestern University Press, 1968.

Deckker, T., ed. *The Modern City Revisited.* New York: Routledge, 2000.

El Nasser, Haya. "Mega-mansions' upside: They help reduce sprawl." *USA Today*, March 13, 2002.

El Nasser, Haya. "Gated communities are not just for the wealthy." *USA Today*, December 12, 2002.

Fagan, B. *The Little Ice Age.* New York: Basic Books, 2000.

Felsenstein, D., Schamp, E. W., and Shachar, A., eds. *Emerging Nodes in the Global Economy: Frankfurt and Tel Aviv Compared.* Dordrecht: Kluwer Academic Publishers, 2002.

Ford, Larry R. *Cities and Buildings: Skyscrapers, Skid Rows, and Suburbs.* Baltimore, Md.: Johns Hopkins University Press, 1994.

Ford, Larry R. "Continuity and Change in the American City." *Geographical Review*, 85, no. 4 (1995), 552–569.

Ford, Larry R. "A New and Improved Model of Latin American City Structure." *Geographical Review*, 86 (1996), 437–440.

Ford, Larry R. "Cities and Urban Land Use in Advanced Placement Human Geography." *Journal of Geography*, 99, no. 3–4 (2000), 153–168.

Freeman, L., & Braconi, F. "Gentrification and Displacement: New York City in the 1990s." *Journal of the American Planning Association*, 70, no. 1 (2004), 39–52.

Gaubatz, P. R. *Beyond the Great Wall: Urban Form and Transformation on the Chinese Frontiers.* Palo Alto, Calif.: Stanford University Press, 1996.

Gilbert, A., & Gugler, J. *Cities, Poverty and Development: Urbanization in the Third World.* 2nd ed. New York: Oxford University Press, 1992.

Grant, Richard and Jan Nijman. "Globalization and the Corporate Geography of Cities in the Less-Developed World." *Annals of the Association of American Geographers*, 92, 2 (2002), 320–341.

Griffin, E., & Ford, L. "A Model of Latin American City Structure." *Geographical Review*, 70, 4 (1980), 397–422.

Gugler, J., ed. *The Urbanization of the Third World.* New York: Oxford University Press, 1988.

Guldin, G. E., ed. *Urbanizing China.* Westport, Conn.: Greenwood Press, 1992.

Hall, T. *Urban Geography.* 2nd ed. New York: Routledge, 2001.

Harris, C. D. "A Functional Classification of Cities in the United States." *Geographical Review*, 33 (1943), 86–99.

Harris, C. D., & Ullman, E. L. "The Nature of Cities." *Annals of the American Academy of Political and Social Science*, 242 (1945), 7–17.

Hartshorn, T. *Interpreting the City: An Urban Geography.* 2nd ed. New York: John Wiley & Sons, 1992.

Harvey, David. "The New Urbanism and the Communitarian Trap." *Harvard Design Magazine* (1997), 1–3.

Hoyt, H. *The Structure and Growth of Residential Neighborhoods in American Cities* Washington, D.C.: U.S. Federal Housing Administration, 1939.

Huang, Youquin. "Collectivism, Political Control and Gated Communities in Chinese Cities." *Abstracts*, Annual Meeting of the Association of American Geographers, 2005.

Hughes, C. J. "Bringing Down the House in Fairfield County." *The New York Times*, September 19, 2004.

Jefferson, M. "The Law of the Primate City." *Geographical Review*, 29 (1939), 226–232.

Jones, G. W., ed. *Urbanization in Large Developing Countries.* London: Oxford University Press, 1998.

Kesteloot, Christian, and Cortie, Cees. "Housing Turks and Moroccans in Brussels and Amsterdam: The Difference between Private and Public Markets. *Urban Studies*, 35, no. 10 (1998), 1835–1853.

Kesteloot, Christian, and Mistiaen, Pascale. "From Ethnic Minority Niche to Assimilation: Turkish Restaurants in Brussels." *Area*, 29, no. 4 (1997), 325–3343.

Kim, W. B., ed. *Culture and the City in East Asia.* New York: Oxford University Press, 1997.

King, L. *Central Place Theory.* Beverly Hills, Calif.: Sage Publications, 1984.

Knox, P. L. *Urbanization: An Introduction to Urban Geography.* Englewood Cliffs, N.J.: Prentice-Hall, 1994.

Knox, P. L., ed. *The Restless Urban Landscape.* Englewood Cliffs, N.J.: Prentice-Hall, 1993.

Knox, P. L., & Taylor, P. J., eds. *World Cities in a World-System.* Cambridge: Cambridge University Press, 1995.

Landman, Karina, and Schonteich, Martin. "Urban Fortresses: Gated Communities as a Reaction to Crime." *African Security Review*, 11, no. 4 (2002), 71–85.

Lea, J., and Connell, J. *Urbanization in the Pacific.* New York: Routledge, 2001.

Ley, D. *A Social Geography of the City.* New York: Harper & Row, 1983.

Ley, D. *The New Middle Class and the Remaking of the Central City.* Oxford: Oxford University Press, 1996.

McGee, T. G. *The Southeast Asian City: A Social Geography of the Primate Cities of Southeast Asia.* New York: Praeger, 1967.

McGee, T. G., & Robinson, I. R., eds. *The Mega-Urban Regions of Southeast Asia.* Vancouver, BC: UBC Press, 1995.

Miao, Pu. "Deserted Streets in a Jammed Toan: The Gated Community in Chinese Cities and Its Solution." *Journal of Urban Design*, 8, no. 1 (2003), 45–66.

Muller, P. O. *Contemporary Suburban America.* Englewood Cliffs, N.J.: Prentice-Hall, 1981.

Newman, Oscar. Creating Defensible Space. U. S. Department of Housing and Urban Development, Office of Policy Development and Research. April 1996, http://humanics-es.com/defensible-space.pdf. Last accessed August 2005.

Olds, K. *Globalization and Urban Change.* London: Oxford University Press, 2001.

Pacione, M., ed. *Britain's Cities: Geographies of Division in Urban Britain.* New York: Routledge, 1997.

Portnov, B. A., & Erell, E. *Urban Clustering.* Burlington, Vt.: Ashgate, 2001.

Roost, Frank. "Recreating the City as Entertainment Center: The Media Industry's Role in Transforming Potsdamer Platz and Times Square." *Journal of Urban Technology*, 5, no. 3 (1998), 1–21.

Rotenberg, R., & McDonogh, G., eds. *The Cultural Meaning of Urban Space.* Westport, Conn.: Bergin & Garvey, 1993.

Scott, A. J., ed. *Global City—Regions.* London: Oxford University Press, 2001.

Short, John R. *The Urban Order: An Introduction to Cities, Culture, and Power.* Oxford: Basil Blackwell, 1996.

Sjoberg, G. *The Preindustrial City: Past, and Present.* Glencoe, Ill.: Free Press, 1960.

Skinner, G. W. "Marketing and Social Structure in Rural China." Part I, *Journal of Asian Studies*, 24 (1964), 3–43.

Slater, T., ed. *Towns in Decline, ad 100–1600.* Burlington, Vt.: Ashgate, 2000.

Smith, D. W. *Third World Cities.* 2nd ed. New York: Routledge, 2000.

Smith, M. P. *Transnational Urbanism: Locating Globalization.* Oxford: Basil Blackwell, 2000.

Stilgoe, J. R. *Borderland: Origins of the American Suburb, 1820–1939.* New Haven, Conn.: Yale University Press, 1988.

Stren, R. E., & White, R. R., eds. *African Cities in Crisis: Managing Rapid Urban Growth.* Boulder, Colo.: Westview Press, 1989.

Taylor, Peter J. "Recasting World-Systems Analysis: City Networks for Nation-States."

In W. A. Dunaway, ed. *Emerging Issues in the 21st Century World-System*. Vol. II *New Theoretical Directions for the 21st Century World-System*. Westport, Conn.: Greenwood Press, 2003), 130–140.

Taylor, Peter J. and Lang, R. E. "The Shock of the New: 100 Concepts Describing Recent Urban Change." *Environment and Planning A*, 36, no. 6 (2004), 951–958.

United Nations Population Fund. *State of World Population 2001*. New York: United Nations, 2001.

Wright, H. T. & Johnson, G. A. "Population Exchange and Early State Formation in Southwest Asia." *American Anthropologist*, 77 (1975), 267–289.

Yeates, Maurice. *The North American City*. New York: Longman, 1998.

Chapter 10

Agnew, John. *The United States in the World Economy: A Regional Geography*. New York: Cambridge University Press, 1987.

Allen, J., & Hamnett, C., eds. *A Shrinking World? Global Unevenness and Inequality*. Oxford: Oxford University Press, 1995.

Bailey, Adran J. "Industrialization and Economic Development in Advanced Placement Human Geography." *Journal of Geography*, 99, no. 3/4 (2000), 142–152.

Bater, J. *Russia and the Post-Soviet Scene: A Geographical Perspective*. New York: John Wiley & Sons, 1996.

Berry, B. J. L., Conkling, E. C., & Ray, D. M. *The Global Economy in Transition*. 2nd ed. Upper Saddle River, N.J.: Prentice-Hall, 1997.

Birdsall, S. S., & Florin, J. W. *Regional Landscapes of the United States and Canada*. 5th ed. New York: John Wiley & Sons, 1999.

Blouet, B. W., & Blouet, O. M., eds. *Latin America and the Caribbean: A Systematic and Regional Survey*. 4th ed. New York: John Wiley & Sons, 2002.

Borthwick, M. *Pacific Century: The Emergence of Modern Pacific Asia*. Boulder, Colo.: Westview Press, 1992.

Boserup, E. *Economic and Demographic Relationships in Development*. Baltimore, Md.: Johns Hopkins University Press, 1990.

Bryson, J. R. *The Economic Geography Reader: Producing and Consuming Global Capitalism*. Chichester: John Wiley & Sons, 1999.

Burks, A. W. *Japan: A Postindustrial Power*. 3rd ed. Boulder, Colo.: Westview Press, 1991.

Chowdhury, A., & Islam, I. *The Newly Industrializing Economies of East Asia*. New York: Routledge, 1993.

Cole, J. P., & Cole, F. J. *The Geography of the European Community*. New York: Routledge, 1993.

Corbridge, S. *Debt and Development*. Cambridge, Mass.: Blackwell, 1993.

Dicken, P. *Global Shift: The Internationalization of Economic Activity*. 2nd ed. London: Paul Chapman, 1993.

Dicken, P. *Global Shift: Transforming the World Economy*. New York: Guilford Press, 1998.

Dottridge, Mike. "Trafficking in Children in West and Central Africa." *Gender and Development*, 10, no. 1 (2002), 38–42.

Drakakis-Smith, D. *Pacific Asia*. New York: Routledge, 1992.

"The other government in Bangladesh." *The Economist*, 23 July 1998.

"With the wolf at the door." *The Economist*, 30 May 2002.

"El Salvador learns to love the green back." *The Economist*, 26 September 2002.

England, Andrew. "Corruption Thrives in Kenya Despite New Regime's Brave Promises." *Financial Times*. 4 November 2004.

Freeman, M. *Atlas of the World Economy*. New York: Simon & Schuster, 1991.

Gleave, M. B., ed. *Tropical African Development: Geographical Perspectives*. New York: Wiley/Longman, 1992.

Hanink, D. M. *The International Economy: A Geographical Perspective*. New York: John Wiley & Sons, 1994.

Hart, Gillian. "Geography and development: critical ethnographies." *Progress in Human Geography*, 28 (2004), 91–100.

Hodder, R. *Development Geography*. New York: Routledge, 2000.

Hugill, P. J. *World Trade Since 1431: Geography, Technology, and Capitalism*. Baltimore, Md.: Johns Hopkins University Press, 1993.

Hussey, A. "Rapid Industrialization in Thailand, 1986–1991." *Geographical Review*, 83 (1993), 14–28.

Knox, P., & Agnew, J. *The Geography of the World Economy: An Introduction to Economic Geography*. 3rd ed. London: Edward Arnold, 1998.

Leeming, F. *The Changing Geography of China*. Cambridge, Mass.: Blackwell, 1993.

Lewis, R. A., ed. *Geographic Perspectives on Soviet Central Asia*. New York: Routledge, 1992.

Lösch, A. *The Economics of Location*. Trans. W. Woglom & W. Stolper. New York: Wiley Science Editions, 1967; originally published in 1940.

Massey, D. *Spatial Divisions of Labor: Social Structures and the Geography of Production*. 2nd ed. New York: Routledge, 1995.

Murphy, A. B. "Economic Regionalization and Pacific Asia: Problems and Prospects." *Geographical Review*, 85, no. 2 (1995), 127–140.

Murphy, R. T. *The Weight of the Yen*. New York: W. W. Norton, 1996.

Porter, P. W., & E. S. Sheppard. *A World of Difference: Society, Nature, Development*. New York: Guilford Press, 1998.

Pounds, N. J. G. *A Historical Geography of Europe, 1800–1914*. New York: Cambridge University Press, 1985.

Rivoli, Pietra. *The Travels of a T-Shirt in the Global Economy: An Economist Examines the Markets, Power, and Politics of World Trade*. New York: John Wiley & Sons, 2005.

Rostow, W. W. *The Stages of Economic Growth*. 2nd ed. New York: Cambridge University Press, 1971.

Sheppard, E., & T. J. Barnes. *A Companion to Economic Geography*. Oxford: Blackwell, 2000.

Silvey, Rachael. "Sweatshops and the Corporatization of the University." *Gender, Place and Culture*, 9, 2 (2002), pp. 201–207.

Silvey, Rachael. "A Wrench in the Global Works: Anti-sweatshop Activism on Campus." *Antipode* (2004), pp. 191–197.

Smith, D. M. *Industrial Location: An Economic Geographical Analysis*. 2nd ed. New York: John Wiley & Sons, 1981.

Smith, N. *Uneven Development: Nature, Capital and the Production of Space*. New York: Blackwell, 1984.

Songqiao, Z. *Geography of China: Environment, Resources, and Development*. New York: John Wiley & Sons, 1994.

Stewart, J. M., ed. *The Soviet Environment: Problems, Policies and Politics*. New York: Cambridge University Press, 1992.

Szekely, G., ed. *Manufacturing Across Borders and Oceans: Japan, the United States and Mexico*. La Jolla, Calif.: Center for U.S.-Mexican Studies, University of California, San Diego, 1991.

Taylor, Peter J. "Understanding Global Inequalities: A World-Systems Approach." *Geography*, vol. 77 (1992), 10–21.

Taylor, P., and Colin Flint, C. *Political Geography: World Economy, Nation-State, and Locality*, 4th ed. New York: John Wiley & Sons, 2000.

United Nations Convention to Combat Desertification, http://www.unccd.int/ last accessed September 2005.

Vogel, E. F. *The Four Little Dragons: The Spread of Industrialization in East Asia*. Cambridge, Mass.: Harvard University Press, 1991.

Wallerstein, Immanuel. *Historical Capitalism*. London: Verso, 1983.

Weber, A. *Theory of the Location of Industries*. Trans. C. Friedrich. Chicago: University of Chicago Press, 1929; originally published in 1909.

Wheeler, J. O. *Economic Geography*. 3rd ed. New York: John Wiley & Sons, 1998.

World Bank. *World Development Report 2000/2001*. Oxford: Oxford University Press, 2001.

Chapter 11

American Farmland Trust. *Farming on the Edge: High Quality Farmland in the Path of Development.* http://www.farmland.org/farmingontheedge/map.htm, last accessed November 2005.

Blaikie, P. *The Political Economy of Soil Erosion in Developing Countries.* London: Longman, 1985.

Blaikie, P., & Brookfield, H. *Land Degradation and Society.* London: Methuen, 1987.

Boserup, E. *The Conditions of Agricultural Growth: The Economics of Agrarian Change under Population Pressure.* Chicago: Aldine, 1966.

Bowen, Dawn. "Agricultural Expansion in Northern Alberta." Geographical Review, 92, no. 4 (2002), 503–526.

Bowler, I. R., ed. *The Geography of Agriculture in Developed Market Economies.* New York: Wiley, 1992.

Bunting, A. H., ed. *Change in Agriculture.* New York: Praeger, 1970.

Carney, J. A. "Converting the Wetlands, Engendering the Environment: The Intersection of Gender with Agrarian Change in Gambia." in R. Peet & M. J. Watts, eds. *Liberation Ecologies.* London: Routledge, 1996.

CNN. "Other Agricultural Reform Efforts." http://www.7.cnn.com/SPECIALS/2000yourbusiness/Stones/labor.conditions/

Dalal-Clayton, D., ed. *Black's Agricultural Dictionary.* 2nd rev. ed. Totowa, N.J.: Barnes & Noble, 1986.

de Blij, H. *Wine: A Geographic Appreciation.* Totowa, N.J.: Rowman & Allanheld, 1983.

de Blij, H. *Wine Regions of the Southern Hemisphere.* Totowa, N.J.: Rowman & Allanheld, 1985.

de Souza, A. *World Space-Economy.* 2nd rev. ed., Columbus, Ohio: Charles E. Merrill, 1989.

Diamond, Jared. *Guns, Germs and Steel: The Fates of Human Societies.* New York: W.W. Norton & Company, 1997.

Dimitri, Carolyn and Greene, Catherine, "Recent Growth Patterns in the U.S. Organic Foods Market." U.S. Department of Agriculture, Economic Research Service, Market and Trade Economics Division and Resource Economics Division. Agriculture Information Bulletin Number 777, September 2002.

Duckham, A. N., & Masefield, G. B. *Farming Systems of the World.* New York: Praeger, 1970.

The Economist. "One Puff at a Time." September 26, 2002.

The Economist. "The War on the Border Streets." June 30, 2005.

Goodman, D., & Redclift, M. *Refashioning Nature: Food, Ecology, and Culture.* London: Routledge, 1991.

Gourou, P. *The Tropical World: Its Social and Economic Conditions and Its Future Status* 5th rev. ed. Trans. S. Beaver. London and New York: Longman, 1980.

Grigg, D. *Population Growth and Agrarian Change.* London: Cambridge University Press, 1980.

Grigg, D. *An Introduction to Agricultural Geography.* 2nd ed. London: Routledge, 1995.

Gritzner, J. A. *The West African Sahel: Human Agency and Environmental Change.* Chicago: University of Chicago Geography Research Paper No. 226, 1988.

Harris, D., ed. *Human Ecology in Savanna Environments.* New York: Academic Press, 1980.

Hart, J. F. *The Land That Feeds Us: The Story of American Farmers.* New York: W. W. Norton, 1991.

Hart, John Fraser and Mayda, Chris, "Pork Palaces on the Panhandle." *Geographical Review,* 87, no. 3 (1997), 396–401.

Heiser, C., Jr. *Seed to Civilization: The Story of Food.* Cambridge, Mass.: Harvard University Press, 1990.

Higgins, Kenneth F., Naugle, David E., and Forman, K. J. "A Case Study of Land Use Practices in the Northern Great Plains, U.S.A.: An Uncertain Future for Watershed Conservation." *Waterbirds,* 25, sp. issue 2 (2002), 42–50.

Higgins, Marguerite. "Poultry in Motion. Eastern Shore Industry Strives to Stay Alive" *Washington Times,* March 14, 2004, p. A01.

Horvath, R. "Von Thünen's Isolated State and the Area Around Addis Ababa, Ethiopia." *Annals of the Association of American Geographers,* 59 (1969), 308–323.

Hudson, John. *Plains Country Towns.* Minneapolis: University of Minnesota Press, 1985.

Ilbery, B. W. *Agricultural Geography: A Social and Economic Analysis.* Oxford: Oxford University Press, 1985.

Ilbery, B. W., et al., eds. *Agricultural Restructuring and Sustainability: A Geographical Perspective.* New York: CAB International, 1997.

Keen, E. A. *Ownership and Productivity of Marine Fishery Resources.* Blacksburg, Va.: McDonald & Woodward, 1988.

Klee, G., ed. *World Systems of Traditional Resource Management.* New York: Halsted Press, 1980.

Klooster, Daniel J. "Producing Social Nature in the Mexican Countryside." *Cultural Geographies,* 12 (2005), 321-344.

Knox, P., & Agnew, J. *The Geography of the World Economy.* 2nd ed. London: Edward Arnold, 1994.

Lanegran, D. A. "Modern Agriculture in Advanced Placement Human Geography." *Journal of Geography,* 99, no. 3/4 (2000): 132–141.

Levi, J., & Havinden, M. *Economics of African Agriculture.* Harlow, U.K.: Longman, 1982.

Little, P. D., & Watts, M. J. *Living under Contract: Contract Farming and Agrarian Transformation in Sub-Saharan Africa.* Madison: University of Wisconsin Press, 1994.

Liu, Lee. "Labor Location, Conservation, and Land Quality: The Caser of West Jilin, China." *Annals of the Association of American Geographers,* 89, no. 4 (1999), 633–657.

Moris, J. R., & Thom, D. J. *Irrigation Development in Africa: Lessons of Experience.* Boulder, Colo.: Westview Press, 1990.

Nelson, T. "Urban Agriculture." *World Watch,* 9 (1996), 10–17.

Polak, Paul. "The Big Potential of Small Farms" *Scientific American.* September (2005), 84–91.

Sauer, C. O. *Agricultural Origins and Dispersals.* 2nd rev. ed. Cambridge, Mass.: MIT Press, 1969.

Shiva, Vandana. "The Violence of the Green Revolution: Ecological Degradation and Political Conflict in Punjab." *The Ecologist,* 1991, 21(2), 57–60.

Spencer, J., & Horvath, R. "How Does an Agricultural Region Originate?" *Annals of the Association of American Geographers,* 53 (1963), 74–82.

Spencer, J. E., & Thomas, William H. *Cultural Geography: Introduction to Our Humanized Earth.* Artography by R. E. Winter. New York: Wiley, 1969.

Troughton, M. J. "Farming Systems in the Modern World." In M. Pacione, ed. *Progress in Agricultural Geography* (1986), pp. 90–97.

United Nations Office on Drugs and Crime. "United Nations Calls for Greater Assistance to Afghans in Fight Against Opium Cultivation." 24 October 2002. http://www.unodc.org/unodc/press_release_2002-10-24_1.html, last accessed November 2005.

Von Thünen, J. H. *Der Isolierte Staat.* Trans. C. M. Wartenberg. In P. Hall, ed., *Von Thünen's Isolated State.* Elmsford, N.Y.: Pergamon, 1966.

Whittlesey, D. "Major Agricultural Regions of the Earth." *Annals of the Association of American Geographers,* 26 (1936), 199–240.

Yellen, J. E. "The Transformation of the Kalahari !Kung." *Scientific American,* April 1990, pp. 96–105.

Chapter 12

Agnew, John. *The United States in the World Economy: A Regional Geography.* New York: Cambridge University Press, 1987.

Allen, J., & Hamnett, C., eds. *A Shrinking World? Global Unevenness and Inequality.* Oxford: Oxford University Press, 1995.

Awotona, A., ed. *Housing Provision and Bottom-Up Approaches*. Burlington, Vt.: Ashgate, 1999.

Bailey, Adran J. "Industrialization and Economic Development in Advanced Placement Human Geography." *Journal of Geography*, 99, no. 3/4 (2000), 142–152.

Bater, J. *Russia and the Post-Soviet Scene: A Geographical Perspective*. New York: John Wiley & Sons, 1996.

Berry, B. J. L., Conkling, E. C., & Ray, D. M. *The Global Economy in Transition*. 2nd ed. Upper Saddle River, N.J.: Prentice-Hall, 1997.

Birdsall, S. S., & Florin, J. W. *Regional Landscapes of the United States and Canada*. 5th ed. New York: John Wiley & Sons, 1999.

Blakeley, E. J., & Stimson, R. J., eds. *New Cities of the Pacific Rim*. Monograph 43. Berkeley: University of California, Institute of Urban and Regional Development, 1992.

Blouet, B. W., & Blouet, O. M., eds. *Latin America and the Caribbean: A Systematic and Regional Survey*. 4th ed. New York: John Wiley & Sons, 2002.

Borthwick, M. *Pacific Century: The Emergence of Modern Pacific Asia*. Boulder, Colo.: Westview Press, 1992.

Boserup, E. *Economic and Demographic Relationships in Development*. Baltimore, Md.: Johns Hopkins University Press, 1990.

Brown, L. R., et al. *State of the World 2001*. New York: W. W. Norton, 2001.

Bryson, J. R. *The Economic Geography Reader: Producing and Consuming Global Capitalism*. Chichester : John Wiley & Sons, 1999.

Burks, A. W. *Japan: A Postindustrial Power*. 3rd ed. Boulder, Colo.: Westview Press, 1991.

Castells, M. *The Power of Identity*. 3 vols. Vol. II. The Information Age: Economy, Society and Culture. Malden: Blackwell, 1997.

Castells, M. *The Rise of the Network Society*. Oxford: Blackwell Publishers, 1996.

Castells, Manuel; Hall, Peter; Hutriyk, John. "Technopoles of the World: The Making of 21st Century Industrial Complexes." *The Sociological Review*, 43, no. 4: 895–900.

Castles, S. "Globalization and Migration: Some Pressing Contradictions." *International Social Science Journal*, 156 (1998), 179–199.

Charlier, Jacques. "The Benelux seaport system." *Tijdschrift voor economische en sociale geografie*, 87, no. 4 (1996), 310–321.

Chowdhury, A., & Islam, I. *The Newly Industrializing Economies of East Asia*. New York: Routledge, 1993.

Cole, J. P., & Cole, F. J. *The Geography of the European Community*. New York: Routledge, 1993.

Corbridge, S. *ebt and Development*. Cambridge, Mass.: Blackwell, 1993.

de Blij, H. J. *Mombasa: An African City*. Evanston, Ill.: Northwestern University Press, 1968.

Dicken, P. *Global Shift: The Internationalization of Economic Activity*. 2nd ed. London: Paul Chapman, 1993.

Dicken, P. *Global Shift: Transforming the World Economy*. New York: Guilford Press, 1998.

Domosh, M. "Cultural Patterns and Processes in Advanced Placement Human Geography." *Journal of Geography*, 99, no. 3/4 (2000), 111–119.

Drakakis-Smith, D. *Pacific Asia*. New York: Routledge, 1992.

Duncan, J. S., and Ley, D. *Place/Culture/Representation*. London: Routledge, 1993).

The Economist. "China's Economy: Growth Spreads Inland," 18 November 2004.

Featherstone, M. "Global Culture: An Introduction." In Mike Featherstone, ed. *Global Culture: Nationalism, Globalization and Modernity*, pp. 1–14. London, Newbury Park: Sage in association with Theory, Culture & Society, 1990.

Freeman, M. *Atlas of the World Economy*. New York: Simon & Schuster, 1991.

Friedmann, J. "The World City Hypothesis." *Development & Change*, 17 (1986), 69–83.

Glasmeier, A. K., & Howland, M. *From Combines to Computers: Rural Services in the Age of Information Technology*. Albany: State University of New York Press, 1995.

Gleave, M. B., ed. *Tropical African Development: Geographical Perspectives*. New York: Wiley/Longman, 1992.

Graham, S., & Marvin, S. *Splintering Urbanism*. New York: Routledge, 2001.

Grant, R., & Nijman, J. "The Corporate Geography of Cities in the Less Developed World." *Annals of the Association of American Geographers*, 92, no. 2 (June 2002).

Hanink, D. M. *The International Economy: A Geographical Perspective*. New York: John Wiley & Sons, 1994.

Harvey, D. *The Condition of Postmodernity: An Enquiry into the Origins of Cultural Change*. Cambridge, Mass.: Blackwell, 1989.

Herb, G., and Kaplan. D. *Nested Identities: Nationalism, Territory, and Scale*. Lanham, Md.: Rowman & Littlefield, 1999.

Hodder, R. *Development Geography*. New York: Routledge, 2000.

Hotelling, Harold. *The Collected Economics Articles of Harold Hotelling*. Adrian Darnell, ed. Springer-Verlag, 1990.

Hugill, P. J. *World Trade Since 1431: Geography, Technology, and Capitalism*. Baltimore, Md.: Johns Hopkins University Press, 1993.

Hussey, A. "Rapid Industrialization in Thailand, 1986–1991." *Geographical Review*, 83 (1993), 14–28.

Ioannides, D. & Debbage, K., eds. *The Economic Geography of the Tourist Industry: A Supply-Side Analysis*. London: Routledge, 1998.

Jackson, P. *Maps of Meaning: An Introduction to Cultural Geography*. London: Routledge, 1994.

Jameson, F., & Miyoshi, M., eds. *The Cultures of Globalization, Post-Contemporary Interventions*. Durham, N.C.: Duke University Press, 1998.

Johnson, J. H., ed. *Suburban Growth: Geographical Perspectives at the Edge of the Western City*. London: John Wiley & Sons, 1974.

Johnston, R. J., et al., eds. *Geographies of Global Change*. Oxford: Blackwell, 1995.

Journal of Commerce. "Nike, Inc.: Fancy Footwork," May 30, 2005.

Kelly, P. *Landscapes of Globalization*. New York: Routledge, 2000.

Kiely, R., and Marfleet, P. *Globalisation and the Third World*. New York: Routledge, 1998.

King, A. D. *Culture, Globalization, and the World-System: Contemporary Conditions for the Representation of Identity*. [Rev.] ed. (Minneapolis: University of Minnesota Press, 1997).

King, R., et al. *Writing across Worlds: Literature and Migration*. London: Routledge, 1995.

Knight, D. B. "People Together, Yet Apart: Rethinking Territory, Sovereignty, and Identities." In George J. Demko and William B. Wood, eds. *Reordering the World: Geopolitical Perspectives on the Twenty-First Century*, pp. 200–225. Boulder, Colo.: Westview Press, 1999.

Knox, P., & Agnew, J. *The Geography of the World Economy: An Introduction to Economic Geography*. 3rd ed. London: Edward Arnold, 1998.

Knox, P., & Taylor, P. J., eds. *World Cities in a World-System*. Cambridge: Cambridge University Press, 1995.

Kotler, P., et al. *Marketing Places: Attracting Investment, Industry, and Tourism to Cities, States, and Nations*. New York: Free Press, 1993.

Leeming, F. *The Changing Geography of China*. Cambridge, Mass.: Blackwell, 1993.

Lewis, R. A., ed. *Geographic Perspectives on Soviet Central Asia*. New York: Routledge, 1992.

Lösch, A. *The Economics of Location*. Trans. W. Woglom & W. Stolper. New York: Wiley Science Editions, 1967; originally published in 1940.

Massey, D. B. *Space, Place, and Gender*. Minneapolis: University of Minnesota Press, 1994.

Massey, D. *Spatial Divisions of Labor: Social Structures and the Geography of Production*. 2nd ed. New York: Routledge, 1995.

Muller, P. O. "The Suburban Transformation of the Globalizing American City." *Annals of the American Academy of Political and Social Science*, 551 (May 1997), 44–58.

Muller, P. O. *Contemporary Suburban America.* Englewood Cliffs, N.J.: Prentice-Hall, 1981.

Murphy, A. B. "Economic Regionalization and Pacific Asia: Problems and Prospects." *Geographical Review,* 85, no.2 (1995), 127–140.

Murphy, R. T. *The Weight of the Yen.* New York: W.W. Norton, 1996.

O'Brien, R. *Global Financial Integration: The End of Geography.* New York: Council on Foreign Relations Press, 1992.

Pacione, M. *Urban Geography.* New York: Routledge, 2001.

Porter, P. W., & E. S. Sheppard. *A World of Difference: Society, Nature, Development* New York: Guilford Press, 1998.

Pounds, N. J. G. *Historical Geography of Europe, 1800–1914.* New York: Cambridge University Press, 1985.

Rostow, W. W. *The Stages of Economic Growth.* 2nd ed. New York: Cambridge University Press, 1971.

Sassen, S. *Losing Control?: Sovereignty in an Age of Globalization, University Seminars/Leonard Hastings Schoff Memorial Lectures.* New York: Columbia University Press, 1996.

Sheppard, E., & Barnes, T. J. *Companion to Economic Geography.* Oxford: Blackwell, 2000.

Smith, A. D. *Nations and Nationalism in a Global Era.* Cambridge, Mass.: Polity Press, 1995.

Smith, D. M. *Industrial Location: An Economic Geographical Analysis.* 2nd ed. New York: John Wiley & Sons, 1981.

Smith, J. Russell. *North America.* New York: Harcourt Brace and Company, 1925.

Smith, N. *Uneven Development: Nature, Capital and the Production of Space.* New York: Blackwell, 1984.

Songqiao, Z. *Geography of China: Environment, Resources, and Development.* New York: John Wiley & Sons, 1994.

Stewart, J. M., ed. *The Soviet Environment: Problems, Policies and Politics.* New York: Cambridge University Press, 1992.

Storey, J. *Cultural Studies & the Study of Popular Culture.* Athens: University of Georgia, 1996.

Szekely, G., ed. *Manufacturing Across Borders and Oceans: Japan, the United States and Mexico.* La Jolla, Calif.: Center for U.S.-Mexican Studies, University of California, San Diego, 1991.

Timmons Roberts, J., & Hite, A. *From Modernization to Globalization.* Oxford: Blackwell, 2000.

Toffler, A. *Future Shock.* New York: Random House, 1970.

Vogel, E. F. *The Four Little Dragons: The Spread of Industrialization in East Asia.* Cambridge, Mass.: Harvard University Press, 1991.

Wallerstein, I. M. *Geopolitics and Geoculture: Essays on the Changing World-System.* Cambridge: Cambridge University Press, Editions de la Maison des Sciences de l'Homme, 1991.

Waters, M. *Globalization, Key Ideas.* London: Routledge, 1995.

Weber, A. *Theory of the Location of Industries.* Trans. C. Friedrich. Chicago: University of Chicago Press, 1929; originally published in 1909.

Wheeler, J. O. *Economic Geography.* 3rd ed. New York: John Wiley & Sons, 1998.

World Bank. *World Development Report 2000/ 2001.* Oxford: Oxford University Press, 2001.

World Trade Organization. "Regional Trade Agreements." http://www.wto.org/english/ tratop_e/region_e/region_e.htm, last accessed October 2005.

Chapter 13

Bennett, R., & Estall, R., eds. *Global Change and Challenge: Geography for the 1990s.* New York: Routledge, 1991.

Botkin, D. B. *Forces of Change: A New View of Nature.* Washington, D.C.: National Geographic Society, 2000.

Brown, L., & Wolf, E. *Soil Erosion: Quiet Crisis in the World Economy.* Washington, D.C., Paper No. 60, 1984.

Brown, L. R., et al. *State of the World.* New York: W. W. Norton, Annual.

Burroghs, W. J. *Does the Weather Really Matter?: The Social Implications of Climate Change* New York: Cambridge University Press, 1997.

COHMAP members. "Climatic Changes of the Last 18,000 Years: Observations and Model Simulations." *Science,* 241 (1988), pp. 1043–1052.

Davis, M. *Late Victorian Holocausts: El Niño Famines and the Making of the Third World.* London: Verso, 2001.

Diamond, J. *Guns, Germs and Steel: The Fates of Human Societies* New York: W. W. Norton, 1997.

Douglas, I., Huggett, R., & Robinson, M., eds. *Companion Encyclopedia of Geography: The Environment and Humankind.* New York: Routledge, 1996.

Ehrlich, P., & Ehrlich, A. *Healing the Planet: Strategies for Resolving the Environmental Crisis.* Reading, Mass.: Addison-Wesley, 1991.

Energy Information Administration (EIA). *International Energy Annual 1999.* February 2001.

Fagan, B. *Floods, Famines and Emperors: El Niño and the Fate of Civilizations.* New York: Basic Books, 1999.

Fagan, B. *The Little Ice Age: How Climate Made History, 1300–1850.* New York: Basic Books, 2000.

Gray, Leslie C. and Moseley, William G. "A Geographical Perspective on Poverty—Environment Interactions." *The Geographical Journal,* 171, no. 1 (2005), 9–23.

Grove, J. *The Little Ice Age.* London: Routledge, reprint, 1990.

Heywood, V. H., ed. *Global Biodiversity Assessment.* Cambridge: Cambridge University Press, 1995.

Intergovernmental Panel on Climate Change. *Climate Change 1995: The Science of Climate Change.* Edited by J. T. Houghton et al. Cambridge: Cambridge University Press, 1996.

Intergovernmental Panel on Climate Change. *Climate Change 2001: Impacts, Adaptation, and Vulnerability; Contribution of Working GroUniversity Press II to the Third Assessment Report.* J. J. McCarthy et al., eds. New York: Cambridge University Press, 2001.

Intergovernmental Panel on Climate Change. *Climate Change 2001: The Scientific Basis; Contribution of Working GroUniversity Press I to the Third Assessment Report.* J. T. Houghton et al., eds. New York: Cambridge University Press, 2001.

Johnston, R. J. *Nature, State, and Economy: A Political Economy of the Environment.* 2nd ed., (New York: John Wiley & Sons, 1996).

Johnston, R. J., Taylor, P. J., & Watts, M. J., eds. *Geographies of Global Change: Remapping the World in the Late Twentieth Century.* Oxford: Blackwell, 1995.

Jordan, A. "Paying the Incremental Costs of Global Environmental Protection: The Evolving Role of GEF." *Environment,* 36 (1994), 12–20, 31–36.

Kates, R. W. "Sustaining Life on the Earth." *Scientific American,* 271 (1994), pp. 114–122.

Krasnapolsky, V. A., & Feidman, P. D. "Detection of Molecular Hydrogen in the Atmosphere of Mars." *Science* 294, November 30, 2001, p. 1914.

Lamb, H. H. *Climate, History, and the Modern World.* 2nd ed. London: Methuen, 1995.

Marsh, G. P. *Man and Nature.* Cambridge, Mass.: Belknap Press of Harvard University Press, 2000, originally publ. 1865.

McCoy, F., & Heiken, G., eds. *Volcanic Hazards and Disasters in Human Antiquity.* Boulder, Colo.: Geological Society of America, Special Paper, 2000.

Michaels, P. J., & Balling, R. C. *The Satanic Gases: Clearing the Air about Global Warming.* Washington, D.C.: Cato Institute, 2000.

Moseley, William G. "Global Cotton and Local Environmental Management: The Political Ecology of Rich and Poor Small-Hold Farmers in Southern Mali." *The Geographical Journal,* 171, no. 1 (2005), 36–55.

Narendra, P. S., Rietbergen, S., Heimo, C. R., & Patel, J., eds. *A Strategy for the Forest Sector in Sub-Saharan Africa.* World Bank Technical Paper no. 251, Africa Technical Department Series. Washington, D.C.: The World Bank, 1994.

Park, C. C. *Tropical Rainforests*. New York: Routledge, 1992.

Philander, G. *Is the Temperature Rising?: The Uncertain Science of Global Warming*. Princeton, N.J.: Princeton University Press, 1998.

Pimm, Stuart L. and Jenkins, Clinton. "Sustaining the Variety of Life." *Scientific American*. September (2005), 66–73.

Radford, Tim. *Soil erosion as big a problem as global warming, say scientists*. The Guardian. February 14, 2004.

Rosendal, G. K. *The Convention on Biological Diversity and Developing Countries*. Boston: Kluwer Academic, 2000.

Rotberg, R. I., & Rabb, T. K. *Climate and History: Studies in Interdisciplinary History*. Princeton, N.J.: Princeton University Press, 1981.

Ryan, W., & Pitman, W. *Noah's Flood: New Scientific Discoveries about the Event That Changed History*. 1st Touchstone ed. New York: 2000.

Schrijver, N. *Sovereignty over Natural Resources: Balancing Rights and Duties*. Cambridge: Cambridge University Press, 1997.

Shafer, S., & Murphy, A. B. "The Territorial Strategies of International Governmental Organizations: Implications for Environment and Development." *Global Governance*, 4 (1998), 257–274.

Simmons, I. G. "Humanity's Resources." In I. Douglas, R. Huggett, & M. Robinson, eds., *The Companion Encyclopedia of Geography: The Environment and Humankind* New York: Routledge, 1996.

Stahle, D. W., et al. "The Jamestown and Lost Colony Droughts." *Science*, 280 (1998), pp. 564–567.

Stevens, W, K. *The Change in the Weather: People, Weather, and the Science of Climate*. New York: Dell Pub., 2001.

Thomas, W. L., Sauer, C. O., Bates, M. & Mumford, L. *Man's Role in Changing the Face of the Earth*. Chicago: University of Chicago Press, 1956.

Tuan, Y.-F. *Topophilia: A Study of Environmental Perception, Attitudes, and Values*. Englewood Cliffs, N.J.: Prentice-Hall, 1974.

Turekian, T. K. *Global Environmental Change: Past, Present, and Future*. Upper Saddle River, NJ: Prentice Hall, 1996.

Turner, B. L., II, Clarke, W. C., Kates, R. W., Richards, J. F., Mathews, J. T., & Meyer, W. B., eds. *The Earth as Transformed by Human Action: Global and Regional Changes in the Biosphere over the Past 300 Years*. Cambridge:

Cambridge University Press with Clark University, 1990.

United Nations Development Programme. *Human Development Report*, 2004. http://www.undp.org.in/hdr2004/#HDR2004, last accessed September 2005.

United Nations. *World Population Prospects: The 2000 Revisions*. New York: United Nations, 2001.

Wind Power "Spain— The World's No.2 Market" May/June 2003. http://www.ewea.org/documents/WDmay_june_focus.pdf, last accessed September 2005.

World Bank. *Natural Resource Management Strategy: Eastern Europe and Central Asia*. Washington, D.C.: World Bank, 2000.

World Bank. *World Development Report* New York: Oxford University Press, Annual.

Young, O. R. *International Governance: Protecting the Environment in a Stateless Society*. Ithaca, N.Y.: Cornell University Press, 1994.

Young, O. R., ed. *Global Governance: Drawing Insights from the Environmental Experience*. Cambridge, Mass.: MIT Press, 1997.

Zebrowski, E. *Perils of a Restless Planet: Scientific Perspectives on Natural Disasters*. Cambridge; Cambridge University Press, 1997.

Chapter 14

Castells, Manuel. "Materials for an Exploratory Theory of the Network Society." *British Journal of Sociology*, 51, no. 1 (2000), 5–24.

Coe, Neil M., Peter Dicken, & Martin Hess. "Introduction: Global Production Networks—Debates and Challenges." *Journal of Economic Geography*, 8 (2008), 267–269.

Coe, Neil M., Peter Dicken, & Martin Hess. "Global Production Networks: Realizing the Potential." *Journal of Economic Geography*, 8 (2008), 267–269.

Corbridge, Stuart. "The Asymmetry of Interdependence: The United States and the Geopolitics of International Financial Relations." *Studies in Comparative International Development*, Spring 1988, 3–29.

The Economist. Lula's message for two worlds, January 30, 2003.

Foote, Kenneth E. *Shadowed Ground: America's Landscapes of Violence and Tragedy*. Austin: University of Texas Press, 2003.

Henry, Leroi, Mohan, Giles, & Yanacopulos, Helen. "Networks as Transnational Agents of Development." *Third World Quarterly*, 25, no. 5 (2004), 839–855.

Hughes, Alex. "Geographies of Exchange and Circulation: Alternative Trading Spaces." *Progress in Human Geography*, 29, no. 4 (2005), 496–504.

Kirby, Andrew. "The Global Culture Factory." In John O'Loughlin, Lynn Staeheli, and Edward Greenberg, eds. *Globalizaton and Its Outcomes*. New York: Guillford Press, 2004: 133–158.

Kumar, Sanjay, & Corbridge, Stuart. "Programmed to Fail? Devlepment Projects and the Politics of Participation." *Journal of Development Studies*, 39, no. 2 (2002), 73–103.

Maskus, Keith E. "A System on the Brink: Pitfalls in International Trade Rules on the Road to Globalization." In John O'Loughlin, Lynn Staeheli, and Edward Greenberg, eds. *Globalizaton and Its Outcomes*. New York: Guillford Press, 2004, 98–116.

O'Loughlin, John, Staeheli, Lynn, & Greenberg, Edward, eds. *Globalizaton and Its Outcomes*. New York: Guilford Press, 2004.

Pacione, Michael. "Local Exchange Trading Systems as a Response to the Globalization of Capitalism." *Urban Studies*, 34, no. 8 (1997), 1179–1199.

Pereira, Miguel Mendes, EU competition law, convergence, and the media industry. European Commission, Media and Music Publishing Unit, April 23, 2002.

Rose, Gillian. "Place and Identity: A Sense of Place" in *A Place in the World? Places, Cultures, and Globalization*, Doreen Massey and Pat Jess, eds. New York: Oxford University Press, 1995.

Taylor, Peter J., & Lang, Robert E. *U.S. Cities in the World City Network*. Washington, D.C.: Brookings Institute, 2005), Access at: http://www.brookings.edu/dybdocroot/metro/pubs/20050222_worldcities.pdf

Veron, Rene, Corbridge, Stuart, Williams Glyn, & Srivastava, Manoj. "The Everyday State and Political Society in Eastern India: Structuring Access to the Employment Assurance Scheme." *Journal of Development Studies*, 39, no. 5 (2003), 1–28.

World Social Forum, www.forumsocialmundial.org, last accessed September 2005.

World Economic Forum, http://www.weforum.org/, last accessed September 2005.

Wrigley, Neil, Coe, Neil M., & Currah, Andrew. "Globalizing Retail: Conceptualizing the Distribution-Based Transnational Corporation (TNC)." *Progress in Human Geography*, 29, no. 4 (2005), 437–457.

Index